Cracking the
AP*
EUROPEAN
HISTORY Exam

2008 Edition

Cracking the
AP*
EUROPEAN
HISTORY Exam
2008 Edition

Kenneth Pearl, Ph.D.

PrincetonReview.com

Random House, Inc. New York

The Princeton Review, Inc.
2315 Broadway
New York, NY   10024
E-mail: editorialsupport@review.com

ISBN: 978-0-375-42845-6
ISSN: 1522-6409

AP and Advanced Placement Program are registered trademarks of the College Entrance Examination Board.

Editor: Melody Marcus
Production Editor: Tighe Wall
Production Coordinator: Kim Howie

Printed in the United States of America.

10   9   8   7   6   5   4   3   2   1

2008 Edition

ACKNOWLEDGMENTS

Everyone at The Princeton Review was extremely helpful and encouraging throughout the course of this project. In particular, I would like to thank Gretchen Feder for all of her hard work and for the countless improvements she made to the original manuscript. I would also like to thank Evan Schnittman, Gabrielle Maisels, Katie O'Neill, Tighe Wall, Stephen White, Kim Howie and Ellen Mendlow. My current editor, Melody Marcus, has been a tremendous help in getting the 2008 edition of the book in order. Thanks should also be given to Rainer Feldt of Northwood High School in Irvine, California and Thomas Kucharski of New Trier High School in Winnetka, Illinois, both of whom provided a very close reading of the text and many useful suggestions for its improvement.

The first edition of this book was written while I was taking care of my infant daughter, Stephanie, making the project both more difficult and pleasurable at the same time. Whatever hardships there were will be well worth it when I make her feel guilty about the ordeal during those difficult teenage years. Finally, the good fortune of getting to write this book is one more example of the wonderful things that have happened to me since the best thing of all—meeting my wife, Ronit, 15 years ago.

CONTENTS

Introduction

WHAT IS THE PRINCETON REVIEW?

The Princeton Review is an international test-preparation company with branches in all major U.S. cities and several abroad. In 1981, John Katzman started teaching an SAT prep course in his parents' living room. Within five years, The Princeton Review had become the largest SAT prep program in the country.

The Princeton Review's phenomenal success in improving students' scores on standardized tests is due to a simple, innovative, and radically effective philosophy: Study the test, not what the test *claims* to test. This approach has led to the development of techniques for taking standardized tests based on the principles the test writers themselves use to write the tests.

The Princeton Review has found that its methods work not just for cracking the SAT but for any standardized test. We've already successfully applied our system to the GMAT, LSAT, MCAT, and GRE, to name just a few. Although in some ways, the AP European History Test is a very different test from those mentioned above, in the end, a standardized test is a standardized test. This book uses our time-tested principle: Crack the system based on how the test is written.

We also offer books and online services that cover an enormous variety of education and career-related topics. If you're interested, check out our website at **PrincetonReview.com**.

PART I

How to Crack the System

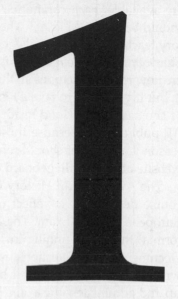

About the Advanced Placement Program

WHAT IS THE ADVANCED PLACEMENT PROGRAM?

The fact that you are reading this book means that you probably already know something about the Advanced Placement (AP) program. After all, how many people pick up a test-preparation guide for a little light reading? So, you probably already know that the AP courses at your high school are supposed to be the toughest available and also that at the end of the school year, you can take an AP exam that may allow you to earn college credit for your work in the course. However, you probably don't know the answers to the following questions: Who decides what constitutes an AP course? Are AP courses the same at every high school? Who writes and grades the AP exam? This section of the book answers these and other related questions.

The Advanced Placement program is coordinated by an organization called **the College Board**. The College Board oversees college admissions examinations. It also publishes test and course materials from previous years, holds seminars on college admissions, and sponsors educational research. Its membership is made up of college administrators, educators, and admissions officers, as well as high school administrators, guidance counselors, and teachers.

The College Board appoints a **development committee** for each of the subjects in which AP exams are available. Each committee meets to decide what should be covered in an AP course and what should be on the AP exam. The AP European History committee is made up of three high school history teachers and three college history teachers. Its decisions are included in a publication called *AP European History Course Description*, which is available online from the College Board. The book you are now reading includes all the pertinent information from that publication, so you don't really need it, but if you want to take a look at this booklet, download it online or ask your history teacher if he or she has a copy. Good history departments should have copies of all the important College Board AP publications. Because those publications are available for sale to the general public, there's no reason your teacher should refuse to let you see them. You can also find them on the College Board's website at **www.collegeboard.com**.

The AP European History development committee performs two important jobs: It updates the course description to reflect recent events and trends in historical analysis, and it writes the AP European History Exam. The committee very rarely makes major changes to the course or the test format, though beginning in 1998, the committee decreased the number of documents used in the Document-Based Questions from around 14 to approximately 10 to 12. When the committee finishes writing each year's exam, it hands it over to the **Educational Testing Service (ETS)**, which prints up and administers the exam. Yes, these are the same folks who administer the SAT and many other admissions exams.

Most AP European History teachers have a copy of the development committee's course requirements, which include an outline of everything a thorough European History course should cover (as well as suggested drills, reading assignments, paper topics, etc.). However, no one forces teachers to teach AP European History in a particular way; the committee's requirements are actually more like suggestions. If you discuss your AP European History course with a friend taking the same course at a different school, you will likely find that his or her course is noticeably different from yours (especially if you are using different textbooks). Don't worry about these differences. There is no one right way to teach European History. Different teachers will interpret the meaning and importance of events differently. In that way, your AP European History course is similar to a college course.

SHOULD I TAKE AP CLASSES? SHOULD I TAKE AP EXAMS?

There's an obvious downside to taking AP classes: They're more difficult than regular classes. Compared with regular classes, AP classes involve more detailed lectures, more homework, more research papers, more tests, and, possibly, a lower grade. So, why take an AP course?

First, if you're looking to go to college, you want as many AP courses on your transcript as you can handle. These classes indicate to your prospective schools that you're serious about studying and challenging yourself. Many admissions offices will give your AP grade a one-level "bump"—that is, they will consider your C a B. (That's how some high school students end up with GPAs above 4.0: They get almost all A's, including their AP courses.) College admissions officers are more favorably disposed to students who take AP courses.

Second, AP courses help you develop skills you will need in college. A good AP teacher will assign research papers and essay tests; require you to study primary source material, maps, census data, and lots of other resources beyond your textbook; encourage discussion of course material; and lecture in such a way that you have to take good notes to pass the course. All of these aspects of AP courses will help prepare you for your college courses.

Third, AP courses are supposed to prepare you for AP exams, which can be quite helpful in getting your college degree. Some schools award college credit for good grades on AP exams. Because college credits cost money, success on AP exams could save you and/or your parents a lot of money. Some schools will admit you as a sophomore if you get high enough marks on three (or more—it varies from school to school) AP exams. It is important to note that *you do not have to take an AP course* to take an AP exam. If you feel that you are up to speed in a subject, you should take the AP exam regardless of the course you took. Remember also that it is the individual college, and not the College Board, that decides whether to grant advanced placement for AP scores. The schools themselves also determine what is considered a satisfactory grade. (AP exams are graded on a scale of 1–5, with 5 being the highest possible score.) Before committing to an AP exam, contact your prospective schools and find out their AP policies. You can also check the school's course catalog. Almost all schools print their AP policies in their catalogs, which are often available at local libraries. Ask the reference librarian for assistance.

Taking AP tests can help your college application in other ways as well. The College Board confers a number of awards on students who excel on three or more AP exams. The **AP Scholar Awards** are given to students who exceed an average grade of 3 on three or more exams; more prestigious awards are given to students who take more tests and receive higher grades. These awards are noted on the score reports that are sent to your prospective colleges.

How Do I Sign Up for the Exam? What Should I Expect on Test Day?

If you want to take one or more AP exams, the first thing you should do is talk to your guidance counselor. He or she will direct to you to the **AP Coordinator** for your school. The AP Coordinator is usually a teacher or a counselor; he or she is the one in charge of collecting your money and telling you when and where the exam will be held. If for some reason you can't take the test through your school—for example, if you're the only student who wants to take an AP exam, so your school has not designated a coordinator—you can still take the test through another school. To find out which schools in your area offer the test, call the College Board's AP Services office at 609-771-7300 or toll free at 888-225-5427, send an e-mail to **apexams@info.collegeboard.org,** or write the College Board by March 1 at: P.O. Box 6671, Princeton, NJ 08541-6671.

It costs $83 to take each exam, with a few exceptions for half-year courses. This fee is expensive, but it's still much cheaper than a college course. Your school keeps $8 for administrative fees, and the College Board suggests that the school refund that money to you if you and your family have financial difficulties. You may also apply to the College Board for a $22 fee reduction based on financial need. If extreme circumstances exist that prevent you from taking an AP exam on its scheduled day, at its set time, contact your AP Coordinator to see if you are eligible for late testing. Be aware that if you test late, your grades may be delayed up to a month and your free-response booklets will not be available. See the College Board website for more information on fees and grade-reporting services.

What Do I Do And When?

Before you do anything, go see your AP European History teacher and your guidance counselor to discuss whether you should take the exam.

- **January**—If you decide to take the test, go see the AP Coordinator and pay your fees. If you need to make special arrangements because of a disability, do so at this time. If your school does not offer AP exams, contact the College Board and ask for the location of the nearest school offering the tests.

- **Early March**—If you need to take the exam at another school and you still have not yet made plans to do so, DO IT NOW!

- **May**—AP European History Exam is administered.

- **Early to Mid-June**—AP exams are graded. If you want your score report sent to colleges other than those you provided with your test registration, or if you want to cancel your test scores, you have until **June 15** to contact the College Board with your request. (There's more about canceling your test scores on the next page, under the heading Special Circumstances.)

- **July 1**—Your grades will be available by phone, and they will be sent to you and your school.

The AP European History Exam is usually given at 8:00 A.M. The test may start a little earlier or later at your school, but not much: College Board rules prohibit starting before 6:00 A.M. or after 10:00 A.M. On test day, you will need to bring

- several number-two pencils (for the multiple-choice section). Make sure you have an eraser.

- a dark-blue or black pen (with which to write your essays).

- a watch (in case you can't see the one in the room or there's no clock in your testing room). Do not bring a watch with an alarm or a calculator. It will be confiscated by the proctor.

- an AP-authorized calculator, if you're also taking one of the Calculus exams, Chemistry, Physics, and/or Statistics.

- a photo ID if you are taking the AP at a school other than your own.

HERE ARE SOME THINGS YOU MAY **NOT** BRING TO THE EXAM

- Textbooks, notebooks, a dictionary, or a pocket encyclopedia. In short—no books!

- Any kind of computer or typewriting equipment.

- A ruler or straightedge, unless you're taking AP Physics.

- A camera (to prevent you from photographing the exam and giving the pictures to someone writing a test-prep book, like me).

- Portable listening devices such as radios, MP3 players, or PDAs.

The AP European History Exam consists of three sections. First, you will fill out a bunch of forms; this takes 10–15 minutes. Then, you will take an 80-question multiple-choice section, for which you are given 55 minutes. Afterward, you will be given a break of approximately 15 minutes. This break is the only one you get during the test. Then there is the Document-Based Question (DBQ), which consists of a 15-minute reading period, followed by a 45-minute writing period. Finally, there are two free-response essay questions. You have 70 minutes to complete both. We will discuss each of these sections in detail in the following chapters.

SPECIAL CIRCUMSTANCES

Special Conditions for Students with Disabilities

Students who seek special testing conditions to accommodate disabilities should have either a current Individualized Education Program (IEP) on file at their school OR a signed letter from an appropriate professional (doctor, psychologist, reading specialist, etc.) describing the disability and verifying the need for different testing arrangements. Qualified students have several options: Students with poor or no vision may take large-type tests and Braille tests. Poor-sighted students may also use a reader or amanuensis. Qualified students also have the right to take the exam at a different, more accommodating location. Take note: You must present documentation of your disability in order for your score report to indicate "Certified Disability." Otherwise, your test report will simply indicate a "Nonstandard Administration," which is the same indication given on the test of a non-disabled student who takes the exam untimed. As an untimed exam may give the appearance of an advantage, admissions officers are not always sympathetic to the "Nonstandard Administration" report. Therefore, contact your AP Coordinator as soon as possible, but no later than April 1, about arranging your test, and make sure your documentation is in order long before test day. Alternatively, if possible, take the test under standard conditions.

Problems on Test Day

On rare occasions, the College Board writes a lousy question. Sometimes, ETS misprints a question, misprints a page of the exam (or leaves it blank!), or makes some other error. If, during the test, you believe that one or more of the questions on the test don't work, you should contact the College Board as soon as possible after the test. Provide the test title, the question number, and a description of what you think was wrong with the question. (This, however, is extremely unlikely to happen in the AP European History Exam. Such errors are almost invariably on tests in math or science.) If you see a misprint, you should report it immediately to the proctor and then again after the exam to the College Board. The phone number, address, and e-mail address to use appear at the end of this chapter.

More common are problems in test administration. Maybe your proctor gave the directions incorrectly. For you, that should be no big deal, as you will know all the directions well before test day (because you read this book!). The big problem is if your proctor mistimes the exam, particularly if he or she gives you too little time. (You *could* report an error if your proctor gave you too *much* time, but why would you want to?) In the case of a timing error, notify the school's AP Coordinator immediately. If the coordinator does not help (he or she might *be* the proctor who screwed up the timing), go see the principal. If you wait too long, you may get stuck with the score you got on the mistimed exam.

That covers what happens when the College Board, ETS, or your proctor screws up. What about when you screw up? If you think (or know) that you blew the exam, you have until June 15 to contact the College Board and cancel your score. June 15 is also the date by which you have to contact the College Board if you want to withhold your grades from certain colleges or add schools to the list of those receiving your grades. Unless you're reasonably certain you got a 1 on an AP exam, you probably shouldn't cancel your grade.

Finally, here's a list of things that will get you thrown out of the testing center, result in your scores being canceled, and raise serious suspicion that you are a cheater.

- leafing through the exam booklet before the exam begins

- trying to give answers to or receive answers from someone else during the exam

- working on the wrong section of the exam

- continuing to work on the exam after you have been instructed to stop

- tearing a page out of your test booklet, or trying to sneak the entire exam out of the test site

- looking in a textbook, notebook, encyclopedia, and so on during the exam or during the break

- failing to obey any other testing regulation

- behaving disruptively by screaming, whooping, dancing, singing, smacking your lips with pleasure or disgust, throwing things, pacing around the room, performing auto-surgery, and so on

FINALLY...

Most of the information in this chapter appears in a College Board publication called *Bulletin for AP Students and Parents*. It's free, and you should be able to get a copy of it from your guidance counselor. You can also download it online at **www.collegeboard.com**. Should those options fail, e-mail **apexams@info.collegeboard.org** or pick up the phone and call 609-771-7300 or 888-225-5427 (toll-free in the U.S. and Canada).

If your guidance counselor doesn't have this publication, your Internet service is down, and you don't have access to a phone (can you imagine?), then write to:

AP Services
P.O. Box 6671
Princeton, NJ 08541-6671

Even if you don't need to go to **www.collegeboard.com** for the bulletin, the College Board website is worth a visit as you prepare for the exams. It includes sample test questions and updated information about all AP exams. It also contains some test-taking suggestions that you should ignore. The good suggestions have already been incorporated into this book!

2

Being a Good Test Taker

Very few students stop to think about how to improve their test-taking skills. Most assume that if they study hard, they will test well, and if they do not study, they will do poorly. Most students continue to believe this even after experience teaches them otherwise. Have you ever studied really hard for an exam, then blown it on test day? Have you ever aced an exam for which you thought you weren't well-prepared? Most students have had one, if not both, of these experiences. The lesson should be clear—factors other than your level of preparation influence your final test score.

This section will provide you with some insights that will help you perform better on the AP European History Exam and on other exams as well.

TEST ANXIETY

Everybody experiences anxiety before and during an exam. To a certain extent, test anxiety can be helpful. Some people find that they perform more quickly and efficiently under stress. If you have ever pulled an all-nighter to write a paper and ended up doing good work, you know the feeling.

However, *too much* stress is definitely a bad thing. Hyperventilating during the test, for example, almost always leads to a lower score. If you find that you stress out during exams, here are a few preemptive actions you can take.

- **Take a reality check.** Evaluate your situation before the test begins. If you have studied hard, remind yourself that you are well prepared. Remember that many others taking the test are not as well prepared, and (in your classes, at least) you are being graded against them, so you have an advantage. If you didn't study, accept the fact that you will probably not ace the test. Make sure you get to every question you know something about. Don't stress out or fixate on how much you don't know. Your job is to score as high as you can by maximizing the benefits of what you do know. In either scenario, it is best to think of a test as if it were a game. How can you get the most points in the time allotted to you? Always answer questions you can answer easily and quickly before you answer those that will take more time. When confronted with a choice, answer those questions that are worth more points rather than those that are worth fewer.

- **Try to relax.** Slow, deep breathing works for almost everyone. Close your eyes, take a few, slow, deep breaths, and concentrate on nothing but your inhalation and exhalation for a few seconds. This is a basic form of meditation, and it should help you to clear your mind of stress and, as a result, concentrate better on the test. If you have ever taken yoga classes, you probably know some other good relaxation techniques. Use them when you can (obviously, anything that requires leaving your seat and, say, assuming a handstand position won't be allowed by any but the most free-spirited proctors).

- **Eliminate as many surprises as you can.** Make sure you know where the test will be given, when it starts, what type of questions are going to be asked, and how long the test will take. You don't want to be worrying about any of these things on test day or, even worse, after the test has already begun.

The best way to avoid stress is to study both the test material and the test itself. Congratulations! By reading this book, you are taking a major step toward a stress-free AP European History Exam.

PACING

A big part of scoring well on an exam is working at a consistent pace. The worst mistake made by inexperienced or unsavvy test takers is that they come to a question that stumps them, and, rather than just skipping it, they panic and stall. Time stands still when you're working on a question you cannot answer, and it is not unusual for students to waste five minutes on a single question because they are too stubborn to cut their losses.

Don't make that mistake. Tests are like marathons—you do best when you work through them at a steady pace. You can always come back to a question you don't know. When you do, very often you will find that your previous mental block is gone, and you will wonder why the question perplexed you the first time around (as you gleefully move on to the next question). Even if you still don't know the answer, you will not have wasted valuable time you could have spent on easier questions.

This is particularly true on multiple-choice tests like the SAT or Part A of the AP European History Exam. On these tests, *all questions are worth the same value toward your final score*. Remember, when all the questions on a test are of equal value, no one question is that important. *You should always skip questions that give you trouble* until you have answered every question to which you know the answer.

Finally, you should set a realistic goal for your final score. Depending on the score you need, it may be in your best interest *not* to try to answer every question. In trying to do too much, you can easily hurt your score with careless mistakes. Check with the schools to which you are applying. Do you need a 3 to earn credit for the test? If you get a **raw score** of 48 (out of 80) on the multiple-choice section *and* do as well on the essays, you will get a 3. Your raw score is determined by adding up the number of questions you answer correctly, then subtracting the number of questions you answer incorrectly times 0.25 (more on this "guessing penalty" later). In other words, you could answer 60 questions, get 51 right and 9 wrong, *leave 20 blank*, and still be on pace for a 3. Only students who intend to get a 5 should try to answer every question on the multiple-choice section; everyone else should go slower and spend more time on each question to avoid careless mistakes.

Because the College Board has not recently released its grading statistics, the following is an approximation of how to pace yourself on the AP exam:

If you want to get a:	You can answer this many:	And you can leave this many blank:
3	60	20
4	70	10
5	as many as you can	as few as possible

We will talk more about pacing on the multiple-choice section in the next chapter.

IN THE WEEKS BEFORE THE TEST...

There are a few things you should start doing any time after January 1 (but certainly before May 1). One of them is to read this book. Here are some others:

- **Ask your teacher for copies of old AP European History Exams**. The College Board releases copies of at least one, and sometimes two, old exams. The College Board also publishes a book that contains every Document-Based Question (DBQ) that has appeared on the test since 1974 and another that contains all the free-response questions asked during the last five years. Your school history department probably has copies of all of these.

- **Commit a little time every night to test preparation**. A little studying every night is much better than a lot of cramming in the week before the exam. Starting in late March or early April, try to set aside thirty to forty-five minutes three or four times a week to review this book, the textbook you use in class, your notes on your teacher's lectures, and any other class materials.

IN THE FINAL WEEK BEFORE THE EXAM...

In a best-case scenario, you should not cram for the test. However, cramming is better than not studying at all. If it's one week before the test and you haven't started studying yet, you should devote as many hours as possible to studying.

If, on the other hand, you have been preparing, you should

- **Maintain your usual routine.** Try not to go to bed a lot later or a lot earlier than usual. Don't start a new diet or a new exercise program. In other words, stay the course.

- **Do a general history review.** Stop concentrating on details this week. Focus instead on "big picture" issues, such as political, social, and economic trends. In other words, stop asking yourself questions like, "What was the Diet of Speyer?", and start asking yourself questions like, "What were some of the fundamental causes of the Protestant Reformation of the sixteenth century?"

- **Read all the directions for the exam.** They're all in this book. Don't waste valuable time during the exam reading instructions. Know what you're supposed to do on each section of the test long before test day.

ON TEST DAY...

- **Start the day with a reasonable, but not huge, breakfast.** You'll need energy for the exam. Have a nice breakfast, but nothing so big that it will put you to sleep. Beware of coffee, tea, or anything else that will send you to the restroom during the test.

- **Bring everything you need.** Those things would be: two or more number-two pencils (for the multiple-choice section), an eraser, a dark-blue or black pen (for the essay sections), and a watch. Do not bring a watch with an alarm or one that beeps; it will be taken from you.

- **Wear comfortable clothing.**

- **Bring a snack.** A piece of fruit or a candy bar during the break can give you a much-needed energy boost. A kind proctor might even let you munch on a noiseless snack (e.g., a banana or a candy bar) during the test, but don't count on it.

FINALLY...

Learn everything you can about the exam. The more you know, the less you will be surprised during the test. To learn everything you need to know about the AP European History Exam, read on. The following chapters will tell you all about the exam's multiple-choice section and the two essay sections.

SUMMARY

- Start studying for the test a month or more in advance. Just 30 to 45 minutes a few nights a week will make a huge difference.

- Ask your teacher for copies of old AP European History Exams. Write some practice essays and review them with your teacher.

- Don't change your regular routine in the week leading up to the test. Do, however, refocus your studies from details to "big picture" questions.

- On test day, wear something comfortable. Have a nice breakfast. Bring pencils, a pen, and a watch to the test. Bring a snack.

- Beat test anxiety. Prepare for the test so that there will be few surprises on test day. Take deep, slow breaths to relax during the test.

- Maintain a steady pace throughout the exam. Don't get hung up on any one question. Set a target score, and pace yourself to achieve your goal.

3

Cracking the
Multiple-Choice Section

THE BASICS

The directions for the multiple-choice section of the AP European History Exam are pretty simple. They read:

Directions: Each of the questions or incomplete statements below is followed by five suggested answers or completions. Select the one that is best in each case, and then fill in the corresponding oval on the answer sheet.

In short, you are being asked to do what you have done on lots of other multiple-choice exams. Pick the right answer and then fill in the appropriate bubble on a separate answer sheet. You will *not* be given credit for answers you record in your test booklet (e.g., by circling them) but not on your answer sheet. The section consists of 80 questions. You will be given 55 minutes to work on the section.

The College Board provides a breakdown of the exam's questions by era and by general subject matter. This breakdown will *not* appear in your test booklet. It comes from the preparatory material the College Board publishes. Here it is:

Breakdown by Era

	Percent of Questions	*Number of Questions*
1450 to 1815	50	40
1815 to present	50	40

Breakdown by General Subject

	Percent of Questions	*Number of Questions*
Political and diplomatic themes	30-35	24–28
Cultural and intellectual themes	30-35	24–28
Social and economic themes	30-35	24–28

As you can see, the test seeks to achieve a measure of balance between the period from the High Renaissance to Napoleon and the period after 1815. Also, note that equal emphasis is placed on political/diplomatic history, cultural and intellectual questions, and social and economic themes. Remember this as you study.

TYPES OF QUESTIONS

The majority of questions on the multiple-choice section of the test are similar to this:

3. The Dreyfus Affair had political repercussions that lasted well into the twentieth century because

(A) it helped deepen the religious and political
conflicts that plagued the Third Republic
(B) it created a consensus in French politics which
eventually led to a strengthening of the
Third Republic
(C) it reminded people of the German threat
(D) it ultimately helped the French army get ready
for the First World War
(E) it led to a fundamental overhaul of the French
political system

(Answers to sample questions appear near the end of this chapter, just before the Summary.)

Sometimes, the College Board makes the questions a little trickier. One way it does this is by phrasing a question so that four answers are correct and one is incorrect. We call these questions "NOT/EXCEPT" questions because they usually contain one of those words (in capital letters, so they're harder to miss). Look at the example on the following page.

6. All of the following led to the Russian Revolution
   of 1917 EXCEPT

   (A) the outbreak of World War I
   (B) the failure of autocratic government
   (C) growing disenchantment of the intellectual
       class
   (D) decline in the rate of industrialization in the
       decade leading up to 1917
   (E) the failure of the 1905 revolution to bring about
       genuine political reform

Once or twice during the multiple-choice section, you will be asked to interpret an illustration—often a map, political cartoon, painting, or poster. These questions are usually easy. The key is *not* to try to read too much between the lines.

Here is an example:

Source: Daily Mail

45. The political cartoon above implies that

   (A) Hitler broke his promise not to destroy the
       German Communist Party
   (B) Hitler betrayed his 1939 nonaggression pact
       with Stalin
   (C) Stalin was warned by the Western Allies that
       Hitler was dangerous
   (D) a nonaggression pact with Germany was
       fraught with problems
   (E) Hitler and Stalin deserved one another

Finally, one or two questions on the test will ask you to interpret a graph or chart. Again, these are usually very straightforward, and the most important thing for you to do is *not* over-interpret the data. The correct answer will be indisputably supported by the information in the chart.

Here's an example:

Rate of Industrial Production in Great Britain
(percentage increase per decade)

1800 to 1810	22.9
1810 to 1820	38.6
1830 to 1840	47.2
1840 to 1850	37.4
1850 to 1860	39.3
1860 to 1870	27.8
1870 to 1880	33.2
1880 to 1890	17.4
1890 to 1900	17.9

13. Which of the following conclusions can be drawn from the information presented in the chart above?

(A) The drop in industrial production in the 1860s was due to the American Civil War.

(B) The rate of industrial production remained steady throughout the century.

(C) Great Britain's industrial production remained higher than the rest of Europe's.

(D) By the last decades of the century, the rate of industrial production was in an irreversible decline.

(E) The period between 1830 and 1860 witnessed the greatest increase in industrial production.

No Military History and No Trivial Pursuit

Here's some good news. The AP European History Exam doesn't ask specifically about military history. You will *never* see a question on the AP exam like the one below:

16. During the First World War, the Battle of Passchendaele

(A) was a British defeat due to the weakening of their right flank at a critical time

(B) ended with a German counterattack and breakthrough of the British lines

(C) was a British defeat due to insufficient artillery support

(D) witnessed the last attempt by the British to blast their way through the German lines without the element of surprise

(E) was postponed for four weeks due to the inclement weather

Although the British assault on German positions at the Battle of Passchendaele serves as an important example of the foolhardiness of Britain's military leadership, you won't be asked about it on the test. The AP European History Exam does not ask about military strategy per se. When it asks about war, the questions concern the political or social implications of a war or the introduction of new technology rather than strategic questions. (The correct answer, by the way, is (D). If you tried it and got it wrong, so what? It won't be on the test.)

Also, AP European History questions never test rote memorization *only*. You have to know your facts to do well on this test; the questions, however, always ask for information in the context of larger historical trends. Therefore, you will *never* see a question like this one:

21. The treaty that marked the end of the Thirty Years War was called the

   (A) Peace of Ghent
   (B) Peace of Versailles
   (C) Peace of Paris
   (D) Peace of Westphalia
   (E) Peace of Augsburg

CHRONOLOGICAL ORDER AND THE ORDER OF DIFFICULTY

Here's some more good news: The folks who write the AP European History Exam organize the multiple-choice section in a predictable way:

- Questions will be organized in groups of approximately four to seven. Each group of questions will be presented in roughly chronological order. For example, the first question in a group may ask about the Renaissance and Reformation; the second, about the Industrial Revolution and its effect on society; the third, about the French Revolution and Napoleon; and so on. You will notice a sharp break in chronology when you move from one group of questions to another. When you see a question about the Brezhnev Doctrine followed by a question on Renaissance humanism, you will know that you have moved on to a new grouping.

Remember that easy questions have easy answers. Do not choose an obscure or trivial answer for an easy question. Remember also that all questions are worth an equal amount toward your final score. Therefore, it is important that you go slowly enough in the beginning so that you do not make careless mistakes on the easier questions. The points you lose early in the test will be much harder to make up later on when the questions get more difficult.

Ask yourself how you can use this information to your advantage as you look at the following three questions (the answer choices have been omitted purposely):

17. The Prussian victory over Austria in 1866 helped pave the way for

18. The Paris Commune came in the wake of the collapse of

19. By the end of the nineteenth century, British politics were dominated by

Here's what you may have figured out: Because the test goes in order of difficulty, and because these are questions 17, 18, and 19 out of 80, these three questions are relatively easy. When you actually answer these questions, this information should give you confidence. Second, from reading the first and third questions, you should have realized that the Paris Commune took place some time between 1866 and the end of the nineteenth century. If you had forgotten about the Paris Commune, this information should help you find the correct answer, or at least eliminate a few incorrect answers. Now let's look at those three questions *with* the answer choices:

17. The Prussian victory over Austria in 1866 led to

   (A) the reentry of Great Britain into European
         affairs to check Prussian expansion
   (B) Prussian domination over the Northern
         German states
   (C) an alliance between France and Austria
   (D) Serbian attacks on Austria
   (E) the loss of Alsace and Lorraine

18. The rise of the Paris Commune was the result of

   (A) the fall of the Orleans monarchy in 1848
   (B) political disagreements that arose following the
         collapse of the French Second Empire
   (C) a large influx of unemployed agricultural
         workers into the capital
   (D) anger and fear following the outbreak of a
         massive cholera epidemic in the city
   (E) the collapse of the Paris stock exchange

19. By the end of the nineteenth century, British politics
    were dominated by

   (A) the Liberal and Conservative parties
   (B) extraparliamentary pressure groups
   (C) a series of coalition governments
   (D) the Conservative and Labour parties
   (E) political infighting within the House of Lords

Here's How to Crack It

Because you know that these are relatively easy questions, you can eliminate any answers that would require you to know something trivial. Furthermore, the correct answers will affirm a basic principle of European history during the era in question, and the incorrect answers should contain information that clearly identifies them as incorrect.

Consider **question 17**. We know that one of the main themes in nineteenth-century European history is the development of nation-states in Italy and Germany. The last stage of German unification was the Franco-Prussian War of 1870, at which time France was defeated, in part because it was diplomatically isolated and therefore had to face Prussia alone. That would eliminate choices (A) and (C) as well as (E), because the loss of Alsace and Lorraine followed the French defeat. Choice (D) would also not be the likely answer because it does not address this larger theme of German unification. The correct answer is (B).

Now, let's look at **question 18**. The chronological order of the questions reveals that the Paris Commune occurred sometime between 1866 and the end of the nineteenth century. Therefore, we can easily eliminate (A) because it occurred prior to the period in question. To successfully answer this question, you need to be aware of one of the most critical events that took place in France during this period—the rise of the French Third Republic following the collapse of the Second Empire of Napoleon III after the Franco-Prussian War of 1870. This Republic, you may recall, was beset with a host of problems including, in its earliest days, a radical revolution in the streets of Paris following the Franco-Prussian War. Therefore, we should choose (B).

Question 19 asks about the state of British politics in the late-Victorian period. One of the things you should be aware of concerning this time period is that British politics were remarkably stable. You can eliminate (B) because, although there were extraparliamentary groups at work during this time, such as organizations to bring about women's suffrage, there is no indication that they dominated British politics. Answer (C) implies that British politics rested on a precarious balance of power among assorted political parties, something that was simply not the case. Choice (E) also implies a measure of instability, while (D) is not correct because the Labour party did not emerge as a major player in British politics until the twentieth century. The correct choice is (A).

THE BIG PICTURE

In the explanations for questions 17–19 above, we hinted at one of the most important characteristics of AP European History multiple-choice questions. The questions and answers are designed to illustrate **basic principles** of European history. Multiple-choice questions will NOT ask about exceptions to historical trends; the test ignores these, because the test writers are trying to determine whether you have mastered the important generalizations that can be drawn from history. They do not want to know whether you have memorized your textbook (they already know that you haven't).

Therefore, you should always keep the **big picture** in mind as you take this exam. Even if you cannot remember the specific event or concept being tested, you should be able to answer the question by remembering the general social and political trends of the era.

Let's look at this illustrative example:

68. In his *Institutes of the Christian Religion*, Calvin argued that from the beginning of time, God

    (A) allowed humans to select their own path to salvation, provided that it included some degree of faith
    (B) knew few would be granted salvation unless they performed charitable works
    (C) selected those who would be saved and those who would be condemned, and that human actions play no role in this
    (D) operated as the divine creator but played no real role in the daily workings of this world
    (E) had prevailed upon the Catholic Church to do his heavenly bidding here on Earth

Here's How to Crack It

The first thing you should notice is that this is question number 68, so it's pretty difficult. At first glance, this question appears to assume that you have read Calvin's *Institutes*, something I doubt you got around to doing. (You probably didn't even read the CliffsNotes.) The question, however, is not really that tricky. What it is really asking you is whether you understand the fundamentals of John Calvin's theology. Calvin believed that God selected only a very few individuals to be saved. Nothing these individuals did affected their own ultimate salvation, because to imply they had a role in it would mean that God's authority was not total, something that Calvin did not accept. Choices (A) and (B) are therefore incorrect, as they both imply some measure of human free will. Choice (D) could not be correct; it represents the Deist point of view dating from the eighteenth-century Enlightenment and bears little resemblance to what a sixteenth-century theologian like Calvin would have believed. (E) is clearly incorrect; Calvin was a Protestant and therefore rejected the teachings of the Catholic Church. The correct answer is (C), which illustrates a "big picture" principle, the primacy for Protestants of faith over works.

THE GUESSING PENALTY AND PROCESS OF ELIMINATION

There will be times, however, when you can eliminate one or more clearly wrong answers and still have more than one reasonable answer choice left over. You may not be able to decide which one is right. When this happens, you should guess. Does this advice take you by surprise? Lots of students think that they should never guess on an exam. But even the College Board will tell you that that's not true. This passage appears on the first page of the AP European History Exam:

> "Many candidates wonder whether or not to guess the answers to questions about which they are not certain. In this section of the examination, as a correction for haphazard guessing, one-fourth of the number of questions you answer incorrectly will be subtracted from the number of questions you answer correctly. It is improbable, therefore, that mere guessing will improve your score significantly; it may even lower your score, and it does take time. If, however, you are not sure of the best answer but have some knowledge of the question and are able to eliminate one or more answer choices as wrong, your chance of getting the right answer is improved, and it may be to your advantage to answer such a question."

The only thing wrong with this advice is that it understates the value of guessing once you have eliminated one or more answer choices. Statistically speaking, guessing after you have eliminated one or more incorrect answer choices *will* improve your final score on the multiple-choice section.

Here's why. Suppose you guess randomly on five questions. Probability tells you that you should get one correct and four incorrect. Your raw score for those five questions would be +1 for the correct answer and –1 for your four incorrect answers ($-4 \times \frac{1}{4} = -1$). Your guesses would net exactly 0 points. That's the exact same score you would have received if you had skipped all five questions! There is, then, no guessing penalty. Random guesses cancel each other out, unless you are either very lucky or very unlucky.

However, you will rarely be faced with a question on which you can't eliminate at least one of the answer choices. In many cases, you will be able to eliminate two or even three incorrect answers. Whenever you get this far but can go no further, you *must* guess from among the remaining answer choices.

Consider this scenario. Billy and Cal are both taking the AP European History Exam. Each one knows the answers to 48 of the 80 multiple-choice questions. Each has time to look at most of the other questions—let's say, 24 of the remaining 32—and in each case, each could eliminate two incorrect answers but could go no further. Billy doesn't guess on those 24 questions, and he ends up with a raw score of 48. He's right on pace for a final score of 3. Cal, on the other hand, guesses on all 24. Because he is guessing from among three answer choices, he will probably get one out of every three correct. He winds up with +8 for his correct answers and $16 \times \frac{1}{4} = -4$ for his incorrect answers. Cal's raw score of 52 gives him a boost toward the final score of 4 that he is shooting for.

Had Billy and Cal been able to eliminate three answer choices on each of the 24 questions, the results would have been even more dramatic. Billy, who didn't guess, would have still gotten a 48. Cal, however, would have gotten 12 of the 24 correct for a +12, while losing only $-12 \times \frac{1}{4} = -3$ for his incorrect answers. His final raw score of 57 would have sent him well on his way to that 4.

Does this mean you should take a guess on every question on the test? No. Because you have only a limited amount of time to spend on the multiple-choice section, you have to maximize that time. The first thing you want to do is make sure you have answered every question to which you know the answer. Only then do you want to guess on questions to which you don't know the answers. However, once you have worked on a question, eliminated some answers, and convinced yourself that you cannot eliminate any other incorrect answers, you should guess and move on to the next question.

If it seems that we are focusing more on eliminating incorrect answers than on finding the correct answers, it is because that is the most efficient way to take a multiple-choice exam. Use **Process of Elimination** to whittle down the answer choices to one on all but the easiest questions (on easy questions, the correct answer will be obvious), because incorrect answers are much easier to identify than the correct one is. When you look for the correct answer among the answer choices, you have a tendency to try to justify how each answer *might* be correct. You'll adopt a forgiving attitude in a situation in which tough assertiveness is rewarded. Eliminate incorrect answers. Terminate them with extreme prejudice. If you have done your job well, only the correct answer will be left standing at the end.

This all probably sounds pretty aggressive to you. It is. The fact is—aggressiveness pays on this test. Sift through the answer choices, toss incorrect answers into the bin, guess without remorse, and prowl the test searching for questions you can answer—all with the tenacity and ruthlessness of a shark. Okay, maybe that overstates the case a *little*, but you get the point. Guess if you don't know the answer but can eliminate at least one answer choice.

COMMON SENSE CAN HELP

Sometimes, an answer on the multiple-choice section contradicts common sense. Eliminate those answers. Common sense works on the AP European History Exam. Which of the answer choices to the question below don't make sense?

26. During the period when England was a republic (1649–1660), which of the following applied to Ireland?

(A) Ireland became primarily Protestant.
(B) Ireland won its independence.
(C) Ireland obtained extensive military assistance from the French.
(D) An army led by Cromwell invaded Ireland and solidified English control.
(E) Ireland underwent a brief but glorious cultural renaissance.

Here's How to Crack It

Common sense should allow you to eliminate answer choice (A) immediately, since you are probably aware that the whole of Ireland has never been primarily Protestant. (B) can be eliminated because independence only came for the Republic of Ireland in the early twentieth century. If (C) actually occurred, then perhaps (B) would have taken place, but that was not what happened. Also, while there is a wonderful Irish literary tradition, there was no "renaissance" during the Cromwellian wars. That leaves (D) as the only correct answer.

CONTEXT CLUES

Some questions contain context clues or vocabulary words that will either lead you to the correct answer or at least help you eliminate an incorrect answer. Look at the question below:

60. In his *Economic Consequences of the Peace* (1919), John Maynard Keynes

(A) supported the reparations payments by the Germans as a necessary evil
(B) argued that the reparations amount was too low to seriously compromise the German economy
(C) charged that by punishing the Germans with a large reparations bill, the entire European economy was threatened
(D) urged that the issue of reparations be postponed for a decade so that the post-war economies could adjust to peace
(E) argued that reparations should be tied to a more stable currency like that of the United States

Here's How to Crack It

Again, you are dealing with a book and an author that you might be less than familiar with, but don't panic—the question itself contains a major clue. The word "consequences" in the title of Keynes's work provides you with the hint that Keynes was possibly critical of the reparations component of the Treaty of Versailles. This bit of information allows you to eliminate (A), (B), (D), and (E), because these answers indicate at least some level of support by Keynes for reparations. The one that stands out from the others is choice (C); it alone seems to be critical of the very concept of German reparations.

DRILL

Here is a group of five questions that could have come from the multiple-choice section of the AP European History Exam. As you work through them, try to apply everything you have learned in this chapter. Use the chronological ordering of the questions to eliminate impossible answers. Keep the big picture in mind as you consider the answer choices. Use Process of Elimination. If you can get rid of one or more answer choices and go no further, guess and move on. Use common sense and context clues. The answers and explanations of how to attack these questions follow the drill. Good luck!

33. Fascism emerged triumphant in Italy in 1922 following

   (A) an armed coup
   (B) a political compromise worked out by the Italian monarch authorizing the Fascists to form a government
   (C) a civil war involving Communists and Fascists
   (D) the assistance of German Fascists
   (E) the emergence of Mussolini as sole leader of the Fascist party following an internal party struggle for power

34. During the Spanish Civil War, the British and French governments

   (A) encouraged the Soviet Union to come to the aid of the Spanish Republic
   (B) refused to offer assistance to the Spanish Republic
   (C) encouraged the League of Nations to intervene to stop the fighting
   (D) waited to see what position the United States would take
   (E) discreetly organized volunteers to go to Spain to aid the Republic

35. The Great Purges eliminated from the Soviet Union

   (A) the Romanovs
   (B) the kulaks
   (C) the Old Bolsheviks
   (D) the intelligentsia
   (E) the Russian Orthodox Church

36. The Truman Doctrine emerged in response to the

   (A) building of the Berlin Wall
   (B) Korean War
   (C) death of Joseph Stalin
   (D) Berlin blockade
   (E) Greek Civil War

37. At the Council of Trent (1545–1563), the Catholic Church

(A) agreed to work with Protestant theologians to work for an acceptable compromise
(B) accepted Protestant positions on most issues but still refused to allow for clerical marriage
(C) decided to wait to formulate a position on most of the issues addressed by the Protestants
(D) rejected Protestant positions on the sacraments, the giving of wine to the laity during communion, and clerical marriage
(E) placed certain constraints on the papacy to limit its ability to implement reforms

Here's How to Crack It

The five questions in the drill are of medium difficulty. On average, between 50 and 70 percent of those taking the test will get each one right. As we discuss how to take your best guess on the following questions, it should go without saying that, if you know the correct answer to the question, you should simply select it and move on. Also, chronological order should have told you that the drill began in the middle of one grouping of questions and that question 37 started a new grouping.

Question 33 has a "big picture" idea that is critical to your understanding of twentieth-century European history. Fascists in both Italy and Germany came to power not through the violent seizure of power but through the democratic process, though once in power, they destroyed all traces of democracy. With this in mind, you can instantly eliminate choices (A) and (C). Choice (D) can also be eliminated because the question provides you with a hint that makes that choice clearly incorrect when it states the year was 1922. Fascism became a significant presence in German political life only following the Depression in 1929, while Hitler became German Chancellor in 1933. Since Mussolini was the founder and undisputed leader of the Fascist Party of Italy, choice (E) is rather unlikely, which leads us to the correct answer, (B).

Question 34 also has one of those "big picture" ideas, this time on the issue of appeasement, the attempt by Britain and France to give in to German demands to avoid war. (E) might have led to a provoking of Hitler, who was openly supporting Franco and the rebels, so it must be wrong; the volunteers from the European democracies and the United States who fought in Spain in support of the Republic did so without any support from their governments. The United States was in isolationist mode at this time, so there was no need to wait for what the Americans would do, because there was never any doubt that they would do nothing. Therefore, (D) is incorrect. By 1936, the year of the start of the Spanish Civil War, the League of Nations had shown itself to be a paper tiger, so (C) is unlikely. It would take a real stretch of the imagination to think that Britain and France, two nations that greatly mistrusted the intentions of the Soviet Union, would encourage the latter's participation in the Spanish Civil War. Therefore, choice (A) is not correct. This leaves us with (B), a tragic mistake by the French and British, though quite in keeping with their desire for appeasement.

Question 35 can be answered by thinking in terms of the chronology of the four questions in this group. Question 33 deals with 1922 and question 34 with 1936. Question 36 can take place no earlier than 1945, because that marks the first year of the presidency of Harry Truman, and in fact, the Truman Doctrine was announced in 1947. This means that question 35 takes place roughly between 1936 and 1945. With this in mind, you can eliminate (A) and (E), because both the old aristocracy and the established church were immediate targets following the Bolshevik Revolution in 1917. You may not have recalled that the collectivization of Soviet agriculture, which led to the mass destruction of the kulaks (wealthy peasants), took place between 1929 and 1933, though if you didn't, at least you could have made an educated guess between this choice and the correct one, (C).

Question 36 requires you to think which provocation led President Truman to state that the United States would come to the aid of nations being subverted either internally or externally by Communists. The death of Stalin was not exactly an act of provocation, so choice (C) is out, and the Berlin Wall was built in 1961, some time after the Truman presidency. You are then left with three events that are close in date and are thematically linked. Although you might want to guess at this point, you may recall that events in Greece were pivotal in shaping an American response to what they saw as the subverting of legitimate regimes in Eastern Europe, and that the Berlin airlift and the entry of the United States into the Korean conflict were examples of the United States carrying out the ideas contained in the Truman Doctrine. The correct answer is therefore (E).

Question 37 jumps back in time several centuries. You have moved up to a slightly more difficult set of questions. Again, think "big picture." What was the Catholic response to the Protestant Reformation? Did the Catholics decide to accept Protestant demands on certain key religious tenets? Certainly not. Therefore, the answer that captures the correct Catholic response can only be choice (D).

Finally, here are the answers to the questions that appear in the first part of this chapter. 3: (A); 6: (D); 45: (B); 13: (E); 16: (D); 21: (D).

SUMMARY

- Don't overextend yourself. If all you need is a final score of 3, don't even try to finish the exam. Take your time and work on the first sixty questions only. If you are shooting for a 4, take your time and work on the first seventy questions only.

- Familiarize yourself with the different types of questions that will appear on the multiple-choice section. Be aware that you will see almost an even split between questions on political and diplomatic history, cultural and intellectual trends, and social and economic themes. Tailor your studies accordingly.

- Look for "big picture" answers. Correct answers on the multiple-choice section confirm important trends in European history. The test will not ask you about weird exceptions that contradict those trends. It also will not ask you about military history. You will not be required to perform miraculous feats of memorization; however, you must be thoroughly familiar with all the basics of European history. There are a lot of them! See our history review in Part II of the book.

- Use the chronological ordering of questions to figure out about which time period you are being asked. Be aware that the questions are presented in groups of four to seven, that each group maintains chronological order, and that each group is a little more difficult than the one that precedes it.

- Use Process of Elimination on all but the easiest questions. Once you have worked on a question, eliminated some answers, and convinced yourself that you cannot eliminate any other incorrect answers, you should guess and move on to the next question.

- Use common sense. Look for context clues.

Cracking the Essay Questions

There are two types of essay questions on the AP European History Exam. The first is the Document-Based Question (DBQ), which requires you to answer a question based on ten to twelve primary-source documents and whatever outside knowledge you have about the subject. The second is the free-response question, which is more like a typical essay question on a history exam. For the free-response section, you are given six questions, three about the period from the Renaissance to the Napoleonic era and three about the period following it. You are required to answer two of these essay questions, one from each group. We will discuss each of these question types in greater detail in the next two chapters. First, let's talk about the basics of writing a successful AP essay.

WHAT ARE THE AP ESSAY GRADERS LOOKING FOR?

In conversations with those who grade AP European History Exams, it is clear that what they want above all else is for you to address the question. In some of your classes, you may have gotten into the habit of throwing everything but the kitchen sink into an essay without truly addressing the question at hand. Do not try to fudge your way through the essay. The graders are all experts in history, and you will not be able to fool them into thinking you know more than you actually do.

It is also very important to focus on the phrasing of the question. Some students are so anxious to get going that they start writing as soon as they know the general subject of the question, and many of these students lose points because their essays do not answer the question being asked. Take, for example, an essay question that asks you to discuss the effects of fascism on the daily life of the average German in the 1930s. If you are an overanxious test taker, you might start rattling off everything you know about German fascism—the reasons for its electoral success in the years leading up to 1933, the personality cult around Adolf Hitler, the Holocaust, and so on. No matter how well this essay is written, you will lose points for one simple reason—not answering the question!

Second, a good essay does more than rattle off facts. Just as the multiple-choice questions seek to draw out certain general principles or the "big picture" of European history, the essay questions seek to do the same. The readers are looking to see that you understand some of the fundamental issues in European history and that you can successfully discuss this material in a coherent manner.

If all this sounds intimidating, read on! There are a few simple things you can do to improve your grade on the AP essays.

REASONS TO BE CHEERFUL

AP graders know that you are given only 15 minutes to prepare and 45 minutes to write about the DBQ and only 70 minutes to write both of your free-response questions. They also know that is not enough time to cover the subject matter tested by the question. The fact is, many very long books have been written about any one subject that you might be asked about on the DBQ and the free-response questions.

The College Board's *AP European History Course Description* advises students to write an essay that has a well-developed thesis, provides support for the thesis with specific examples, addresses all parts of the question, and is generally well organized. Therefore, expressing good ideas and presenting valid evidence in support of those ideas are important. Making sure you mention every single relevant piece of historical information is not so important.

Also, you should remember that graders are not given a lot of time to read your essays. When they gather to read the exams, they each go through more than one hundred per day. No one could possibly give detailed attention to all points in your essay when he or she is reading at such a fast clip. What he or she can see in such a brief reading is whether you have something intelligent to say and whether you have the ability to say it well. Also, as I know from my own career as a professor, when you read many bad essays (and there will be quite a few even among AP students), you tend to give those that are not completely awful more credit than they possibly deserve. Just hope that the essay being read before your own was written by someone who didn't buy this book and was therefore completely unprepared.

THINGS THAT MAKE ANY ESSAY BETTER

There are two essential components to writing a successful timed essay. First, plan what you are going to write before you start writing! Second, use a number of tried-and-true writing techniques that will make your essay appear well organized, well thought-out, and well-written. This section is about those techniques.

BEFORE YOU START WRITING

Read the question carefully. Underline key words and circle dates. Then, brainstorm for one or two minutes. Write down everything that comes to mind in your test booklet. (There is room in the margins and at the top and bottom of the pages.) Look at your notes and consider the results of your brainstorming session as you decide what point you will argue in your essay; that argument is going to be your thesis. Tailor your argument to your information, but by no means choose an argument that you know is wrong or with which you disagree. If you do either of these things, your essay will be awful. Finally, sort the results of your brainstorm. Some of what you wrote down will be "big picture" conclusions, some will be historical facts that can be used as evidence to support your conclusions, and some will be garbage.

Next, make an outline. You should plan to write five paragraphs for each of the three essay questions, and plan to go into special detail in each of the paragraphs on the DBQ. (Remember, you will have the documents and your outside knowledge to discuss on the DBQ. Plus, you will have more time.) Your first paragraph should contain your thesis statement, in which you directly answer the question in just a few sentences. Your second, third, and fourth paragraphs should contain three arguments that support that statement, along with historical evidence to back those arguments. The fifth paragraph should contain your conclusion and reiterate your answer to the question.

Before you start to write your outline, you will have to decide what type of argument you are going to make. Here are some of the classics.

1. MAKE THREE GOOD POINTS

This is the simplest strategy. Look at the results of your brainstorming session, and pick the three best points supporting your position. Make each of these points the subject of one paragraph. Make the weakest of the three points the subject of the second paragraph, and save the strongest point for the fourth paragraph. If your three points are interrelated and there is a natural sequence to arguing them, then by all means use that sequence, but otherwise, try to save your strongest point for last. Begin each paragraph by stating one of your three points, and then spend the rest of the paragraph supporting it. Use specific, supporting examples whenever possible. Your first paragraph should state what you intend to argue. Your final paragraph should explain why you have proven what you set out to prove.

2. MAKE A CHRONOLOGICAL ARGUMENT

Many questions lend themselves to a chronological treatment. Questions about the development of a political, social, or economic trend can hardly be answered any other way. When you make a chronological argument, look for important transitions and use them to start new paragraphs. A five-paragraph essay about the events leading up to the French Revolution, for example, might start with an introductory discussion of France and the role of royal absolutism. This is also where you should state your thesis. The second paragraph might then discuss the economic crisis that led to the calling of the Estates General. The third paragraph could deal with concern among members of the third estate that their interests might not be represented at Versailles, despite the vital economic role they played in eighteenth-century France. The fourth paragraph could be concerned with the events leading up to and including the King's agreement to meet the three estates as a National Assembly. Your conclusion in this type of essay should restate the essay question and answer it. For example, if the question asks whether the French Revolution was inevitable, you should answer "yes" or "no" in this paragraph.

3. IDENTIFY SIMILARITIES AND DIFFERENCES

Some questions, particularly on the free-response section, ask you to compare events, issues, and/or policies. Very often, the way the question is phrased will suggest the best organization for your essay. Take, for example, a question asking you to compare the impact of three events and issues on the decision to execute the English monarch Charles I in 1649. This question pretty much requires you to start by setting the historical scene prior to the three events/issues you are about to discuss. Continue by devoting one paragraph to each of the three, and conclude by comparing and contrasting the relative importance of each. Again, be sure to answer the question in your final paragraph.

Other questions will provide options. If you are asked to compare Italian and Northern humanism during the Renaissance, you might open with a thesis stating the essential similarity or difference between the two. Then, you could devote one paragraph each to a summary of certain trends and authors, while in the fourth paragraph you could point out the major similarities and differences between Italian and Northern humanism. In the final paragraph, you could draw your conclusion (e.g., "their similarities were more significant than their differences," or vice versa).

Or, using another angle altogether, you might start with a thesis, then discuss in the body of your essay three pertinent philosophical, religious, or political issues, then discuss how Italian humanists dealt with such questions, then move on to the Northern humanists, and wrap up with an overview of your argument for your conclusion.

4. USE THE STRAW DOG ARGUMENT

In this essay-writing technique, choose a couple of arguments that someone taking the position opposite yours would take. State their arguments, and then tear them down. Remember that proving your opposition wrong does not mean that you have proved you are correct; that is why you should choose only a few opposing arguments to refute. Summarize your opponent's arguments in paragraph two, dismiss them in paragraph three, and use paragraph four to make the argument for your side. Or, use one paragraph each to summarize and dismiss each of your opponent's arguments, and then make the case for your side in your concluding paragraph. Acknowledging both sides of an argument, even when you choose one over the other, is a good indicator that you understand that historical issues are complex and can be interpreted in more than one way, something teachers and graders like to see.

CONCLUSION

No matter which format you choose, remember to organize your essay so that the first paragraph addresses the question and states how you are going to answer it. (That is your thesis.) The second, third, and fourth paragraphs should each be organized around a single argument that supports your thesis, and each of these arguments must be supported by historical evidence. Your final paragraph ties the essay up into a nice, neat package. Your concluding paragraph should also answer the question. And remember, stay positive!

As You Are Writing, Observe the Following Guidelines

- **Keep sentences as simple as possible.** Long sentences get convoluted very quickly and will give your graders a headache, putting them in a bad mood.

- **Throw in a few big words.** But don't overdo it, because it will look like you are showing off. Remember that good writing does not have to be complicated; some great ideas can be stated simply. NEVER use a word if you are unsure of its meaning or proper usage. A malapropism (misuse of a word) might give your graders a good laugh, but it will not earn you any points, and it will probably cost you.

- **Write clearly and neatly.** As long as we are discussing your graders' moods, here is an easy way to put them in good ones. Graders look at a lot of chicken scratch; it strains their eyes and makes them grumpy. Neatly written essays make them happy. When you cross out, do it neatly. If you are making any major edits—if you want to insert a paragraph in the middle of your essay, for example—make sure you indicate these changes clearly.

- **Define your terms.** Most questions require you to use terms that mean different things to different people. One person's "liberal" is another person's "conservative," and yet another person's "extremist." What one person considers "expansionism," another might call "colonialism," or "imperialism." The folks who grade the test want to know what you think these terms mean. When you use them, define them. Take particular care to define any such terms that appear in the question. Almost all official College Board materials emphasize this point, so do not forget it. Be sure to define any term that you suspect can be defined in more than one way.

- **Use transition words to show where you are going.** When continuing an idea, use words such as "furthermore," "also," and "in addition." When changing the flow of thought, use words such as "however" and "yet." Transition words make your essay easier to understand by clarifying your intentions. Better yet, they indicate to the graders that you know how to make a coherent, persuasive argument.

- **Use structural indicators to organize your paragraphs.** Another way to clarify your intentions is to organize your essay around structural indicators. For example, if you are making a number of related points, number them ("First…Second…And last…"). If you are writing a compare/contrast essay, use the indicators "on the one hand" and "on the other hand."

- **Stick to your outline.** Unless you get an absolutely brilliant idea while you are writing, do not deviate from your outline. If you do, you will risk winding up with an incoherent essay.

- **Try to prove one "big picture" idea per paragraph.** Keep it simple. Each paragraph should make one point and then substantiate that point with historical evidence.

- **Back up your ideas with examples.** Yes, we have said it already, but it bears repeating: Do not just throw ideas out there and hope that you are right (unless you are absolutely desperate). You will score big points if you substantiate your claims with facts.

- **Try to fill the essay form.** An overly short essay will hurt you more than one that is overly long.

- **Make sure your first and last paragraphs directly address the question.** Nothing will cost you points faster than if the graders decide you did not answer the question. It is always a safe move to start your final paragraph by answering the question. If you have written a good essay, that answer will serve as a legitimate conclusion.

- **Always place every essay into a historical context.** For example, if you are given an essay "comparing and contrasting Newton's and Einstein's ideas on the universe," don't make it an essay on science. Instead, show how each of these men was a product of his respective time period, and show how their ideas influenced their contemporaries as well as future generations.

SUMMARY

- Read questions carefully. Be sure you are answering the question that is asked. You must answer the question in order to get full credit.

- Do not start writing until you have brainstormed, chosen a thesis, and written an outline.

- Follow your outline. Stick to one important idea per paragraph. Support your ideas with historical evidence.

- Write clearly and neatly. Do not write in long, overly complex sentences. Toss in a couple of "big" words you know you will not misuse. When in doubt, stick to simple syntax and vocabulary.

- Use transition words to indicate continuity of thought and changes in the direction of your argument.

- Provide a strong historical context. You may be faced with questions focusing on science, economics, philosophy, literature and art, religion, etc. Always remember this is a *history* exam.

- Remember also that this is a *European* history exam (not an *American* history exam). So, for example, if you get a question on technological changes in the nineteenth century, you should focus on Marconi, Siemens, or Bessemer, *not* on Edison or Bell. Similarly, on Cold War questions, don't avoid the U.S., but have your answer reflect Europe's situation as much as possible.

- Study the question. Make sure you understand what it is asking you to write about. Address all parts of the questions. If it asks for "social, political, and economic changes," make sure you discuss all three. If you cannot address the whole question, either choose another question or fake it. If you don't know anything about the social impact, then try to use logic—how would something like this affect society?

- Have at least two concrete facts to support each of your themes (e.g., two themes of social change, two of economics, and two of politics).

5

Cracking the Document-Based Question (DBQ)

WHAT IS THE DBQ?

DBQ stands for "Document-Based Question." The DBQ is an essay question that requires you to interpret *primary-source* documents. (There are typically ten to twelve documents in a DBQ.) These documents will include many, if not all, of the following: newspaper articles and editorials, letters, diaries, speeches, excerpts from legislation, political cartoons, charts, and graphs. The documents will *not* include excerpts from current textbooks. Occasionally, one or two of the documents will be taken from something "classic" that you may have seen previously, but generally, the documents will be new to you. However, they will discuss events and ideas with which you should be familiar. All the documents will pertain to a single subject. The average document is about six lines long, although occasionally you will see something longer.

The 45-minute DBQ is the second part of the AP European History Exam; it is administered immediately after the five- to ten-minute break that follows the multiple-choice section. At the beginning of the DBQ, you will be handed a green booklet in which the essay question and documents are printed, as well as a separate form on which to write your essay. The DBQ session begins with a 15-minute mandatory reading period, during which you are allowed to read the documents and take notes in the DBQ booklet. You may not start recording your essay on the essay form until the 45-minute writing period begins. However, if you finish taking notes and outlining your essay before the reading period is over, you should write a first draft of your opening paragraph in your DBQ booklet; then, when the writing period begins, you can transcribe it into your essay booklet and continue.

To give you an idea of what you can expect on your DBQ, let's look at what appeared on a previous test. The question asked students to describe and analyze problems in the relationship between the English and Irish in the period from 1800 to 1916. The documents included excerpts from the following:

- A quote from English Prime Minister William Pitt, the creator of the Act of Union of 1801, in which he states that "Ireland must be governed in the English interest."

- A parliamentary speech by a Protestant Irish leader dating from 1805 demanding the continuation of exclusive Protestant political rights within the United Kingdom.

- A poem written in 1842 by an Irish Nationalist that speaks of the commonality of interests between Irish Protestants and Catholics.

- An article in the English Conservative Party newspaper from 1848 that claims that anything good in Ireland is due to the influence of England, while the Irish have only themselves to blame for all their problems.

- A declaration of principles from 1879 by the National Land League that states that the "land of Ireland belongs to the people of Ireland."

- A piece of writing from 1900 by Maud Gonne, founder of the Daughters of Ireland, in which she declares that her organization wants to help establish Irish independence in part through a revival of indigenous Irish culture.

- A map showing the distribution in 1901 of Protestants and Roman Catholics in the Irish population.

- A 1907 speech by a Nationalist politician stating that in the long run, the Protestants cannot expect more than the rights enjoyed by minorities in other countries.

- An impassioned speech from a 1911 rally in which Edward Carson, the leader of the Ulster Unionists, warns that, should Home Rule be granted, Protestants must seize the reigns of power in Ulster.

- A proclamation issued during the Easter Rebellion of 1916 declaring the establishment of an independent Irish republic.

As you can see, a typical DBQ may contain documents you have seen prior to the exam. (The proclamation from the Easter Rebellion is often quoted in textbooks.) However, the DBQ also includes documents you certainly have not seen before. Each of the documents, though, represents a political position you have studied. Although you may not know much about the authors of these documents, with the exception of William Pitt the Younger, the tensions between England and Ireland might be familiar to you. In other words, you will not be starting from square one, even when the documents are new to you. Also, the writers of the AP European History Exam provide a paragraph summary of the historical background of the question being asked, which may also provide you with much needed information.

Is There a "Right" Answer to Each DBQ?

No. DBQs are worded in such a way that you can argue any number of positions. In the previous example, the documents provide evidence for various issues that stand at the heart of the Irish-English conflict, such as religious bigotry and questions concerning Home Rule. As long as you support your argument with evidence, you can argue whatever thesis you want.

Graders are supposed to take into account the strength of your argument and the evidence you offer in support of it. In other words, if you forget to mention a good, illustrative historical event but manage to back your point up in some other way, you will not be penalized.

However, in order to earn the most credit for your essay, you must include *outside information*. You will notice that your DBQ contains a phrase that looks something like this:

Using the Documents AND Your Knowledge of the Subject...

"Your knowledge of the subject" is the outside information. It includes historical facts and ideas that are relevant to the question but that are not mentioned in the DBQ documents. For example, in the England and Ireland DBQ described above, any information offered about the writers' backgrounds would count as outside information, as would information concerning, for example, Charles Stuart Parnell and the Land League. Some students make the mistake of throwing everything they know about a subject into their essays, whether or not it pertains to the question. That type of information receives partial credit at best.

HOW IS THE DBQ SCORED?

The College Board uses a "core-scoring method" that is graded on a 1–9 scale. This means that for each DBQ, you can earn up to six points by performing what the graders consider basic tasks, such as using the majority of documents or displaying a point of view or bias in at least three of the documents. In addition, you can earn up to three more points in what they call the "expanded core," by excelling in more difficult areas. To earn any points from the expanded core, students must earn all six points in the basic core.

The following chart might make this scoring system somewhat more comprehensible.

BASIC CORE POINTS

Students may earn a total of six points by earning one point in each of the following areas:

Core Skill	Points
1) Provides a clearly stated and appropriate thesis that addresses all parts of the question. **This thesis should not merely be a restating of the question.**	1
2) Discusses a majority of the documents individually and specifically	1
3) Demonstrates an understanding of the basic meaning of the documents (you may misinterpret no more than one document)	1
4) Supports thesis with an appropriate interpretation of the majority of the documents	1
5) Shows point of view or bias in at least three documents	1
6) Analyzes documents by organizing them into at least three appropriate groups	1

EXPANDED CORE POINTS

If students earn a 6 on the Basic Core, they can then earn up to *three* additional points by displaying some of the following skills:

> 7) Having a clear, analytical, and comprehensive thesis
>
> 8) Using every document or almost every document
>
> 9) Skillfully using documents as evidence
>
> 10) Displaying an understanding of the nuances within the documents
>
> 11) Discussing bias or point of view in at least four documents
>
> 12) Analyzing documents by creating additional groupings or using some other advanced method
>
> 12) Incorporating outside historical knowledge in the essay
>
> 13) Addressing all aspects of the question thoroughly

GETTING THE POINTS

Here are concrete ways to earn the points for each of the skills.

The Basic Core 6 Points

Skill 1

Study the question carefully; make sure you are writing about what the question is actually asking. Misinterpreting the question is the most common mistake students make and results in a zero on the essay. Also, be careful to provide a thesis that is not a regurgitation of the exam question. Failure to come up with your own thesis will also result in a zero.

Skill 2

Try to use every document either explicitly or implicitly.

Skill 3

Show your reader that you understand the basic meaning of the documents. This doesn't mean that there won't possibly be a number of ways of interpreting the document, but make it clear that you understand the connection of your document to the topic at hand.

Skill 4

Write each of your body paragraphs about one of your document groups. Start off with a topic sentence, and write an analysis of the information drawn from the documents in that group. Use quotes or examples to support your analysis. Just quoting for the sake of quoting is a common error among students. Do not assume that quotations can simply stand on their own without any elaboration. Be sure to show the graders that you understand what the quotation means and use the quote in a manner that furthers your argument.

Skill 5

The documents are not fact; they are **opinions.** Write the essay in such a way that this is made clear to the reader.

1) Make a big effort to find Point of View, and keep in mind that *tone* can also present a point of view: e.g., outrage, contempt, or concern. Before you read the document, look at who the author is and when he or she made this statement. Why did the author have this particular point of view? What about the author's background or the time, place, or historical circumstance under which the document was written shaped the writer's outlook on life? Is there an ulterior motive behind the statements made? Do not hesitate to use logic. For example: If the DBQ is about the various views on German unification in the 1860s, why would a German poet, the Italian Foreign Minister, and Otto von Bismarck support unification, while an ethnically French citizen of Alsace-Lorraine, a French socialist politician, and Napoleon III all oppose it?

2) Demonstrate that you are aware that certain documents are more credible than others. A document giving statistics from a government census, for example, is considered more credible than claims made by an editorialist for a party newspaper.

Skill 6

Have three or more groupings. A group cannot contain just one document, and it's safest to use more than two (in case one is used incorrectly). It is fine to use a document more than once.

How to group will vary according to the question. Some DBQs, for example, may ask you to show how various segments of society view a particular issue; some will ask how views on a particular issue have changed over time. Find the documents that have similar points of view and write about those views; in other words, pro versus con, German versus French, liberal versus conservative, nineteenth century versus twentieth century.

You may group according to the reasons and motives behind the arguments. Your groups might be, for example, individuals influenced by nationalist idealism, individuals representing the power politics of the era, and groups representing the internationalism promoted by Karl Marx.

The Additional 3 Points

Skills 8, 10, 11, and 12 ask you simply to take the Basic Core skills even further. Skills 7, 9, and 13 are discussed below.

Skill 7

The thesis is not simply restating the question. It must also answer the question and indicate the various groupings into which the essay is divided.

Skill 9

Use attribution as much as possible. Attribution means that you give credit to the authors of the statements used. It is also useful to cite the document you are quoting. For example, you might write "British Prime Minister William Gladstone stated in his address to Parliament 'blah-blah-blah' (Document 8)." (Citing the document is not mandatory, but it makes it easier for the reader to see which documents you used.) Never write an essay that says, "In document 8, such-and-such is said, which is contradicted by document 13." Your essay is not about the documents; it is about the opinions of the people quoted in the documents.

Skill 13

Unlike the AP U.S. History Exam, the AP European History Exam does not require students to bring in outside information. The topics of the DBQs are often outside the scope of what students have studied. However, if it is possible to bring in any outside information, such as comments about the time period your essay addresses, or historical events that may have been affected by the issue being discussed, this could show a greater historical understanding and give you an extra point in the expanded core (provided, of course, the additional information is correct and relevant).

GETTING STARTED ON THE DBQ: READ THE QUESTION

Start by reading the question. This direction may seem obvious, but it really is not, given how many students write essays on subjects that are only marginally related to the question being asked. Students miss the question because they get anxious during the exam. They panic. They think they are going too slowly. In an effort to speed up, they read half the question, say to themselves, "A-ha! I know what they're going to ask!" and stop reading. Do NOT make this mistake! The question is probably the shortest thing you have to read on the DBQ. Take your time; savor it. Explore its nuances. Essays that address the question fully earn huge bonuses; those essays that ignore parts of the question are doomed to a grade of 5 or lower.

Here's a sample question:

1. "Analyze and discuss why the year 1848 brought about an explosion of revolutionary activity throughout Europe."

As you look over the question, you should ask yourself two questions.

- Do I have an opinion about this subject?
- What must I discuss in order to write a successful essay?

Of the two questions, the second is much more important. You can construct a position later, after you have gathered the information you want to include in your essay. First, you need to figure out what issues you must address and what data you will use in your discussion.

To begin, you might want to break down the question in a variety of ways. Perhaps focus first on economic issues, such as the economic downturn of the 1840s, a decade that some referred to as the "hungry forties." Then move on to critical political issues such as a backlash against the repressive nature of politics in the decades after 1848 or the role of nationalism in the revolutions of 1848. Others might find it more useful to discuss events in 1848 on a nation-by-nation basis, beginning with the collapse of the Orleans monarchy in France and moving on to the revolutionary movements in places such as the German states, the Austrian Empire, Italy, and so on. Finally, you must include a discussion of the given documents and your outside knowledge in the essay.

However you decide to approach the question, it is essential that you take your time. Read carefully to make sure that you understand what issues must be addressed in your essay. Then, determine how to organize the information you plan to collect from the documents and from memory for inclusion in the essay.

ORGANIZING YOUR ESSAY: USE GRIDS AND COLUMNS

Many DBQs ask you to draw comparisons. For those questions, you can always organize your thoughts about a DBQ in a grid. Drawing a grid helps in seeing all sides of an argument, which is important because DBQ graders will reward you for acknowledging arguments other than your own.

For the DBQ question on the revolutions of 1848 (on the previous page), you may find it useful to create a grid like the one shown below. Such a grid will allow you to see the complexity of the events of 1848 and how economics, domestic politics, and nationalism all played a role in fanning the flames of revolution across Europe.

	Economics	Politics	Nationalism
France			
Prussia			
Austria			
Italian States			

As you remember appropriate outside information and as you read the documents, take notes in the appropriate boxes. When it comes time to write your essay, you will find it easier to compare and contrast because your information will already be organized in a way that makes similarities and differences more obvious.

If you cannot draw a grid for a question, you can instead set up column headings. Because every DBQ can be argued from at least two different positions, you can always set up two (or more) columns, designating one for each position. Consider the DBQ about Ireland, which we discussed at the beginning of the chapter. You could create one column, entitled "England," where you can provide examples of English justification for holding onto Ireland. A second column, labeled "Unionist," will give the Unionist argument for remaining part of the United Kingdom, and a third, labeled "National-ist," can provide their argument for creating an independent Irish state, free from British domination. You might even want a fourth column, for information that you know belongs in your essay but that you cannot yet classify (give that the title "To be classified").

Good essays do not just flow out of your pen by accident. They happen when you know what you are going to say *before you start writing*. Although it is difficult (if not impossible) to prepare your entire DBQ essay before you begin writing, given the time constraints, pre-organization and a good outline will get you much closer to that goal.

A Sample Question

Let's take a look at another possible DBQ question.

1. Discuss whether Napoleon was a supporter of the ideas espoused in the eighteenth-century Enlightenment or whether he was an enemy of individual liberty. Answer this question by using BOTH the documents AND your knowledge of the Enlightenment and Napoleonic era.

Your essay will have to show whether you understand certain basic tenets of the Enlightenment and also show your knowledge of the period of Napoleon's domination over France (1799–1815). You will, of course, have to include both analysis of the documents and outside information. Since the question is asking for a basic comparison, you might want to make a simple three-column grid like the one below:

Ideals of Enlightenment	Napoleon pro	Napoleon con

Once you have created your grid, begin organizing information for your essay. At this point, you are probably anxious to start reading the documents. Resist the temptation. You have one more important job to do before you start reading.

GATHER OUTSIDE INFORMATION

Most students read the DBQ documents first and *then* try to think of outside information to supplement their essays. This is a mistake. The reason? *The power of suggestion.* Once you have read the documents—a chore that can take from six to eight minutes—those documents will be on your mind. If you wait until after you have read them to think of outside information, you will not be able to get the documents out of your head. Invariably, you will think of things you have already read about, rather than things you *have not* read about, which is precisely what outside information means.

Plus, reading and processing the documents is a big task. Once you have accomplished that, you will want to get started right away on organizing and writing your essay while the documents are fresh in your mind. You *do not* want to stop to think of outside information to include in your essay. And you certainly do not want to be trying to come up with outside information *while* you are writing your essay. So, do it quickly *before* you read the documents.

Here's what you do. Look at your grid or columns and brainstorm. In a separate blank space in your green booklet (*not* in your grid/columns), write down everything you can think of that relates to the question. Spend just two or three minutes on this task, and then look at what you have written. Cross out what you know you cannot use, and enter the rest into your grid/columns in the appropriate spaces.

Chances are that some of the "outside information" you think of will be mentioned in the documents, which means that it will not be outside information any more. That is no big deal. In fact, you should think of it as something good. If some of what you remembered shows up in the documents, that means you are on the right track toward answering the question!

This is what a brainstorming grid for the Napoleon question might look like.

Ideals of Enlightenment	Napoleon pro	Napoleon con
religious tolerance	• extended religious freedom throughout the empire • concordat	
rational government	• codex Napoleon • increased centralization of government	
equality of individuals	• favored meritocracy	• created imperial title and a new aristocracy • placed relatives on foreign thrones
freedom from repression		• created secret police censorship • jailed and executed political opponents

READ THE DOCUMENTS

After you have gathered outside information to include in your essay, you are ready to read the documents. As you read, keep the following things in mind:

- **The order in which documents appear is almost always helpful.** Very often, the documents in the DBQ appear in chronological order. When they do, it often indicates that you are expected to trace the historical development of the DBQ subject. On such questions, you do not have to write an essay that adheres strictly to chronological order, but chronology should play an important part in the development of your thesis. When the documents appear in an order other than chronological, they are usually organized so that you can easily compare and contrast different viewpoints on a particular event or issue. On these questions, one of your main goals should be to draw those comparisons.

- **Watch for inconsistencies within and among the documents.** The documents will not necessarily agree with one another. In fact, they are almost certain to present different viewpoints on issues and almost as certain to present conflicting accounts of a historical event. Some documents might even contradict themselves! This is intentional. The exam is testing your ability to recognize these contradictions. You are expected to resolve these conflicts in your essay. To do so, you will have to identify the sources of the documents. (See below.)

- **Identify the sources of the documents.** Why do two accounts of the same event contradict each other? Why do two historians, looking at the same data, come up with dissimilar interpretations of their significance? Is it because the people giving these accounts—the sources of the documents—have different perspectives? Identify the sources and explain why their opinions differ. As you explain these differences, look for the following differences between sources:

  - political ideology
  - class
  - race
  - religion
  - gender

  Consider the question on Napoleon. A supporter of the exiled Bourbons would offer a very different point of view on this question than a member of Napoleon's inner circle. The graders will be looking specifically to see if you have tried to explain those differences.

- **Look for evidence that could refute your argument.** Once you have decided what your thesis will be, you will be looking through the documents for evidence to support your argument. Not all the documents will necessarily back you up. Some may appear to contradict your argument. *Do not simply ignore those documents!* As you read them, try to figure out how you might incorporate them into your argument.

  Again, let's consider the Napoleon DBQ. Suppose you argue that Napoleon was a supporter of the ideals of the Enlightenment. Now suppose that one of the documents presents evidence that Napoleon kidnapped a Bourbon prince living in exile in one of the German states and then had him killed. You might be tempted to pretend that the document does not exist. However, you will be better off if you incorporate the document into your essay. By doing this you are acknowledging that this historical issue, like all historical issues, is *complex*. This acknowledgment is good. AP essay graders are instructed to look for evidence that you understand that history has no simple answers and to reward you for it.

As you read the documents, be aware that each one holds a few morsels of information for your essay. Do not fixate on any one document, but at the same time, do not ignore any. Also, as you read the documents, take note of any "outside information" that the document reminds you of and enter it into your grid/columns.

DRILL

Below is a "mini-DBQ" (it has only four documents, instead of the usual ten to twelve). Read through the documents, taking notes in the margins and blank spaces.

1. Discuss the roles of women in the religious conflicts of the sixteenth century.

Document A

Source: a printed pamphlet addressed to Katherine von Bora, the wife of Martin Luther

Woe to you, poor fallen woman, not only because you have passed from light to darkness, from the cloistered holy religion into a damnable shameful life, but also that you have gone from the grace to the disfavor of God, in that you have left the cloister in lay clothes and have gone to Wittenberg like a chorus girl. You are said to have lived with Luther in sin.

Document B

Source: Letter written in 1523 by Agrula von Grumbach, the daughter of a Bavarian noble, to the faculty of the University of Ingolstadt after they had forced a young member of the teaching staff to recant his belief in Luther's theology

What have Luther and Melanchthon taught save the Word of God? You have condemned them. You have not refuted them. Where do you read in the Bible that Christ, the apostles, and the prophets imprisoned, banished, burned, or murdered anyone? You tell us that we must obey the magistrates. Correct. But neither the pope, nor the Kaiser, nor the princes have any authority over the Word of God.

Document C

Source: Examination of Elizabeth Dirks before a Catholic court in 1549 on the charge of being an Anabaptist

Examiner: We understand that you are a teacher and have led many astray. We want to know who your friends are.

Elizabeth: I am commanded to love the Lord my God and honor my parents. Therefore I will not tell you who my parents are. That I suffer for Christ is damaging to my friends.

Examiner: What do you believe about the baptism of children, seeing that you have had yourself baptized again?

Elizabeth: No my Lords, I have not had myself baptized again. I have been baptized once on my faith, because it is written, "Baptism belongs to believers."

Document D

Source: *The Way of Perfection* by St. Teresa of Avila (1515–1582), a prominent Catholic reformer and author of spiritual books

At about this time there came to my notice the harm and havoc that were being wrought in France by these Lutherans and the way in which their unhappy sect was increasing. I felt that I would have laid down a thousand lives to save a single one of all the souls that were being lost there. And, seeing that I was a woman, and a sinner, I determined to do the little that was in me—namely, to follow the evangelical counsels as perfectly as I could, and to see that these few nuns who are here should do the same.

Here's How to Crack It

The writers of the exam have provided you with four different examples of the ways in which women participated in the religious disputes of the sixteenth century. **Document A** may initially look somewhat confusing until you take a moment to think about the source: It is a pamphlet addressed to the wife of Martin Luther. If you forgot about the story of Katherine von Bora and her marriage to Luther, you're in luck, since the document provides you with some background. You should be aware, however, that the position taken in the pamphlet is entirely hostile to both Katherine and Martin Luther. Therefore, it does not take much of a leap of faith to conclude that the document was written by a Catholic who was horrified by Katherine's leaving the cloistered life and by her marriage to Luther.

Document B reveals another side of the participation of women in the religious debates of the Reformation. It is from a woman who actively participated in such questions by championing a young Lutheran teacher. The author, Argula von Grumbach, will not be a familiar name to you, but you can see from the document that she was fully aware of the major issues of the conflict, such as Luther's emphasis on the Bible as the sole source of faith and his rejection of papal authority. Challenging the authorities on behalf of this young man is an interesting example of open defiance, something not usually expected from women in the sixteenth century.

Document C is part of a transcript of a trial of a woman who was accused of being an Anabaptist. Don't panic if you have forgotten what the Anabaptists believed in, since the document explains that Anabaptists believed in adult baptism. As the accused woman Elizabeth Dirks says, "Baptism belongs to believers," implying that it's not appropriate for unaware infants. There are other things that you can pull from this document. One of the accusations that the Catholic authorities mentioned is that she was a teacher, albeit one who was leading people astray. Considering that women were rarely literate in this age, her profession is something to be noted, as should her intense loyalty to her friends, whom she refuses to betray by revealing their presence at her rebaptism. She must have been aware that such a refusal would bring her additional torture, the typical means of extracting a confession.

Document D can be compared with Document B, since once again, a woman actively threw herself into the religious debates of the period. This time, however, our author, St. Teresa of Avila, used her pen not to challenge the Catholic Church but to defend it. She revealed that she found herself as a defender of the church in response to Lutheranism taking root in France. She also grappled with the question as to how, as a woman, she could best serve her church. She would have liked, if the opportunity arose, to "have laid down a thousand lives to save a single one of all the souls that were being lost there," but since that cheery prospect was not open to her, she had to find some other outlet for her anger. So she organized the nuns who still remained in the monastery and recommitted them to the Catholic Church.

That's it for the documents. Now, formulate a thesis, figure out how and where to fit all your information into your argument, and write an essay. Relax. It is easier than it sounds.

DEVELOPING A THESIS

Before you decide on your thesis, GO BACK AND READ THE QUESTION ONE MORE TIME! Make sure that your thesis addresses all the pertinent aspects of the question. Your thesis should not simply restate the prompt; it also has to answer the question. It should include a mention of the groups you have chosen for this question.

For this sample question, your thesis might state that women played an active role in the religious debates of the sixteenth century, both as supporters of a break with Rome and as defenders of the Catholic Church. You can then bring in the variety of experiences revealed in the four sources above to buttress this thesis.

BEFORE THE WRITING PERIOD BEGINS...CREATE AN OUTLINE

At this point, you should still have time left in the mandatory 15-minute reading period. Create an outline with one Roman numeral for each paragraph. Decide on the subject of each paragraph and on what information you will include in each paragraph. Do not rely on your grid/columns if you do not have to. The grid/columns are good for organizing your information but are less efficient for structuring an essay.

If you *still* have time after writing an outline, write a rough draft of your first paragraph in your green booklet, then transcribe it to your essay form once the writing period starts.

WRITE YOUR ESSAY

Go back and read the chapter on "Cracking the Essay Questions" to review good essay-writing techniques. The most important advice when writing your exam is to stay confident. Everyone else taking the test, all across the country, is at least as nervous about it as you are.

SUMMARY

- The DBQ consists of an essay question and ten to twelve historical documents. Most likely, you will not have seen most of the documents before, but they will all relate to major historical events and ideas. The DBQ begins with a 15-minute reading period, followed by a 45-minute writing period.

- There is no single "correct" answer to the DBQ. DBQs are framed so that they can be successfully argued from many different viewpoints.

- Read the essay question carefully. Circle and/or underline important words and phrases. Once you understand the question, create a grid or columns in which to organize your notes on the essay.

- Before you start reading the documents, brainstorm about the question. This way you will gather the all-important "outside information" before you submerge yourself in the documents.

- Read the documents. Read them in order, as there is usually a logic to the order in which they are presented. Pay attention to contradictions within and among the documents and also to who is speaking and what sociopolitical tradition he or she represents. If you have decided on a thesis, keep an eye out for information that might refute your thesis, and be prepared to address it in your essay.

- Decide on a thesis; then write an outline for your essay.

- Do not use the historical background provided as part of your essay.

- Your introductory paragraph should set the historical scene and include a thesis.

- Try to include as many of the documents as you can in your essay.

- When you write the essay, do not be concerned with literary merit. Be sure your essay is logically organized, easy to understand, and always focused on the thesis.

- Know the core. Be sure you address each of the six basic criteria.

- Stay positive. Do not panic. Everyone else is as nervous as you are.

6

Cracking the Free-Response Questions

WHAT ARE THE FREE-RESPONSE QUESTIONS?

The free-response questions consist of six questions grouped into two sections. The first group of three contains questions covering the period from the Renaissance to the Napoleonic era, and the second group of three covers the period from the end of the Napoleonic era to the present. You are required to answer two of these essay questions, one from each group. These questions are probably very similar to the essays your AP teacher has given you on tests throughout the academic year.

The free-response questions are the final section of the AP European History Exam. This section is administered immediately following the DBQ. (You do not get a break between sections.) You are given 70 minutes to write both free-response essays.

The free-response questions, like the DBQ, have no single "correct" answers. Unlike the DBQ, though, the free-response questions are not accompanied by documents; *everything* you include in your free-response answer will be outside information. Also, because you have less time to plan and write the free-response essays, these essays can be shorter and not as comprehensive as your DBQ essay. A simple, defensible thesis, accompanied by an organized essay discussing as much relevant information as you can remember, should earn a top grade. Most free-response questions ask you to *analyze*, *assess*, or *evaluate* the causes and effects of a historical subject, allowing you to write an essay that is primarily descriptive. Here are two examples:

1. Assess the impact of any THREE of the following on the growth of industrialization in Great Britain in the first half of the nineteenth century:

   Choose three: the rise in population
   the entrepreneurial ethic
   plentiful natural resources
   political and social stability

2. Analyze the ways in which Renaissance humanism affected the concept of the individual.

As you can see, the free-response questions allow you to recite what you have learned in class. The subjects should be familiar; the questions are straightforward.

These essays are graded on a 1–9 scale like the DBQ. The DBQ is worth more on your final grade, however, than each free-response essay. When computing your final score, the College Board multiplies your DBQ score by 4.5 and each of your free-response essays by 2.75. Yes, it's confusing, but don't sweat it. All you need to know is the end result: The DBQ is worth 45 percent of your essay grade, and each free-response question is worth 27.5 percent.

WHICH QUESTIONS TO CHOOSE

Choose the questions about which you know the most specific details, NOT the ones that look easiest at first glance. The more you know about the subject, the better your final grade will be.

HOW TO WRITE THE ESSAYS

Since we have covered this information already in the previous two chapters, here are brief directions for how to structure your essay.

- First, read the question and analyze it.

- Second, create a grid or columns and take notes.

- Third, assess your information and devise a thesis.

- Fourth, write a quick outline.

- Lastly, write your essay.

If any of these instructions are unclear, reread the previous two chapters.

As best you can, *split your time evenly between the two essays*. Too many students spend most of their time on the first essay, then do not have enough time to write a decent second essay. Both essays are worth the same amount of points. Treat them equally. Pace yourself, watch the clock, and make sure you are finishing (or, better yet, have finished) your first essay when 35 minutes have passed. Then move directly on to the next essay.

A FINAL NOTE

This chapter is short, not because the free-response questions are unimportant, but because we have already discussed in previous chapters what you need to know to write successful AP essays. The free-response questions are worth more than one-quarter of your grade; they are VERY important. Many students are tempted to ease up when they finish the DBQ because it is so challenging. Do not make that mistake. Reach down for that last bit of energy like a long-distance runner coming into the home stretch. When you reach the free-response questions, you have only a little more than one hour to go. *Then*, you can take it easy.

SUMMARY

- The free-response section consists of two groups of three questions. You must answer one question from each of the groups. The first group covers the period up to the end of the Napoleonic era, and the second group covers the post-1815 period.

- Choose the questions about which you know the most specific details, not the ones that look easiest.

- Study each question carefully. Make sure you are answering the question exactly. If you misinterpret a question and write about something other than what the prompt asks, you will receive a 0 for that question.

- Circle all key words. Consider the dates given; they are clues to what you are to write about. If, for example, a question asks, "How did the nature of the Soviet regime change after 1924?", the question is in fact asking you to show the differences between the leadership and policies of Lenin and Stalin.

- Do not ignore any part of the question. If a question asks you to "Compare and contrast the different personalities and leadership styles of Henry V, Holy Roman Emperor, and his son Philip II, King of Spain, and how these influenced the methods they used to counter the Protestant movement," be sure to address *personalities*, *leadership styles*, and *the ways these influenced policy toward the Reformation*. If you find yourself in a situation in which you do not know enough to answer a part of the question, do not ignore that part. Use the historical knowledge you have, combined with logic, to guess at the answer.

- Once you understand the question, create a grid or columns in which to organize your notes.

- Decide on a thesis, and then write an outline for your essay.

- Follow your outline. Stick to one important idea per paragraph. Provide concrete examples to support the point you are making. We recommend at least two examples per issue.

- Stay focused on the question, and don't go off on tangents. Only write about what the question asks, and carefully choose the evidence to support it. You have very little time to throw together these essays. Do not spend time including information that isn't directly relevant.

- Your introductory paragraph is more than just your thesis. It should also set the historical scene (time, place, historical situation) so that the reader can more clearly understand what your essay is about. In your thesis, do not simply restate the question; be sure to also *answer* the question. The thesis tells the reader what the main points of the essay are.

- Remember: This is a European history exam. If you write about the Cold War, for example, put as much focus as possible on what the Europeans are doing. If your essay deals with literature, art, philosophy, science, economics, social issues, and so on, place the discussion in the correct historical context.

- Do not be concerned with literary merit. Be sure your essay is logically organized, easy to understand, and **always focused on the thesis.** Each paragraph should have a topic sentence, and the essay should close with a concluding paragraph.

- Write clearly and neatly. Do not write in overly complex sentences. Toss in a couple of "big" words that you know you will not misuse. When in doubt, stick to simple syntax and vocabulary.

- Use transition words to indicate continuity of thought and changes in the direction of your argument.

- Keep a close watch on the time. Spend approximately 45 minutes writing the DBQ and 30 minutes on each free-response question. This will ensure that you don't suddenly find yourself with 10 minutes left and an entire essay still to write.

- Stay positive. Do not panic. Everyone else is at least as nervous as you are.

PART II

HISTORY REVIEW

OVERVIEW

The history review on the following pages is meant to serve as a *supplement* to the textbook you use in class, not a *substitute* for your textbook. However, it does cover all major subjects and terms that are likely to appear on the AP European History Exam. If you are familiar with everything in this section, you should do very well on the test.

This review covers some subjects more perfunctorily than they would be covered in a serious treatment of European history. We have weighted this review not toward what we think is most important or most interesting about the history of Europe, but rather toward what we know the AP exam is likely to cover. Please do not be offended if your favorite subject receives short shrift in this book. It does not mean that your interests are unimportant; they simply may not be important *in the context of preparing for the AP exam.* What is summarized here are those events and actions that the writers of the AP exam consider important. Because historical events often exemplify social, political, and economic trends, and because that's what makes those events important to historians (and to test writers), this review focuses on those connections. We have tried to make this section as interesting and brief as possible while remaining thorough.

You'll notice that several names, events, etc. are in **bold** type. This is to facilitate your study when you go back to review particular periods and want to quickly locate specific people, places, or things. There are also some words in *italics* and others in ***bold italics***. Foreign terms and titles of works (such as books, art, etc.) are always in italics and sometimes in bold italics if deemed especially important.

The Renaissance and Reformation
(1350–1600)

Fifteenth- and sixteenth-century intellectuals and artists believed that they were part of a new golden age. **Georgio Vasari**, a sixteenth-century painter, architect, and writer, used the Italian word *rinascità*, meaning **"rebirth,"** to describe the era in which he lived. Vasari and other artists and intellectuals believed that their achievements owed nothing to the backwardness of the Middle Ages and instead were directly linked to the glories of the Greek and Roman world. History tells us that they were kidding themselves. The **Renaissance** artisans owe far more to the cultural and intellectual achievements of the medieval world than they cared to acknowledge. Nevertheless, the Renaissance was a time in which significant contributions were made to Western civilization, with particular gains in literature, art, philosophy, and political and historical thought. Our modern notion of **individualism** was also born during the Renaissance, as people sought to receive personal credit for their achievements, as opposed to the medieval ideal of all glory going to God.

These intellectual and artistic developments first took place in the vibrant world of the Italian **city-states**. Eventually, the invention of the **printing press** in the mid-fifteenth century allowed these cultural trends to spread to other parts of Europe, which resulted in the creation of the **Northern Renaissance** movement. The Italian Renaissance writers were primarily interested in secular concerns, but in the north of Europe, the Renaissance dealt with religious concerns and ultimately helped lay the foundation for the movement known as the **Protestant Reformation**.

THE ITALIAN CITY-STATES

The Italian States During the Renaissance

The city-states of Renaissance Italy were at the center of Europe's economic, political, and cultural life throughout the fourteenth and fifteenth centuries. During the Middle Ages, the towns of northern Italy were nominally under the control of the **Holy Roman Empire**; residents, however, were basically free to decide their own fate, which resulted in a tremendously vibrant—and at times violent—political existence. The old nobility, whose wealth was based on land ownership, often conflicted with a new class of merchant families who had become wealthy in the economic boom times of the twelfth and thirteenth centuries. Both groups had to contend with an urban underclass, known as the *popolo*, or "the people," who wanted their own share of the wealth and political power.

In Florence in 1378, the *popolo* expressed their dissatisfaction with the political and economic order by staging a violent struggle against the government that became known as the **Ciompi Revolt**. The revolt shook Florence to its very core and resulted in a brief period in which the poor established a tenuous control over the government.

This struggle reverberated in the other city-states throughout Italy. In Milan, the resulting social tensions led to the rise of a tyrant or *signor*, and the city eventually came to be dominated by the family of a mercenary (*condottiero*) named Sforza. Florence and Venice remained republics after the revolt, but a few wealthy families dominated them. The most noteworthy of these families was the **Medici**, who used the wealth gained from banking to establish themselves first as the behind-the-scenes rulers of the Florentine republic and later as hereditary dukes of the city.

The internal tensions within the city-states were matched by external rivalries as the assorted city-states were engaged in long-term warfare among themselves. By the mid-fifteenth century, these external wars had effectively narrowed the numerous city-states of the medieval age to just a few dominant states—Florence, Milan, and Venice in the north, the **papal states** in central Italy, and the Kingdom of Naples in southern Italy.

In addition to every city-state's internal and external tensions that may have helped stir the creative energy that was so important to the Renaissance, economic factors were also a significant energy-creating agent. The Italian city-states were far more economically vibrant than the rest of Western Europe, with merchants carrying Italian wool and silk to every part of the continent, and with Italian bankers providing loans for money-hungry European monarchs. Wealthy Italian merchants became important **patrons** of the arts and insisted on the development of secular art forms, such as portraiture, that would represent them and their accumulated wealth to greatest effect.

Geography also played a role in the vibrant cultural life of the Italian Renaissance. Italy's central location in the Mediterranean was ideal for creating links between the Greek culture of the east and the Latin culture of the west. Additionally, southern Italy had been home to many Greek colonies and later served as the center for the Roman Empire. In essence, classical civilization had never totally disappeared from the Italian mainland, even following the collapse of the western half of the Roman Empire in the fifth century.

HUMANISM

Humanism is a highly debated term among historians. Most would characterize it not as representing a particular philosophical viewpoint but rather as a program of study, including rhetoric and literature, based on what students in the classical world (c. 500 B.C.E.–500 C.E.) would have studied. **Francesco Petrarch** (1304–1374) is often considered the father of humanism. Petrarch became dissatisfied with his career as a lawyer and set about to study literary classics. It was Petrarch who coined the phrase **"Dark Ages"** (c. 400–900) to denote what he thought was the cultural decline that took place following the collapse of the Roman world in the fifth century.

While literate in *medieval* Latin from his study of law, Petrarch learned *classical* Latin as preparation to study these important literary works. In a task that was to become exceedingly important during the Renaissance, Petrarch sought out classical texts that had been largely unknown during the Middle Ages. It was common in the Middle Ages to become familiar with classical works not by directly reading the original manuscripts but rather by reading secondary commentaries about the works. Petrarch set out to read the originals and quickly found himself engaged with such works as the letters of **Cicero**, an important politician and philosopher whose writings provide an account of the collapse of the Roman Republic. Cicero was a brilliant Latin stylist. To write in the Ciceronian style became the stated goal of Petrarch and those humanists who followed in his path.

Although his contemporaries accused him of turning to the pagan culture of ancient Greece and Rome, Petrarch—despite his fascination with classical culture—did not reject Christianity. Instead, he argued for the universality of the ideas of the classical age. Petrarch contended that classical works, although clearly written by pagans, still contained lessons that were applicable to his own Christian age.

Although Petrarch was not interested in investigating how his studies of the classics could be used to educate others, his work did prove inspirational to a group of wealthy young Florentines known as the "**civic humanists**." They viewed Cicero's involvement in political causes as justification to use their own classical education for the public good. They did this by serving Florence as diplomats or working in the chancellery office, where official documents were written. They also went beyond Petrarch's achievements by studying a language that had almost been completely lost in Western Europe—classical Greek.

The revival of Greek is one of the most important aspects of the Italian Renaissance. It allowed Westerners to become acquainted with that part of the classical heritage that had been lost during the Middle Ages—most significantly the writings of the ancient Greek philosopher **Plato** (427–348 B.C.E.). Plato held a great deal of interest for Renaissance writers. In particular, they were fascinated by his belief that ideals such as beauty or truth exist beyond the ability of our senses to recognize them, and that we can train our minds to make use of our ability to reason and thus get beyond the limits imposed by our senses. This positive Platonic view of human potential is found in one of the most famous passages from the Renaissance, **Pico della Mirandola's** *Oration on the Dignity of Man*.

Renaissance humanist scholarship branched out in a number of different directions. Some writers strove to describe the ideal man of the age. In **Castiglione's** *The Courtier* (1528), such a person would be a man who knew several languages, was familiar with classical literature, and was also skilled in the arts—what we might label today as a "Renaissance Man." Other contributions were made in the new field of critical textual analysis. **Lorenzo Valla** was one of the critical figures in this area. Working in the Vatican libraries, he realized that languages can tell a history all their own. In 1440, he proved that the *Donation of Constantine*, a document in which Constantine, the first Christian Emperor, turned control of the western half of his empire over to the papacy, could not have been written by Constantine. Valla noticed that the word fief was used by Constantine in describing the transfer of authority to the pope, a word that Valla knew was not in use until the eighth century, around four hundred years after Constantine's death. In another work that influenced the humanists in northern Europe, Valla took his critical techniques to the Vulgate Bible, the standard Latin bible of the Middle Ages, and showed that its author, Jerome, had mistranslated a number of critical passages from the Greek sources.

Women were also affected by the new humanist teachings. Throughout the Middle Ages, there were women, very often attached to nunneries, who learned to read and write. During the Renaissance, an increasing number of wealthy, secular women picked up these skills. The humanist scholar **Leonardo Bruni** even went so far as to create an educational program for women, but tellingly left out of his curriculum the study of rhetoric or public speech, critical parts of the male education, since women had no outlet to make use of these skills. **Christine de Pisan**, an Italian who was the daughter of the physician to the French King Charles V, received a fine humanist education through the encouragement of first her father and later her husband. She wrote *The City of Ladies* (1405) to counter the popular notion that women were inferior to men and incapable of making moral choices. Pisan wrote that women have to carve out their own space or move to a "City of Ladies" in order for their abilities to be allowed to flourish. (This idea would later be espoused by Virginia Woolf in her early twentieth-century work, *A Room of One's Own*.)

RENAISSANCE ART

It is arguably in the area of **fine arts** that the Renaissance made its most notable contribution to Western culture. A number of different factors drove Renaissance art. In a reflection of the shift toward individualism, Renaissance artists were now considered to be important individuals in their own right, whereas in the Middle Ages they toiled as anonymous craftsmen. These artists sought prestige by competing for the patronage of secular individuals such as merchants and bankers, who wanted to sponsor art that would glorify their achievements rather than tout the spiritual message that was at the heart of medieval art.

These patrons demanded a more naturalistic style, which was aided by the development of new artistic techniques, including the rejection of the old practice of hierarchical sealing, in which figures in a composition were sized in proportion to their spiritual significance. In the Middle Ages, painting consisted of **fresco** on wet plaster or tempera on wood. In the fifteenth century, oil painting, which developed in the north of Europe, became the dominant method in Italy. Artists also began to make use of *chiaroscuro*, the use of contrasts between light and dark, to create three-dimensional images. Perhaps the most important development was in the 1420s with the discovery of **single-point perspective,** a style in which all elements within a painting converge at a single point in the distance, allowing artists to create more realistic settings for their work.

In architecture, one can see the increasing influence of classical motifs, such as the use of simple symmetrical decorations and classical columns. Perhaps the most noteworthy architectural achievement of the Early Renaissance period was the building of a dome over the Cathedral of Florence by **Filippo Brunelleschi**, the first dome to be completed in western Europe since the collapse of the Roman Empire.

The end of the fifteenth century marked the beginning of the movement known as the **High Renaissance.** During the High Renaissance, Rome replaced Florence as the great center of artistic patronage. Florence had experienced a religious backlash against the new style of art, while in Rome, a series of popes (most notably **Michelangelo**'s great patron **Julius II**) were very interested in the arts and sought to beautify their city and their palaces. The High Renaissance lasted until around the 1520s, when art began to move in a different direction. We sometimes label this art as Late Renaissance or **Mannerism**, an art that showed distorted figures and confusing themes and may have reflected the growing sense of crisis in the Italian world due to both religious and political problems.

There are three major High Renaissance artists with whom you should be familiar.

LEONARDO DA VINCI

While it is a bit of a cliché to label **Leonardo da Vinci** (1452–1519) as a Renaissance man, the label is accurate. Leonardo was a military engineer, an architect, a sculptor, a scientist, and an inventor whose sketchbooks (now owned by Bill Gates) reveal a remarkable mind that came up with workable designs for submarines and helicopters. Oh yes, he was also a painter, as the hordes of tourists snaking their way through the Louvre to see the *Mona Lisa* will attest.

RAPHAEL

In an age of artistic prima donnas, **Raphael** (1483–1520), a kindly individual, stands out for not being despised by his contemporaries. He came from the beautiful Renaissance city of Urbino and died at the early age of 37, but in his brief life, he was given some very important commissions in the Vatican palaces. Besides his wonderfully gentle images of Jesus and Mary, Raphael links his own times and the classical past in *The School of Athens*, which shows Plato and Aristotle standing together (in a crowd that also features the images of Leonardo and Michelangelo) in a fanciful classical structure and uses the deep, single-point perspective characteristic of High Renaissance style.

MICHELANGELO

Like Leonardo, **Michelangelo** (1475–1564) was skilled in numerous areas. His sculptural masterpiece *David* was commissioned by Michelangelo's native city, Florence, as a propaganda work to inspire the citizens in their long struggle against the overwhelming might of Milan. Four different popes commissioned works from him, most notably the warlike Julius II, who gave Michelangelo the task of creating his tomb. Julius II also employed Michelangelo to work on the **Sistine Chapel** in the Vatican, a work that Julius II began to have doubts about as he rushed to have the revealing anatomy of some of the figures covered up with fig leaves, much to the anger of its creator. Michelangelo, who enjoyed a very long life, lived to see the style of art in Italy change from the harmony and grace of the High Renaissance to the more tormented style of the Late Renaissance, as viewed in his final work in the Sistine Chapel, the brilliant yet disturbing *Final Judgement*.

THE NORTHERN RENAISSANCE

By the late fifteenth century, Italian Renaissance humanism began to affect the rest of Europe. Although the writers of the Italian Renaissance were Christian, they thought less about religious questions than their northern counterparts. In the north, questions concerning religion were paramount. Christianity had arrived in the north later than in the south, and northerners at this time were still seeking ways to deepen their Christian beliefs and understanding and display what good humanists they were. They believed they could achieve this higher level by studying early Christian authors. Eventually, northern writers such as Erasmus and More, often referred to as **Christian Humanists**, criticized their mother church, only to find to their horror that more extreme voices of dissent—for example, that of Martin Luther—had not used their methodology to find ways to better the Catholic Church, but to justify why the church had strayed from the will of God.

ERASMUS AND SIR THOMAS MORE

The greatest of the northern humanists was **Desiderius Erasmus** (1466?–1536). You can thank Erasmus the next time you use such tired clichés as "Where there's smoke, there's fire," since he collected this and many other ancient and contemporary proverbs in his *Adages*. Erasmus's *In Praise of Folly* used satire as a means of criticizing what he thought were the problems of the church. His *Handbook of the Christian Knight* emphasized the idea of inner faith as opposed to the outer forms of worship, such as partaking of the sacraments. Erasmus's Latin translation of the New Testament also played a major role in the sixteenth-century movement to better understand the life of the early Christians through its close textual analysis of the *Acts of the Apostles*. Erasmus was at first impressed with Luther's attacks on the church and even initiated a correspondence with him. Eventually, however, the two men found that they had significant disagreements. Unlike Luther, Erasmus was committed to reforming the church, not abandoning it, and he could never accept Luther's belief that man does not have free will.

Another important northern humanist was the Englishman **Sir Thomas More** (1478–1535). A friend of Erasmus, he wrote the classic work *Utopia* (1516). More, who coined the term *utopia*, which literally means "nowhere," was critical of many aspects of contemporary society and sought to depict a civilization in which political and economic injustices were limited by having all property held in common. More, like Erasmus, was highly critical of certain practices of his church, but in the end he gave his life for his beliefs. In 1534, Henry VIII had More, who was serving the King as his chancellor, executed for refusing to take an oath recognizing Henry as Head of the Church of England.

NORTHERN RENAISSANCE CULTURE

The Northern Renaissance also represented more than simply the Christian humanism of individuals such as More and Erasmus. Talented painters from the north, while clearly influenced by the artists of the Italian Renaissance with whom they often came into contact on visits to the Italian peninsula, also created their own unique style. This is seen, for example, in the work of **Albrecht Durer**, a brilliant draftsman, whose woodcuts powerfully lent support to the doctrinal revolution brought about by his fellow German, Martin Luther.

The greatest achievement in the arts in northern Europe in the sixteenth and early seventeenth centuries took place in England, a land that had, up until then, been a bit of a cultural backwater, with the notable exception of **Geoffrey Chaucer**, whose *Canterbury Tales* were based on *The Decameron* by **Boccaccio** (both works written during the fourteenth century). There is perhaps no way to explain the emergence of the sheer number of men possessing exceptional talent during the reign of Queen Elizabeth, since providing her with much credit for this cultural awakening seems to be unwarranted. In fact, much of what we refer to as the **Elizabethan Renaissance** occurred during the reign of her cousin and heir, James I.

Although **Christopher Marlowe** and **Ben Jonson** are both writers of significant repute, the age produced an unrivaled genius in **William Shakespeare** (1564–1616). Though little is known of Shakespeare's life and the question of the provenance of his plays will never be answered to the satisfaction of all, apparently this man, who received little more than a primary school education, was able to author plays such as *Hamlet* and *King Lear*, works that reveal an unsurpassed understanding of the human psyche as well as a genius for dramatic intensity.

THE PRINTING PRESS

The search for new ways to produce text became important in the late medieval period, when the number of literate individuals rose considerably as the number of European universities increased. The traditional method of producing books, via a monk working dutifully in a monastic scriptorium, was clearly unable to meet this heightened demand. Although the question as to who was actually first to print using movable type is much debated, **Johannes Gutenberg**, from the German city of Mainz, is generally given the honor. Between 1452 and 1453, Gutenberg printed approximately 200 bibles and spent a great deal of money making his bibles as ornate as any handwritten version. He eventually went broke. The significant increase in literacy in the sixteenth century supports the theory that few inventions in human history have had as great an impact as the printing press. It is hard to imagine the Reformation spreading so rapidly without the books that informed people of the nature of the religious debate.

THE PROTESTANT REFORMATION

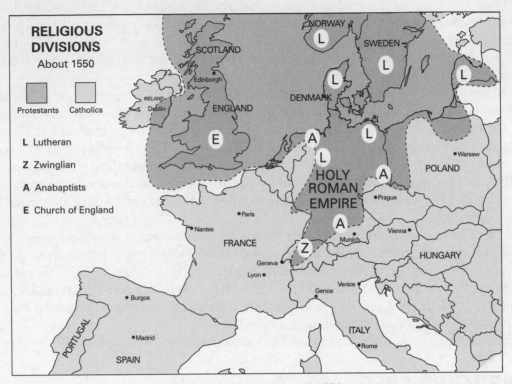

RELIGIOUS DIVISIONS
About 1550

☐ Protestants ☐ Catholics

L Lutheran
Z Zwinglian
A Anabaptists
E Church of England

Religious Divisions Around 1550

In western Europe in the year 1500, the simple declarative sentence, "I went to church on Sunday," could mean only one thing, as only one church existed in the West. At the top of this hierarchical church sat the pope in Rome, to whom all of Europe looked for religious guidance. Several decades later, the **Protestant Reformation** movement resulted in the great split in western Christendom, which dethroned the pope as the single religious authority in Europe. Although it took several decades, eventually there was a Catholic response to this challenge known as the **Catholic Reformation**.

In part, the Reformation of the sixteenth century was a reflection of the ways in which Europe was changing. The humanism of the Renaissance, particularly in the north of Europe, had led individuals to question certain practices such as the efficacy of religious relics and the value to one's salvation of living the life of a monk. In addition, the printing press had made it possible to produce bibles in ever greater number, which made the church's exclusive right to interpret the scriptures seem particularly vexing to those who could now read the text themselves. The rise of powerful monarchical states also created a situation in which some rulers began to question why they needed to listen to a distant authority in Rome.

> One important thing to keep in mind is that on the AP exam, the College Board will not be playing the role of your Sunday school teacher. You are not looking for absolute religious truths, so when dealing with religious questions, leave your personal beliefs at the door and think as a historian.

PROBLEMS FACING THE CHURCH ON THE EVE OF THE REFORMATION

It is important for the student of the sixteenth-century Reformation to remember that the Reformation is far more than just the story of **Martin Luther** (1483–1546). While Luther is a central figure in the story, to reduce it simply to his own struggles against the Catholic Church simplifies what is a complex and compelling story.

The church was facing a number of significant problems on the eve of the Reformation. Some of these problems resulted from the crisis of the fourteenth century, when the **Black Death,** a ferocious outbreak of plague, struck the population of Europe. These problems included a growing **anticlericalism**—a measure of disrespect toward the clergy, stemming in part from what many perceived to be the poor performance of individual clergymen during the crisis years of the plague. Geoffrey Chaucer's *The Canterbury Tales* and Boccaccio's *The Decameron* reveal some of the satirical edge with which society now greeted clergymen. Additionally, this period witnessed a rise in **pietism**, or the notion of a direct relationship between the individual and God, thereby reducing the importance of the hierarchical church based in Rome. The fourteenth century was undoubtedly a disaster for the church, with the papacy under French dominance in the city of Avignon for almost 70 years. It was further damaged by the **Great Schism**, which for a time resulted in the sad specter of three competing popes excommunicating each other.

Other problems on the eve of the Reformation included a poorly educated lower clergy. Peasant priests, who in many cases knew just a bit of Latin, proved to be unable to put forward a learned response to Luther's challenge to their church. **Simony**, the selling of church offices, was another considerable problem, as was the fact that some clergy held multiple positions, thus making them less than effective in terms of ministering to their flocks.

In response to some of these problems, a number of movements arose in the late Middle Ages that would be declared heretical by the church. In England, **John Wycliffe** (1329–1384) questioned the worldly wealth of the church, the miracle of transubstantiation, the teachings of penance, and, in a foretaste of the ideas of Luther, the selling of indulgences. Wycliffe urged his followers (known for unclear reasons as the **Lollards**) to read the Bible and to interpret it themselves. To aid in this task, Wycliffe translated the Bible into English.

In Bohemia (the modern-day Czech Republic), **Jan Hus** (1369–1415) led a revolt that combined religious and nationalistic elements. Hus, the rector of the University of Prague, argued that it was the authority of the Bible and not the institutional church that ultimately mattered. Like Wycliffe, he was horrified by what he saw as the immoral behavior of the clergy. This antagonism toward the clergy and its special role in administering the sacraments led Hus to argue that the congregation should be given the cup during the mass as well as the wafer, something that only clergymen were allowed. Hus was called before the **Council of Constance** in 1415 by **Pope Martin V**, and while promised safe passage, he was condemned as a heretic and burnt at the stake. In response, his followers in Bohemia staged a rebellion, which took many years to put down.

MARTIN LUTHER

The initial issue that first brought attention to Martin Luther (1483–1546) was the debate over indulgences. The **selling of indulgences** was a practice that began during the time of the Crusades. To get knights to go on crusades, the papacy sold indulgences, which released the buyer from **purgatory**. Eventually, long after the crusading movement had ended, the church began to grant indulgences as a means of filling its treasury. In 1517, **Albert of Hohenzollern**, who already held two bishoprics, was offered the Archbishopric of Mainz. He had to raise 10,000 ducats, so he borrowed the money from the great banking family of the age—the **Fuggers**. To pay off his debt, the papacy granted him permission to raise money from the preaching of an indulgence, with half of the money going directly to Rome, where the papacy was in the midst of a program to finally complete St. Peter's Basilica. **Johann Tetzel**, a Dominican friar, was sent to preach the indulgence throughout Germany with the famous phrase: "As soon as gold in the basin rings, the soul to heaven rings."

Luther was horrified by the behavior of Tetzel and tacked up his *95 Theses* on the Castle Church at **Wittenberg**, which was the medieval way of indicating that an issue should be debated. Part of Luther's complaints dealt with German money going to Rome. Another major point involved control over purgatory. If the pope had control over it, Luther wondered, why didn't he allow everyone out? Luther believed that a pope could only remit penalties that he himself had placed on someone. Therefore, the pope had no right to sell misleading indulgences.

In a reflection of the power of the printing press, the *95 Theses* were quickly printed all over Germany. At first, the papacy was not concerned. **Pope Leo X** reportedly said he was not interested in a squabble between monks. The Dominicans wanted to charge Luther with heresy, but Luther soon found himself with a large number of supporters.

Luther began to move in a more radical position. In part, a great deal of his attack on the church was based on his own fears that he was unworthy of salvation. Back in 1505, he was caught in a thunderstorm and a bolt of lightning struck near him. He cried out, "St. Anne help me; I will become a monk." Unlike many of you who will make many promises to God for help on your AP exam, Luther kept his promise and joined the Augustinian order. However, Luther was dissatisfied leading the life of a monk. In later years, he claimed that if any monk could have been saved by what he termed "monkery," it was he:

> Though I lived as a monk without reproach, I felt that I was a sinner before
> God with an extremely disturbed conscience. I could not believe that He was
> placated by my satisfaction. I did not love, yes, I hated the righteous God
> who punishes sinners, and I was angry with God.

Still troubled, Luther went on to be appointed Professor of Scriptures in Wittenburg in Electoral Saxony.

Following the publication of his *95 Theses*, Luther engaged in a public debate on these issues in Leipzig, where **John Eck**, a prominent theologian, challenged him. Eck was to call Luther a Hussite, while Luther claimed that Hus had been unjustly condemned at the Council of Constance. After this debate, Luther spent the year 1520 writing three of his most important political tracts.

1) In his *Address to the Christian Nobility*, he urged that secular government had the right to reform the church;

2) In his *On the Babylonian Captivity of the Church*, Luther attacked other teachings of the church such as the **sacraments**.

3) Finally, in *Liberty of a Christian Man*, he hit on what would become the basic elements of Lutheran belief: Grace is the sole gift of God; therefore, one is saved by faith alone, and the Bible is the sole source of this faith.

In response to these works, Pope Leo X finally decided he had to act. He issued a papal bull (an official decree) that demanded that Luther recant the ideas found in his writings or be burnt as a heretic. In a highly symbolic gesture, Luther publicly burned the bull to show that he no longer accepted papal authority. In turn, the pope excommunicated Luther.

Luther was fortunate in that, unlike Hus, he had some important patrons. Some German princes, such as **Frederick the Elector of Saxony**, were either sympathetic to Luther's ideas or at least wanted him to be given a public hearing. To that end, in 1521 Luther appeared before the **Diet of Worms**, a meeting of the German nobility. In one of the most famous scenes in history, Luther was asked by **Charles V, the Holy Roman Emperor**, "Do you or do you not repudiate your books and the errors they contain?" Luther began to answer with a quivering voice but then gathered his courage and said:

> Unless I am convicted by Scripture and plain reason—I do not accept the authority of popes and councils, for they have contradicted each other—my conscience is captive to the Word of God. I cannot and I will not recant anything, for to go against conscience is neither right nor safe. God help me. Amen.

In response, Luther was placed under the ban of the Empire but was safely hidden over the next year in Wartburg Castle by the Elector of Saxony. In the castle, Luther continued to write prolifically and finished some of his most important works, including a translation of the Bible into German.

Since he now considered papal authority to be a human invention, Luther and his friend Philip Melanchthon decided to form a new church based on his revolutionary ideas free from papal control. Instead of the seven sacraments of the Catholic Church (Marriage, Ordination, Extreme Unction, Confirmation, Penance, Communion, Baptism), he reduced them to two—baptism and communion. Luther changed the meaning of the latter (also called The Holy Eucharist) by rejecting the Catholic idea of **transubstantiation**, the miraculous transformation of the bread and wine into the flesh and blood of Christ, an act that could be performed only by an ordained priest. Instead, Luther claimed that Christ was already present in the sacrament. Luther also did away with the practice of monasticism and the insistence on the celibacy of the clergy. He himself went on to have a happy marriage with a former nun with whom he had several children.

WHY DID THE REFORMATION SUCCEED?

Within three decades after Luther posted his *95 Theses*, **Protestantism**[1] had spread to many of the states of northern Germany, Scandinavia, England, Scotland, and parts of the Netherlands, France, and Switzerland. There are a number of possible explanations for its phenomenal success.

Luther and the church that he founded were socially conservative and therefore not a threat to the existing social order. Luther's conservatism can be seen clearly in the **German Peasant's Revolt** of 1525. The revolt was the result of the German peasants' worsening economic conditions and their belief, articulated in the **Twelve Articles**, that Luther's call for a **"priesthood of all believers"** was a message of social egalitarianism. It certainly was not. The revolt and the distortion of his ideas horrified Luther. He published a violently angry tract entitled "Against the Robbing and Murderous Hordes of Peasants," in which he urged that no mercy be shown to the revolutionaries.

---

[1] The term today is used very broadly and means any non-Catholic or non-Eastern Orthodox Christian. Initially it referred to a group of Lutherans who in 1529 attended the **Diet of Speyer** in an attempt to work out a compromise with the Catholic Church and ended up "protesting" the final document that was drawn up at its conclusion.

Luther was willing to subordinate his church to the authority of the German princes. Political questions were not of great importance to Luther, who felt that what occurred on this Earth was secondary to what truly mattered—the Kingdom of Heaven. He was not critical of the German princes who created state churches under their direct control. Luther also encouraged German princes to confiscate the lands of the Catholic Church, and many rulers did not have to be asked twice, in part because one-quarter of all land in the Holy Roman Empire was under church control.

Political issues within the Holy Roman Empire (see Chapter 8) produced turmoil. When the **Emperor Maximilian** died in 1519, his grandson and heir **Charles V** was caught in a struggle with the French King **Francis I** to see who would sit on the Imperial throne. Although Charles V was able to muster enough bribe money, borrowed from the Fuggers, to convince the rulers of the electoral states to select him, he was ultimately unable to effectively control his empire. Also, as ruler of a vast multinational empire that included Spain and its possessions in the New World, the Netherlands, southern Italy, and the Habsburg possessions in Austria, Charles had huge commitments. He was unable to deal with the revolt in Germany for several critical decades because he was involved in extended wars with France as well as with the powerful **Ottoman Empire** to the east. In the 1540s, the **Schmalkaldic Wars** were fought between Charles and some of the Protestant princes. While for a time Charles had the upper hand, by 1555 he was forced to sign the **Peace of Augsburg**. This treaty granted legal recognition of Lutheranism in those territories ruled by a Lutheran ruler, while a Catholic ruler ensured that the territory remained Catholic.

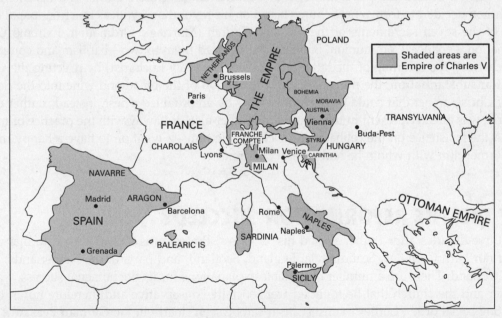

The Empire of Charles V

RADICAL REFORMATION

Historians sometimes use the term **"Radical Reformation"** to describe a variety of religious sects that developed during the sixteenth century, inspired in part by Luther's challenge to the established church. Many felt that Luther's Reformation did not go far enough in bringing about a moral transformation of society.

One such group was the **Anabaptists**, who upon reading the Bible, began to deny the idea of infant baptism. Instead they believed that baptism only works when it is practiced by adults who are fully aware of the decision they are making. Eventually, rebaptism, as the practice became known, was declared a capital offense throughout the Holy Roman Empire, something on which both the pope and Luther heartily agreed. Attacks against Anabaptists became even worse following the Anabaptist takeover of the city of Munster in 1534, during which time they attempted to create an Old Testament theocracy in which men were allowed to have multiple wives. Following the capture of Munster by combined Catholic and Protestant armies, Anabaptism moved in the direction of pacifism under the leadership of Menno Simons.

Besides Anabaptists, other groups such as the **Antitrinitarians**, who denied the scriptural validity of the Trinity, were part of the Radical Reformation. Both Catholics and Lutherans hunted down those who held such beliefs.

ZWINGLI AND CALVIN

Shortly after the appearance of Luther's *95 Theses*, **Ulrich Zwingli's** (1484–1531) teachings began to make an impact on the residents of the Swiss city of Zurich. Many of his ideas were similar to Luther's, with some important differences. Zwingli was a strict sacramentarian in that he denied all the sacraments. To him, the Last Supper was a memorial of Christ's death and did not entail, as it did for Luther, the actual presence of Christ. Zwingli was also a Swiss patriot in ways that Luther could not be called a German patriot. Zwingli was far more concerned with this world and called for social reform. He died leading the troops of Zurich against the Swiss Catholic cantons in battle.

John Calvin (1509–1564) was born in France, although he eventually settled in Geneva, Switzerland. His main ideas are found in his *Institutes of the Christian Religion*, in which he argued that grace was bestowed on relatively few individuals, and the rest were consigned to hell. Since God was all-powerful and had already predestined our fate, there was no room for free will. Calvin was a strict disciplinarian who did his best to make Geneva the new Jerusalem. He closed all the taverns and inflicted penalties for such crimes as having a gypsy read your fortune.

Calvinism began to spread rapidly in the 1540s and 1550s, becoming the established church in Scotland, while in France—where the Calvinists were known as **Huguenots**—only a significant minority joined. In many ways, it can be said that Calvinism saved the Protestant Reformation, since in the mid-sixteenth century, it was a dynamic Calvinism—rather than the increasingly moribund Lutheranism—that stood in opposition to a newly aggressive Catholic Church during the Catholic Counter-Reformation.

THE ENGLISH REFORMATION

The English Reformation was of a different nature—a political act rather than a religious act as in other parts of Europe. **Henry VIII** (r. 1509–1546), the powerful English monarch, was supportive of the Catholic Church. He even criticized Martin Luther in a pamphlet that he wrote, *The Defence of the Seven Sacraments*. Henry was never comfortable with Protestant theology. He did not believe in salvation by faith and saw no need to limit the role of the priest. The story of the English Reformation begins with what became known as the **"King's Great Matter,"** which involved King Henry VIII's attempt to end his marriage to his Spanish wife, **Catherine of Aragon**. Henry had grown concerned that he did not have a male heir, and he began to question whether Catherine's failure to produce sons (a man of his times, he blamed his wife) was a sign of God's displeasure at his marriage to Catherine, who had earlier been married to Henry's deceased older brother. Because the Catholic Church did not recognize divorce, Henry would have to go through the process of getting an annulment. During this time, Henry fell in love with a young woman at his court, **Anne Boleyn**, who virtuously refused to sleep with him unless he made her his queen.

When the papacy showed no signs of granting the annulment, primarily because Catherine was the aunt of the powerful Charles V, Henry decided to take authority into his own hands. Starting in November 1529 and continuing for seven years, he began what became known as the **Reformation Parliament**, which Henry used as a tool to give him ultimate authority on religious matters. This parliament would come to be very useful, since by 1533, Henry was on a short timetable. He had bribed Anne Boleyn into joining him in bed by making her the Marchioness of Pembroke and by giving her an annual income of £1,000. Three months later she was pregnant and had secretly married Henry, although Henry was still married to Catherine as well. If Henry was to be saved from bigamy, and if his child was to be legitimate, he had only eight months to end his marriage to Catherine. Henry decided the only way to do this was by cutting off the constitutional links that existed between England and the papacy. In April 1533, Parliament enacted a statute known as the **"Act in Restraint of Appeals,"** which declared that all spiritual cases within the Kingdom were within the King's jurisdiction and authority and not the pope's. A month later, Henry appeared before an English church tribunal headed by the man he selected to be Archbishop of Canterbury. The tribunal declared that his marriage to Catherine was null and void and that Anne Boleyn was his lawful wedded wife. That September, a child was born, but it was a baby girl, **Elizabeth Tudor**, instead of the boy Henry so desperately wanted. Eventually, Henry would marry a total of six times; his third wife, **Jane Seymour**, provided him with a son, Edward. In 1534, the English Reformation was capped off by the **Act of Supremacy,** which acknowledged the King of England as the Supreme Head of what became known as the Church of England.

While Henry may have been merely interested in creating what we might call Catholicism without the pope—in that he wanted to keep all the aspects of Catholic worship without acknowledging the primacy of the pope—it proved to be difficult to stem the tide of change. Henry himself played a role in this by closing all English monasteries and confiscating their lands. The brief reign of his son **Edward VI** (r. 1547–1553) saw an attempt to institute genuine Protestant theology into the church that Henry had created.

During the similarly short reign of his half-sister **Mary Tudor** (r. 1553–1558), the daughter of Catherine of Aragon and wife of the fanatically Catholic Philip II of Spain, there was an attempt to bring England back into the orbit of the Catholic Church. While succeeding to restore the formal links between England and the papacy, Mary found that many still held to their Protestant beliefs. To end this heresy, she allowed for several hundred Englishmen to be burnt at the stake, thus earning her the sobriquet **"Bloody Mary."** It was only during the long, successful reign of her half-sister Elizabeth (r. 1558–1603), the daughter of Anne Boleyn, that a final religious settlement was worked out, one in which the Church of England followed a middle-of-the-road Protestant course.

THE COUNTER-REFORMATION

Although it took several decades to be effective, eventually there was a Catholic response to the Protestant Reformation. Initially historians referred to this movement as the **Counter-Reformation**, although today it is more commonly known as the **Catholic Reformation**. To a certain extent, both labels are appropriate. It was Counter-Reformation in the sense that the Catholic Church was taking steps to counteract some of the successes of the Protestant side. Among these steps was the creation of the notorious **Index of Prohibited Books**, including works by writers such as **Erasmus** and **Galileo**. Also, the medieval institution of the **papal Inquisition** was revived, and individuals who were deemed to be heretics were put to death for their religious beliefs. The term Catholic Reformation is also apt in that the Catholic Church has a long tradition of adjusting to changed conditions, whether it was the papal Reform Movement of the High Middle Ages or, more recently, the Second Vatican Council of the 1960s.

The centerpiece of the Catholic Reformation was the **Council of Trent** (1545–1563). Unlike the medieval conciliar movement, which sought to place the papacy under the control of a church council or parliament, the Council of Trent was dominated by the papacy and, in turn, enhanced its power. The council took steps to address some of the issues that had sparked the Reformation, including placing limits on the **selling of church offices**. Recognizing that the poorly educated clergy were a major problem, the council mandated that a seminary for the education of clergy should be established in every diocese. The Council of Trent refused to concede any point of theology to the Protestants. Instead they emphatically endorsed their traditional teachings on such matters as the sacraments, the role of priests, and the belief that salvation comes from faith as well as works, and that the source for this faith was the Bible and the traditions of the church. Although it is incorrect to say that the council created the idea of the **Baroque** style of art, the council was critical of what it deemed to be the religious failings of the Mannerist style and urged that a more intensely religious art be created, something that did play a role in the development of the early Baroque.

Perhaps the greatest reason for the success of the Catholic Reformation was the founding of the **Society of Jesus (Jesuits)** organized by **Ignatius Loyola** (1491–1556), a Spanish noble who was wounded in battle and spent his recuperation time reading various Catholic tracts. After undergoing a religious conversion, he attempted, not unlike Luther, to reconcile himself to God through austere behavior. He became a hermit but still felt that something was amiss. While Luther, in his search for spiritual contentment, decided that the Bible was the sole source of faith, Loyola hit on the idea that even if the Bible did not exist there was still the spirit.

Loyola's ideas are laid out in his *Spiritual Exercises*; one passage in particular states his belief in total obedience to the church:

> To arrive at complete certainty, this is the attitude that we should maintain: I will believe that the white object I see is black if that should be the desire of the hierarchical church, for I believe that linking Christ our Lord the Bridegroom and His Bride the church, there is one and the same Spirit, ruling and guiding us for our souls' good. For our Holy Mother the church is guided and ruled by the same Spirit, the Lord who gave the Ten Commandments.

This total and complete loyalty is why the Jesuit order, although at first under suspicion by a cautious papacy uncomfortable with Loyola's mysticism, would be accepted as an official order of the church in a papal bull in 1540. The Jesuits began to distinguish themselves as a teaching order and also worked as Catholic missionaries in places where Lutheranism had made large inroads, such as Poland.

CHAPTER TIMELINE

Just before the Review Questions at the end of each chapter in Part II, you'll find a timeline of events for the relevant period. The timeline below includes events not only mentioned in this chapter but also ones discussed in the next chapter. This is due to the overlap in time frames between chapters. Use the timelines simply as a quick review of key events and don't obsess over memorizing every date.

Year(s)	Event
1341	Petrarch crowned Poet Laureate
1378	Ciompi Revolt
1378	Black Death hits Europe
1387	Chaucer starts *The Canterbury Tales*
1397	Establishment of the Medici Bank
1403	Alberti begins work on the doors of the baptistery in Florence
1405	Christine de Pisan's *City of Ladies*
1406	Florence conquers Pisa
1415	Burning at the stake of Jan Hus at the Council of Constance
1415	Prince Henry the Navigator participates in capture of Ceuta
1417	Great Schism comes to an end
1420s	Development of single-point perspective
1440	Lorenzo Valla's *On the Donation of Constantine*
1440s	Donatello's *David*
1452	Gutenberg prints bible
1453	End of the Hundred Years War
1453	Fall of Constantinople
1454	Treaty of Lodi
1469	Marriage of Ferdinand of Aragon to Isabella of Castile

Year(s)	Event
1485	Henry VII begins Tudor dynasty following Battle of Bosworth
1486	Pico's *Oration on the Dignity of Man*
1487	Bartholomew Dias sails around Cape of Good Hope
1490	Ludovico il Moro becomes despot of Milan
1492	Columbus leaves Spain for what he believes will be Asia
1492	Expulsion of the Jews from Spain
1492	Reconquista of Spain completed
1492	Lorenzo de Medici dies
1494	King Charles VIII of France invades Italy
1494	The Treaty of Torsedillas divides the discoveries in the New World between Spain and Portugal
1498	Vasco da Gama reaches the coast of India
1498	Burning of Savonarola
1501	Michelangelo's *David*
1503	Leonardo's *Mona Lisa*
1509	Raphael's *School of Athens*
1513	Machiavelli writes *The Prince*
1515	Erasmus' *In Praise of Folly*
1516	More's *Utopia*
1517	Luther's *95 Theses*
1519	Charles V becomes Holy Roman Emperor
1519	Ferdinand Magellan sets out to circumnavigate the globe
1519	Hernán Cortés lands on the coast of Mexico

Year(s)	Event
1521	Luther called before the Diet of Worms
1522	Ignatius Loyola begins *The Spiritual Exercises*
1525	German Peasant Revolt
1528	Castiglione's *The Courtier*
1529	Diet of Speyer
1529	Henry VIII summons the "Reformation Parliament"
1531	Zwingli dies in battle
1531	Francesco Pizarro sets out for Peru
1534	Henry VIII's Act of Supremacy
1534	Anabaptists seize Munster
1535	Sir Thomas More executed by Henry VIII
1536	Calvin publishes first edition of his *Institutes*
1540	Jesuits receive official papal sanction as religious order
1540	Henry VIII marries Ann Boleyn
1540s	Schmalkaldic Wars
1543	Copernicus publishes his *Concerning the Revolutions of the Celestial Spheres*
1543	Andreas Vesalius writes *De humani corporis fabrica* with its critique of the anatomical work of Galen
1545	Council of Trent convenes
1553	End of reign of Edward VI
1553	Michael Servetus burnt at the stake in Geneva

Year(s)	Event
1555	Peace of Augsburg
1556	Philip II becomes King of Spain
1558	Death of Queen Mary of England
1558	Beginning of reign of Elizabeth Tudor
1559	Frederick III of the Palatinate converts to Calvinism
1559	Death of King Henry II of France
1559	Elizabethan religious settlement
1562	Beginning of the French Wars of Religion
1571	Battle of Lepanto
1572	St. Bartholomew's Day Massacre
1587	Execution of Mary, Queen of Scots
1588	Failure of the Spanish Armada
1589	Henry Bourbon becomes King Henry IV
1593	Henry IV converts to Catholicism
1598	Edict of Nantes
1602	First known performance of Shakespeare's *Hamlet*

REVIEW QUESTIONS

Answers and explanations are in Chapter 15.

1. Humanist scholars broke with the medieval
    scholarly tradition

    (A) in declaring that all knowledge was
         relative
    (B) by insisting on reading the original
         manuscript and not a second-hand
         commentary
    (C) by challenging the existence of God
    (D) by supporting the idea of scientific
         experimentation
    (E) by rejecting the central authority of the
         church

2. All of the following are characteristics of
    Renaissance art EXCEPT

    (A) the use of oil paints
    (B) the emphasis on naturalism
    (C) the desire to create three-dimensional
         images
    (D) secular portraiture
    (E) hierarchical scaling

3. What was the initial reaction of Pope Leo X
    to the posting of Luther's *95 Theses*?

    (A) He declared Luther to be a heretic.
    (B) He immediately summoned Luther to
         Rome.
    (C) He recalled Tetzel from Germany
         in order to have him stop selling
         indulgences.
    (D) He declared that Luther's action was a
         significant threat to the unity of the
         church.
    (E) He claimed he was not interested in a
         squabble among monks.

4. Which of the following best describes
    Luther's position on the social questions of
    his day?

    (A) He wanted to see marked
         improvements in the lives of the
         peasantry.
    (B) He was deeply concerned about these
         questions but feared antagonizing
         his aristocratic supporters.
    (C) He was a deeply conservative man who
         did not want to upset the traditional
         social order.
    (D) He feared that his religious reforms
         would fail unless they were
         combined with a program to address
         social concerns.
    (E) He blamed the Catholic Church for
         maintaining a spiritual as well as
         social hierarchy.

5. Following the death of her half-sister Mary,
    Queen Elizabeth of England pursued which
    of the following religious policies?

    (A) She followed her father's example
         and refused to embrace either
         Protestantism or Catholicism.
    (B) She followed Mary's policy by keeping
         England within the Catholic Church.
    (C) She began a massive persecution of
         Catholics on the charge of heresy.
    (D) She broke with Rome and established a
         moderate Protestant church.
    (E) She waited to make a decision on
         religious matters until many years
         into her reign.

6. Family life was directly influenced during the Protestant Reformation by

   (A) the doctrine of salvation by grace alone
   (B) changes in land-holding patterns by German peasants
   (C) Protestant emphasis on primogeniture
   (D) Martin Luther's decision to marry and start a family
   (E) women who led Anabaptist congregations

7. For most Florentines, work was tied to

   (A) banking
   (B) the production of wool cloth
   (C) mercenary activities
   (D) the church
   (E) the manufacture of leather goods

8

The Age of Expansion and the Rise of Monarchical States

(1415–Early 1700s)

THE PORTUGUESE AND SPANISH EMPIRES

If geography is destiny, then it is not surprising that the Portuguese would look to the sea. Living in a land that was not well suited to farming, the Portuguese had always looked to distant lands for sources of wealth. In 1415, **Prince Henry the Navigator**, a younger son of the King of Portugal, participated in the capture of the North African port of Ceuta from the Muslims. This conquest spurred his interest in Africa. It also inspired him to sponsor a navigational school in Lisbon and a series of expeditions, manned mainly by Italians, which aimed not only to develop trade with Africa but also to find a route to India and the Far East around Africa.

In 1487, a Portuguese captain, **Bartholomew Dias**, sailed around the **Cape of Good Hope** at the tip of Africa. A decade later, in 1498, **Vasco da Gama** reached the coast of India. The Portuguese defeated the Arab fleets that patrolled the Indian Ocean by being the first to successfully mount cannons on their ships and also by deploying their ships in squadrons rather than individually, which gave them a huge tactical advantage. The Portuguese established themselves on the western coast of India and for a while controlled the lucrative spice trade.

With the Portuguese controlling the African route to the Indian Ocean, the Spanish decided to try an Atlantic route to the east. **Christopher Columbus**, a Genoese sailor, set sail on August 2, 1492, certain that he would find this eastern route. Although there is no truth that Columbus was unique in insisting that the world was round (this fictional story dates from the nineteenth century), he did believe he would fulfill medieval religious prophesies that spoke of converting the whole world to Christianity. After a 33-day voyage from the Canary Islands, Columbus landed in the eastern Bahamas, which he insisted was an undeveloped part of Asia. He called the territory the "Indies" and the indigenous population "Indians" and noted ominously in his diary that they were friendly and gentle and therefore easy to enslave.

Although Columbus's failure to locate either gold or spices during his voyages was a disappointment, within a generation, others built on Columbus's discoveries. The most important of the journeys was undertaken by **Ferdinand Magellan** in 1519, who set out to circumnavigate the globe. Although Magellan did not live to see the end of his voyage (he died in the Philippines), he did prove that the territory where Columbus landed was not part of the Far East but rather an entirely unknown continent, a continent that the Spanish planned to conquer.

In 1519, **Hernán Cortés** landed on the coast of Mexico with a small force of 600 men. He had arrived at the heart of the **Aztec Empire**, a militaristic state, which through conquest had carved out a large state with a large central capital, **Tenochtitlán** (modern-day Mexico City). The Aztecs were less than popular with the people they conquered, primarily because they practiced human sacrifice to appease their gods. These conquered people felt no loyalty to the Aztec state and were willing to cooperate with the Spanish.

The Aztecs viewed the light-skinned Spaniards, who were riding on horses (unknown at this time in North and South America), wearing armor, and carrying guns, as gods. At first, Montezuma, the Aztec ruler, tried to appease them with gifts of gold. Unfortunately for the Aztecs, this just further whetted the appetite of the Spanish, who seized the capital city and took Montezuma hostage. He died mysteriously while in Spanish captivity. While rebellions against Spanish rule continued, the Aztec ability to fight was sapped by smallpox and other European diseases foreign to the indigenous peoples. By 1521, Cortés declared the former Aztec Empire to be New Spain.

The Spanish also succeeded in destroying another great civilization, the **Inca Empire of Peru**. Like the Aztecs, the Incas had carved out a large empire by conquering and instigating harsh rule over many other tribes. In 1531, **Francisco Pizarro,** a Spanish soldier, set out for Peru with a tiny force of approximately 200 men. Pizarro, following Cortés's brutal example, treacherously captured the Inca Emperor Atahualpa, who then had his subjects raise vast amounts of gold for ransom. By 1533, Pizarro had grown tired of ruling through Atahualpa, and he had him killed. Once again, Western technology and diseases sapped the indigenous population's ability to fight back, and while it took longer for the Spanish to secure their hold over the Inca territories, by the 1560s, they had stamped out the last bit of resistance.

The impact of this age of exploration and conquest was immense, not just for Europe but for the entire globe. The Spanish set out to create *haciendas*, or plantations, to exploit both the agricultural and mineral riches of the land. The indigenous population, compelled to work under a system of forced labor called *encomienda*, continued to die at an incredible pace from both disease and overwork. So to provide labor for their estates, the Spanish and Portuguese began to take captured Africans from their homeland to serve on the farms and in the mines of the **New World**. It has been estimated that by the time the slave trade ended in the early nineteenth century, almost 10 million Africans were abducted from Africa, with countless numbers dying as a result of the inhumane conditions on the difficult overseas passage.

THE DEVELOPMENT OF MONARCHICAL STATES

Although tools of statecraft, such as permanent embassies in foreign lands, were first developed in the city-states of Renaissance Italy, in northern Europe during the Early Modern period, large, unified nation-states began to develop. These city-states ultimately came to dominate the Italian peninsula and contributed to the transition away from the medieval notion of feudal kingship. Prior to the sixteenth century, the king was not an absolute ruler; instead he had to rule with the consent of his great vassals. In the age of the new monarchical state, it was deemed that monarchical power was God-given and therefore by its very nature absolute. Although in the Middle Ages, parliamentary institutions developed throughout Europe as a means of placing limits on kings, in the Early Modern period, thought shifted. The sixteenth-century French philosopher **Jean Bodin** wrote of this new style of monarchy:

> It is the distinguishing mark of the sovereign that he cannot in any way be subject to the commands of another, for it is he who makes law for the subject, abrogates laws already made, and amends absolute law.

The French monarchy is the most important example of how this power shift came about. It was not an easy victory for the French monarchy, which had to deal with assorted aristocratic and religious conflicts that threatened to destroy the state. Eventually, under **Louis XIV,** France created a centralized monarchy in which the power of the king was absolute, although it came at a high price as it helped pave the way for the late eighteenth-century French Revolution. England serves as a very different model. In England, the **Stuart monarchs,** who reigned for most of the seventeenth century, were interested in adopting French-style royal absolutism but found that the English Parliament stood in their way. Eventually, England became embroiled in what one historian has labeled as a "century of revolution," which eventually resulted in the supremacy of Parliament over the monarchy.

Be aware of these important characteristics of the new nation-states:

1. GROWING BUREAUCRATIZATION

Across Europe, salaried officials began to depend on the monarchy for their livelihood. In France, the monarchy established the new office of *intendant*, which employed individuals to collect taxes on behalf of the monarch. Corruption was still a part of this system, as was the practice of buying and selling royal offices to satisfy the short-term financial needs of the monarch. England was the exception to this trend. In England, the older system of cooperation between the crown and its leading subjects continued.

2. EXISTENCE OF A PERMANENT MERCENARY ARMY

In the Late Medieval/Early Modern periods, a **revolution in warfare** came about. In the fourteenth century, Swiss mercenary infantrymen lined up in a phalanx of 6,000 men and used their pikes to kill aristocratic horsemen, but by the end of the century, gunpowder further eroded the dominance of the mounted knight and made feudal castles far easier to conquer. The rising cost of warfare, most particularly the need to provide for an army on an annual (as opposed to occasional) basis, played into the hands of the developing monarchical state, which alone could tap into the necessary resources. Again, England was the exception, since it did not establish a permanent army until the end of the seventeenth century when it was firmly under parliamentary control.

3. GROWING NEED TO TAX

Clearly this is an instance where 1 + 2 = 3. Countries like France basically faced a vicious circle: Monarchs were in constant need of taxes to pay for their permanent armies, while it was the army that the monarchy needed to ensure control over a rebellious peasantry who resented the high rate of taxation. Traditionally, medieval monarchs were supposed to live off their own incomes, although in the Early Modern period this was becoming impossible due to the Price Revolution and the increased costs of managing a centralized state.

ITALY

Not every part of Europe followed this process of national consolidation under a centralizing monarchy. The Italian peninsula remained divided throughout this period, and thus it became an easy target for ambitious monarchs of centralized states such as France and Spain.

The **Treaty of Lodi** (1454) had provided for a balance of power among the major Italian city-states. It created an alliance between long-term enemies Milan and Naples and also included the support of Florence. Their combined strength was enough to ensure that outside powers would stay out of Italian affairs. This system came to an end in 1490, when **Ludovico il Moro**, upon becoming despot of Milan, initiated hostilities with Naples and then four years later invited the French into Italy to allow them to satisfy their long-standing claims to Naples. **Charles VIII**, the King of France, didn't have to be asked twice; he immediately ordered his troops across the Italian Alps.

Charles and his forces crossed into Florence, where a radical Dominican preacher, **Savonarola** (1452–1498), had just led the Florentine population in expelling the **Medici** rulers and then had established a puritanical state. This complete religious and political transformation of the city marked the end of Florence's leading role in Renaissance scholarship and art. Eventually, by 1498, Ludovico il Moro recognized the folly of what he had wrought and joined an anti-French Italian alliance that ultimately succeeded not only in expelling the French but also in restoring the Medici in Florence. The Medici promptly burnt Savonarola at the stake with the support of the papacy, which hated the Dominican friar because of his pre-Lutheran call for a complete overhaul of the church, including the institution of the papacy.

The damage to the independence of the Italian city-states had already been done. Throughout the sixteenth century, Italy became the battlefield in which Spain and France fought for dominance. The collapse of Italian independence was the historical context in which **Niccolò Machiavelli** wrote what is generally seen as the first work of modern political thought, *The Prince* (1513). Machiavelli had happily served his beloved Florentine Republic as a diplomat and official in the chancellery. When the Republic was overthrown by the Medici, Machiavelli was forced into exile to his country estate. *The Prince* is a résumé of sorts in which Machiavelli tried to convince the Medici to partake of his services. Although some scholars have debated whether he was serious about his ideas, it does appear that Machiavelli was genuinely horrified by the increasing foreign domination of the Italian peninsula and believed that only a strong leader using potentially ruthless means could unify Italy and expel the foreigners.

SPAIN

Prior to the fifteenth century, Spain was divided into several Christian kingdoms in the north, while the south had been under Islamic control since the eighth century. The 1469 marriage of **Ferdinand, King of Aragon**, and **Isabella, Queen of Castile**, laid the groundwork for the eventual consolidation of the peninsula, with the final stage of the *Reconquista* taking place in 1492, when their armies conquered the last independent Islamic outpost in Spain—the southern city of Grenada. The same year also marks the beginning of a new wave of religious bigotry, as the ardently Catholic Ferdinand and Isabella began to demand religious uniformity in their lands and formally expelled the Jewish population that had been established in Spain since the time of the Roman Empire. Those Jews and Moors who converted so they could remain in Spain were later hounded by the **Spanish Inquisition**, an effective method that the Spanish monarchy would later use to root out suspected Protestants.

Through a series of well-planned marriages, Ferdinand and Isabella's grandson, **Charles V**, eventually controlled a vast empire that dominated Europe in the first half of the sixteenth century. His Spanish possessions were the primary source of his wealth and also supplied him with the tough Castilian foot soldiers who were the best in Europe. When Charles V—exhausted from his struggles to destroy Protestantism in the Holy Roman Empire—abdicated in 1556, he gave his brother **Ferdinand** (whom he disliked intensely) the troublesome eastern Habsburg lands of Austria, Bohemia, and Hungary as well as his title of Holy Roman Emperor, while Charles's son **Philip** (r. 1556–1598) received the more valuable part of the empire—Spain and its vast holdings in the New World, along with southern Italy and the Netherlands.

Philip gained a vast wealth from the New World's silver mines. Yet surprisingly, Philip spent most of his reign in debt as he used his riches to maintain Spanish influence. In the Mediterranean, the Spanish fought for supremacy against the Ottoman Empire and won a notable success against that eastern power at the **Battle of Lepanto** in 1571. In northern Europe, however, Philip was caught in a quagmire when he attempted to put down a revolt in the Netherlands. This revolt combined religious and nationalistic ideas and began in 1568 following an attempt by Philip to impose the doctrines of the Council of Trent and the Inquisition in a land where Calvinism had made significant inroads, particularly among key members of the aristocracy. For the next several decades, Philip expended huge amounts of money to try to restore Spanish control. Inquisition-based efforts such as the **Duke of Alva's Council of Troubles** (aka the "Council of Blood") failed, as did the effort of military hero **Don Juan**. It was for this reason that Philip launched the great **Spanish Armada** in 1588 as an attempt to conquer England, which, under Queen Elizabeth's rule, was aiding the Dutch rebels. By 1609, an exhausted Spain conceded virtual independence to the northern provinces of the Netherlands (while still maintaining control over the southern part of the country) and in 1648 formally acknowledged their independence.

The sixteenth and early seventeenth centuries were a cultural golden age that featured the writings of **Cervantes** (1547–1616), possibly Spain's greatest writer, whose masterpiece, *Don Quixote*, bemoans the passing of the traditional values of chivalry in Spain. It was also a period of remarkable Spanish painters such as the Greek-born **El Greco** (1541–1614), whose magnificent yet somber works reveal much about a Spain that appeared to have it all, only to find it could not maintain its preeminent European position. In fact, the golden age of Spain did prove to be short-lived. The constant wars, the effects of the **Price Revolution**, and the economic collapse of the Castilian economy led to a decline in Spain's power by the end of the seventeenth century.

THE HOLY ROMAN EMPIRE

The Holy Roman Empire, a large state that straddled central Europe, can be said to date back to 962, when the Saxon King Otto I was crowned emperor in Rome by the pope. In the late tenth and eleventh centuries, the Empire was the most powerful state in Europe, but it was eventually weakened as a result of a series of conflicts with the papacy. While lacking the soldiers to stem the ambitions of the Holy Roman emperors, successive popes were able to find support among the German nobility, who chafed under strong imperial leadership. By 1356, the practice of electing the emperor was formally defined in the **Golden Bull** of **Emperor Charles IV**. This document, which granted to seven German princes the right to elect an emperor, made it clear that the emperor held office by election rather than hereditary right. The electors usually chose weak rulers who would not stand in the way of their own political ambitions.

In the ensuing centuries, the empire continued to splinter into numerous semi-autonomous territorial states so that by 1500 it consisted of more than 300 semi-autonomous entities over which the emperor ruled but had very little actual authority. Charles V, the powerful Habsburg (also spelled Hapsburg) ruler who was elected emperor in 1519, attempted to establish genuine imperial control over the state. He soon found that the Lutheran Reformation provided a new weapon for those German princes and cities that wanted to avoid losing their independence.

The **Peace of Augsburg** (1555) signified the end of the religious wars in the time of Charles V, who now agreed to adhere to the basic principle that the prince decides the religion of the territory. The treaty, however, did not grant recognition to Calvinists, thus creating a problem when **Frederick III**, the ruler of the Palatinate, converted to Calvinism in 1559. What further complicated the situation was that as the ruler of the Palatinate, Frederick was one of the seven electors of the Holy Roman Emperor.

Within the next two decades, several other German princes followed Frederick's lead and aggressively challenged the religious status quo achieved by the Peace of Augsburg. The tremendous success of the Catholic Counter-Reformation in Southern Germany further stoked religious tensions in Germany. In areas such as Bavaria, all traces of Protestantism were stamped out as Jesuits were invited to take charge of Bavarian schools and universities. Although Charles V failed in his attempt to create a unified German state, the dream would continue. The **Thirty Years War (1618–1648),** a struggle that combined political and religious issues, marked one final attempt within the Holy Roman Empire to make that dream a reality.

THE THIRTY YEARS WAR (1618–1648)

The Thirty Years War began in **Bohemia** (the modern-day Czech Republic), where in 1617 Ferdinand of Styria, an avid Catholic, was crowned King of Bohemia. The majority of Bohemians were Protestant, and they were angered with their new King Ferdinand's intolerance toward their religious beliefs. In May of 1618, a large group of Bohemian Protestant nobles surrounded two of Ferdinand's Catholic advisors and threw them out of a window (the Defenestration of Prague). They survived by landing in a dung heap. The next year, Matthias, the Holy Roman Emperor, passed away, and his cousin Ferdinand, the King of Bohemia, was elected Emperor in his stead. A few hours after being elected, Ferdinand learned to his horror that rebels in Bohemia had deposed him and elected **Frederick**, the **Calvinist Elector of the Palatinate**, as their king. Since he did not have an army, Ferdinand had to turn to the Duke of Bavaria, who agreed to lend his support in exchange for the electoral right enjoyed by the Palatinate. At the **Battle of White Mountain**, the Bavarian forces won a major victory, and Frederick became known as the Winter King since he held onto the Bohemian throne for only that season. By 1622, he had lost not only Bohemia but also the Palatinate.

The question now arises as to why the Thirty Years War didn't end in 1622 (and force historians to give it a different name). Part of the problem was that there were still private armies throughout the Empire that wanted to fight to keep earning a living. Also, because of the perceived threat to Protestants in Germany, outsiders such as the King of Denmark became involved. Additionally, both Catholic and Protestant rulers were concerned that the traditional constitution of the Holy Roman Empire had been dramatically altered when the Palatinate's electoral vote was given to Bavaria. Taking away this vote from the Palatinate was deemed an attack on what contemporaries called "German liberties," by which they meant the independence and political rights enjoyed by territories within the Holy Roman Empire.

This issue of liberties also came to the foreground when Emperor Ferdinand confiscated defeated Protestant princes' land in the north and created the genuine opportunity to forge a unified state under Habsburg control. Given this opportunity, Ferdinand first had to find a new army, since he could no longer rely on the Duke of Bavaria, who began to fear Habsburg domination. He turned to a Bohemian noble by the name of **Albrecht von Wallenstein** for this second phase of the war, who promised to create a vast mercenary army. By 1628, Wallenstein controlled an army of 125,000 and had won a series of major victories in the north.

The high-water mark for Habsburg success in the Thirty Years War came with the **Edict of Restitution** of 1629. The edict outlawed Calvinism in the Empire and required Lutherans to turn over all property seized since 1552—16 bishoprics, 28 cities and towns, and 155 monasteries and convents. This led the king of Sweden, **Gustavus Adolphus,** to enter the war, triggering a third phase. Although he claimed that he became involved to defend Protestant rights in Germany, Adolphus was also interested in German territory along the Baltic. To make matters even more confusing, the French government financially supported the Swedish army, because France's chief minister, **Cardinal Richelieu,** was concerned about the increase of Habsburg strength in Germany. Clearly this skirmish had ignited far beyond a religious war.

The Swedes rolled back the Habsburgs until 1632, when Adolphus died in battle. The next year, Wallenstein was murdered on orders of the Emperor, since Ferdinand began to fear that his general was negotiating with his opponents. The final phase of the war consisted of the French and Swedes fighting against the Austrian Habsburgs and their Spanish allies. This was the most destructive phase of the war; German towns were decimated, and a general agricultural collapse and famine ensued. By the end of the war in 1648, the Empire had 8 million fewer inhabitants than it had in 1618.

The **Peace of Westphalia** (1648) marked the end of the struggle. Thirty years of war had brought about very little. The Holy Roman Empire maintained its numerous political divisions, and the treaty ensured that the Emperor would remain an ineffectual force within German politics. The treaty also reaffirmed the Augsburg formula of each prince deciding the religion of his own territory, although the new formula now fully recognized Calvinism.

FRANCE

By the end of the reign of the powerful **Francis I**, it appeared as if the struggle between the feudal aristocracy and the monarchy had been settled in favor of the newly powerful centralized monarchy. However, the **French Wars of Religion** (1562–1598) revealed that the struggle was not quite over. Although ostensibly concerned with religious ideas, this series of civil wars were part of a long tradition, dating back to the very roots of French history, in which the aristocracy and monarchy battled one another for supremacy.

Partially owing to Calvin himself being French, Calvinism had made early inroads in France (Calvinists in France were known as **Huguenots**). Religious conflicts rose to the surface following the French monarch Henry II's 1559 death when his eye was pierced with a lance while celebrating the end of the wars between the Habsburgs and the French Valois monarchs. On Henry's death, his sickly 15-year-old son Francis II came to the throne, only to be replaced the next year by his brother, who reigned as Charles IX (r. 1560–1574) and then 14 years later by a second brother, the last of the Valois kings, Henry III (r. 1574–1589). All three boys would be dominated by their mother, one of the most remarkable women of the age, **Catherine de Medici**.

Behind the scenes of the French monarchy, a power struggle began to emerge among three prominent families. The rise of the nation-state in France had contributed to a decline in the power of the old aristocratic families. These three families hoped that with a weak monarch on the throne they could reverse this trend. The **Guises**, the most powerful of the three, turned toward a militant, reactionary form of Catholicism. Meanwhile, partly through religious convictions and partly out of political opportunism, **Admiral Coligny**, the leader of the Montmorency family, and the **Prince of Conde**, the leading Bourbon, both converted to Calvinism.

The Wars of Religion began in 1562 when the Duke of Guise was infuriated to see a group of Huguenots worshipping in a barn and had them killed. After ten years of combat, in which both the Duke of Guise and the Prince of Conde were killed, the Huguenots had the upper hand. As a sign of this Calvinist ascendancy, **Henry of Navarre**, a young Bourbon prince, married King Charles IX's sister. The political eclipse of the Valois family greatly concerned Catherine de Medici, who, although not the religious bigot of legend, constantly sought to balance out the power of the aristocratic families to protect the interest of her sons. When the cream of the Huguenot aristocracy gathered in Paris in 1572 to celebrate the wedding, Catherine encouraged her son the king to set in motion the **St. Bartholomew's Day Massacre,** in which an estimated 3,000 died in Paris. Possibly 20,000 Huguenots in total were killed in organized attacks throughout France. Admiral Coligny was killed, but Henry of Navarre's life was spared when he promised to return to Catholicism.

In 1574, Henry III, the last of the Valois kings, turned to the Huguenots to defeat the powerful Catholic League that the Guise family had formed to serve their interests. He eventually made Henry of Navarre his heir and in 1589, following the assassination of Henry III, Henry became **King Henry IV**, thus beginning the **Bourbon** dynasty that would rule France up to the time of the French Revolution. Above all else, the new king wanted peace in his kingdom. Faced with a struggle with Spain, a nation that sought to keep France both politically weak and Catholic, and because most Parisians remained fiercely Catholic, Henry IV—having switched numerous times for political reasons between Calvinism and Catholicism—in 1593 converted permanently to Catholicism. He marked this occasion with the noteworthy words: "Paris is worth a Mass."

In many ways, Henry's actions instigated a new way of thinking in France, the idea of the *Politique*, putting the interests of France before the goal of religious unity. Although his Calvinist allies were horrified by Henry's final religious conversion, he did not forget them. In 1598, he issued the **Edict of Nantes**, granting the Huguenots freedom of worship and assembly as well as the right to maintain fortified towns for their protection.

ROYAL ABSOLUTISM

Until his assassination in 1610, Henry IV worked to revitalize his kingdom. With his finance minister, the **Duke of Sully**, Henry established government monopolies over a number of key commodities such as salt to restore the finances of the monarchy. He also limited the power of the French nobility by reining in its influence over regional parliaments. Despite this strengthening of monarchical power, Henry's assassination in 1610 and the ensuing ascension of his nine-year-old son Louis XIII made France once again vulnerable to aristocratic rebellion and the potential of religious wars. Louis needed a strong minister, and he found one in **Cardinal Richelieu**. Richelieu defeated the Huguenots and took away many of the military and political privileges granted them by the Edict of Nantes. He brought France into the Thirty Years War, not as the defender of Catholic interests, but on the side of the Protestants in order to counter the traditional French enemy, the Spanish Habsburgs.

The death of Louis XIII in 1643 once again left France with a minor on the throne; the five-year-old **Louis XIV** was unable to benefit from Richelieu's guidance because the great minister had predeceased Louis XIII by one year. Louis XIV's mother, Ann of Austria, selected **Cardinal Mazarin** to be the regent during the king's childhood. Mazarin had a less sure political hand than Richelieu, and once again, France had to grapple with a series of rebellions known as the *Fronde* in the period between 1649 and 1652. These events were to scar the young Louis XIV, who at one point during the rebellion had to flee from Paris. Following the death of Mazarin, Louis decided to rule without a chief minister and to finally grapple with the central issue that had dominated France for more than a hundred years— how to deal with an aristocracy that resented the ever increasing powers of the French monarchy.

One way that Louis achieved this goal was to advocate a political philosophy that had been developing in France since the sixteenth century—the notion that the monarch enjoyed certain **divine rights**. Using Old Testament examples of divinely appointed monarchs, Louis's chief political philosopher, **Bishop Bossuet**, wrote that since the king was chosen by God, only God was fit to judge the behavior of the king, not parliamentary bodies or angry nobles. Although it is unclear whether Louis ever said the famous line, *"L'etat, c'est moi"* ("I am the state"), the statement does assert Louis's belief that no political or religious authority existed, either within or beyond the borders of France, that had any right to encroach on his sovereignty.

Louis built the palace of **Versailles** 12 miles outside of Paris as another way to dominate the French nobility and the Parisian mob. Although his grandfather had converted to Catholicism to appease the people of Paris, Louis felt he could safely ignore the people from the confines of his palace. Eventually, 10,000 noblemen and officials lived at Versailles, a palace so immense that its facade was a third of a mile long, with grounds boasting 1,400 fountains. While it cost a huge amount of money to maintain Versailles, Louis thought it was worth it. Instead of plotting against the king, the aristocrats were involved with court intrigue and gossip and with ceremonial issues such as who got to hold the king's sleeve as he got dressed. Those members of the aristocracy who did not live at Versailles were pleased with their tax exemptions as well as their high social standing.

To administer his monarchy, Louis made use of the upper bourgeoisie. No member of the high aristocracy attended the daily council sessions at Versailles. Instead, his most important minister was **Jean-Baptiste Colbert**, the son of a draper. Colbert centralized the French economy by instituting a system known as **mercantilism**. The central goal of mercantilism was to build up the nation's supply of gold by exporting goods to other lands and earning gold from their sale. To do this, Colbert organized factories to produce porcelains and other luxury items. He also tried to abolish internal tariffs, ultimately creating the **Five Great Farms** which were large, custom-free regions.

Part of mercantilism was a reliance on foreign colonies to buy the mother country's exports. To that end, Colbert succeeded in helping to create France's vast overseas empire. By the 1680s, Louis controlled trading posts in India, slave-trading centers on the west coast of Africa, and several islands in the Caribbean, while the largest colonial possession was New France, the territory we know today as Quebec. Colbert particularly wanted to strike at the rich commercial empire of the Dutch, so he organized the **French East India Company** to compete with the Dutch. It enjoyed only limited success as a result in part of excessive government control and a lack of interest in such ventures by the French elite.

Louis XIV touted religious unity in France as a means of enhancing royal absolutism. While during the reign of his father the rights of Huguenots had declined due to the hostility of Richelieu, the Edict of Nantes was still in effect. Louis decided that the time had come to eradicate Calvinism in France. In 1685, he **revoked the Edict of Nantes**. He demolished Huguenot churches and schools and took away their civil rights. Some remained underground, but as many as 200,000 were exiled to England and the Netherlands. The Huguenots were an important part of the French economy; by fleeing to enemy lands, they aided the two countries that were at war with Louis. For Louis, however, such economic considerations meant little in comparison to what he thought was the more important goal and the one most pleasing to God—the elimination of religious heresy from France.

During the reign of Louis XIV, France was involved in a series of wars as a means to satiate Louis's desire for territorial expansion. In the early part of his reign, this policy was quite successful, as France conquered territories in Germany and Flanders. This success lasted until 1688, when the English—in a move that marked the Glorious Revolution—replaced the king who had received subsidies from the French with a new monarch, **William of Orange**, who as leader of the Netherlands was committed to waging total war against Louis. After 1688, another series of wars erupted that lasted for 25 years, including the **War of Spanish Succession** between the French and the English and Dutch allies, which lasted from 1702 to 1713 and concluded with the **Treaty of Utrecht**, which left a Bourbon (Louis's grandson) on the throne of Spain but forbade the same monarch from ruling both Spain and France. These wars ultimately resulted in the containment of Louis XIV's France but left the French peasantry hard pressed to pay the taxes to support Louis's constant desire for glory.

ENGLAND

THE TUDORS

Although seventeenth-century France witnessed the rise of royal absolutism and the diminishing importance of the Estates General (the French national parliament, which met for the last time in the seventeenth century in 1614), the English experienced a very different course of events. In England, during this same period, a long, drawn-out conflict between the English monarchy and Parliament pervaded, which ultimately resulted in a parliamentary triumph. The victory did not result in the end of the monarchy (except for a brief interregnum in the middle of the century); however, by 1700, it was Parliament that dominated the political scene. The following paragraphs outline the events that led to the parliamentary triumph.

England had achieved a measure of unity under a centralized monarchy in the medieval period, well before its continental counterparts. The fifteenth-century **Wars of the Roses** (commonly known to us, although a bit inaccurately, through the plays of Shakespeare) were not aristocratic attempts to break the power of the monarchy but rather a series of civil wars to determine which aristocratic faction, York or Lancaster, would dominate the monarchy. In the end, it was a junior member of the Lancastrian family, **Henry Tudor (Henry VII)**, who won central authority in England when he established the Tudor dynasty following his defeat of Richard III in 1485 at the battle of Bosworth Field.

Following the death of his autocratic father in 1509, **Henry VIII** became king and maintained his father's policies to strengthen the crown. The near total decimation of aristocratic opponents during the Wars of the Roses and an expanding economy, which benefited the Tudor dynasty throughout the sixteenth century, helped the king to restore royal authority. Henry created a small but efficient bureaucracy which made the king's will known throughout the land. Henry, however, believed that his sovereignty would not be manifest so long as England was under the religious leadership of the papacy. In 1534, he made a political—not a religious—decision when he broke with Rome and created the Church of England. Although their tenures on the throne were short and full of religious tension, Henry VIII's children, Edward VI and Mary Tudor, enjoyed the benefits of the restored prestige of the monarchy, which resulted from the efforts of Henry VII and Henry VIII.

The greatest of all the Tudors was **Queen Elizabeth** (r. 1558–1603), Henry VIII's daughter with **Anne Boleyn**. Elizabeth was an intelligent woman who had been educated in the Italian humanist program of classical studies. She was a diligent worker and had excellent political instincts like her father. Also like her father, Elizabeth knew how to select able ministers who would serve the crown with distinction—men such as William Cecil (Lord Burghley)—but she always kept herself as the ultimate decision maker in the land. Elizabeth used the prospect of marriage as a diplomatic tool and allowed almost every single ruler in Europe to imagine that he could possibly marry her—a powerful way to build alliances whenever the need arose. Whether she truly was the **"Virgin Queen"** is a question that no one—not even the wise folks who write the questions for the AP exam—could ever answer. She did seem to regard marriage as incompatible with her sovereignty. Yet by staying single, she exposed England to the risk of religious war, since as long as she remained single, the Catholic **Mary Stuart**, the ruler of Scotland, was her legal heir.

The relationship between England and Scotland was a complex affair that continued to plague both lands throughout the sixteenth and seventeenth centuries. For years, Mary lived as Elizabeth's prisoner, following a rebellion by Scottish nobles that forced her from the throne. Elizabeth treated Mary as the rightful ruler of Scotland and the probable heir to the English crown, though she kept her under house arrest because she feared that Mary was intriguing against her. Only after Mary plotted with Philip II of Spain did Elizabeth decide to settle relations with the Scots and distance herself from Mary. In the Treaty of Berwick in 1586, she entered into a defensive alliance with Scotland; recognized James, Mary's son who was being raised as a Protestant, as the lawful king; gave him an English pension; and, while she never specifically said so, let it be known that James was the heir to her throne. In 1587, Elizabeth finally took a step that she had been reluctant to take: She ordered the execution of **Mary, Queen of Scots**.

In 1588 came the greatest moment in Elizabeth's reign—the defeat of Philip II's **Spanish Armada**, which ensured that England would remain Protestant and free from foreign dominance. Although as she grew older, at least part of Elizabeth's authority gradually eroded and people began to look beyond her reign to the future, the decades that followed the Armada conquest were also a period of an incredible cultural flourishing. This was the age of **Shakespeare**, **Christopher Marlowe**, **Ben Jonson**, and **Edmund Spenser**; and while Elizabeth may not have been a significant direct patron of this **English Renaissance**, the stability that she provided England during her reign allowed it to take place.

THE STUARTS

When Elizabeth died childless in 1603, as promised, her cousin **King James VI of Scotland** inherited the throne. To a certain extent, James was ill suited for the role of English king. The Scottish Parliament was a weak institution that did not inhibit the power of the monarch. James's interest lay in asserting his divine notion of kingship, which he had been exposed to by reading French writings on the subject. He told the English Parliament the following during the first session with them:

> The state of monarchy is the supremest thing upon Earth: for Kings are not only God's lieutenants upon Earth and sit upon God's throne, but even by God Himself they are called gods. As to dispute what God may do is blasphemy, so it is sedition in subjects to dispute what a King may do in height of his power. I will not be content that my power be disputed on.

Such words could not have pleased his audience. In the relationship between the king and Parliament at the start of the seventeenth century, the monarch held the upper hand—only the king could summon a parliament, and he could dismiss them at will. James did, however, have to consult the two-house English Parliament, the **House of Commons** and the **House of Lords**, when he needed to raise additional revenue beyond his ordinary expenses. This parliamentary control over the financial purse strings in an age when the cost of governing was dramatically increasing played a crucial role in Parliament's eventual triumph over royal absolutism.

Religious issues further complicated James's reign. The religious settlement worked out by Elizabeth in 1559 was no longer adequate in an age in which English religious passions grew increasingly intense. It failed to satisfy the radical Calvinist Protestants, known as **Puritans**, who emerged during the **Stuart period**. In 1603, most Puritans still belonged to the Church of England, although they were a minority within the church. For the most part, what distinguished the Puritans was that they wanted to see the church "purified" of all traces of Catholicism. Although raised in Calvinist Scotland, James, on his arrival in England, found the Church of England with its hierarchical clergy and ornate rituals more to his taste. He believed its Episcopal structure was particularly well suited to his idea of the divine right of kings. In 1604, when a group of Puritans petitioned the new king to reform the Church of England, James met them with the declaration: "I will have one doctrine, one discipline, one religion, both in substance and in ceremony." He added words that would prove to be rather prophetic for his son: **"No Bishop, No King,"** meaning that by weakening the church, the monarchy in turn weakens. James's opposition to the Puritan proposal drove the more moderate of the Puritans—individuals who just wanted to rid the Church of England of its last traces of Catholic ritual—onto a more extreme track. Some Puritans even decided to leave England; one such group founded the colony of Plymouth, Massachusetts, in 1620.

James's three-part program—to unite England with Scotland, to create a continental-style standing army, and to set up a new system of royal finance—met with little support from Parliament. James's son, **Charles I** (r. 1625–1641), did not possess even the somewhat limited political acumen of his father. Like his father, Charles felt that the Anglican Church provided the greatest stability for his state, and he further enflamed passions by lending his support to the so-called **Arminian** wing of the Anglican Church. **Arminius** was a Dutch theologian of the early seventeenth century who argued in favor of free will as opposed to the Calvinist doctrine of **predestination**. In 1633, Charles named **William Laud**, a follower of this doctrine, his Archbishop of Canterbury. The Arminians, although certainly not pro-Catholic, refused to deny that Catholics were Christians; this philosophy greatly angered the Puritans. The Arminians further antagonized Puritan sentiment by advocating a more ornate church service.

The relationship between Charles and Parliament got off to a bad start when Parliament granted him **Tonnage and Poundage** (custom duties) for a one-year period rather than for the life of the monarch, as had been the custom since the fifteenth century. Charles, however, was committed to the war against Spain, so he cashed in his wife's dowry and sent an expedition to the Spanish port of Cadiz; the mission was a complete failure. To pay for these military disasters, Charles requested a forced loan from his wealthier subjects. Several members of Parliament refused to pay this loan and were thrown in jail. Parliament was called in again in 1628, at which time it put forward a **Petition of Rights**, which Charles felt forced to sign. It included provisions that the king could not demand a loan without the consent of Parliament. The petition also prohibited individuals from being imprisoned without published cause and the government from housing soldiers and sailors in private homes without the owner's permission. Finally, it outlawed using martial law against civilians, which Charles had used to collect his forced loan.

In August 1628, Charles's chief minister, the dashing but incompetent **Duke of Buckingham**, was murdered by an embittered sailor who blamed him for England's recent military disasters. Charles, on the other hand, blamed the leaders of the House of Commons, most notably John Eliot, for inflaming passions against Buckingham. When Parliament was again called in January 1629, both sides felt that the issue of prerogative rights would lead to a conflict between Parliament and the king. In March 1629, the issue came to the foreground when Eliot proposed three resolutions.

1. High churchmen and anyone suspected of popery (practicing Catholicism) should be branded as capital enemies of the state.

2. Any of the king's advisors who recommended that he raise funds without Parliament's approval should be tried as capital enemies of the state.

3. Anyone who paid tonnage and poundage, which the King was still illegally collecting, would be betraying the "liberties of England."

After hearing these (what he thought were) outrageous demands, the king summoned the Speaker of the House of Commons and ordered him to dissolve parliament. Two members of Parliament held the Speaker in his chair, a treasonable act because it disputes the right of the king to dissolve parliament. Once Eliot's resolutions were passed, the king's messengers announced that he had dissolved parliament.

For the next 11 years, what is known as the **Personal Rule of Charles** was the law of the land. Charles decided to govern England without calling a parliament. Charles could have carried this off successfully and brought about the end of Parliament, as this occurred in France during the same period of time. The major problem of how to raise enough revenue was solved by extending the collection of ship money throughout the kingdom, a politically explosive decision. Traditionally, certain coastal cities were responsible for raising funds for naval defense during times of national emergency. In 1634, Charles declared an emergency (although England was at peace), and two years later he extended this tax to inland cities and counties, areas that had never before paid ship money. This was such a substantial source of income that it could possibly have freed the king from ever having to call a parliament. The collection of ship money led to a famous legal case involving John Hampden, a Puritan Member of Parliament, who having already challenged the legality of the forced loan, now questioned Charles's raising of ship money. While the judges found against Hampden by a vote of seven to five, he was viewed as having achieved a moral victory.

By 1637, Charles was at the height of his power. He had a balanced budget, and his government policies and restructuring appeared to be effective. Yet within four years of this peak, the country would be embroiled in a civil war. Charles ultimately ruined his powerful position by insisting that Calvinist Scotland adopt not only the Episcopal structure of the Church of England, but also follow a prayer book based on the English *Book of Common Prayer*. The Scots rioted and signed a national covenant that pledged their allegiance to the king but also vowed to resist all changes to their church.

In 1640, Charles called an English Parliament for the first time in 11 years, because he believed it would be willing to grant money to put down the Scottish rebellion. This became known as the **Short Parliament** because it met for only three weeks and was dissolved after it refused to grant funds prior to Charles addressing their own grievances. Charles was still determined to punish the Scots; after he dissolved parliament, he patched together an army with the resources he could muster. The Scots were the victors on the battlefield and invaded northern England. They refused to leave England until Charles signed a settlement and, in the meantime, forced him to pay £850 per day for their support.

To pay this large sum, Charles was forced to call another parliament. This became known as the **Long Parliament,** since it met for an unprecedented 20 years. The House of Commons launched the Long Parliament by impeaching Charles's two chief ministers, the Earl of Strafford and Archbishop Laud (Strafford was executed in 1641 and Laud in 1645). Parliament abolished the king's **prerogative courts,** like Henry VIII's Court of Star Chamber, which had become tools of royal absolutism. Tensions grew even higher when a rebellion broke out in Ireland, which had been ruled with a strong hand since the time of the Tudors.

Parliament took the momentous step of limiting some of the king's prerogative rights. They supported what was known as the **Grand Remonstrance**, a list of 204 parliamentary grievances from the past decade. They also made two additional demands: that the king name ministers whom Parliament could trust and that a synod of the Church of England be called to reform the Church of England. In response Charles tried to seize five of the leaders of the House of Commons, an attempt that failed, resulting in Charles leaving London in January 1642 to raise his royal standard at Nottingham. This marks the beginning of the **English Revolution**.

The English Revolution

During the initial stage of the English Revolution, things went poorly for Parliament. Their military commander, the Earl of Manchester, pointed out the dilemma when he noted: "If we beat the King 99 times, he is still the King, but if the King defeats us, we shall be hanged and our property confiscated." Individuals such as **Oliver Cromwell**, who were far more dedicated to creating a winning war policy, soon replaced the early aristocratic leaders. It was Cromwell who created what became known as the **New Model Army**, a regularly paid, disciplined force with extremely dedicated Puritan soldiers. By 1648, the king was defeated, and in the following year, Cromwell made the momentous decision to execute the king, a move that horrified most of the nation.

From 1649 to 1660 England was officially a republic, known as **The Commonwealth**, but essentially it was a military dictatorship governed by Cromwell. Cromwell had to deal with conflicts among his own supporters, such as the clash between the **Independents** and the **Presbyterians**. The Independents, who counted Cromwell among their ranks, wanted a state church, but were also willing to grant a measure of religious freedom for others (although Catholics were to be excluded from this tolerant policy). On the other side of the divide were the Presbyterians, who wanted a state church that would not allow dissent. Cromwell also had to deal with the rise of radical factions within his army, groups like the **Levellers and Diggers**, who combined their radical religious beliefs with a call for a complete overhaul of English society. They touted a philosophy that included such radical ideas as all men should be allowed to vote for members of the House of Commons, not just those who owned land.

Cromwell destroyed the Leveller elements in his army in 1649 after several regiments with large Leveller contingents revolted against his rule. In the following year, Cromwell led an army to Ireland, where he displayed incredible brutality in putting down resistance by supporters of the Stuarts.

Cromwell would find, as Charles I had earlier, that Parliament was a difficult institution to control. In 1652, he brought his army into London to disperse a Parliament that dared to challenge him only to replace them with hand-selected individuals who still earned his displeasure within a matter of months. Over the next year, a group of army officers wrote the "Instrument of Government," the only written constitution in English history and a document that provided for republican government (the Protectorate) with a head of state holding the title **Lord Protector** and a parliament based on a fairly wide male suffrage. Cromwell stepped into the position of Lord Protector, but still found Parliament difficult to control. Finally in 1655, Cromwell gave up all hope of ruling in conjunction with a legislature, and divided England into 12 military districts, each to be governed by a major general.

By the time Cromwell died, an exhausted England wanted to bring back the Stuart dynasty. In 1660, the eldest son of the executed monarch became **Charles II**. The return of the Stuarts turned back the clock to 1642 as the same issues that had led to the revolution against Charles's father remained unresolved: What is the proper relationship between king and Parliament? What should be the religious direction of the Church of England? These issues were not fully addressed during Charles's reign although they came to the forefront during the reign of his younger brother, **James II**, who succeeded Charles on the throne in 1685.

James, a Catholic, immediately antagonized Parliament by demanding the repeal of the **Test Act**, an act that effectively barred Catholics from serving as royal officials or in the military (there was no law at this time barring Catholics from the monarchy). James also issued a **Declaration of Indulgence**, which suspended all religious tests for office holders and allowed for freedom of worship. On the surface, James appeared to have been a champion of religious freedom; this was deceptive. What James really wished to achieve in England was royal absolutism; however, the steps that he took to achieve this goal were illegal. The final stages of this conflict took place in 1688. Early in the year,

James imprisoned seven Anglican bishops for refusing to read James's suspension of the laws against Catholics from their church pulpits, the usual way of informing the community of royal edicts in an age before modern communications. James also unexpectedly fathered a child in June 1688 and now had a male heir who would be raised as a Catholic, in contrast to his previous heir, his daughter Mary, who was a Protestant. These moves to create a Catholic England created unity among previously contentious Protestant factions within England. One faction of this political and religious elite invited **William, the Stadholder** of the Netherlands and the husband of Mary, to invade England. When his troops landed, James's forces collapsed in what was basically a bloodless struggle (except for in Ireland, where there was tremendous violence over the next several years), known as the **"Glorious Revolution."** James was overthrown, and William and Mary jointly took the throne.

What followed was a constitutional settlement, which attempted to finally address the pervasive issues of this century of revolution. The settlement consisted of the following acts:

1. **The Bill of Rights** (1689) forbade the use of royal prerogative rights as Charles and James had exercised in the past. The power to suspend and dispense with laws was declared illegal. Armies could not be raised without parliamentary consent. Elections to parliament were to be free of royal interference. The monarchs also had to swear to uphold the Protestant faith, and it was declared that the monarchy could not pass into the hands of a Catholic.

2. **The Act of Toleration** (1689) was in many ways a compromise bill. To get nonconformists' (Protestants who were not members of the Church of England) support in the crucial months of 1688, Whigs and Tories had promised them that an act of toleration would be granted when William became king. The nonconformists could have achieved liberty of worship from James II's act of toleration, but an act from a popular Protestant monarch would prove to be a better safeguard to their liberties. The Act of Toleration granted the right of public worship to Protestant nonconformists but did not extend it to Unitarians or to Catholics (those two groups were also left alone, although legally they had no right to assemble to pray). The Test Act remained, which meant nonconformists, Jews, and Catholics could not sit in Parliament, until the law was changed in the nineteenth century.

3. **The Mutiny Act** (1689) authorized the use of martial law to govern the army. But the act was only in effect on a year-by-year basis, which meant that a parliament had to be summoned annually if for no other reason than to pass this act.

4. **The Act of Settlement** (1701) was passed to prevent the Catholic Stuart line from occupying the English throne. In 1714, when Queen Anne, the second Protestant daughter of James II, died childless, the throne passed to George I, the Elector of Hanover, a Protestant prince and a distant kinsman of the Stuarts.

5. **The Act of Union** (1707) marked the political unification of England and Scotland, forming the entity known as Great Britain. This union was by no means a love match and, in fact, primarily occurred because relations between the two previously independent states were so bad that on his deathbed, William III urged that union take place to forestall Scotland from going to war with England as an ally of France. As part of the agreement, Scotland gave up its parliament but was allowed to maintain the state-sponsored Presbyterian Church and its Roman-based legal system.

THE NETHERLANDS

A Center of Commerce and Trade

The relative decline of Spain as an economic power was in part due to the growing competition from the Netherlands. The Netherlands had already achieved a central role in inter-European trade due to its geographic position and large merchant marine fleet. For example, it was the Netherlands that provided a connection between the raw material producers in the Baltic region and the rest of Europe. Beyond Europe, control over the lucrative spice trade in Asia was wrested out of the hands of the Portuguese, a situation which was made worse when Spain took control over Portugal in 1580 and found itself without the resources to rival the Dutch in Asia.

Increasingly, it was the city of Amsterdam (the capital of the Netherlands), rather than the Spanish controlled city of Antwerp, that became the center of commerce in northern Europe. The sacking of the city of Antwerp in 1576 during the **Dutch War for Independence** and the permanent closing of the Scheldt River that led to its harbor, as part of the Peace of Westphalia, also aided in the decline of Antwerp and its replacement as an economic center by Amsterdam.

Dutch dominance in part came from technological achievements such as the development of less expensive but ocean-worthy cargo ships, but the Dutch also proved to be creative in their establishment of financial and commercial institutions. The **Bank of Amsterdam**, founded in the early part of the seventeenth century, issued its own currency and increased the amount of available capital, while also making Amsterdam the banking center of Europe. In 1602, the **Dutch East India Company** was established. The company operated under quasi-government control and was capitalized by both public and private investment. Risks and profits would now be shared among many more individuals, and the large capitalization behind the company allowed for the purchasing of more ships and warehouses. The Dutch also proved to be very nimble businessmen, so that when the prices of spices decreased due to oversupply, they quickly turned to other commodities such as coffee, tea, and fabrics, although by the beginning of the eighteenth century, Dutch commercial power, although continuing down to this day, would lose its preeminent place in Europe to the English.

This **"Golden Age"** in the Netherlands produced a high standard of living, with wealth being more equally distributed than any other place in Europe. The Netherlands also stood out from the rest of Europe for its **tolerant attitude towards religious minorities**, with Jews fleeing from the Spanish Inquisition and Anabaptists as well as Catholics finding a place among the majority Calvinist population.

Political Decentralization

Dutch exceptionalism also extended to the political realm, because politically, the Netherlands didn't look like any other state in Europe. For most of the seventeenth century, it was politically decentralized, with each of the seven provinces retaining extensive autonomy. Wealthy merchants dominated the provincial Estates, which retained powers far more extensive than the national Estates General, particularly in the area of taxation. Executive power, such as it was, came from the noble **House of Orange**, whose family members had achieved prominence for leading the revolt against Spain. The male head of this family held the title of *stadholder*, an office with primarily a military function, no mere formality as the Netherlands switched from fighting for its independence from Spain to economic wars against the English and a long-term struggle for survival against France. During the struggle with Louis XIV's France, the power of the provincial Estates went into decline, while the authority of **William of Nassau**, the head of the House of Orange, increased tremendously, particularly when William became King of England after the Revolution of 1688.

A GOLDEN AGE OF ART

Culturally, the seventeenth century proved to be a golden age as well. Dutch artists, reflecting the fact that the majority of the population was Calvinist, didn't receive large commissions to be placed in churches, although the Baroque style of painting penetrated the Netherlands through Catholic Flanders. Instead, Dutch artists painted for private collectors, who supported an incredibly large numbers of painters and a wide range of styles, including the production of a large number of landscapes, which may have been popular because the Netherlands occupied little actual land. Like so much else in the Netherlands, pictures were treated as commodities, with prices at times reaching speculative rates.

The art market didn't just flourish in Amsterdam, as shown by the thriving career of **Franz Hals** (c. 1580–1666), the great portrait painter from Haarlem. Another gifted Dutch painter, **Jan Vermeer** (1632–1675), had initially thought of being a painter of historical scenes, but when he received no commissions, he turned to the carefully composed genre scenes of everyday Dutch life, for which he has become justifiably famous. The greatest genius of the Dutch golden age was **Rembrandt Van Rijn** (1606–1669), whose paintings, which were initially influenced by the High Baroque and were later in his career more subtly painted, are fraught with a deep emotional complexity. One of his masterpieces, *The Night Watch* (1642), transforms a standard group portrait of a military company into a revealing psychological study.

ECONOMIC AND SOCIAL LIFE IN EARLY MODERN EUROPE

It's a little difficult to generalize about life in Early Modern Europe, because conditions varied from region to region, but general trends do emerge for the period.

ECONOMIC EXPANSION AND POPULATION GROWTH

By the end of the fifteenth century, Europe was ushering in an age of economic expansion that sharply contrasted with the decline that had taken root in the fourteenth century with its disastrous famines and plagues.

The key development in the period was the **growth in population.** To use France as a typical example, the population doubled from 10 million to 20 million from 1450 to 1550. This significant population expansion was very important for economic productivity, in an age in which manpower was still far more important than labor-saving technology. The expansion of Europe's population also provided for additional consumers, which meant that there was greater incentive to bring more food and other essentials to market.

The growth of population also had an impact on another important development, the significant increase in prices in the Early Modern period, which has become known as the **Price Revolution**. Initially, historians thought that this increase came from the influx of precious metals from the New World and the debasement of their coinage by money-hungry monarchs, but it is now apparent that it was population growth that put pressure on the prices of basic commodities such as wheat. This inflation did not increase at a rate that would impress a modern consumer, with grain prices increasing 500 percent—which sounds much more impressive until you take into account that this increase took place in the 150-year period from 1500 to 1650. Nevertheless, for a society that was accustomed to stable prices, a price increase of this magnitude came as a shock. Historians have even tried to find ways of connecting the Price Revolution to the political and religious struggles of the age, based on the theory that periods of high inflation can be an important factor behind the development of social tensions.

Rural Life and the Emergence of Economic Classes

One way in which rural life was transformed in this period, in part due to the Price Revolution, was the emergence of a class of wealthy individuals, located socially below the aristocracy, who began to buy significant amounts of newly valuable landholdings. In England, this class of individuals, who often had their economic roots in fortunes made in towns and cities, were known as the **gentry**, and would play a major role in the political struggles that the English Parliament would wage against the monarchy in the seventeenth century. The land-buying habits of the gentry forced up the price of land. In addition, the gentry were able to use their social connections to get local authorities to accept the **enclosure** of lands for their own personal use, land that had previously been available for the grazing of animals by the entire community. In Book 1 of *Utopia*, Sir Thomas More refers to the notion of sheep devouring men, a criticism of the displacement of the small farmer by valuable herds of sheep.

The problem of rural poverty became significantly worse in the Early Modern period, with many small farmers reduced to the role of beggars, spending their days tramping from one locale to another. Increasingly, the problem of poverty weighed on the political elite; in Catholic lands, the Church remained the major provider of social services, while in Protestant countries it became the task of the state to provide for the destitute, such as in the example of the first **English Poor Law** during the reign of Queen Elizabeth. Although rural overpopulation was a problem throughout most of western Europe, in eastern Europe, low population density was a much more serious problem, leading wealthy landowners to solve their labor shortages by binding the formerly free peasantry to the land in a process of enserfment.

Farm Life

For the majority of individuals in Europe, who lived in rural areas as small-scale farmers, life was fairly dismal and centered on a constant struggle to find the resources to survive. Life centered around the small village, often with fewer than 50 households, with most never traveling a few miles beyond the location of their birth. Housing in rural villages offered little protection from the cold and wet winters. Homes were generally made of wood, with packed mud on the walls and straw on the floor and lacking windows and adequate ventilation. For the most part, they consisted of one main room that possessed a stone hearth that provided heat. The possessions that went into these houses were as simple as their surroundings, with a few cooking utensils, a table, and some stools. The worldly possessions of most rural households could fit in a single chest, which could double as a table and could be carried away by the family in case they had to flee during an emergency, such as the arrival of mercenaries looking for plunder.

The workdays were long during the summer harvests, and shorter in the winter, with late winter offering the rural household the terrifying prospect of not having enough resources to tie them over until the coming of spring. Although farming began to change by the end of the seventeenth century in the Netherlands and in England with the beginnings of what we may refer to as scientific methods, for the most part, Europeans were farming in 1800 the same way they had farmed going back to the High Middle Ages, with the **three-field system** used in the north of Europe and the two-field system predominating in the Mediterranean region. Farmland in most rural areas was set out in long strips, with individual peasant families owning a portion of land in each of the strips. Because animals such as cows or sheep needed copious amounts of food, common lands in each village were shared, although the wealthy rural elite was increasingly coveting this common land. Most of what was grown was used by the farmers for the use of their own households, leaving very little to be brought to market. The diet of the average European peasant farmer was incredibly monotonous, with most calories coming from grain in various forms, ranging from dark bread to gruels and beer.

Life in the Cities and Towns

Although towns and cities held scarcely more than 10 percent of the overall population, they provided for some variation from what Karl Marx would call "the idiocy of rural life." Townspeople in general lived better than their rural counterparts, with better housing and a more varied diet, although urban poverty was also increasing in this period.

There was also a much greater variety of occupations, with a much greater emphasis on specialization, with specific tasks such as baking or brewing taking place in specific quarters of the town. **Guilds**, which began to dominate the urban economy during the High Middle Ages, continued to play a role in the production of commodities down to the time of the French Revolution.

However, the guild method of production was being supplanted by a new means of production that was in part directed by the expansion of population and the growth of markets. Cloth production was now done on a much larger scale by a new group of **capitalist entrepreneurs** and required a large outlay of money to get started. These individuals would provide the money and the organizational skills, which they used to direct every stage of the production of broad cloth, beginning with the cleaning of the wool and ending with the weaving. This work provided a benefit in some rural households (where the various stages of production would now take place), adding an important source of revenue particularly during the long winter months.

For guild members, however, this new competition created great hardships. Also, for those apprentices and journeymen who had expected at some point to become full-fledged guild masters, such dreams were becoming increasingly rare, and they became essentially wage earners with little hope of rising up the economic and social ranks. Dissatisfied journeymen and apprentices would play an important role in the urban revolts of the period.

Family Life and Family Structure/Hierarchy

Although we tend to assume that some notion of the extended family existed in the past, with several generations living under one roof, the family in the Early Modern period would not look significantly different from today's nuclear family. Family size was smaller than what one might have imagined for the period, with the average family consisting of no more than three or four children. The relatively small number of children was partly the result of fewer childbearing years resulting from later marriages, with women on average marrying around 25 and men two years later. Traditionally, marriages were either arranged by the parents or at least formally approved, in part because even in the poorest of rural communities, marriage involved some transfer of property. Weddings were important community events, because the married couple was now considered to be full-fledged members of society, and in general, single adults were looked on as potential thieves or troublemakers if they were male and as prostitutes if they were female.

The Role of Men in the Family

In many ways, the family with the father as the patriarchal head served as a reflection in miniature of the larger hierarchical ordering of Early Modern society. In wealthier families, the father had to ensure that the family's wealth remained intact, which meant that the oldest male child inherited most of the estate **(primogeniture)**, with younger sons being guided towards careers in the church, military, or in the increased opportunities offered by the burgeoning administration of the Early Modern state.

The Role of Women

The only claim that daughters would have on the parental estate would come with the **dowry** that they would receive upon marriage. Wives could usually determine who should receive their dowry upon their death, although during their own lifetime their husbands would manage the dowry. Among the poor, arrangements would be different, with boys apprenticed off to a trade or as servants at the age of seven, and domestic service being the only opportunities for girls, who in the poorest of families were left with the difficult task of trying to raise their own dowry.

The Family as Economic Unit

Families, whether rich or poor, should be seen as an economic unit, with tasks divided by both gender and age, and child labor (which would be much deplored during the Industrial Revolution) passed without comment in this period. Men were in what might be called the "public" sphere, which might mean handling the plowing of the family's plot in the strip fields or managing the family's commercial interests if they lived in a town. Women took care of the domestic sphere, the cooking, cleaning, and childrearing, although in wealthier households, they would more likely be in a supervisory role. Life for women centered around their pregnancies, which in wealthier families were an annual occurrence, whereas it was less frequent among the poor. The wealthy were also, due to their better diet, more likely to see their children survive.

How the Protestant Reformation Changed Family Life

Although one can scarcely talk about a revolution taking place in family life in this period, the Protestant Reformation did usher in some changes. In Protestant lands, the household became the center of Christian life, rather than the church or monastery. Arguably, paternalism increased, as the father now assumed a spiritual role as the chief intermediary between the family and God, while also more strictly enforcing moral standards and the value of hard work. For women who wanted to avoid marriage and constant childrearing, the option of convent life came to an end, and frugal fathers lost the opportunity to save dowry money. In some places, divorce was allowed, something that was anathema to the Catholic Church.

Although women in Protestant lands were conceivably freer in the sense of being able like any man to directly communicate with God without relying on a male priest as an intermediary, those women who wanted to take a more active role by leading congregations and preaching—as seen in some of the more radical Protestant sects such as the Anabaptists—were going to be brutally persecuted.

CHAPTER TIMELINE

In addition to the events discussed in this chapter, the timeline below includes many events mentioned in the previous and next chapters. This is due to the overlap in time periods. The benefit is that you will have a complete picture of events taking place concurrently in a variety of areas (art, religion, government, etc.). As advised earlier, try not to get caught up in memorizing each and every date, as the point here is simply to give you a feel for the flow of major events in European history and to help you recognize potential cause and effect relationships between the timing of one event and another.

Year(s)	Event
1415	Prince Henry the Navigator participates in capture of Ceuta
1415	Burning at the stake of Jan Hus at the Council of Constance
1417	Great Schism comes to an end
1420s	Development of single-point perspective
1440	Lorenzo Valla's *On the Donation of Constantine*
1440s	Donatello's *David*
1450	Ludovico il Moro becomes despot of Milan
1452	Gutenberg prints bible
1453	End of the Hundred Years War
1453	Fall of Constantinople
1454	Treaty of Lodi
1469	Marriage of Ferdinand of Aragon to Isabella of Castile
1485	Henry VII begins Tudor dynasty following Battle of Bosworth
1486	Pico's *Oration on the Dignity of Man*
1487	Bartholomew Dias sails around Cape of Good Hope
1492	Columbus leaves Spain for what he believes will be Asia
1492	Expulsion of the Jews from Spain
1492	Reconquista of Spain completed

Year(s)	Event
1492	Lorenzo de Medici dies
1494	King Charles VIII of France invades Italy
1494	The Treaty of Torsedillas divides the discoveries in the New World between Spain and Portugal
1498	Vasco da Gama reaches the coast of India
1498	Burning of Savonarola
1501	Michelangelo's *David*
1503	Leonardo's *Mona Lisa*
1509	Raphael's *School of Athens*
1513	Machiavelli writes *The Prince*
1519	Ferdinand Magellan sets out to circumnavigate the globe
1519	Hernán Cortés lands on the coast of Mexico
1519	Charles V becomes Holy Roman Emperor
1521	Luther called before the Diet of Worms
1522	Ignatius Loyola begins *The Spiritual Exercises*
1525	German Peasant Revolt
1528	Castiglione's *The Courtier*
1529	Diet of Speyer
1529	Henry VIII summons the "Reformation Parliament"
1531	Zwingli dies in battle
1531	Francesco Pizarro sets out for Peru
1534	Henry VIII's Act of Supremacy

Year(s)	Event
1534	Anabaptists seize Munster
1535	Sir Thomas More executed by Henry VIII
1536	Calvin publishes first edition of his *Institutes*
1540	Jesuits receive official papal sanction as religious order
1540	Henry VIII marries Ann Boleyn
1540s	Schmalkaldic Wars
1543	Copernicus publishes his *Concerning the Revolutions of the Celestial Spheres*
1543	Andreas Vesalius writes *De humani corporis fabrica* with its critique of the anatomical work of Galen
1545	Council of Trent convenes
1553	End of reign of Edward VI
1553	Michael Servetus burnt at the stake in Geneva
1555	Peace of Augsburg
1556	Philip II becomes King of Spain
1558	Beginning of reign of Elizabeth Tudor
1559	Frederick III of the Palatinate converts to Calvinism
1559	Death of King Henry II of France
1559	Elizabethan religious settlement
1562	Beginning of the French Wars of Religion
1571	Battle of Lepanto
1572	St. Bartholomew's Day Massacre
1587	Execution of Mary, Queen of Scots

Year(s)	Event
1588	Failure of the Spanish Armada
1589	Henry Bourbon becomes King Henry IV
1593	Henry IV converts to Catholicism
1598	Edict of Nantes
1600	Giordano Bruno burned at the stake
1602	Dutch East India Company established
1603	James II becomes king following death of Elizabeth
1603	Michael Romanov begins new dynasty in Russia
1605	Cervantes publishes first part of *Don Quixote*
1607	Founding of colony at Jamestown
1610	Assassination of Henry IV
1610	Galileo begins astronomical observations with his telescope
1613	Galileo publishes *Letters on Sunspots*
1616	William Harvey announces his discovery of the circulatory system
1618	Johannes Kepler reveals his third and final law of planetary motion
1618	Beginning of the Thirty Years War
1620	Battle of White Mountain
1620	Founding of Plymouth Colony
1620	Francis Bacon publishes *Novum Organum*
1624	Cardinal Richelieu becomes Louis XIII's chief minister
1625	Charles I becomes king upon death of James I
1628	Petition of Right

Year(s)	Event
1628	Murder of the Duke of Buckingham
1629	Edict of Restitution
1629	Personal Rule of Charles I begins and will last 11 years
1632	Gustavus Adolphus dies at the Battle of Lutzen
1632	Galileo's *Dialogue on the Two Chief Systems of the World*
1633	Trial of Galileo
1633	Murder of Albrecht von Wallenstein
1633	France enters the Thirty Years War
1637	Charles introduces the Book of Common Prayer into Scotland
1637	Rene Descartes publishes *Discourse on Method*
1640	Beginning of reign of Frederick William (Great Elector)
1640	Charles forced to summon Parliament to deal with Scottish revolt
1641	Rebellion in Ireland
1642	Execution of the Earl of Strafford
1642	Issuing of Grand Remonstrance
1642	Beginning of English Revolution
1643	Five-year-old Louis XIV becomes king of France
1645	Execution of Archbishop Laud
1648	Peace of Westphalia
1649	Beginning of the *Fronde*
1649	Execution of Charles I and establishment of English republic
1653	Oliver Cromwell becomes Lord Protector

Year(s)	Event
1659	Death of Cromwell
1660	Restoration of Charles II
1660	Thomas Hobbes publishes *Leviathan*
1661	Death of Cardinal Mazarin; Louis XIV becomes own chief minister
1662	Royal Society established by Charles II
1664	Chartering of the French East India Company
1669	Louis XIV begins construction of the Palace of Versailles
1669	Posthumous publication of Pascal's *Pensées*
1682	Beginning of the reign of Peter the Great
1682	Rembrandt paints *The Night Watch*
1685	Revocation of the Edict of Nantes
1685	James II, a Catholic, becomes king of England
1687	Newton publishes his *Principia*
1688	John Locke's *Two Treatises on Government*
1688	Glorious Revolution
1689	Act of Toleration
1690	John Locke's *Essay on Human Understanding*
1701	Prussia becomes a kingdom
1701	Act of Settlement passed to bypass potential Catholic kings
1703	Cornerstone laid for the new city of St. Petersburg
1707	Act of Union brings about political unification of England and Scotland
1713	Treaty of Utrecht marks end of the War of the Spanish Succession

REVIEW QUESTIONS

Answers and explanations are in Chapter 15.

1. Which of the following European states was the first to send sailors into the Indian Ocean?

   (A) France
   (B) Great Britain
   (C) Portugal
   (D) Spain
   (E) Genoa

2. The Spanish term *Reconquista* refers to which of the following?

   (A) Spain's victory over the French in northern Italy
   (B) The defeat of the Islamic states on the Spanish peninsula
   (C) The long sought rapprochement with Portugal
   (D) The beginnings of Habsburg rule in Spain
   (E) The sailing of the Armada against England

3. King Gustavus Adolphus of Sweden entered the Thirty Years War in 1629 in order to

   (A) forestall the entry of France into the conflict
   (B) aid the Habsburg cause
   (C) neutralize the potential threat from England
   (D) defend Protestant interests in the Holy Roman Empire
   (E) keep Habsburg troops from directly entering Swedish territory

4. Which of the following individuals said, "Paris is worth a Mass"?

   (A) Cardinal Richelieu
   (B) Henry IV
   (C) Louis XIII
   (D) Catherine de Medici
   (E) Louis XIV

5. King Charles I of England was forced to call a parliament in 1640 following

   (A) the outbreak of a rebellion in Scotland
   (B) the declaration of war between France and England
   (C) the demands of Parliament to be called into session
   (D) a mass public outcry demanding that a new parliamentary session be called
   (E) a declaration of royal bankruptcy

6. In the Early Modern era, urban disturbances among journeymen and apprentices were most often related to

   (A) resentment by apprentices against the socially higher journeymen
   (B) the banning of guilds by increasingly centralized monarchies
   (C) a decline in population leading to falling prices
   (D) growing social tensions between various guilds
   (E) social tensions stemming from the inability to enter the rank of masters

7. Which of the following best describes the Early Modern family as an economic unit?

   (A) Males were in the "public" sphere while females were in the "domestic."
   (B) Male and female roles were largely interchangeable among the peasantry but not among the bourgeoisie.
   (C) The family as an economic unit was collapsing following the introduction of capitalist production methods.
   (D) Larger immediate families meant that extended families were no longer part of the same economic unit.
   (E) Child labor was no longer as essential a component in an age of economic expansion.

The Scientific Revolution and Enlightenment

(Mid Sixteenth Century–Late Eighteenth Century)

In 1611, the English poet John Donne wrote *The Anatomy of the World*, in which he reflected on the multitude of ways that his world had changed as a result of the new discoveries in science.

> New philosophy calls all in doubt
> The element of fire is quite put out;
> The sun is lost, and th' Earth, and no man's wit
> Can well direct him where to looke for it.
> And freely men confesse that this world's spent,
> When in the Planets, and the new firmament
> They seeke so many new; then see that this
> Is crumbled out againe to his Atomies
> 'Tis all in peeces, all coherance gone;
> All just supply, and all Relation.

EVENTS LEADING TO THE SCIENTIFIC REVOLUTION

As Donne understood, the scientific discoveries of the sixteenth and seventeenth centuries brought about a fundamental change in the way Europeans viewed the natural world. To call this change a revolution may be misleading in light of the length of time over which it occurred, but the implications from these discoveries were truly revolutionary. Not only did it change the way Europeans viewed the world around them, but it also had significant implications in such areas as religion and political thought.

Why was it that seventeenth-century thinkers challenged the medieval view of the natural world? What possibly occurred in that age that led them to question ideas that previously had been readily accepted? The following are some possibilities.

DISCOVERY OF THE NEW WORLD

The period of exploration and conquest led to the discovery of new plant and animal life and possibly encouraged greater interest in the natural sciences. Also, the traditional link between navigation and astronomy and the great advances made by Portuguese navigators in the fifteenth century helped fuel an interest in learning more about the stars.

INVENTION OF THE PRINTING PRESS

Scientific knowledge could spread much more rapidly because of the printing press. By the second half of the seventeenth century, there were numerous books and newsletters keeping people informed about the most recent scientific discoveries. It is because of the printing press that Thomas Hobbes, sitting in England, was cognizant of scientific discoveries coming out of Italy.

RIVALRY AMONG NATION-STATES

The constant warfare between the various nation-states may have pushed scientific development by placing an increasing importance on technology, or applied science. In China, by comparison, a land previously well ahead of Europe in terms of achievements, the lack of an external threat during the sixteenth and seventeenth centuries may have helped create a complacency that stood in the way of scientific and technological advancement.

REFORMATION

The historian Robert K. Merton suggested a number of years ago that the English who professed Calvinist beliefs were somehow linked to those who were active in the new science. Even earlier than Merton, one of the fathers of sociology, Max Weber, argued that the worldly asceticism found in Protestantism helped create capitalism, which in turn helped propel the Scientific Revolution. These theories, however, ignore the fact that much of the Scientific Revolution came from Catholic Italy. The telescope and microscope, for example, were Italian in origin, as was the new botany. Nevertheless, the Protestant Reformation, by encouraging people to read the Bible, did help create a larger reading public. And although Luther, Calvin, and the like were not interested in challenging the traditional scientific worldview, their opposition to the religious hegemony of Rome did provide a powerful example of challenging established authority.

RENAISSANCE HUMANISM

Humanist interest in the writings of the classical world also extended to the scientific texts of the ancient Greeks. Certain texts, such as Archimedes's writings on mathematics and Galen's anatomical studies, were rediscovered in the Renaissance. Although the Scientific Revolution ultimately rejected the ideas contained in such works, this basic familiarity with the past was a necessary stage in order for modern scientific thought to mature.

MEDIEVAL WORLD VIEW PRIOR TO THE SCIENTIFIC REVOLUTION

The medieval world view was based on **scholasticism**, a synthesis of Christian theology with the scientific beliefs of the ancient authors. The great architect of this synthesis was **Thomas Aquinas** (1225–1274), who took the works of **Aristotle** and harmonized them with the teachings of the church. Knowledge of God remained the supreme act of learning and was to be attained through both reason and revelation. The value of science, for those living in the Middle Ages, was that it offered the possibility of a better understanding of the mysterious workings of God. To view science without this religious framework was simply inconceivable in the Middle Ages.

Influenced by the work of Aristotle, medieval people thought that the material world was made up of four elements: Earth, air, fire, and water. Earth was the heaviest and the basest of the elements and therefore tended toward the center of the universe. Water was also heavy but lighter than Earth, so its natural place was covering the Earth. Air was above water, with fire as the lightest element of all. It was this notion of the four elements that gave rise to the idea of **alchemy**, or the perfect compound of the four elements in their perfect proportions. Less perfect metals such as lead might be transformed by changing the proportion of their elements. The four-element approach also dominated the practice of medicine. The four elements combined in the human body to create what were known as the four humours: blood, phlegm, yellow bile, and black bile. An excess of any one of the humours produced one's essential personal characteristics.

People in the Middle Ages did not have a great interest in astronomy; the popular work of the Greek astronomer **Ptolemy** (c. 85–165 A.D.) was not questioned. The Ptolemaic, or Geocentric, system placed the Earth as a stationary object around which heavenly bodies moved, while the stars were fixed in their orbits. One problem with this system was addressed rather early: How does one explain the unusual motion of the planets in relation to the fixed stars? At times planets even appeared to be moving backward. To cope with these problems, epicycles—planetary orbits within an orbit—were added to the system.

THE COPERNICAN REVOLUTION

In 1543, **Nicholas Copernicus** (1473–1543), a Polish mathematician and astronomer, wrote *Concerning the Revolutions of the Celestial Spheres*. Copernicus was a cleric, and since he was afraid of the implications of the ideas contained in the work, he waited many years before he finally decided to publish it. When he finally took that step, Copernicus cautiously dedicated the book to **Pope Paul III** and included a preface that claimed that the ideas contained on those pages were just mathematical hypotheses. Even the language of the work was moderate as Copernicus merely suggested that should the Earth revolve around the sun, it would solve at least some of the problematic epicycles of the Ptolemaic system. However, since the Copernican, or **Heliocentric**, system explains that the planets move in a circular motion around the sun, it did not completely eliminate all the epicycles. Despite his book's famous reputation, Copernicus's ideas did not stir a revolution in the way in which people viewed the planets and the stars.

AFTER COPERNICUS

The Earth-centered system would not go away that quickly. The Danish astronomer **Tycho Brahe** (1546–1601) tried to come up with a different Earth-centered system rather than just rely on the Ptolemaic system. Brahe had plenty of time on his hands to construct the best astronomical tables of the age, as his social life was nonexistent after he lost part of his nose in a duel and rebuilt it with a prosthetic made of silver and gold alloy. Brahe proposed a system in which the moon and the sun revolved around the Earth, while the other planets revolved around the sun.

Brahe's student, **Johannes Kepler** (1571–1630), disagreed with his teacher concerning Copernicus's findings. Kepler ended up using Brahe's own data to search for ways to support Copernicus and eventually dropped Copernicus's "planets move in a circular motion" theory, instead proposing that their orbits were elliptical. However, it would take the greatest mind of the next age, **Isaac Newton**, to explain why this elliptical motion was in fact possible.

GALILEO

The first scientist to build on the work of Copernicus was a Florentine by the name of **Galileo Galilei** (1564–1642). In 1609, he heard about a Dutchman who had invented a spyglass that allowed distant objects to be seen as if close up. Galileo then designed his own telescope that magnified far away objects thirty times the naked eye's capacity. Using this instrument, he noticed that the moon had a mountainous surface very much like the Earth. For Galileo, this provided evidence that it was composed of material similar to that on Earth and not some purer substance as Aristotle had argued. Galileo also realized that the stars were much further away than the planets. He saw that Jupiter had four moons of her own. This challenged the traditional notion of the unique relationship between Earth and her moon. Sunspots and rings around Saturn also put the whole Ptolemaic construct into doubt.

Galileo was also interested in the question of motion. He may not have really thrown a ten-pound weight and a one-pound weight from the top of the Leaning Tower of Pisa, but he did notice that heavier weights do not fall any faster. He also noticed that under ideal conditions a body in motion would tend to stay in motion. It was therefore relatively easy for him to deduce from this the possibility that Earth is in perpetual motion.

Following the publication of his *Dialogues on the Two Chief Systems of the World* (1632), the Catholic Church began to condemn Galileo's work. In 1616, the Catholic Church labeled the Copernican theory as "foolish and absurd, philosophically false, and formally heretical." The church authorities warned Galileo not to publish any more writings on astronomy. Throwing caution to the wind, he wrote a book that compared the new science with the old; an ignorant clown Simplicio represented the old science. Pope Urban VIII thought the book was making fun of him, and he put Galileo under house arrest for the remainder of his life. This did not stop Galileo from writing, although he was forced to send his manuscripts to Holland where the mood was more tolerant.

Galileo proved to be far more fortunate than his fellow Italian, **Giordano Bruno** (1548–1600), a Dominican friar who was executed by the **papal Inquisition** in 1600 for arguing that there may be a plurality of worlds in the universe. The Church took this as an implication that there might be a multiplicity of redeeming Christs—an intolerable heresy.

SIR ISAAC NEWTON

The greatest figure of the Scientific Revolution was **Isaac Newton** (1642–1727). Newton wanted to solve the problem posed by the work of Copernicus, Kepler, and Galileo: How do you explain the orderly manner in which the planets revolve around the sun? Newton worked for almost two decades on the problem before he published his masterpiece, *Principia*, in 1687. Galileo's work on motion influenced Newton, a sign of the intellectual link between southern and northern scientists. Newton wondered what force kept the planets in an elliptical orbit around the sun, when theoretically they should be moving in a straight line. Supposedly Newton saw an apple drop from a tree and deduced that the same force that drew the apple to the ground may explain planetary motion. Newton finally posited that all planets and objects in the universe operated under the effects of gravity.

It is important to remember that Newton was an extremely religious man and often wondered why, when he delivered public talks, his audiences were more interested in his scientific discoveries than in theology. He spent a great deal of time making silly calculations of biblical dates and practicing alchemy. More important, he began to experiment with optics, thus making the study of light a new scientific endeavor. It was Newton who showed that white light was a heterogeneous mixture of rays rather than the pure light many believed it to be. Newton is also the father of differential **calculus** (much to the regret of those of you who will have to take it in high school). Finally, Newton also eventually became head of the British Royal Society, an organization committed to spreading the new spirit of experimentation.

THE IMPACT OF THE SCIENTIFIC REVOLUTION ON PHILOSOPHY

Among the philosophers affected by the new science was **Francis Bacon** (1561–1626). Bacon led an extraordinarily varied life. He was a lawyer, an official in the government of James I, a historian, and an essayist. The one thing he did not do in his life, it seems, was perform scientific experiments. What he did contribute to science was the experimental methodology. In his three major works, *The Advancement of Learning* (1605), *Novum Organum* (1620), and *New Atlantis* (1627), Bacon attacked medieval scholasticism with its belief that the body of knowledge was basically complete and that the only task left to scholars was to elaborate on existing knowledge. Instead, Bacon argued that rather than rely on tradition, it was necessary to examine evidence from nature. In France, this debate over the new learning became known as the conflict between the ancients and the moderns, while in England it was known as the "Battle of the Books."

RENÉ DESCARTES

The French philosopher **Descartes** (1596–1650) can in some ways be seen as the anti-Bacon. For Descartes, deductive thought—using reason to go from a general principle to the specific principle—provided for a better understanding of the universe as opposed to relying on the experimental method. However, like Bacon, Descartes believed that the ideas of the past were so suffocating that they all must be doubted. In his famous quote, **"I think, therefore I am,"** Descartes stripped away his belief in everything except his own existence. Another way that Descartes broke with the past was by writing in French rather than Latin, which had been the language of intellectual discourse in the Middle Ages. Descartes was also a highly gifted mathematician who invented analytical mathematics.

Descartes's system can be found in his *Discourse on Method* (1637). In the work, he reduced nature to two distinct elements: mind and matter. The world of the mind involved the soul and the spirit, and Descartes left that world to the theologians. The world of matter, however, was made up of an infinite number of particles. He viewed this world as operating in a mechanistic manner, as if in a constant whirlpool that provided contact among the various particles.

BLAISE PASCAL

Pascal (1623–1662) saw his life as a balancing act. He wanted to balance what he saw as the dogmatic thinking of the Jesuits with those who were complete religious skeptics. His life's attempt to achieve this balance is found in his *Pensées*, particularly in the idea that became known as **Pascal's Wager**, in which Pascal concluded that it was better to wager on the existence of God than on the obverse, since the expected value that comes from believing is always greater than the expected value of not believing. Pascal became involved with the **Jansenists**, a Catholic faction that saw truth in St. Augustine's idea of the total sinfulness of mankind and the need for salvation to be achieved through faith because we are predestined—ideas that were also followed by the Calvinists.

THOMAS HOBBES

Thomas Hobbes (1588–1679) personally knew Galileo, Bacon, and Descartes and was also friends with **William Harvey** (1578–1657), who, rather than relying on the writings of the Ancient Greeks, used dissections to show the role the heart plays in the circulation of blood through the body. His contact with the leading figures in the world of science influenced Hobbes to apply the experimental methods they used in the study of nature to the study of politics. Hobbes' willingness to think scientifically shows the way in which the world had changed from the time of Machiavelli, whose work reflects the world as it was during the pre–Scientific Revolution. Hobbes was horrified by the turmoil of the English Revolution and was convinced of the depravity of human nature; man was like an animal in that he was stimulated by appetites rather than by noble ideas. Hobbes wrote in his classic work, *Leviathan*, that life was "nasty, brutish, and short."

Hobbes's view of the depravity of human nature led him to propose the necessity for **absolutism**. Man formed states, or what Hobbes called the great Leviathan, because they were necessary constructs that worked to restrain the human urges to destroy one another. Out of necessity, the sovereign has complete and total power over his subjects. The subjects are obliged never to rebel, and the sovereign must put down rebellion by any means possible. When the parliamentary side won the civil war, Hobbes went back to England and quietly went on with his life. He readily accepted any established power, and therefore he could live under Cromwell's firm rule. His theories did not please traditional English royalists, since his brand of absolutism was not based on the divine right theory of kingship.

JOHN LOCKE

Like Hobbes, **John Locke** (1632–1704) was interested in the world of science. His *Two Treatises on Government*, written before the Revolution of 1688, was published after William and Mary came to the throne and served as a defense of the revolution as well as a basis for the Bill of Rights. It also proved critical for the intellectual development of the founders of the United States. Locke argued that man is born free in nature, although as society gets more advanced, government is needed to organize this society. Because man is a free and rational entity, when he enters into a **social contract** with the state, he does not give up his inalienable rights to life, liberty, and property. Should an oppressive government challenge those rights, man has a right to rebel.

Locke was an opponent of religious enthusiasm. In his *Letter Concerning Toleration*, Locke attacked the idea that Christianity could be spread by force. His influential *Essay on Human Understanding* contained the idea that children enter the world with no set ideas. At birth, the mind is a blank slate or *tabula rasa*, and infants do not possess the Christian concept of predestination or original sin. Instead, Locke subscribed to the theory that all knowledge was empirical in that it comes from experience.

THE EIGHTEENTH-CENTURY ENLIGHTENMENT

Although his response has become a bit of a cliché, there is no better answer to the question, "What is the Enlightenment?" than that offered by the German philosopher **Immanuel Kant** (1724–1804). For Kant, the answer was clear: "Dare to know." By this, he meant that it was necessary for individuals to cast off those ideas of the past that had been accepted simply because of tradition or intellectual laziness and instead use one's reason to probe for answers to questions on the nature of mankind. The ultimate reward, stated Kant, would be something that all previous generations had so woefully lacked—freedom. This freedom would extend to the political and religious realms and would also lead the writers of the Enlightenment to cast doubt on such ancient human practices as slavery.

Traditionally, the Enlightenment has been associated with France, where they use the term *philosophes* to describe the thinkers of the age. These *philosophes* were not organized in any formal group, although many of the most prominent displayed their erudition at salons, which were informal discussion groups organized by wealthy women. Others would hang around the print shop putting the final touches on their pamphlets. No matter where their ideas were produced, French thinkers helped produce the so-called **"Republic of Letters,"** an international community of writers who communicated in French. This Republic of Letters extended throughout much of western Europe and of course to the American colonies, where the ideas of the Enlightenment would play a significant role in the founding of the United States.

The direction of the Enlightenment changed over the course of the eighteenth century. The early Enlightenment was deeply rooted in the Scientific Revolution and was profoundly influenced by Great Britain, which appeared to continental writers as a bastion of freedom and economic expansion, while also providing the world with such inestimable thinkers as John Locke. Locke's idea, expressed in his *Essay Concerning Human Understanding*, that the individual is a blank slate at birth, provided a powerful argument for the potential impact of education as well as for the inherent equality among all people. Locke also greatly influenced eighteenth-century thought through his contention that every person has the right to life, liberty, and property, and that there is a contractual relationship between the ruler and the subjects.

As the age of Enlightenment continued, it moved beyond the influence of Locke, who had refused to see how freedom could be granted to slaves in the Americas. Writers such as **Voltaire** and **David Hume** would offer a powerful challenge to established religion. By the end of the century, people such as **Adam Smith** had veered into other areas such as economic thought. **Jean-Jacques Rousseau** inspired people of the age to seek to find truth not through the cold application of reason, but rather through a thorough examination of their inner emotions. Meanwhile, in places such as Russia, Prussia, and Austria, rulers sought to find ways to blend their royal absolutism with some of the ideas of the Enlightenment, although little would come out of this attempt except perhaps a further enhancement of their absolute authority.

VOLTAIRE

Perhaps the greatest of the *philosophes* was **Voltaire** (1694–1778). After writing a number of rather forgettable volumes of poetry and drama, Voltaire went to England, a trip that would forever change his life. He was struck by the relative religious tolerance practiced there as well as the freedom to express one's ideas in print—far greater than that which existed in France. Voltaire was also struck by the honor the English showed Newton when the scientist was buried with great aplomb at a state funeral. To Voltaire, England seemed to offer those things that allowed for the happiness of the individual, which seemed so desperately lacking in his own land of France.

Although educated by the Jesuits, Voltaire hated the Catholic Church and despised what he thought was the narrowness and bigotry that was at the heart of all religious traditions. Voltaire was a **deist**, one who believes that God created the universe and then stepped back from creation to allow it to operate under the laws of science. Voltaire felt that religion crushed the human spirit and that to be free, man needed to *Écrasez l'infame!* (Crush the horrible thing!)—his famous anti-religious slogan.

Voltaire's most famous work is *Candide* (1759), which he was inspired to write following an earthquake that completely leveled the city of Lisbon in 1755. Voltaire was particularly struck by the story of a group of parishioners who, following the earthquake, went back into their church to give thanks to God for sparing their lives, only to have the weakened foundations of the church collapse on them. One of the false stereotypes concerning the ideas of the Enlightenment is that it was fundamentally optimistic. *Candide* is a deeply pessimistic work, as young Candide and his traveling companions meet with one disaster after another. The book basically touts the idea that humans cannot expect to find contentment by connecting themselves with a specific philosophical system. Instead, the best one can hope for is a sort of private, inner solace, or as Voltaire put it, "one must cultivate one's own garden."

Voltaire became an intellectual celebrity across Europe following his involvement in the case of Jean Calas, a French Protestant who was falsely accused of murdering his son after learning that the son was planning to convert to Catholicism. In 1762, the Parliament of Toulouse ordered Calas's execution, and he was brutally tortured to death. In the following year, Voltaire published his *Treatise on Toleration* and pushed for a reexamination of the evidence. By 1765, the authorities reversed their decision, and while it was obviously too late to aid the unfortunate Calas, Voltaire was able to use the case as a lynchpin in his fight against religious dogmatism and the struggle for religious toleration, one of the greatest legacies of the Enlightenment.

MONTESQUIEU

Charles Louis de Secondat, **Baron de Montesquieu** (1689–1755), wrote what was perhaps the most influential work of the Enlightenment, *Spirit of the Laws* (1748). Montesquieu, who became president of the Parlement of Bordeaux, a body of nobles that functioned as the province's law court, was, like Voltaire, inspired by the political system found in Great Britain. Also, similar to Voltaire, he believed that societies and their political institutions could be studied in a scientific manner. He incorrectly interpreted the British constitution, and in the *Spirit of the Laws*, Montesquieu wrote of the English **separation of powers** among the various branches of government providing for the possibility of **checks and balances**, something that in fact did not exist in the British system. In many ways Montesquieu was a political conservative who did not believe in a republic—which he associated with anarchy—but rather he wanted France to reestablish aristocratic authority as a means of placing limits on royal absolutism.

In an earlier work, *Persian Letters* (1721), Montesquieu critiques his native France through a series of letters between two Persians traveling in Europe. To avoid royal and church censorship, Montesquieu executed a deeply satirical work that attacked religious zealotry, while also implying that despite the differences between the Islamic East and the Christian West, a universal system of justice was necessary. Another aspect of Montesquieu's universal ideals was his anti-slavery sentiment; he deplored slavery as being against natural law.

DIDEROT AND THE ENCYCLOPEDIA

The *Encyclopedia*, the brainchild of **Denis Diderot** (1713–1784), was one of the greatest collaborative achievements of the Enlightenment and was executed by the community of scholars known as the Republic of Letters. The *Encylopedia* offers an example of the eighteenth century belief that all knowledge could be organized and presented in a scientific manner. The first of 28 volumes appeared in 1751, with such luminaries as Voltaire, Montesquieu, and Rousseau contributing articles. Diderot, the son of an artisan, also had a great deal of respect for those who worked with their hands, and included articles on various tools and the ways in which they made people more productive.

The *Encyclopedia* was also important for spreading Enlightenment ideas beyond the borders of France; copies were sent to places as far away as Russia and Scandinavia, and on the American shores, Thomas Jefferson and Benjamin Franklin purchased their own sets. In various parts of Europe, the work was attacked by the censors, particularly in places like Italy where the Catholic Church was highly critical of what it viewed as thinly veiled attacks on its religious practices. In France, the work was at various times placed under the censor's ban, since it was highly critical of monarchical authority. Ironically, Diderot had to turn to the throne for protection of his copyright when printers published pirated copies.

JEAN-JACQUES ROUSSEAU

Enlightenment thought did not consist of a single intellectual strand. The work of **Rousseau** (1712–1778) provides one of the best examples of this fact. He lived a deeply troubled and solitary existence, and at one point or another antagonized many of the other leading *philosophes*, including Voltaire, who hated Rousseau's championing of emotion over reason. Rousseau was perhaps the most radical of the *philosophes*. Unlike many of the *philosophes* who believed in a constitutional monarchy as the best form of government, Rousseau believed in the creation of a direct democracy. Although during his lifetime his works were not widely read, following Rousseau's death, his ideas became far more influential, and many of the leading participants in the more radical stages of the **French Revolution** studied his work.

His greatest achievement, *The Social Contract* (1762), begins with the classic line: "All men are born free, but everywhere they are in chains." He once again differed from many of the other *philosophes*, however, in that he had little faith in the individual's potential to use reason as a means of leading a more satisfactory life. Instead, Rousseau explained that the focus needed to be placed on reforming the overall community, since only through the individual's attachment to a larger society could the powerless people hope to achieve much of anything. Sovereignty would be expressed in this ideal society not through the will of the king but rather via the **general will** of the populace; only by surrendering to this general will could the individual hope to find genuine freedom.

Rousseau helped set the stage for the **Romantic Movement** of the late eighteenth and nineteenth centuries. His pedagogical novel *Émile* (1762) deals with a young man who receives an education that places higher regard on developing his emotions over his reason. To achieve this, the character Émile is encouraged to explore nature as a means of heightening his emotional sensitivity. Rousseau was also important for emphasizing the differences between children and adults. He argued that there were stages of development during which the child needed to be allowed to grow freely without undue influence from the adult world.

THE SPREAD OF ENLIGHTENMENT THOUGHT

Although originally rooted in France, over the course of the eighteenth century, the Enlightenment spread to other parts of Europe.

GERMANY

The greatest figure of the German Enlightenment, **Immanuel Kant** (1724–1804), argued in his *Critique of Pure Reason* (1781) against the idea that all knowledge was empirical, since the mind shaped the world through its unique experiences. Like Rousseau, Kant's emphasis that other, possibly hidden layers of knowledge exist beyond the knowledge that could be achieved through the use of reason served to inspire a generation of Romantic artists, who felt stifled by the application of pure reason.

ITALY

In Italy, **Cesare Beccaria** (1738–1794), in his work *On Crimes and Punishment* (1764), called for a complete overhaul in the area of **jurisprudence**. For Beccaria, it was clear that those who were accused of perpetrating crimes should also be allowed certain basic rights, and he argued against such common practices of the day as the use of torture to gain admissions of guilt as well as the application of capital punishment. Beccaria's work can be seen as part of the overall theme of humanitarianism found in the Enlightenment, which extended from such areas as the push to end flogging in the British navy to the call for better treatment of animals.

SCOTLAND

One of the most vibrant intellectual centers of the eighteenth century was Scotland, a place that hitherto had not been at the center of European intellectual life. The philosopher **David Hume** (1711–1776) pushed his thinking further than French deists and delved directly into the world of atheism. In *Inquiry into Human Nature*, Hume cast complete doubt on revealed religion, arguing that no empirical evidence supported the existence of those miracles that stood at the heart of Christian tradition.

Another Scottish author, **Edward Gibbon** (1737–1794), reflected the growing interest in history that was first seen during the Enlightenment with his monumental *Decline and Fall of the Roman Empire*. His work criticized Christianity in that he viewed its rise within the Roman Empire as a social phenomenon rather than a divine interference. He also asserted that Christianity weakened the vibrancy of the Empire and contributed to its fall.

The Scottish Enlightenment also made a huge impact on economic thought through the work of **Adam Smith** (1723–1790), a professor at the University of Glasgow. In 1776, Smith published *Inquiry into the Nature and Causes of the Wealth of Nations*, in which he argued against mercantilism, a term that refers to the system of navigation acts, tariffs, and monopolies that stood as the economic underpinnings for most of the nations of Europe. Smith became associated with the concept of *laissez-faire*, literally to "leave alone," since he argued that individuals should be free to pursue economic gain without being restricted by the state. Rather than producing economic anarchy, such a system would produce an **"invisible hand,"** which would lead to the meeting of supply and demand. Smith's thinking proved influential for both the **Manchester School** of economists in England and the **Physiocrats** in France.

WOMEN AND THE ENLIGHTENMENT

Women figured prominently in the Enlightenment; most of the Parisian **salons** were organized by women. At times, these wealthy and aristocratic individuals would use their social and political connections to help the *philosophes* avoid trouble with the authorities or perhaps aid them in receiving some sort of government sinecure to allow them greater freedom to work. Perhaps surprisingly, given the great help that women proffered to the *philosophes*, these male thinkers for the most part were not tremendous advocates of the rights and abilities of women. The *Encyclopedia* barely bothered to address the condition of women, although the work may never have reached the reading public without the aid of the **Marquise de Pompadour**, Louis XV's mistress, who played a critical role in helping Diderot avoid censorship.

Some writers were more sympathetic to women's issues than others. Montesquieu, in his *Persian Letters*, included a discussion of the restrictive nature of the Eastern harem, which by implication, was an indictment of the treatment of women in western Europe. Rousseau, on the other hand, while a radical on many issues, was an advocate of the idea that men and women occupied separate spheres and that women should not be granted an equal education to men. By the end of the century, inspired partially by the French Revolution and partially by the Enlightenment, the Englishwoman **Mary Wollstonecraft** (1759–1797) wrote in her *Vindication of the Rights of Women* that women should enjoy the right to vote as well as to hold political office, the first openly published statement of such ideas.

EUROPEAN POWERS IN THE AGE OF ENLIGHTENMENT

The eighteenth century witnessed a number of significant developments for the European nation-states. Two major powers, Prussia and Russia, emerged over the course of the century, while Austria, France, and Great Britain adjusted to changing political, economic, and social circumstances.

The century would also be noteworthy for the monarchs who sought to govern using ideas taken from the writings of the French *philosophes*. Rulers such as **Catherine the Great** of Russia, **Joseph II** of Austria, and **Frederick II** of Prussia are generally referred to as **"Enlightened Absolutists."** They could safely toy with the ideas of the *philosophes* without threatening their own power because most of the *philosophes* were not republicans but were believers in monarchical authority (although they felt that the power of the monarchy should be wielded in a more rational manner). These monarchs found that the writings of the *philosophes* on economics and education could mesh with their own desires to enhance the power of their states within the community of European nations and their personal authority within the state. What made this even more appealing for these Enlightened Absolutists was that this would be achieved at the expense of those elements in society, such as the nobility or the church that had previously stood in the way of this centralizing tendency.

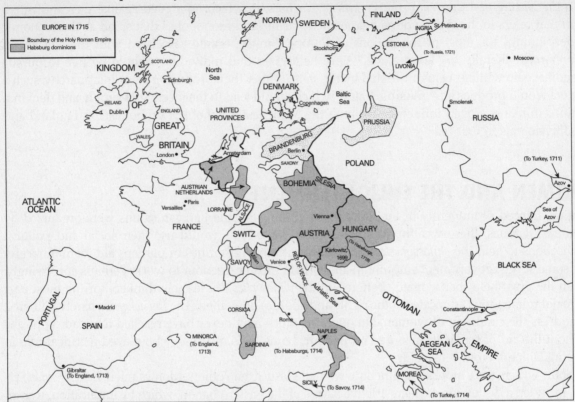

Europe in 1715

PRUSSIA AND AUSTRIA

It is perhaps rather surprising that Prussia would emerge in the eighteenth century as one of the dominant European powers and a rival to Austria for hegemony in Germany. In the seventeenth century, Prussia was a poor German state that was devastated by various marauding armies during the **Thirty Years War**, although in the **Peace of Westphalia**, marking the end of the conflict, Prussia did receive some minor territorial gains. Relatively poor agricultural land and labor shortages led to the establishment of serfdom by the sixteenth century. This led to the state receiving some badly needed support from the Prussian nobility, the **Junkers**, who looked to the ruler to ensure control over their serfs.

The first ruler to tap into whatever potential the Prussian state possessed was **Frederick William** (r. 1640–1688), often referred to as the **"Great Elector,"** since in his capacity as ruler of Brandenburg he served as one of the electors of the Holy Roman Emperor. Because his state consisted of three noncontiguous chunks of land without natural borders, Frederick William wanted to build an army.

As he was without significant resources of his own, he worked out an agreement with the Junkers, according to which they would provide him with revenue in exchange for his acceptance of their control over the serfs. This was the beginning of a long and mutually beneficial relationship between the Prussian monarchy and the Junkers, who found that Frederick's expanded army offered them the opportunity to leave their poor agricultural lands and engage in more appealing careers as officers. The Great Elector left his son Frederick III (r. 1688–1713) a well-organized army, an expanded territorial base, and arguably the most efficient civil service in all of Europe. Frederick III was to take this inheritance and make Prussia into a kingdom in 1701, gaining the title of **King Frederick I**.

Prussian power would reach its zenith in the eighteenth century with the reign of **Frederick the Great** (r. 1740–1786). Frederick is often cited as an example of an Enlightened Absolutist, since he was fascinated by the intellectual current from France. At his palace of Sans Souci, Frederick established a glittering intellectual center, where Voltaire would live for a time and where the king himself participated by writing philosophical tracts and also by playing his flute, which may have led Voltaire to make an early exit from the court. Frederick freed the serfs on the royal estates, though to ensure the continual support of the Junker class he refused to emancipate the serfs living on private estates. He also brought an end to capital punishment and limited the use of corporal punishment on serfs, though he did not emancipate the Jews living within his kingdom. Like his royal colleagues who have received the label of enlightened absolutists, Frederick used the rational thought of the age as a tool for greater royal centralization and absolutism, rather than as a means of ensuring individual rights or establishing participatory political institutions.

A more thoroughgoing series of reforms inspired by the Enlightenment took place in Austria, where the Empress **Maria Theresa** pushed a series of reforms that removed some of the hardships that had been placed on the serf population. Her son **Joseph II** (r. 1765–1790) was impressed with the idea of religious toleration, particularly as he wished to reduce the power of the Catholic Church within his own domains, since he viewed the Church as hostile to his plan for greater centralized authority. In 1781, he issued the first of a series of Edicts of Toleration granting Jews, Lutherans, and Calvinists freedom of worship. Civil liabilities were still left in place for Jews—while Protestants could enter into the Habsburg civil service, Jews were still barred and were forced to pay special taxes for the right to worship. Joseph antagonized his aristocracy by making them responsible for taxes and by abolishing serfdom. Following his death in 1790, his brother and heir, Leopold II (r. 1790–1792), was forced to back away from some of Joseph's enlightened policies in order to put an end to a series of aristocratic and peasant revolts.

Unfortunately, when they were not perusing the writings of the *philosophes*, the rulers of Prussia and Austria were often engaged in violent conflict. The roots of the **War of the Austrian Succession** (1740–1748) began during the reign of the Holy Roman Emperor **Charles VI** (r. 1711–1740), who, because he lacked a male heir, pushed the other European states to accept what was known as the **Pragmatic Sanction**, allowing for the assorted Habsburg lands under his control to remain intact under one ruler and granting the right of a female to succeed to the throne of Austria if there was no direct male heir.

When Charles died without leaving a son, his daughter Maria Theresa came to the throne. While both France and Prussia had promised to respect the Pragmatic Sanction, both nations viewed the death of Charles as an opportunity to gain territory at the expense of the Austrians. Frederick immediately launched an attack to seize **Silesia**, the richest part of the Austrian empire. Regaining Silesia was to prove impossible for Maria Theresa, but with the help of Hungarian nobility, which had agreed to the Pragmatic Sanction in exchange for recognition of Hungary as an independent kingdom, she was able to put down a dangerous revolt in Bohemia and remain on the throne.

The conflict became a general European war with Austria gaining support from Russia, Sweden, Denmark, and eventually Great Britain, which feared French territorial gains in the Austrian Netherlands. Opposing them was an alliance made up of Prussia, France, and Spain. By the time the war came to a close in 1748 with the signing of the **Treaty of Aix-la-Chapelle**, the Austrian throne was ultimately saved for the Habsburgs. (Because women remained ineligible to head the Holy Roman Empire, Maria Theresa's husband was to hold that position as Emperor Francis I.)

One result of the war was that Prussia emerged as a German state and a major rival to Austria. Understanding that Prussia under its aggressive King Frederick would continue to be a threat, in 1756, Maria Theresa's able foreign minister, Count Kaunitz, brought about what became known as the **Diplomatic Revolution** (or reversal of alliances) by working out an alliance with France, the traditional enemy of the Austrian Habsburgs and a state that was increasingly wary of growing Prussian power. France also demanded the Austrian Netherlands as their price for this alliance. Sweden and Russia signed on as part of an alliance that increasingly looked as if it would result in significant territorial gains at the expense of the Prussians.

The other side of this Diplomatic Revolution was that Great Britain broke off its ties with Austria and became allies with Prussia, and while the British did not contribute men to the war on the continent, their financial subsidies were vital in enabling Frederick to continue fighting. The Diplomatic Revolution led directly to the **Seven Years War** (1756–1763), which started when Frederick launched an attack in 1756 in order to quickly put down his enemies before they had an opportunity to form a cohesive military plan to defeat Prussia. Initially, the bold Prussian plan paid off as Frederick first defeated a French and then an Austrian army, but disaster struck when a massive Russian army arrived from the east and took Frederick's capital of Berlin. Only the crowning of a new Russian tsar, **Peter III**, in 1762 staved off the complete destruction of the Prussian state, since Peter, an admirer of Frederick, wanted no part in the conflict and brought his army home. So Frederick, by preserving the Prussian state, was the clear winner on the continent, while his British allies had won a series of tremendous victories overseas against the French, particularly in the **French and Indian War**, resulting in the confiscation of French colonies in India and Canada.

RUSSIA

Until the eighteenth century, Russia remained largely closed off to western Europe as a result of the Mongol invasion of the thirteenth century. Some trade did exist; for instance, Elizabethan England imported Russian timber for the building of ships, but for the most part Russia was not affected by developments in the west, most notably missing out on the humanistic culture of the Italian Renaissance.

By the sixteenth century, the Duchy of Muscovy would emerge as the dominant state within the Russian steppe, an area that had absorbed a number of other rival states while pushing the Mongols back to the east. During the reign of the appropriately named **Ivan the Terrible** (r. 1533–1584), there was a significant expansion of the territory under the control of Muscovy, while Ivan also sought, often through staggeringly violent means, to gain control over a recalcitrant nobility. Following his death in 1584, Russia entered into the period known as the **"Time of Troubles,"** which lasted until the selection of a tsar from the **Romanov family** in 1603, the dynasty that would continue to rule Russia until the Revolution of 1917.

The individual who did the most to transform the Russian state into a major European power was **Peter the Great** (r. 1682–1725). As a young man, Peter traveled to the West where he became fascinated by the work done in Dutch shipyards and other examples of Western technology. Upon his return to Russia, Peter was determined to Westernize his backward state, beginning with his nobles, whom he famously forced to shave their beards, as was the style in the West. Peter expanded the revenue available to the monarchy by imposing head taxes on Russian serfs while also establishing monopolies on essential commodities such as salt. Peter used this expanded revenue to follow the lead of the absolutist states in Europe and establish a centralized bureaucracy. In order to ensure the loyalty of his nobility as well as use them for governance, Peter established a Table of Ranks, in which all positions in the state had graduated rankings, which also provided an opportunity for commoners to rise up the ranks and reach a coveted position as a noble. Just as in Prussia, the nobility were to be used as an essential tool of royal absolutism. In keeping with his desire to keep a **"window on the West,"** Peter established the eponymous city of **St. Petersburg** in 1703. The city was built on what seemed to be unpromising marsh land, and thousands of serf laborers would lose their lives in the building of a grand city with architecture that mimicked the newest styles from France.

At the start of World War I, many of the Russian officers had German names, the descendents of the Western military experts that Peter invited to Russia to help him establish a standing army. To ensure that he had enough soldiers, Peter conscripted serfs to serve in his force for the interminable period of 20 years. Peter also built the first Russian navy. Peter used his army to greatly expand Russian territory, and in achieving this goal, he was fortunate that his state was becoming more powerful at the same time that the major states on his borders, the Ottoman Empire and the Kingdom of Poland-Lithuania, were in relative decline. Most notably, he defeated the Swedes in the **Great Northern War** (1700–1721), which marked the end of the brief period going back to the age of Gustavus Adolphus in the seventeenth century when Sweden was a great European power.

The westward outlook of Russia during the reign of Peter would continue under his successors. Western thought, particularly the writings of the French *philosophes*, would play a role in inspiring the reign of **Catherine the Great** (r. 1762–1796). While the story of Catherine and the horse is most likely the stuff of legend, she was a robust, sexually active woman who read Montesquieu and Voltaire and toyed with ways to apply their ideas to her still semi-barbaric state. Catherine began the process of revising and codifying Russian law, but for the most part, she only dabbled with bringing about actual reform. Once she became convinced later on in her reign that enlightened thought could pose a challenge to her monarchy, she dropped the idea entirely. While few practical results stemmed from Catherine's infatuation with Enlightenment thought, it did help establish the primacy of French culture and ideas among the Russian aristocracy.

Catherine didn't hesitate to mix love and politics. Her affair with **Stanislaw Augustus Poniatowski** resulted in not only the birth of Catherine's second child, Anna, but also the election of Poniatowksi as King of Poland-Lithuania.

Poland

The story of Poland in the eighteenth century consists of the complete eradication of a nation that had previously played a critical role in the affairs of Central Europe. The traditional starting date for the history of Poland is 966, when Prince Mieszko, who was to be the founder of a dynasty (Piast) that would rule Poland for four centuries, accepted Roman Catholicism, firmly tying Poland to the culture of western Europe. Vulnerable to attacks due to a lack of natural borders, the Poles in the Middle Ages had to deal with threats from the Mongols from the East as well as the Teutonic Knights from the West. In order to deal with the threat from the crusading order, a new dynasty was established in 1385 (Jagiellon) through the uniting of Poland with Lithuania, when the Lithuanian Grand Duke Jagiello, the ruler of the last pagan state in Europe, married the Polish Queen Jadwiga. This newly created **Polish-Lithuanian Commonwealth** met its initial goal of defeating the Teutonic Knights by securing an important victory at the Battle of Grunwald (Germans refer to it as the Battle of Tannenberg).

The fatal flaw for the Polish-Lithuanian state was the failure to create a strong, centralized government in the face of a recalcitrant nobility that feared the loss of authority. By the end of the sixteenth century, the nobles had greatly weakened the crown by making it an elective position and often selecting foreign princes to further ensure it would remain a weak title. This policy became increasingly dangerous in the seventeenth century, as new threats appeared from the Swedes and the Russians. The Polish-Lithuanian state still remained a significant player in Europe up until the end of the century, when King Jan Sobieski played a critical role in driving the Turks from the gates of Vienna in 1683, but by the middle of the eighteenth-century, Poland was so weak that she maintained her independence only by the good graces of Russia. Her luck ran out, however, eventually resulting in the loss of a great deal of land.

When Poniatowski became King in 1764, he displayed an independent streak that Catherine the Great did not expect from her former lover, and this did not bode well for Poniatowski's attempt to move the nation's political system in a more centralized direction, an attempt that was met with displeasure by all of Poland's neighbors. In 1772, Russia, Prussia, and Austria forced Poland to accept a **partition** that cost her 30 percent of her territory. In some ways, this first partition provided the nudge to finally get her political house in order. Influenced by the ideas of the Enlightenment, in 1791, the Polish-Lithuanian parliament (*Sejm*) produced Europe's first written **constitution**. The constitution, which was never fully implemented (although it remained a beacon for later generations of Polish reformers), angered many nobles who saw their influence reduced as well as Poland's neighbors who feared a national revival. The anti-Poniatowski nobles applied to the Russians for assistance, and Catherine, with the aid of Prussia, was more than willing to intercede.

Russia and Prussia insisted on the removal of the constitution and also carried out the **Second Partition** in 1793. This led to the loss of vast lands in the eastern part of the nation and reduced Poland to a rump state. In a heroic, last ditch effort to retain statehood, a Polish revolt broke out in 1794 under the military leadership of **Tadeusz Kosciuszko**, who had fought with distinction in the American Revolution. Overwhelmed by more powerful enemies, Poniatowski was forced to abdicate, and a **third and final partition** took place in 1795 wiping Poland off the map. Despite the best hopes of Polish nationalists throughout the nineteenth-century, an independent Polish state would only be revived in the aftermath of World War I.

GREAT BRITAIN

After the turmoil of the seventeenth century, Great Britain became the most stable nation in Europe in the eighteenth century. The triumph of Parliament in its struggle against Stuart absolutism put Great Britain in a position of political stability that would provide one of the critical foundations for the establishment of a vast overseas empire, as well as the industrial transformation that would begin by the middle of the century.

With the death of Queen Anne in 1714, the throne passed to George I (r. 1714–1721), the ruler of the German state of Hanover, whose sole qualification was that he was a Protestant cousin of the late queen. Like his son George II (r. 1727–1760), he was far happier spending time in Hanover, where he could reign as an unquestioned absolutist, rather than having to deal with the independent-minded British Parliament. While there is a historical debate over the strength of support within Great Britain for the Stuart cause, the eighteenth century did experience two pro-Stuart revolts, in 1715 and 1745, the latter one famous for the involvement of "Bonnie Prince Charles," who saw his dream of being restored to the throne dashed at the Battle of Culloden in 1746.

While it was clear that after 1688 the Houses of Parliament would dominate political life within the country, how that power was to be utilized in an efficient manner remained one of the significant questions in the early part of the eighteenth century. The most significant development in this regard was the evolution of the office of Prime Minister, which, while not officially recognized until 1905, became a political reality in all but name during **Robert Walpole's** tenure as Chancellor of the Exchequer from 1721 to 1741. The fact that both George I and George II were less than attentive to British domestic politics meant that Walpole had a free hand to mold the political system to his advantage. Walpole used a complex system of political patronage to maintain his control over the House of Commons. This support in the lower house became the vital component for ministerial power, and when Walpole lost that support in 1741 over a conflict over the direction of British foreign policy, he resigned his post as Chancellor of the Exchequer even though he still enjoyed the support of George II.

Another development that shaped British politics in the eighteenth century was the formation of two parliamentary blocks: **Tories** and **Whigs**. While Tories stood for the prerogative rights of the monarch and support of the Church of England, the Whigs were more closely allied to the spirit of the Revolution of 1688 and the idea of religious tolerance. When George III (r. 1760–1820) came to the throne, he claimed that he wanted the throne to rise above party strife, though **Edmund Burke** in his *Thoughts on the Cause of the Present Discontent* (1770) argued that parties were essential to parliamentary government and were a fundamental component for political stability. George III's desire to choose his own chief minister during the first ten years of his reign remained problematic until Lord North assumed the mantle of chief minister in 1770 and held the position for the next 12 years.

The problems stemming from the first ten years of George III's rule were to have important consequences as the colonists in the 13 American colonies became increasingly restless, laying the groundwork for the **American Revolution**. The British government ended the Seven Years War with a tremendous victory over the French but also with an enormous deficit. In order to pay for the increasing costs of administering their far-flung empire, the British government looked for new sources of revenue. The passage of the Stamp Act in 1765, during the ministry of George Grenville, was probably a mistake, since it ticked off the two groups in society you don't want to anger: publishers and lawyers. While the British government continued to assert its right to tax the colonists as it pleased, the colonists responded that without parliamentary representation, no taxes could ever be acceptable. By 1774, American anger at what was viewed as high-handed British policies led to the establishment of the First Continental Congress, with open hostilities breaking out the following year at Lexington and Concord in Massachusetts. Eighteenth-century wars seemingly always brought about curious alliances, and the Americans were eventually to win their independence by 1783 with the help of France and Spain, with both states seeking to deliver a major blow to the British as payback for the Seven Years War.

The struggle for independence by the American colonists also helped to inspire a movement for parliamentary reform in Great Britain. Voting in eighteenth-century Britain was primarily the prerogative of the landed classes, but there were plenty of anomalies in the system, including a fairly wide franchise in London, while in other areas there were "rotten" boroughs such as Old Sarum, where no one had lived since the Middle Ages but which still duly provided two members to the House of Commons. The arrest in 1763 of John Wilkes, a member of the House of Commons and part-time pornographer, for publishing a satirical attack on George III in his newspaper *The North Briton* provided an outlet for those Englishmen who, by shouting "Wilkes and Liberty" in the streets, saw the possibility of bringing about what they viewed to be much needed reforms in the political system, including greater freedom of the press and an expansion of the suffrage. The parliamentary reform movement was to emerge as a significant factor in British political life in the 1780s, but the advent of the French Revolution and, more specifically, its increasing violence and radicalism, by 1792, brought about a backlash against political reform in Great Britain, so that any expansion of suffrage would have to wait until the Great Reform Bill of 1832.

FRANCE

Perhaps not surprising given the increased power of the throne during the reign of Louis XIV, a backlash against royal absolutism set in during the following century. Compared to its fellow absolutist states in central and eastern Europe, French absolutism seemed to hardly deserve the term at times, but for some Frenchmen, particularly those influenced by Enlightenment thought, the powers of the crown were seen as increasingly despotic.

An opportunity to challenge the throne came about at mid-century, when a papal decree attacked the **Jansenists**, a Catholic sect that held beliefs on predestination that were similar to the Calvinist point of view. **Louis XV** (r. 1714–1774) wished to support the papal decree and ban the group, but found himself blocked by the various provincial *parlements*, law courts primarily made up of nobles that had the prerogative right of registering royal edicts before they could be enforced. Many of those who sat in these parlements, while opposed to Jansenist teachings, also opposed registering the edicts since they felt it was emblematic of royal despotism.

During the long reign of Louis XV, the financial troubles of the monarchy increased, particularly as a result of the disastrous Seven Years War, but once again, the parlements stood in the way of any significant reform in the revenue system. Finally, in frustration, Louis XV abolished the parlements, but Louis XVI (r. 1774–1792) felt forced to bring them back in an attempt to curry favor with the nobility. The recalcitrance of the parlements in allowing the establishment of a more rational revenue system was to play a significant role in bringing France to the point of revolution by 1789.

CHAPTER TIMELINE

Another chapter, another timeline! As with the previous timelines, this one includes some items you read about earlier to help you build connections between significant events and possibly identify trends over time. Remember: You don't need to memorize every line. Use the timeline as a quick review and a means to getting the big picture.

Year	Event
1543	Copernicus publishes his *Concerning the Revolutions of the Celestial Spheres*
1543	Andreas Vesalius writes *De humani corporis fabrica* with its critique of the anatomical work of Galen
1545	Council of Trent convenes
1553	End of reign of Edward VI
1553	Michael Servetus burnt at the stake in Geneva
1555	Peace of Augsburg
1556	Philip II becomes King of Spain
1558	Beginning of reign of Elizabeth Tudor
1559	Frederick III of the Palatinate converts to Calvinism
1559	Death of King Henry II of France
1559	Elizabethan religious settlement
1562	Beginning of the French Wars of Religion
1571	Battle of Lepanto
1572	St. Bartholomew's Day Massacre
1587	Execution of Mary, Queen of Scots
1588	Failure of the Spanish Armada
1589	Henry Bourbon becomes King Henry IV
1593	Henry IV converts to Catholicism

Year	Event
1598	Edict of Nantes
1600	Giordano Bruno burned at the stake
1602	Dutch East India Company established
1603	James II becomes king following death of Elizabeth
1603	Michael Romanov begins new dynasty in Russia
1605	Cervantes publishes first part of *Don Quixote*
1607	Founding of colony at Jamestown
1610	Assassination of Henry IV
1610	Galileo begins astronomical observations with his telescope
1613	Galileo publishes *Letters on Sunspots*
1616	William Harvey announces his discovery of the circulatory system
1618	Johannes Kepler reveals his third and final law of planetary motion
1618	Beginning of the Thirty Years War
1620	Battle of White Mountain
1620	Founding of Plymouth Colony
1620	Francis Bacon publishes *Novum Organum*
1624	Cardinal Richelieu becomes Louis XIII's chief minister
1625	Charles I becomes king upon death of James I
1628	Petition of Right
1628	Murder of the Duke of Buckingham
1629	Edict of Restitution
1629	Personal Rule of Charles I begins and will last 11 years

Year	Event
1632	Galileo's *Dialogue on the Two Chief Systems of the World*
1632	Gustavus Adolphus dies at the Battle of Lutzen
1633	Trial of Galileo
1633	Murder of Albrecht von Wallenstein
1633	France enters the Thirty Years War
1637	Rene Descartes publishes *Discourse on Method*
1637	Charles introduces the Book of Common Prayer into Scotland
1640	Beginning of reign of Frederick William (Great Elector)
1640	Charles forced to summon Parliament to deal with Scottish revolt
1641	Rebellion in Ireland
1642	Execution of the Earl of Strafford
1642	Issuing of Grand Remonstrance
1642	Beginning of English Revolution
1643	Five-year-old Louis XIV becomes king of France
1645	Execution of Archbishop Laud
1648	Peace of Westphalia
1649	Beginning of the *Fronde*
1649	Execution of Charles I and establishment of English republic
1653	Oliver Cromwell becomes Lord Protector
1659	Death of Cromwell
1660	Restoration of Charles II
1660	Thomas Hobbes publishes *Leviathan*

Year	Event
1661	Death of Cardinal Mazarin; Louis XIV becomes own chief minister
1662	Royal Society established by Charles II
1664	Chartering of the French East India Company
1669	Louis XIV begins construction of the Palace of Versailles
1669	Posthumous publication of Pascal's *Pensées*
1682	Beginning of the reign of Peter the Great
1682	Rembrandt paints *The Night Watch*
1685	Revocation of the Edict of Nantes
1685	James II, a Catholic, becomes king of England
1687	Newton publishes his *Principia*
1688	John Locke's *Two Treatises on Government*
1688	Glorious Revolution
1689	Act of Toleration
1690	John Locke's *Essay on Human Understanding*
1701	Prussia becomes a kingdom
1701	Act of Settlement passed to bypass potential Catholic kings
1703	Cornerstone laid for the new city of St. Petersburg
1707	Act of Union brings about political unification of England and Scotland
1713	Treaty of Utrecht marks end of the War of the Spanish Succession
1714	George I becomes first Hanoverian king of England
1721	End of the Great Northern War between Russia and Sweden
1721	Start of Robert Walpole's tenure as Prime Minister

Year	Event
1739	Hume's *Inquiry into Human Nature*
1740	Frederick the Great becomes king of Prussia
1740	Start of the War of the Austrian Succession
1746	Battle of Culloden
1748	Montesquieu's *Spirit of Laws*
1748	Treaty of Aix-la-Chapelle marks end of War of the Austrian Succession
1751	The first volume of Diderot's *Encyclopedia* appears
1755	Lisbon earthquake
1756	Marie Theresa carries out the "Diplomatic Revolution"
1756	Beginning of the Seven Years War
1759	Voltaire's *Candide*
1762	Rousseau's *The Social Contract*
1762	Rousseau's *Emile* is published
1762	Start of reign of Catherine the Great
1763	Voltaire pushes for reexamination in the trial of Jean Calas
1763	Peace of Paris marks end of Seven Years War
1764	Beccaria's *On Crime and Punishment*
1765	Stamp Act
1770	Burke writes *Thoughts on the Cause of the Present Discontent*
1770	Marriage of the future Louis XVI to Marie Antoinette
1774	Louis XVI becomes king of France
1774	First Continental Congress

Year	Event
1775	Fighting begins between American colonists and British
1776	Jefferson writes the *Declaration of Independence*
1776	The first volume of Edward Gibbon's *The History of the Decline and Fall of the Roman Empire* is published
1776	Adam Smith's *Wealth of Nations*
1778	France goes to war against Britain in support of the American colonists
1781	Kant's *Critique of Pure Reason*
1781	Joseph II of Austria issues Edicts of Toleration
1786	Calonne, finance minister to Louis XVI, informs him that the crown is bankrupt
1787	Assembly of Notables meets
1788	Louis XVI decides to call the Estates General
1788	Abbé Siéyès writes *What is the Third Estate?*
1792	Mary Wollstonecraft's *Vindication of the Rights of Women*

REVIEW QUESTIONS

Answers and explanations are in Chapter 15.

1. Medieval science was primarily based on

   (A) close observations of nature
   (B) pure superstition
   (C) the experimental method
   (D) a blending of Christian theology and the writings of classical authors
   (E) decrees emanating from the papacy

2. Which of the following individuals was responsible for first describing the elliptical motion of the planets around the sun?

   (A) Newton
   (B) Galileo
   (C) Copernicus
   (D) Kepler
   (E) Brahe

3. In *Leviathan*, Thomas Hobbes became an advocate for which of the following types of government?

   (A) Absolute monarchy
   (B) Parliamentary government
   (C) Divine-right monarchy
   (D) Constitutional monarchy
   (E) Democracy

4. Women played their most prominent role during the Enlightenment by

   (A) serving as a major topic for the philosophes
   (B) writing books and political tracts
   (C) declining to participate in any social events
   (D) sponsoring salons
   (E) rejecting enlightened ideals

5. Deists such as Voltaire believe that

   (A) God reveals himself through miracles
   (B) there is no God
   (C) God created the universe but then played no additional role in shaping the course of events
   (D) a state church is necessary
   (E) limited religious toleration should be encouraged

6. Rousseau's *Émile* influenced the way people viewed childhood

   (A) by emphasizing the need to teach emotional restraint
   (B) by suggesting it as the time in which to instill the benefits of a rational education
   (C) by emphasizing that children were not merely small adults
   (D) by positioning it as the critical focus for the family dynamic
   (E) by framing it as a mirror to adult behaviors

7. Mary Wollstonecraft's *Vindication of the Rights of Women*

   (A) focused primarily on economic issues such as property rights
   (B) served as the inspiration for a small group of eighteenth century women who formed the first female suffrage organization
   (C) was the first work to openly state the need for women to enjoy the full political rights of men
   (D) failed to find a publisher during her lifetime
   (E) directly influenced the "women's question" during the French Revolution

10

The French Revolution, Napoleon, and the European Reaction

(1789–1815)

PHASES OF THE FRENCH REVOLUTION

Before 1789	Pre-revolutionary period (*Ancien Régime*)
1789–92	Liberal Phase (Constitutional Monarchy)
1792–93	Moderate Republic (Girondins)
1793-94	Radical Republic (Jacobins)
1795–1799	Directory (Moderate Republic)
1799–1804	Consulate
1804–1815	Napoleonic Empire

BACKGROUND TO THE REVOLUTION—THE *ANCIEN RÉGIME*

Under different circumstances, **Louis XVI** might have made a decent constitutional monarch. He possessed the two main qualities needed for success in that job—he was rather kindly and quite stupid. Unfortunately, France at this time was an absolute monarchy, and Louis's personal limitations were significant. Louis was not helped by the tremendous unpopularity of his wife, **Marie-Antoinette**, an Austrian princess who was extremely unhappy with her marriage to the sexually impotent Louis; theirs was an arranged marriage meant to aid relations between France and Austria. We'll never know whether she truly said, "Let them eat cake," when told that the people were starving, but the fact that she and her ladies-in-waiting enjoyed playing peasant at a specially created peasant village situated at Versailles points to her general insensitivity. Rumors regarding acts of infidelity on her part continued to plague the monarchy and helped to widen the gap between the court and the rest of the country.

The major problem facing the monarchy was financial. France was not bankrupt in 1789, although the same could not be said for the French monarchy. Throughout the eighteenth century, the country had been at war, mostly with Great Britain, a conflict that dated back to the Glorious Revolution of 1688. The ignoble defeat of French forces in the Seven Years War and the more successful involvement of French forces in the American Revolution helped exacerbate the financial difficulties facing the monarchy. The debt grew so large that interest and payments on the debt absorbed slightly more than half the annual budget. While all European nations in the eighteenth century had racked up large debts, and by comparison the French debt was not particularly onerous given the great wealth of France, the problem was that the French monarchy was unable to tap into the wealth of the nation.

In the seventeenth century, the French monarchy, in an attempt to pacify a potentially rebellious nobility, had basically granted the nobility freedom from most taxation. It would be the task of Louis XVI (r. 1774–1792) to try to convince the nobility to give up their cherished tax-free status. This meant that Louis, a weak man, would have to break the back of the Paris and regional *parlements*, royal law courts that claimed the right of judicial review of all royal edicts, therefore empowering them to veto any attempt to tax the nobility. These parlements had gained influence throughout the eighteenth century and were a bastion of aristocratic intransigence on the taxation question.

THE CALLING OF THE ESTATES GENERAL AND THE DEMAND FOR A NATIONAL ASSEMBLY

By 1787, the financial situation grew so bad that Louis XVI called an **Assembly of Notables** made up of leading aristocrats and churchmen to see if they would willingly pay a new land tax that would apply to all, regardless of social status. The notables at the meeting refused to consider the tax and instead demanded that they be granted a greater share in governing the nation. This refusal by the nobility marks the start of the process by which France would be enveloped by the Revolution. Ironically, it is the nobles who set the stage for their own downfall with their demand for the **Estates General**, an institution from medieval times that consisted of a three-house body made up of clergy (the first estate), nobility (the second estate), and commons (the third estate). "Commons" referred to everyone from bourgeoisie to peasants who were neither clergy nor nobility. Traditionally, each house received one vote, so the clergy and nobility dominated the proceedings. The notables assumed that calling the Estates General, which had last met in 1614, would be an effective means of ensuring that the monarchy would not implement any economic reform that would place limits on their privileges. It also ensured that the bourgeoisie would not be able to limit the rights of the nobility.

By 1788, Louis XVI decided that in the following year he would call the Estates General. To the chagrin of the conservative nobles, the question of the assembly's voting structure immediately arose. Increasingly, writers began to declare that the **Third Estate,** consisting of all nonclergy and non-aristocracy (the majority of Frenchmen), was the true embodiment of the political will of the nation. Though the clergy were officially the **First Estate,** many simple parish priests felt more aligned with the Third Estate. Indeed, the most famous pamphlet from this period was written by the **Abbé Siéyès** (1748–1836), an obscure lower clergyman, who wrote:

> What is the Third Estate? Everything.
> What has it been in the political order up to the present? Nothing.
> What does it ask? To become something.

By the end of 1788, the king agreed to double the number of representatives to the Third Estate, which meant little since voting would still be cast by each estate as a unit and not as individuals. Since no one has ever followed Shakespeare's sage advice on what to do with lawyers, a large portion of the 600 members of the Third Estate were from that profession. No peasants attended the sessions, which would be held in the very home of royal absolutism—Versailles.

This sense of wanting change but ultimately not knowing what direction this change should take can be seen in the thousands of *cahiers de doléances*, or lists of grievances, that were presented to the king by the various electoral assemblies at the start of the meeting of the Estates General. Many of these documents survive, and they reveal an assortment of grievances, such as the demand for a tax system that would be more equitable and the call for regular meetings of the Estates General, along with some more practical notions, such as the need to limit the size of sheep herds, since their bad breath was destroying French pastures. While many of the *cahiers de doléances* demanded a lessening of royal absolutism, all were loyal to the idea of monarchy and to the concept that the monarchy would continue to lead the French state.

May 5, 1789, marked the first day of the meeting of the Estates General. Immediately, Louis XVI angered the members of the Third Estate by keeping them waiting for several hours as he formally received the credentials of members of the first two estates. Since it was clear that the king would not compromise on voting as individuals, the members of the Third Estate delayed formally submitting their credentials for several weeks. On June 17, in a momentous decision, the Third Estate declared that it would not meet as a medieval estate based on social status but instead would only assemble before the king as a national assembly representing the political will of the entire French nation.

From this point on, things moved rapidly. The First Estate, although it included great clerics like the Bishop of Paris who were a part of the nobility, also included those simple parish priests who saw themselves as having more in common with the members of the Third Estate. These parish priests voted to join the Third Estate and to meet as a national assembly. Rumors began to swirl that the king was preparing to take action against leading members of the Third Estate, and they also found that their meeting hall was closed off. In one of the famous scenes from the Revolution, members of the Third Estate gathered at a tennis court on the grounds of Versailles and, in what became known as the **Tennis Court Oath**, promised to continue to meet "until the constitution of the kingdom is established and consolidated upon solid foundations." In response, the king granted a number of concessions, such as promising to periodically call the Estates General and to drop some of the more onerous taxes on the Third Estate. Just one year earlier, such acts would have been greatly welcomed, but by this point, events had gone well past the point where this gesture was enough. Finally, on June 27, a desperate Louis XVI formally agreed to the consolidation of all three estates into a new national assembly.

THE STORMING OF THE BASTILLE AND THE GREAT FEAR

The implications from these momentous events would extend far beyond the confines of Versailles. Indeed, the Revolution was about to see the first incident of violence. In Paris, panic began to set in as people continued to try to cope with a shortage of food that many blamed on the rapacious nobility and the acts of hoarders. The populace believed the rumors that the king was not interested in meeting with the National Assembly and was instead organizing troops that would be used to scatter the National Assembly and to reestablish royal absolutism. This created a panic in Paris as people searched for weaponry to defend themselves against the royal troops.

There is an ongoing debate among historians as to whether the crowds that gathered around the **Bastille**, a fortress prison in Paris famous as a symbol of royal despotism since it had held critics of the monarchy, were there spontaneously or whether they were organized by bourgeois elements. Regardless, the crowd of around 80,000 demanded the surrender of the fortress so they could confiscate the arms they believed were inside. Although the rebels promised safe passage to the small garrison inside, the crowd eventually surrounded them, cut off the head of the commander of the troops, and marched around the city with his head on a pike. When Louis heard about the storming of his fortress he asked, "Is this a revolt?" In response he was told, "No sire, it is a revolution."

Once again, Louis quickly made concessions. He sent away some of the troops that he had possibly planned to use to disperse the National Assembly. He formally recognized the **Commune of Paris**, the new municipal government that would come to play a pivotal role in the later stages of the Revolution. He also agreed to the formation of a National Guard under the leadership of the **Marquis de Lafayette** (1757–1834), who was already known as a champion of liberty because of his involvement in the American Revolution.

In the countryside, things also began to spiral out of control. Just as rumors had spurred on events in Paris, rumors in the countryside brought about further changes in the direction of the Revolution. For the peasants, the decade of the 1780s had been a period of poor harvests. This, combined with a crushing tax burden, had resulted in a resentful and fearful peasantry. A general panic set in known as the **Great Fear**, which consisted of rumors that the nobility were using the increasingly anarchical situation both at Versailles and in Paris to organize groups of thugs to steal from the peasants. In response, peasants began to attack some of the great noble estates, carefully burning documents that verified some of their old manorial obligations.

The Great Fear contributed to one of the most remarkable moments in the Revolution. On August 4, aristocrats in the National Assembly decided that the only way to halt the violence in the countryside was by renouncing their feudal rights. In a highly emotional scene, aristocrat after aristocrat stood up—some sincerely, others out of peer pressure—to renounce those rights that had made them a separate caste in French society. Peasants were no longer obligated to work on the local lord's land, nor were they barred from fishing in common streams or hunting in the forests, restrictions that the hungry peasantry found particularly onerous. As a result of the events of August 4, all the people of France were subject to the same laws and obligations to society.

THE CONSTITUTIONAL MONARCHY

Because there was no time to write a constitution, the National Assembly decided to put forward a document that would declare the rights of the new French citizen. Lafayette, aided by Thomas Jefferson, wrote the **Declaration of the Rights of Man and Citizen**, one of the most influential documents in European history. Using the language of the Enlightenment, the work declared that political sovereignty did not rest in the hands of a monarch but rather in the nation at large. It also stated that all citizens were equal before the law and in their enjoyment of all rights and responsibilities of the society. Because all men were "born and remain free and equal in rights," they were entitled to enjoy freedom of religion, freedom of the press, and the freedom to engage in the economic activity of their choice. Befitting the bourgeois audience for whom this document was primarily intended, it also offered that property was inviolable and sacred.

Lafayette was being quite literal when he referred to the "Rights of Man." He, like most other males, believed that women were clearly not entitled to the same rights as men because their domestic role precluded the possibility of a life beyond the household. Nevertheless, the language of liberty tugged at women's sense of independence and by 1791, **Olympe de Gouges** wrote *The Rights of Women*, in which she argued that women should enjoy such fundamental rights as the right to be educated, to control their own property, and to initiate divorce. She did not, however, go so far as to demand full political rights for women. During this stage of the Revolution, women did gain certain rights over their property and the right to divorce, although these rights would be rolled back in the backlash that took place during the rule of the Directory and the reign of Napoleon. De Gouges's book would be the inspiration for Mary Wollstonecraft's *Vindication of the Rights of Women*. De Gouges's herself would be executed during the Reign of Terror.

The events of the summer of 1789 had left Louis XVI unsure as to how to respond. He hesitated to accept the dramatic changes posed by the renunciation of aristocratic privileges on August 4. Although Louis vacillated, events would once again overtake him. On October 5, a large crowd of women, angry over the shortage of bread in Paris, decided to go to Versailles to meet with "the baker, the baker's wife, and the baker's little boy" (or as they were previously known, the royal family). At first, unsure of how to proceed, the crowd decided the surest way to hold the king to his promise to respect the decrees of the National Assembly was to escort him back to Paris where they could watch him more closely. This proved to be a pivotal decision; the king was now under the control of the people of Paris, whose revolutionary zeal far outstripped that of the rest of the country.

Another reason for the increasingly radical moves of the French revolutionaries was the steps taken by the National Assembly to control the Catholic Church in France. Part of the incentive for taking control of the church was that the assembly now had to address the financial crisis that was initially the monarchy's undoing and was now their responsibility. To pay for the financing of the French debt, the assembly took the very risky step of confiscating and selling the property of the church. The assembly decided to issue *assignats*, government bonds that were backed by the sale of church lands.

Along with the confiscation of the church's property, it was decided that the entire constitutional status of the Catholic Church needed to be altered. In July 1790, the king was forced, to his horror, to accept the passage of the **Civil Constitution of the Church**, legislation that basically made the church a department of state. Bishops were to be chosen by assemblies of parish priests, who themselves were to be elected by their parishioners. Clergy were now civil servants with salaries to be paid by the state. In addition, clergy had to swear an oath of loyalty to the French state and to uphold the Civil Constitution of the Church.

In response, **Pope Pius VI** denounced the Civil Constitution and the Declaration of the Rights of Man. This set in motion a major nineteenth century conflict, the dispute between church and state. In France, these attacks on the privileges of the church instigated a counter-revolutionary movement comprised of people who were committed to undoing what they thought was the sacrilegious treatment of their church.

With the king and the National Assembly safely ensconced in Paris, steps were taken by the National Assembly to establish a workable system of government. In 1791, a constitution for France was promulgated, creating a constitutional monarchy. The king had the right to delay legislation passed by the unicameral, or single house, legislature, for at most four years, although the monarch retained significant powers including control over foreign policy and command of the army. Because the framers of the constitution feared how popular influence would affect the political process, a complex system of indirect elections was set up. The men of France were split into two different categories: active and passive citizens. Only those men who paid taxes that equaled three days of a laborer's wages were allowed to vote for electors. Electors had to meet higher property requirements to qualify to vote for members of the assembly. Women were not given any sort of franchise, so out of a population of roughly 25 million, only 50,000 qualified as electors.

The National Assembly brought about other significant changes. The old French system of provinces was abandoned and replaced by 83 departments, which, making use of the rational spirit of the Enlightenment, were each roughly equal in size and are still in use today in France. In a stunning development for the cause of religious liberty, Jews and Protestants were granted full political rights. Slavery, although still practiced in the colonies, was abolished in France. This led to a slave rebellion led by Toussant L'Ouverture, a former slave, on the Caribbean island of Hispaniola. By 1794, slavery was abolished throughout the empire, although by that time, Haiti, the eastern half of the island of Hispaniola, had broken free from France and was the first independent black state in the Caribbean.

THE END OF THE MONARCHY

By 1791, not only was there a growing counter-revolutionary movement within France, but on the borders of France resided thousands of nobles who had fled their country and were actively working to restore the ancient regime and their feudal privileges. The leader of these *émigrés* was the **Count of Artois**, the youngest brother of Louis XVI, and it was he who made the fatal decision to encourage his brother to flee France. On June 20, 1791, the royal family reached the French border town of Varennes, where the king was exiled and escorted back to Paris. Because the leaders of the National Assembly were still interested in maintaining the constitutional monarchy, they lied and said that the king had not fled Paris but instead had been abducted. Despite this attempt to keep Louis on the throne, the stage was set for the eventual collapse of the constitutional monarchy.

Although the new legislative assembly that was created out of the Constitution of 1791 stayed in existence for only one year, it was crucial for changing the course of the Revolution. The contentious debate within the assembly was matched by the factious debates that took place within the hundreds of political clubs that emerged throughout France. The most famous and popular of these clubs were the **Jacobins**, so named because they met in the Jacobin monastery in France. The Jacobins were represented in the National Assembly, although at this time, the **Girondins** faction primarily filled the leadership role in the assembly. The Girondins, named for the Gironde department north of Paris where many in the faction came from, favored starting a revolutionary war to free from tyranny those people living in absolutist states, such as Austria and Prussia, the two nations on which France declared war in April 1792. This declaration of war ultimately sealed the fate of the royal family and helped further radicalize the Revolution.

Despite Girondin assurances that victory would be easy, the early stages of the war did not go well for France, which was forced to cope with an officer corps that was depleted by aristocratic defections. The war brought about an increasingly radical situation in Paris where the *sans-culottes* (literally those who did not wear the fancy breeches—culottes—worn by the aristocracy) tried to deal with the scarce supply of bread and feelings of chagrin at being labeled passive citizens without the right to vote. They were also fearful following a manifesto issued by the Prussian commander, the **Duke of Brunswick**, which promised to destroy Paris if the royal family was harmed. In Paris, this helped create a political transformation that led to a demand for wider political participation and the establishment of a radical government, the Commune, in the city.

On August 10, a large mob of *sans-culottes* stormed the Tuileries palace, where the king and the queen were living, and slaughtered 600 of the king's Swiss guards. This was followed by another act of horrendous violence. In September, following a series of defeats by French armies, around 1,200 individuals who had been arrested as potential counter-revolutionaries were slaughtered by a frenzied mob who were reacting to rumors that the prisoners were about to escape and attack French armies from behind. The Paris Commune then forced the National Assembly to call for elections for a new legislative body using universal male suffrage. This body, known as the Convention, was given the task of drawing up a new constitution ending the constitutional monarchy. Meanwhile, the military acts that had spurred on these developments began to change. The threat to Paris, which had spurred on the September massacres, ended quickly when a French army, inflamed by revolutionary passion, stopped the combined Austrian and Prussian advance at the battle of Valmy. With the Revolution apparently saved from the combined threat of foreign armies and counter-revolution, France officially became a republic on September 21, 1792, and the royal family was placed under arrest. Following the discovery of a cache of letters that Louis XVI had exchanged with his brother-in-law, the Austrian Emperor, Louis was tried and in early 1793 guillotined before a large crowd yelling for his blood.

EUROPEAN REACTIONS TO THE FRENCH REVOLUTION

The French Revolution had a huge impact on the rest of Europe. For those on the continent who had been influenced by the ideas of the Enlightenment, the events in France seemed like a breath of fresh air, and they eagerly created radical political associations of their own in places like the Italian states and the German states. At first, Austria and Prussia thought that the Revolution would be useful for bringing about the eclipse of France as the major power on the continent. They soon came to regret their initial complacency and began to see the Revolution for its potential to spread to other areas and possibly to threaten their own thrones.

In Great Britain, the immediate reaction to the fall of the Bastille and the abolition of French feudalism, along with the establishment of a constitutional monarchy, was quite friendly. For many, it appeared as if the violent rivalry between the two nations would finally come to a peaceful conclusion. **William Pitt the Younger**, the British Prime Minister, stated, "The present convulsions in France must sooner or later culminate in general harmony and regular order and thus circumstanced, France will stand forth as one of the most brilliant powers of Europe. She will enjoy just that kind of liberty which I venerate." His chief political opponent, Charles Fox, was even more enthusiastic. He called the revolt "the greatest event that ever happened in the history of the world."

Only **Edmund Burke**, a leading British politician attached to the Whig faction, was cautious. In 1790, he wrote *Reflections on the French Revolution*, which expressed his opposition to the Revolution. Burke was not against reform; he himself had been interested in the reform of certain aspects of English political life. He feared, however, that once you remove the traditional system of deference and alter dramatically the role of such institutions as the monarchy and the church, eventually force will rule. To that end, he predicted that the Revolution would take a more violent direction, something that was rather prescient considering he was writing in only 1790. Burke believed that reform could take place only by keeping the present political structure and seeking to achieve evolutionary rather than revolutionary change. His work serves as the foundation piece for modern political conservatism.

Britain was eventually brought into the European-wide war sparked by the Revolution. By the fall of 1792, French armies, following initial setbacks, were pushing the enemy back and began to occupy territories, such as the Austrian Netherlands. They also captured much of the Rhineland and the important city of Frankfurt. Wherever French armies went they brought with them the ideas of the Revolution. Although the National Convention promised "fraternity and assistance to peoples who want to recover their liberties," the French armies soon became more of an occupying force than liberators.

THE REIGN OF TERROR

In the Convention, the Girondins and Jacobins continued to disagree over the direction of the Revolution. The radical Jacobins sat on the left side of the hall where the Convention met on a raised platform; this seating arrangement earned them the label **"the Mountain."** On the right sat the more conservative Girondins. This configuration was the origin of our modern political designations of left and right. In the middle of the hall sat those who were not directly tied to either faction; this section became known as **"the Plain."** It was this group that held the key to the Revolution, since whichever side they aligned with would ultimately triumph.

Both the Girondins and Jacobins were republicans, although the Girondins had favored exile for the king rather than subscribing to the Jacobin argument that the king was a traitor and therefore deserved to be executed. The Girondins were also believers in *laissez-faire*, the idea that the government should not play an active role in regulating the economy, while the Jacobins began to favor the idea that the government would have to regulate such things as the wheat trade to fight against wild inflation. The Girondins were fearful of establishing too much centralized authority in Paris and preferred the maintenance of some degree of local autonomy. The Jacobins believed that the only way to fight against counter-revolution and to maintain the ideals of the Revolution was through the creation of a powerful centralized government. In addition, the Girondins were fearful of the political influence of the *sans-culottes* and favored the continuation of voting rights based on property ownership, while the Jacobins found increasing support among the *sans-culottes* for opposing any such restrictions on the franchise.

The spring of 1793 marked the beginning of what became known as the **"Reign of Terror."** In part, it was inspired by the counter-revolutionary revolt that began in March in a western region of France known as the **Vendée**, a counter-revolution that was largely inspired by anger toward the restrictions placed on the church. French armies met a major defeat that same month in the Austrian Netherlands, followed by the betrayal of their commanding officer, General Dumouriez, who fled to join the Austrians. In response to these provocations, the Convention created two committees, the Committee of General Security and the **Committee of Public Safety**; the latter assumed virtually dictatorial power over France throughout the following year. The leaders of the security committee included **Danton**, **Carnot**, and **Robespierre**, a lawyer whose anti-monarchical sentiments may have started at the age of 11, when a coach carrying the royal family splashed him with mud just as he was about to read some Latin verses he had written in their honor. These men were associated with the Jacobin faction, which was becoming more influential at the expense of the Girondins. The Girondins were tainted by having made the traitor Dumouriez commander of French forces in the Netherlands and by their perceived lack of sympathy toward the Parisian masses.

The *sans-culottes* continued to be a useful tool for the Jacobins, and it was a mob of the former who stormed the hall where the Convention met and successfully demanded the expulsion of Girondin members. This allowed the Mountain to further consolidate its control, which had already been enhanced following the uproar in July, when Charlotte Corday, a Girondin sympathizer, stabbed to death the radical journalist **Marat**, a hero of the *sans-culottes*, while he lay in his bath. To appease the *sans-culottes'* sensibilities, the Mountain-led Convention established a law of maximum prices, which placed limits on the price of bread and taxed the wealthy to pay for the war effort.

In August 1793, **Lazare Carnot**, the head of the military, issued his famous proclamation calling for a *levée en masse*, drafting the entire population for military service. This marks the first time that all citizens of a nation were called on to serve their country. According to the proclamation, men were expected to go into battle; women should "make tents and clothing and…serve in the hospitals." Children were to "turn old linen into lint," and the old folks were to go to public places and "arouse the courage of the warriors and preach the hatred of kings and the unity of the Republic." The armies created out of this levée en masse proved to be surprisingly successful against the well-trained but unmotivated soldiers of Austria and Prussia, and the war once again began to turn in the French favor.

Once in power, the Jacobins worked to create what they considered to be a **Republic of Virtue**. To achieve this ideal, they felt that they had to obliterate all traces of the old monarchical regime. To that end they came up with a new calendar based on weeks made up of ten days, which must have angered workers who found they now had only one day off in ten as opposed to one in seven. The months were renamed to reflect the seasons, and 1792, the first year of the Republic, was labeled as year one. There was also an attack on Christianity and churches, and those in power forced the removal of religious symbols from public buildings. To move people away from what he thought was the corrupting influence of the church, Robespierre established a **Cult of the Supreme Being**, turning the cathedral of Notre Dame into a Temple of Reason. Most of these steps proved to be quite unpopular and eventually led to a political backlash against the Committee of Public Safety.

From the summer of 1793 to the following summer, France was embroiled by the workings of the Reign of Terror. Because the Revolution was believed to be threatened by both internal and external enemies, niceties such as the rule of law—or fair trials—were thrown out the window. The Committee of Public Safety first began by banning political clubs and popular societies of women. Next, they executed leading Girondin politicians who were accused of being traitors, and the **guillotine** became a symbol of the age. In the end, around 20,000 individuals were executed. Approximately 15 percent of these were nobles and clergy; the majority were peasants who had been involved in counter-revolutionary activities.

Eventually, the Terror began to turn on those who had first set it in motion. By March 1794, under the leadership of Robespierre, it had an extreme radical faction known as the **Hébertists**, who were violently anti-Christian and wanted to see the government implement further economic controls. Soon afterward, Danton, one of the Jacobin Committee leaders, and his followers were brought to the guillotine for arguing that it was time to bring the Terror to a close. The surviving followers of Hébert and

Danton were joined by members of the National Convention who feared that they were next in line for the guillotine. The end was fairly anticlimactic: On 8 *Thermidor* (July 26, 1794), Robespierre spoke before the Convention about the need for one more major purge. Someone in the assembly shouted "Down with the tyrant," and for once, Robespierre seemed at a loss for words and left the building. The next day, he and his leading supporters were arrested by the **Thermidorians**, the label for those who were opposed to Robespierre, and after a quick trial that very same day, 100 leading Jacobins were escorted to the guillotine.

THE DIRECTORY (1795–1799)

Following the execution of the leading members of the Convention and the Committee of Public Safety, the Thermidorians abolished the Paris Commune, a hotbed of radical sentiment, along with the Committee of Public Safety. They produced a government known as the **Directory**, because it was led by an executive council of five men who possessed the title of director. The new constitution provided for a two-house legislature, made up of a **Council of the Ancients**, which discussed and voted on legislation proposed by the second house, the **Council of Five Hundred**.

As part of the backlash against the radical republic established by Robespierre, the franchise was limited to those men who possessed property, and only those who possessed significant property were allowed to hold public office. In general, the Directory witnessed the triumph of men of property over the *sans-culottes*. One sign of this was the revival of ornate dress, which members of the *sans-culottes* had been proud to not possess, along with the removal of all price ceilings on staples such as bread. Another part of this backlash against the radical phase of the Revolution was the attack on Jacobin club meetings by wealthy young men whose families had grown rich by providing French troops with supplies or through the confiscation of church property.

The Directory also had to be concerned with the possibility of a royalist reaction, and on 13 *Vendémiaire* (October 5, 1795), a royalist rebellion did break out in parts of Paris. A young general named **Napoleon Bonaparte** was told to put down the rebellion, and with a "whiff of grapeshot," his cannon dispersed the rebels. The Directory had been saved, but soon it was to be destroyed by its savior.

NAPOLEON

Domestically, the Directory did little to solve the economic problems still facing the French nation, nor did it solve the ongoing conflict with the Catholic Church. Its armies, however, did meet with tremendous success on the battlefield. Among the rising generation of new French generals, the most important was Napoleon Bonaparte. Napoleon was born in 1769 to a family of minor nobles on the island of Corsica, which had been annexed by France the year prior to his birth. He attended a French military academy, and in 1785 he was commissioned as an artillery officer.

Had it not been for the French Revolution, Napoleon would have remained a junior officer for the remainder of his military career owing to his relatively humble birth and Corsican background. However, the Revolution offered tremendous opportunities to young men of ability, and Napoleon became a strong supporter of the Revolution and was aligned with the Jacobin faction. In 1793, after playing a major role in the campaign to retake the French port of Toulon from the British, he was made a general. Napoleon was nothing if not lucky during his career, and while other Jacobins were dragged off to the guillotine during the Thermidor reaction, Napoleon was left unscathed.

Desperate for military victories that might take the people's minds off the dismal conditions at home, the Directory sent Napoleon to Italy. In a series of stunningly quick victories, Napoleon destroyed the combined Austrian and Sardinian armies, and before long, France controlled northern and central Italy. With the Austrians and the Prussians now out of the war, the only enemy was Great Britain. Instead of trying to cross the English Channel with an invasion force, a battle that Napoleon knew would have limited chance of success due to the powerful British navy, he decided to invade Egypt in order to cut Britain's ties with its colony of India. Napoleon succeeded in conquering Egypt (and ushered in a new age of appreciation for Ancient Egyptian civilization, in part inspired by the discovery of the Rosetta Stone). He was unable to do much with his victories on land because a British fleet under the command of **Admiral Horatio Nelson** defeated a French fleet at the Battle of Abukir on August 1, 1798.

Seeing that the situation in Egypt was doomed, Napoleon abandoned his army and rushed back to France where he had received word that the Directory was increasingly unstable. On 19 *Brumaire* (November 10, 1799), Napoleon joined the Abbé Siéyès, who at the time was one of the five Directors, staged a coup d'état, and overturned the Directory. Siéyès, who thought Napoleon could be controlled, established a new constitution with a powerful executive made up of three consuls, which included one of the sitting directors, Roger-Ducos, and Siéyès and Napoleon as the other two. One month after the coup, the politically ambitious Napoleon set up a new constitution with himself as **First Consul**. This structure granted universal male suffrage to satisfy republican sentiment but left Napoleon firmly in control over the real workings of the state. Using a technique that he would find increasingly useful, Napoleon staged a **plebiscite** (a vote by the people) for his new constitution to show popular support, and they passed it overwhelmingly.

Napoleon attempted to end some of the bitterness that had arisen out of the Revolution. A general amnesty was issued, and émigrés began to stream back to France. Since Napoleon only required that public servants be loyal to him, he was able use the talents of those Jacobins and monarchists who were willing to accept his dominance over the French state. Napolean treated those who were not willing with brutal cruelty. He established a secret police force to root out his opponents. Following a plot on his life, Napoleon purged the Jacobins, and he kidnapped and executed the Bourbon Duke of Enghien after falsely accusing the Duke of plotting against him.

Napoleon recognized that a major problem during the course of the Revolution was the ongoing hostility of French Catholics. He himself was not religious, but he recognized that religion could be a useful tool for maintaining political stability and that the church would continue to be important for many French people. In 1801, Napoleon created a **concordat** with Pope Pius VII. Basically, the settlement worked to the benefit of Napoleon. The concordat declared that "Catholicism was the religion of the great majority of the French"; it did not, however, reestablish the Catholic Church as the official state religion, and it remained tolerant toward Protestants and Jews. The papacy would select bishops, but only on the recommendation of the First Consul. The state would pay clerical salaries, and all clergy had to swear an oath supporting the state. In addition, the church gave up its claims to those lands confiscated during the Revolution. The church was able to get Napoleon to do away with the calendar that had been established during the period of Jacobin dominance, which the church particularly hated since it did away with Sundays and religious holidays.

Following a plebiscite in 1802 that made him Consul for Life, Napoleon set about to reform the French legal system. **The Civil Code of 1804**, commonly known as the **Napoleonic Code**, provides the framework for the French legal system to this day. The code provided for a single unitary legal system for all of France, rather than the hundreds of localized codes that had been in existence under the monarchy. The code enshrined the equality of all people before the law and safeguarded the rights of property holders. Reversing the advances made by women during the Revolution, the code reaffirmed the paternalistic nature of French society. Women and children were legally dependent on their husbands and fathers. A woman could not sell or buy property without the approval of her father or husband, and divorce, while still legal, became much harder for women to obtain.

In 1804, Napoleon decided to make himself Emperor. Once again, he held a plebiscite as a means of trying to show popular support, and again his wishes were overwhelmingly affirmed by vote. He invited the pope to take part in the ceremony, which took place in Notre Dame, rather than in Rheims Cathedral, the traditional place where French kings had been crowned. During the point in the ceremony at which the pope was about to place the crown on the Emperor's head, Napoleon yanked it out of the pope's hands and placed it on his own head and then took a second crown and placed it on the head of his wife, Josephine. Napoleon wanted to make it clear that he was Emperor of the French not based on the will of God or through accident of birth, but rather as a result of the weight of his own achievements. Napoleon also created a new aristocracy that was based on service to the state rather than birth. Members of the new aristocracy did not enjoy any special privileges before the law, nor could their titles be passed on to their children.

FRANCE AT WAR WITH EUROPE

Constant warfare was a hallmark of the reign of Napoleon. Although he is considered to be one of the geniuses in the history of warfare, in many ways his greatest skill was in taking advantage of certain developments that were taking place in eighteenth-century warfare. In 1792, with the *levée en masse*, French armies became larger than their opponents' forces, and Napoleon became masterful at moving these large armies to outmaneuver his opponents. In part, he could do this because he could trust his highly motivated citizen-soldiers, unlike his opponents, who employed unreliable mercenaries who were given little independence on the battlefield for fear of desertion. Napoleon certainly did not invent the new lighter artillery found in the eighteenth century, but he skillfully recognized that this new artillery could be fully integrated with the infantry and cavalry as a very effective fighting tool. Although Napoleon supposedly said that an army "moves on its stomach," he did little to feed those stomachs. He encouraged his men to live off the land, rather than using costly time to provide adequate provisions through the maintenance of a supply line, something that added to the great unpopularity of French occupying armies.

Although France was officially at peace with Great Britain as a result of the **Treaty of Amiens (1802)**, Napoleon saw it only as a temporary measure as he sought for means to limit British influence. To antagonize the British, who had colonies in the Caribbean, he sent troops to Haiti, where a slave rebellion had created an independent republic. After most of the French troops died from disease, Napoleon turned his interest away from the colonies and even sold the **Louisiana Territory** to the United States for the paltry sum of around $11 million. Napoleon refocused on Europe and readied plans to invade England, but first the powerful Royal Navy would have to be defeated. At the **Battle of Trafalgar** on October 21, 1805, Admiral Nelson died in the struggle that ultimately destroyed the French fleet and with it any hope of the French landing in England.

On land, however, Napoleon was in his element. Following the formation of the **Third Coalition**, in which Austria and Russia joined Great Britain, Napoleon set out to first destroy the Austrians, a goal which he achieved at the **Battle of Ulm** in October 1805, and then he won his greatest victory over a Russian force at **Austerlitz**. Following these battles, Napoleon decided to abolish the Holy Roman Empire and created the **Confederacy of the Rhine**, a loose grouping of 16 German states that were placed under the influence of France. Ironically, just as in Italy, Napoleon's victories in Germany resulted in the redrawing of the map, although with long-term consequences not favorable to the French nation. When the Prussians, who had previously worked out a treaty with France, saw the extent of French control over German territories, they hastily joined the Third Coalition. To punish them, Napoleon quickly gathered his forces, and at the **Battle of Jena** he obliterated the Prussian army and occupied their capital city of Berlin.

Following the complete collapse of the Prussian army, the Russian Tsar **Alexander I** (r. 1801–1825) decided that it was necessary to make peace with France. He met with Napoleon on a raft on the Nieman River, and on July 7, 1807, the two monarchs signed the **Treaty of Tilist**, with the Prussian monarch eagerly waiting on the shore to see what Alexander and Napoleon cast as the fate of his defeated kingdom. Because of the insistence of Alexander, Prussia was saved from extinction, but it was reduced to half its previous size and was forced to become an ally of France in its ongoing struggle against Great Britain. Seeing that he could not defeat the British navy, Napoleon decided to wage economic war. He established the **Continental System**, an attempt to ban British goods from arriving on the continent. Rather than damaging Great Britain, however, the Continental System weakened the economies of those states that Napoleon had conquered and achieved little to advance French economic interests.

The Continental System and the resentment it caused throughout Europe helped galvanize support against French rule. Initially, wherever French troops went, they brought with them the ideals of the Enlightenment and the French Revolution. French troops arriving in Venice broke down the walls of the ghetto where Jews had been forced to live since the High Middle Ages and established full religious toleration. They also brought about the end of social distinctions wherever they went and imposed the Civil Code as the basic rule of law. Despite this, the French were still occupiers, and as time went on, increasingly harsh ones. Napoleon placed his generally worthless family on the various thrones of Europe essentially as figureheads because all authority came from Paris.

THE DEFEAT OF NAPOLEON

Napoleon's eventual defeat came about for three reasons: the peninsula war in Spain, growing nationalism in French-occupied Europe, and the fateful 1812 invasion of Russia.

THE WAR IN SPAIN

In 1807, a French army passed through Spain on its way to conquer Portugal, an ally of Great Britain. When a revolt broke out against the incompetent Spanish King Charles IV the next year, bringing his son, the almost as incompetent Ferdinand VII (r. 1808–1833) to its throne, Napoleon decided to take the opportunity to occupy Spain and place his brother Joseph on its throne. Almost immediately, the Spanish nation rose up in a nationalistic fervor to expel the French, who in turn used tremendous brutality against the Spanish people. Napoleon was eventually forced to leave 350,000 troops in Spain where they were tied down in a costly struggle against Spanish patriots who fought with guerilla tactics against the more static French troops.

GROWING NATIONALISM IN EUROPE

While Napoleon continued to struggle with what he called his "Spanish ulcer," stirrings of nationalism also began to churn in other parts of Europe. In the German states, intellectuals began to see that a struggle against the French might be just the tool to create that unified German state for which they longed. These writers looked to Prussia for leadership, while within Prussia, there were stirrings of reform as the nation began to grasp the magnitude of its defeat at Jena. Fortunately for Prussia, it was blessed with two administrators who possessed immense abilities: **Baron von Stein** (1757–1831) and Count von Hardenberg (1750–1822). These men were hardly democratic reformers; they wanted to see the continuation of monarchical power and aristocratic privilege. They did, however, bring about much-needed reforms, such as ending the Junker (Prussian noble) monopoly over the ownership of land and the abolition of serfdom. To create an army of motivated soldiers led by competent leaders like the French model, Stein appointed some bourgeois officers and removed some of the more incompetent Junker officers. He also established a professional ministry of war. Stein eliminated some of the harsher elements of military discipline to encourage the peasant soldiers to fight loyally for the state, and he established a large reserve army made up of part-time soldiers.

THE 1812 INVASION OF RUSSIA

Some of Napoleon's advisors warned him that the constant wars came at a high cost to the French nation. Napoleon, however, still looked for new lands to conquer. Russia seemed a suitable target, particularly because after the defeat of Prussia and Austria, only Russia was still standing as a strong continental rival. In June 1812, Napoleon took his **"Grand Army"** of 600,000 men into Russia, where he fully expected to defeat the Russians in open battle. To his great annoyance, the Russians merely retreated within their vast landscape. When Napoleon took Moscow in September, he found the city a smoking ruin, with fires set by the retreating army of the tsar. Since there was no enemy to fight and few supplies left in the part of Russia occupied by French troops, Napoleon decided to withdraw his army in one of the most famous retreats in military history. The combination of Russian attacks and the brutal winter made the withdrawal a disaster; only 40,000 of the original Grand Army finally returned to France.

The Russian retreat marked the beginning of the end. In 1813, Russia, Prussia, Austria, and Great Britain formed a coalition to fight together until all of Europe was freed from French forces. While British forces under the **Duke of Wellington** pushed forward toward France through Spain, a combined Russian, Prussian, and Austrian force entered eastern France. By March of 1814, they were in Paris, and in the following month, after learning that the allies would not accept his young son on the French throne, Napoleon abdicated.

THE CONGRESS OF VIENNA, THE BOURBON RESTORATION, AND THE HUNDRED DAYS

In victory, the allies demanded the restoration of the **Bourbon monarchs** as outlined in the Treaty of Chaumont, which brought the Count of Provence, a brother of the executed Louis XVI, to the French throne as Louis XVIII. Meanwhile, Napoleon was exiled to the Mediterranean island of Elba, although the allies generously paid off his debts and allowed him to maintain the title of Emperor and keep a small army on his tiny island state.

To create a lasting peace and to try to put the revolutionary genie back in the bottle, the allies met at the **Congress of Vienna** beginning in September 1814. The four great powers, Great Britain, Austria, Prussia, and Russia dominated the proceedings, although the great architect of the Congress settlement was the Austrian Chancellor, **Prince Metternich** (1773–1859). Metternich was aware that the social and political changes brought about by the French Revolution had been detrimental to his own state and that it was necessary to turn back the clock. Metternich and the other representatives wanted to make sure that such ideas emanating out of the French Revolution, such as **nationalism** and **liberalism**, would have no place in a redrawn Europe. To that end, they made sure that Polish demands for a free and independent Poland went unanswered and gave the territory to the Tsar of Russia as the Duchy of Poland.

The great powers also wanted to ensure that no nation, least of all France, should ever dominate Europe again. To keep order in France, and to ensure that the Bourbons' subjects would not greatly resent them, France walked away with rather generous peace terms, including the right to hold onto all territorial gains made prior to November 1, 1792. The great powers also erected a series of states that would serve as a barrier to future French expansion. They created the Kingdom of the Netherlands by incorporating the Dutch territory with the Austrian Netherlands to the south, gave Prussia important territories along the Rhine River to block future French expansion to the east, and gave Piedmont the territory of Genoa.

While the victors debated the future course of Europe, the past came back to haunt them. On March 15, 1815, Napoleon returned to France having escaped from Elba. He found many in the army and in the country at large willing to support him, particularly since the return of the Bourbons had led to an unleashing of a violent **white terror** against Jacobins and Bonaparte supporters. Louis XVIII was once again forced to flee his homeland as Napoleon was rapidly reinstalled as Emperor. Although he promised France a liberal constitution and the end to foreign aggression, he knew that the allies would not allow him to maintain the throne, so once again he raised an army. At the **Battle of Waterloo** (June 18, 1815), Wellington, the British commander, aided by Marshal Blucher, the leader of the Prussian forces, defeated Napoleon. Following the **Hundred Days**, the name given to Napoleon's remarkable return, he was exiled once again, although this time to the distant island of St. Helena, in the middle of the Atlantic, where he died in 1821.

CHAPTER TIMELINE

You've probably got the hang of this by now. I'll say no more.

Year	Event
1787	Assembly of Notables meets
1788	Louis XVI decides to call the Estates General
1788	Abbé Siéyès writes *What is the Third Estate?*
1789	Estates General meets for the first time (May 5)
1789	Third Estate declares that they will only meet as a National Assembly (June 17)
1789	Tennis Court Oath (June 20)
1789	Storming of the Bastille (July 14)
1789	Lafayette selected as commander of the National Guard
1789	Great Fear (July–August)
1789	Renunciation of aristocratic privileges (August 24)
1789	Declaration of Rights of Man is adopted by the Constituent Assembly (August 26)
1789	Women's march on Versailles (October 5)
1789	Jeremy Bentham's *Introduction to the Principles of Morals and Legislation*
1790	Civil Constitution of the Clergy
1790	Edmund Burke's *Reflections on the Revolution in France*
1791	Constitution promulgated
1791	Revolt breaks out in French colony of St. Domingue
1791	Louis XVI attempts to flee Paris (June 20)
1792	Mary Wollstonecraft's *Vindication of the Rights of Women*
1792	France declares war on Austria (April 20)

Year	Event
1792	Mob of *sans-culottes* storm the Tuileries Palace (August 10)
1792	September Massacres
1792	Battle of Valmy (September 20)
1792	France becomes a republic (September 21)
1793	Execution of Louis XVI (January 21)
1793	Universal conscription for the French armies begins (February 24)
1793	Execution of Marie Antoinette (October 16)
1793	Britain enters the war against France
1793	Counter-Revolution breaks out in the Vendee (March)
1793	Establishment of the Committee of Public Safety (April)
1793	Expulsion of Girondins from the Convention (June 2)
1793	Ratification of new republican constitution (June 24)
1793	Murder of Marat by Charlotte Corday (July 13)
1793	Napoleon retakes Toulon from counter-revolutionaries
1794	Execution of Danton (April 6)
1794	Festival of the Supreme Being (June 8)
1794	Fall of Robespierre and the Jacobins (July 27)
1795	Establishment of the Directory
1795	Napoleon puts down royalist revolt (October 5)
1796	Napoleon launches invasion of northern Italy
1798	Napoleon begins invasion of Egypt
1798	French fleet defeated at the Battle of the Nile (August)

Year	Event
1798	Thomas Malthus' *Essay on Population*
1799	Napoleon involved in coup overthrowing Directory
1799	Napoleon becomes First Consul
1800	Eli Whitney's cotton gin
1801	Napoleon and Pope Pius VII sign Concordat
1802	Plebiscite establishes Napoleon as Consul for Life
1802	Treaty of Amiens between Britain and France
1803	Napoleon sells the Louisiana territory to the United States
1804	Napoleon crowned Emperor
1804	Murder of the Duke of Enghien
1804	Promulgation of the Civil Code
1805	British victory over French-Spanish fleet at Trafalgar
1805	Defeat of the Prussians at the Battle of Jena
1805	Formation of the Third Coalition
1805	Defeat of the Austrians and Russians at Austerlitz
1806	Abolition of the Holy Roman Empire
1807	Napoleon and Alexander I sign Treaty of Tilsit
1807	Continental System implemented
1807	Invasion of Spain by French forces
1807	British Parliament votes for the end of the slave trade
1807	First passenger train line
1812	Napoleon's invasion of Russia

Year	Event
1812	Occupation of Moscow (September)
1813	Retreat from Russia
1813	Battle of Leipzig (October)
1814	Napoleon forced to abdicate and the reign of Louis XVII begins
1814	Congress of Vienna convenes (September)
1815	Napoleon escapes from Elba (March 15)
1815	Battle of Waterloo marks end of the Hundred Days (June 18)
1815	Napoleon sent into exile on St. Helena
1821	Death of Napoleon

REVIEW QUESTIONS

Answers and explanations are in Chapter 15.

1. At the start of the Estates General, members of the Third Estate refused to have their credentials officially recognized because

   (A) they resented that the three estates met and voted separately
   (B) they doubted that decisions would be made by fully democratic means
   (C) the aristocracy also refused to show credentials
   (D) they resented the attempt to include peasants within the Third Estate
   (E) the king refused to hold future meetings of the Estates General

2. The Bastille was a symbol of royal power because

   (A) the king used it as his residence in Paris
   (B) it had housed political prisoners
   (C) wheat for bread was stored there
   (D) it was located at Versailles
   (E) it was built by Louis XVI with forced labor

3. The significance of the women's march on Versailles on October 5, 1789 was that

   (A) it led to cheaper bread prices
   (B) it resulted in the king being brought back to Paris
   (C) the leaders of the march were immediately arrested
   (D) it was used by the Jacobins as justification for the elimination of the Girondins
   (E) it marked the only instance in which women participated in the events of the revolution

4. The Continental System represented Napoleon's attempt to

   (A) lead the continent in a potential struggle with the United States
   (B) close off the continent to British trade
   (C) create a continent-wide parliament
   (D) issue a new code of law
   (E) draft soldiers throughout Europe into his Grand Army

5. Napoleon's Civil Code allowed for

   (A) the elimination of private property
   (B) full property rights for women
   (C) special rights for those holding aristocratic titles
   (D) taxation of all social classes
   (E) the rights of the accused to be considered innocent until proven guilty

6. The *sans-culottes*

   (A) were tied to the Girondins
   (B) recoiled from the use of violence
   (C) failed to recognize the legitimacy of the National Guard
   (D) were primarily peasants
   (E) consisted of the working-class people of Paris

7. Baron von Stein challenged the traditional social structure in Prussia by

   (A) allowing the bourgeoisie to enter the officer corps
   (B) advocating for a constitutional monarchy
   (C) pushing for a bourgeois-led government
   (D) ending agricultural subsidies for the Junkers
   (E) eliminating the rights of the free peasantry

11

Europe from 1815 to 1871

RESTORATION AND REVOLUTION

Following the final fall of Napoleon in 1815 and the restoration of the Bourbons to the throne of France, the rulers of Europe were faced with a daunting task—restoring stability in the relationships between the nations of Europe while also ensuring that the specter of revolution did not reappear within their domains. To aid in this task, one aspect of Napoleon's reign was widely copied throughout Europe—France's efficiency in controlling its population. In the period following the Napoleonic wars, states created larger and more efficient bureaucracies, secret police forces, and more efficient censorship offices. In an undeveloped nation such as Russia, these oppressive institutions were the only well-functioning part of the state.

States used another strategy to try to turn back the clock—attacking the legacy of the Enlightenment. No institution had suffered as much from the Enlightenment and the French Revolution as the church. The German Romantic poet Novalis wrote in 1799, "Catholicism is almost played out. The old papacy is laid in the tomb, and Rome for the second time has become a ruin." Despite this prediction, the churches of Europe, both Catholic and Protestant, witnessed a remarkable recovery in the Restoration period (1815–1830). States viewed religion as a useful tool to aid in repression. In England, the Anglican clergy worked in the House of Lords to block parliamentary measures such as the bill in favor of Catholic emancipation and the Great Reform Bill. In Russia, the Orthodox clergy remained a bulwark of the reactionary policies of the state. The same was true in Catholic lands such as Spain, where the Inquisition was once again allowed to operate following its disappearance during the Napoleonic domination of Spain.

AN AGE OF COMPETING IDEOLOGIES

The Restoration period was a highly ideological period in which ideas inspired either from support or approbation of the French Revolution played a role in whether one was committed to the restored order that emerged after 1815 or wanted to see its demise.

CONSERVATISM

Modern conservatism is rooted in the writings of **Edmund Burke**, whose *Reflections on the Revolution in France* (1790) was widely read throughout Europe. Two components of Burke's work were extremely popular in the Restoration period: his attack on the principle of the rights of man and natural law as fundamentally dangerous to the social order and his emphasis on the role of tradition as the basic underpinning for the rights of those in positions of authority. Burke, a member of the English House of Commons, proposed a conservatism that was not reactionary in nature. He believed in the possibility of slow political change over the passage of time.

On the continent, however, a more extreme form of conservatism appeared in the writings of such men as *Joseph de Maistre* (1753–1821), an émigré during the French Revolution. The church, argued de Maistre, should stand as the very foundation of society because all political authority stemmed from God. De Maistre advocated that monarchs should be extremely stern with those who advocated even the slightest degree of political reform and that the "first servant of the crown should be the executioner."

NATIONALISM

Nationalism is based on the idea that all people's identities are defined by their connection with a nation and that it is to this nation that they owe their primary loyalty. The roots of nationalism date back to the Early Modern period; however, nationalism emerged as an important ideology during the French Revolution. At this time, developments like national conscription, the calling of all young men for military service, helped create the idea of a citizen whose primary loyalty lies not to a village or province but to the nation instead.

Nationalism became important in other parts of Europe in reaction to the expansion in France. In the German and Italian states, the desire to rid their lands of French soldiers created a unifying purpose that helped establish a national identity. This growing national identity also had a literary component. Writers such as the **Grimm brothers** recorded old German folk tales to reveal a traditional German national spirit that was part of a common past, whether one lived in Bavaria, Saxony, or any of the other German states. Early nineteenth-century nationalism was often, though not exclusively, tied to liberalism because many nationalists, like the liberals, wanted political equality and human freedom to serve as the bedrock for the new state.

LIBERALISM

The foundations for nineteenth-century liberalism can be found in the writings of the philosophers of the Enlightenment, with their emphasis on the **individual's natural rights** and support for limits on political authorities through the writing of **constitutions** and the formation of **parliamentary bodies**. Liberalism was also connected to the events of the early stages of the French Revolution with the establishment of the constitutional monarchy and with Lafayette's *Declaration of the Rights of Man* serving as a basic foundational document. Liberals hoped to protect the rights of individuals by limiting the power of the state and by emphasizing the individual's right to enjoy religious freedom, freedom of the press, and equality under the law.

Besides being a political theory, liberalism was also a school of economic thought. The most important of the early liberal economists—individuals who collectively formed what became known as the **classical school**—was **Adam Smith** (1723–1790), who published his most important work, *An Inquiry into the Nature and Causes of the Wealth of Nations*, in 1776. Smith believed that it was necessary to break the control that eighteenth-century states generally wielded over their national economies. Smith was a critic of mercantilism, where the state played a role in setting prices, granted exclusive economic privileges, and actively sponsored business enterprises. Smith believed governments should practice *laissez-faire* ("to leave alone"), and that instead of providing economic guidance, they should allow, for example in the setting of prices, an **"invisible hand"** that would provide balance between supply and demand.

Economics is sometimes referred to as "the dismal science," which has nothing to do with the difficulty of getting a 5 on the AP Economics exam. The expression was applied to economics because the classical economists—men such as **Thomas Malthus** (1766–1834) and **David Ricardo** (1772–1823)—reached conclusions that can only be viewed as deeply depressing. Malthus, a country parson, argued in his *Essay on Population* that the population was growing at a rate that would eventually outstrip the food supply. Factory owners were pleased to read in Malthus a justification for the payment of miserable wages to their workers, because according to Malthus, if they were better compensated, they would be more likely to produce more children, ultimately leading to only more misery as increasing numbers of workers competed for fewer jobs and less food. According to Ricardo, the only way factory owners could find an advantage over their competitors was by offering lower wages, resulting in a steady downward spiral in their earnings. This "iron law of wages" must also have pleased factory owners, because once again, their parsimony could be presented as if it were actually essential for the public good. Ironically, Malthus and Ricardo were both writing at a time when the dramatic expansion of production brought on by the Industrial Revolution was making their negative predictions obsolete.

Some writers, although we still apply to them the label of "liberal," began to question certain classical, liberal orthodoxies on the workings of the economy as well as the role of the state. **John Stuart Mill** (1806–1873) began as a disciple of **Jeremy Bentham** (1748–1832), who had provided a justification for an expanded role for government by suggesting that governments should seek to provide "the greatest happiness for the greatest number." Bentham's views, which are given the label of **utilitarianism**, were taken further by Mill, who wrote in his *Principles of Political Economy* that it may be necessary for the state to intervene and help workers achieve economic justice.

In some of Mill's later works, he began to move into a direction that brought him ever closer to socialism, with his questioning of the absolute right to hold private property while also suggesting that there needed to be a more equitable way for societies to distribute their wealth. Mill's most famous work, *On Liberty*, was a clarion call for personal freedom. Although in the past, the struggle for liberty involved placing constraints on monarchs, today the danger was that in democratic governments, the majority could deny liberty to the minority, thus squashing the personal liberty that Mill cherished in the name of majority rule.

Unlike other male liberals who saw political liberty solely as a male domain, Mill was greatly influenced by the feminist thought of his wife, **Harriet Taylor** (1807–1856). Inspired by her, *On the Subjugation of Women* consists of arguments in favor of granting full equality to women.

SOCIALISM

Socialism, like the other ideologies discussed above, was also partly rooted in the French Revolution, with a number of radical Jacobins taking the idea of political equality for all and moving it to the next step: economic equality for all through the common ownership of all property. The early socialist writers are sometimes given the label **"Utopian Socialists,"** a phrase coined by **Karl Marx**, who viewed these early writers with contempt because he felt they offered non-scientific, unrealistic solutions to the problems of modern society. Utopian Socialists believed that expansive possibilities were available to mankind and that poor environments corrupted human nature. The utopians also believed that capitalism over-emphasized production, under-emphasized distribution, and possessed other serious flaws such as unemployment and the suffering brought about by low wages.

These early Socialists provided no single answer to society's problems. **Henri de Saint-Simon** (1760–1825) argued that society needed to be organized on a scientific basis. He argued for the creation of a hierarchical society led by an intellectual class that improved society and, most important, the lot of those on the bottom of the social ladder. Contemporary events in Europe are currently heading in a direction that Saint-Simon imagined: He hoped to witness the rise of a community of European nations that would have a common currency, transportation, and a parliament, among other things.

Another Utopian Socialist was **Charles Fourier** (1772–1837) who created a blueprint for a cooperative community. The blueprint consisted of a self-contained group of precisely 1,620 people living on 5,000 acres of land. Fourier hoped to make the workday more satisfying by rotating tasks so that everyone would do the boring tasks but not exclusively—Fourier thought that because children liked to play with dirt, they should take care of the community's garbage.

Another individual who designed a planned community—and unlike Fourier he actually built it—was **Robert Owen** (1771–1858), a self-made manufacturer. Like Fourier, he blamed the environment for man's corruption and in response built New Lanark, a mill town in Scotland, where workers were housed decently and children received an education. These early Socialists had relatively little impact in comparison with Karl Marx's proletarian socialism which came later.

POLITICAL RESTORATION AND REFORM

FRANCE

The term restoration literally refers to the events in France, where the Bourbons were restored to the throne following the final defeat of Napoleon at Waterloo. The throne that **Louis XVIII** returned to was different from the one his older brother had enjoyed up until 1789. The Charter of 1814—a hastily written constitution—contained many of the freedoms from the revolutionary period, such as freedom of religion, even though it was presented to the French people by the king and contained no notion of popular sovereignty. The charter angered many royalists by confirming land purchases made from nationalized church property. Politically, it allowed for a constitutional monarchy with a chamber of peers and a chamber of deputies made up of a very restricted franchise. The king held the firm reins of power, however, because only he could introduce legislation, and ministers were responsible to him instead of to the assembly.

In 1820, the son of the younger brother of Louis, Duke de Berry, who was thought to be the last male Bourbon, was assassinated. The ultra-royalists, individuals who wanted to see the revival of absolute monarchy, used the assassination to pressure the king to clamp down on the press and to give more rights to the aristocracy, including compensation for nobles who had lost land during the Revolution.

Political repression increased after the death of Louis XVIII in 1824. At that time, Louis's younger brother **Charles X** came to the throne. Charles felt more bitter about the Revolution than his brother Louis had. A year after taking the throne, he introduced a Law of Sacrilege, which ruled death as the penalty for any attack on the church. In 1829, Charles appointed the Prince of Polignac as his chief minister, a man disliked throughout the country for being a leading ultra-royalist. In the following year, Polignac issued what became known as the **July Ordinances,** which dissolved the newly elected assembly, took away the right to vote from the upper bourgeoisie, and imposed rigid censorship.

That same month, revolution broke out in Paris. Leading liberals were afraid of the Parisian mob and wanted to avoid the creation of a republic, because they associated republics with the violence of the first French republic dating back to 1792. Instead, they turned to Louis Phillipe, the Duke of Orleans, a liberal who had stayed in France during the Revolution. The **July Revolution** of 1830, which sparked revolutions throughout Europe, ended with the crowning of Louis Phillipe and the creation of what became known as the bourgeois, or **July monarchy**.

REVOLUTIONARY MOVEMENTS

By the third decade of the century, people across Europe showed signs that to stem their desire for change would be impossible.

Spain and Portugal

In Spain, King Ferdinand VII had been restored to the throne following the collapse of French control in 1814. Ferdinand was restored on the condition that he honor the liberal constitution of 1812 drawn up by the Cortes, the Spanish parliament, which had met in Cadiz—the one part of Spain that was not conquered by Napoleon. Once restored to his throne, Ferdinand dissolved the Cortes and persecuted those liberals who had drawn up the constitution.

In 1820, a rebellion began among army divisions that were about to be sent to South America to put down the rebellions against the Spanish Empire. The small Spanish middle class soon joined the army divisions in the rebellion. Although the king agreed to rule under the laws of the constitution to end the rebellion, Austria, France, Prussia, and Russia wanted to intervene to stem the tide of the revolt. The British, however, refused to directly intervene; they did not want the five great powers of Europe to be involved in putting down internal rebellions in other nations. Two years later, a French army acted unilaterally—although with the tacit support of Russia, Prussia, and Austria—and restored Ferdinand to absolute power.

A similar revolt took place in Portugal, where a group of army officers wanted to draw up a constitutional monarchy under John VI who had fled to Brazil during the Napoleonic Wars.

Italy

A more serious revolt broke out in Naples, a revolt that the Austrian statesman Metternich labeled as the "greatest crisis" of his career. Similar to the situation in Spain, King Ferdinand of Naples had made promises while in exile to rule as a constitutional monarch, although once restored to the throne, he refused to give up any of his absolute powers. Neapolitan army officers, perhaps inspired by French ideas, joined with members of the bourgeoisie and began, with the assistance of secret nationalistic societies such as the **Carbonari,** to oppose the monarch. The revolt led to nationalistic stirrings throughout Italy and to another revolt in the Kingdom of Sardinia, which ultimately came to nothing.

Metternich wanted to put down the revolt in Naples, but once again, the British refused to participate in a joint attack. Metternich wanted the support of the other great powers, so he called the rulers of Austria, Prussia, and Russia to the Austrian town of Troppau to create what became the **Troppau Protocol**, which stated that the great European powers had the right to intervene in revolutionary situations. The following year, the rebellion in Naples was put down with the help of Austrian troops.

Greece

With the forces of repression appearing to be in the ascendancy, liberals throughout Europe looked with hopeful eyes to the Greek revolt of 1821. Liberals felt passionate about this revolt because Greece was the birthplace of democracy. The romantic poet **Lord Byron** (1788–1824) went to Greece to aid the rebels in their struggle against the Ottoman Empire and died not on the battlefield but from a fever.

The Greek revolt was also tied to what became known as the **"Eastern Question"**—what should be done regarding the increasing weakness of the Ottoman Empire? By 1827, Britain, France, and Russia organized a combined naval force to intervene on the side of the Greek revolutionaries, and in the following year, the Russians attacked the Ottomans on land. By 1832, Greece declared its independence from the Ottoman Empire, although it became a monarchy with an imported Bavarian prince and was hardly a bastion of liberalism. Around the same time, the Ottoman Emperor granted independence to Serbia, which was protected by Russia. The Russians saw themselves as Serbia's champion because both Russia and Serbia were populated by ethnic Slavs.

Russia

Russia had emerged as a great European power as a result of the Napoleonic Wars, although in many ways, Russia was a much more backward nation than the other European countries. **Alexander I** (r. 1801–1825) had ruled Russia and at various times had toyed with the idea of political reform, although in the latter part of his reign he grew increasingly reactionary.

Alexander's death in 1825 produced confusion as to the succession; Constantine, the older of his two surviving brothers, turned down the throne, so **Nicholas I** (r. 1825–1855) stepped up. In the confusion, a small group of military officers decided to stage a revolt in support of Constantine, who they wrongly thought was in favor of a constitutional monarchy and had been unfairly removed from the succession. This **"Decembrist" revolt** was put down rapidly and with great brutality. In the following years, Nicholas ruled with an iron fist, making sure to stamp out any additional movements for reform within his vast empire.

Great Britain

The French Revolution and the wars against Napoleon had created a backlash against the idea of political reform in Great Britain. The governing elite were also wary of possible social unrest owing to the economic downturn that occurred following the end of the Napoleonic Wars. Such fears were realized in a catastrophe in 1819 when a large crowd of 60,000 people gathered in St. Peter's field in Manchester to demand fundamental political changes, including universal male suffrage and annual parliaments. Although those who attended the meeting were for the most part peaceful, the soldiers on hand shot eleven members of the crowd. This became known as the **Peterloo Massacre**, an obvious play on the Battle of Waterloo. Soon after this disgraceful event, Parliament passed the repressive **Six Acts**, which banned demonstrations and imposed censorship.

The mood in Great Britain became more conducive to reform beginning in 1824 with the repeal of the **Combination Acts**, which had banned union activity. In 1829, restrictions dating back to the seventeenth century on the rights of Catholics to hold political office and government posts were lifted. In 1832, the **Great Reform Bill** was passed. The bill was hardly radical. Although it expanded the electorate to include those who had become wealthy as a result of industrialization, only one in five males in Great Britain could vote. It reduced but did not completely eliminate the number of so-called rotten boroughs, which were sparsely populated electoral districts. The Bill succeeded in showing that political reform was possible in Great Britain without having to resort to the barricades as in continental Europe.

The new electorate created out of the Great Reform Bill undertook additional reforms. Although inspired by the middle-class members of Parliament, they showed a new harshness toward the poor. The **Poor Law of 1834** forced the destitute to enter into workhouses where conditions were purposefully miserable to discourage people from seeking assistance.

On a more humanitarian level, in 1833, slavery was banned in the British Empire, and the **Factory Act of 1833** reduced the number of hours that children could work in factories and established government inspectors to ensure adequate working conditions. One sign that the new political order in Great Britain was now dominated by manufacturing interests as opposed to the old landed class was the 1846 elimination of the **Corn Laws**, which had imposed high tariffs on imported grain to support domestic growers. Manufacturers had long supported the end of the Corn Laws, believing that lower food prices would allow them to pay lower wages to their factory workers.

THE REVOLUTIONS OF 1848

On January 12, 1848, there was a rebellion in the Kingdom of the Two Sicilies against King Ferdinand II. This rebellion was to be the first of approximately 50 revolts that convulsed Europe in the first four months of that year. Nationalistic desires throughout the Italian and German states and the Austrian Empire partly fueled the revolutionary tensions, although economic problems—including issues raised by industrialization, which had created a whole new class of working poor—also contributed to the tensions. The 1840s were a terrible decade for agriculture and have accordingly been labeled the **"hungry forties."** The Irish experienced the most terrible conditions, even though Ireland had not been convulsed by revolution. The Irish **potato famine** of 1846 led to the death of 1 million individuals and the emigration of an additional million out of Ireland.

FRANCE

There is an old saying that when France coughs, the rest of Europe catches a cold. In 1848, a rebellion in France, not the Sicilian rebellion, created the spark for revolution throughout Europe. In France, the revolution of 1830 brought about only slight changes. The wealthy bourgeoisie dominated the July Monarchy, while the workers who had played such a pivotal role in the revolution of 1830 felt that they had received little for their efforts. Louis Phillipe's chief minister, Francoise Guizot (1787–1874), believed that France had evolved politically as far as it should and that anyone who resented their lack of political rights should simply "get rich." With the rise of censorship and the banning of openly political meetings, opponents of the regime turned to the practice of holding banquets that were thinly disguised political meetings. Over the winter, there had been more than 70 of these banquets with the largest one scheduled for February 22, 1848 to honor George Washington, a great hero to continental liberals. On the day of the banquet, Guizot issued an order banning it, which resulted in four days of revolution in the streets of Paris. After the first day, Louis Phillipe forced the resignation of Guizot, which may have been enough to placate the liberals; however, the workers on the barricades were not satisfied until they forced Louis Philippe to flee to England.

Political disagreements between the liberals and the radicals plagued this revolution in France from the start, with the liberals focusing on political issues such as an expansion of suffrage. The radicals, led by socialist journalist **Louis Blanc** (1811–1882), spoke of the need for fundamental social and economic change. Blanc's supporters successfully pressured the provisional government to set up **national workshops** to provide jobs for the unemployed.

Outside of Paris, however, the nation was more conservative, as seen by the national assembly election held on April 23, which elected an assembly made up primarily of moderate republicans. The election, which had employed universal male suffrage, created a government run by a five-man executive committee comprised of moderates. Anger over the election results led to a **workers' revolt** that May in Paris that was quickly put down. In the following month, the government now believed itself in a strong enough position to do away with the national workshops, which they had felt pressured to support.

The termination of the workshops led to what became known as the **"June Days,"** essentially a violent class struggle in the streets of Paris in which 10,000 people died. The June Days further strengthened the hands of the moderate republicans, and in November, they felt confident enough to create the French **Second Republic**, headed by a president who would be elected by a universal adult male body of voters and who would not be responsible to the legislature.

The surprising outcome of this year of revolution came in December when the first election for president was held and the victor was **Louis Napoleon** (1808–1873), a nephew of the Emperor. Louis Napoleon was able to capitalize on the appeal of his name and made vague promises to aid the embittered workers. After being elected, he created a rather conservative government, and by 1851, during a constitutional crisis, he assumed dictatorial powers. In 1852, seeking to emulate his famous relative, he made himself **Emperor Napoleon III**.

THE GERMAN STATES

Events in France had huge repercussions in the German states. In Prussia, **Frederick William IV** (r. 1840–1861) had promised to promote moderate reform for many years, but he never implemented any changes. In March 1848, disturbances erupted in the streets of Berlin. The crowd got angry when two shots rang out and struck two people. Horrified by the bloodshed, Frederick ordered his army to leave the city, which left him without any defense against the crowd. The king then allowed for an election for a constituent assembly, which would have the task of drawing up a new constitution for Prussia. Several months later, the king was confident enough to call back the troops, and the constituent assembly was dissolved. Nevertheless, in December 1848, the king did draw up his own constitution, which was rather close to what the assembly had planned. It allowed for personal rights such as freedom of the press and created a two-house legislature with adult-male universal suffrage for the lower house, although in the end, this provision was watered down by giving weighted votes to those who paid more taxes.

In Austria, news of the revolution in France inspired assorted nationalists to break free from the control of the Austrian monarchy. In Hungary, **Lajos Kossuth** (1802–1894) demanded a constitution that would provide for responsible government for Hungary. In Prague, a similar revolt called for the creation of a semi-autonomous Czech homeland. From May to October, Vienna was under the control of students and workers who demanded freedom of the press, an end to censorship, and also the removal from office of the hated Metternich. As in Prussia, the Emperor did not want bloodshed and called off his troops. By June, the revolt in Prague was put down by military force, and in November, the Emperor was firmly in control in Vienna, although he needed Russian help to put down the Hungarian rebellion.

Another notable event in 1848 was a concerted effort to establish a unified German state. On May 18, elected representatives from all the German states gathered in Frankfurt to participate in what they thought was going to be the birth of a nation. From the start, the **Frankfurt Parliament** was hampered by the political inexperience of its participants and by conflicting aims; while all wanted to see a unified German nation, major disagreements arose over whether it should be a monarchy or a republic.

A paralyzing dispute also emerged over the question of where to draw the borders of the new Germany. Those who favored the **Grossedeutsch** plan wanted to see all German lands, including German sections of Austria and Bohemia, united under German rule. **Kleindeutsch** supporters felt that the more realistic solution would be to include only Prussia and the smaller German states. Eventually, the delegates settled on the Kleindeutsch, and they offered the German Imperial throne to William IV, the King of Prussia. He responded that he did not want a "crown picked up from the gutter" and declined the offer.

This was a lost opportunity to build a German nation under a liberal parliament rather than by a militaristic Prussian state, as would be the case in 1871. Perhaps the future course of German history would have been very different had Germany united under a liberal parliament. The German liberals at Frankfurt, however, had proven to be quite militaristic when they helped put down a revolt in some of Prussia's Polish territories and had also been completely unconcerned with the rights of those Czechs who had no desire to see their lands included in the new Germany.

THE ITALIAN STATES

In the Italian states, the revolt that first broke out in Sicily led Ferdinand II to grant a liberal constitution. Eventually, similar revolts broke out and terrified monarchs granted charters in Tuscany, Sardinia, and even the papal States, where in the following year, a short-lived Roman Republic was created. In the north of Italy, revolts broke out in the Austrian-dominated provinces of Lombardy and Venetia. This led to a call by Italian liberals for a war of unification, with **Charles Albert**, the ruler of the Kingdom of Sardinia, reluctantly taking up the banner of Italian nationalists and attacking Lombardy, only to be easily defeated by the Austrians.

For Italy, the lesson for the future was that unification would not take place under the auspices of the papacy, as some Italian liberals prior to 1848 had assumed. On the other hand, the possibility of the Kingdom of Sardinia serving as the foundation for a unified state improved, because in the group of Italian states that were granted constitutions in 1848, only Sardinia governed via the constitutional monarchical course in the following years. A final important lesson that had future ramifications: the Italians could not eject Austria from its possessions within Italy without the aid of another European power.

RUSSIA AND GREAT BRITAIN

Two nations avoided the turmoil of revolution in 1848: Russia and Great Britain. Repression in Russia was so complete under the reign of Nicholas I that the nation passed the year with hardly a yawn. In Great Britain, the story was quite different, since 1848 marked the peak year for a movement known as **Chartism**, which dated back to the previous decade. Chartism centered on the belief that the problems of the working class could be corrected by changes in the political organization of the country. The **People's Charter of 1838**, from which the movement received its name, contained six points.

- universal adult-male suffrage (some Chartists did favor female suffrage as well)
- the secret ballot
- abolition of property requirements for members of Parliament
- payment to members of Parliament
- equal electoral districts
- annual parliaments with yearly elections

In many ways, working-class dissatisfaction with the House of Commons after the passage of the Great Reform Bill was a motivating factor behind the Chartist movement, because working-class citizens believed that the reformed Parliament was completely unresponsive to their demands.

In April 1848, a mass meeting was scheduled in London for the presentation of the Charter to the House of Commons. If the petition were once again rejected by Parliament, the Chartist Convention planned to transform itself into a National Assembly that would take over the government of the country. The mood in the capital was apprehensive. One middle-class man wrote to his wife:

> London is in a state of panic from the contemplated meeting of the Chartists, 200,000 strong on Monday; for myself, nothing that happened would in the least surprise me: I expect a revolution within two years: there may be one within three days. The *Times* is alarmed beyond all measure. I have it from good authority that the Chartists are determined to have their wishes granted.

In London, there were preparations for a violent conflict, and Queen Victoria was sent out of London for safety. On April 10, the day of the mass meeting, the situation was tense as 200,000 individuals gathered to sign the petition. The petition was presented to the House of Commons, and basically, everyone went home peacefully. The House of Commons, however, refused to even debate the clauses contained in the petition. At this point, Great Britain appeared to be on the verge of revolution, but the country emerged far more fortunate than its continental counterparts. Reform did eventually come about in incremental stages; by the early twentieth century, five of the six acts of the Charter (the annual parliaments didn't pass) were established parts of the British Constitution.

THE INDUSTRIAL REVOLUTION (1750–1850)

Historians had formerly placed the beginning of the Industrial Revolution at 1760, when a group of new inventors appeared from nowhere and began to develop factories, bringing an end to the **domestic system** of production that had guided manufacturing since the Early Modern period. Experts have modified this belief over the last several decades; some historians even avoid the term "Industrial Revolution," which they claim implies far too dramatic a change. We now know that technological progress did not begin in 1760; it had been occurring for centuries. This much is true: The second half of the eighteenth century saw a quickening of an age-old evolutionary process rather than a fresh break with the past. By the middle of the nineteenth century, particularly with the advent of the railroad, industrialization was beginning to reshape the European landscape and to dramatically alter the way in which people lived.

GREAT BRITAIN'S INDUSTRIAL LEAD

Great Britain was the first European nation to begin the process of industrialization. What motivated England to change so dramatically? Although numerous books and articles have dealt with this question, conclusive or definitive answers for queries of this sort are rare. Several possible factors may have contributed to England's role as the leader of the industrialization of Europe:

- In the years following the Glorious Revolution of 1688, Great Britain achieved a degree of **political stability** that created an environment friendly to economic investment.

- Compared to most other European states (the exception being the Netherlands), Great Britain permitted a much greater degree of **religious toleration**. For example, the Quakers, while closed off by law from parliamentary careers, had no such restrictions placed on their economic activities and were able to play a central role in the Industrial Revolution.

- **Expanding population**—that almost doubled in Great Britain over the course of the eighteenth century, due in large part to a lower death rate thanks to better diet and hygiene—is of particular importance to the Industrial Revolution. Britain's increased population size produced not only a large body of potential low-wage workers for the factories but also a steady supply of consumers.

- The **Agricultural Revolution** of the eighteenth century, initiated by men like Jethro Tull (who also played a mean flute), introduced scientific farming to Great Britain. Their observations led them to realize that continuous rotation of crops, instead of the traditional method of allowing land to lay fallow, allowed for an increase in crop yield while also leading to the growth of turnips and beets that could be used to feed larger quantities of animals during the difficult winter months.

- The **Enclosure Act** of the early eighteenth century forced small-scale farmers into urban areas, both increasing the efficiency of the now larger farms and providing a low-paid workforce for the factories.

- The increased prosperity of English farms led to an **increase in capital** that could be used to invest in the new industries. Great Britain also had a central bank (The Bank of England, chartered in 1694), that encouraged the flow of money in the economy. Interest rates were lower in Great Britain than in any other part of Europe in this period.

- The eighteenth century witnessed a significant increase in Great Britain's **overseas trade**. Besides supplying additional investment capital, it provided the nation with the world's largest merchant marine. It is important to remember, however, that the eighteenth century also witnessed the height of the Atlantic slave trade, although the valiant efforts of individuals such as William Wilberforce finally paid off when Parliament brought the brutal trade to an end in 1807.

- **Transportation** within Great Britain was enhanced by the fact that the entire nation lies within close proximity to the sea. Internally, a network of navigable rivers and the creation of canals made water transport efficient. Turnpike trusts built new roads in Great Britain on a scale not seen since the end of Roman rule.

- Availability of the two critical natural resources of the Early Industrial Revolution: **coal** and **iron**.

The first eighteenth-century technological advances occurred in cotton manufacturing. In 1733, **John Kay** (1704–1764) invented the flying shuttle, which greatly increased the speed at which weavers could make cloth. Kay's invention created a problem: Cloth could be made so rapidly that it outstripped the supply of thread. By 1765, **James Hargreaves** (d. 1778) solved this problem by inventing the **spinning jenny**, a machine that initially spun 16 spindles of thread at one time, and by the end of the century, improvements allowed it to spin as many as 120 spindles at once. Kay's and Hargreaves's machines were small enough that they could still be used in the traditional location of cloth manufacturing—the home. If what was truly revolutionary about the Industrial Revolution was the displacement of domestic manufacturing by the factory system, then it was **Richard Arkwright's** invention of the **water frame** that marked the beginning of this development. The water frame was a huge apparatus that combined spindles and rollers to create a spinning machine to spin cloth. By 1770, Arkwright employed 200 individuals under one roof in what is known to be the first modern factory, and in so doing, made a half-million-pound fortune for himself.

The first factories were originally located along streams and rivers so that water could provide the energy needed to work the machinery. The invention of the **steam engine** made it possible to build factories in other locations. The ancestor of the steam engine was the steam pump, which was used to remove water from mines. **James Watt** (1736–1819) studied the steam pump and adapted it for use in industry. His invention was the first true steam engine, as opposed to a steam pump, since it worked by pushing steam into each end of a closed cylinder, resulting in the upward and downward movement of the pistons. A decade later, Watt invented an engine that turned a wheel. This made factories independent of waterpower and dramatically increased the pace of industrial change.

Another factor that increased the pace of industrialization was the greater ability to **smelt iron**. Traditionally, iron was smelted in extremely hot ovens fueled by charcoal, but by the eighteenth century, England was devoid of forests, and the resulting lack of charcoal seriously limited the production of iron. **Abraham Darby** (1677–1717) discovered a means of smelting iron using coal. Like the inventions discussed earlier, the economy experienced a multiplying factor as a result of Darby's invention, as more productive machines made of iron replaced those previously made from wood.

Iron and steam were the combination behind perhaps the most important invention of the nineteenth-century Industrial Revolution—the **railroad**. The first passenger railroad traveled between Liverpool and Manchester in 1830, and by the middle of the century, Britain was crisscrossed with railroad tracks that carried passengers and goods throughout the land. The railroads had an immense impact on the economy. Engines, tracks, stations, tunnels, and hotels for travelers were just some of the machines and structures that were connected with the railroads. It is estimated that by 1880, one in ten jobs in Great Britain was in some way connected either directly with the railroads or with services tied to rail transportation.

The British took the lead in manufacturing, but it wasn't long before methods pioneered by the British appeared on the continent. Belgium was the first to industrialize, possibly because, like Great Britain, it had a plentiful supply of coal and iron. Other nations industrialized with varying degrees of rapidity. The German states were hampered by numerous tolls and tariffs, making the transportation of goods extremely expensive. To aid in the spread of trade and manufacturing, Prussia in 1834 took the lead by creating the *Zollverein*, a customs union that abolished tariffs between the German states.

As certain German states, most notably Prussia, achieved significant industrial growth by the middle of the century, France lagged behind by comparison. Historians often make telling comparisons between Great Britain and France. Unlike Great Britain, France was wracked by political instability in the first half of the nineteenth century. France also lacked the centralized banking structure enjoyed by British entrepreneurs. Additionally, French population growth was only half that of the other European nations during this period. French peasants remained relatively content to stay on the land, unlike their British counterparts who had little choice but to go to the cities in search of low-paying factory jobs. In certain industries, however, such as in the manufacturing of luxury goods, the French took the lead, and while their economic growth was not quite as dramatic as the British and Prussian models, it remained constant throughout most of the nineteenth century.

THE IMPACT OF INDUSTRIALIZATION

Industrialization dramatically changed life in Europe. Because the location of factories tended to be concentrated in certain areas, it fueled the growth and development of cities. By the middle of the century, Great Britain became the first nation to have more people living in the cities than in the countryside, one of the most dramatic transformations in the history of humankind. Unfortunately, the cities that grew from the ground up as a result of industrialization tended to be awful places for the working poor. Poor ventilation and sanitation led to conditions in which the mortality rates were significantly higher for urban dwellers than for those who resided in the countryside. Because people had to use a water supply that came into direct contact with animal and human feces, cholera became part of the early nineteenth-century urban landscape, killing tens of thousands of individuals.

Industrialization greatly affected the family structure. The fact that the entire family was working was not new; the earlier domestic system had relied on the family as a cohesive working unit. What was different was that the family no longer worked together under one roof, with women and children now often working under conditions even more deplorable than the men, since factory owners thought they were less likely to complain. Great Britain's **Sadler Committee** exposed that children were being beaten in the factories. As a result, the House of Commons passed the Factory Act (1833), which mandated that children younger than nine could not work in textile mills, that children younger than 12 could work no more than nine hours per day, and that children younger than 18 couldn't work more than 12 hours each day, while also providing for seven inspectors to ensure compliance.

Interestingly, many workers were against placing constraints on child labor. It was not that they were monstrous parents; it was simply that wages were so low that children were providing funds that were an essential part of the family budget. There has been a long-standing—and perhaps tired—historical debate about the wages earned by industrial workers and the type of life such wages provided. The "optimist" school on this standard-of-living debate argues that in the first half of the nineteenth century, wages did rise somewhat for workers while prices remained steady or in fact declined, thus allowing for improved living conditions. The "pessimists," on the other hand, claim that horrible working conditions and miserably low wages provided for an increasingly bleak existence for the working poor.

WORKING-CLASS RESPONSES TO INDUSTRIALIZATION

At first, workers were befuddled as to how to grapple with the economic and social problems caused by industrialization. For some individuals, such as handloom weavers, complete economic dislocation ensued, and their traditional way of life was threatened by machinery. Some laborers tried to destroy the machines, which they blamed for their problems. Their fictional leader was Ned Lud, and the term **Luddite** has stayed in the modern vocabulary in reference to those who refuse to embrace new technologies. Machinery also caused hardship for many laborers on the farms. They created an imaginary character known as "Captain Swing," who righted the wrongs imposed on hardworking individuals by the advent of technology. After these rather primitive means of dealing with industrialization proved to be ineffective, workers sought out to create **cooperative societies**, small associations within a given trade that provided funeral benefits and other services for their members.

Despite government disapproval, workers in Great Britain in the late eighteenth century organized what first were known as "friendly societies," and these eventually evolved into full-blown unions once the ban on such activities was lifted in 1824. On the continent, it was not until the 1860s that unions were allowed to freely operate in France and in Prussia. Great Britain also took the lead in establishing the first unions that represented more than a single industry. In 1834, Robert Owen helped form the Grand National Consolidated Trades Union, which several decades later evolved into the Trade Union Congress, pulling together workers from disparate industries. Skilled laborers formed the first unions; by the end of the nineteenth century, however, unions were being formed by dockworkers and other non-skilled workers. Unions were a critical reason for the steady improvement in wages and factory conditions that took place in the second half of the nineteenth century.

Socialism and Karl Marx

Some workers—particularly on the continent—found that although the unions' emphasis on gradual improvements in wages and hours worked, it was at best only a partial solution to the problems caused by industrialization. Many turned to **socialism**, believing that it offered a complete overhaul to an oppressive society. Socialism had early roots in the writings of such individuals as Saint-Simon, Robert Owen, and Charles Fourier; the most significant strand in socialist thought, however, was the so-called **scientific socialism** offered by **Karl Marx** (1818–1883).

Marx was born in the German city of Trier and eventually received a university education at Jena. As a young man, he became the editor of a Cologne newspaper, the *Rheinische Zeitung*, but he soon found that his political views were considered too radical by the authorities who banned the newspaper, leading Marx to seek out the freer intellectual climate of Paris. The French, however, quickly grew tired of Marx, so he left Paris for London where he spent the remainder of his life.

Marx and his colleague **Friedrich Engels** (1820–1895) organized a **Communist League** to link the far-flung German Socialists, many of whom, like Marx, were living in exile. In 1848, they teamed up to write a pamphlet that was to serve as a basic statement of principles for the organization. This document was *The Communist Manifesto*, one of the most influential political tracts in history. The very first line contains Marx and Engels's view that all history from the beginnings of time consists of the struggle between social classes, an idea that was labeled as historical materialism, or the material dialectic. The origin of this idea can be found in the writings of the German philosopher Georg Wilhelm Friedrich Hegel, whose dialectic differed from Marx's in that it saw economic conditions emanating from ideas rather than the reverse. Hegel's thinking influenced Marx and many others, as it seemed to suggest a means toward analyzing historical events. Marx posited that the feudal age was supplanted by the triumph of the bourgeois class in the nineteenth century. The development of capitalism led to the creation of a new class, the **proletariat** (the working class), who would one day arise and supplant those capitalists who had exploited them. In the beginning of this supplantation, the state would dominate in what Marx admitted would be a violent, though triumphant, struggle by the workers; eventually, the state would wither away when it was no longer needed as a result of the elimination of all other classes besides the proletariat. Marx is also known for *Das Kapital*, an enormous treatise on capitalism that explains the mechanics by which capitalists extract profit from labor.

Marx brought a revolutionary dynamism to the class struggle, since he believed that the working class had to constantly prepare itself by organizing socialist parties. In 1864, he organized the **First International**, which Marx said was created to "afford a central medium of communication and cooperation" for those organizations whose aim was the "protection, advancement, and complete emancipation of the working classes." This First International was not a completely Marxist organization—Trade Unionists, Mazzini Republicans, Marxists, and Anarchists were all members. Internal conflicts eventually led the First International to dissolve in 1876. After Marx's death, Engels helped organize the **Second International**, a loose federation of the world's socialist parties heavily influenced by Marxism that met for the first time on July 14, 1889.

THE AGE OF NATIONAL UNIFICATION (1854–1871)

Metternich once remarked that Italy was "a mere geographical expression." He could have said the same for Germany, because up until the second half of the nineteenth century, both lands consisted of a number of independent territories, a disunity that dated back to the Middle Ages. In the late Middle Ages (c. 1100–1500) and the Early Modern period (c. 1500–1789), the rulers of France, Spain, and Great Britain successfully expanded their authority. In France, this expansion resulted in the monarchy destroying the independence of the rulers of Normandy, Brittany, and Aquitaine and incorporating them into the domains of the French king. Such a process did not take place in either the German territories or on the Italian peninsula. However, by the early nineteenth century, individuals in both the German and Italian states sought to create a nation-state that would unite all Italians or all Germans under one political banner because they shared either a common culture or a fear of foreign domination. This process of national unification would have a tremendous impact on the future course of European history.

THE CRIMEAN WAR (1854–1856)

The Crimean War was critical to the formation of centralized states in both Italy and Germany, though initially it was impossible to foresee such a result when the war began in 1854. Several factors led to the outbreak of hostilities, including a controversy over which nation would control access to the religious sites sacred to Christians in Jerusalem. The main issue, however, was the fear among British and French statesmen that Ottoman weakness was encouraging Russian adventurism in the Balkans and the possibility that the Russians might gain access to the Mediterranean by occupying the port city of Istanbul.

Following a naval defeat by the Ottomans, who had declared war on the Russians in 1853 with British encouragement, France and Great Britain declared war on the Russians. Most of the fighting took place in the Crimean region and was notable for the incredible incompetence of all participants. Alfred Lord Tennyson's famous poem, *The Charge of the Light Brigade*, captures just one instance of battlefield stupidity. Most of the half-million casualties did not die in battle but perished due to disease in filthy field hospitals, something that inspired **Florence Nightingale** (1820–1910) to revolutionize the nursing profession.

The war came to an ignominious end after the fall of the Russian fortress of **Sevastopol**. Though reluctant to quit, the Russians were forced to reconsider when the Austrians threatened to enter the war on the side of the British and the French unless Russia accepted the offered peace terms. Russia was forced to cede some territories on the Danube River and to accept a ban on warships in the Black Sea region.

The real cost of the war, however, was that the **Concert of Europe**, the idea that the great powers (France, Prussia, Austria, Russia, and Great Britain) should work together—a concept that emerged from the Congress of Vienna—was finally shattered. This conflict was the first European war since the Napoleonic era. Previously, Russia and Austria had worked together to resist the trend toward nation-building. During the Crimean War, the Germans and other Europeans had no sense of unity on such questions. Additionally, the British public was horrified by the course of events in the Crimean region; as a result, Great Britain became more isolationist regarding European affairs. This meant that when Austria stood in opposition to the building of states in Germany and Italy, it received no support from an embittered Russia, and when France found itself confronting Prussia in 1870, it would find little sympathy across the English Channel.

THE UNIFICATION OF ITALY

The Unification of Italy

In 1848, Italian liberals made an aborted attempt to create an Italian state. Although the attempt failed, the dream for a state never disappeared. Following the collapse of the short-lived Roman Republic, **Pope Pius IX**—when his authority in Rome was restored—instilled increasingly reactionary policies. Liberals no longer saw any potential for the realization of a federation of Italian states headed by the pope. Although some liberals wanted nothing less than the creation of an Italian republic, an increasing number looked with hope to the Kingdom of Piedmont-Sardinia,[1] the one Italian state that had preserved its liberal constitution since the year of revolutions.

The true architect of Italian unification, or what is referred to in Italian as the *Risorgimento*, was not the king of Piedmont-Sardinia, Victor Emmanuel (r. 1849–1878), but **Count Camillo di Cavour** (1810–1861), his chief minister. Cavour was quite different from earlier Italian nationalists like **Giuseppe Mazzini** (1805–1872), who saw state-building in romanticized terms. Cavour was a far more practical individual who primarily sought ways to enhance the power of the Sardinian state.

Cavour realized that creating an Italian state would require the expulsion of Austria from the Italian peninsula. Events in 1848 foreshadowed the impossibility of succeeding in this expulsion without the aid of some other European state, so Cavour entered into a secret alliance with France. Cavour had set the groundwork for this relationship by cleverly entering the Kingdom of Piedmont-Sardinia in the Crimean War on the side of France and Great Britain, and although its participation was minimal, it earned Napoleon III's gratitude. Napoleon III was additionally interested in aiding the Sardinians, because Austria was a traditional enemy of the French state. Napoleon III also periodically looked for foreign military adventures, so that he could live up to his famous namesake, something that would eventually lead to his downfall.

The war began in April 1859. The combined French and Sardinian forces won a series of battles against the Austrians, but Napoleon decided to bring the conflict to a close before expelling the Austrians from all Italian lands. He was horrified by the high number of casualties from the conflict (something that never seemed to bother his uncle) and was threatened by Prussia who was massing troops on the Rhine to come to the aid of the Austrians. Cavour was so angered over Napoleon's abortion of the war and his betrayal of the treaty with Sardinia that he resigned as Prime Minister, though a year later he resumed the office.

Both Cavour and Napoleon sought to create a state that would unite northern Italy. Napoleon did not want to see the entire Italian peninsula unified for fear that a large Italian state could be a threat to France. But to Cavour's and Napoleon's surprise and to the latter's great displeasure, the war against Austria helped inspire popular rebellions throughout the Italian peninsula. In the Austrian-dominated regions of Tuscany, Parma, and Modena, revolts led plebiscites to join with Sardinia.

Meanwhile, in the south of Italy, one of the most intriguing characters in Italian history, **Giuseppe Garibaldi** (1807–1882), emerged. Garibaldi was a link to the old romantic tradition of Italian nationalism; he had at one time been a member of Mazzini's **Young Italy** movement. Horrified by the terms of the treaty between Sardinia and France, which required Italy to hand over Savoy and Nice to the French, Garibaldi at first threatened to attack France over the loss of what he considered to be Italian territories. Cavour instead encouraged Garibaldi to invade the Kingdom of the Two Sicilies, thinking that it would be a suicide mission. To everyone's surprise, Garibaldi led his famous army of 1,000 **"red shirts"** and conquered this southern Italian kingdom, which had been ruled with great incompetence by the Bourbons. Garibaldi wanted to march on Rome and make it the new capital of a unified Italy, but this threat to papal control of the city would have greatly antagonized Napoleon III, who found it useful for his popularity among the French to portray himself as a defender of the church.

Cavour was horrified by the idea that the vastly popular Garibaldi might seek to unify Italy under his own charismatic leadership rather than under the Piedmont's control. To curtail this possibility, Cavour rushed troops to Naples to block Garibaldi from his march. Cavour was interested in the papal lands, however, and he shrewdly waited for a popular revolt in the papal states to commence, and only then, under the pretext of restoring order, moved Sardinian troops into all of the lands controlled by the pope except for the city of Rome. This was followed by the declaration of **Victor Emmanuel**

---

[1] The Kingdom of Piedmont-Sardinia consisted of the island of Sardinia and Piedmont, a northern Italian territory that borders France and Switzerland. In some of your textbooks you may see this Kingdom labeled as the Kingdom of Sardinia, or sometimes simply as Piedmont, though all these labels refer to the same state.

as the first king of Italy on March 17, 1861. After the successful invasion of papal lands, only Venetia and Rome were not under the unified Italian flag. In 1866, after Prussia's victory over Austria, the Italians used the opportunity of Austria's vulnerability to seize Venetia. Rome was added to Italy in 1870 and named as its new capital following the withdrawal of French troops from the city as a result of the **Franco-Prussian War**.

The new Italian nation was beset with problems. For more romantically oriented nationalists like Garibaldi, the new Italy was a cold bureaucratic state led by petty officials from Sardinia, inspiring little of the passion that they had felt for the cause of statehood. To this day, there is an economic divide between the north of Italy, which is highly industrialized, and the far more economically backward south. A major problem for the new state was the continuing hostility of the Catholic Church, which banned Catholics from participating in national elections, even though Catholics widely ignored this order. In fact, the church would not fully reconcile with the Italian state until 1929 when Mussolini agreed to restore the sovereignty of Vatican City to the papacy.

GERMAN UNIFICATION

Although Italian unification had important implications for the rest of Europe, the rise of a unified German state in 1871 totally altered the balance of power in Europe owing to the great military and economic strength of this new state. The story of German unification is rooted in the Napoleonic era. Napoleon's domination of large parts of Germany not only increased the demand among German patriots for the creation of a unified nation but also reduced the sheer number of independent German states, which eventually aided in the actual process of unification.

Following the fall of Napoleon, Austria and Prussia were the two dominant states within the German Confederation. In 1848, it appeared as if German unification would be achieved when the Frankfurt Parliament offered the crown to the Prussian king, but Frederick William's refusal delayed the process until it was achieved through means that the Prussians found more conducive to their interests.

Although it was not a foregone conclusion that it was to be Prussia rather than Austria that would take the lead in creating a unified Germany, Prussia did enjoy a number of significant advantages. Prussia, through its creation of the *Zollverein*, had achieved an economic preeminence over the other member states, while Austria was specifically excluded by Prussia for membership in the *Zollverein* customs union. By mid-century, Prussia had achieved a significant measure of industrialization while Austria remained a primarily agricultural state. In addition, the Austrian Empire was a polyglot state made up of numerous nationalities while Prussia was primarily a German state. Perhaps most important to its dominance, Prussia enjoyed the services of one of the most remarkable statesmen of the nineteenth century, **Otto von Bismarck** (1815–1898).

On taking the throne of Prussia, **William I** (r. 1861–1888) made the most important decision of his reign when he selected Bismarck as his Prime Minister. William was engaged at the time in a fight with his parliament over military reforms that he wanted in order to challenge Austrian supremacy in the German Confederation. To break the impasse, William turned to Bismarck, a Junker (Prussian noble), who was known for his arch-conservative views. Standing before the parliamentary budget commission, Bismarck delivered his **"Blood and Iron"** speech in which he said, "Germany is not looking to Prussia's liberalism but to her power...it is not by speeches and majority resolutions that the great questions of the time will be decided—that was the mistake of 1848 and 1849—but by iron and blood." Despite the colorful speech, the parliament still refused to vote in favor of the military budget. Never one to bother with constitutional niceties, Bismarck simply ignored them and collected the taxes and implemented the reforms. To their great discredit, the Prussian liberals did nothing to oppose this blatant disregard for their authority.

The key to his plan to create a unified German state was to modernize the Prussian army by giving it the latest weapons. The first stage in this plan took place in 1864 and involved an alliance with Austria against Denmark over the disputed territories of Schleswig and Holstein. After easily defeating the Danes (the **Danish War**, also known as the German-Danish War or Danish-Prussian War), Schleswig came under Prussian control while Holstein was administered by the Austrians. Bismarck cunningly set up this system, since he wanted the Danish dispute to help achieve his next goal—war with Austria.

In 1866, after securing an alliance with Italy (who wanted to see the final removal of Austria from Italian lands) and securing a promise of non-participation from the French, Prussia, under Bismarck's orders, declared war on Austria, citing the petty dispute over the governance of Holstein as the reason for the attack. The modernization program undertaken by the Prussian army proved to be astonishingly successful, as Prussian forces brought about the defeat of Austria in a matter of seven weeks (the **Seven Weeks War,** or Austro-Prussian War). Ignoring the advice of both his king and the generals who wanted to stage a victory parade through the streets of Vienna and to annex large pieces of the Austrian Empire, Bismarck wisely treated Austria with leniency to keep her out of the next stage of his plan—a war with France.

After the defeat of the Austrians, Bismarck annexed those small German states in the north that had supported Austria in the conflict. Other northern German states were convinced to join Prussia in the creation of what became known as the North German Confederation. The states of southern Germany, while remaining independent, concluded a military alliance with Prussia in case of French aggression.

In 1870, the final stage of Bismarck's plan was set in motion when he provoked a war with the French. Bismarck, with great cunning, made France the outward aggressor in a conflict that began when a prince, who was a kinsman of the Prussian king (a Hohenzollern), was invited to take the vacant throne of Spain. To Napoleon III, the thought of Hohenzollern rulers on two fronts was too much to contemplate. Napoleon III initially won a diplomatic victory when William I agreed to withdraw his cousin's name. However, Bismarck, who desperately wanted war, rewrote the so-called **"Ems dispatch,"** a telegram sent by the Prussian king to Bismarck informing him of what had transpired in the conversation between the king and the French ambassador, to make it appear as though the king had insulted France. Bowing to the demands of an outraged French public, Napoleon III declared war on Prussia. Following the decisive battle of Sedan, France, who many believed had the finest army in the world, was soundly defeated by Prussia. Using Prussia's new-found prestige earned by achieving this victory, Bismarck was able to either convince or bribe the rulers of the other German states to accept the creation of a Germany under Prussian leadership. On January 18, 1871, William I was proclaimed in the palace of Versailles as German Emperor.

The creation of a German Empire completely changed the direction of European history. For example:

- The new German state created a bitter enemy of France, who lost the territories of Alsace and Lorraine and was forced to pay a huge indemnity to Germany for having started the war.

- The economic power of this new German state created rising tensions with Great Britain and helped set into motion the rush to build colonial empires in the last quarter of the nineteenth century. The mad scramble began when Bismarck encouraged the French to build an empire in Africa to take her mind off the loss of Alsace-Lorraine.

- Eventually, all the nations of Europe sought to create overseas empires as a means to further their political and economic interests within a Europe that was trying to adjust to the tensions that arose from the development of a powerful German state.

This new Germany was also not necessarily a very stable entity. Created by military might, its military commanders had a great influence over the nation at large, particularly following the forced retirement of Bismarck in 1890. Prior to being put out to pasture, Bismarck had worried about the internal dangers facing the new nation and therefore attacked two groups he deemed to be a threat to the internal cohesion of the Reich—the Catholics and the Socialists.

Fearful that Catholics owed an allegiance to a church that extended beyond nationalism to Germany, Bismarck responded with an attack on the Catholic Church in a conflict known as the **"Kulturkampf,"** in which he insisted on controlling all church appointments and on gaining complete supervision over Catholic education. Eventually, because of Catholic resentment toward such policies, Bismarck backed away from this struggle.

He turned to another perceived enemy—the **Socialists**—and in 1878, Bismarck called for the passage in the Reichstag of a ban on Socialists' right to assemble and to publish materials. Bismarck also attempted to limit the political appeal of the Socialists by establishing old-age pensions and other social benefits for all Germans. However, as in the case of the Catholics, Bismarck found that oppressing the German Social Democratic Party merely increased its appeal.

FRANCE

France seemed to have a tortured existence throughout the nineteenth century as it continued to grapple with the legacy of the French Revolution. A measure of stability finally emerged with the rise of the **Third French Republic** (1870–1940), though it too had to deal with a past that still divided segments of the French public.

Following his victory in the December 1848 election, **Louis Napoleon** became the first and only president of the short-lived Second Republic. He used a tool developed by his uncle, Napoleon. Following a constitutional dispute with the legislature, he staged a plebiscite in 1851 that polled the people about whether to grant him dictatorial powers for a ten-year period. After winning this vote, Napoleon moved on in the following year to stage another plebiscite, this time on the question of whether to create a second French empire. Although there were numerous electoral irregularities, apparently large numbers of Frenchmen were perfectly content to see the revival of the empire in the hope of once again seeing France take the dominant position in Europe.

France prospered greatly during the first ten years of the reign of **Napoleon III**. Cheap credit provided by the government allowed for a significant economic expansion during this period. The city of Paris underwent a remarkable transformation from a medieval city to a modern one under the guidance of **Georges Haussmann** (1809–1891), who cleared many of the slums of the city and in their place built the wide avenues that have become a hallmark of Paris. Besides making the city more attractive visually, this new Paris was a much cleaner and sanitary place, with aqueducts to bring fresh water into the city and sewers to remove waste, resulting in the elimination of one of the great scourges of the earlier part of the century—cholera. One British visitor told the Emperor with a bit of sarcasm, "May it be said of you that you found Paris stinking and left it sweet."

Despite the economic improvements during the first decade of his reign, politically Napoleon III led an authoritarian regime. Beginning in 1860, Napoleon began to make a number of concessions such as the easing of censorship, in part because of the unpopularity of his wars in the Crimean region and the Italian states. However, this liberalization had the opposite effect of what he intended; it led the people to openly display their disenchantment with his reign. Napoleon was, nevertheless, an effective politician, and he took a bold gamble in 1859 when he declared the creation of a **"liberal empire,"** making his state a constitutional monarchy. This intriguing experiment never had the opportunity to succeed. Napoleon blundered into the Franco-Prussian War and was captured in battle. Eventually, he was sent into exile in Britain where he soon died.

Following the collapse of the Second Empire, France created what became known as the **Third Republic**. Right away, the Republic had to deal with the daunting task of putting down a revolt in Paris, which resulted in the rise of the **Paris Commune**, a radical government created out of the anarchy brought about by the Franco-Prussian War. The republican government restored order in Paris only after winning an armed struggle that resulted in the massacre of 25,000 Parisians. By 1875, the republic was firmly established and consisted of a two-house parliamentary body, with a chamber of deputies, or lower house, elected by a universal male pool of voters and a senate chosen by indirect elections. The president, or head of government, was a relatively weak office, directly responsible to the chamber of deputies. Although the Third Republic was marked by significant problems, such as tensions between the state and the Catholic Church and significant anti-Semitism, it proved to be the most durable of all the French republics.

GREAT BRITAIN

In contrast to events in France, Great Britain enjoyed remarkable stability and prosperity in the second half of the nineteenth century. A general sense of self-satisfaction pervaded in Victorian England. Nowhere was this more apparent than in the **Great Exhibition of 1851**, which boasted more than 13,000 exhibitors displaying the variety of British goods that were now available as a result of industrialization. To accommodate the exhibits and the millions of visitors, the architect John Paxton constructed the first prefabricated building, which became known as the **Crystal Palace**. One contemporary wrote that because buildings represent the society that builds them, the Crystal Palace revealed "the aesthetic bloom of its practical character, and of the practical tendency of the English nation."

Politically, the nation was slowly evolving in the direction of increased democracy. The Great Reform Bill of 1832 was only the first in a number of steps that were taken to expand the franchise. In 1867, under the direction of Prime Minister **Benjamin Disraeli** (1804–1881), one of the most remarkable men to ever hold that post, the **Second Reform Bill** passed, which extended the vote to urban heads of households. In 1884, during the Prime Ministership of Disraeli's great rival, **William Gladstone** (1809–1898), the vote was further extended to heads of households in the countryside. The rivalry between Disraeli and Gladstone was emblematic of another important aspect of Victorian politics—the evolution of a political system dominated by two political parties, in this case, Disraeli's Tory or Conservative party and Gladstone's Liberal party. The long reign of **Queen Victoria** (r. 1837–1901) saw a continuing deterioration in the political power of the monarchy, resulting in the crown's inability to play a significant role in the selection of a prime minister, which meant that at times Victoria had to live with Gladstone as her chief minister, even though she detested him and adored Disraeli, who knew how to flatter her vanity.

RUSSIA

The stresses of war can show a nation at its best or they can reveal significant problems. For Russia, the poor showing in the Crimean War, fought in her own backyard, revealed the backwardness of her society in comparison to the nations of western Europe. Although Nicholas I was far too reactionary to contemplate reform, his successor **Alexander II** (r. 1855–1881) recognized that the greatest problem facing Russia was the continuation of the institution of serfdom. In 1861, he issued a proclamation freeing the serfs, though the former serfs had to buy their freedom with payments that were to extend over fifty years (a practice that was stopped following the Russian Revolution of 1905). The peasants were also generally given the poorest lands by their former owners, which meant that life remained harsh for many agricultural laborers.

Administratively, to cope with a Russia that faced a burgeoning population throughout its far-flung empire, Alexander introduced *zemstvos*, or district assemblies, that had mandates to deal with local issues such as education and social services. The *zemstvos* were dominated by the local gentry and were hardly bastions of democracy, though some Russian reformers saw their exist333333ence as the potential for greater political freedoms. Alexander enacted further reforms, such as a revision of the legal system, although at heart he remained an autocrat and saw no need to implement fundamental changes like the introduction of a written constitution and parliamentary bodies. His intransigence on these points led to a rise in revolutionary organizations such as the **People's Will**, which succeeded in assassinating Alexander in 1881. The succession to the throne of his reactionary son Alexander III (r. 1881–1894) brought about a new round of repression and an attempt to weaken even the tentative reforms of Alexander II.

AUSTRIA

The nineteenth century was not kind to the Austrian Empire, a multinational empire in an age of growing nationalist sentiment. By 1866, the Habsburgs had lost all their territories in Italy, and their shattering defeat by the Prussians at the Battle of Sadowa made Austria no longer a factor in German affairs. In 1867, the government in Vienna found it necessary to sign an agreement with the Magyars in Hungary, creating a dual Austrian-Hungarian empire. Each state was to be independent but united under the mutual leadership of **Francis Joseph**, who became Emperor of Austria and King of Hungary. Perhaps not surprisingly, the Magyars, having achieved a measure of independence, turned around and did their best to ensure that the Croats, Serbs, Romanians, and other nationalities located within Hungary were denied any form of self-rule. As a result of a lessening influence in western Europe, Austria-Hungary attempted to become more influential in the Balkan region, ultimately with disastrous consequences.

THE OTTOMAN EMPIRE

Another multinational empire at the crossroads was the Ottoman Empire. Commonly referred to as "the sick old man of Europe," the Ottoman state attempted in the second half of the nineteenth century to implement a process of modernization. This reform program, which began during the reign of **Sultan Abdul Mejid** (r. 1839–1861) and was known as the *Tanzimat*, was an attempt to adopt Western methods of waging wars, to bring about a much needed overhaul of the Ottoman economy, and to introduce such notions as equality before the law and freedom of religion.

The introduction of Western education played a significant role in forming a group of liberal intellectuals known as the **"Young Turks."** The Young Turks were eventually able to push reform further than the government had ever planned and in 1876 helped establish the Ottoman state as a constitutional monarchy. However, when the brutal **Sultan Abdul Hamid II** (r. 1876–1909) came to the throne, the constitution was scrapped as part of his attempt to subjugate the non-Muslim peoples within his empire. His policies led to the deaths of thousands of Armenians and general repression throughout the state, although by the end of his reign, the Young Turks once again restored a measure of constitutional rule.

Ottoman weakness, however, continued to plague the empire up until it sided with the Central Powers in the First World War. The Ottomans could do little but sit idly by when, at the **Congress of Berlin** (1878), after another humiliating defeat at the hands of the Russians (the **Russo-Turkish War**), the other European powers recognized the independence of Serbia, Montenegro, Romania, and Bulgaria—all former Ottoman territories.

CHAPTER TIMELINE

Year(s)	Event
1717	Abraham Darby smelts iron using partially burnt coal
1733	John Kay's flying shuttle
1764	James Hargreave's spinning jenny
1769	Richard Arkwright patents the water frame
1774	James Watt patents the first steam engine
1776	Adam Smith's *An Inquiry into the Nature and Causes of the Wealth of Nations*
1779	First iron bridge completed
1785	Power loom invented by Edmund Cartwright
1789	Jeremy Bentham's *Introduction to the Principles of Morals and Legislation*
1790	Burke's *Reflections on the Revolution in France*
1793	Eli Whitney's cotton gin
1798	Thomas Malthus' *Essay on Population*
1807	British Parliament votes for the end of the slave trade
1807	First passenger train line
1815	Napoleon escapes from Elba (March 15)
1815	Battle of Waterloo marks end of the Hundred Days (May 15)
1815	Napoleon sent into exile on St. Helena
1817	David Ricardo's *Principles of Political Economy*
1819	Peterloo Massacre in Great Britain
1819	Combination Acts ban union activity
1820	Troppau Protocal
1820	Rebellion in Spain put down with French support in 1824

Year(s)	Event
1821	Beginning of Greek Revolt
1821	Death of Napoleon
1823	Revolt in Naples
1824	Charles X becomes king of France
1825	Decembrist revolt in Russia
1829	George Stephenson invents the Rocket
1830	Charles X issues July Ordinances
1830	July Revolution topples the last Bourbon monarch
1830s	Cholera outbreak in Europe
1831	Charles Darwin leaves on five-year voyage that will take him to the Galapagos Islands
1832	Sadler Committee looks into child labor
1832	Great Reform Bill
1833	Slavery banned within the British empire
1833	Factory Act
1833	English Poor Law
1834	Robert Owen establishes the Grand National Consolidated Union
1835	David Friedrich Strauss's *The Life of Jesus Critically Examined*
1835	Daguerreotype invented
1837	Beginning of the reign of Queen Victoria
1838	Beginning of the Chartist movement
1839	First in a series of Opium Wars between Great Britain and China
1840	Napoleon's body brought back to France for reburial

Year(s)	Event
1840	Joseph Proudhon writes the anarchist tract *What is Property?*
1842	British gain control over Hong Kong
1846	Repeal of the Corn Laws
1846	Irish potato famine
1847	Liberia established as independent African republic
1848	*The Communist Manifesto* by Karl Marx and Friedrich Engels (February)
1848	Overthrow of Louis Philippe (February)
1848	Unrest in various German states (March)
1848	Nationalist revolts breakout throughout the Austrian Empire (beginning in March)
1848	Charles Albert of Savoy goes to war against Austria (March)
1848	Meeting of the Frankfurt Parliament (May)
1848	"June Days" uprising in Paris
1848	Louis Napoleon elected President of the Second Republic (December)
1851	Louis Napoleon stages coup against the Second Republic Crystal Palace exhibition
1852	Development of the safety elevator
1852	David Livingstone begins exploring the African interior
1852	Commodore Perry arrives in Japan
1852	Establishment of the Second Empire by Napoleon III
1854	Charles Dickens publishes *Hard Times*
1854	Start of the Crimean War
1856	Development of Bessemer process for manufacturing steel
1856	Synthetic dyes developed

Year(s)	Event
1857	Flaubert publishes his masterpiece, *Madame Bovary*
1857	Indian Mutiny
1858	Jews allowed to enter the British Parliament
1859	Darwin's *Origins of Species*
1859	France and Piedmont-Sardinia go to war against Austria
1859	Garibaldi invades the Kingdom of the Two Sicilies
1861	Victor Emmanuel II becomes the first king of Italy
1861	Otto von Bismarck becomes Prussian chancellor
1861	Alexander II emancipates the serfs
1863	Opening of the *Salon des Refusés*
1864	Establishment of the First International in London
1864	Prussia and Austria go to war against Denmark
1866	Italians seize Venetia from Austria
1866	Austro-Prussian War
1867	Establishment of the Austro-Hungarian Empire
1867	Alfred Nobel patents dynamite
1869	Suez Canal completed
1869	Johns Stuart Mill's *On Liberty*
1870	Doctrine of Papal Infallibility
1870	Rome becomes capital of Italy
1870	Franco-Prussian War
1870	French Third Republic created

Year(s)	Event
1871	Establishment of the German Empire
1871	End of the French Second Empire
1871	Paris Commune
1871	Darwin's *The Descent of Man*
1881	Assassination of Alexander II

REVIEW QUESTIONS

Answers and explanations are in Chapter 15.

1. The end of the Corn Laws in Great Britain in 1846 was an indication that

   (A) the government was fully responsive to the needs of workers
   (B) the industrial revolution was beginning to slow down
   (C) grain was now available in abundance
   (D) the role of the monarchy was in decline
   (E) the old landed classes no longer fully dominated British politics

2. During the 1848 revolution in France, liberals and radicals differed over

   (A) whether to establish a republic
   (B) allowing Louis Napoleon to return to France
   (C) whether political changes or social and economic changes should take priority
   (D) what to do concerning Louis Philippe and his family
   (E) universal male suffrage

3. All of the goals of the Chartist movement were eventually achieved in Great Britain EXCEPT

   (A) the secret ballot
   (B) annual parliaments
   (C) equal electoral districts
   (D) abolition of property requirements for Members of Parliament
   (E) salaries for Members of Parliament

4. The first nation to industrialize on the continent was

   (A) Prussia
   (B) France
   (C) Belgium
   (D) Russia
   (E) Denmark

5. Rome became the capital of the new Italian nation

   (A) immediately upon the creation of Italy in 1861
   (B) after the withdrawal of French troops from the city during the Franco-Prussian War
   (C) as a result of its conquest by Garibaldi
   (D) after Cavour successfully negotiated the surrender of the city to the Italian government
   (E) with the approval of the papacy

6. The significance of the Sadler Committee of 1832 was that it

   (A) eradicated the practice of child labor
   (B) refused, for political reasons, to come to firm conclusions
   (C) was the first parliamentary commission
   (D) revealed to a larger public the extent of child labor
   (E) committed Great Britain to easing labor shortages through immigration

7. The freeing of Russia's serfs in 1861

   (A) led to an agricultural depression
   (B) required Russia to pay for the serfs' freedom in annual payments over fifty years
   (C) was met with firm opposition by the Tsar
   (D) led to a large emigration of Russian peasants to the United States
   (E) provided former serfs with adequate landholdings

12

Europe from 1871 to 1914

THE SECOND INDUSTRIAL REVOLUTION

By the middle of the nineteenth century, Europe had undergone a dramatic process of economic expansion. These economic changes—sometimes referred to as the Second Industrial Revolution—and their impact on human lives may have been even greater than what occurred during the initial stages of industrialization.

STEEL

The label **"Age of Steel"** is an apt one for the second half of the century. Previously, the high costs of steel production were prohibitive to its use. In 1856, an Englishman, **Henry Bessemer** (1813–1898), introduced a method that became known as the Bessemer Process that produced steel in far greater quantities without increasing costs. A few years later, **William Siemens** (1823–1883), a German, introduced an even better method of making steel that produced a higher quality product at significantly reduced costs. Because of its strength and durability, steel became the metal of choice for buildings and ships, resulting in a revolution in architecture and shipbuilding.

ELECTRICITY

Few developments have affected the way people live their lives as significantly as the invention of the means to harness **electrical power**. In 1879, Thomas Edison invented the incandescent lamp. Two years later, the first electrical power station was built in Great Britain. Soon after that, European cities began to be lit after dark, and populations moved through the streets of the city more effectively with the introduction of electric tramways. Electric lights made cities far safer and even led to the expansion of nighttime activities in London and Paris, where the late nineteenth century saw a tremendous growth in the number of public opera houses and theaters.

TRANSPORTATION

The second half of the nineteenth century witnessed many significant developments in all forms of transportation.

- Europe's rail network expanded dramatically. By the end of the century, well over 100,000 miles of track had been laid.

- In 1869, the French built the **Suez Canal**, though it was the British who gained control over the canal in 1875, eager to ensure their continued use of a waterway that almost halved the amount of time it took to travel from Great Britain to India.

- Speedy clipper ships began to set records for crossing the Atlantic Ocean, though by the end of the century they were to be replaced by steamships.

- Trains and steamships, using the ice-making machines that were introduced in the 1870s, were able to transport perishables around the world and made the United States, Australia, and Argentina major providers of European provisions.

- In 1885, Karl Benz invented an internal combustion engine powered by gasoline. Automobiles, however, would remain a plaything of the very wealthy until Henry Ford built his first Model T in 1903.

- Finally, a whole new area of transportation was opened up when Orville and Wilbur Wright, brothers whose background was in the building of bicycles, launched the first successful airplane at Kitty Hawk, North Carolina, in 1903.

COMMUNICATION AND EDUCATION ADVANCES

Britain was the first European nation to establish a national postal system, with users able to send a letter for a penny, affordable to almost all.

- The development of universal public education also meant that more people were inclined to communicate in writing.

- In 1830, the telegraph was invented, and by the second half of the century, Europe was covered with telegraph lines.

- In 1876, Alexander Graham Bell invented the telephone, and Germans were making 700 million calls per year by 1900.

- Some of those calls might have been to make social arrangements around the new entertainment options of the age, such as attending motion pictures, first shown publicly in the 1890s, while stay-at-home sorts could enjoy the phonograph, invented by the incredibly prolific Thomas Edison in 1876.

OTHER SCIENTIFIC DEVELOPMENTS

Science began to play an increasingly important role in industrial expansion. In particular, the second half of the nineteenth century produced a series of major developments. While this trend was to continue into the first decades of the twentieth century, in many ways, the optimism that one could sense in the 1880's concerning the world of science was not to be found some forty years later. Even before the First World War delivered a terrible blow to the belief in rational progress, scientists were revealing that nature was incredibly complex and that many questions would remain unanswered while at least some of the basic assumptions concerning the workings of the universe were under attack.

- The introduction of synthetic dyes revolutionized the textile industry.

- Science also played a role in the invention of such things as man-made fertilizers, leading to increased crop yields.

- The invention of dynamite by the Swedish chemist **Alfred Nobel** (1833–1896) made it possible to blast tunnels through rock and to remove those hills that nature had placed in inconvenient spots. Nobel, however, was horrified by the potentially destructive uses of his invention, and in his will he entrusted money for a prize to be given in his name to those who served the cause of peace.

Increasingly, the nineteenth and early twentieth centuries witnessed greater specialization in the sciences, as scientists provided some of the key foundational work in areas such as physics and chemistry.

- Some of these developments include Michael Faraday's work on electricity and electromagnetism.

- The amateur scientist and deeply religious James Joule defined many of the laws of thermodynamics.

- In chemistry, Dimitri Mendeleev developed the periodic table, arranging the known elements by atomic weight while leaving empty spaces in his table for those elements then unknown.

- In 1895, Wilhelm Röntgen made an accidental discovery of X-rays.

- In the following year, in another fortuitous accident, Antoine Henri Becquerel discovered radioactivity, although he did not follow this up with additional work. That task would be undertaken by the Curies—Marie and her husband, Pierre—who would spend their lives studying radioactivity. In 1910, four years after the death of her husband, **Marie Curie** isolated radium.

- In England, **Ernest Rutherford** laid the groundwork for an understanding of atomic structure by showing that atomic particles had a central core called the nucleus. Rutherford had once famously said that a theory in physics wasn't any good unless it could be explained to a barmaid, yet his own work became part of an increasingly complex body of knowledge that left many ordinary people feeling alienated from the world as revealed by science.

- As a young student, **Max Planck** was told that there was nothing further to be discovered in physics, yet his work was to revolutionize the field. In 1901, he devised a theory based on the idea that energy did not flow in a steady continuum but rather was delivered in discrete units, or quanta. His quantum physics spelled an end to the dominance of the mechanistic interpretation of physics that stemmed from the work of Newton.

- Further undermining Newton's concept of the universe was **Albert Einstein's** special theory of relativity, where time, space, and movement are not absolute entities but are understood to be relative in accordance with the position of the observer.

Philosophy

Just as scientific inquiry was revealing ideas and principals that appeared to be less than rational, philosophers such as **Friedrich Nietzsche**, for a time a professor of classical languages at the University of Basel, began to question and even to reject the ideas of the eighteenth-century Enlightenment. In Nietzsche's most influential work, *Thus Spake Zarathustra*, he argued that it was necessary to break free from traditional morality, which is why he famously proclaimed that "God is dead." It was necessary, according to Nietzsche, to "kill" God, since religion was at the center of a Western model of civilization that he despised. Nietzsche hated the Germany created by Bismarck, a nation he saw as being populated by the masses and instead yearned for the emergence of the artist-warrior superman. Unfortunately, after his death in 1900, his pro-Nazi sister was in charge of his literary estate, and she edited his writings to make them supportive of Hitler's extreme nationalism and anti-Semitism, two modern chauvinisms that he, in fact, despised.

Psychoanalysis

Sigmund Freud, the father of psychoanalysis, took the methods of modern science and proposed to find a way to treat mental disorders by delving into the human subconscious, using what he referred to as the "talking cure." As he spelled out in *The Interpretation of Dreams*, Freud believed that dreams revealed the inner workings of a subconscious world and devised a list of Freudian symbols—items or events that appear in dreams that actually represent other items or events stored in the unconscious. In *Civilization and Its Discontents*, a book written in his more pessimistic later years, Freud questioned the very premise of continuous progress for the human race and instead posited that despite attempts to suppress it, violence lies at the very core of our being.

Advances in Medicine

The beginnings of modern Western medicine took root in the nineteenth century, marking the first time in history that going to the doctor was not such a bad idea.

- Surgery, which was previously dominated by practitioners who bragged about their ability to remove a leg in under 90 seconds, was transformed in 1846 when American dentist William Morton began to introduce anesthesia in the form of ether, followed by the use of chloroform anesthesia a few years later.

- Overall, the most significant change in medicine in the period was that the experimental method found in the sciences was applied to medicine. Applying the experimental method, **Louis Pasteur** discovered that microbes—small, invisible organisms—caused diseases.

- Pasteur also explained how vaccines, which had been in use since the eighteenth century to fight against smallpox, worked within the body, producing antibodies after coming into contact with a weak form of the bacilli.

- The English surgeon Joseph Lister, building on Pasteur's discoveries, initiated the use of carbolic acid as a disinfectant during surgery.

- A Hungarian doctor, Ignaz Semmelweis, made labor much safer for women, demonstrating that if doctors and nurses thoroughly washed their hands prior to delivery, it could dramatically reduce the number of women who died from what was known as "childbed fever."

Darwin

Few individuals had a greater impact on the intellectual world of the nineteenth century than **Charles Darwin** (1809–1882), an English naturalist who traveled on the *H.M.S. Beagle* to the Galápagos Islands off the coast of South America. Prior to Darwin, there were some, including his grandfather, who had challenged the biblical account of creation found in Genesis, which states that creation was a one-time event and that species therefore never undergo a process of change (evolvution), since God created the world in six days and then stopped. In addition, geologists, like **Charles Lyell** (1797–1875), claimed that geological evidence proved that the Earth was much older than the biblical age of approximately 6,000 years.

Although Darwin was not operating in an intellectual vacuum, he was the first to offer an explanation for the process of change. Darwin argued that certain members of a species inherit traits that over time may make them more successful in the struggle for survival. These traits are then passed down, while those members of the species who lack such characteristics ultimately do not reproduce. Darwin labeled this process **"natural selection"** in his epochal book *The Origin of Species* (1859). It was not until more than a decade after the publication of his first book that Darwin, a cautious man, would take his idea to its natural conclusion. In *The Descent of Man* (1871), Darwin argued that humans were not exempt from this process of evolutionary change and that human beings have therefore evolved from simpler forms of life. The opposition to Darwin was swift and vehement, particularly from religious groups, who saw such ideas as a direct threat to the very basis of their beliefs.

Darwin did attract a number of followers. Although Darwin was always calculating in his own speculative thought, many of his followers pursued his ideas with wild abandon. It was **Herbert Spencer** (1820–1903) who first used the phrase **"survival of the fittest,"** a phrase never in fact uttered by Darwin. For Spencer, such an idea provided justification for governments to abandon the poor; he believed that giving aid on their behalf would upset the natural order of survival. Such ideas, which received the label **"Social Darwinism,"** were used to justify the idea that Europeans were superior to Africans and Asians and therefore should dominate them. Across Europe, ardent nationalists used the concept of survival of the fittest to explain the constant state of tensions between nations and why some states thrived while others didn't. Social Darwinism also played a role in the heightened anti-Semitism found across Europe in the last quarter of the nineteenth century, as some argued that Jews were a lesser race and could never be integrated within the larger fabric of society.

SOCIAL CLASS AND THE SECOND INDUSTRIAL REVOLUTION

Such far-reaching industrial developments played a significant role in changing the social dynamic in western Europe. One group in decline was the traditional aristocracy. The French Revolution created the concept of a meritocracy, thereby eliminating any special privileges based on birth. In Great Britain, the development of refrigerated railcars meant that less expensive agricultural products could be imported from the United States, Argentina, and Australia, which resulted in the propitious decline in the wealth of many of the great noble families, whose wealth was primarily based on land. The implementation of competitive examinations for civil service and military positions served to reduce the aristocracy's role in two of their traditional endeavors: government administration and command of the military.

The second half of the nineteenth century has sometimes been called the **"Age of the Middle Class,"** and in many ways it is an apt designation. At this time, the term "middle class" was of relatively recent origin, because it referred to a group that simply did not exist in the pre-industrial world. Initially, this class was the exclusive provenance of manufacturers and merchants, although as the century progressed, professionals such as lawyers, doctors, engineers, and teachers became part of the middle class.

As a group, the middle class enjoyed new luxuries such as fresh running water and central heating. All families that were considered middle class had at least one servant, while wealthier families had large staffs to attend to their every need. Department stores began to cater to the increasing taste for consumer goods that became a hallmark of middle-class existence. Travel in the eighteenth century had been the preserve of the extremely wealthy, when it was considered an essential part of a young gentleman's education to go on a "Grand Tour" of the capitals of Europe. However, this too changed. **Thomas Cook** (1808–1892) popularized travel among the middle class when he organized day trips to the Great Exhibition in London, thus giving rise to the tourist trade. For those seeking less vigorous relaxation than seeing ten countries in as many days, spas and resorts became common vacation destinations.

Another sign that the middle class enjoyed preeminence at this time was that its standards of behavior became the societal norms. In some instances, this trend produced positive results; for example, certain barbaric forms of popular entertainment, such as animal fights, ceased. Unfortunately, the middle class often obeyed a rather priggish, or what we today refer to as "Victorian," morality. This sense of propriety also greatly affected middle-class women: Victorian sensibilities seemed to preclude them from living fulfilled lives. Women were excluded from the professions and from enrollment in institutions of higher education. The late Victorian period did witness the development in Great Britain, the United States, and, to a lesser extent, France and Germany, of a women's rights movement that sought to dramatically change the status of women.

For workers, the Second Industrial Revolution brought about some improvements in their standard of living. One example of this is the development of popular entertainment such as dance halls and professional sports leagues, a sign that the working-class income was not entirely consumed by survival necessities, such as food and housing. Yet, for many workers across western Europe, the improvements were slight at best. Many still saw socialism as the best means to change their dreary existence. Socialism itself underwent some significant developments in the latter part of the nineteenth century. **Edward Bernstein** (1850–1932), a German intellectual, challenged some of Marx's basic ideas in *Evolutionary Socialism* (1898). He and his followers, who were labeled **"revisionists,"** argued that capitalism was not, as Marx claimed, about to collapse. Because capitalism was firmly rooted in society, it was necessary for Socialists to work toward the progressive improvement of working-class conditions within a capitalist framework rather than focus on revolutionary upheaval. Their more radical views had been mollified in part due to the development of parliamentary democracy and universal male suffrage in parts of western Europe, which led them to believe that socialism could be achieved through the ballot box.

Radicals such as the German **Karl Kautsky** (1854–1938) held firm to the validity of Marx's "laws" and were harsh toward the revisionists, whom they considered heretics, although Kautsky himself in fact altered some of Marx's ideas. Unlike Marx, he claimed that the proletarian revolution would not be a bloody affair but a civilized process. A socialist movement could be a passive evolution since it was inevitable. Such views were in turn declared heretical by more extreme Socialists such as **Lenin** and **Rosa Luxemberg**.

Another political ideology that began to attract some workers by the end of the century was anarchism. **Joseph Proudhon** (1809–1865), a self-educated typesetter, is often considered to be the father of anarchism. In 1840, he wrote *What Is Property?*, and his answer to that question was simply that "property is theft." Proudhon, who was the first to use the term **"anarchist,"** believed that the true laws of society had little to do with authority and came from the nature of society itself. Anarchism touted the idea that bringing these laws to the surface should be the ultimate goal of any society. Anarchists like Proudhon wanted workers to organize small groups of independent producers that would govern themselves without interference from the state, an institution that anarchists wanted to see abolished. Anarchism never gained the support of as many workers as socialism, but in certain regions, such as in the Spanish province of Andalusia, the movement had a significant following.

SOCIAL AND CULTURAL DEVELOPMENTS

RELIGION

Religious beliefs and institutions made a significant recovery in the period after 1815, particularly considering the extent of the challenges posed to organized religion by the Enlightenment, the French Revolution, and the Napoleonic era. Secular rulers saw religion as an important bulwark for the existing social order, with the revolutions of 1848 further spurring this trend toward state support of religion.

Catholicism

Spain, in 1851, declared Catholicism the only religion of the Spanish people, while in Austria, the reforms that Joseph II had imposed on the Catholic Church in the late eighteenth century over areas such as the training of priests were repealed.

Nowhere were the events of 1848 felt more than in Rome, where a revolution forced Pius IX to flee his city. Restored to power with the help of French troops, he issued the encyclical *Syllabus of Errors*, which listed liberalism as one of the errors of modern life. In 1870, Pius put forward the doctrine of **"papal infallibility,"** which posits that when making an official statement on matters of faith, the pope could not be in error, a controversial doctrine that alarmed moderate Catholics.

Perhaps inevitably, there was a backlash against religious institutions where they appeared to be standing in the way of change. Such criticism could be clearly expected from liberal circles, but even conservative politicians could be antagonistic toward religious bodies. In the newly unified Germany, Bismarck saw Catholicism as a force that could rip the nation apart, because Catholics were tied to a supranational institution that would be the object of their primary loyalties. To deal with this purported threat, Bismarck, with the support of German liberals, attacked Catholic institutions in what was known as the *Kulturkampf* (cultural war), taking control over Catholic schools and the appointment of bishops. After seeing that this was having little effect, Bismarck stopped this harassment in 1878.

In the last quarter of the nineteenth century, there was a growing sentiment among both Catholic and Protestant clergy that religion needed to address the social issues of the day. In 1891, **Pope Leo XIII** (r. 1878–1903) issued *Rerum Novarum* ("Of New Things"), and although the encyclical reaffirmed the right of private property and bashed socialism, it said that Christians in general and the Church specifically had a responsibility toward the poor. In primarily Catholic countries such as France and Italy, this message led to the establishment of the **Catholic Social** movement, while in Protestant lands, churches expanded their efforts on behalf of the poor.

The Bible as History

In the German states in the early nineteenth century, a group of theologians began to study the Bible as history in search of the **"historical" Jesus**. A critical step in this effort was the publication in 1835 of *The Life of Jesus Critically Examined* by **David Friedrich Strauss** (1808–1874). For Strauss, the Bible consisted of a series of myths formulated by the early Christians, ultimately providing for a scripture that contained, in his famous phrase, a "Christ of faith, rather than the Jesus of history." The work of these German theologians was brought to England by Samuel Taylor Coleridge as well as by George Eliot, who translated Strauss's *Life* as well as Ludwig Feuerbach's (1804–1872) *Essence of Christianity*, which argued that God was a man-made device that reflected our own inner sense of the divine.

Religion for the Working Class and Peasants

In Great Britain, a religious census taken in 1851 revealed that attendance at church (it assumed everyone was Christian) was much less than expected and that the working class in particular had very little connection with organized religion. On the other hand, the nineteenth century was not without some interesting examples of the continuing strength of popular religious sentiment. One well-known incident dates back to 1858, when a young French peasant girl named Bernadette saw a vision of the Virgin Mary, an event that was repeated eighteen more times. The waters from the grotto at Lourdes where she saw the vision became an important religious shrine, and to this day, the grotto remains a place where those who are infirm drink the waters in the hope of a cure.

Judaism, Anti-Semitism, and Zionism

For Jews, the nineteenth century presented new opportunities as well as new pressures. The legal status of Jews improved throughout the century. In 1858, Jews were allowed to enter the House of Commons in Great Britain, and in the following decade, Jews received full political rights in Austria-Hungary and Germany. Despite their newly enhanced legal status, social discrimination remained endemic. Those Jews who wanted to rise in certain professions or in government often found the path blocked to them unless they converted.

The last quarter of the nineteenth century was a period of increasing hardships for Jews. For many, Jews were seen as responsible for new and troubling trends in modern economic life, such as the creation of the department store, which put small shopkeepers out of business. The economic depression of 1873, which lasted for most of the remainder of the decade, led to an increase in prejudice. Economic resentment was combined with a new form of **anti-Semitism** (the word was first used in 1879) based on Social Darwinist notions of Jews being part of a distinct and foreign race and not just members of a religious denomination.

Hitler's early years in Vienna were spent in a city governed by Karl Lueger (1844–1928), who was elected mayor of the city on an openly anti-Semitic platform. Anti-Semitic political parties formed in Germany, while in France, the **Dreyfus Affair** helped give rise to *Action Française*, a monarchist group that was also virulently anti-Semitic.

In Russia, the monarchy used attacks on Jews, or *pograms*, as a tool for redirecting popular anger, which might otherwise have been directed toward the throne. Several millions Jews left Russia at the turn of the century to escape the persecution that grew worse after the 1905 Revolution.

For many Jews, the optimism they felt at mid-century that the future would bring ever greater social acceptance was by the end of the century being destroyed by a wave of hatred. For some, this would lead to the conclusion that the only hope to live in peace would be through the establishment of a Jewish homeland. The leading advocate for **Zionism**, as this idea was called, was **Theodore Herzl** (1860–1904), an Austrian journalist who was horrified over the anti-Semitism that bubbled over the surface as a result of the Dreyfus Affair. In *The Jewish State*, he argued that Jews must have a state of their own and began to form a worldwide organization to achieve this goal, with the First Zionist Congress meeting in Switzerland in 1897.

THE RIGHTS AND ROLE OF WOMEN

The role of the family changed in the nineteenth century, with one of the most significant developments being that families, which at one time operated as a cohesive economic unit, no longer functioned in such a manner. Increasingly, there were now separate spheres for both male and female endeavors, with the male going off to earn the money that provided for the family's support.

If man's place was in the workforce, the woman's place was in the home, a place that was seen as a haven in an ever-changing world. This idealization of the household and the female's place within it led in the Victorian period to the rise of what is known as the **"cult of domesticity."** Women were expected to exhibit certain traits that were to make the home a blissful paradise. Submissiveness was one of the traits that women were expected to exhibit, along with sexual purity and religious piety, because women were expected to be responsible for the religious life of the family. Books were written to provide women with tips on running their households and raising their children, the most famous being Mary Mayson Beeton's (1836–1865), *Book of Household Management*, a book that was second in sales in Great Britain only to the Bible. Publications like Beeton's were not written with working-class women in mind, although the working class would sometimes receive visits from well-meaning but patronizing middle-class women offering to instruct them in the new ways of home economics.

Limits to Women's Education and Work

Keeping women in the home was in part ensured by outside institutions that limited the opportunities that were available to females. Higher education was generally reserved for men, although cracks began to appear, with women being allowed to attend the University of Zurich by 1865 and the University of London in 1878. With the development of professional societies in areas such as medicine and law, women found an additional barrier, as the bylaws of these societies generally excluded women. For those middle-class women who did work outside the home, certain professions such as primary school teacher, nurse, secretary, and librarian became almost completely female, which also ensured that they were poorly paid jobs in comparison to those held by men.

Some women were able to move beyond the bounds of convention. Frances Power Cobbe (1822–1904) was one of the first women to make a living as a journalist and later became an active campaigner against medical vivisection, and Josephine Butler (1828–1906) challenged a basic Victorian prohibition simply by talking about sex publicly. Butler helped found the Ladies National Association in 1869, an all-female organization that fought against the Contagious Diseases Act, which allowed for women, who were deemed to possibly be infected by sexually transmitted diseases, to be dragged off the street for examination while males went unaccosted.

Women's Struggles for Increased Rights

As the century continued, a growing number of women began to be critical of the civil disabilities under which they lived, such as the lack of right to divorce or to possess property rights. These women, who adopted the French word **"feminist"** to describe themselves, began to organize a litany of organizations to help bring about change. Even where one wouldn't necessarily expect it, such as in a conservative society like Greece, a feminist newspaper existed that advocated for both professional and civil rights and survived for over 20 years with a circulation of 20,000.

Cross-national cooperation existed among the various feminist groups, and there were also transatlantic links with feminists in the United States. Although there was a general desire for cooperation, these first-generation feminists tended to split over the issue of whether the primary struggle should be for the vote or to work for the improvement of social conditions.

Some progressive women scorned feminism altogether, as was the case with the German Marxist Clara Zetkin (1857–1933), who saw socialism as offering women the only possibility for ending their oppression. In Great Britain, there was a split among those women who were working to achieve the vote. **Suffragists,** women who worked peacefully for the vote, were at times overshadowed in the public consciousness by the individuals who joined the **Women's Social and Political Union** formed by **Emmeline Pankhurst** (1858–1928). With her daughter Christabel (1880–1958) at her side, Emmeline and her followers pursued a militant campaign of heckling political speakers, breaking church windows, and committing arson.

In 1918, women were given the vote in Great Britain, leaving a continuing historical debate over whether it was the suffragettes or the suffragists who deserve pride of place in the struggle for the female franchise, although there is also a third factor to be considered: that the vote was achieved as a result of the significant contribution that women made to the war effort during the First World War. Women received the vote in the newly created Weimar Republic in 1918, whereas in France, the vote would not be achieved until the end of World War II.

CULTURE CHANGES

Although political rights were slowly being advanced, there were also cultural changes taking place at the turn of the century that provided the foundations for the emergence of the so-called **"new woman."** Factors such as the increased availability of birth control and greater educational and professional opportunities seemed to offer new horizons for women. For some men, this all remained a bit much, with the British novelist D. H. Lawrence noting in an essay that women, who used to "see themselves as a softly flowing stream of attraction," were now "pointed and they want everything."

EMERGENCE OF THE SOCIAL SCIENCES

History

In the nineteenth century, there was a new impetus to take the methodology established in the sciences and apply it to the workings of society. One result of this was the emergence of history as a modern academic discipline. One of the pioneers in the new historical methods was Barthold Niebuhr (1776–1831), who introduced the close examination of primary source documents into the writing of classical history. His *Roman History* influenced **Leopold von Ranke** (1795–1886) and led von Ranke to challenge the traditional way of looking at history as revealing some grand design, whether that design was the revealed work of God or led to a more secular purpose. He wanted to reconstruct the past by presenting it as it actually was rather than viewing the past in the same manner we view the present. Ranke felt that the historical texts of his day were unreliable and instead felt that it was necessary, like Niebuhr, to go to original sources.

Anthropology

Another social science, anthropology, was born out of the sudden expansion of European dominance over large parts of the globe as a result of the new imperialism. Across Europe, national anthropological societies were established, although unfortunately, due to the endemic "scientific" racism of the age, such societies often spent their time exploring the "inferiority" of non-Europeans.

Sociology

Sociology, the study of human social behavior (or as we historians like to say, the study of the obvious), was in part inspired by the growing tendency of governments to keep statistics on the conditions of their citizenry. Émile Durkheim (1858–1917) held the first chair in sociology at the University of Bordeaux, an appointment that was met with skepticism by the more traditional faculty.

Archeology

Scientific principles were also used in the field of archeology, which in the nineteenth century still remained the preserve of dedicated amateurs such as Heinrich Schliemann, a German businessman who searched for the ruins of ancient Troy, and the Englishman Sir Arthur Evans (1851–1941), who excavated the Minoan culture of Crete.

THE ARTS

Romanticism began in the second half of the eighteenth century as a rejection of what was viewed as the cold rationalism of eighteenth century Neo-Classicism and instead placed a much higher value on the primacy of emotions and feeling.

Romanticism in Literature

Part of the inspiration for Romanticism came from the writer **Jean-Jacques Rousseau**, who in his novel *Émile* proposed an educational program for a young man in which the education was derived from nature and not from rote memorization of facts.

The most important of the early Romantic writers is arguably **Wolfgang von Goethe** (1749–1832). In his *Sorrows of Young Werthe*, an epistolary novel, young Werthe kills himself when his love for a woman is not returned. The novel proved to be so popular that young men throughout Europe began to dress in clothes similar to Werthe and, in some extreme cases, killed themselves. Goethe was the greatest figure of the *Sturm und Drang* (Storm and Stress) generation of German Romantic writers of the 1770s and 1780s, who were introduced to an interested French public by the author Madame de Staël (1766–1817), who was living in exile in Switzerland after angering Napoleon.

Artists who worked in the Romantic tradition extolled both the beauty and mystery of nature. They also exhibited a great deal of interest in the supernatural, as for example in Goethe's *Faust*, which deals with a man who sells his soul to the devil in order to achieve worldly success.

Romantics explored folklore and traditional peasant life, because such people were idealized as living closer to nature. Romantics also found it necessary to break with the traditional styles of the past. In their jointly written *Lyrical Ballads*, the English poets **William Wordsworth** (1770–1850) and **Samuel Taylor Coleridge** (1772–1834) completely ignored the rules of punctuation, revealing their rejection of classical poetic forms.

Many of the artists who worked in the Romantic tradition became fascinated with the Middle Ages. Although their glorification of the medieval past, an age of theocratic kingship, would have seemingly pointed them into a more conservative direction, many of the Romantics were political liberals. **Sir Walter Scott** (1771–1832) and **Victor Hugo** (1802–1885) in many ways invented the popular image of the Middle Ages in novels such as *Ivanhoe* and *The Hunchback of Notre Dame*. Their influence can be felt when you look at almost any church in the United States from the second half of the nineteenth century; the odds are that it's built in the Gothic style.

Many in the Romantic movement not only rejected traditional literary and artistic styles, but also rejected the traditional political order. **Percy Bysshe Shelley** (1792–1827), an English Romantic poet, rebelled against the conservative values found in his country. In *Prometheus Unbound*, a lyrical drama, the mythical protagonist challenges the established order by stealing fire from the gods, and *Mask of Anarchy* was written as a political protest after the Peterloo massacre. George Gordon, **Lord Byron** (1788–1824), challenged the political status quo and ended up dying in Greece fighting in the rebellion against the Ottoman Turks. Amandine-Aurore Dupin (1804–1892), who wrote under the male-sounding pen name **George Sand**, challenged the endemic oppression that weighed down women. Sand was involved in a famous affair with Frederic Chopin, who initially said about her to his family, "Something about her repels me." In *Indiana*, we have the story of a woman who is desperate for love but finds herself abused by both her husband and a selfish lover. Sand broke with stereotypes not only with her pen name but by smoking cigars, dressing like a man, and engaging in affairs with married men.

Music

Besides its impact on literature and art, Romanticism influenced the world of nineteenth-century music. **Ludwig von Beethoven** (1770–1827) began to write compositions that broke with earlier classical forms by adjusting their length and doing unheard-of things such as putting a vocal soloist toward the end of the last movement of a composition. Beethoven was able to break with tradition because he was the first composer to earn his living directly with proceeds from compositions and performances, earning enough to not have to rely on either aristocratic or religious patrons.

Other innovative composers include **Franz Schubert** (1797–1828), who invented the *lied*, or art song, which involves a solo voice performing a melody to piano accompaniment. **Hector Berlioz** (1803–1869) wrote pieces in which for the first time there was an attempt to tell a story without the use of singers and a written text, such as when he set Goethe's *Faust* to music. Some composers made use of traditional oral tales or folksongs: **Frederic Chopin** (1810–1849) was influenced by the music of the peasants of his native Poland, and **Franz Liszt** (1811–1886) wrote music based on traditional gypsy music. **Giuseppi Verdi** (1813–1901) was the leading operatic composer of the Romantic movement, and in his Carmen, one finds the seduction of a young soldier by a passionate yet ruthless gypsy.

At the turn of the century, a self-styled avant-garde sought to break with convention, so that when Sergei Diaghilev presented his ballet *The Rite of Spring* in 1913, the odd costumes, peculiar dancing, and jarring music by **Igor Stravinsky** seemed to be an utter rejection of every element of classical ballet. The artists were often well ahead of their skeptical audiences, and the premiere performance of *The Rite of Spring* was famous for the mayhem that ensued among the proper bourgeois crowd.

Art

Romantic artists became fascinated with what they deemed to be "exotic," and leading painters traveled to North Africa and to the Middle East in search of subjects. Also, like their literary counterparts, many artists rejected the political order in their works. For example, **Eugène Delacroix's** (1798–1863), *Liberty Leading the People*, painted one year after the overthrow of Charles X, captures the stirring events of the revolution in the streets of Paris.

By the mid-century mark, **photography** was beginning to have a significant impact on painting while also serving as a new art form in its own right. One of the pioneers was **Louis Daguerre** (1789–1851), who in 1835, accidentally discovered that he could produce an image when he put an exposed plate in a chemical cupboard where mercury vapor was present. It still took him several years to find a way to fix the image, a process that received the name of **daguerreotype**. Photography would enter into the mainstream with the introduction of celluloid film, and in the 1880s, **George Eastman** introduced flexible film and the first box camera, which made photography into something far less expensive that could be enjoyed by many.

The development of photography made it increasingly clear to painters that there would be less demand for realistic landscapes and portraits. Some artists began to look to new subjects, such as those we refer to as the **Realists**, who sought to paint the world around them without any illusions. In part inspired by the revolutionary upheavals of 1848, **Gustave Courbet** (1819–1877) began to paint works like *The Stone-Breakers* that rejected the romantic traditions of the day and instead focused on showing the world of the peasants in all its grim reality. **Jean-Francois Millet** (1814–1875) is most famous for *The Sowers*, which shows hardscrabble peasants who seem, like the wheat, to be growing out of the Earth. Millet was himself from the peasant class and refused to paint them in an idealistic manner, nor did he seek to show that hard labor brought happiness. The artist **Honoré Daumier** (1808–1879) is best known for his cartoons that lifted the curtain on the corrupt politicians and legal system of the July Monarchy. In his later years, he turned to painting and sculpture, with one of his most famous works being *The Third Class Carriage*, focusing on a group of French peasants, their faces creased with the legacy of their difficult lives, sitting in the obviously uncomfortable setting of the railcar.

Realism in Literature

Realism was also an important movement in literature. Just as Realist painters wanted to show the world the actual conditions of those on the bottom of the social order, so too did novelists like **Charles Dickens** (1812–1870), who used his brief experience in a blacking factory as the basis for his critique of industrialized society. In *Hard Times*, the noble workingman Stephen Blackpool struggles against forces over which he has no control. He can't divorce his drunken wife and marry his beloved Rachael, because divorce is available only to the wealthy. Meanwhile, he's falsely accused of being a troublemaker at work and finds himself unable to make a living. Such works, although at times a shade maudlin, introduced many middle-class individuals in Great Britain to the hardships of working-class life.

Other Realist authors focused on what they perceived to be the barrenness of middle-class domestic life and most notably the institution of marriage. One such writer was Mary Ann Evans (1819–1880), who wrote under the name **George Eliot**. In *Middlemarch*, her most important work, Eliot deals with English provincial life on the eve of the Great Reform Bill. Her main character, Dorothea Brooke, despite her own beauty, marries an unattractive older cleric named Casaubon, in the failed hope that his scholarly ways will broaden her world. Although her second marriage, to Casaubon's young cousin, is a happy one, frustration still remains over her inability to realize her dream of improving the living conditions for their tenant farmers. Emma Bovary, the title character in **Gustave Flaubert's** (1821–1880) *Madame Bovary*, marries a mediocre village doctor only to find that reality is far different from the romantic notions of marriage she received from books. In search of excitement, she engages in a series of affairs, but the emptiness continues, and finally disappointment in love and financial failure lead her to commit suicide by taking arsenic. In **Leo Tolstoy's** (1828–1910) *Anna Karenina*, once again we have a beautiful but bored woman who engages in an affair that also meets with disastrous results.

Tolstoy's masterpiece, *War and Peace*, takes the grand events of Napoleon's 1812 invasion of Russia and reveals how ordinary people can get caught up in the swirl of events over which they have no control. Tolstoy's fellow Russian, **Fyodor Dostoyevsky** (1821–1881), was almost executed for his participation in an illegal political group, after which he was forced to spend ten years in Siberia. The experience transformed him, pushing in a conservative direction both his politics and his interest in the psychological and moral obligations of man, an interest that was revealed in his classic novels, *Crime and Punishment* and *The Brothers Karamazov*.

Back in France, **Émile Zola** (1840–1902) found himself applying the social sciences to the novel. Using this "naturalistic" technique, he wrote a series of novels dealing with a family over several generations, showing how environment and heredity were the critical factors in explaining their moral and physical degeneration. Zola also defended Alfred Dreyfus from charges of treason in his open letter entitled *"J'accuse,"* which appeared on the front page of the French daily, *L'Aurore*.

Post-Realist Art: The Impressionists and Expressionists

Although some painters, such as **Édouard Manet** (1832–1883), were inspired by the Realists, they wished to push their techniques in new directions. Manet's *Luncheon on the Grass* shows a rather peculiar picnic, with two fully clothed males and a nude female. The work was in part startling to contemporaries because nudes were acceptable only if they were figures from classical mythology and not the people who packed the peanut-butter sandwiches. But besides the perplexing subject matter, Manet was changing the way we look at art. Dating back to the Renaissance and the introduction of single-point perspective, paintings served to open the window into another world. Now, however, instead of looking through the painting, Manet has us stop at the surface of the canvas, something that was to be pivotal for the development of Modern art.

Although Manet was a quiet man who was not looking to be controversial, he and other innovative artists of the day were to find themselves at the center of a controversy when they were not allowed to show their work at the official 1863 *Salon*, an annual public exhibition held in Paris. In response to the public outcry over the hanging committee's refusal to show these paintings, Napoleon III decided that the public should be given an opportunity to see them and make their own judgments, which led to the establishment of the *Salon des Refusés,* or "exhibition of the rejected."

Those artists who took the techniques of Manet are labeled **Impressionists**, although the term was initially used as one of derision after a critic first used it in 1874 to blast a work by **Claude Monet** (1840–1926) entitled *Impression: Sunrise*. Instead of shying away from the label, painters embraced it, with the exception of Manet who refused to use it for his own work. Impressionists wanted to capture the shimmering effects of light, and to do this, they were the first to take their easels outdoors. They were aided in this desire to leave their studios by the invention of portable paint tubes. Monet would take the same theme, such as a haystack or the Cathedral of Rouen, and paint it at different times of day or different seasons to show how the impact of light would transform it. Although Monet is most famous for his landscapes, he didn't shy away from scenes of modern life such as railroad stations. Other impressionists, like **Auguste Renoir** (1841–1919), captured everyday scenes such as couples flirting in a dance hall, or in the case of **Edgar Degas** (1834–1917), numerous works showing the behind-the-scenes world of the ballet.

By the end of the 1880s, Impressionism, which had once seemed so revolutionary, had become widely accepted. Some artists, while acknowledging their debt to the Impressionists, wanted to push things even further. **Paul Cézanne** (1839–1906) challenged traditional perspective, composition, and the use of color. His work had a great influence on twentieth-century artists; he is therefore often referred to as the "father of modern art." Cezanne said that he wanted to make Impressionism into "something solid and durable, like the art of the museums." Taking the forms of geometry that he believed were most commonly found in nature—the cylinder, sphere, and cone—he took the somewhat abstract technique used in his landscapes and applied it to numerous still-lifes of fruit.

If Cézanne became the inspiration for artists who would completely challenge the traditional three-dimensional picture frame, artists like Pablo Picasso who said of Cézanne that he was his "one and only master," then **Vincent Van Gogh** (1853–1890) would influence those twentieth-century Expressionists who sought to put their deepest emotions on canvas. Van Gogh, a native of Holland, had a very brief, ten-year career ended by his tragic suicide. Although his dark early paintings, such as *The Potato Eaters*, reveal his deep sensitivity to those who were economically struggling, his style changed following a trip to Paris where he met a number of leading artists through his brother Theo's gallery. In Arles, in the south of France, he painted his most famous works, landscapes of sunflowers or cypress trees, using bright colors and broad brush strokes to provide them with a deep emotional intensity.

Painters such as **Edvard Munch** (*The Scream*) also sought to reveal the emotions rather than portray the way things looked on the surface. In Vienna, one of the centers of the avant-garde movement, artists such as **Gustave Klimt** saw themselves as rejecting the values of mass society and proceeded to find ways to shock their viewers through the vibrant use of color or by showing classical images in strange, unfamiliar ways.

The most revolutionary artist of the age was **Pablo Picasso**, who, with his nearly abstract *Les Demoiselles d'Avignon* (1907), made an irreparable break with the single-point perspective that had been central to Western art since the time of the Italian Renaissance. Later on, Picasso became famous as the co-founder (with Georges Braque) of cubism.

THE NEW IMPERIALISM: COLONIZATION OF AFRICA AND ASIA

In the 1880s, the nations of Europe began an expansion into Africa and Asia that was unprecedented both for its speed and its scale. This period of conquest and the establishment of colonies is referred to as the **"new imperialism."** The term is used in part to separate the period from earlier periods of overseas conquest, such as the Spanish conquest of Central and South America but also to denote the fundamental ways in which life was transformed in those regions that were now under the sway of Europeans.

The new imperialism was built on a foundation of **technological advances:**

- Breech-loading rifles, which allowed the user to fire from a prone position, offered a significant advantage over the nuzzle loaders still in use by those Africans who had guns. Even greater firepower was provided by the introduction of rapid-fire weapons such as the Gatling gun.

- Steamships allowed for rapid transport across oceans without having to deal with the vagaries of wind power, and smaller steam-driven river boats allowed Europeans to penetrate into the heart of Africa. The construction of the **Suez Canal**, which was finished in 1869, significantly reduced the time it took to go to Asia.

- One of the most important technological developments for imperialism was the telegraph, which allowed for the exchange of messages between India and London over the course of a day—a dramatic decrease over the two years it took at the start of the century.

- The discovery in 1820 of quinine, a drug made from the bark of the cinchona tree, was found to be an effective treatment for the great scourge of the tropics—malaria.

Although technology was vital for the new imperialism, it would have made little difference without the various motivating factors that stirred Europeans to conquer foreign lands. One important factor was the search for profits that were assumed to be had from imperialism. With the establishment of higher tariff barriers in Europe in the last quarter of the century, nations began to look to colonies as potential free trade zones. Raw materials, such as the palm oil that was used as an industrial lubricant, or precious metals such as gold and silver led individuals to the African heartland.

Yet those imperialists who saw colonies as a source of unimaginable wealth were going to be disappointed, because many colonies lacked any economic value, or if they did, the extensive investments necessary to make them economically viable never arrived from Europe. The exception to this was India, where the British were able to extract enough wealth for it to be justifiably referred to as the "jewel in the crown."

Other motivating factors came from **social imperialists**, who viewed imperialism as a means of relieving certain domestic social problems such as overpopulation. This would also prove to be disappointing, because, for example, in the case of Italy, those who left the country much preferred to go to the United States, rather than to an uncertain existence in the Italian colonies in East Africa.

Nationalism also played a major role in empire building. European states believed that the only way they could matter on a global scale would be through the establishment of colonies. For France, building an overseas empire was a way of showing she still mattered, even after her horrific defeat by the Prussians in 1870.

Religion also served as a motivating factor, and Christian missionaries were actually the first Europeans to penetrate central Africa. Some skeptics questioned the actual motivation behind the missionaries, as can be seen in a German political cartoon from the period, which showed an English preacher droning on while behind a curtain, a businessman involves himself in the real business of empire—financially squeezing the Africans.

Social Darwinism also influenced the new imperialism. There was a genuine belief that the white races were destined to have sovereignty over the inferior peoples of Asia and Africa. Paintings would often show colonists with local children, the implied message being that all Africans were children who would benefit from the guidance of Europeans in the role of parents. Elements of this *noblesse oblige* can be found in Rudyard Kipling's (1865–1936) famous poem *The White Man's Burden*, in which he writes that Europeans have a moral obligation to "bind your sons to exile, To serve your captives' need." The so-called moral imperative behind imperialism was also discussed at the **Berlin Conference** (1884–1885), ostensibly called to deal with the control of the Congo, where it was stated that one of the goals for the imperialist nations was "to care for the improvement of the conditions of their [the Africans] moral and material well-being and to help in suppressing slavery, and especially the slave trade."

Balance of Power politics was perhaps the most significant reason for the acquisition of even unprofitable pieces of land. Nations wanted colonies so that other nations would not get them. Great Britain in particular, led by the adventurer **Cecil Rhodes**, attempted to gain colonial advantage from the Cape of Good Hope to Cairo.

In what has become known as the **"mad scramble"** for colonies, little concern was shown for local tribal and cultural differences, with borders being drawn up in Europe. The Berlin Conference ended up setting up rules for the establishment of colonies. Organized by Bismarck, nations had to prove that they established sufficient authority in a territory to protect existing rights, such as freedom of trade and transit. This set off the mad dash that left every square inch of Africa divided among the European powers, with the exception of **Ethiopia**, which repelled an Italian invasion in 1896, and the small state of **Liberia** on the west coast of Africa, which remained independent as a result of its unique historical link to the United States.

British dominance over **India** began to take shape following the withdrawal of the French from the Indian subcontinent as a result of the Seven Years War (1756–1763). As the nineteenth century continued, additional, formerly independent Indian territories fell under British control, with the last being the Punjab region in 1849. Following what the British refer to as the **"Indian Mutiny"** or **"Sepoy Rebellion"** of 1857, colonial control became more centralized with the establishment of an administrative structure to replace the British East India Company. By 1877, Prime Minister Disraeli went so far as to make Queen Victoria the Empress of India, thus flattering an empty-headed queen while perhaps more importantly issuing a warning to the other European powers on the significance of India for Great Britain.

In **China,** Great Britain was the first European state to practice what is referred to as **"informal empire,"** where a state has significant influence over another nation's economy without actual territorial or political control. After fighting and losing a series of wars with assorted European powers in the second half of the century, China was forced to grant European states sovereign control over a series of **"treaty ports"** along the coast. In Southeast Asia, although Thailand was able to maintain its independence, the French seized control over **Indochina** with its vital rubber plantations.

Other nations involved in colonialism in Asia included the Dutch, who controlled Indonesia, and the United States, who seized the Philippines in the aftermath of the **Spanish-American War**. **Japan**, who had imitated Britain and Germany in her economic transformation into an industrial power, would also mimic their taste for colonial expansion by seizing control over **Korea** in 1910 after the **Russo-Japanese War**.

Violence was often a part of the colonial enterprise. The German explorer Carl Peters (1856–1914), whom Hitler admired, established a German colony in East Africa where he was referred to by the local population as the "man with blood on his hands." The most horrific example of colonial exploitation took place in the Belgian Congo. **King Leopold II** (r. 1876–1909), one of the pioneers in the scramble for Africa, personally established this massive colony many times the size of Belgium and expected the proceeds from this wealthy land to line his own pocket. Millions were enslaved, maimed, or killed in the crazed pursuit of profits. Eventually, there was an international outcry over these atrocities, including the publication of Mark Twain's sarcastic *King Leopold's Soliloquy*, forcing the king to concede control to the Belgian government, which corrected some of the worst abuses.

Colonialism could also provide certain benefits. Again, the example of India stands out because here, the British made actual investments in infrastructure. Irrigation systems, railways, and cities were all byproducts of British rule. Concepts such as nationalism and political liberty, which were later to be used by colonial people as a tool for their own liberation, were also European exports. It was those Africans or Asians who had the most contact with the West, often through study abroad in Europe, who were the most committed nationalists.

In recent years, historians have asked whether imperialism was ever actually popular among the mass of population, and the question has not been fully answered. Newspaper editors, who enjoyed an enlarged readership in this age of growing literacy, apparently saw imperialism as a topic of interest to their readers because they filled their pages with colonial exploits. In Britain, the pro-Imperial Primrose League had more than a million members, and in Germany, Italy, and France, similar organizations existed, although with far fewer members. The **Boer War** (1899–1902) possibly helped dim public support in Great Britain for empire, although across Europe, the working class seemed to have little interest in such affairs.

Although some hoped that the building of colonies would lead to a diminishing of tensions on the European continent, the opposite was the case. Rivalries among the European powers led to further imperial expansion, as in the case with British establishment of a protectorate over Egypt and the Suez Canal in 1882 in order to ensure Britain's dominance over India. Both the British and Russians were involved in what was referred to as the **"great game"**—a struggle over the generally worthless territory of Afghanistan—because for the Russians, British control over this region would put Russia's recent expansion into Central Asia in jeopardy, whereas the British were once again concerned for the security of India.

Also, Britain and France almost went to war over **Fashoda** in the Sudan in 1898, and France and Germany twice almost went to war over Morocco in 1905 and 1911. One of the problems that helped bring about the First World War was the sense among leading German political and military figures that their country did not have a colonial empire commensurate with its position in Europe. The problem dated back to Bismarck's lack of interest in colonies, which he once displayed by pointing to a map of Europe and stating, "This is my Africa" to show his true object of fascination. Bismarck's lack of interest was opposed by those Germans who joined the Society for German Colonization (1884). When **Kaiser Wilhelm II** pushed Bismarck into retirement in 1890, one of his reasons for removing the chancellor was his lack of interest in colonies, something by which the new Kaiser simply couldn't abide.

CHAPTER TIMELINE

Year	Event
1871	Establishment of the German Empire
1871	End of the French Second Empire
1871	Paris Commune
1871	Darwin's *The Descent of Man*
1874	Typewriters invented
1874	Claude Monet paints *Impression: Sunrise*
1875	Constitution establishes the French Third Republic
1876	Serbia becomes independent
1876	Alexander Graham Bell's telephone
1876	Thomas Edison's phonograph
1877	Queen Victoria becomes Empress of India
1877	Russo-Turkish War
1878	Congress of Berlin
1879	Dual Alliance between Germany and Austria-Hungary
1879	Thomas Edison invents the incandescent lamp
1881	Assassination of Alexander II
1882	Great Britain seizes control over the Egyptian government
1884	Berlin Conference
1885	Introduction of the internal combustion engine
1885	First meeting of the Indian National Congress
1885	Friedrich Nietzsche's *Thus Spake Zarathustra*

Year	Event
1887	Reinsurance Treaty between Germany and Russia
1890	Kaiser Wilhelm II forces Bismarck to retire as Chancellor
1890	Germany fails to renew Reinsurance Treaty
1891	Pope Leo XIII issues *Rerum Novarum*
1894	Beginning of the Dreyfus Affair
1894	Russo-Japanese War
1894	Russian-French alliance
1896	Italians defeated by the Ethiopians at the Battle of Adowa
1897	First Zionist Congress meets in Switzerland
1898	Edward Bernstein publishes *Evolutionary Socialism*
1898	Spanish-American War
1898	France and Britain almost go to war over incident at Fashoda
1899	Start of the Boer War
1900	Sigmund Freud's *The Interpretation of Dreams*
1901	Max Planck introduces quantum physics
1902	J. A. Hobson's *Imperialism: A Study*

Year	Event
1903	Henry Ford's Model T
1903	Emmeline Pankhurst forms the Women's Social and Political Union
1903	First successful airplane flight by the Wright brothers
1904	Herero War
1904	British-French entente (Entente Cordial)
1905	Revolution in Russia leads to granting of a Duma
1905	First Moroccan Crisis
1905	Separation of church and state in France
1906	H.M.S. *Dreadnaught* launched
1907	British–Russian entente
1908	Austria-Hungary annexes Bosnia
1910	Madame Curie isolates radium
1911	Agadir Crisis in Morocco (aka Second Moroccan Crisis)
1913	Sergei Diaghilev revolutionizes ballet with *The Rite of Spring*
1913	Socialists become largest political party in Germany

REVIEW QUESTIONS

Answers and explanations are in Chapter 15.

1. The development of national postal services in the nineteenth century reveals all of the following EXCEPT

   (A) an increased role for government
   (B) the growth of the rail network
   (C) an increase in privatization of previously public services
   (D) an expansion of public education
   (E) the existence of large overseas émigré communities

2. The nature of anti-Semitism changed in the late nineteenth century

   (A) in that it became primarily tied to the working class
   (B) through the idea that Jews were a separate race
   (C) in that socialist parties directed their energies toward fighting it
   (D) in that Jewish communities didn't respond to it
   (E) as shown by a general decline in anti-Semitic attacks

3. The term "informal empire" best describes the situation in

   (A) Rhodesia
   (B) the Congo
   (C) Indochina
   (D) India
   (E) China

4. All of the following were invented during the Second Industrial Revolution (1850–1914) EXCEPT

   (A) synthetic dyes
   (B) dynamite
   (C) the power loom
   (D) the Bessemer process of steel production
   (E) the safety elevator

5. The literary works of Charles Dickens, Émile Zola, and Gustave Flaubert are all considered to be part of which movement of literature?

   (A) Modernist
   (B) Gothic
   (C) Neo-Classicism
   (D) Romanticism
   (E) Realism

6. The Berlin Conference of 1885 was called to address the status of

   (A) India
   (B) the Congo
   (C) the Balkans
   (D) South Africa
   (E) Morocco

7. The Thomas Cook company

   (A) developed the idea of the "Grand Tour"
   (B) was the first firm to sell rail tickets
   (C) received a parliamentary charter in 1887
   (D) introduced package tours to Britain's middle class
   (E) was the first mass cruise company

13

Global Wars
(1914–1945)

THE FIRST WORLD WAR (1914–1918)

CAUSES OF THE WAR

Although the Versailles Treaty, which marked the end of the First World War, stated emphatically that the Germans and their allies were responsible for starting the war, the reality is a bit more complicated. The following are some of the major reasons why Europe exploded in 1914, setting the stage for a conflict that would shatter the very foundations of the continent.

Political and Social Tensions in Europe

The first decade of the twentieth century witnessed a number of political and social crises around Europe that may have led politicians to willingly pursue a foreign war with the hope that it would divert attention from domestic issues.

Great Britain and Ireland

Great Britain faced the contentious issue of Ireland, particularly after the famine years of the 1840s, which threatened to explode as Nationalist forces began to press for independence while their political opposites, the Unionists, expressed their increasingly determined desire to remain a part of Great Britain. Great Britain was also shaken, as was France, by a growing number of labor conflicts that resulted from the overall stagnation of wages during this period.

France

In France, the Third Republic was in crisis over the **Dreyfus Affair** that began in 1894 and involved a Jewish officer who was falsely accused of telling military secrets to the Germans. The incident revealed the virulence of French **anti-Semitism** while also showing the extent to which many in France despised the very idea of a republican form of government.

The "Affair" was also tied to another contentious issue splitting the French public—the question concerning the proper role of the Catholic Church in a democratic French state. Increasingly, by the end of the century, the individuals who governed France were openly hostile to the Catholic Church which they considered to be anti-republican. These politicians worked to exclude the church from French life by enacting laws such as one that eliminated the church from primary and secondary education.

Russia

Russia rang in the twentieth century with the **Russo-Japanese War** in 1904, which once again revealed the complete bankruptcy of the Tsarist state. This led to a revolution in the following year. Initially, the goal of the revolution was met—the creation of the **Duma,** or parliament— that would transform Russia into a constitutional monarchy. Tsar **Nicholas II** agreed to rule in conjunction with the Duma. Throughout the following years, the Tsarist regime recovered and once again functioned primarily as an unwieldy autocracy.

Germany and Austria-Hungary

The other imperial regimes, Germany and Austria-Hungary, also saw war as a possible means of escaping from a relatively bleak domestic political situation. In Germany, worker agitation was on the rise, and the kaiser and his inner circle dreaded the possibility of a Socialist revolution, although the threat did not really exist.

Austria-Hungary had to deal with its constant, seemingly insurmountable nationality problems. In the Hungarian part of the empire, the process of "Magyarization," the mandatory dominance of the Magyar language and culture, created great hostility among the other nationalities, who in fact made up the majority of the Hungarian population. As the Austro-Hungarian Empire lumbered from one crisis to the next, it appeared as though the union's demise was always just around the corner.

Entangling Alliances

In 1879, Bismarck created the **Dual Alliance**, a military treaty with the Austro-Hungarians. However, because Bismarck correctly foresaw that it would be suicidal for Germany to face a war on two fronts, he signed the **Reinsurance Treaty** with Russia in 1887 in order to make it clear that the treaty with Austria-Hungary was purely defensive in nature and not meant to show possible hostile intent toward Russia. Unfortunately, once Kaiser Wilhelm II (r. 1888-1918), an inordinately pigheaded man, pushed Bismarck out of office, the Russians began to view the Germans with increased trepidation, particularly since Wilhelm didn't bother to renew the Reinsurance Treaty in 1890.

While France had remained diplomatically isolated after 1870, Germany's diplomatic missteps led the Russians to join the French in a military treaty that pledged that the two countries would fight together in the event of an attack on either state by the Germans. German fears of being encircled were enhanced when in 1904 Great Britain signed an **Entente Cordiale** with France, resolving certain contentious colonial issues. German fears were further increased when three years later, Great Britain signed another entente with the Russians. This is why during the First World War, Britain, France, and Russia were referred to as the **"Entente" powers**.

Increased Militarization

One of the worst decisions that the kaiser and his officers made was to build a high seas fleet in 1897. Britain and Germany were not necessarily natural enemies, with the British readily accepting the fact that Germany possessed the most powerful army on the continent. Navies, however, were a completely different matter for the British, because they saw their fleet as their only means to protect their vast colonial empire. The British were particularly horrified given that the Germans took advantage of a revolution in battleship design and built powerful new ships known as Dreadnoughts, thus making the British fleet suddenly obsolete. The rivalry between Great Britain and Germany now became far more openly hostile, as each side scrambled to enhance its fleets. In the end, navies were not particularly significant in the outcome of the First World War; the Battle of Jutland in 1916 was the only major naval battle of the war. Across Europe, the production of vast stores of weapons by the Great Powers dramatically increased tensions and played a critical role in the advent of the war.

Crisis in the Balkans

The immediate crisis that led to the war was the assassination on June 28, 1914, in Sarajevo, the capital of Bosnia, of **Archduke Franz Ferdinand**, heir-presumptive to the Austrian and Hungarian thrones. Ferdinand was murdered by a Bosnian Serb who wanted to see Bosnia become part of an enlarged Serbian state.

The crisis in the Balkans had brought Europe to the brink of war in 1908, following the annexation of Bosnia and Herzegovina, previously Ottoman territories, by Austria-Hungary. The weakness of the Ottoman state allowed Bosnia and Herzegovina to be taken away from it. The Austro-Hungarians annexed these territories, not because they wanted more Serbs within their empire, but because they feared the lands would be taken by the Serbian state, a national state that the Austro-Hungarians saw as the greatest threat to their own survival as a multinational empire. Gavrilo Princip (1895–1914), the Archduke's assassin, had operated with the full cooperation of the **Black Hand**, a secret Serbian nationalist group with strong ties to Serbian officials in both the government and the army. Seeing that Serbian authorities were tied to the bloodshed, the Austrians issued an ultimatum that was clearly designed to provoke a Serbian refusal and achieve what the Austrians truly wanted—war with the Serbian state.

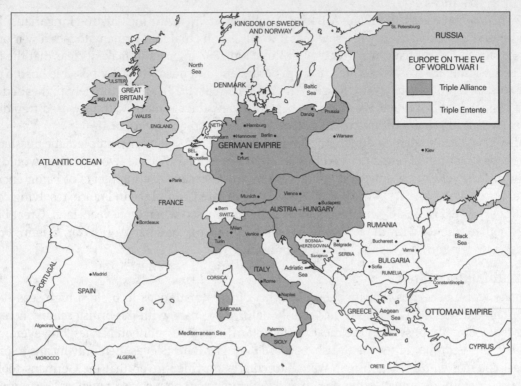

Europe on the Eve of World War I

THE COURSE OF THE WAR

On July 28, 1914, Austria-Hungary declared war against Serbia, knowing that it risked setting off a larger European conflict. Russia had guaranteed to protect the Serbs, but despite this pact, the Austrians felt that they had to take the risk or their multinational empire would collapse. Additionally, Austria had the backing of Germany, the "blank check," which bears significant responsibility for the start of the war because it was the one power that could have possibly restrained the Austrians from taking such an aggressive stance.

As a precautionary measure, Russia responded to the Austrian declaration on Serbia by beginning the process of mobilization. Germany demanded that Russia stop the process, which the Russians refused to do, in part because they knew that their own mobilization would take much longer than that of the Germans. They also feared that if the war spread beyond just the struggle between Austria-Hungary and Serbia, they could be caught unprepared. The Germans, seeing the continuation of Russian mobilization, decided that they had to declare war on the Russians, which they did on August 1. The whole net of entangling alliances began to fall into place as France started to mobilize on that same day, which led the Germans to respond with a declaration of war on the French.

When the shelling began in August 1914, there was tremendous enthusiasm among the citizens of the combatant nations. To their great discredit, the parties of the Second International, which for years had claimed that they would not support a capitalist European war and spoke glowingly of international brotherhood, voted in each of their respective nations to support the war effort. One of the few Socialists who spoke out against the war was the idealistic leader of the French Socialist Party, **Jean Jaurès** (1859–1914). He was shot on the eve of the war by a fanatical French nationalist who hated Jaurès's pacifist posture. French Socialist leaders attended his funeral and on the same day voted in the Chamber of Deputies to support the government in the war with Germany and Austria-Hungary.

Part of the enthusiasm for war stemmed from the misbegotten belief that the struggle would be a short one. This premise was based on observations made from such admittedly quick conflicts as the **Austro-Prussian War** (1866) and the **Franco-Prussian War** (1870), both of which lasted only a matter of weeks. Unfortunately, the decades following those conflicts had witnessed the rise of new weapons that favored soldiers on the defensive, such as machine guns, barbed wire, mines, and more powerful artillery shells, all of which created the eventual stalemate on the western front. Even the introduction of airplanes possibly made the war a more defensive affair because the planes were used for spotting the enemy's positions, making it harder to stage surprise offensives. Also, the economic expansion, industrial strength, and national wealth wrought by the Second Industrial Revolution allowed the participants to stay in the war much longer than before.

The Germans began the war by attempting to implement the **Schlieffen Plan**, which relied on a rapid advance through northern France, with the expectation that France would be knocked out of the war in six short weeks, allowing Germany's military might to be transported by rail to the east where it would be used to defeat the Russians. The German plan required the invasion of Belgium, a nation created in 1830 with the promise that its neutrality would be guaranteed by the major European powers. The German sweep through Belgium, which broke this guarantee, brought Great Britain into the war on the side of the French and Russians. The brutal German occupation of the small nation inflamed public opinion in the United States.

The German plan had succeeded in the early weeks of the war, although, with hindsight, the Belgians' spirited defense would prove very costly to the Germans, who were operating on a strict timetable. By the first week of September, German troops had threatened Paris, leading the French government to flee the capital. After the Germans crossed the Marne river, a French army under General Joffre (1852–1931) counterattacked and stopped the Germans at what became known as the **First Battle of the Marne**. For the remainder of the fall season, the various armies to the northern coast of Flanders made a mad scramble to see if either side could be outflanked. By the first winter of the war, both sides settled down to what now looked like a much longer contest. Both sides would hold positions that would remain virtually unchanged for the next three years.

Although everyone expected the war to be a glorious affair, trench warfare proved to be anything but glamorous. At first, the trenches were just rapidly dug ditches, but as the stalemate continued, huge networks of defensive fortifications were built. Life in the trenches was a series of horrors as the men had to deal with rats bloated from chewing on readily available corpses, noise from artillery, and extreme boredom as the war dragged way past the time that soldiers had expected to be heading home. The soldiers were fairly well protected in their trenches, but unfortunately, both sides insisted on periodically sending their soldiers "over the top" into no man's land to stage assaults on enemy trenches. These excursions often became little more than suicide missions, as soldiers got caught on the barbed wire or found that their artillery did little to break the fighting spirit of the opposing side.

Another horror was soon introduced into the war. In early 1915, **poison gas** began to be used by both sides. The petrochemical revolution of the Second Industrial Revolution had unleashed a new weapon on the battlefield, and while the introduction of gas masks cut down on the losses from these gases, it was another sign that modern warfare was an increasingly inhumane affair.

The war in the east was rather different than in the west. At first, the Russians met with success against the Austro-Hungarians, but as the fighting began to stalemate in the west, German forces shifted to the east, where they began to pile up victories against the brave but poorly equipped Russians. The eastern front never became bogged down with trenches like in the west, in part because the huge size of the theater of war made the much easier to maneuver.

Attempting to break the stalemate in the east, the British decided to launch an attack on Turkey, who had entered the war on the side of the central powers. **Winston Churchill** (1874–1965), who at the time was the First Lord of the Admiralty, organized the plan, which was such a disaster that it almost led to the complete obliteration of his political career. Churchill reasoned that knocking the Turks out of the war would allow the British to send supplies to the hard-pressed Russians through the Black Sea. In April 1915, five divisions landed on the beach of **Gallipoli**. Unfortunately for the soldiers, who were for the most part from Australia and New Zealand, the Turks were well dug in and the attack failed. By January, the British withdrew after suffering withering losses.

The British were not the only ones who sought the pivotal breakthrough that would end the stalemate. In 1916, the Germans decided to launch a massive offensive against the French fortress of **Verdun**, a fortress that France would have to defend at all costs or risk creating a disaster in French public opinion. The Germans organized a huge number of artillery pieces, including some "Big Bertha" guns that fired shells weighing more than a ton. While it appeared as though the Germans might take the fortress, the French were able to put up a spirited defense under **General Philippe Pétain** (1856–1951), who unfortunately survived the battle to later become the disgraced leader of the defeated Vichy French state following the German victory in 1940. While the Germans hoped to bleed France dry by attacking Verdun, in the end, both sides together lost 600,000 troops in one of the most costly battles of the war. The French and British, however, learned little from the failure of the German offensive. Each side was convinced that it held the secret to breaking the stalemate, and over the next year, both Entente powers launched wasteful and ineffective offensives, such as the **Battle of the Somme** and the **Battle of Passchendaele**, in an attempt to break the German lines.

THE END OF THE WAR

The year 1917 turned out to be the critical turning point in the war. The war in the eastern front came to a close as Russia became embroiled in revolution, and by December 1917, the leaders of the new Bolshevik state sued Germany for peace. For the Germans, this looked like it could be the turning point, enabling them to focus all their forces on breaking the impasse in the west. This German advantage was never to occur because of the entry of the United States into the war on April 6, 1917, a result of Germany's policy of unrestricted submarine warfare and the ill-considered **Zimmermann Telegram**. In 1915, the Germans declared that the waters around Great Britain were a war zone and warned that they would sink any ship—either British vessels or those from neutral lands—that tried to enter into British ports. Although this policy may appear to have been inhumane, at that time, the British were blockading German ports, but because of their powerful surface fleet, they did not have to rely on using submarines to indiscriminately sink ships. In May 1915, a German U-boat sank the *Lusitania,* a British passenger ship, stirring tremendous anger in the United States, from which 120 of the ship's passengers hailed. As a result of an American warning, the Germans agreed to end their attacks on neutral shipping, but as the war continued to drag on, the Germans decided in early 1917 to resume the practice.

Although it would take roughly a year for the Americans to make an impact in the war, their entry turned out to be a decisive factor. The Germans decided in 1918 that they had to move quickly if they hoped to achieve victory before the Americans could send in large numbers of fresh troops. Beginning in March, the Germans decided to gamble everything on victory. For four months, German troops met with the kind of success they had enjoyed in the first months of the war. Paris was once again evacuated, but Germany lacked the manpower and raw materials to exploit their initial victory, and by the summer, large numbers of Americans played a critical role in blocking any further German advance. By August, the German offensive was turning into a retreat, as Germany increasingly revealed how absolutely exhausted it was from the fighting.

After realizing that there was little it could do to block the Entente powers from marching all the way to Berlin, the German high command informed the kaiser that Germany had to sue for peace. A new German government, led by **Prince Max von Baden** (1867–1929), a man known for his moderate political views, contacted the American President, **Woodrow Wilson** (1856–1924), and asked for an armistice that would be based on Wilson's **Fourteen Points**—an idealistic document that sought to reduce future tensions between nations by maintaining free trade and an end to secret negotiations. Events in Germany, however, were spiraling out of control, and throughout November, soldiers and workers began to form soviets, or councils, and to demand that these loosely organized political debating societies be given authority to rule the state. Fearing that Germany would follow Russia's example and undergo a Bolshevik Revolution, the kaiser was convinced to abdicate, leading to the creation of a republic, which was empowered for the signing of the armistice that brought the war to a close on November 11, 1918.

THE WAR ON THE HOME FRONT

The First World War was the first armed struggle to witness the complete mobilization of society at large. This was total war—something that would be experienced again during the Second World War—in that no segment of the population within any of the participating nations could avoid its impact.

Once people realized that their initial expectation of a quick war was wrong, political leaders began to understand that they would have to mobilize all national resources. The war, therefore, was a major contributing factor to the increased role that government played in the twentieth century. All aspects of the economy became regulated to support the war effort, including price controls, the banning of strikes, rationing, and the planned use of national resources such as coal. In Great Britain, the government regulated pub hours, ensuring that they closed in the afternoon to prevent factory workers from staggering back to work drunk.

Governments also began to play a larger role in trying to manipulate public opinion. Censorship became a basic task for all governments. They read and censored the letters soldiers sent home to shield the public from the full extent of the horrors of trench warfare. The governments believed that if the people realized the true nature of the war, support for it would rapidly diminish. Governments also set up **propaganda** offices to create films and posters to help boost morale. One reason why so many Germans were later willing to believe Hitler's claims that Germany had not lost the war on the battlefield but had been "stabbed in the back" by Jews and other so-called enemies of the German people was that they had been told by their government, up until the day that Germany surrendered, that all was going well at the front and that victory was just around the corner.

War has a way of quickening long-term trends. In the United States, the Second World War helped pave the way for the Civil Rights movement, and the First World War helped bring about the greater emancipation of women. Prior to the war, Great Britain saw an expanding female suffrage movement. The Women's Social and Political Union, better known as the **Suffragettes**, under the leadership of **Emmeline Pankhurst** (1858–1928), organized a militant campaign to win the vote. The Suffragettes disturbed political meetings, destroyed stained-glass windows in historical churches, and set fires to draw attention to their cause. Once the war began, the Suffragettes supported the war effort and encouraged women to do their share for the nation. By the end of the war, more than 5 million British women were employed, many in dangerous jobs such as those in munitions factories. At the end of the war, British women were rewarded for their contribution to victory by being granted the **right to vote** in 1918. At the same time, in Germany, the Weimar Republic granted complete female suffrage as well.

THE VERSAILLES TREATY AND THE COSTS OF THE WAR

It is impossible to determine a precise count of the human costs of the war. Around 9 million men lost their lives in battle, and approximately 23 million more were wounded. Many men who came home from the front were permanently affected by gas and the other vices of modern war. Germany suffered about 6 million casualties (killed and wounded combined). France's losses were 5.5 million, proportionally much greater than Germany's losses, as France's pre-war population had been less than two-thirds that of Germany's. Very few French families escaped losing a loved one, and today, if you travel to France, you'll find a memorial in every town to those lost in the war. Incredibly, the loss of life from the war was soon dwarfed by an outbreak of **influenza**, which claimed an estimated 30 million lives worldwide.

Besides the loss of lives, the economic costs of the war were unprecedented. Hundreds of towns and villages in France and Belgium were destroyed, and even today, an occasional Belgian farmer is killed while plowing over an unexploded shell dating back to the trench wars in Flanders fields. Economically, both victors and vanquished were shattered. The nations of Europe, which had been the creditors to the rest of the world, were now heavily in debt to the United States, the only participant that still had a fully functioning economy. After the war, the Carnegie Endowment for International Peace attempted to discern the war's actual cost and estimated a figure of $338 billion. The wealth accumulated from the unprecedented economic growth of the Second Industrial Revolution dissipated in a matter of five years.

The terrible human and economic costs of the war must be considered when looking at the negotiations marking the end of the conflict. Five separate settlements were reached at the peace conference that took place in Paris, though the first and most famous of them was the **Treaty of Versailles**, signed on June 28, 1919, in the Hall of Mirrors, the same place that the German Empire had been declared back in 1871. This event witnessed several competing visions on how to reshape the postwar world:

- Wilson wanted to reshape the world on the basis of the principles outlined in his **Fourteen Points**, a peace that would allow for national self-determination and an international body, the **League of Nations**, that would work to settle disputes between nations. Yet it was easy for an American President to be conciliatory, particularly because none of the fighting had taken place on American soil, and the loss of American lives, though significant, paled beside that of France and Great Britain.

- The French Premier, **Georges Clemenceau** (1841–1929), represented a completely different outlook from Wilson's. No nation had suffered during the war more than France, and Clemenceau had to satisfy a French public that wanted to ensure that Germany would never again be a threat.

- The third major participant, the British Prime Minister **David Lloyd-George** (1863–1945), while not as intransigent as Clemenceau, also wanted to see Germany punished. England was, as usual, interested in naval superiority and colonies. In the end, the treaty represented the triumph of Clemenceau's position over Wilson's.

To justify the demand for German payment of reparations, the victorious allies included Article 231 in the final treaty, which forced Germany to accept all responsibility for the outbreak of the war on behalf of herself and her allies. Although Germany may have had an additional measure of blame, all the nations of Europe bore some guilt, so Article 231 was quite unfair. Germany also had to pay a huge reparation sum of 132 billion gold marks to the Entente powers. Other clauses of the treaty included the return of **Alsace-Lorraine** to France and the occupation of French troops in those parts of Germany on the western bank of the Rhine and a strip of land on the right bank. These territories, while still German, were to remain demilitarized. France would maintain economic control over the coal and iron mines of the Saar border region for 15 years. Additionally, Germany was to have an army of no more than 100,000 men, was banned from having an air force, and could maintain only a tiny navy to protect its coastal waters.

Other treaties signed in Paris in 1919 reordered the map of Europe. With the demise of the Austro-Hungarian Empire and the reduction in size of Germany, new nations began to emerge in central Europe.

- Czechoslovakia was born, combining the lands of the Czechs and Slovaks and also including a significant number of Germans.

- Hungary became fully independent, though it was somewhat reduced in size.

- An independent Romania was also created out of former Austro-Hungarian lands.

- Serbia was rewarded with additional territories for being on the victorious side; the resulting enlarged state, Yugoslavia, was what the Serbs had dreamed of and had been one of the root causes of the war.

- For the first time since the eighteenth century, there was an independent Poland.

- The Baltic states of Lithuania, Latvia, Estonia, and Finland were carved out of parts of the former Russian Empire.

- Although most of these states started as democracies, within a short time span, a host of problems, including economic and social issues, led all of them—with the exception of Czechoslovakia—to become dictatorships.

One place where nationalist sentiments were not satisfied was in the Middle East following the collapse of the Ottoman Empire. During the war, the British made numerous promises to both Arabs and Jews to gain their support for the war effort. With the advent of peace, the British ignored these hasty wartime promises, and Great Britain and France divided the area into colonial spheres of influence. Also, despite the contributions that colonial soldiers made to the war effort, the French and British made no move to reward their African colonies with independence.

THE RUSSIAN REVOLUTION

Though it is hard to imagine, some Russian soldiers were thrown into battle during the First World War without guns, having been told to pick up rifles from their fallen comrades. This is just one indication of how the First World War revealed the complete incompetence of the tsarist regime. Although it is hard to imagine any autocratic state functioning well during an unprecedented crisis like a world war, the problem was made more severe by the sheer stupidity of Russia's last tsar, **Nicholas II** (1868–1918), who decided during the second year of the conflict that he should emulate the warrior tsars of the past and assume personal command of the army.

In his absence, Nicholas left his wife **Empress Alexandra** in charge of the state. Alexandra turned out to be completely ignorant in matters of statecraft and was personally under the influence of a mystical Russian monk named **Gregory Rasputin** (1872–1916), who, she believed, had the power to control the bleeding of her son Alexis, a hemophiliac. Rasputin took advantage of Nicholas's absence to encourage the Empress to place his friends in important state offices despite their obvious incompetence. With the war going badly for the Russians, false rumors began to spread that Alexandra and Rasputin were lovers and that the German-born Empress was doing her best to make sure that Russia was defeated. (Similar rumors were spread about the British royal family, who also had German roots, leading them to change their family name from Saxe-Coburg to the more English sounding Windsor.) Rasputin met his end in 1916 when he was killed by a group of arch-monarchists, who feared he was destroying the prestige of the throne. The problems in Russia, however, extended well beyond what could be solved by removing the monk from his position of influence.

THE PROVISIONAL GOVERNMENT

Two revolutions occurred in Russia in 1917. The first was in March, when order collapsed in the capital city of Petrograd (formerly and currently St. Petersburg) as the population grappled with a severe shortage of food. Troops were called out to disperse the demonstrations, but instead of following their orders, the solders joined with the strikers. On March 14, the tsar abdicated. What became known as the Provisional Government took over authority. This government was made up of members of the **Duma**—the Russian parliament that arose out of the 1905 revolution—and was provisional because it was supposed to only exist long enough to establish a constituent body which would then write a constitution for the new Russian republic.

One sign of future trouble was that workers and soldiers continued to form soviets, as was the case in the revolution of 1905. These soviets consisted primarily of assorted Russian socialists, with the majority belonging to the **Menshevik** and **Socialist Revolutionary** wings, while only a minority belonged to the most extreme of the social groups, the **Bolsheviks**. Russian socialism had split into assorted factions back in 1903 when **Vladimir Lenin** (1870–1924) insisted that a small party of professional revolutionaries could seize power on behalf of the working class. His followers became known as the Bolsheviks. The group that insisted that Russia had to proceed through the proven historical stages before it could achieve an ideal socialist society, as Marx had mandated, became known as the **Mensheviks**. This led the Mensheviks, who dominated the Petrograd Soviet, to initially support the Provisional Government, since it fit their idea that a bourgeois revolution needed to precede a socialist revolution.

Tragically for the history of Russia, this short-lived republic faced problems of the greatest magnitude. One controversial decision was made when the provisional government decided to remain in the First World War rather than withdraw from the fighting. This decision stemmed partly from a sense of responsibility to the other Entente powers, but more important to this decision was the presence at that time of German troops on Russian soil. This presence led the Provisional Government to believe that a renewed war effort, led by a democratic regime, would inspire Russian support. The Provisional Government also made the decision to delay the redistribution of the great estates, which were supposed to be broken up to provide land for the peasantry. Seeing that their demands were not being met, the peasants acted on their own initiative and seized the great estates.

THE TRIUMPH OF THE BOLSHEVIKS

In April, Lenin returned from exile in Switzerland, aided by the Germans who transported him through their territory in a sealed railcar. The Germans did this because they thought that Lenin would undermine the Russian war effort, never expecting that he would be able to seize power. Over the ensuing months, the Bolsheviks continued to build up their strength, particularly among the workers and soldiers in Petrograd. By the fall of 1917, the Bolsheviks were the largest party in the soviets.

As the situation in the city became more desperate and unrest continued, Lenin made the decision to seize the moment, and on November 9, the Bolsheviks, led primarily by **Leon Trotsky** (1870–1940), took over key positions in the city, including power stations and communication centers. The revolution came off without much violence as the provisional government simply collapsed. Much violence would ensue, however, over the next three years, as the Bolsheviks had to cope with a bloody civil war to maintain their power.

Lenin and his party operated under the assumption that the revolution in Russia was only the first in a series of Communist revolutions that would begin in Germany and then move on to the remainder of western Europe. Therefore, the Bolsheviks were willing to accept a draconian peace with Germany, because they believed that Imperial Germany would shortly disappear and the territorial settlements would no longer matter. By the end of 1917, the Germans and the new Bolshevik state had signed the **Treaty of Brest-Litovsk**, thus removing Russia from the war. The treaty was exceedingly harsh and involved German confiscation of huge tracts of Russian land (perhaps more unfair than what the Germans were punished with in the Treaty of Versailles). The Treaty of Brest-Litovsk was never fully implemented because of Germany's defeat in the war and the Allies' refusal to allow Germany to gain territories in the east.

THE INTERWAR YEARS

THE GERMAN WEIMAR REPUBLIC

The story of the German Weimar Republic is nothing short of tragic, though its ultimate failure should not be surprising given its problematic birth at the end of a disastrous war. It has sometimes been argued that the death of Weimar came not in 1933 with the triumph of Hitler and his Nazi party, but rather in 1919, in the very early days of the republic, when its leaders were forced to sign the vastly unpopular Versailles Treaty.

Although forces from the extreme political right caused its final demise, in the first years of the republic, the far left was a much greater threat to its stability. The republic was created in November 1918 and was initially led by **Friedrich Ebert** (1871–1925), a moderate Socialist, who served as its first president. To put down a rebellion led by radical Marxists like **Karl Liebknecht** and **Rosa Luxemburg**, and to secure his republican regime, Ebert was forced to rely on the old imperial officer corps. Because the army was in no position to put down the rebellion alone, Ebert gave approval for the formation of **"Free Corps,"** voluntary paramilitary groups often with extreme right-wing leanings. In 1920, some of these Free Corps became involved in an attempt to overthrow the democratic state, but a general strike by workers put an end to what became known as the Kapp Putsch. However, by 1920, it was clear that although the threat from the left was eradicated, the far right was an even greater danger to the long-term viability of the Weimar state.

By 1924, the republic had achieved some degree of stability, despite the continuing effects of the Versailles Treaty penalties. In the postwar years, Germany suffered from terrible inflation as a result of the government's wild printing of money to pay its reparations debt. This insanely high inflation, which eventually led to an exchange rate of 11 trillion marks to the dollar, shattered the German middle class who saw its life savings disappear overnight. In 1923, the Chancellor of Germany was **Gustav Stresemann** (1878–1929), the leader of the German People's Party, a conservative party that supported the Weimar Republic. Although this hyperinflation may have done more than even the Great Depression to damage the long-term possibility of success for the republic, in the short term, Stresemann was able to get the economy back on its feet. He was even able to work out a new agreement on reparations, making them less damaging to the German economy.

By 1925, Germany was slowly rebuilding its relations with the other nations of Europe. Germany signed the **Lucarno Agreement** with France, by which Germany agreed to accept the current borders between France and Germany (and therefore French control over Alsace-Lorraine). They also resolved other issues, such as initiating the withdrawal of French troops from the Rhineland. In the following year, Stresemann capped off these efforts by entering Germany into the **League of Nations**. By 1929, the republic appeared as though it was taking root within Germany, though the outbreak of the Great Depression would reveal how shallow German support for republican government truly was.

THE SOVIET EXPERIMENT

Following the Bolshevik revolution of November 1917, Lenin and his tiny party ruled over a land that had been completely shattered. An indication of how little support they held within the nation can be seen by the elections for the constituent assembly that were finally held a few weeks after the Bolshevik revolution. Despite attempts to intimidate voters at the polls, the best the Bolsheviks could garner was one-quarter of the seats in the assembly. With such a showing, it was not surprising that armed Red Guards dispersed the assembly at the end of its first and only meeting.

Over the next several years, the **Communists** (the name adopted by the Bolshevik party in 1919), worked to solidify their control over the vast Russian state. For three years they had to fight a life-or-death struggle against the **"White" forces**, a loose term for the various anti-Communist factions, including dedicated monarchists and ardent republicans. The Whites received support from a British and American contingent, who nominally were sent to protect supplies the Allies had sent during the war but were really in Russia to keep an eye on events. The Civil War provided justification for Lenin and Trotsky to launch a **"Red Terror"** against their opponents, some of whom were right-wing extremists who were genuine enemies of the Bolshevik state; others were fellow Socialists, like the members of the Menshevik party, who feared the formation of a Communist dictatorship in Russia. By 1920, the Communists had defeated the various White armies and firmly established Bolshevik rule over Russia.

In the early days of the Soviet Union, there was still an expectation that the revolutionary tide would sweep across western Europe. To that end, in 1919, the Russian Communists founded the **Third (or Communist) International** to aid in the cause of revolution. The rise of this body, often referred to as the **Cominterm**, had a major impact on the various Socialist parties of western Europe, as some Marxists turned to the new Soviet state for guidance. The majority of Socialists, however, were horrified by the obviously repressive nature of Lenin's regime. This led to a split across Europe between those who formed Communist parties and those who maintained their ties to the original Socialist parties. In Germany, this split within the ranks of the left played a major role in the eventual rise of the Nazis; the German Communists saw the Social Democratic Party as more of a threat to their eventual success than the Nazis. By 1920, when it was becoming clear that the revolutionary tide across Europe was barely a trickle, the Cominterm shifted its focus more toward aiding the success of the one Marxist state, the Soviet Union, which filled all the leadership posts in the organization.

As the leaders of the Soviet Union increasingly turned their attention to internal questions within Russia, a debate ensued within the party concerning economics. During the Civil War, the party imposed "war communism," extremely tight control over all aspects of the economy. In 1921, anger over the harshness of this program led to a rebellion by the sailors of the Kronstadt Naval Base, once one of the primary strongholds of Bolshevik support. While the rebellion was crushed with stunning brutality, it did lead Lenin to replace war communism with the **New Economic Policy (NEP)**. This policy placed the "heights of industry" in government hands but also allowed a significant scope for private enterprise. Under this program, the economy made a quick recovery to pre-war levels.

The question remained, however, as to how to build a socialist state. This debate became closely intertwined with the issue of who would succeed Lenin as the leader of the party after he died in 1924. One possible candidate for the post was Trotsky, who enjoyed immense prestige as the builder of the Red Army that had won the Civil War. Trotsky thought that the NEP was too much of an ideological compromise, and he envisioned the return of an economic structure more akin to war communism. Trotsky, as the leader of the **"Left Opposition,"** also argued that it was necessary to focus on the spread of revolution to the industrialized nations of western Europe; he believed that communism could not survive unless it spread to other lands. His major opponent in this debate was **Nikolai Bukharin** (1888–1938), the **"Right Opposition"** leader who advocated continuing the NEP and building communism within the Soviet state.

Stalin

In the end, it was neither Trotsky nor Bukharin who took up the mantle of Lenin but **Joseph Stalin** (1879–1953) instead, a Georgian who had joined the party in 1902 but played a relatively minor role in the seizure of power in November 1917. Stalin was completely uninterested in ideological debates; he wanted to establish his own power within the Soviet system. To achieve this power, Stalin cunningly worked with Bukharin to maneuver Trotsky out of authority. In 1927, Trotsky and his ally Gregory Zinoviev (1883–1936) were expelled from the party. Stalin waited two years before he also ousted Bukharin. Eventually, beginning in 1936, Stalin launched a series of show trials in which his former opponents were tortured until they confessed to all sorts of crimes against the state.

While the complete story of Stalin's brutality will never be fully known, close to 10 million Russians were arrested in the late 1930s; several million were executed immediately or eventually died in the brutal detention camps that Stalin set up in Siberia. Stalin eventually decimated the ranks of the "Old Bolsheviks" who had joined the party prior to 1917; he destroyed the officer corps and anyone else he perceived as disloyal to the state. In 1940, an agent sent by Stalin assassinated Trotsky, who had earlier been sent into exile.

Once in a position of undisputed authority, Stalin adopted the policy of the Left Opposition and its program to rapidly turn Russia into an industrial nation. To achieve this goal, in 1928, Stalin implemented the first **Five-Year Plan**, a comprehensive, centrally controlled plan for industrial expansion. To pay for this unprecedented economic growth, Stalin followed Trotsky's plan to extract the necessary money by squeezing the peasantry through the forced **collectivization** of Russian agriculture. The state waged an open war on the *kulaks*—the wealthy peasants—and sent party cadres to the countryside with the order to kill any peasant who refused to join the collective farm. Millions of kulaks were shot or died from starvation, as they destroyed their crops and farm animals rather than turn them over to the hated Communist state. The human cost was staggering; perhaps 10 million people in the countryside died as Stalin moved the available crops to urban areas. The result, however, was that by the end of the 1930s, the Soviet Union emerged as a major industrial power while the Western nations were embroiled in a devastating economic depression.

THE GREAT DEPRESSION

Traditionally, we think of the Great Depression as beginning in October 1929 with the stock-market crash, which was soon followed by people hurling themselves out of windows (though there is little evidence such suicides took place). It should be understood, however, that the roots of the problem were deeper than just a crash of the financial markets, and the worldwide depression would not begin in earnest until the banking crisis in 1931.

Our image of the 1920s is that of the **"Jazz Age,"** a glittering time chronicled in the novels of **F. Scott Fitzgerald**. The reality was far less festive. The war had been incredibly devastating to the worldwide economy. In places such as Great Britain, the 1920s remained a time of economic stagnation. Much of the postwar economic recovery in Germany was dependent on the availability of American bank loans, monies that the Germans in turn used to lend at higher interest to the newly emerging nations of eastern Europe. This led to what looked like solid financial gains in both the United States and Germany from 1924 to 1929, but in many ways it was a false prosperity. The contraction of available credit brought on by the collapse of the American stock market caused the veneer of prosperity to rapidly fade.

In May 1931, the collapse of Vienna's most powerful bank, the Credit-Anstalt, created a domino effect. Banks throughout Germany and eastern Europe started to fail. The economic crisis deepened when the British government took its nation off the gold standard, ending the right to exchange pound notes for gold. This led to a contraction of available money, a problem made worse by the common belief that the way to deal with an economic depression was to further tighten the supply of money, which encouraged governments to cut their expenditures. **John Maynard Keynes** (1883–1946) was almost a singular voice of dissent. He argued that it was necessary for nations embroiled in depression to "prime the pump," that is, increase government expenditures in areas such as public works to get the economy moving again.

The depression worsened as governments took further misguided measures such as raising tariff barriers to protect domestic manufacturing. The United States was the first to take this step when it raised the tariff wall in 1930. All the other nations of Europe soon followed, including Great Britain, where free trade was a doctrine held with almost religious intensity.

The depths of the depression were truly staggering. By 1932, the economies of Europe were performing at only half the 1929 level. The depression hit hardest in the United States and in Germany, where eventually almost one-third of the available workforce was unemployed. In the United States—a stable democracy—those embroiled in the Depression elected **Franklin Roosevelt** as President and subscribed to his **New Deal**. In Germany—a shaky democracy at best—the crisis resulted in the death of republican institutions and the triumph of a political ideology that was anathema to the very spirit of democracy—**fascism**.

FASCISM

During the interwar years, as democracy appeared to be faltering, millions of people across Europe looked to fascism as a movement that offered the means to rebuild their shattered lives. Historians actively debate the definition of fascism; some claim that nothing really can be labeled as a fascist ideology. Fascist parties emerged across Europe and in other parts of the world, including the United States. They did not all possess the exact same set of beliefs; there are certain ideas, however, they all hold in common, which can be useful in defining the movement.

The word fascism comes from the Latin term *fasces*, a reference to a small bundle of sticks the Romans carried as symbols of authority and community. These bound sticks were symbolic of one central goal of fascism—to destroy the notion of the individual and instead push for a common community. In some ways, this sounds similar to what the Communists wanted to achieve—a unified society devoid of class differences. But the fascist concept was not tied to an international identity, as communism was, nor did fascism advocate the end of class distinctions. Instead, fascism pushed for another identity, one that was rooted in both extreme nationalism and often in some mystical racial heritage, such as that found in the Volkish ideology pursued by the German fascists.

Fascists were deeply antagonistic to the idea of parliamentary democracy, which they viewed as anarchical and effete. Instead, fascism favored the idea of a strong leader; the Italian fascists had *Il Duce*, the Germans, the *Führer*, men who, in an almost mystical manner, represented all the desires and dreams of the nation. This antagonism toward democracy is interesting, because in the two nations where fascism triumphed, Italy and Germany, fascist governments were created using the ballot box and not forced by an armed coup. While despising democracy, fascists also rejected all forms of socialism, a significant factor in why the movement rose to power. Many middle-class individuals were fully aware that the Soviet regime had collectivized all private property and saw fascism as the only barrier to the triumph of the hated communism. While many fascists, like Hitler, hardly bothered to contemplate a fascist economic program, Mussolini promised that an Italian fascist state would implement what he called **corporatism**— an association of employers and workers within each industry that would iron out all contentious issues regarding production and wages.

To a certain extent, fascism was antagonistic toward much of what is representative of the modern world. Fascists were against the political emancipation of women, they hated modern art, and they despised a religious faction that had become emancipated in modern times—Jews. **Anti-Semitism** was a key component in fascist movements throughout Europe, except in Italy, in part because Jews were seen as standing outside the arch-nationalistic identity that was so dear to the heart of all Fascists.

Fascism in Italy

The first state to have a fascist government was Italy, and because the empowerment of fascism occurred prior to the Great Depression of 1929, it was not this financial devastation that caused the movement. In Italy, fascism emerged partly out of a deep national dissatisfaction with its participation in the First World War. In 1915, Italy decided to enter the war on the side of the Entente powers, in part because it was interested in extending Italian control over those areas of Austria-Hungary that were home to a significant number of people who spoke Italian as their mother tongue. Italy's military participation was initially disastrous, leading to the almost total collapse of the Italian front in 1917, but Italy stayed in the war and played a role in the eventual triumph of the Entente powers. It was a costly victory, but many Italians thought it would be justified with the gains they would receive at the peace table. In the event, Italy got most of what it had been promised by the British and French, but with the collapse of the Austro-Hungarian state, many Italians believed that they should have been more generously rewarded for their participation.

Following the war, Italy underwent a marked political transformation. In 1919, the political system adopted proportional representation, whereby parties would be rewarded seats in the legislature on the basis of their percentages in the national vote. This new system favored the creation of mass parties such as Mussolini's fascist movement. Italian politics were also transformed by events in 1919 and 1920, years that witnessed a series of factory occupations by angry workers who seemed to portend the advent of a Bolshevik state. This led many landowners and businessmen to turn against democratic politics. They began to look for another political solution and thought they had found it in fascism, a political movement that was just emerging in Italy.

The founder and leader of the Italian Fascists was **Benito Mussolini** (1883–1945). His father was a Socialist, who named his son after the Mexican revolutionary Benito Juarez. Mussolini adopted his father's Socialist beliefs and became the editor of the party newspaper. Interestingly, for a man who would eventually become an extreme nationalist, during his years as a Socialist, Mussolini wrote, "The national flag is a rag that should be placed in a dunghill." His views began to shift during the war when Mussolini broke with his fellow Socialists and supported Italy's entrance into the war, a war in which Mussolini eventually served but without any particular distinction, like Hitler.

Returning to civilian life, Mussolini founded a new party, the **National Fascist Party**. The party quickly formed paramilitary squads (the Blackshirts) to fight leftist organizations, thus earning them the gratitude of factory owners and landowners who filled the party coffers with much-needed cash. By 1921, the party had begun to seat members in the Italian parliament and emerge as a significant presence in Italian political life.

Although his party still only had a few seats in the legislature, by October 1922, Mussolini demanded that **King Victor Emmanuel III** (r. 1900–1946) name him and several other Fascists to cabinet posts. To provide support for his demands, Mussolini organized his black-shirted thugs to march on Rome and possibly attempt to seize power. If the king had declared martial law and brought in the army, there is little doubt that the Fascists would have been easily scattered. The king, however, was a timid man who was not altogether unsympathetic to the fascist program, so he named Mussolini as Prime Minister. The fascist march on Rome turned into a celebration instead of a possible coup.

Fortunately for Mussolini, there was very little opposition to his consolidation of political power. He played at being a parliamentary leader for only several months after taking over in 1922. He then implemented a number of constitutional changes to ensure that the niceties of democracy no longer limited his actions. Mussolini's grip on power in the early years was only shaken in 1924 when he and the party were involved in the murder of a Socialist politician. Mussolini, however, was able to take this crisis and turn it to his advantage: He further consolidated his power by basically banning all non-fascist political activity.

Perhaps because of the nature of the land that he governed, Mussolini found it hard to recast Italy in his fascist image. Rather than achieving the revolution that many of his followers wanted, he made peace with more established institutions, such as the Catholic Church, when in 1929 he signed the **Lateran Pact** with the papacy; for the first time, the papacy officially recognized the Italian state. In the latter part of the decade, Mussolini tried to implement the corporatist economic program that was supposed to be a hallmark of the new Italy, but in practice it never lived up to the promise. Italy did rebound economically in the late 1920s, but then again, so did the rest of the world economy.

German Fascism

A more thorough fascist reordering of the state took place in Germany. While the Nazi regime in January 1933 marks the final stage in the collapse of the Weimar Republic, in many ways the failure of the republic dates back to the first years of the **Great Depression**. In March 1930, a government led by Hermann Müller (1876–1931), a Socialist, resigned over a crisis concerning unemployment insurance, which because of the Depression was beginning to be an unbearable burden for the German government. This was the last truly democratic government in Germany until the end of the Second World War.

The long-term health of the Weimar Republic was shaky in that the president was **Paul von Hindenburg** (1847–1934). If there had been a genuine reordering of German society following the collapse of the imperial regime and the rise of a republic, then a bombastic general like Hindenburg would have been cast aside with scorn. Unfortunately, Weimar never really escaped its recent past. The republic had as its leader a dedicated monarchist, who in 1925, prior to running for the office of president, contacted his former emperor in exile in Denmark to ask the emperor's approval to run for office.

President Hindenburg took the opportunity of the resignation of the Socialist Chancellor to install a more authoritarian government. Hindenburg selected **Heinrich Brüning** (1885–1970), the leader of a middle-of-the-road Catholic party. Brüning proposed an economic program that would have done little to solve the economic crisis and simply led to increased political opposition by the left and the right. Because Brüning could not achieve a parliamentary majority, he took the terrible step of involving Article 48, an emergency decree within the Weimar Constitution that enabled him to govern under presidential decree.

For the remainder of his long life, Brüning would try to defend his next decision, which was to call for new parliamentary elections in September 1930, just as the economic crisis worsened. Brüning thought the electorate would back him on his austerity measures, while what actually happened was that the two most extreme political parties, the Communists and the **Nazis**, emerged as the big winners. The election transformed the Nazis from a tiny party with only 12 seats in the Reichstag to a major force holding 102 seats.

With such a hostile Reichstag, Brüning continued to govern under Article 48. For the next two years he attempted to implement his austerity program, which only served to deepen the economic crisis. By the spring of 1932, Hindenburg removed Brüning and put in his place Franz von Papen (1879–1969), a wealthy anti-parliamentary conservative. In the elections held in November, the Nazis became the largest party in the Reichstag with 196 seats, and in January 1933, Hindenburg, despite a certain measure of personal disgust for Hitler, asked him to become chancellor.

It was a remarkable achievement for the Austrian-born **Adolf Hitler** (1889–1945). As a young man, he had gone to Vienna to study at its Academy of Fine Arts, but unfortunately for the history of Europe, Hitler proved to have little talent as an artist and was rejected. It was while living in Vienna that Hitler developed his virulent anti-Semitism, although the roots of his hatred toward Jews are hotly disputed. Because he had little sympathy for the multinational character of the Habsburg Empire when war began in 1914, he volunteered to serve in the German army where he survived a poison gas attack.

In 1919, he joined the **German Workers Party**, which was renamed the **National Socialist German Workers Party**, one of the small extremist groups that formed in the early days of the Weimar Republic. By 1923, he thought the party was strong enough to seize power, so he launched the **Beer Hall Putsch** in Munich, falsely believing that it would set the stage for a revolt throughout Germany. Following this failure he was put on trial but used this opportunity to stage a spirited defense before the court and to gain greater attention for himself and his movement. In prison, Hitler wrote *Mein Kampf* (*My Struggle*), outlining his extremist views, along with his desire, shared by Germans of assorted political persuasions, to overturn the Treaty of Versailles.

Following the Beer Hall failure in 1923, Hitler decided that in the future he had to use the existing political structure to achieve power rather than use extraordinary means like a coup. The **Nazis**, however, were not just a simple political party politely trying to convince the German electorate of the reasonableness of its views. Like Mussolini's Fascists, the Nazis enlisted a corps of armed thugs to support their political rallies and to disrupt opposing groups' meetings. This helped lead to an increase in political violence in Weimar, as all political parties had begun to sponsor armed factions; street fighting became endemic in the streets of Berlin and other German cities.

When Hitler was named Chancellor in 1933, he rapidly sought to consolidate his power. On February 27, 1933, the Reichstag building in Berlin was set on fire, although to this day it is not entirely clear who set it. The Nazis, who may have set the fire themselves, blamed the Communists for the incident. By claiming that there was a Communist plot against the state, Hitler encouraged the Reichstag to vote to grant him emergency powers, allowing him to eliminate virtually all human rights while granting the executive branch of the government almost total authority. In the last election held in Germany until the end of the Second World War, the Nazis, despite having control over the state, received only 44 percent of the vote. Hitler followed the vote with an **Enabling Act**, which gave the party emergency powers to govern the state and combined the authority of the chancellor and the president into one with a new non-republican sounding title—the Fuhrer. Finally, by the summer of 1933, Hitler banned all political parties except the Nazis and followed with an attack on the independent trade union movement.

Consolidation of power also meant that Hitler had to work out an arrangement with the one institution within the state that was still a threat—the army. The army was highly concerned about the growing size and power of the **S.A.**, the Nazi political army that had played such an important role in the party's rise to power. Once Hitler was in power, the S.A. was expendable. In June 1934, Hitler organized the **"Night of the Long Knives,"** in which he murdered his old ally Ernst Röhm (1887–1934), the leader of the S.A., who had wanted to make it the backbone of a new revolutionary army. Following the attack on the S.A., the members of the German army agreed to give their complete loyalty to the new German state and eventually would swear a personal oath to Hitler.

The Nazification of the German state soon proceeded apace. To create support for such a program, the Nazis put a great deal of effort into creating a Ministry of Propaganda under the leadership of **Joseph Goebbels** (1897–1945). German life had always been chock full of organizations like hiking groups and choral societies. The Nazis did their best to reorganize such groups along lines that the state could control, and huge organizations such as the **Hitler Youth** were established to indoctrinate the young. For those who refused to accept the new state of affairs, the Nazis organized a ruthlessly efficient police apparatus to silence political opposition and to intimidate anyone who even considered dissenting from the party line.

WESTERN DEMOCRACIES IN CRISIS

Woodrow Wilson had promised that the First World War was fought "to make the world safe for democracy," and for a time it looked as if his vision was accurate as democracies began to sprout throughout Europe in such places as the newly emerging nations of eastern Europe and in formerly monarchical states like Germany. Sadly, this democratic renaissance was to be short lived. By the 1930s, not only had democracy faltered in almost all the new states that had been born out of the Versailles Treaty (with the exception of Czechoslovakia), but it also appeared to be in crisis in western Europe, as France and Spain struggled with contentious political issues that threatened the very existence of parliamentary sovereignty.

Great Britain

Just as in the nineteenth century, Great Britain remained politically stable, though it certainly did not remain stagnant. One significant change was the emergence of the **Labour Party**, as it supplanted the liberals to become Britain's second-largest political party. The First World War had revealed fundamental problems within the **Liberal Party**, which was much more comfortable with the trappings of the Victorian world, as opposed to the age of total war. Labour had achieved prominence by more effectively voicing the concerns of the working man. British Prime Minister **David Lloyd-George** had encouraged British soldiers and civilians to fight hard for the war effort by promising to make their country after the war a "land fit for heroes." Unfortunately, unless heroes happen to like high unemployment, urban slums, and a growing number of labor disputes, all of which were endemic in the 1920s and 1930s, they may have been rather disappointed, yet accurate, in thinking this new Britain was much like the old.

France

France had won an incredible victory in the First World War and had achieved such long-term goals as the recapture of Alsace-Lorraine and what she thought was the permanent reduction of the threat posed by Germany. However, just as in Great Britain, the war merely diverted attention from, but did not solve, the tremendous economic and social tensions on the eve of the war. Economically, France did grow in the 1920s, but it could hardly offset the tremendous impact of the Great Depression. The economic crisis helped spur the radicalization of French politics, as groups from the far left and far right gathered support. In February 1934, following a right-wing riot that looked like it was going to shake the French Republic to its core, a number of parties on the center and left began to work together to form a **"Popular Front"** to block the possibility of a fascist victory in France as had occurred the previous year in Germany.

This "Popular Front" proved to be successful in May 1936, when a coalition of Communists, Socialists, and Radicals (the name belies the fact that this was a center-left party) won a majority in the Chamber of Deputies. They selected the leader of the Socialist Party, **Léon Blum** (1872–1950), to be Prime Minister. The new government worked to solve some of the labor issues that had plagued France for decades. In June, they put through the **Matignon Agreement**, allowing workers to collectively bargain with employers, reducing the work week to 40 hours, and granting the right to fully paid vacations. Attention to social problems, however, had to be delayed, as France had to now grapple with an issue that challenged the very existence of the Popular Front, the **Spanish Civil War**.

The Spanish Civil War

Spain had become a parliamentary democracy only in 1931, following the fall of the Spanish monarchy in that year. The first elections in the Spanish republic brought about a victory for a coalition of liberals and socialists. Unfortunately, the problems facing Spain were extremely severe, and the new government had trouble finding solutions. Many landless farm laborers waited in vain as the government failed to implement a promised land reform that would break up the vast estates of the rich. Increasingly, the failings of the government created more radical sentiments among the workers, which was matched by equally aggressive action from the parties of the far right.

In February 1936, a Popular Front coalition of the leftist parties—created to avert what they felt was a threat from Spanish Fascists—won a narrow electoral victory. This government attempted to achieve what the earlier socialist government could not, including significant reforms such as land redistribution. They still did not operate quickly enough to satisfy the disaffected masses who seized land and factories. This failure to maintain order was used by the far right to stage a coup to overturn the government.

In the summer of 1936, a group of army officers under the leadership of **General Francisco Franco** (1892–1975) took control of large parts of Spain. Their belief that the republic would simply collapse proved to be false, as republican loyalists bravely organized to defend the state against the nationalist insurgents. Spain was swept into an incredibly brutal civil war, which soon brought about the participation of German and Italian support for the nationalists, although Franco was not a Fascist but rather a more traditional conservative.

The fascist states of Germany and Italy were interested in testing out their new armaments, thus leading to one of the most brutal events in the war. On market day, in the city of **Guernica**, German and Italian planes bombed and strafed the civilian population. Guernica was not a military target in the least; it was targeted simply to instill fear among republican supporters. As a reflection of his horror over the attack, the Spanish artist **Pablo Picasso** painted his masterpiece, *Guernica*, which he willed to Spain. The painting was only to be handed over to the government when the nation was once again a republic, something that happily occurred in the years following Franco's death in 1975.

Although the Fascists willingly offered their support to those on the Spanish right, France and Great Britain refused to come to the aid of their fellow democracy. Instead of assistance, they promoted a nonintervention policy, which meant that the Spanish Loyalists had to make a Mephistophelean pact with the Soviet Union, whereby the Soviets would provide desperately needed arms in exchange for Spanish gold. Because of Soviet support, the Communists, who were initially a small faction on the Spanish left, began to play the preeminent role on the republican side. Tragically, the Communists, having received their marching orders from Stalin, put as much effort into destroying their allies on the left as they did to defeating the nationalists. George Orwell wrote a fascinating firsthand account of these events in his story *Homage to Catalonia*, which details how the Communists destroyed the anarchist movement in Catalonia in June 1937. After reading Orwell, you will not be surprised to learn that by 1939, the nationalists had captured Madrid and triumphed over the republic.

THE ROAD TO THE SECOND WORLD WAR

From the very beginning of his political career, Hitler had made clear his desire to overturn the Versailles Treaty. Once in power, he set about to keep that promise. In 1935, he openly began the rearmament of Germany, something that was prohibited by Versailles. Seeing that France and Britain did not respond to such an act of provocation, in the following year, the Germans remilitarized the Rhineland. While the French contemplated an aggressive response to this act, they knew that since they lacked British support, they would have to act unilaterally, and so they did nothing. Rather than satisfying Hitler, these steps convinced him of the weakness of the democracies, so he continued with his plans.

Germany Invades Austria

The very first sentence of *Mein Kampf* states Hitler's desire to absorb Austria into the larger **German Reich**. In March 1938, this became a reality as German troops moved into Vienna. Despite postwar claims by the Austrians that they were the first victims of Nazi aggression, the *Anschluss* was welcomed by a majority of Austrians who celebrated by wildly greeting Hitler on his arrival in the city and by attacking their Jewish neighbors.

Germany Invades Czechoslovakia

Hitler next set his sights on Czechoslovakia. Czechoslovakia was the singular success story of eastern Europe; it was a thriving democracy, had a strong industrial base, and a relatively strong army. It was burdened with nationality problems, most particularly the animosity toward the state from the 3.5 million Sudenten Germans who lived in the western part of the nation. France had assured the Czechoslovak state that in the event of German aggression it would come to its aid. Unfortunately, these assurances, which also included guarantees for its security from the Soviet Union, ultimately came to nothing.

Great Britain Tries to Appease Germany

The British eventually settled on a policy known as **Appeasement**. In 1937, **Neville Chamberlain** (1869–1940) became British Prime Minister and head of a conservative government. Chamberlain recognized that events in 1936 had been detrimental to British interests. These events included the German occupation of the Rhineland, the creation of the **Rome-Berlin Axis**, and even the Olympic games that had been held that year in Berlin, which were a propaganda victory for Germany. Chamberlain was not a fool, and he certainly had little sympathy for the brutality of the Nazi state, but he believed that it was impossible for Great Britain to fully rearm against the combined strength of Germany and Italy. As a result, he wanted to work out some sort of understanding with either Mussolini or Hitler.

Appeasement began with British recognition of Italy's annexation of Ethiopia. The British did nothing when Hitler annexed Austria. However, the policy of appeasement would stand a real test over the question of Czechoslovakia, which Germany threatened to invade unless the **Sudentenland**, the western part of the Czechoslovak state that was largely inhabited by ethnic Germans, was turned over to the Reich. In a radio address during this crisis, Chamberlain said it was "fantastic and incredible to be involved in a war because of a quarrel in a faraway country between people of whom we know nothing." In September, with Europe on the verge of war, Chamberlain flew to Munich to attend a four-power summit with France, Italy, and Germany to discuss the future of Czechoslovakia, who was not even invited to attend. At this summit, the powers signed the **Munich Agreement**, which led to the transfer of all Sudenten territories to Germany. In return, Hitler promised to respect the sovereignty of what remained of Czechoslovakia. Chamberlain returned home to London and was met by a huge crowd that roared with joy as Chamberlain announced that there would be "peace in our time." Rather than peace, his actions led to destruction in Czechoslovakia one year later when the Germans ignored the Munich agreement and seized most of what remained of the nation.

Before we are too quick to criticize the appeasers, we need to remember several things.

- First, politicians such as Chamberlain saw it as almost a sacred responsibility to remove the specter of war from Europe. The scars from the First World War were still burnished by all who had lived through it.

- Also, from the British point of view, the Versailles Treaty was unjust, and part of what Hitler wanted appeared to be self-determination for nationalities, an idea that the respected President Wilson had promoted in his Fourteen Points.

- Finally, with hindsight, it is clear that Hitler never intended to maintain any of his promises. It may be unfair to have expected that the appeasers would have been able to foresee Hitler's intentions. In 1938, few individuals in Great Britain other than Winston Churchill fully understood that Hitler had to be stopped at all costs.

Germany and the Soviet Union Invade Poland

Following the dismemberment of Czechoslovakia, Hitler's attention was now drawn to the next contentious area—Poland. The Polish nation born out of Versailles included land that had once been part of the German Empire. To allow Poles access to the sea, the new nation was given a strip of territory that split East Prussia from the rest of Germany. Now that he realized Hitler's intentions following the complete occupation of Czechoslovakia, Chamberlain was determined to stop further German aggression. He worked out an arrangement with France whereby the two nations would respond in the event that Poland's borders were threatened.

At the same time, the Soviet Union was inquiring as to whether the British and French would consider forming a military alliance directed against the Germans. The British and French rebuffed the Soviets in part because, after Stalin's purge of the officer corps, they questioned the effectiveness of the Soviet military, and they found little evidence that Stalin was any more a man of his word than Hitler. Once Stalin realized that he was getting nowhere with the British and French, he announced on August 22, 1939—to the shock of the rest of the world—that Germany and the Soviet Union had signed a **nonaggression pact**. The way was now open for Germany to invade Poland, while the Soviets were able to seize eastern Poland, Finland, and the Baltic states, all lands that Russia had lost in the First World War.

THE SECOND WORLD WAR (1939–1945)

The war began on September 1, 1939, with an attack on Poland. The Poles fought bravely; however, the Germans had learned critical lessons from the First World War and practiced *blitzkrieg* warfare, swift attacks using tanks and other highly mobile units, supported by warplanes. Within a month, the Polish army was routed and the British and French forces to the west maintained their defensive positions.

Over the winter of 1939–1940 little warfare occurred, earning the time period the nickname the **"Phony War."** This lull came to a shattering end in April 1940 when the Germans attacked Norway and Denmark to secure necessary iron ore supplies for Germany. In May, the Germans followed up these successes with an invasion of Belgium and the Netherlands before launching their ultimate goal, an attack on France. In six short weeks, the French army, considered after the First World War to be the finest in the world, was destroyed.

THE FALL OF FRANCE

Part of the problem for the French was that in 1940, their hearts were just not in the war. The *Blitzkrieg* attacks in the east and the quick defeat of the Scandinavian countries bred tremendous pessimism among the French political and military leadership. The French were still following a military strategy that was tied to the way the First World War had been fought. During the interwar period, they built the **Maginot Line**, a series of seemingly impregnable defenses to protect their soldiers during what they automatically assumed would be another war of stagnant positions. The Germans simply bypassed the fortifications, which were not extended to the Belgian frontier, and encircled the French armies. The British, seeing that France was about to fall, staged a heroic retreat from the Belgian beaches at **Dunkirk**, in which every available British ship, no matter the size, was used to take the British army back to Great Britain so that she might fight another day.

Following the military debacle, a new government was formed in France under the elderly **Marshal Pétain**, the hero of the Battle of Verdun. Pétain had been a bit of a defeatist in the First World War, and those pessimistic tendencies rose to the forefront once again as he decided to pull France out of the war and use the opportunity to create a more authoritarian French government. Pétain's **Vichy** regime brought to an end the Third Republic that was blamed for France's defeat.

Although almost the entire officer corps had been defeatists, one charismatic general, **Charles de Gaulle** (1890–1970), arrived in London and from there issued a call for French forces in the colonies to form a new French army to retrieve the national honor. Vichy authorities immediately labeled de Gaulle a traitor and began to happily assist the Germans. Nevertheless, a free French force did flourish under de Gaulle's leadership. On French soil, the *Maquis*, or French resistance, found itself fighting against both the Germans and against the Vichy state.

GERMANY AGAINST GREAT BRITAIN

Hitler always believed that the British shared similar traits with the German Aryans. Because of such foolish racial theories, he thought that the British would see the folly of their ways after the fall of France and make peace with Germany. Great Britain, however, was gearing up for what would be its most dangerous moment in its history. Fortunately for the survival of the nation, it had an extraordinary leader in **Winston Churchill**, who had replaced Chamberlain as prime minister. Churchill committed the nation, which he inspired through a series of stirring speeches, to continue the war no matter what may come. In the House of Commons, Churchill declared, "I have nothing to offer but blood, toil, tears, and sweat" and that the only goal for Britain was to "wage war against a monstrous tyranny, never surpassed in the dark, lamentable catalogue of human crime." In response to Britain's refusal to sue for peace, Hitler decided to attack.

The **Battle of Britain** was not the one-sided struggle that is often portrayed. It is true that the *Luftwaffe*, the German air force, had many more planes and trained pilots. But the British had radar, which had been developed at Cambridge University and could detect oncoming German attacks. The British Spitfires and Hurricanes were better planes than the German Messerschmits. Unbeknownst to the Germans, the British had also cracked the German secret military code. Furthermore, there was no comparison in terms of military leadership. Hitler was convinced that he was a military genius following the rapid fall of Poland and France, although fortunately for the eventual triumph of the Allies, that was clearly not the case. The German air force was led by the incompetent drug addict **Hermann Göring** (1893–1946), who, after a token group of British planes dropped bombs on Berlin, decided to end the effective raids that had been staged on British air bases and directed the *Luftwaffe* to attack British cities. This strategy created tremendous suffering in the cities (the Blitz), and it also allowed the **Royal Air Force (R.A.F.)** time to recover. By the end of September 1940, Hitler decided to drop the plan to invade Britain and move on to his ultimate dream, the defeat of the Soviet Union.

THE HOLOCAUST

The Holocaust, the slaughter of 6 million Jews, did not begin suddenly, nor is it clear at what point the Nazis made the decision to destroy European Jewry. Anti-Semitism had always been at the heart of Nazi ideology. Soon after taking power, the Nazis implemented the **Nuremberg Laws**, depriving Jews of citizenship and forcing them to wear a yellow Star of David on their clothing whenever they left their homes. Marriage and sex between Jews and gentiles were also forbidden. While some Jews left Germany immediately after these restrictions were implemented, many refused to leave, thinking that things could not get any worse. Nevertheless, the following years would witness only a slow, steady decline for German Jews as they were forced out of all professions and had their stores boycotted and property confiscated. On November 9, 1938, the Nazis launched *Kristallnacht*, the "night of broken glass," so called because of the resonating sound of shattered glass from Jewish stores and homes that rung out throughout that night. The events of that night proved that the Germans were interested in eliminating the Jews, as several hundred people were killed and 30,000 Jews were shipped to concentration camps.

One sign that demonstrates the Nazi obsession with the so-called **"Jewish Question"** is that when the Russians were putting up stiff resistance and Germany had not been able to defeat them, the Nazis still chose to direct resources that could have been used in the war effort to exterminate European Jewry instead. The conquest of Poland had placed the largest concentration of Jews in the world directly under German control. To deal with them, as well as with the large numbers of Jews from the other conquered territories, Hitler had his top lieutenants organize the **"Final Solution."** By the end of 1941, 1 million Jews were slaughtered, most in mobile vans poisoned by carbon monoxide gas or machine-gunned by specially designated S.S. troops. This was not efficient enough for the Germans, however, and so in January 1942, the top leadership met in **Wannsee**, a suburb of Berlin, to plan a more efficient slaughter.

The Nazis organized a camp system throughout Poland, including concentration camps, where Jews from around occupied Europe were gathered, and extermination camps, the most notorious of these being **Auschwitz**. Upon arrival in the camps, the prisoners would be subject to a sorting process, where S.S. doctors, including the notorious **Doctor Mengele**, selected who would be sent to work camps and who would be sent immediately to die in the gas chambers. Besides Jews, the camps also contained Gypsies, homosexuals, Jehovah's Witnesses, Russian prisoners of war, Communists, and others considered by the Nazis to be "undesirables." Approximately 7 million such individuals were slaughtered, in addition to 6 million Jews.

There has always been a debate over what the Allies knew about the Holocaust and what they could have done to stop the German death machine. Although the S.S. took every precaution to hide the Final Solution, which was partly why the Nazis chose Poland as the site of the camps, word of the terror reached the west right from the beginning. Such reports were initially doubted: Who could believe such monstrosities were taking place? The sheer bulk of reports, many from eyewitnesses to the slaughter, however, made it clear that an unprecedented event in human history was taking place. The debate on what could have been done will never be resolved. Many believe that attacks on the German rail network used to bring Jews to the camps could have possibly been of help, although Allied military leaders always claimed that the planes that could have been used for such raids were needed for more immediate military targets.

One reason why two-thirds of European Jews were so effectively rounded up for slaughter was that the Nazis never lacked help among the conquered peoples of Europe to assist in this task. Yad Vashem, the Holocaust museum and memorial in Israel, has a special row of trees in honor of those gentiles who risked their lives to help rescue Jews; however, a forest would be needed to represent the sheer number of people who aided the Germans in implementing the Holocaust. In France, Vichy officials rounded up Jews and turned them over to the Nazis before the Germans even asked for their help. In the Ukraine, Croatia, and in other parts of eastern Europe, the local population set off on their own initiative to exterminate their Jewish neighbors. Anti-Semitic feelings obviously ran deep throughout European society in the early twentieth century.

THE TURNING OF THE TIDE

The Second World War had three critical turning points. The Battle of Britain was certainly one, as was the eventual entry of the United States into the war. The third turning point may be the most important of all—Operation Barbarossa, the German attack on the Soviet Union on June 22, 1941.

Germany Invades the Soviet Union

Initially, the attack went according to plan, as German forces drove deep into Russian territory, catching the Soviet forces completely unprepared, even though Stalin had been warned by numerous sources, including his own intelligence agency, that such an attack was imminent. By the end of

1942, the Germans had reached the outskirts of Stalingrad and Leningrad, but both cities were held owing to the Russian forces' dogged defense and the extraordinary sacrifices of the citizens of the Soviet Union. Because of their common enemy—Germany—Great Britain, the United States, and the Soviet Union were to form a rather unlikely alliance that would not only destroy the Third Reich but also shape the postwar world.

The War in North Africa

By 1941, the war had become a global conflict. The Italians under Mussolini had entered the war as allies of Germany just as France was about to collapse. The Italians also extended the war to North Africa, as they attempted to push the British out of Egypt. The Italians were hard-pressed to achieve this goal, forcing the Germans to come to their aid. The Germans had one of their best officers, **Erwin Rommel** (1891–1944), the "Desert Fox," positioned in this theater of the war. For a while he met with remarkable success, eventually proceeding within 60 miles of the Egyptian city of Alexandria. However, at the **Battle of El Alamein** in November 1942, a British army under the leadership of General Montgomery (1887–1976) pushed the German and Italian forces back to Tunisia.

U.S. Involvement

Following the Japanese attack on Pearl Harbor and Hitler's declaration of war on the United States in 1941, the United States was involved in the conflict with the Axis powers (Germany, Italy, and Japan). The entry of the United States into the war sparked a new energy to the war in the west, as the United States landed troops in Africa and joined with the British in pushing back the Germans and Italians. By 1943, the **Allies** had pushed the last of the **Axis forces** out of Africa and sent troops to Italy, the "soft underbelly" of the Axis. By 1943, Italy was knocked out of the war, although in many ways, the Italian campaign did not have a huge impact on the eventual course of the war.

Following a meeting between Stalin, Churchill, and Roosevelt in Teheran in November 1943, the decision was made that the British and Americans should stage an invasion of western Europe from Great Britain. On June 6, 1944, the Allies launched the **D-Day** invasion. While another year of brutal fighting was yet to be experienced, the landing of the Allied forces in Europe and the Russian counterattack following the lifting of the siege of Leningrad marked the beginning of the end for Nazi Germany.

On May 8, 1945, a week after the suicide of Hitler, Germany surrendered unconditionally. Japan had entered the Second World War with the goal of creating a vast empire in the Pacific where it would be able to exploit the natural resources of the conquered lands and use these territories as a market for Japanese manufactured goods. Such dreams of hegemony over the Pacific ended violently with the dropping of the first **atomic bomb** on the city of **Hiroshima** on August 6, 1945, which was followed two days later by a second atomic bomb, this time on the city of **Nagasaki**. On August 14, the Japanese surrendered (signing the formal surrender document on September 2), thus bringing to an end the bloodiest conflict in human history.

THE AFTERMATH

The Second World War was even more staggering in its destructiveness than the First World War. Civilian casualties—rather than military deaths—made up the majority of the **50 to 60 million** people who lost their lives during the conflict. For the Soviet Union alone, although the precise numbers remain the subject of debate and will ultimately never be fully known, losses were upwards of 25 million. Cities across the continent were leveled as brutal attacks on civilian targets, initiated when the Germans bombed Warsaw in 1939 and then followed up in places such as Rotterdam and London, were eventually thrown back on the Germans, with 50,000 killed in the **fire bombing of Dresden** and with almost every German target of any military, economic, or administrative value laying in ruin. In Berlin and in other German cities, one found the *Truemmerfrauen*, or "rubble ladies," who in the absence of men and machinery began the slow process of removing the wreckage by hand.

In 1945, it seemed as if all of Europe was on the move. The roads were clogged with displaced persons, including Jews who had survived the death camps and couldn't go back to their homes but also seemingly had no place to go. In many cases, Jews would live for the next several years under difficult conditions in camps the British set up in places such as Cyprus, unable to follow their dream and go to Palestine.

Russian POWs returned to the Soviet Union and immediately faced rearrest under the orders of Stalin, who thought their failure to die in battle may be an indication they were spies or had seen too much of life in the West to be satisfied with conditions in the Soviet Union. This was in spite of the fact that Soviet POWs had been treated with incredible brutality by the Germans, who saw them as subhuman.

Millions of Germans also poured west, fleeing from the forces of the Soviet Union, who were extracting their revenge through mass rape. Other Germans were forced from their homes in Poland and Czechoslovakia, as the civilians in those countries refused to countenance living with ethnic Germans they blamed for the start of the war.

At the end of the First World War, cries of "Hang the Kaiser!" could be heard in the capitals of the victors, but in the end, nothing was done to punish those individuals who were blamed for the war. However, by 1945, with the liberation of the Nazi death camps and the realization of the unspeakable scale of the slaughter, it was agreed by the Allies that Germany would not only have to undergo a process of **deNazification,** but that the perpetuators of these crimes would have to be punished as well.

The new legal concept of **"crimes against humanity"** was applied to the defendants who took part in the first **Nuremberg Trial** that began on November 20, 1945 and ended on October 1, 1946. With the suicide of Hitler and Goebbels, the leading Nazi to stand trial was Hermann Göring, who escaped the hangman's noose by swallowing poison that was smuggled into his cell, while eleven others were sentenced to death. Other trials were held for leading industrialists, military commanders, judges, and those involved in the Final Solution. Many Nazis escaped justice by fleeing to the Middle East and South America, such as the infamous **Dr. Josef Mengele**, while some, such as Gestapo officer Adolf Eichmann, were eventually brought to justice. Questions arose over what to do about the rank-and-file Nazi party members, and although millions were investigated, relatively few received punishment. By June 1946, the Americans transferred responsibility for deNazification to the German legal authorities, who quietly brought the process to a close.

In the years following the war, West Germans would refer to 1945 as **"Zero Hour,"** marking the darkest point in their national history. Many commentators thought that not only Germany but all of Europe would remain on its back, with minimal economic development and the renewed threat of war. Remarkably, Europe staged a thorough recovery over the next 20 years and in the process transformed the lives of people throughout the region and ushered in an age of political and social stability.

CHAPTER TIMELINE

There are a couple of events listed below that are not discussed in this chapter (but they take place during the same period). Don't be alarmed; you'll find them covered in the next one.

Year	Event
1914	Assassination of Franz Ferdinand (June 28)
1914	Austria-Hungary issues ultimatum to Serbia (July 23)
1914	Austria-Hungary declares war on Serbia (July 28)
1914	Russia begins mobilization (July 29)
1914	Germany declares war on Russia (August 1)
1914	Germany declares war on France (August 3)
1914	Germans defeat Russians at Tannenberg (August 26-30)
1914	First Battle of the Marne (September 5-10)
1914	Completion of the Panama Canal
1915	Gallipoli campaign begins (April 25)
1915	Sinking of the *Lusitania* (May 7)
1916	Germans begin attack on Verdun (February 21)
1916	British launch attack at the Somme (July 1)
1917	Zimmermann Telegram (January 19)
1917	Germany resumes unrestricted submarine warfare (February 1)
1917	Bolsheviks sign armistice with Germany (December 3)
1917	United States declares war on Germany (April 6)
1917	Provisional Government established in Russia (February)
1917	Bolshevik seizure of power (November)
1918	Worldwide influenza outbreak
1918	Female suffrage begins in Great Britain

Year	Event
1918	Germany Republic established after abdication of Kaiser Wilhelm II (November 10)
1918	Armistice bring the war to a close
1919	Treaty of Versailles
1919	Mussolini organizes first Fascist party
1919	Weimar constitution established
1920	Formation of Communist International
1922	Mussolini becomes Prime Minister of Italy
1923	German hyperinflation
1923	Beer Hall Putsch
1924	Death of Lenin
1924	Dawes Plan
1925	Treaty of Lucarno
1928	First Soviet Five-Year Plan
1929	Beginning of collectivized farms in Soviet Union
1929	Lateran Accord between Mussolini and the Catholic Church
1929	Young Plan
1929	Stock market crash
1930	Nazis make huge electoral gains
1931	Bank failures
1932	Hindenburg defeats Hitler for the German presidency
1932	Nazis become largest party in Reichstag
1933	Hitler becomes Chancellor

Year	Event
1933	Reichstag fire
1933	Enabling Act
1933	Germany withdraws from League of Nations
1933	German boycott of Jewish businesses
1934	Beginning of the Great Terror—the Soviet Union
1934	Night of the Long Knives
1934	Hitler becomes Fuhrer after death of Hindenburg
1935	Germany openly begins rearmament
1935	Italian invasion of Ethiopia
1935	Nuremberg Laws directed against German Jews
1936	Berlin Olympics
1936	German remilitarization of the Rhineland
1936	Beginning of the Spanish Civil War
1938	Germany absorbs Austria in Anschluss
1938	Munich accord leads to dismemberment of Poland
1938	*Kristallnacht* (November 9)
1939	Nazi-Soviet nonaggression pact
1939	Invasion of Poland
1939	Britain and France declare war on Germany
1940	Fall of France
1940	Winston Churchill replaces Chamberlain as Prime Minister
1940	Battle of Britain (July–October)
1940	Germans begin Blitz on British cities (September to May 1941)

Year	Event
1941	Germany launches Operation Barbarossa
1941	Japanese attack on Pearl Harbor
1941	30,000 Jews killed at Babi Yar over two days
1941	Atlantic Charter
1942	German advance stopped at Stalingrad
1942	Battle of Midway (June)
1942	Wansee Conference organizes the Final Solution
1943	Battle of Kursk
1943	Allies land in Italy
1943	Mussolini's government falls
1943	Warsaw ghetto uprising
1944	Percentages Agreement between Churchill and Stalin
1944	D-Day
1944	Germans launch Battle of the Bulge (December 16)
1945	Yalta Conference (February 4–11)
1945	Hitler commits suicide (April 30)
1945	V-E Day (May 8)
1945	Victory of British Labour Party over Conservatives (July)
1945	Potsdam Conference (July 17–August 2)
1945	Atomic bomb dropped on Hiroshima (August 6)
1945	V-J Day (August 14)
1945	United Nations created as charter is ratified (October)
1945	Nuremberg Trials for crimes against humanity begin (November)

REVIEW QUESTIONS

Answers and explanations are in Chapter 15.

1. During the first years of the Great Depression, governments responded to the economic crisis by

   (A) increasing their support for higher unemployment payments
   (B) supporting the economic ideas of John Maynard Keynes
   (C) launching major public works projects
   (D) committing their countries to a laissez-faire economic policy
   (E) reducing their expenditures in order to balance their budgets

2. Mussolini attempted to improve the relationship between the Italian state and the Catholic Church by

   (A) mandating that all Italians attend mass
   (B) placing loyal fascists in key clerical positions
   (C) emphasizing his own path towards religious belief
   (D) signing the Lateran Treaty, which resolved some of the longstanding issues between the Church and the Italian state
   (E) returning all confiscated church property

3. The British won a major propaganda victory at the start of the First World War because of

   (A) the sinking of the *Lusitania*
   (B) the Zimmerman telegram
   (C) German atrocities in Belgium
   (D) the destruction by the Germans of major Parisian landmarks
   (E) the Battle of the Marne

4. The term "popular fronts" refers to the idea of

   (A) political parties of the center and the left working together to block the triumph of fascism
   (B) communists uniting with unions to oppose bourgeois governments
   (C) the elimination of class conflict
   (D) using German and Italian forces to support Spanish nationalists
   (E) coalition governments in Great Britain between the Labour Party and the Conservatives

5. The Nuremberg Trials of 1945/1946 were the first tests in international law of the concept of

   (A) collective guilt
   (B) the natural rights of victims
   (C) crimes against humanity
   (D) genocide
   (E) supranational legal authority

6. The Matignon Agreements in France (1936)

   (A) failed to lead to the forty-hour work week
   (B) provided the legal right for unions to organize and strike
   (C) led to the end of the Popular Front government
   (D) ended the informal practice of owner-employee cooperation stemming from the Great War
   (E) satisfied the French far right while antagonizing the moderates and the left

7. The British government had an impact on private life during the First World War in all of the following ways EXCEPT

   (A) the regulation of pub hours
   (B) rationing
   (C) conscription
   (D) billeting of soldiers in civilian residences
   (E) mass propaganda

Postwar Europe

EUROPEAN STABILITY

The most important factor in European affairs in the period after 1945 was the emergence of political, economic, and social stability. Even while the war was raging, Allied statesmen began to think about ways of rebuilding Europe and creating lasting peace.

In 1941, President Roosevelt put forward the **Atlantic Charter**, advocating the establishment of an international organization to replace the ineffective League of Nations. Four years later, this dream became a reality when delegates from 50 nations met in San Francisco to formally create the **United Nations**. To ensure the participation of the United States, whose nonparticipation in the League of Nations doomed it to failure, the new organization was to be based in New York. In July 1945, the U.S. Senate ratified the agreement (with others signing onto it in October), indicating that the United States was not going to return to its interwar isolationism and would instead remain committed to European recovery and stability.

Besides the significance of America's commitment to European affairs, other reasons help account for the development of stability in Europe. The level of destruction brought by Germany and Italy in a war they initiated and the extent of their atrocities against civilians led to a discrediting of Fascism as a political movement. *Revanchism*, a French word for revenge and often applied to the desire to regain so-called lost territories, was a major factor in destabilizing European affairs during the interwar period, as many nations—besides the most prominent example of Germany—sought to regain territories lost in the peace treaties following the Great War. In part due to the mass expulsion of ethnic Germans from Poland and Czechoslovakia, *revanchism* became the cry of fringe groups in the postwar period rather than the stated policy of national governments.

Probably the most important factor in explaining postwar European stability was the emergence of **democratic governments** that were able to carry out policies that dramatically improved the economic conditions for their citizenry. Class conflict, which had been a destabilizing factor in the 1920s and 1930s, was replaced by a new **social contract** in which workers, in exchange for giving up their most extreme demands, received promises of full employment, living wages, and social welfare.

THE BEGINNING OF THE COLD WAR

There have been three major schools of thought on the causes of the Cold War.

1. For the **Traditionalists** (a position that emerged in the earliest days of the Cold War), the Soviet Union, under the brutal dictatorship of Joseph Stalin, was fundamentally responsible for the development of hostilities between the East and West.

2. Beginning in the 1960s (in part a reflection of the challenges that were being posed to all forms of established authority and anger over the Vietnam War), a new school of Cold War thought, known as **Revisionism**, began to appear. For the Revisionists, fear of a postwar economic downturn (as was the case after 1918) meant that, in 1945, the United States was not seeking to make the world safe for democracy but was instead seeking to make it safe for American trade.

3. By the 1980s, a third position began to emerge, that of the **Post-Revisionists**, which perhaps not surprisingly took a middle ground. For the Post-Revisionists, even if the Soviet Union bore the brunt of the responsibility, the United States was more active than the Traditionalists might argue.

In many ways, the views of historians have not been altered all that fundamentally by the collapse of the Soviet Union and the opening, if at times tentatively, of their archives. What is often today referred to as the neo-Traditionalist point of view is currently in the ascendancy, although one can easily find in scholarly books and journals writings reflecting the other two traditions.

One can make the argument that the Cold War rivalry was largely inevitable. In an often-quoted passage, Alexis de Tocqueville, in *Democracy in America*, wrote,

> "There are now two great nations in the world, which starting from different points, seem to be advancing toward the same goal: the Russians and the Anglo-Americans... Each seems called by some secret design of Providence one day to hold in its hands the destinies of half the world."

When de Tocqueville wrote that passage in 1835, he certainly wasn't thinking about ideological differences, but such differences did emerge dating back to the establishment of the Communist state in 1917, which was followed by limited Allied involvement in the Russian Civil War. Even during the war, although cooperation certainly existed, mistrust played a role in the relationship between the Soviet Union and its Western allies, ranging from Soviet anger over the delay in opening a second front to fears that the British and Americans were seeking to negotiate a separate peace with the Germans.

THE YALTA CONFERENCE ON THE FUTURE OF GERMANY

Once the war came to an end and cooperation was no longer necessary for victory, mutual antagonism came out, beginning with the debate over the future of Germany. At **Yalta,** the Big Three agreed to the **temporary division of Germany,** and in the aftermath of the war, Germany was divided into four zones (France was given a zone at the insistence of the British), with an **Allied Control Council** to make joint decisions. None of the Allies apparently wanted or expected dismemberment. Nevertheless, Yalta had provided each of the Allies with the opportunity to affect the transformation in their own zone, with the end result that the Soviet Union would obviously transform their zone in a far different manner than the Western Allies. Ultimately, Germany would become a Cold War showcase for the rival ideologies.

The method chosen by the Soviet Union to gain control over political life in its zone was the subversion of a democratic structure it pretended to support. The Soviets began in their zone by allowing for the reestablishment of all non-right-wing parties that had existed in the Weimar Republic. **Walter Ulbricht**, the Soviet-selected leader of the German Communist Party (KPD), thought that because most Germans didn't want to go back to the world of Weimar and its capitalist crises, there would be genuine support for the KPD. The problem was that mass rape, dismantling of factories to be sent back to the Soviet Union, and the failure of land reform led to anger at the Soviets and their clients in the KPD. Seeing that no groundswell of electoral support would be forthcoming, Ulbricht brought about the forced merger of the KPD and the more popular Social Democratic Party (SPD) in 1946 and created a one-party state, a technique the Soviets were to find useful as they sought to gain control over other governments in Eastern Europe.

While these political developments were taking place, tensions were increasing over the issue of **reparations**. Neither the Americans nor British were diametrically opposed to reparations, and an agreement had been reached at Yalta with an amount set at 20 billion dollars. At Potsdam, further negotiations led to the agreement that each occupying power would collect reparations in its own zone, with the hard-pressed Soviets receiving 25 percent from the amount collected by the other three.

The problem was that the Western Allies began to fear that carrying out a reparations program would leave the German economy prostrate, with the British and American public left paying the bill to feed the Germans. Even President Truman had been shaken by what he saw when he traveled to Germany for the Potsdam conference and noted, "Unless we do what we can to help, we may lose next winter what we won at such terrible cost last spring." On his own initiative, in May 1946, General Lucius Clay, the commander of the American zone, ended the collection of reparations, which was soon to be followed by the other two Western Allies, which meant that goods stopped flowing to the Soviet Union.

INCREASING TENSIONS OUTSIDE OF EUROPE

Tensions were also increasing between the American and Soviets in regions outside of Europe. Back in 1941, the Soviets and British jointly divided and occupied **Iran**, with an agreement that they would both leave at the end of the war. In 1945, the British promptly left, but the Soviets refused and demanded oil concessions. When Truman heard that Soviet tanks were heading to the capital of Teheran, he sent warships into the Persian Gulf, and Stalin responded by removing his troops.

Stalin also tried to intimidate **Turkey**, which was neutral in the war, into granting the Soviets naval bases along the straits to give the Soviet fleet access to the Mediterranean. To show the Turks he was serious, Stalin massed troops along their common border, and it was only when he understood that the U.S. would fight to protect Turkey that he backed down and withdrew his forces.

American foreign policy towards the Soviet Union was in a state of flux in the immediate postwar period. In part, this reflected the replacement of Franklin Roosevelt, who felt that his good wartime relationship with Stalin could serve as the basis of postwar ties, with the no-nonsense Harry S. Truman, who saw Stalin in a more wary light.

American policy was also influenced by the writings of **George Kennan**, an official in the State Department. In 1947, Kennan wrote what became known as the **Long Telegram**, in which he indicated that in our relationship with the Soviets, we were dealing with a state that viewed us as an ideological enemy and would never seek to find the means for coexistence. In this and in articles that appeared under the pseudonym "X" in the journal *Foreign Affairs*, Kennan became the architect of the policy of **Containment**, in which our goal needed to be the "long-term, patient but firm and vigilant containment of Russian expansive tendencies."

CONTAINMENT AND THE CREATION OF NATO

Containment as an actual policy was first tested in **Greece**, where a Communist-led insurgency was fighting against the newly reestablished Greek government. Great Britain, which had assumed a watchdog position in Greece at the end of the war, informed the U.S. in 1947 that it lacked the economic resources to continue to support the Greek government. Seeing this as a major Soviet attempt to gain control over a strategically important nation (even though Soviet aid to the Greek Communists would later be shown to be quite minimal), Truman went before a joint session of Congress on March 12, 1947 and stated in what is known as the **Truman Doctrine** that, "it must be the policy of the United States to support free peoples who are resisting attempted subjugation by armed minorities or by outside pressures." He then proceeded to ask for money, which eventually reached the amount of $400 million to be given to the Greek and Turkish governments.

Containment was also going to figure into one of the most important decisions made by the United States in the postwar period. Rejecting George Washington's admonition in his farewell address to stay clear of permanent alliances with foreign powers, the United States directly decided to counter the threat posed by the millions of Soviet soldiers based in Eastern Europe by establishing the **North Atlantic Treaty Organization (NATO)** in 1949. Joining the United States as initial members were Great Britain, France, Canada, Denmark, Belgium, Iceland, Italy, the Netherlands, Portugal, and Norway, with Greece and Turkey joining the alliance in 1952.

SOVIET DOMINANCE OVER EASTERN EUROPE

In 1944, seeing that Soviet troops were advancing through Eastern Europe, Winston Churchill traveled to Moscow to meet with Stalin. As Churchill recalled years later, after pushing a piece of paper in front of Stalin, "There was a slight pause. Then he [Stalin] took his blue pen and made a large tick upon it, and passed it back to us. It was all settled in no more time than it takes to set down." This document became known as the **Percentages Agreement**, because it divided the various nations of Eastern Europe into spheres of influence based on percentages, with for example, Soviet influence being at 90 percent in Romania and only 50 percent in Hungary. Serious flaws in the agreement included the fact that Poland was left out entirely and the United States refused to accept any such agreement at this time.

The fact that Churchill in 1944 rushed to get an agreement signed reveals his growing concern that Eastern Europe would become dominated by the Soviet Union and that there was not that much that the Western Allies could do to block this development. Several years later, it was Churchill who delivered his famous speech at Westminster College and used a metaphor that would represent Soviet control over Eastern Europe when he decried the fact that "From Stettin in the Baltic to Trieste in the Adriatic, an **iron curtain** has descended across the Continent."

With the war in Europe winding down, Stalin expected to be able control the future of those areas liberated by the Red Army. With the enormity of Soviet losses in the war in mind and unwilling to see Roosevelt's Atlantic Charter as a source of future peace, Stalin wanted to establish a protective shield to protect the Soviet Union from any future invasion from the west. Meeting in **Yalta**, on the Crimean Sea, the British and Americans were able to get the Soviets to accept a high-minded **Declaration of Liberated Europe**, stating that in those countries that were Axis or liberated, governments were to be formed that were "broadly representative of all democratic elements in the population" and that free elections were to be held at the earliest possible time.

POLAND

On the question of **Poland,** Stalin was going to continue with his plans to establish a government dominated by Polish Communists; the only concession he granted was that an undetermined number of anticommunist Poles based in London would be added to this provisional government. This aspect of the Yalta conference has proven to be very controversial, with Roosevelt being accused of selling out the Poles. The tragic reality was that the Soviets had troops on the ground in Poland, and there was little that the United States and Great Britain could do about it short of war. There was going to have to be a price for having the Soviet Union for an ally against Germany.

When the promised elections in Poland were finally held under conditions of intimidation in 1947, the Communists received 80 percent and proceeded to bring any sign of a multiparty state to an end. The Soviets understood that they would have to use force to maintain Communist control over Poland because they were hated in that nation—a loathing that grew worse when the role of the Soviets was revealed in the murder of 15,000 Polish officers in the forests of **Katyn** at the start of the war.

ELSEWHERE IN EASTERN EUROPE

Nevertheless, in the rest of Eastern Europe, the Soviets hoped that control could be achieved through less recourse to violence. The Soviet Union seemingly had a number of advantages in this goal, including the economic and social failure of the states of Eastern Europe during the interwar period (with the exception of Czechoslovakia), which meant that few were advocating a return to the politics of the past, although in most of Eastern Europe, the Soviets were viewed as liberators from the horrors of German dominance. With the exception of Poland, the Soviet Union initially tried to establish **"People's Democracies"** in Eastern Europe. For the Communists, this was a go-slow program, with governments that were more proletarian than in the bourgeois West but were still not ready for a full-fledged Communist system as found in the Soviet Union.

In many ways, the push for tighter control over Eastern Europe came about in reaction to the offer of **Marshall Plan** money to all the nations of Europe. Stalin saw the Marshall Plan as a threat to informal Soviet control over countries like Hungary or Czechoslovakia, because by taking the money, those countries would automatically be drawn toward the capitalist West, so Stalin moved to assert more direct control. In Hungary, the Communists practiced "salami" tactics, where intimidation and false plots against non-Communist political leaders sliced them away from the body politic. Using such tactics, the Hungarian Communist Party forced its competitor, the Smallholder's Party, out of existence by 1948 and in the following year won a tainted election with 95 percent of the vote.

CZECHOSLOVAKIA

In Czechoslovakia, the situation was different, because in the immediate postwar period, the government was dominated by men like President Eduard Benes, who although a non-Communist understood that it would be necessary to maintain a pro-Soviet foreign policy if Czechoslovakia were to retain her national independence. Also, the Czechs were more favorably disposed toward the Soviet Union, whom they gratefully saw as liberators, while feeling they didn't owe anything to the West, which had sold them out at Munich in 1938. This balancing act failed in the wake of Czech desire to accept badly needed Marshall Aid monies. To put pressure on Benes's government, the Czech Communists formed a "People's Militia," which intimidated Benes into forming a new government dominated by Communists.

When the body of Foreign Minister Jan Masaryk, the son of the founder of Czechoslovakia, was found shattered outside his window—either a suicide or a murder victim—it was clear that a multi-party Czechoslovak state was coming to an end. The Social Democrats were forcibly absorbed into the Communist party, and in controlled elections in May 1948, the Communists won a complete victory and proceeded to set up a Soviet-style state.

YUGOSLAVIA

The major exception to Soviet control over Eastern Europe took place in Yugoslavia. Initially, Yugoslavian resistance was based on a broad alliance against the brutal Croatian puppet government established by the Germans. As the war continued, however, a civil war broke out among the partisan groups with the Communists, led by **Josip Tito** fighting against the royalist Chetniks. The civil war ended with the triumph of Tito's Communists, but Stalin never trusted Tito, in part because of the assistance he received during the war from the British and Americans, as well as the fact that Stalin never liked indigenous Communist movements that he couldn't directly control. Relations between the two states remained poor in the ensuing years, and by 1948, a formal break took place. Although Tito became the West's favorite Communist due to his independent foreign policy, at home he maintained a brutal, Communist-style police state.

THE END OF IMPERIALISM

The British had hoped to maintain their vast empire following the war. The United States, however, was extremely reluctant to allow this, and Great Britain, which was dependent on American loans, was forced to concede the point. The beginning of decolonization took place on August 15, 1947 when India declared independence, initiating a domino effect throughout the rest of the Empire.

ISRAEL

In 1947, the British announced that they were withdrawing from Palestine, leaving the United Nations to determine its fate. Demands for a Jewish homeland had grown louder following the Holocaust, and Arabic nationalist sentiment also had increased. In response, the United Nations agreed to partition Palestine into Jewish and Arab homelands. On May 14, 1948, the Jewish state of Israel was founded, but it was immediately attacked by its Arab neighbors. Surprisingly, the small Jewish state pushed back its enemies and the proposed Arab Palestinian state never left the drawing boards.

EGYPT AND AFRICA

In Egypt, Great Britain maintained significant influence even though it had been an independent nation since 1922. This began to change when **Abdul Nasser** (1918–1970) became president. In 1956, he announced the nationalization of the Suez Canal, which the British still controlled. In response, Britain, France, and Israel planned a surprise attack on Egypt. The immediate outcry from the American and Soviet governments made it quite clear to Britain and France exactly who were the dominant powers in this postwar world. They bowed to the American and Soviet demands to withdraw.

Soon after, the British saw the writing on the wall, and they began the process of decolonization in sub-Saharan Africa. In 1957, the nation of Ghana declared its independence from Great Britain, and in the ensuing years Nigeria, Sierra Leone, Uganda, and Kenya followed Ghana's lead. Because these territories all contained few British settlers, independence came about without too much trouble. In Rhodesia, on the other hand, in 1965, the large number of British settlers formed their own white-supremacist government and declared their independence from Britain. Not until 1980 would Africans win control over that land, which they renamed Zimbabwe.

INDONESIA, VIETNAM, AND ALGERIA

For nations such as France and the Netherlands that had a less-than-sterling military record in the Second World War, holding on to their colonies became an important part of restoring national honor. The Dutch maintained a costly and ultimately unwinnable struggle in the East Indies to keep the land they had first occupied in the seventeenth century. By 1949, the Netherlands reluctantly agreed to recognize Indonesian independence.

France almost ripped itself apart in its attempt to hold on to Algeria. This followed a bitter loss in Indochina (Vietnam), where a nationalist movement under the leadership of **Ho Chi Minh** (1890–1969) fought first against the Japanese during the Second World War and then against the French, as the latter attempted to restore its colonial authority. By 1954, France realized it was an impossible task and agreed to divide Vietnam into two states: a northern communist-led nation and a republic in the south dominated by the United States.

Although the French could accept the loss of Indochina, Algeria was different; it had been a French possession since 1830 and more than a million native French lived in the territory. France almost erupted in civil war over the Algerian question in 1958, until de Gaulle took the helm of the French government and used his immense prestige four years later to grant Algerian independence.

THE CREATION OF A EUROPEAN UNION

In the aftermath of the war, there were several factors that contributed to the goal of establishing greater European cooperation. For the French in particular, pan-European cooperation would provide a means for keeping an eye on its traditional enemy, Germany. There was also a growing sense that economic rationalization and cooperation were needed to end wasteful competition and ease tensions between nations. Additionally, concern over the Soviet Union, which led to military cooperation through the establishment of NATO, aided the cause of European unity.

The first stage in this process took place in the realm of economic cooperation, with the establishment of the **Organization for European Economic Cooperation (OEEC)**, which had the task of handling the money provided by the United States through the Marshall Plan. The United States made it clear when providing the money that it did not want to see it used to revive unprofitable industries in order to salvage national pride, and the U.S. insisted that Europeans use the money in a cooperative manner. The OEEC also began the initial work on lowering tariffs and eliminating trade barriers among those states receiving assistance.

The next development was the creation in 1951 of the **European Coal and Steel Community (ECSC)**. The ECSC combined and administered the steel and coal resources of its member states: France, West Germany, Italy, Belgium, the Netherlands, and Luxemburg. The main architect of the ECSC, Frenchman **Robert Schuman**, stated that one byproduct of this form of economic cooperation was that "any war between France and Germany becomes not merely unthinkable, but materially impossible." The ECSC also provided certain models that were important for the future development of European unity, such as the establishment of a supranational assembly to guide the ECSC (which was renamed the **European Parliament** in 1962), a court of justice, and direct income for the Community in the form of taxes.

In 1957, the original members of the ECSC signed the **Treaty of Rome** establishing the **European Economic Community** (more commonly referred to as the **Common Market**). The members of the EEC, who were joined by Britain, Ireland, and Denmark in 1973 in the first expansion of the Community, lifted almost all trade restrictions among member states. In 1986, in the first major revision to the Treaty of Rome, the **European Single Act** provided for the free movement among member nations of capital, labor, and such services as banking and insurance.

The **Maastricht Treaty** of 1992 led to the establishment of a common currency, the **Euro**, with banknotes and coins going into circulation in January 2002, with the exception of Denmark, Sweden, and most significantly the United Kingdom, who refused to give up the pound. The Maastricht Treaty also introduced new areas where there was supposed to be increased cooperation, such as in defense, justice, and environmental affairs, which resulted in a name change from the EEC to the **European Union (EU)**.

RECENT AND FUTURE EXPANSION OF THE EUROPEAN UNION

The European Union has undergone a number of expansions in its list of member states (the largest crop of entrants joined in 2004), notably with nations that were formally members of the Warsaw Pact or part of the Soviet Union, such as the Czech Republic, Estonia, Hungary, Latvia, Lithuania, Poland, Slovakia, and Slovenia. Bulgaria and Romania joined in 2007, and Turkey entered into negotiations for membership back in 2005. Turkey's European Union bid has been controversial for a number of reasons. Some EU officials doubt that Turkey can meet economic targets required for membership, or they question Turkey's commitment to human rights. Some have expressed concern about admitting a Muslim state into the EU with a large population that would make it second only to Germany.

EU expansion has also led to the desire to make it work more efficiently, which led to the writing of a **European Constitution**, the caveat being that all EU members had to approve the constitution for it to go into effect. France, however, a nation that has been at the forefront of European cooperation, voted "no" in May 2005 in a national referendum. What this will mean for further European integration is not yet clear.

POST-WWII DEVELOPMENTS IN WESTERN EUROPEAN STATES

GREAT BRITAIN

The postwar period in Great Britain began with what at the time was considered to be one of the greatest political upsets in electoral history—the replacement of Prime Minister Winston Churchill and his Conservative Party with the **Labour Party** and its leader, **Clement Attlee**. It probably shouldn't have come as such a surprise, because although many in Britain were deeply grateful to Churchill for the steely leadership he provided during the war, there was a sense that he was not the man to lead them in times of peace.

Economic and Social Reforms

Even while the war was in full swing, there was a sense that when the war ended, Britain had to move beyond the dismal economic and social conditions that had prevailed during the interwar years. **Sir William Beveridge**, a member of the Liberal Party, had produced in 1942 (at the request of the government) a report that recommended that all adults should pay a weekly contribution, and in return benefits would be paid to people who were sick, unemployed, retired, or widowed. For Beveridge, the benefit of such a system was that it would provide for a minimum standard of living "below which no one should be allowed to fall." The electoral triumph of the Labour Party was due to the belief within the British public that it was the party most committed to implementing this far-reaching plan for reform, and with its victory in 1945, Labour began the establishment of a cradle-to-grave social welfare program—the highlight being the establishment of the **National Health Service (NHS)**, which provided for a comprehensive system of free health care.

Nationalization of Industries

Attlee and the Labour party were also committed to a program of nationalization of major industries. Beginning in 1945, the government took control of the Bank of England, the railroads, and the electric, iron, and steel industries. This was not as revolutionary as it might appear, because in many cases, these industries had already been placed under government control during the war years. Fair compensation was paid to the existing owners, and company management (which some of the more radical members of the Labour Party wanted to see handled by the workers through committees) remained in the hands of professional managers, in many cases the same individuals who had led the firm prior to the takeover.

Economic conditions remained fairly grim in the immediate postwar years. Britain was now a major debtor to the United States, because its own gold and foreign currency reserves had been depleted to save the nation from the Nazi onslaught. The Labour party remained committed to sizeable military expenditures, because Britain still had large military commitments overseas, and the advent of the Cold War also impacted on spending. Although the standard of living improved for many people in the immediate postwar years due to the increase in social services, this period is generally referred to as the **"Age of Austerity"** and lasted until 1954, when the wartime rationing of butter and sugar finally came to an end.

By the 1951 general election, the Labour Party and the public were fairly exhausted from the pace of change, which provided a renewed opportunity for Churchill and the Conservatives. Aside from reversing the nationalization of the iron and steel industries, the Conservatives did not return the remaining industries to private hands and continued to support the social service network implemented by the Labour Party. This has come to be known as the **"Politics of Consensus,"** because although the two major parties may have differed on details such as funding levels, they were in general agreement on the need to provide social services and that government should play a large role in the management of the economy.

Economic Decline

Although one can refer to a postwar **"economic miracle"** in Germany and Italy, such talk for Great Britain would be wide off the mark. Britain's economic growth by the 1950s was clearly less than that achieved by the nations of Western Europe. The reasons for **Britain's economic decline** in the postwar period remain controversial, but one can generally see factors such as the reliance on older factories, whereas plants in places like Germany were rebuilt with the latest technology following the destruction brought by the war. Britain also lacked the central economic planning that was to prove to be critical for French economic growth, and Britain had to deal with aggressive unions that wanted higher wages without agreeing to produce gains in productivity. Some scholars have even looked to cultural reasons for Britain's decline suggesting, for example, that the study of the sciences in British universities took a back seat to the pursuit of the humanities.

Following a period of Conservative dominance in the period after 1951, the Labour Party re-emerged as the dominant political party in the period from 1964 to 1974. Although Prime Minister Harold Wilson was leading a party that would prove to be successful at the polls, he was not able to strengthen the position of Britain in the global economy.

Violence in Ireland

During these same years, the situation in **Northern Ireland** worsened, with the British government sending troops into the troubled province in 1969. On January 30, 1972, thirteen Catholics were killed when British soldiers fired on civil rights marchers. The day became known as **Bloody Sunday** and led to a renewed surge of violence by groups such as the **Irish Republican Army** that were opposed to the British presence in Northern Ireland.

Margaret Thatcher and the Post-Thatcher Years

In 1979, Prime Minister James Callaghan's Labour government proved unable to deal with a wave of strikes that negatively affected road transport and public services, known as the "winter of discontent." This provided an opportunity for the triumph of the Conservative Party and its leader **Margaret Thatcher**, who became Britain's first female prime minister. Thatcher had made it clear that she wanted to break with what she viewed as the failed policies of the past and stated, "I am not a consensus politician, I am a conviction politician." **Thatcherism,** the eponymous term for her economic policies, included tight control over the money supply to reduce inflation, sharp cuts in public spending, and a cut in taxes, particularly for higher earners.

Thatcher sought to make Britain more competitive in the global market by reducing the power of the trade unions and by reprivatizing those parts of the British economy still under the control of the government. Thatcher was a very divisive leader, and her career might have come to an early end if it had not received a boost following the successful war that Britain fought with Argentina in 1982 over the **Falkland Islands**. Thatcher ran into trouble during her third term when she tried to introduce market principles into the running of the NHS and education system, and her hostility to working toward further European integration created dissent within her own party. In 1990, she resigned and was replaced by **John Major**. Major continued with most of Thatcher's domestic policies, though perhaps without some of the vindictive gusto that she had brought to British politics. Because he was more pro-European than Thatcher, he signed the Maastricht Treaty.

In 1997, after being out of government for 18 years, the Labour Party triumphed under its youthful leader **Tony Blair**. Blair, who had become the leader of his party in 1994, had moved Labour away from its socialist roots, creating what he referred to as **"New Labour."** Rather than renationalizing the economy, Labour under Blair focused on improving Britain's social services, reform of the House of Lords, and the devolution of power away from Westminster and toward regional parliaments in Wales and Scotland. Blair received a second term in 2001 and a third in 2005, although the margin of Labour's victory in the 2005 election was significantly reduced because of anger over Blair's support for the war in Iraq.

Blair resigned as Labour Leader in May of 2007, and Gordon Brown, who served as Chancellor of the Exchequer under Blair for many years, rose to become both leader of the Labour Party and Prime Minister of the United Kingdom.

FRANCE

France in 1945 had to deal with the grim aftermath of what one writer has termed the "Strange Defeat" of 1940. France largely chose to deal with the difficult Vichy years by propagating certain myths, including the idea that France was a nation of resisters against German occupation, that few supported Marshal Pétain and Vichy, and that the tragic fate of the Jews in France was entirely the responsibility of the Germans. Marcel Ophuls's powerful documentary *The Sorrow and the Pity* (1969) helped open the door to questioning these national myths, although it remained several years before French television was willing to show the film. Under President **Jacques Chirac**, the nation finally began to address France's role in the deportation of 66,000 Jews to Germany, along with other issues involving collaboration activities during the war.

Charles de Gaulle, the leader of the French government-in-exile, expected to dominate political life in postwar France, but he stepped away from politics when the newly established **Fourth Republic** refused to establish the strong presidency that de Gaulle felt was needed if France was not going to repeat the mistakes of the politically contentious Third Republic. French political life was also transformed, if in a more positive manner, by the granting of the vote to women. It was left to the Fourth Republic to grapple with a series of colonial problems, including the disastrous defeat in Indochina in 1954 and in the same year a revolt that broke out in **Algeria**.

The crisis in Algeria, which led to fears that a military coup would take place in France itself, brought about the return of de Gaulle to politics, and he led the vote for a plebiscite in 1958 establishing the **Fifth Republic**, which contained the powerful presidency whose office de Gaulle now held. Although his enemies saw him as dictatorial, de Gaulle was committed to restoring France to a leading place on the global stage. To do this, he committed France to taking a leading role in Europe, which meant vetoing Britain's attempt to enter the Common Market in 1962.

To ensure that she could provide for her own defense, France refused to sign the **Limited Test Ban Treaty** and exploded its first hydrogen bomb in 1968. France also maintained an independent foreign policy marked by its withdrawal from NATO's unified command in 1966 and its recognition, over the strong objections of the United States, of the Communist government in China.

Economic Struggles

France's economy in the 1950s and 1960s made significant strides from the serious economic difficulties it faced at the end of the war. In 1945, five million men returned home from Germany and needed jobs, the transport system was shattered during the heavy fighting in the last year of the war, and the country had limited supplies of coal and food. This dire situation favored the **French Communist Party**, which had a good wartime resistance record (although it only turned against the German occupiers following the invasion of the Soviet Union in 1941) and appeared to offer answers to these economic problems. Although the Communists were part of the first postwar coalition government, they were pushed out of the coalition in 1947, in part with the support of the United States, which made it clear that economic assistance would not be forthcoming if the Communists remained in the government.

In that same year, France began the implementation of an economic program designed by **Jean Monnet**, who was also one of the founders of the European Community. The **Monnet Plan** established the Commissaritat General du Plan (CGP), which provided for nonpolitical technocrats to run the economy. With increased foreign investment and rational central planning, the French economy, which had traditionally lagged behind Germany and Great Britain, began to take off. This transformed life in France as newly prosperous consumers began to buy cars, televisions, and dishwashers. It also, however, created a sense that their unique way of life was being transformed by what its critics referred to as **Americanization**, embodied most directly by the newfound popularity of that most American of products, Coca-Cola.

By 1968, disenchantment among the young over what they considered to be the sterile course of French life, as well as anger over classrooms, laboratories, and libraries that were bursting at the seams as more students pursued higher education, led to student revolts at every major French university, with the most serious situation taking place in Paris. In May of that year, students forged an alliance with workers, but this soon petered out as the students' demand for a thorough reordering of French society clashed with the more limited demands of the workers for wage increases and better working conditions. Although de Gaulle survived this crisis, in the next year he resigned.

France continued to be led by members of the Gaullist party until the electoral victory in 1981 of Socialist leader **François Mitterrand**, the longest-serving president of France. A moderate within his party, Mitterrand focused on social reform programs and reducing unemployment rather than radical plans for the socialization of the French economy. Mitterrand, who was reelected in 1988, retired from politics in 1995 and was replaced in office by **Jacques Chirac**, the Gaullist mayor of Paris.

Chirac served two full terms as president of France for a total of 12 years, the second longest tenure in the job after Mitterand. He ran on a platform committed to healing social ills (such as racism and labor strikes), providing tax cuts, and instituting job programs. Unfortunately, social unrest grew in his second term with some of the worst rioting seen in France since the late 1960s. Chirac also came under fire during his presidency for several instances of corruption that took place while he was mayor of Paris and for general wastefulness in spending, particularly where his own palace services were concerned.

Conservative **Nicolas Sarkozy** succeeded Chirac in May of 2007, winning a runoff against Socialist Segolene Royal. He vows to implement a controlled immigration policy and an ambitious development plan to modernize the country.

Italy

The fall of Mussolini's government in 1943 presaged a violent civil war that lasted until the end of the Second World War. Because the Italian monarchy was tainted by its association with the fascists, a referendum in 1946 led to the establishment of a republic. The **Christian Democrats** became the party of government, dominating political life in Italy until the 1990s. In Italy, unlike the rest of Western Europe, the Communists remained a significant opposition party. In part, this was due to the influence of **Antonio Gramsci** (1891–1937), one of the founders of the Italian Communist party, whose writings encouraged a measure of political flexibility that was certainly not found within the more doctrinaire French Communist Party.

Italy made outstanding economic progress in the 1950s and 1960s, to the point that it is referred to as the **"economic miracle."** In part, this was achieved through the large role played by the state in the Italian economy through the **Institute for Industrial Reconstruction (IRI)**, which was created in 1931 during the fascist years. The IRI controlled shipbuilding, airlines, metallurgy, and the chemical industry, with the automaker Fiat being the only large manufacturer to remain in private hands.

Italy benefited from its early commitment to the Common Market, as well as from the cheap labor supply provided by the 6 million southern Italians who moved to the north in the 1960s. Attempts were made to address the longstanding poverty of the south, with an interest in the **"southern question"** emerging as a peculiar byproduct of Mussolini's exile of political opponents to the south. This meant that a number of postwar Italian political leaders had a firsthand acquaintance with the economic plight of that region. Land reform broke up the large estates, and money was pumped into the region through a series of five-year plans, but to this day, there is a significant economic gap between north and south.

By the 1970s, economic problems were increasing, including high unemployment, inflation, and the loss of a staggering number of workdays to strikes. The Christian Democrats limped on as the party in power, in part because despite their own failings, there was seemingly no other option. A revival of the mafia took place in the south, while political terrorism from the extreme left led to frequent attacks on politicians, judges, and business leaders. The most brazen of these terrorist attacks took place in 1978 when the **Red Brigade** kidnapped former Prime Minster Aldo Moro and eventually murdered him when the government refused to negotiate his release.

Although Italy remains politically stable, frequent changes of government remain a part of the political landscape as do charges of corruption, which after years of being ignored, shook the Christian Democratic Party in the late 1990s. In 2006, questions regarding corruption led to the defeat of Prime Minister **Silvio Berlusconi**, a conservative media magnate who controls most of the major media outlets in Italy outside of government control. **Romano Prodi** of the Olive Tree party became Prime Minister in May of 2006, his second time assuming the position (first was in 1996).

GERMANY

The first years after the war were extremely difficult in Germany, as the nation dealt with the sheer magnitude of its defeat and the incredible destruction from the war; in 1947, industrial production was still only half the prewar level. Adding to the problems was the reality that if there was one place where Cold War tensions could flare up into actual fighting, then that location was **Berlin**, a city that was divided, like the country at large, into four occupation zones.

A series of crises would periodically flare up over the divided city, the first taking place in June 1948, when the United States and Britain introduced a new currency into their occupation zones without seeking Soviet approval. Stalin retaliated by **blockading** the city of Berlin, completely cutting off the city from the west. Why Stalin took this step is not entirely clear, but perhaps he felt that this was a way to push for negotiations on the status of the city. An odd quirk from the negotiations at Potsdam was that, although there was no written agreement on access to Berlin by rail, road, or water, there were three officially designated air corridors. Seeing this as an opportunity, U.S. General Clay once again showed personal initiative and began to send supplies by air, with President Truman soon offering his full support. The **Berlin Airlift** went on for ten-and-a-half months and came to an end in May 1949, when Stalin lifted the blockade with no preconditions.

A Divided Country: East and West Germany

Seizing on the momentum achieved by the successful airlift, in 1949, the United States, Great Britain, and France agreed to combine their zones to create the **Federal Republic of Germany**, with the city of Bonn as its capital. The Soviet Union responded several months later and decreed that its zone in eastern Germany would become the Communist-dominated **German Democratic Republic**. Possible reunification was suggested by Stalin in a note he sent in 1952 to the West German government, in which he implied that Germany could be reunified and exist as an unarmed and neutral state. There has been a historical debate over how sincere Stalin was in his offer, though he may have been willing to allow for German unification because he desperately wanted to forestall West German rearmament. In any event, the offer was rejected, and West Germany rearmed and entered NATO in 1955.

Germany would remain at the center of the Cold War, with the city of Berlin as the critical hotspot. In 1958, Soviet Premier Nikita Khrushchev gave an ultimatum to the West saying that they could stay six months and then had to pull out all their troops and allow Berlin to become a free city with access controlled by East Germany. President Eisenhower refused to budge and made it clear that he would launch another Berlin airlift if necessary.

The Building of the Berlin Wall

The next stage in the conflict over Berlin began at the ungodly hour of 2:00 A.M. on August 13, 1961, when East German border police began to string a barbed-wire barrier between East and West Berlin. This was followed over the next several days by the building of a concrete barrier, the infamous **Berlin Wall**. For the East German Communists, this was deemed to be necessary because they were suffering a serious brain drain as the educated elite were leaving the country in droves, with more than 2.5 million having passed to West Germany by 1949.

The reaction of the Western Allies was fairly mild, because putting up the wall did not impact on what the West thought was essential to its Berlin policy: the presence of Western troops, free access to the city, and political self-determination for West Berliners. Kennedy's critics said he should have done something when the barrier was just barbed wire, but short of war, there was little to be done. As proof that there may be something to the old adage "good fences make for good neighbors," the building of the Berlin Wall proved beneficial, in that it meant that the constant crises over Berlin would now come to an end with the acceptance by both sides of a divided city.

Political, Social, and Economic Reforms

The early years in the history of the Federal Republic of Germany were dominated by **Konrad Adenauer**, who served as chancellor from 1949 to 1963 as the head of the **Christian Democratic Union** party. Adenauer, an anti-Nazi German conservative who had been mayor of Cologne in the Weimar Republic, greatly feared the Soviet Union and therefore preferred to see a West German state tied to the West rather than a unified Germany that was forced into neutrality. Adenauer's government also attempted to address the terrible crimes committed by the Germans during the Nazi period by paying compensation to Jewish victims of the Holocaust as well as making direct payments to the state of Israel.

Adenauer's government also ushered in a period of economic growth, aided in the immediate postwar years by the influx of millions of Germans who had fled west from Poland, Czechoslovakia, and East Germany. In the most dramatic example of **a postwar economic miracle**, the West German economy grew from $23 billion in 1950 to $103 billion in 1964. Equally significant, this newfound prosperity trickled down through the population so that workers experienced increased wages from higher productivity, which they used on hitherto-unimagined luxuries like new cars and foreign vacations. The main government architect of this economic boom, which was notably achieved without high inflation, was **Gerhard Ritter**, Adenauer's Minister of Economics and chancellor following Adenauer's retirement in 1961.

During the Adenauer/Ritter years, the **Social Democrats** looked like they were going to remain in a position of permanent opposition. Electoral success arrived through a combination of two elements: dropping the Marxist language of class struggle, which the party did in 1955, and the emergence of the charismatic **Willy Brandt** as the leader of the party. Brandt, who rose to national prominence as Mayor of Berlin, became chancellor in 1969, the first time a Socialist led a German government since 1930.

Although remaining firmly tied to the West, Brandt felt it necessary to reach out to the Soviets and their satellite states in Eastern Europe. This policy of contact, known as *Ostpolitik*, led to the signing of treaties with the Soviet Union, Poland, and Czechoslovakia and provided for de facto recognition of the East German state. In a famous display of national contrition, Brandt, on a visit to Poland in 1970, kneeled before a monument to those who fell during the Warsaw Ghetto uprising. Despite the international acclaim that he received, including the awarding of a Nobel Prize in 1972, the end of Brandt's term as chancellor occurred swiftly in 1974, when a member of his staff was arrested as an East German spy.

Brandt's successor as Chancellor was **Helmut Schmidt**, who despite having to face economic problems stemming from the oil crisis of 1973 was still able to lead the Social Democrats to an electoral victory in 1976. As in Great Britain and the United States, the early 1980s seemed to represent a surge in conservative politics, and in 1982, the CDU achieved an electoral comeback under **Helmut Kohl**.

German Reunification

It was Kohl, however, who would move with speed and determination to bring about **German reunification in 1990**. He also worked with French President Francois Mitterand to promote the Maastricht Treaty which created the European Union. Kohl's tenure as Chancellor of Germany, at sixteen years, was longer than that of any German chancellor since Otto von Bismarck. The aura surrounding him eventually wore off amid continuing problems in the newly reunified Germany, including high unemployment. In 1998, the German electorate turned once again to the Social Democrats under the leadership of **Gerhard Schröder**.

Schröder had promised more jobs during the 1998 election, and during his first term, unemployment did go down, only to rise back up to the level he had inherited from Kohl and later to a record-breaking level. After narrowly winning reelection in 2002, in large part because of his strong opposition to the looming U.S.-led invasion of Iraq, Schröder introduced several reforms that many perceived as a dismantlement of the welfare state. These reforms were very unpopular with the core constituency of the Social Democrats. In July of 2005, Schröder intentionally lost a vote of confidence in the Bundestag (German parliament) paving the way for early elections in September of that year.

Angela Merkel of the CDU became the first female chancellor of Germany in November of 2005 after striking a coalition deal with the Social Democrats, brought about by the extremely close election in September of that same year whereby no party received a majority of seats in the Bundestag. So far, the German economy under Merkel is booming and her approval rating is high. As any politician will tell you, however, what goes up can just as easily come down. Time will tell how successful Germany is in dealing with its tough domestic issues.

THE COLLAPSE OF THE COMMUNIST BLOC

Having suffered two foreign invasions in the twentieth century, the Soviet Union set as its priority the establishment of a system of satellite states in Eastern Europe. The Soviet Union created the Warsaw Pact in 1955 to establish military ties with its satellite states and the COMENCON to link their economies. From the start, however, there was tension.

REFORM IN HUNGARY

In 1953, East German workers went to the streets first to criticize the government's plan to increase productivity, then later to demand greater political freedom. By 1961, life was so grim in East Germany that millions of individuals fled to the West, which led the Soviets to construct the **Berlin Wall**.

EAST GERMANY AND THE BERLIN WALL

In 1956, similar strikes in Poland set off an even more important movement for change in Hungary, where reform-minded communists led by Imre Nagy took the helm of government and began a liberalizing process. The Hungarians wanted to create a multiparty system, pull themselves out of the Warsaw Pact, and reestablish Hungary as a neutral nation. By late 1956, the Soviets grew tired of such demands that threatened the whole system of satellite states and crushed the reform movement, killing thousands along the way.

POWER STRUGGLES IN THE SOVIET UNION

Within the Soviet Union, significant developments followed the death of Stalin in 1953. The winner of the power struggle for his replacement was **Nikita Khrushchev** (1894–1971), who, in a significant reversal from the previous regime, did not execute the losers in this political contest. At the Communist Party's twentieth national congress in 1956, Khrushchev, standing before a secret session, made a speech in which he attacked the many crimes of Stalin. Khrushchev claimed that Stalin's government had deviated from the political program of Marxist-Leninism, rather than being a natural outgrowth of it, and that the only reforms that would be acceptable would be those that stayed within the guidelines offered by Marxist-Leninism. Although Khrushchev made a successful visit to the United States in 1959 (and was disappointed when he was not allowed to visit Disneyland due to security concerns), tensions between the two nations were heightened in the following year when the Soviet Union shot down an American U-2 spy plane over Russia. By October 1962, the two nuclear superpowers nearly went to war when the Soviets placed missiles in Cuba. President Kennedy's skillful handling of the crisis, however, allowed both nations to avoid the specter of a nuclear nightmare.

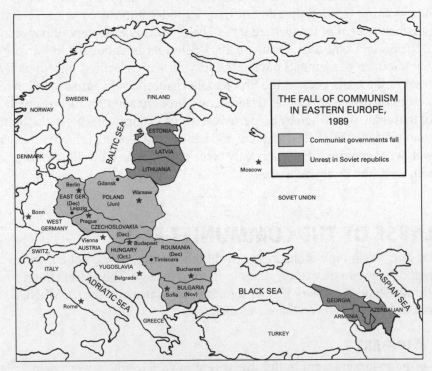

The Fall of Communism in Eastern Europe

The relative liberalization of the Khrushchev years came to an end with his forced retirement in 1964. His successor, Leonid Brezhnev (1906–1982), did not reinstate the terror of the Stalin years, but he did seek to once again strengthen the role of the party bureaucracy and the **KGB** and encouraged the further clamp down on reform in the satellite states.

By 1968, disaffection with this step backward led to the emergence in 1968 of a reform movement in Czechoslovakia. The goal of this **"Prague Spring"** was to bring about a more humanistic socialism within certain limits, such as keeping the nation within the Soviet Bloc. Brezhnev still saw this as a threat to the entire Warsaw Pact and initiated what became known as the **"Brezhnev Doctrine,"** declaring that the Soviet Union would support with all the means at its disposal (including military intervention) any established communist state in Eastern Europe that was threatened by internal strife. The reform movement was crushed and its leader, Alexander Dubĉek, was replaced by someone more to Brezhnev's liking.

REFORM IN POLAND AND EASTERN EUROPE

The most significant challenge to the Brezhnev Doctrine came in Poland, a land whose people were deeply stirred when in 1978 Karol Wojtyla, a Polish Cardinal, was elected **Pope John Paul II**. Two years later, led by Lech Walesa, an electrician, a massive strike took place at the Lenin shipyard in Gdansk, where workers demanded the right to form an independent trade union. **Solidarity**, as the new union was called, survived the declaration of martial law and being outlawed by going underground, in part with the aid of the Catholic Church. By 1989, the Polish economy was in such a shambles that the government was forced to negotiate with Walesa and his union. Surprisingly, the negotiations resulted in the promise for multiparty elections, which when they took place in that same year, resulted in the defeat of all Communist candidates.

When the reform-minded **Mikhail Gorbachev** (b. 1931) took charge of the Kremlin, he indicated his opposition to the "Brezhnev Doctrine." With reform looming overhead, 1989 proved to be one of the most remarkable years of the century, as Communist-led regimes peacefully collapsed in Hungary, Czechoslovakia, Bulgaria, and Albania. In East Germany, the collapse of the regime in that same year was followed in 1990 by the reunification of East and West Germany and the destruction of the Berlin Wall. Romania proved to be an exception to this peaceful transformation, as the violent dictator **Nicolae Ceausescu** (1918–1989) desperately tried to hold on to power. In the end, his government collapsed, and he and his wife, Elena, were executed on Christmas Day 1989.

THE COLLAPSE OF THE SOVIET UNION

As their satellite states underwent a complete political transformation, people within the Soviet Union expressed their desire for change. Disasters like the Soviet invasion of Afghanistan and the nuclear accident at Chernobyl revealed the deplorable state of affairs within the nation. Gorbachev wanted to limit the extent of this change; he accepted the need for *glasnost*, or openness in debate, as well as *perestroika*, an economic restructuring of the state, but he was no democrat and still wanted to see the Communist Party lead these reforms. Events, however, went beyond his control, and in 1990, the government was forced to allow the political participation of non-Communist parties. Nationalist movements throughout the Soviet Union also popped up, beginning with the declaration of independence by Lithuania, followed by the insistence of the Russian Republic, another Soviet state, that its laws superceded those of the Soviet Union.

By the end of 1990, Gorbachev appointed some hard-liners to government positions to make the prospect of future reform far less likely. Instead, the whole system collapsed. In part, this was the result of the rivalry between Gorbachev and **Boris Yeltsin** (b. 1931), who served as chairman of the Russian Parliament. In August 1991, hard-line communists decided that Gorbachev's policies were threatening the existence of the Communist Party and staged a coup while Gorbachev was on vacation, placing him under arrest in his Crimean home. This turned out to be the last gasp of the Soviet Union, as Yeltsin bravely defied the plotters when he stood on a tank outside the parliament building and led the resistance. The coup failed and with it any hope of preserving communist control. One by one, the assorted republics left the Soviet Union, and by the end of 1991, the Soviet Union was dissolved; soon after, Gorbachev resigned.

A New Russian Republic

In 1991, Yeltsin was elected president of the newly created Russian Federation with 57 percent of the vote amid heightened expectations among Russians following the end of the Soviet Union. Sadly, when he resigned from office in 1999, Yeltsin acknowledged that his time in office was a lost opportunity, and in his resignation speech, he went so far as to say to his nation, "I want to ask you for forgiveness, because many of our dreams have not been realized."

Beginning his first term in office, Yeltsin decided to rapidly move the economy from centralized state control to free-market capitalism, a policy recommended by many foreign economists, including advisors from the International Monetary Fund. This policy, which supporters and skeptics both referred to as "shock treatment," was based on significant short-term economic dislocation followed by greater economic stability and expansion. Unfortunately, the pain proved even harsher than expected and was marked by the seizure of state assets by a handful of well-placed oligarchs and hyperinflation, which created turmoil for millions of Russians who depended on fixed state pensions. Official corruption and the emergence of vast mafia-style criminal organizations also became mainstays of the new Russian state and greatly contributed to a diminishment of Yeltsin's popularity.

The transition to political democracy was equally troubled. Conflict with the Congress of People's Deputies (the parliament of the Russian Federation) over his economic policies brought about a series of confrontations with parliament, leading to a serious crisis in October 1993 when the Congress began impeachment proceedings against the president. Yeltsin responded by ordering tanks to shell the building where the Congress met and ordered the legislature to be dissolved. Without a recalcitrant parliament to block his plans, Yeltsin was able to impose a new constitution providing enhanced power for the presidency and the establishment of the Duma, a new parliamentary body.

In 1996, Yeltsin surprised many Kremlin observers by running for reelection, despite having suffered several strokes and also publicly displaying occasional incapacity due to possible problems with alcohol. When his reelection seemed about to be derailed by a growing electoral threat from a resurgent communist party, Yeltsin turned to the business oligarchs who agreed to fund a lavish campaign for him in exchange for greater access to the remaining state assets, although the oligarchs were also fearful that the election of a communist government would hinder their economic activities. Yeltsin comfortably won reelection, but except for working out a peace treaty that brought an end to the fighting with separatists in Chechnya, there were few other significant accomplishments during his second term.

Just prior to his resignation in December 1999, Yeltstin chose the relatively unknown Vladimir Putin as his prime minister. A former officer in the KGB, one of Putin's first acts upon assuming the presidency was to protect Yeltsin and his family from prosecution for corruption. Because other possible presidential candidates were surprised by the rapid promotion of Putin and the resignation of Yeltsin, Putin had a tremendous political advantage over his rivals and was easily elected to his own term as president in 2000.

Democracy, which never truly thrived under Yeltsin, has received further blows during Putin's presidency, such as in the aftermath of the Beslan massacre of September 2004, when Chechen terrorists seized control of a school leading to the death of over three hundred hostages. The tragedy was used by Putin as an excuse for enacting a law that ended the practice of popular elections for governors in Russia's provinces, with the spurious claim that it would be more efficient to fight terror with a more centralized government. The suspicious deaths of several Russian journalists and the poisoning in London of former spy and Putin critic Alexander Litvinenko has further chilled the political climate in Russia.

In sharp contrast with Yeltsin, Putin has garnered significant popular support among Russians and he would have been easily reelected in 2004 even if he did not have control over most media outlets. Part of his popularity stems from the rise in worldwide oil prices, which has provided a huge boost to the Russian economy, although once again, Russia is in danger of repeating the Soviet mistake of the 1970s when it became too dependent on the proceeds from this one commodity.

Many Russians have also embraced Putin's attempt to restore Russia to a higher place on the world stage. After a sharp military decline in the 1990s, Putin is seeking to restore Russia's military might, although against what threat is not clear. He has also at times made use of the sort of rhetoric denouncing the West that has not been used since the Cold War and has ordered the resumption of regular patrols of strategic bombers, which were suspended in 1991.

Putin's second term comes to an end in 2008. The Russian constitution limits the president to two consecutive terms, although there is no barrier to Putin running in 2012. Whether Putin will alter the constitution and remain in office beyond 2008 or will seek to wield power behind the scenes is the major political question facing Russia today.

ETHNIC WARFARE IN THE FORMER YUGOSLAVIA

Uncertainty has been the hallmark of the former Yugoslavia. Its former leader, Josip Tito (1892–1980), led a successful resistance force against the Germans during the Second World War and after the war helped establish a Yugoslav state that avoided being tied to the Soviet Bloc. His strong leadership limited the intense ethnic rivalries within the country, but after he died in 1980, Slovenia and Croatia broke away from Yugoslavia to create their own states.

In 1992, a majority of the Muslim and Croat populations living in the Yugoslavian province of Bosnia wanted to follow suit. Bosnia's Serbs, however, refused to allow themselves to become part of a Bosnian state in which they would be a minority, and with the help of Yugoslavian President **Slobodan Milosevic**, they carried out "**ethnic cleansing,**" the forced removal and, at times, execution, of Muslims in certain regions under their control. One of the last great atrocities of a century that has known so many was the Serb shelling of the Bosnian capital of Sarejevo, particularly the firing of shells on market days, when more people would be out on the streets. Such horrors led to the American-brokered **Dayton Accords** of 1995, which provided for a precarious peace for a time.

The next stage of the conflict in the Balkans centered on the Yugoslav province of **Kosovo**, a territory that the Serbs saw as the cradle of their national identity, stemming from their defeat in the Battle of Kosovo against the Ottoman Turks in 1389. In 1998, Milosevic ordered an assault on Kosovo, using as his justification the attacks made on Serbs living in the province by the Kosovo Liberation Army (K.L.A.), a small militant group that wanted to see the creation of an independent Kosovo. When the Serbs refused to sign a treaty that would have granted the Kosovars greater autonomy, NATO in March 1999 launched an aerial bombardment on Serbia that lasted for 74 days. This was the first offensive action taken by NATO against a sovereign nation in the alliance's history and resulted in the withdrawal of Serbian troops from Kosovo.

For Milosevic, this was the beginning of the end of his dominance over Yugoslavian politics. In 2000, he was forced to call new elections, which he lost to Vojislav Kostunica. While Milosevic was reluctant to turn over the reins of government to Kostunica, his hand was forced when hundreds of thousands of Serbs went into the street to demand he honor the election results. Though initially President Kostunica said that he would not turn Milosevic over to the **War Crimes Tribunal** in The Hague, he changed his mind in 2001 in order to receive badly needed economic assistance from the West.

CHAPTER TIMELINE

Year	Event
1941	Atlantic Charter
1944	Percentages Agreement between Churchill and Stalin
1945	Yalta Conference (February 4–11)
1945	Hitler commits suicide (April 30)
1945	V-E Day (May 8)
1945	Victory of British Labour Party over Conservatives (July)
1945	Potsdam Conference (July 17–August 2)
1945	Atomic bomb dropped on Hiroshima (August 6)
1945	V-J Day (August 14)
1945	United Nations' charter is ratified (October)
1945	Nuremberg Trials for crimes against humanity begin (November)
1946	Establishment of French Fourth Republic
1946	Referendum establishes the Italian Republic
1946	Churchill delivers Iron Curtain speech at Westminster College
1947	George Kennan writes the "Long Telegram"
1947	Truman Doctrine
1947	Introduction of the Marshall Plan
1947	India and Pakistan become independent states
1948	Break between the Soviet Union and Yugoslavia
1948	Establishment of the State of Israel
1948	National Health Service established in Great Britain

Year	Event
1948	Soviet dominance in Eastern Europe solidified
1949	Formation of NATO
1949	Berlin Airlift leads to ending of blockade after 11 months
1949	Establishment of the Federal Republic of Germany
1949	Establishment of Democratic Republic of Germany
1951	Establishment of the European Coal and Steel Community
1953	Death of Stalin
1954	French suffer defeat in Indochina
1954	Algerian revolt begins
1955	Establishment of the Warsaw Pact
1956	Soviets send in troops to put down Hungarian uprising
1957	Ghana declares its independence from Great Britain
1957	Signing of the Treaty of Rome establishing the EEC
1958	French plebiscite leads to creation of the Fifth Republic
1961	East Germany begins construction of wall dividing Berlin
1962	France vetoes Britain's attempt to join the European Community
1962	Cuban missile crisis
1968	Wave of student protests in Europe and the United States
1968	Prague Spring
1969	Willy Brandt becomes German chancellor
1972	Irish Troubles begin with the shooting of 13 Catholic peace marchers on "Bloody Sunday"
1973	Oil crisis

Year	Event
1978	Red Brigades kidnap and murder former Prime Minister Aldo Moro
1978	Papal election of John Paul II
1979	Margaret Thatcher becomes Prime Minister
1981	Francois Mitterand elected president of France
1985	Mikhail Gorbachev becomes leader of the Soviet Union
1989	End of Communist rule in Eastern Europe
1990	Reunification of Germany
1991	End of the Soviet Union
1992	Maastricht Treaty
1992	Beginning of a series of violent conflicts in the former Yugoslavia
1997	Tony Blair becomes Prime Minister
2002	Introduction of the Euro
2004	Entry into NATO of former Warsaw Pact nations

REVIEW QUESTIONS

Answers and explanations are in Chapter 15.

1. The Atlantic Charter was the founding document behind what entity?

   (A) The World Bank
   (B) The International Monetary Fund
   (C) The World Court
   (D) The European Union
   (E) The United Nations

2. The Percentages Agreement signed between Stalin and Churchill dealt with

   (A) Yugoslavia's future under Tito
   (B) the political future of Poland
   (C) spheres of influence in Eastern Europe
   (D) the question of postwar reparations
   (E) the opening of a second front by 1944

3. The Truman Doctrine came about as a direct result of

   (A) the conflict over Iran
   (B) remaining issues from the Potsdam conference
   (C) the presence of Soviet troops in Poland
   (D) the issue of the status of Berlin
   (E) Britain's withdrawal from Greece

4. During the "Prague Spring" of 1968, Czechoslovakia attempted to

   (A) break completely free from the influence of the Soviet Union
   (B) end military links with the Warsaw Pact nations
   (C) introduce a capitalist economy
   (D) allow freedom of the press
   (E) end the practice of forced food exports to the Soviet Union

5. The German "Economic Miracle" was in part due to

   (A) socialization of the means of production
   (B) a labor force enlarged by Germans fleeing from the east
   (C) a high degree of central planning
   (D) limiting overseas investment
   (E) tight monetary policies

6. All of the following are true concerning the student revolts in Paris in 1968 EXCEPT

   (A) they involved student organizations with differing ideological agendas
   (B) they stemmed from overcrowding in French universities
   (C) they helped spark a general strike by French workers
   (D) they caused the fall of Charles de Gaulle's government
   (E) they were partly in reaction to the Vietnam War

7. Mikhail Gorbachev's Perestroika program

   (A) ended the practice of central economic planning
   (B) failed to improve the average Russian's standard of living
   (C) provided the economic foundation for improved foreign ties with the West
   (D) focused on heavy industry at the expense of consumer products
   (E) was primarily aimed at addressing the extreme shortage of housing

15

Answers and Explanations for Review Questions

CHAPTER 7

1. Humanist scholars broke with the medieval scholarly tradition

   (A) in declaring that all knowledge was relative
   (B) by insisting on reading the original manuscript and not a second-hand commentary
   (C) by challenging the existence of God
   (D) by supporting the idea of scientific experimentation
   (E) by rejecting the central authority of the church

1. **B** While medieval scholars read second-hand commentaries on ancient works, the humanists, inspired by the example of Petrarch, sought out the manuscripts in their original form.

2. All of the following are characteristics of Renaissance art EXCEPT

   (A) the use of oil paints
   (B) the emphasis on naturalism
   (C) the desire to create three-dimensional images
   (D) secular portraiture
   (E) hierarchical scaling

2. **E** Renaissance artists rejected the practice of hierarchical scaling, in which the size of figures in a composition is proportionate to their spiritual significance, in favor of a greater emphasis on realism. For example, Leonardo, in his *Last Supper*, emphasized Christ's significance not by rendering him as larger than his disciples but by placing him at the center of the painting.

3. What was the initial reaction of Pope Leo X to the posting of Luther's *95 Theses*?

   (A) He declared Luther to be a heretic.
   (B) He immediately summoned Luther to Rome.
   (C) He recalled Tetzel from Germany in order to have him stop selling indulgences.
   (D) He declared that Luther's action was a significant threat to the unity of the church.
   (E) He claimed he was not interested in a squabble among monks.

3. **E** Pope Leo X made the assumption that since Luther was an Augustinian monk and Tetzel the main seller of indulgences was a Dominican, the *95 Theses* were simply a typical squabble between religious orders. Leo had not counted on the fact that the printing press would enable Luther to reach an audience far beyond his native city of Wittenberg. The lack of a more determined response by the Catholic Church in the early stages of the Reformation played a major role in the successful spread of Luther's ideas.

QUESTIONS	EXPLANATIONS

4. Which of the following best describes Luther's position on the social questions of his day?

(A) He wanted to see marked improvements in the lives of the peasantry.

(B) He was deeply concerned about these questions but feared antagonizing his aristocratic supporters.

(C) He was a deeply conservative man who did not want to upset the traditional social order.

(D) He feared that his religious reforms would fail unless they were combined with a program to address social concerns.

(E) He blamed the Catholic Church for maintaining a spiritual as well as social hierarchy.

4. C Luther had very little interest in social issues and was furious when German peasants tied some of his theological ideas to certain social goals such as the elimination of serfdom. His lack of interest in challenging the existing social order encouraged some German rulers to support his religious ideas because they didn't pose a challenge to their primacy in the social hierarchy.

5. Following the death of her half-sister Mary, Queen Elizabeth of England pursued which of the following religious policies?

(A) She followed her father's example and refused to embrace either Protestantism or Catholicism.

(B) She followed Mary's policy by keeping England within the Catholic Church.

(C) She began a massive persecution of Catholics on the charge of heresy.

(D) She broke with Rome and established a moderate Protestant church.

(E) She waited to make a decision on religious matters until many years into her reign.

5. D In 1559, one year after coming to the throne, Elizabeth worked out a religious settlement that led to a formal break with Rome and the creation of a Church of England that emphasized middle-of-the-road Protestant beliefs.

6. Family life was directly influenced during the Protestant Reformation by

   (A) the doctrine of salvation by grace alone
   (B) changes in land-holding patterns by German peasants
   (C) Protestant emphasis on primogeniture
   (D) Martin Luther's decision to marry and start a family
   (E) women who led Anabaptist congregations

6. **D** While many were surprised by his decision, the 42-year-old Luther's marriage to Katherine von Bora emphasized his refusal to accept the need for clerical celibacy. By marrying the 26-year-old former nun and having six children, Luther placed the family at the center of religious faith rather than the institutional church.

7. For most Florentines, work was tied to

   (A) banking
   (B) the production of wool cloth
   (C) mercenary activities
   (D) the church
   (E) the manufacture of leather goods

7. **B** The majority of Florence's population of 60,000 in the fifteenth century was involved in the most important commodity produced in Florence, wool cloth, which it exported to the rest of Europe.

CHAPTER 8

1. Which of the following European states was the first to send sailors into the Indian Ocean?

   (A) France
   (B) Great Britain
   (C) Portugal
   (D) Spain
   (E) Genoa

1. **C** In 1498, Vasco da Gama, a Portuguese captain, reached the coast of India.

2. The Spanish term *Reconquista* refers to which of the following?

   (A) Spain's victory over the French in northern Italy
   (B) The defeat of the Islamic states on the Spanish peninsula
   (C) The long sought rapprochement with Portugal
   (D) The beginnings of Habsburg rule in Spain
   (E) The sailing of the Armada against England

2. **B** 1492 marked the final stage of the *Reconquista*, the long struggle by the Christian states in the north of the Spanish peninsula against the Muslims. In that year, Grenada, the last Islamic outpost in Spain, fell to the armies of Ferdinand and Isabella.

3. King Gustavus Adolphus of Sweden entered the Thirty Years War in 1629 in order to

   (A) forestall the entry of France into the conflict
   (B) aid the Habsburg cause
   (C) neutralize the potential threat from England
   (D) defend Protestant interests in the Holy Roman Empire
   (E) keep Habsburg troops from directly entering Swedish territory

3. **D** Bankrolled by a French monarchy that wished to see its rivals the Habsburgs weakened, Gustavus Adolphus entered the conflict in part to seek territorial gains for Sweden along the Baltic coast but also to defend Protestant interests in the Empire that had recently come under attack following the issuing of the Edict of Restitution.

QUESTIONS	EXPLANATIONS
4. Which of the following individuals said, "Paris is worth a Mass"? (A) Cardinal Richelieu (B) Henry IV (C) Louis XIII (D) Catherine de Medici (E) Louis XIV	4. **B** After becoming King of France in 1589, Henry IV, a Calvinist, found that he was unable to gain control over Paris due to the strong Catholic sentiments of the inhabitants of the city. Never one to take his religious beliefs all too seriously, Henry decided it would be expeditious to convert to Catholicism in order to control the French capital.
5. King Charles I of England was forced to call a parliament in 1640 following (A) the outbreak of a rebellion in Scotland (B) the declaration of war between France and England (C) the demands of Parliament to be called into session (D) a mass public outcry demanding that a new parliamentary session be called (E) a declaration of royal bankruptcy	5. **A** King Charles was able to rule without calling a parliament so long as he kept his expenditures to a minimum. This proved to be impossible in 1640, when a rebellion broke out in Scotland following Charles's insistence on placing the *Book of Common Prayer* in Scottish churches. In order to raise an army to put down the rebellious Scots, Charles was forced to call his first parliament in 11 years.

6. In the Early Modern period, urban disturbances among journeymen and apprentices were most often related to

   (A) resentment by apprentices against the socially higher journeymen
   (B) the banning of guilds by increasingly centralized monarchies
   (C) a decline in population leading to falling prices
   (D) growing social tensions between various guilds
   (E) social tensions stemming from the inability to enter the rank of masters

6. **E** While urban riots stemmed from a variety of causes, those disturbances that saw the extensive participation of journeymen and apprentices were often tied to their growing frustration over a glass ceiling that now limited their opportunities. With the guild method of production being replaced by large-scale production featuring capitalist entrepreneurs, the economically hard-pressed guilds were increasingly reluctant to see further competition and therefore limited the number of entrants into the ranks of guild master.

7. Which of the following best describes the Early Modern family as an economic unit?

   (A) Males were in the "public" sphere while females were in the "domestic."
   (B) Male and female roles were largely interchangeable among the peasantry but not among the bourgeoisie.
   (C) The family as an economic unit was collapsing following the introduction of capitalist production methods.
   (D) Larger immediate families meant that extended families were no longer part of the same economic unit.
   (E) Child labor was no longer as essential a component in an age of economic expansion.

7. **A** While both rich and poor families in the Early Modern period can be viewed as an economic unit, there were significant gender differences within this unit. While men served in the "public" sphere, such as working the family's plot of land or handling commercial transactions, women were expected to remain exclusively tied to the "domestic" sphere by either doing the housework themselves or, if wealthier, supervising such activities.

CHAPTER 9

1. Medieval science was primarily based on

    (A) close observations of nature
    (B) pure superstition
    (C) the experimental method
    (D) a blending of Christian theology and the writings of classical authors
    (E) decrees emanating from the papacy

1. **D** Medieval science consisted of a synthesis of Christian theology and classical authors. The Scientific Revolution would bring about a rejection of this synthesis in favor of a new brand of science in which the experimental method would predominate.

2. Which of the following individuals was responsible for first describing the elliptical motion of the planets around the sun?

    (A) Newton
    (B) Galileo
    (C) Copernicus
    (D) Kepler
    (E) Brahe

2. **D** In his *Concerning the Revolutions of the Celestial Spheres*, Copernicus hypothesized that the planets moved around the sun in perfect circles. It was Johannes Kepler, however, who was the first to explain that the planets moved in an elliptical orbit around the sun.

3. In *Leviathan*, Thomas Hobbes became an advocate for which of the following types of government?

    (A) Absolute monarchy
    (B) Parliamentary government
    (C) Divine-right monarchy
    (D) Constitutional monarchy
    (E) Democracy

3. **A** After viewing the horrors of the English Revolution, Thomas Hobbes wrote *Leviathan* to show that men were naturally depraved and therefore required an absolutist state in order to rein in their evil passions.

QUESTIONS	EXPLANATIONS

4. Women played their most prominent role during the Enlightenment by

    (A) serving as a major topic for the philosophes
    (B) writing books and political tracts
    (C) declining to participate in any social events
    (D) sponsoring salons
    (E) rejecting enlightened ideals

4. **D** Women played an important role in the Enlightenment by sponsoring salons, where philosophes could speak on an informal basis with the elite of society.

5. Deists such as Voltaire believe that

    (A) God reveals himself through miracles
    (B) there is no God
    (C) God created the universe but then played no additional role in shaping the course of events
    (D) a state church is necessary
    (E) limited religious toleration should be encouraged

5. **C** Deists such as Voltaire believe that God created the world but then played no additional role in overseeing his creation. Science must therefore be used to explain the workings of the universe.

6. Rousseau's *Émile* influenced the way people viewed childhood

   (A) by emphasizing the need to teach emotional restraint
   (B) by suggesting it as the time in which to install the benefits of a rational education
   (C) by emphasizing that children were not merely small adults
   (D) by positioning it as the critical focus for the family dynamic
   (E) by framing it as a mirror to adult behaviors

6. **C** As surprising as it may seem, prior to the eighteenth century, children were viewed simply as smaller versions of adults (something that is quite apparent when looking at medieval images of Mary holding an infant Christ looking like an adult in miniature). The change in this perception owes a great deal to Rousseau's *Émile* and his description of three distinct stages on the road to adulthood: infancy, childhood, and adolescence.

7. Mary Wollstonecraft's *Vindication of the Rights of Women*

   (A) focused primarily on economic issues such as property rights
   (B) served as the inspiration for a small group of eighteenth century women who formed the first female suffrage organization
   (C) was the first work to openly state the need for women to enjoy the full political rights of men
   (D) failed to find a publisher during her lifetime
   (E) directly influenced the "women's question" during the French Revolution

7. **C** Angered by a 1791 report to the French Revolutionary government that stated women should only receive an education geared toward their domestic duties, Mary Wollstonecraft wrote her *Vindication of the Rights of Women* in response to what she saw as sexual double standards. While the primary focus of the book is on the issue of equality of education, Wollstonecraft does state the need for equality in political rights.

CHAPTER 10

1. At the start of the Estates General, members of the Third Estate refused to have their credentials officially recognized because

   (A) they resented that the three estates met and voted separately
   (B) they doubted that decisions would be made by fully democratic means
   (C) the aristocracy also refused to show credentials
   (D) they resented the attempt to include peasants within the Third Estate
   (E) the king refused to hold future meetings of the Estates General

1. **A** The members of the Third Estate realized that if voting was done by estate they would consistently be outvoted by the clergy and aristocracy. Therefore, they refused to show their credentials unless the king met all attendees of the Estates General in a National Assembly, a new legislative body where there would be no further distinctions based on social class.

2. The Bastille was a symbol of royal power because

   (A) the king used it as his residence in Paris
   (B) it had housed political prisoners
   (C) wheat for bread was stored there
   (D) it was located at Versailles
   (E) it was built by Louis XVI with forced labor

2. **B** The Bastille was traditionally the place where prisoners of conscience were kept for opposing the Bourbon monarchy. Though by 1789, the year the prison was stormed, it no longer housed political prisoners, it still stood as a symbol of royal repression.

3. The significance of the women's march on Versailles on October 5, 1789 was that

   (A) it led to cheaper bread prices
   (B) it resulted in the king being brought back to Paris
   (C) the leaders of the march were immediately arrested
   (D) it was used by the Jacobins as justification for the elimination of the Girondins
   (E) it marked the only instance in which women participated in the events of the revolution

3. **B** The march of the women of Paris on Versailles was one of the turning points of the French Revolution since the march ended with Louis XVI and his family returning to Paris with the women. Paris was far more radical than any other locality in France, and with the king now within the confines of the city, the revolution would advance much further than if the king had remained at Versailles.

QUESTIONS	EXPLANATIONS

4. The Continental System represented Napoleon's attempt to

    (A) lead the continent in a potential struggle with the United States
    (B) close off the continent to British trade
    (C) create a continent-wide parliament
    (D) issue a new code of law
    (E) draft soldiers throughout Europe into his Grand Army

4. B After realizing that he could not defeat the British navy, Napoleon decided to wage economic war on Britain through his Continental System, which closed the European continent to British imports and exports.

5. Napoleon's Civil Code allowed for

    (A) the elimination of private property
    (B) full property rights for women
    (C) special rights for those holding aristocratic titles
    (D) taxation of all social classes
    (E) the rights of the accused to be considered innocent until proven guilty

5. D The Napoleonic Code enshrined one of the fundamental ideas of the French Revolution: There were no special rights based on social class and therefore everyone was responsible for the payment of taxes.

6. The *sans-culottes*

    (A) were tied to the Girondins
    (B) recoiled from the use of violence
    (C) failed to recognize the legitimacy of the National Guard
    (D) were primarily peasants
    (E) consisted of the working-class people of Paris

6. E The *sans-culottes*, who proudly wore pants rather than the silk breeches of wealthier Parisians, were members of the working class and played a vital role in the growing radicalization of the French Revolution. It was support from the *sans-culottes* that allowed the Jacobins to push the Girondins out of the National Assembly and assume control over the Revolutionary government.

7. Baron von Stein challenged the traditional social structure in Prussia by

    (A) allowing the bourgeoisie to enter the officer corps
    (B) advocating a constitutional monarchy
    (C) pushing for a bourgeois led government
    (D) ending agricultural subsidies for the Junkers
    (E) eliminating the rights of the free peasantry

7. A While abhorring what he felt was the anarchism of the French Revolution, Baron von Stein recognized that there were new forces being introduced into Europe by the power of nationalism. To that end, von Stein directly challenged one of the key rights of the Prussian Junkers—their exclusive hold over the officer corps by placing members of the bourgeoisie within their ranks.

CHAPTER 11

1. The end of the Corn Laws in Great Britain in 1846 was an indication that

   (A) the government was fully responsive to the needs of workers
   (B) the industrial revolution was beginning to slow down
   (C) grain was now available in abundance
   (D) the role of the monarchy was in decline
   (E) the old landed classes no longer fully dominated British politics

1. E The Corn Laws provided for high tariffs for wheat imported into Great Britain. While the law was hailed by the landed classes, who wanted to keep foreign grain out of the country so they could have exclusive rights to the British market, it was hated by the middle-class manufacturers, who believed that expensive bread forced them to pay higher wages. Getting rid of the Corn Laws was a sign that the middle class, which had entered Parliament as a result of the Great Reform Bill of 1832, was now a force to be reckoned with in British politics.

2. During the 1848 revolution in France, liberals and radicals differed over

   (A) whether to establish a republic
   (B) allowing Louis Napoleon to return to France
   (C) whether political changes or social and economic changes should take priority
   (D) what to do concerning Louis Philippe and his family
   (E) universal male suffrage

2. C While the middle-class liberals viewed the revolution as a means to securing political rights, the more radical workers hoped that the revolution would provide increased economic opportunities. Their demands led to the creation of national workshops that provided jobs for unemployed workers, this over the objections of the liberals, who viewed the workshops as a costly and unnecessary intrusion by the government into the economy.

3. All of the goals of the Chartist movement were eventually achieved in Great Britain EXCEPT

   (A) the secret ballot
   (B) annual parliaments
   (C) equal electoral districts
   (D) abolition of property requirements for Members of Parliament
   (E) salaries for Members of Parliament

3. B The Chartists believed that annual parliamentary elections were necessary in order to create a government more responsive to the needs of the people. This was the one point within the Six Acts of the People's Charter that was never implemented. Today the life of a British parliament is five years.

4. The first nation to industrialize on the continent was

   (A) Prussia
   (B) France
   (C) Belgium
   (D) Russia
   (E) Denmark

4. C Belgium, like Great Britain, was blessed with a ready supply of coal and iron as well as a stable government. With these advantages, it was able to become the first industrialized nation on the continent.

5. Rome became the capital of the new Italian nation

   (A) immediately upon the creation of Italy in 1861
   (B) after the withdrawal of French troops from the city during the Franco-Prussian War
   (C) as a result of its conquest by Garibaldi
   (D) after Cavour successfully negotiated the surrender of the city to the Italian government
   (E) with the approval of the papacy

5. **B** With the advent of the Franco-Prussian War in 1870, Napoleon III was forced to remove from Rome the French troops who were protecting the city on behalf of the papacy. Following this withdrawal, Italian troops entered the city, which became the new capital of the Italian state.

6. The significance of the Sadler Committee of 1832 was that it

   (A) eradicated the practice of child labor
   (B) refused for political reasons to come to firm conclusions
   (C) was the first parliamentary commission
   (D) revealed to a larger public the extent of child labor
   (E) committed Great Britain to easing labor shortages through immigration

6. **D** Collecting first hand testimony from adults who began their working lives as child laborers in factories and mines, the Sadler Committee brought child labor to the attention of the British public. The investigations of the committee would eventually lead to the passage of the Factory Act in 1833.

7. The freeing of Russia's serfs in 1861

   (A) led to an agricultural depression
   (B) required them to pay for their freedom in annual payments over fifty years
   (C) was met with firm opposition by the Tsar
   (D) led to a large emigration of Russian peasants to the United States
   (E) provided former serfs with adequate landholdings

7. **B** The emancipation decree signed by Tsar Alexander II in 1861 required the newly emancipated serfs to pay for their freedom in annual payments extending over fifty years. This practice was brought to an end as part of a series of concessions by the monarchy in the aftermath of the Revolution of 1905.

CHAPTER 12

1. The development of national postal services in the nineteenth century reveals all of the following EXCEPT

   (A) an increased role for government
   (B) the growth of the rail network
   (C) an increase in privatization of previously public services
   (D) an expansion of public education
   (E) the existence of large overseas émigré communities

1. **C** In the second half of the nineteenth century, governments throughout Europe began to develop postal systems, reflecting such factors as increased literacy through the expansion of public schools and the ability to move large quantities of letters through an ever increasing rail network. This clear cut expansion of the role of government is the direct opposite of choice C, which posits that European governments were stepping away from providing such services and expected private concerns to pick up the task.

2. The nature of anti-Semitism changed in the late nineteenth century

   (A) in that it became primarily tied to the working class
   (B) through the idea that Jews were a separate race
   (C) in that socialist parties directed their energies toward fighting it
   (D) in that Jewish communities didn't respond to it
   (E) as shown by a general decline in anti-Semitic attacks

2. **B** While anti-Semitism was certainly not new to the eighteenth century, its increased vehemence in part reflected a growing conviction among many that Jews were a separate racial category and as a result could never be properly integrated into society at large.

3. The term "informal empire" best describes the situation in

   (A) Rhodesia
   (B) the Congo
   (C) Indochina
   (D) India
   (E) China

3. **E** "Informal empire" refers to when a nation controls the economy and politics of another nation or territory. Prior to the expansion of direct colonial control in the period after 1870, nations such as Britain sought to secure their trading privileges without feeling the need to step in directly and rule. The situation in China serves as the best description of informal empire, since Britain, France, Germany, and other nations insisted on certain economic rights without directly controlling the vast Chinese state.

QUESTIONS	EXPLANATIONS

4. All of the following were invented during the Second Industrial Revolution (1850–1914) EXCEPT

    (A) synthetic dyes
    (B) dynamite
    (C) the power loom
    (D) the Bessemer process of steel production
    (E) the safety elevator

4. C While the other items on the list were all invented in the second half of the nineteenth century, the power loom was invented in 1785 by Edmund Cartwright and was one of the most important inventions of the Early Industrial Revolution.

5. The literary works of Charles Dickens, Émile Zola, and Gustave Flaubert are all considered to be part of which school of literature?

    (A) Realism
    (B) Gothic
    (C) Neo-Classicism
    (D) Romanticism
    (E) Modernism

5. A All of these writers are considered to be part of the realist tradition in literature. Realism was a movement in the nineteenth century that focused on depicting the relatively ordinary lives of the middle and working classes without relying on traditional embellishments such as the romanticization of their subject.

6. The Berlin Conference of 1885 was called to address the status of

    (A) India
    (B) the Congo
    (C) the Balkans
    (D) South Africa
    (E) Morocco

6. B While establishing the rules that European states needed to follow to show their control over the various parts of Africa, the Conference was initially called to deal with the status of the Congo, a territory that King Leopold II of Belgium was seeking to control for economic exploitation through the formation of what would eventually be known as the Congo Free State.

7. The Thomas Cook company

    (A) developed the idea of the "Grand Tour"
    (B) was the first firm to sell rail tickets
    (C) received a parliamentary charter in 1887
    (D) introduced package tours to Britain's middle class
    (E) was the first mass cruise company

7. D Thomas Cook's career as a travel agent began when he came up with the idea of providing travel arrangements for a group of fellow temperance advocates who were in need of transportation to a rally. By the 1860s, Cook was selling group tours to destinations such as Egypt, Italy, France, and Switzerland and introduced packaged foreign travel to the British middle class.

CHAPTER 13

1. During the first years of the Great Depression, governments responded to the economic crisis by

   (A) increasing their support for higher unemployment payments
   (B) supporting the economic ideas of John Maynard Keynes
   (C) launching major public works projects
   (D) committing their countries to a laissez-faire economic policy
   (E) reducing their expenditures in order to balance their budgets

1. **E** When the economic slowdown began, governments responded by following the standard economic theory of the day and reducing their expenditures in order to balance their budgets. Unfortunately, this had the unintended consequence of making the depression far worse, as declines in both governmental and individual consumption dramatically shrunk the global economy.

2. Mussolini attempted to improve the relationship between the Italian state and the Catholic Church by

   (A) mandating that all Italians attend mass
   (B) placing loyal fascists in key clerical positions
   (C) emphasizing his own path toward religious belief
   (D) signing the Lateran Treaty, which resolved some of the longstanding issues between the Church and the Italian state
   (E) returning all confiscated church property

2. **D** In 1929, Mussolini, an agnostic, decided to heal the long-term rift between the Papacy and the Italian state. With the Lateran Treaty, Mussolini allowed the pope to become the ruler of Vatican City, a district in the heart of Rome, in exchange for the Church's recognition of his fascist government.

3. The British won a major propaganda victory at the start of the First World War because of

   (A) the sinking of the *Lusitania*
   (B) the Zimmerman telegram
   (C) German atrocities in Belgium
   (D) the destruction by the Germans of major Parisian landmarks
   (E) the Battle of the Marne

3. **C** In the early stages of the war, German atrocities in neutral Belgium provided the British with a powerful propaganda tool both for domestic consumption as well as for the important task of swaying American public opinion.

QUESTIONS	EXPLANATIONS

4. The term "popular fronts" refers to the idea of

    (A) political parties of the center and the left working together to block the triumph of fascism

    (B) communists uniting with unions to oppose bourgeois governments

    (C) the elimination of class conflict

    (D) using German and Italian forces to support Spanish nationalists

    (E) coalition governments in Great Britain between the Labour Party and the Conservatives

4. A Popular front governments were created in France and Spain as a reaction to the triumph of fascism in Germany. Politicians of the left in both nations viewed the conflict between Communists and Social Democrats in Germany as having provided an opportunity for the ascendency of Hitler.

5. The Nuremberg Trial of 1945 was the first test in international law of the concept of

    (A) collective guilt

    (B) the natural rights of victims

    (C) crimes against humanity

    (D) genocide

    (E) supranational legal authority

5. C The term "crimes against humanity" was originally found in the preamble to the 1907 Hague Convention on War. At the conclusion of the Second World War, the Allied states formed an International Military Tribunal charged with prosecuting Nazi war criminals. One of the charges against the accused, "crimes against humanity," was the category used to cover the murder of millions of civilians by the Nazis.

6. The Matignon Agreements in France (1936)

    (A) failed to lead to the forty-hour work week

    (B) provided the legal right for unions to organize and strike

    (C) led to the end of the Popular Front government

    (D) ended the informal practice of owner-employee cooperation stemming from the Great War

    (E) satisfied the French far right while antagonizing the moderates and the left

6. B The Matignon Agreements, named after the hotel where the French government, employers, and the trade unions met and signed the accord, took place in the aftermath of a damaging general strike. The Agreements, the crowning achievement of Leon Blum's Popular Front government, for the first time provided a guarantee for French unions to organize and to strike.

7. The British government had an impact on private life during the First World War in all of the following ways EXCEPT

    (A) the regulation of pub hours

    (B) rationing

    (C) conscription

    (D) billeting of soldiers in civilian residences

    (E) mass propaganda

7. D Perhaps understanding that there's nothing worse than having a soldier as a forced houseguest, the British government did not house soldiers in private dwellings during the war.

CHAPTER 14

1. The Atlantic Charter was the founding document behind what entity?

   (A) The World Bank
   (B) The International Monetary Fund
   (C) The World Court
   (D) The European Union
   (E) The United Nations

2. The Percentages Agreement signed between Stalin and Churchill dealt with

   (A) Yugoslavia's future under Tito
   (B) the political future of Poland
   (C) spheres of influence in Eastern Europe
   (D) the question of postwar reparations
   (E) the opening of a second front by 1944

3. The Truman Doctrine came about as a direct result of

   (A) the conflict over Iran
   (B) remaining issues from the Potsdam conference
   (C) the presence of Soviet troops in Poland
   (D) the issue of the status of Berlin
   (E) Britain's withdrawal from Greece

4. During the "Prague Spring" of 1968, Czechoslovakia attempted to

   (A) break completely free from the influence of the Soviet Union
   (B) end military links with the Warsaw Pact nations
   (C) introduce a capitalist economy
   (D) allow freedom of the press
   (E) end the practice of forced food exports to the Soviet Union

1. **E** Meeting in July 1941 for the first time on a ship off the coast of Newfoundland, Roosevelt and Churchill issued a joint proclamation in which they declared that the struggle against the Axis powers was to "ensure life, liberty, independence, and religious freedom and to preserve the rights of man and justice." The Atlantic Charter served as the foundation for the later establishment of the United Nations, a central postwar goal for Roosevelt.

2. **C** On his own initiative, Churchill traveled to Moscow in October 1944 in an attempt to get Stalin to accept some sort of role for the Western Allies in Eastern Europe. The name of the agreement comes from the numbers that Churchill had scribbled on the piece of paper that he gave to Stalin, listing the various percentages of control that each of the Allies might expect to have in the postwar period.

3. **E** When the Second World War ended, Britain had 40,000 troops in Greece and was providing the military and financial support that allowed for the survival of the Greek government in its struggle with a Communist insurgency. Due to its own dire financial situation, Great Britain informed the United States that it would withdraw from Greece at the end of March 1947. To fill the void left by the British, Truman went before Congress and requested money for the Greeks, using the justification that the United States needed to support any nation that was trying to avoid subjugation by Communists. This later became known as the Truman Doctrine.

4. **D** In 1968, the "Prague Spring," a movement in Czechoslovakia that sought not to overturn the Socialist system but simply to allow greater personal liberties, such as freedom of the press, was brutally put down when the leader of the Soviet Union, Leonid Brezhnev, decided that the reform movement was a threat to Soviet dominance in Eastern Europe.

QUESTIONS	EXPLANATIONS

5. The German "Economic Miracle" was in part due to

   (A) socialization of the means of production
   (B) a labor force enlarged by Germans fleeing from the east
   (C) a high degree of central planning
   (D) limiting overseas investment
   (E) tight monetary policies

5. **B** Millions of Germans expelled from Poland and Czechoslovakia were joined by millions of other Germans fleeing from the approaching Red Army in a mass migration into what later became established as West Germany. These individuals were to provide the low wage—but relatively skilled workforce—that proved essential for the expansion of the German economy in the 1950s.

6. All of the following are true concerning the student revolts in Paris in 1968 EXCEPT

   (A) they involved student organizations with differing ideological agendas
   (B) they stemmed from overcrowding in French universities
   (C) they helped spark a general strike by French workers
   (D) they caused the fall of Charles de Gaulle's government
   (E) they were partly in reaction to the Vietnam War

6. **D** While the mass protests that hit France in the wake of the student revolt of May 1968 shook the government of Charles de Gaulle to its core, the parliamentary elections that took place the following month, in which the Gaullists won 358 of 487 seats, showed that de Gaulle still maintained the support of the majority of Frenchmen.

7. Mikhail Gorbachev's Perestroika program

   (A) ended the practice of central economic planning
   (B) failed to improve the standard of living
   (C) provided the economic foundation for improved foreign ties with the West
   (D) focused on heavy industry at the expense of consumer products
   (E) was primarily aimed at addressing the extreme shortage of housing

7. **B** Perestroika was an attempt to redirect the Soviet economy toward meeting consumer demand, but it was to do so within the continuing structure of central planning. This inability to break away from the limits of central planning led to the clear-cut failure of Perestroika and a general decline in living standards.

PART III

The Princeton Review AP European History Practice Tests and Explanations

16

Practice Test 1

EUROPEAN HISTORY

Three hours and five minutes are allotted for this examination: fifty-five minutes for Section I, which consists of multiple-choice questions, and two hours and ten minutes for Section II, which consists of essay questions. Fifteen minutes of Section II are devoted to a mandatory reading period, primarily for the document-based essay question in Part A. Section I is printed in this examination booklet; all Section II essay questions are printed in a separate green booklet. In determining your grade, the two sections are given equal weight.

SECTION I

Time—55 minutes

Number of questions—80

Percent of total grade—50

Because this section of the examination contains 80 multiple-choice questions, please be careful to fill in only the ovals that are preceded by numbers 1–80 on your answer sheet.

General Instructions

DO NOT OPEN THIS BOOKLET UNTIL YOU ARE INSTRUCTED TO DO SO.

INDICATE ALL YOUR ANSWERS TO QUESTIONS IN SECTION I ON THE SEPARATE ANSWER SHEET. No credit will be given for anything written in this examination booklet, but you may use the booklet for notes or scratchwork. After you have decided which of the suggested answers is best, COMPLETELY fill in the corresponding oval on the answer sheet. Give only one answer to each question. If you change an answer, be sure that the previous mark is erased completely.

Example: Sample Answer

Chicago is a

(A) state
(B) city
(C) country
(D) continent
(E) village

Many candidates wonder whether they should guess the answers to questions about which they are not certain. In this section of the examination, as a correction for haphazard guessing, one-fourth of the number of questions you answer incorrectly will be subtracted from the number of questions you answer correctly. It is improbable, therefore, that mere guessing will improve your score significantly; it may even lower your score, and it does take time. If, however, you are not sure of the best answer but have some knowledge of the question and are able to eliminate one or more of the answer choices as wrong, your chance of getting the right answer is improved, and it may be to your advantage to answer such a question.

Use your time effectively, working as rapidly as you can without losing accuracy. Do not spend too much time on questions that are too difficult. Go on to other questions and come back to the difficult ones later if you have time. It is not expected that everyone will be able to answer all the multiple-choice questions.

SECTION I

Time—55 minutes

80 Questions

<u>Directions:</u> Each of the questions or incomplete statements below is followed by five suggested answers or completions. Select the one that is best in each case, and then fill in the corresponding oval on the answer sheet.

1. Renaissance artists viewed the medieval past with

   (A) the same reverence that they held for the classical past
   (B) tremendous respect for their achievements, though they did not view them as equal to the ancients
   (C) no clear sense that their own age was distinct from the medieval period
   (D) disdain for what they perceived to be its backwardness
   (E) great interest because it served to inspire their own works of art

2. The revolt of the German peasants in 1525 was caused by all of the following EXCEPT

   (A) economic distress of the German peasants
   (B) increasing restrictions on the independence of the German peasantry
   (C) Martin Luther's call for a "priesthood of all believers"
   (D) encouragement by the Catholic Church for the peasants to rebel against Protestant nobles
   (E) the loss of hunting and fishing rights that had been taken by the nobles

3. John Calvin argued in his book, *Institutes of the Christian Religion*, that

   (A) grace could not be achieved without good works
   (B) grace was bestowed on few individuals, and the rest are destined for hell
   (C) salvation was the one topic that he could not fully explore because God's will in that area could never be known
   (D) grace was available to all who had faith
   (E) salvation was a sign of a compact between God and man

4. Before the Europeans invaded these territories, the Americas

   (A) contained powerful empires in both Mexico and Peru
   (B) remained divided into tiny tribal units
   (C) were on the verge of ocean discoveries of their own
   (D) remained for the most part completely without the means to wage war
   (E) were covered by migratory people who left no traces of urban life

5. Artists who worked in the Impressionist style attempted to

   (A) make their images as realistic as possible
   (B) show their disdain for the modern world
   (C) create images that blended with previously held artistic styles
   (D) propel their art into the modern world by refusing to paint nature
   (E) capture the initial fleeting effect that occurs when one first sees an object

6. The "Liberal Empire" of Napoleon III represented an attempt to

   (A) galvanize British support for France's struggle with Prussia
   (B) regain the lost glory of his uncle's reign
   (C) bring about an end of the monarchy with a slow evolution toward a republic
   (D) create a constitutional monarchy in the last years of Napoleon III's reign
   (E) show that France had not been eclipsed on the continent by the other great powers

GO ON TO THE NEXT PAGE

Annual Output of Steel
(in millions of metric tons)

Year	Britain	Germany	France	Russia
1875–1879	0.9	—	0.26	0.08
1880–1884	1.82	0.99	0.46	0.25
1885–1889	2.86	1.65	0.54	0.23
1890–1894	3.19	2.89	0.77	0.54
1895–1899	4.33	5.08	1.26	1.32
1900–1904	5.04	7.71	1.70	2.35
1905–1909	6.09	11.30	2.65	2.63
1910–1913	6.93	16.24	4.09	4.20

7. The table above supports which of the following statements?

(A) Steel was the most important product of the Second Industrial Revolution.
(B) Steel production in Russia was hindered by the incompetence of the tsarist regime.
(C) Steel production in Germany more than doubled in the first 15 years of the twentieth century.
(D) Steel's strength and durability give it a solid advantage over iron.
(E) Steel production in Great Britain increased by nearly 85 percent over the last decade of the nineteenth century.

8. Which of the following describes the reaction of the German kaiser following the assassination of the Archduke Franz Ferdinand?

(A) He urged that a European summit be held to possibly bring about a mediated compromise.
(B) He urged Austria to invade Serbia, because he feared that the crisis could destroy Austria.
(C) The kaiser remained indecisive on what to do and basically waited while events unfurled around him.
(D) The kaiser immediately sent troops into Russia to make sure the Russians could not come to the aid of their Serbian allies.
(E) The kaiser urged France and Great Britain to practice restraint before coming to the assistance of the Serbs.

9. Working and middle class individuals were united in opposition to

(A) the Factory Act
(B) Chartism
(C) the Reform Bill of 1867
(D) the Great Reform Bill of 1832
(E) the Corn Laws

10. At Yalta in February 1945, the Big Three—the United States, Great Britain, and the Soviet Union—agreed to

(A) postpone dealing with the question of what to do concerning Germany
(B) a post-war division of Germany into British, American, Soviet, and French occupation zones
(C) a two-bloc division in Europe, with the West under American domination and the East under Soviet control
(D) commence the distribution of American financial aid under the Marshall Plan
(E) distance themselves from the French, who under de Gaulle were making outlandish demands

11. Machiavelli's *The Prince* represented an attempt to find ways to

(A) blend medieval and Renaissance scholarship
(B) convince the French to intercede in Italian affairs on behalf of his native Florence
(C) show how the rule of princes was clearly inferior to republican forms of government
(D) unify the entire Italian peninsula under a powerful ruler
(E) show how a Christian prince can use religious precepts as a moral guide

12. Which of the following explorers sighted New-foundland in 1497 and on later voyages explored the eastern coastline as far south as New England?

(A) John Cabot
(B) Vasco de Gama
(C) Christopher Columbus
(D) Prince Henry the Navigator
(E) Ferdinand Magellan

GO ON TO THE NEXT PAGE

13. The sixteenth-century revolt in the Netherlands was largely inspired by

   (A) an economy that was mired in recession
   (B) English support for the Dutch rebels
   (C) strict language laws imposed by the Spanish that blocked the use of Dutch for official correspondence
   (D) the failure of the Netherlands and Spain to agree on how best to use the wealth created from the vast Spanish overseas empire
   (E) economic, political, and religious tensions in the relations between the Netherlands and Spain

14. James I agreed to a new translation of the Bible in his one concession to the

   (A) Catholics
   (B) Puritans
   (C) Levellers
   (D) House of Commons
   (E) Arminians

15. The Peace of Westphalia of 1648

   (A) brought about an end of the title of emperor within the Holy Roman Empire
   (B) brought official recognition to Calvinism in the Holy Roman Empire
   (C) officially recognized French absorption of large tracts of German territory
   (D) was brokered by the papacy
   (E) was a temporary measure that within a generation would result in a new conflict in the empire

16. The formation of the Warsaw Pact in 1955 was a sign that

   (A) war was believed to be imminent on the continent
   (B) the Soviet Union saw great military potential in the nations of Eastern Europe
   (C) the Berlin Wall was ineffective
   (D) the Soviet Union was concerned about the advent of NATO in 1949
   (E) the Soviet Union viewed the United States with disdain

17. French existentialism was based on the premise that

   (A) life was essentially absurd
   (B) life represented a Manichaean choice between good and evil
   (C) American culture was destroying traditional European life
   (D) there are absolute moral standards
   (E) a belief in God was essential for any system of morality

18. Britain's economy in the three decades immediately following World War II was hampered by

   (A) a huge debt that was owed to the United States
   (B) obsolete factories and low rates of investment and savings
   (C) the failure of centralized planning
   (D) a poorly educated populace
   (E) too great a reliance on exports

19. The Arab oil embargo of 1973

   (A) led to a dramatic upsurge in the use of alternative energy
   (B) brought about increased tensions among the countries of the European Union
   (C) led to the high inflation that undercut the economies of Europe for the remainder of the decade
   (D) had relatively little impact because fuel reserves throughout Europe remained adequate
   (E) brought about an East-West rapprochement as the Eastern Bloc provided much needed coal

20. The collapse of Communist rule throughout Eastern Europe occurred peacefully in all of the following countries EXCEPT

   (A) Czechoslovakia
   (B) Bulgaria
   (C) East Germany
   (D) Romania
   (E) Hungary

GO ON TO THE NEXT PAGE

21. Sweden emerged as a powerful European nation in the seventeenth and early eighteenth century until

(A) economic and population decline forced the Swedes to implement a more realistic policy concerning foreign conquest
(B) their defeat by the Russians at the Battle of Polotova
(C) the Swedish nobility demanded that their monarchs focus on domestic affairs
(D) the Swedish peasantry refused to either serve in the military or pay the high taxes that were necessary owing to constant warfare
(E) their defeat by the Prussians at the Battle of Narva

22. Elections for the British House of Commons in the eighteenth century were primarily limited to those who

(A) had significant wealth in either land or other forms of property
(B) were male and older than 21
(C) paid taxes equivalent to three days of wages
(D) could prove that in Elizabethan times their ancestors voted
(E) owned significant amounts of land

23. Poland disappeared as an independent nation in the eighteenth century due to all of the following reasons EXCEPT

(A) Russian, Prussian, and Austrian annexations of Polish territories
(B) the Polish nobility reduced the monarchy to a powerless institution
(C) France refused to intervene on behalf of the Poles
(D) the nation was vulnerable due to its exposed lands without natural borders
(E) the Catholic Church was unsympathetic to Polish statehood

24. Which of the following statements is most accurate for those rulers in the eighteenth century who are labeled Enlightened Absolutists?

(A) They undercut the basis of monarchical authority.
(B) They didn't understand many of the nuances of Enlightenment thought.
(C) They implemented serious reforms that had long-term consequences for their countries.
(D) They toyed with the ideas of reform but refused to put limits on their royal prerogatives.
(E) They made their nations into more rational constitutional monarchies.

25. Which of the following cities became the center of High Renaissance (1490–1520) culture?

(A) Rome
(B) Venice
(C) Florence
(D) Naples
(E) Milan

26. Based on his work *Lives of the Artists*, Vasari is considered to be the first

(A) humanist scholar to be interested in art
(B) art historian
(C) to be concerned with the question of aesthetics
(D) to question the seriousness of contemporary artists
(E) art collector

27. The Catholic Church banned the work of which of the following humanist writers?

(A) Sir Thomas More
(B) Ulrich von Hutton
(C) Erasmus
(D) Rabelais
(E) Petrarch

GO ON TO THE NEXT PAGE

28. Subsistence farming in the sixteenth century meant that

    (A) there were significant surpluses
    (B) famine was reduced significantly
    (C) an agricultural revolution was imminent
    (D) farming had changed little since the ancient world
    (E) people consumed what they raised in any given year

29. The majority of victims of the European witch craze were

    (A) Protestants
    (B) children
    (C) women
    (D) Catholics
    (E) men

30. Napoleon's 1801 Concordat with the Catholic Church

    (A) brought to a permanent close the church-state conflict in France
    (B) once again made Catholicism the state church of France
    (C) brought about an expulsion of French Protestants
    (D) led the papacy to support the ideals of the French Revolution
    (E) left the church under the supervision of the state

31. The Congress of Vienna attempted to lessen the possibility of French expansion by

    (A) leaving foreign troops on French soil
    (B) granting Prussia land on the left bank of the Rhine
    (C) demanding that the French dismantle their military
    (D) providing the Russians with a corridor through German territory to reach the French border
    (E) annexing large tracts of French territory

32. The Utopian Socialists were labeled as such by Marx mainly because

    (A) he couldn't imagine how such plans could be funded
    (B) he hated their plans for agricultural communities
    (C) he thought that they were primarily anarchists
    (D) he believed that their ideas were unsystematic and unscientific
    (E) he viewed with disdain any ideas that failed to account for bourgeois avarice

33. The primary purpose of the Chartist movement of the 1840s was to

    (A) get working men the eight-hour day
    (B) convince working men to unionize
    (C) get the House of Commons to pass the Six Acts of the People's Charter
    (D) form a political party that would challenge the Whig and Tory political dominance
    (E) tap into the revolutionary potential of the English working class

34. The Boulanger Affair almost destroyed the

    (A) French Third Republic
    (B) French-British commercial treaty of 1860
    (C) Second Republic
    (D) Fourth Republic
    (E) Second Empire

35. Bismarck's *Kulturkampf* was an attack on which of the following?

    (A) German Social-Darwinists
    (B) The Catholic Church
    (C) The German Social Democratic Party
    (D) German Liberals
    (E) The Lutheran Church

GO ON TO THE NEXT PAGE

36. "To arrive at complete certainty, this is the attitude that we should maintain: I will believe that the white object I see is black if that should be the desire of the hierarchical church, for I believe that linking Christ our Lord the Bridegroom and His Bride the Church, there is one and the same Spirit, ruling and guiding us for our souls' good. For our Holy Mother the Church is guided and ruled by the same spirit, the Lord who gave the Ten Commandments."

This passage comes from the pen of

(A) Martin Luther
(B) Erasmus
(C) Ignatius Loyola
(D) Galileo
(E) John Calvin

37. The French Wars of Religion involved all of the following EXCEPT

(A) aristocratic resentment at royal authority
(B) antagonism between Calvinists and Catholics
(C) a weakened monarchy following the death of Henry II
(D) Spanish interference in French political affairs
(E) the refusal of the *politiques* to view France as anything other than a purely Catholic nation

38. The Restoration of Charles II to the throne in 1660 indicates that many Englishmen

(A) hoped that Calvinism would remain a viable part of English religious life
(B) were unsympathetic to the ideas of John Locke
(C) had never chosen sides in the struggle between king and parliament
(D) had a deep affection for the Stuart dynasty
(E) were tired of what they perceived to be the anarchism of the English Republic

39. Charles de Gaulle encouraged France to develop its own nuclear force because

(A) he remained concerned about Soviet intentions
(B) he wanted France still to be considered a great power
(C) he doubted America's will to use its nuclear weapons in times of war
(D) the conflict in Indochina would hinge on whether the French had nuclear arms
(E) the expense of a nuclear force allowed the French to reduce the size of their conventional forces

40. In the immediate post–World War II period, most Western European states

(A) continued to limit their spending on social service programs
(B) expanded social services only for the poor and elderly
(C) began to scale back on their more generous entitlement programs
(D) greatly expanded their social service programs for all their citizens
(E) focused on industrial expansion at the expense of social spending

41. In the 1970s, one of the biggest threats facing the Italian government was the

(A) escalation of political terrorism
(B) collapse of the lire
(C) reemergence of fascism as a political force
(D) increasing strength of the Italian Communist Party
(E) inability to increase industrial output

42. Following the Conservative Party victory in 1979, the process began in Great Britain of

(A) ending the National Health Service
(B) once again using gold to back up the British pound
(C) trying to loosen some of the ties with the United States
(D) selling off many nationalized industries
(E) trying to revive certain declining industries

43. The Price Revolution of the sixteenth century was primarily caused by

(A) the influx of precious metals from the New World
(B) currency devaluation
(C) counterfeit currency
(D) increased population
(E) increased production

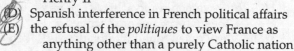

GO ON TO THE NEXT PAGE

44. During the English Revolution, the Levellers advocated the idea that

(A) all private property should be abolished
(B) the economic playing field needed to be leveled to allow for greater opportunities for the poor
(C) the monarchy had to be restored
(D) all men should have the vote regardless of whether they own property
(E) there was a contract between the government and the people

45. Spanish decline by the end of the seventeenth century was primarily caused by

(A) religious zealotry
(B) royal incompetence
(C) too many foreign military commitments
(D) Ottoman aggression in the Mediterranean
(E) a lack of adequate revenue

46. Louis XIV built his great palace of Versailles for all of the following reasons EXCEPT

(A) to control the aristocracy
(B) to show on a grand scale the wealth and power of the French monarchy
(C) to rule outside the confines of Paris
(D) to make it a center of French culture
(E) to allow for better communications with his people

47. Which of the following individuals became known as the father of the experimental method?

(A) Descartes
(B) Francis Bacon
(C) Robert Boyle
(D) John Locke
(E) Richard Hooker

48. The two crises over Morocco in the early twentieth century almost brought about war between

(A) England and France
(B) England and Morocco
(C) France and Germany
(D) Italy and Germany
(E) Italy and France

49. Virginia Woolf's *A Room of One's Own* became an important piece of feminist writing for pointing out

(A) why women needed to advance their own political agenda outside mainstream British politics
(B) why women needed the vote
(C) how women could achieve equality only when the divorce laws are changed
(D) why women found it difficult to be taken seriously as writers and intellectuals
(E) that modern society had opened up new opportunities for women

GO ON TO THE NEXT PAGE

ON HER
THEIR LIVES DEPEND

WOMEN
MUNITION
WORKERS

Enrol at once

Source: Imperial War Museum

50. The preceding poster reveals the extent to which women

(A) were encouraged to leave the factories when their husbands came home
(B) were a critical part of the war effort
(C) needed to be careful while working in munitions factories
(D) were underutilized until the end of the war
(E) needed to be convinced to work in the factories because they were uninterested in the war effort

51. At the start of the First World War, the various Socialist parties in Europe

(A) waited to see if the war would be over quickly before committing to a particular response
(B) refused to vote for war credits for their governments
(C) quickly organized the Third International to rebuild socialism as a political force
(D) supported their nation's war efforts
(E) voted to support the war only if certain critical demands were immediately met

52. Which group was most dramatically affected by the German hyperinflation of 1923?

(A) unionized workers
(B) the peasantry
(C) the urban poor
(D) the middle class
(E) landowning families

53. "Oh highest and most marvelous felicity of man! To him it is granted to have whatever he chooses, to be whatever he wills."

The above quote represents most closely the view of

(A) a Northern humanist scholar
(B) someone from the Middle Ages
(C) a Protestant preacher
(D) a Catholic priest
(E) an Italian Renaissance scholar

54. After a radical beginning marked by violence, Anabaptist communities

(A) fell apart after the execution of their leaders
(B) lost interest in the Reformation when they realized that Luther did not agree with them
(C) turned their attention inward, rejecting violence and the influence of outsiders
(D) attacked the ideas of the Mennonites
(E) fled to England where there was religious toleration

GO ON TO THE NEXT PAGE

55. The fact that the Portuguese were able to dominate in the Indian Ocean was due to their ability to

(A) arrange diplomatic missions
(B) export valuable commodities from home
(C) mount cannons on their ships
(D) use religion as a tool to convert their opponents
(E) defeat the Spanish on the open seas

56. During the reign of Edward VI—Henry VIII's only surviving son—England

(A) continued to reject Protestantism in favor of Catholicism
(B) focused primarily on foreign disputes to limit the domestic impact of religious disputes
(C) became a center for religious toleration
(D) maintained the Church of England as it had been established under Henry VIII
(E) witnessed the introduction of Protestant ideas into the Church of England

57. The Later Baroque style is known for

(A) its restrained use of color
(B) the intensity of its religious message
(C) its rigorous realism
(D) its soothing contemplative qualities
(E) its extreme ornamentation

58. Eduard Bernstein, the father of Marxist revisionism, believed that

(A) Marxism as a political force would be finished unless it learned how to deal with the issue of unemployment
(B) workers would not need to seize power by revolutionary tactics because their goals could be achieved through democratic means
(C) workers needed to primarily think of themselves as wage slaves before they could become proper Marxists
(D) European nations would have to adjust themselves to Marxism and not the other way around
(E) Marxism as a political force was over

59. Anarchists believed that individuals would be free only when

(A) the state is geared toward better meeting the needs of workers
(B) the individual accepted that freedom is in the mind and not possible in a physical sense
(C) the state is abolished
(D) the teachings of Marx are accepted
(E) the individual is free to return to the simple rural life

60. Theodore Herzl argued that because of the increased anti-Semitism in Europe, it would be necessary for Jews to

(A) try to blend into the larger European population
(B) recommit themselves to religious tradition
(C) create a homeland of their own
(D) go to the United States where there was religious freedom
(E) organize associations to come to the aid of their hard-pressed brethren

61. Sigmund Freud believed that humans are

(A) influenced by their subconscious feelings and emotions
(B) not influenced by the subconscious mind though it would be better if they were
(C) sometimes influenced by their sexual drives
(D) capable of making rational choices only when they are free of parental authority
(E) eminently rational and therefore fully aware of their subconscious thoughts

62. Voltaire's *Candide* reveals that Enlightenment thought was not always

(A) tolerant
(B) clearly focused on philosophical matters
(C) light-hearted
(D) opposed to traditional ideas
(E) optimistic

GO ON TO THE NEXT PAGE

63. The loss of significant colonial possessions in the Seven Years War played a role in France's decision to

    (A) impose a mercantilistic system on its remaining colonies

    (B) aid the American colonies in their struggle with the British

    (C) focus its attention on continental affairs

    (D) ally itself with the Austrians to counter the British

    (E) join with Prussia and Russia in an anti-British alliance

64. *The law locks up both man and woman*
Who steals the goose from off the common
But lets the greater felon loose
Who steals the common from the goose.

    This poem is primarily critical of English

    (A) common law

    (B) poaching laws

    (C) hunting and fishing restrictions

    (D) enclosure laws

    (E) royal wealth

65. The appointment of Lord Bute in 1761 as chief minister to George III

    (A) solidified George's hold over the House of Commons

    (B) seemed to violate the idea that the king should select ministers who had a power base in Parliament

    (C) came when the king was suffering from a bout of insanity

    (D) directly caused the American Revolution

    (E) was quickly followed by political stability throughout the following decade

66. During the French Revolution, *assignats*, the new paper money, were backed by

    (A) church property

    (B) noble property

    (C) gold

    (D) silver

    (E) tax revenues

67. "Sire! We must do from above what the French have done from below!"

    Who said the above words?

    (A) Johann Fichte

    (B) Count Steuben

    (C) Friedrich Hegel

    (D) Baron Stein

    (E) General Blucher

Source: Houghton-Mifflin

68. This drawing, which appeared on the cover of a songbook, best reveals

    (A) the Victorian love of music

    (B) Victorian sentimentality

    (C) the Victorian cult of domesticity

    (D) a reverence for the countryside

    (E) Victorian prosperity

GO ON TO THE NEXT PAGE

69. The Black Hundreds

    (A) were armed Russian anarchist bands
    (B) were Socialist revolutionaries
    (C) attempted to restore tsarist authority in Russia following the 1905 Revolution
    (D) were armed bandits who stole to fill Bolshevik coffers prior to the First World War
    (E) attempted to restore the tsar following the November 1917 Revolution

70. In 1924, Ramsey MacDonald became the first British Prime Minister

    (A) who was a Catholic
    (B) who was from Scotland
    (C) from the Labour Party
    (D) who had served in the First World War
    (E) who received a salary

71. Hitler won the support of the German military following

    (A) his promise to remilitarize Germany
    (B) the destruction of the S.A.
    (C) his breaking of the Versailles Treaty
    (D) the destruction of the Communist Party
    (E) his commitment to wipe out European Jewry

72. Which of the following nations was the last to grant women the right to vote?

    (A) France
    (B) Sweden
    (C) Italy
    (D) Switzerland
    (E) Finland

73. The term "Phony War" refers to

    (A) the French response to the German advance in 1940
    (B) the way the British viewed the war in 1940
    (C) the American attitude toward the war until the attack on Pearl Harbor
    (D) the inability of Britain and France to come to the aid of the Poles
    (E) the surprisingly little action on the Western Front following the fall of Poland

74. The government of Venice during the Renaissance may most accurately be labeled a

    (A) constitutional monarchy
    (B) dictatorship
    (C) republic
    (D) autocracy
    (E) democracy

75. Luther's decision to marry Katherine Von Bora was an example of

    (A) the means by which Luther reached the decision to challenge the church on the issue of the sacraments
    (B) how clergy could misinterpret Catholic teachings on the sacrament of marriage
    (C) a personal decision that involved no religious principles
    (D) the changing role of the clergy in Protestant churches
    (E) how traditional matchmaking remained significant in rural German communities

76. At the Council of Trent, the Catholic Church

    (A) agreed to work with Protestant theologians to come to an acceptable compromise
    (B) accepted Protestant positions on most issues, though still refused to allow for clerical marriage
    (C) decided to wait to formulate a position on most of the issues addressed by the Protestants
    (D) rejected Protestant positions on the sacraments, on the giving of wine to the laity during communion, and on clerical marriage
    (E) focused on producing a new catechism that could effectively counteract Protestant ideas

GO ON TO THE NEXT PAGE

77. In the early 1950s, the French government tried to

(A) ban the use of "Americanisms" like *le week-end*
(B) ban the importation of Coca-Cola for fear it would damage the French wine industry
(C) stop stores from using any language other than French in their store windows
(D) ban the importation of American dairy products such as Velveeta
(E) ban all British products from French stores unless they could be reinspected for contaminants

78. German chancellor Willy Brandt resigned in 1974 after it was revealed that

(A) he had failed to acknowledge his Nazi past
(B) his political party had received political funding from the American CIA
(C) the West German economic miracle was fundamentally flawed
(D) one of his aides was a spy for the East Germans
(E) he was hiding a serious illness

79. German unification in October 1990

(A) occurred with remarkably few problems since the West Germans had planned for this moment for decades
(B) was achieved at an economic cost far higher than expected
(C) led to renewed calls to redraw the postwar boundaries of Germany and its Eastern European neighbors
(D) was secretly opposed by the United States
(E) was strongly opposed by the French

80. The formation of the Northern League in the early 1990s is a reflection of

(A) the continuing strength of fascism in Italy
(B) the failure of Italian governments to deal with substantive issues
(C) the strength of separatist tendencies in Italy
(D) the continuing political legacy of Garibaldi
(E) Northern Italy's declining economic influence within the Italian Republic

STOP
END OF SECTION I

IF YOU FINISH BEFORE TIME IS CALLED, YOU MAY CHECK YOUR WORK ON THIS SECTION.
DO NOT GO ON TO SECTION II UNTIL YOU ARE TOLD TO DO SO.

EUROPEAN HISTORY

SECTION II

You will have 15 minutes to read the contents of this essay question booklet. You are advised to spend most of the 15 minutes analyzing the documents and planning your answer for the document-based question in Part A. You should spend some portion of the time choosing the two questions in Part B that you will answer. You may make notes in this booklet. At the end of the 15-minute period, you will be told to break the seal on the free-response booklet and to begin writing your answers on the lined pages of that booklet. Do not break the seal on the free-response booklet until you are told to do so. Suggested writing time is 45 minutes for the document-based essay question in Part A. Suggested planning and writing time is 35 minutes for each of the two essay questions you choose to answer in Part B.

BE SURE TO MANAGE YOUR TIME CAREFULLY.

Write your answers in the <u>free-response</u> booklet with a <u>pen</u>. The essay question booklet may be used for reference and/or scratchwork as you answer the free-response questions, but no credit will be given for the work shown in the essay question booklet.

DO NOT OPEN THIS BOOKLET UNTIL YOU ARE TOLD TO DO SO.

EUROPEAN HISTORY

SECTION II

Part A

(Suggested writing time—45 minutes)

Percent of Section II score—45

<u>Directions:</u> The following question is based on the accompanying Documents 1–10. (Some of the documents have been edited for the purpose of this exercise.) Write your answer on the lined pages of the free-response booklet.

This question is designed to test your ability to work with historical documents. As you analyze the documents, <u>take into account both the sources and the author's point of view.</u> Write an essay on the following topic that integrates your analysis of the documents; in no case should documents simply be cited and explained in a "laundry list" fashion. You may refer to historical facts and developments not mentioned in the documents.

1. Discuss the ways in which the French Revolution sparked debate on the issue of human rights.

Historical Background:

The eighteenth-century Enlightenment made it fashionable to speak of the question of human rights, particularly what were deemed to be natural rights, those universal rights that apply to all people at all times. Following the outbreak of revolution in 1789, a process began in France of extending rights to groups that had previously had few rights or privileges under the French monarchy. There was a question, however, as to how far to extend political rights to groups such as women and Jews, and throughout the revolutionary period there were those who saw human rights as something that should apply only to Christian French males who owned property.

Document 1

It is to the general will that the individual must address himself to learn how to be a man, citizen, subject, father, child, and when it is suitable to live or to die. It fixes the limits on all duties. You have the most sacred *natural right* to everything that is not disputed by the rest of the species. The general will enlightens you on the nature of your thoughts and your desires. Everything that you conceive, everything that you mediate upon will be good, grand, elevated, sublime, if it is in the general and common interest . . . Tell yourself often: I am a man, and I have no other true, inalienable *natural right* than those of humanity.

Diderot, article on "Natural Law" from the *Encyclopedia* (1755)

GO ON TO THE NEXT PAGE

Document 2

. . . The Catholic religion that we have the good fortune to profess will alone enjoy in our kingdom the rights and honors of public worship, while our other, non-Catholic subjects, deprived of all influence on the established order in our state...will only get from the law what natural right does not permit us to refuse them, to register their births, their marriages, and their deaths, in order to enjoy, like all our other subjects, the civil effects that result from this.

Royal Edict of Toleration (1787), granting Calvinists certain rights within France

Document 3

Who therefore dares to say that the Third Estate does not contain within itself all that is needed to form a complete Nation? The Third Estate is like a strong and robust man with one arm still in chains. If we remove the privileged order, the Nation will not be something less but something more. Thus, what is the Third Estate? All but all that is shackled and oppressed. What would it be without the privileged order? All, but an all that is free and flourishing. Nothing can be done without it; everything would be infinitely better without the other two orders.

Abbé Siéyès, leading writer during the French Revolution, *What Is the Third Estate?* (1789)

Document 4

1. Men are born and remain free and equal in rights. Social distinctions may be founded only upon the general good.

2. The aim of all political association is the preservation of the natural and imprescriptible rights of man. These rights are liberty, property, security, and resistance to oppression.

4. Liberty consists in the freedom to do everything which injures no one else; hence the exercise of the natural rights of each man has no limits except those which assure to the other members of the society the enjoyment of the same rights. These limits can only be determined by law.

Declaration of the Rights of Man and Citizen (1789)

Document 5

The Committee proposes that the necessary qualifications for the title of active citizen in the *primary* assembly of the canton be: 1) to be French or to have become French; 2) to have reached the age of one's majority; 3) to have resided in the canton for at least one year; 4) to pay direct taxes at a rate equal to the local value of three days of work . . . ; 5) to not be at the moment a servant.

Report presented to the National Assembly dealing with the question as to who should be allowed to vote, 1789

GO ON TO THE NEXT PAGE ⇨

Document 6

Thus, Sirs, assure each Jewish individual his liberty, security, and the enjoyment of his property. You owe it to this individual who has strayed into our midst; you owe him nothing more. He is a foreigner to whom, during the time of this passage and his stay, France owes hospitality, protection, and security. But it cannot and should not admit to public posts, to the administration, to the prerogative of the family a tribe that, regarding itself everywhere as foreign, never exclusively embraces any region.

> La Fare, Bishop of Nancy, *Opinion on the Admissibility of Jews to Full Civil and Political Rights* (1790)

Document 7

I ask therefore that the decree of adjournment be revoked and that it be declared relative to the Jews that they will be able to become active citizens, like all the peoples of the world, by fulfilling the conditions prescribed in the Constitution. I believe that freedom of worship no longer permits any distinction to be made between the political rights of citizens on the basis of their beliefs.

> Speech by Adrien Jean Françoise Duport, a deputy in the National Assembly, on the issue of granting Jews full political rights, 1791

Document 8

The National Convention declares the abolition of Negro slavery in all the colonies; in consequence it decrees that all men, without distinction of color, residing in the colonies, are French citizens and will enjoy the rights assured by the constitution.

> Decree of the National Convention abolishing slavery in all French colonies, February 4, 1794

Document 9

1. Woman is born free and remains equal to man in rights. Social distinctions may be based only on common utility.

2. The purpose of all political association is the preservation of the natural and imprescriptible rights of women and men. These rights are liberty, property, security, and especially resistance to oppression.

13. For maintenance of public authority and for expenses of administration, taxation of women and men is equal; she takes part in all forced labor service, in all painful tasks; she must therefore have the same proportion in the distribution of places, employments, offices, dignities, and in industry.

> Olympe de Gouges, a self-educated woman who wrote pamphlets and plays on various political topics, *The Declaration of the Rights of Woman* (1791)

GO ON TO THE NEXT PAGE

Document 10

In general, women are hardly capable of lofty conceptions and serious cogitations. And if, among ancient peoples, their natural timidity and modesty did not permit them to appear outside their family, do you want in the French Republic to see them coming up to the bar [to practice law], to the speaker's box, to political assemblies like men, abandoning both the discretion that is the source of all the virtues of this sex and the care of their family?

Decree: The clubs and popular societies of women, under whatever denomination are prohibited.

Jean Baptiste Amar, speech before the National Assembly in favor of a decree banning women's political clubs, 1793

END OF PART A

EUROPEAN HISTORY

SECTION II

Part B

(Suggested writing time—70 minutes)

Percent of Section II score—55

Directions: You are to answer TWO questions, one from each group of three questions below. Make your selections carefully, choosing the questions that you are best prepared to answer thoroughly in the time permitted. You should spend 5 minutes organizing or outlining each answer. In writing your essays, <u>use specific examples to support your answer.</u> Write your answers to the questions on the lined pages of the free-response booklet. If time permits when you finish writing, check your work. Be certain to number your answer as the questions are numbered below.

Group 1:   Choose ONE question from this group. The suggested writing time for this question is 30 minutes.

1.   Analyze how Renaissance art was a reflection of the new humanistic learning of the period.

2.   Describe and analyze at least TWO factors that led to the English Revolution of 1642.

3.   Discuss the impact of the Early Industrial Revolution on the British working class.

Group 2:   Choose ONE question from this group. The suggested writing time for this question is 30 minutes.

4.   Explain how the great powers of Europe attempted to stem the tide of revolution in the period from 1815 to 1830.

5.   Analyze and discuss why governments and workers in Western Europe in the aftermath of the Second World War sought to achieve a new level of cooperation, ushering in a period of economic, political, and social stability as well as an improved standard of living for the working class.

6.   Analyze the reasons behind the collapse of the Eastern Bloc and the demise of the Soviet Union.

END OF EXAMINATION

17

Practice Test 1: Answers and Explanations

QUESTIONS	EXPLANATIONS
1. Renaissance artists viewed the medieval past with (A) the same reverence that they held for the classical past (B) tremendous respect for their achievements, though they did not view them as equal to the ancients (C) no clear sense that their own age was distinct from the medieval period (D) disdain for what they perceived to be its backwardness (E) great interest because it served to inspire their own works of art	1. **D** Artists and intellectuals in the Renaissance felt a sense of contempt for the medieval past, which they viewed as primitive and undeserving of respect. To a great extent, their attitude toward the Middle Ages was mistaken: The world of the Renaissance owes a great deal to the impressive achievements of the High Middle Ages (c. 1000–1350), a time of significant economic and cultural accomplishments. During the Renaissance, there was great reverence for the Classical world and Renaissance artists sought to emulate the achievements of the Classical Greeks and Romans.
2. The revolt of the German peasants in 1525 was caused by all of the following EXCEPT (A) economic distress of the German peasants (B) increasing restrictions on the independence of the German peasantry (C) Martin Luther's call for a "priesthood of all believers" (D) encouragement by the Catholic Church for the peasants to rebel against Protestant nobles (E) the loss of hunting and fishing rights that had been taken by the nobles	2. **D** The German peasants in the decade leading up to the 1525 revolt did suffer from an economic downturn, which to a great extent reversed some of the economic gains they had achieved dating back to the last two decades of the fifteenth century. (A) is therefore one of the causes of the revolt, as is (B), since at the same time they suffered from this economic depression, an increasing number of formerly free peasants found themselves forced into serfdom, which meant that they had lost the right to move off the land and look for work elsewhere. (E) was also a factor in the revolt. One of the rights that the peasants had lost was the right to hunt and fish on lands that the nobles claimed, something that greatly angered the peasants because hunting and fishing provided important sources of protein. Martin Luther was completely unsympathetic toward the Peasant's Revolt and wrote an angry pamphlet denouncing it. Nevertheless, Luther's call for a "priesthood of all believers" (C), which meant that there should not be a separate clerical caste (unlike the Catholic Church) that enjoys special rights and privileges, was mistakenly understood by the peasants to mean that there should also be social equality among all believers.

QUESTIONS	EXPLANATIONS

3. John Calvin argued in his book, *Institutes of the Christian Religion*, that

  (A) grace could not be achieved without good works

  (B) grace was bestowed on few individuals, and the rest are destined for hell

  (C) salvation was the one topic that he could not fully explore because God's will in that area could never be known

  (D) grace was available to all who had faith

  (E) salvation was a sign of a compact between God and man

3. B   In the *Institutes*, Calvin's most important theological work, he spelled out what became one of the central tenets of Calvinism: Grace was limited to only a few individuals. This was different from Martin Luther's position that grace was available to all who had faith. Calvin did agree with Luther's belief that works played absolutely no role in whether one was to be saved because to imply that individuals played a role in their own salvation meant that the power of God was not absolute, something that Calvin could not even begin to contemplate.

4. Before the Europeans invaded these territories, the Americas

  (A) contained powerful empires in both Mexico and Peru

  (B) remained divided into tiny tribal units

  (C) were on the verge of ocean discoveries of their own

  (D) remained for the most part completely without the means to wage war

  (E) were covered by migratory people who left no traces of urban life

4. A   By the time Europeans arrived in Central and South America in the sixteenth century, two powerful empires had developed in this region over the previous two hundred years. The Aztec empire flourished in Mexico and built the impressive capital Tenochtitlán in what today is known as Mexico City. The other great empire was the Inca empire, a huge state that extended from Ecuador to Chile. Both empires were highly centralized states whose leaders built roads and bridges to tie together their vast territories. Both were also highly militaristic empires, although their weapons proved to be no match for the more sophisticated weapons used by the Europeans.

5. Artists who worked in the Impressionist style attempted to

  (A) make their images as realistic as possible

  (B) show their disdain for the modern world

  (C) create images that blended with previously held artistic styles

  (D) propel their art into the modern world by refusing to paint nature

  (E) capture the initial fleeting effect that occurs when one first sees an object

5. E   The Impressionist style flourished in France in the last quarter of the nineteenth century. With the development of photography, some painters found themselves less interested in creating realistic images. Instead, artists such as Édouard Manet and Claude Monet attempted to create art that revealed how the eye responds when it first glances at an object. This is why Monet worked on 40 paintings of Rouen Cathedral to capture how the eye saw this magnificent medieval structure at different times of day and during different seasons of the year.

6. The "Liberal Empire" of Napoleon III represented an attempt to

(A) galvanize British support for France's struggle with Prussia
(B) regain the lost glory of his uncle's reign
(C) bring about an end of the monarchy with a slow evolution toward a republic
(D) create a constitutional monarchy in the last years of Napoleon III's reign
(E) show that France had not been eclipsed on the continent by the other great powers

6. D In 1859, Napoleon III announced his plans to implement a series of reforms that included allowing for greater freedom of the press and granting workers the right to strike. The National Assembly, which previously had been a fairly powerless institution, was given additional powers, including the right to approve the imperial budget. Such steps, which resulted in this period of Napoleon's reign to be labeled the "Liberal Empire," were part of a process by which Napoleon sought to create more of a constitutional monarchy. His goal was to increase the support for his rule, which had dropped sharply by 1859, causing Napoleon to fear that he would not be able to pass on the throne to his son. Ultimately, the Liberal Empire was destroyed by Napoleon's blundering into war with Prussia in 1870.

Annual Output of Steel
(in millions of metric tons)

Year	Britain	Germany	France	Russia
1875–1879	0.9	—	0.26	0.08
1880–1884	1.82	0.99	0.46	0.25
1885–1889	2.86	1.65	0.54	0.23
1890–1894	3.19	2.89	0.77	0.54
1895–1899	4.33	5.08	1.26	1.32
1900–1904	5.04	7.71	1.70	2.35
1905–1909	6.09	11.30	2.65	2.63
1910–1913	6.93	16.24	4.09	4.20

7. The table above supports which of the following statements?

(A) Steel was the most important product of the Second Industrial Revolution.
(B) Steel production in Russia was hindered by the incompetence of the tsarist regime.
(C) Steel production in Germany more than doubled in the first 15 years of the twentieth century.
(D) Steel's strength and durability give it a solid advantage over iron.
(E) Steel production in Great Britain increased by nearly 85 percent over the last decade of the nineteenth century.

7. C Make sure you don't read more into a table than what is really there. The table in fact tells us nothing about the strength and durability of steel (D), nor does it tell us that steel production in Russia was hindered by the incompetent tsarist regime. Choice (A) contains a statement that is arguably true, that steel was the most important product of the Second Industrial Revolution, but there is no information provided in the table to support this claim. Of the two remaining choices, simple mathematics confirms that (E) is not correct, which leaves (C), the only answer that can be supported by the information in the table.

QUESTIONS	EXPLANATIONS

8. Which of the following describes the reaction of the German kaiser following the assassination of the Archduke Franz Ferdinand?

   (A) He urged that a European summit be held to possibly bring about a mediated compromise.

   (B) He urged Austria to invade Serbia because he feared that the crisis could destroy Austria.

   (C) The kaiser remained indecisive on what to do and basically waited while events unfurled around him.

   (D) The kaiser immediately sent troops into Russia to make sure the Russians could not come to the aid of their Serbian allies.

   (E) The kaiser urged France and Great Britain to practice restraint before coming to the assistance of the Serbs.

8. B Although Clause 231 of the Versailles Treaty—which states that Germany and her allies bore sole responsibility for the outbreak of the First World War—may be a bit of an overstatement, the kaiser's actions in the summer of 1914 were important in pushing Europe toward war. Following the assassination of the Austrian Archduke Ferdinand, the heir to the Austrian-Hungarian Empire, the kaiser did inform the Austrians that he would fully back them in their war with the Serbs and urged them to strike quickly, otherwise they would appear weak to the other European states. The kaiser hoped that the war could remain contained within the Balkan region, but he was willing to back the Austrian-Hungarians even if it meant a general European war.

9. Working and middle class individuals were united in opposition to

   (A) the Factory Act

   (B) Chartism

   (C) the Reform Bill of 1867

   (D) the Great Reform Bill of 1832

   (E) the Corn Laws

9. E The working and middle class were united in opposition to the Corn Laws but for different reasons. For the British working class, the Corn Laws kept the price of bread, the basic commodity in its diet, artificially high. For the middle class, lower wages could be paid to factory workers if grain prices were reduced.

10. At Yalta in February 1945, the Big Three—the United States, Great Britain, and the Soviet Union—agreed to

   (A) postpone dealing with the question of what to do concerning Germany

   (B) a postwar division of Germany into British, American, Soviet, and French occupation zones

   (C) a two-bloc division in Europe, with the West under American domination and the East under Soviet control

   (D) commence the distribution of American financial aid under the Marshall Plan

   (E) distance themselves from the French, who under de Gaulle were making outlandish demands

10. B By the time the United States, Great Britain, and the Soviet Union met at Yalta, Soviet troops were only 100 miles from Berlin. The question of what to do with Germany now that its defeat was certain dominated the discussions, although other issues were also on the table, such as whether the Soviet Union should declare war on Japan. Eventually, the Big Three agreed to a four-way division of Germany so that the British, Americans, Soviets, and French would each have their own occupation zone.

QUESTIONS	EXPLANATIONS

11. Machiavelli's *The Prince* represented an attempt to find ways to

(A) blend medieval and Renaissance scholarship
(B) convince the French to intercede in Italian affairs on behalf of his native Florence
(C) show how the rule of princes was clearly inferior to republican forms of government
(D) unify the entire Italian peninsula under a powerful ruler
(E) show how a Christian prince can use religious precepts as a moral guide

11. **D** In 1494, Charles VIII, the King of France, invaded the Italian peninsula with a large army. This was the first stage of a process that lasted throughout the next century in which Italy became the battleground in the struggle between the French and the Spanish, much to the detriment of the independent Italian city-states. In 1513, Machiavelli wrote *The Prince* in which he reflected on the dreary recent history of the Italian peninsula and its relative weakness in comparison to France and Spain. Machiavelli reflected that Italy needed a strong leader—the prince—who would use rather ruthless means to unite the Italian peninsula and kick the foreign armies out of Italy.

12. Which of the following explorers sighted Newfoundland in 1497 and on later voyages explored the eastern coastline as far south as New England?

(A) John Cabot
(B) Vasco de Gama
(C) Christopher Columbus
(D) Prince Henry the Navigator
(E) Ferdinand Magellan

12. **A** John Cabot was a Venetian sailor who went to England to offer his services to King Henry VII. Cabot claimed that he could find a way to the Far East by means of a northern passage. Cabot obviously never found the nonexistent northern passage, but his journeys along the northern coast of North America extending from Newfoundland to New England helped inspire later English explorers such as Henry Hudson and also set the stage for the creation of the permanent settlement at Jamestown in 1607.

13. The sixteenth-century revolt in the Netherlands was largely inspired by

(A) an economy that was mired in recession
(B) English support for the Dutch rebels
(C) strict language laws imposed by the Spanish that blocked the use of Dutch for official correspondence
(D) the failure of the Netherlands and Spain to agree on how best to use the wealth created from the vast Spanish overseas empire
(E) economic, political, and religious tensions in the relations between the Netherlands and Spain

13. **E** A number of issues inspired the revolt in the Netherlands that began in 1567. The Dutch resented the high taxes imposed by Spain and in turn the tight control that the Spanish crown maintained over the Dutch economy. The people of the Netherlands also had little personal affection for the Spanish King, Philip II, who was born in Spain and never in his life set foot in the Netherlands. The Dutch were also greatly concerned over the religious zeal of Philip, who saw it as his God-given mission to quell Protestantism in all his lands. Philip brought the Inquisition to the Netherlands, a land where the majority of the people were Calvinists. All of these economic, political, and religious problems led to the outbreak of a rebellion that lasted until 1648 when Spain finally recognized the independence of the Netherlands.

QUESTIONS	EXPLANATIONS

14. James I agreed to a new translation of the Bible in his one concession to the

(A) Catholics
(B) Puritans
(C) Levellers
(D) House of Commons
(E) Arminians

14. B In 1604, James I, the King of England, met with leading Puritans (the more zealous members of the Church of England) at what became known as the Hampton Court Conference. The Puritans demanded that the church discontinue practices that the Puritans thought were strictly Catholic and should therefore not be part of a Protestant religious ceremony. The Puritans' list of demands included doing away with the ornate robes worn by the clergy, the end of the use of wedding rings in marriage ceremonies, and discontinuing the signing of the cross in baptism. James refused to make such changes in the Church of England, but he did agree that there should be a new translation of the Bible, deeming that the one currently in use was inadequate. James proceeded to have a group of biblical scholars from both Oxford and Cambridge work on the new Bible, which is known to us as the King James Bible, a beautifully written Bible that is still used by the Church of England today.

15. The Peace of Westphalia of 1648

(A) brought about an end of the title of emperor within the Holy Roman Empire
(B) brought official recognition to Calvinism in the Holy Roman Empire
(C) officially recognized French absorption of large tracts of German territory
(D) was brokered by the papacy
(E) was a temporary measure that within a generation would result in a new conflict in the empire

15. B The Thirty Years War (1618–1648) was a terribly bloody conflict that began in part because the earlier Peace of Augsburg (1555) did not officially recognize Calvinism within the Holy Roman Empire. After 30 years of horrific warfare that witnessed the intervention of Spain, France, Denmark, and Sweden, little changed within the Holy Roman Empire except that now Calvinism was granted the same rights as Lutheranism. This did not mean that individuals enjoyed religious freedom; rather, the Peace of Westphalia extended the principle stated in the Peace of Augsburg that the ruler of each territory could determine the religion to be practiced in the territory.

QUESTIONS	EXPLANATIONS

16. The formation of the Warsaw Pact in 1955 was a sign that

(A) war was believed to be imminent on the continent
(B) the Soviet Union saw great military potential in the nations of Eastern Europe
(C) the Berlin Wall was ineffective
(D) the Soviet Union was concerned about the advent of NATO in 1949
(E) the Soviet Union viewed the United States with disdain

16. **D** The formation of NATO in 1949 was a clear sign that the United States intended to stay involved in European affairs following the end of the Second World War. The signatories to the treaty creating NATO agreed to provide for a common defense in case one of the member states was attacked and also created a unified military command under American leadership. In response to the formation of an alliance that the Soviets viewed as being primarily directed against them, they created the Warsaw Pact in 1955, which forced the nations of Eastern Europe into a military alliance with the Soviet Union. The formation of the Warsaw Pact also provided the Soviet Union with justification for stationing troops in Eastern Europe.

17. French existentialism was based on the premise that

(A) life was essentially absurd
(B) life represented a Manichaean choice between good and evil
(C) American culture was destroying traditional European life
(D) there are absolute moral standards
(E) a belief in God was essential for any system of morality

17. **A** The seeds of French existentialism were planted during the Second World War, a war of such tremendous destructiveness that it led the French philosopher Jean-Paul Sartre to conclude that life was essentially absurd. In a series of plays and novels that he published after the war, Sartre argued that life had essentially no meaning and that humans cannot depend on a God that does not exist, nor can they depend on tradition or social mores for ethical guidance. Instead, individuals have the freedom to go out and define their own ethical standards. While Sartre spent the war years hanging around the cafes of Paris, another leading existentialist, Albert Camus (who hated the label existentialist), spent those years living by his ideals by serving in the French resistance. Camus's writings focused on the need for the individual to rebel against the irrationality and tyranny of modern life. In his novel *The Plague*, he wrote of the heroism of those individuals who, despite the fact that they know life is absurd, still aid those who are suffering from the plague.

QUESTIONS	EXPLANATIONS

18. Britain's economy in the three decades immediately following World War II was hampered by

   (A) a huge debt that was owed to the United States
   (B) obsolete factories and low rates of investment and savings
   (C) the failure of centralized planning
   (D) a poorly educated populace
   (E) too great a reliance on exports

18. **B** Unfortunately for the British, many more of their factories survived the Second World War than the factories in Germany and Japan. Even prior to the war, the British were saddled with an industrial base that was desperately in need of new investment. Following the war, as the West Germans and Japanese began to build new factories incorporating the most modern technologies, the British spent their scarce resources on a foolish and ultimately doomed attempt to preserve the British Empire. By the 1960s, the British economy was growing at a much slower rate than those of Italy, France, and West Germany.

19. The Arab oil embargo of 1973

   (A) led to a dramatic upsurge in the use of alternative energy
   (B) brought about increased tensions among the countries of the European Union
   (C) led to the high inflation that undercut the economies of Europe for the remainder of the decade
   (D) had relatively little impact because fuel reserves throughout Europe remained adequate
   (E) brought about an East-West rapprochement as the Eastern Bloc provided much needed coal

19. **C** When the Egyptian and Syrian surprise attack on Israel at the start of the Yom Kippur War began to stall, the oil-producing Arab nations cut off the supply of oil to Western Europe and the United States, with the hope that this would force the Western nations to place pressure on Israel to accept a ceasefire. When the supply of oil was resumed after several weeks, though at much higher prices, the economies of Western Europe were hit with severe inflation as the increased cost of oil drove up the price of other commodities. While some nations (including the United States) began to consider alternative sources of energy, not much was accomplished. Some nations, such as Great Britain and Norway, began to look for other sources of oil with some degree of success: They found large deposits of oil in the North Sea. For the remainder of the 1970s, however, the economies of Europe were still dealing with the effects of the rapid increase in the price of oil, including a surge in unemployment.

20. The collapse of Communist rule throughout Eastern Europe occurred peacefully in all of the following countries EXCEPT

   (A) Czechoslovakia
   (B) Bulgaria
   (C) East Germany
   (D) Romania
   (E) Hungary

20. **D** Fortunately, the fall of Communist rule in Eastern Europe occurred with a remarkable degree of peace. In Czechoslovakia, for example, the fall of communism became known as the "Velvet Revolution" because it occurred without bloodshed. The same is true for all the countries listed above, with the exception of Romania, where the Ceausescu family did their best to hold on to power. Eventually 1,000 Romanians died during the street battles that raged throughout the country.

21. Sweden emerged as a powerful European nation in the seventeenth and early eighteenth century until

   (A) economic and population decline forced the Swedes to implement a more realistic policy concerning foreign conquest
   (B) their defeat by the Russians at the Battle of Polotova
   (C) the Swedish nobility demanded that their monarchs focus on domestic affairs
   (D) the Swedish peasantry refused to either serve in the military or pay the high taxes that were necessary owing to constant warfare
   (E) their defeat by the Prussians at the Battle of Narva

21. **B** Although today it may seem hard to believe, there was a brief period when Sweden was one of the great powers of Europe. In the seventeenth century, under its great King Gustavus Adolphus, Sweden played a major role in the Thirty Years War. Throughout the late seventeenth and early eighteenth centuries, Sweden continued to expand its power at the expense of neighboring states like Denmark, Norway, Poland, and Russia. Eventually it was the rise of a more powerful Russian state under Peter the Great that brought an end to this golden age of Swedish power and influence. In 1709 at the Battle of Polotova, a Russian army soundly defeated the Swedes, bringing to an end the expansion of Sweden throughout the Baltic region.

22. Elections for the British House of Commons in the eighteenth century were primarily limited to those who

   (A) had significant wealth in either land or other forms of property
   (B) were male and older than 21
   (C) paid taxes equivalent to three days of wages
   (D) could prove that in Elizabethan times their ancestors voted
   (E) owned significant amounts of land

22. **E** Although there were some exceptions, for the most part voting in England in the eighteenth century was a right limited to those who owned significant amounts of land. This became an issue by the early nineteenth century when a new class of individuals—men who had become rich as a result of the Industrial Revolution—began to press for the vote. Although they may have possessed significant wealth, this class was still excluded from voting because they did not necessarily own significant amounts of land. In 1832, the Great Reform Bill granted these middle-class men the right to vote.

QUESTIONS	EXPLANATIONS

23. Poland disappeared as an independent nation in the eighteenth century due to all of the following reasons EXCEPT

(A) Russian, Prussian, and Austrian annexations of Polish territories

(B) the Polish nobility reduced the monarchy to a powerless institution

(C) France refused to intervene on behalf of the Poles

(D) the nation was vulnerable due to its exposed lands without natural borders

(E) the Catholic Church was unsympathetic to Polish statehood

23. **E** Poland disappeared as a nation in 1795 and would not reemerge as an independent state until the Treaty of Versailles restored Polish statehood in 1919. Poland had been a powerful state in the seventeenth century, but in the eighteenth century, Poland suffered from the rise of its powerful neighbors, the Russians, Prussians, and Austrians, all of whom craved Polish lands (A). Because Poland lacked natural borders (D), it was hard to defend its territories against these aggressive states. The Polish nobility (B) deserve much of the blame for the fall of the Polish state because they insisted on the expansion of their own rights at the expense of the monarchy, which in turn increasingly was unable to lead the nation, even in times of national crisis. In the 1790s, some Poles became interested in the philosophy behind the French Revolution, and they hoped that the French would intercede on their behalf, but the French sent no aid (C). This leaves choice (E). There is no evidence to suggest that the papacy was unsympathetic to Polish statehood, particularly because Catholic Poland struggled against Eastern Orthodox Russia and Lutheran Prussia.

24. Which of the following statements is most accurate for those rulers in the eighteenth century who are labeled Enlightened Absolutists?

(A) They undercut the basis of monarchical authority.

(B) They didn't understand many of the nuances of Enlightenment thought.

(C) They implemented serious reforms that had long-term consequences for their countries.

(D) They toyed with the ideas of reform but refused to put limits on their royal prerogatives.

(E) They made their nations into more rational constitutional monarchies.

24. **D** For the most part, those rulers who we label as Enlightened Absolutists played with the idea of significant reform. Catherine the Great of Russia allowed for the first private printing presses in Russia, although her government still censored certain works. Catherine also considered providing a written constitution for Russia, although she and the other Enlightened Absolutists, such as Frederick the Great of Prussia and Joseph II of Austria, refused to implement any reforms that would significantly undercut their own authority. They hoped to rationalize government, not to aid those who lived within their lands, but rather to enhance their own authority within the state.

QUESTIONS	EXPLANATIONS

25. Which of the following cities became the center of High Renaissance (1490–1520) culture?

(A) Rome
(B) Venice
(C) Florence
(D) Naples
(E) Milan

25. A Following the invasion of Northern Italy by France in 1494 and in the same year in Florence the rise to power of the radical priest Savonarola, who hated art, the center of Renaissance art moved from Florence to Rome. In Rome, Pope Julius II and a number of other popes over the next 25 years provided important patronage for artists such as Michelangelo, who began work on the Sistine Chapel in the Vatican in 1508. Rome lost its place as a center of the High Renaissance culture around the third decade of the sixteenth century, partially because of Emperor Charles V's troops sacking of Rome in 1527 and also because of the Protestant Reformation and the ensuing crisis that the papacy faced.

26. Based on his work *Lives of the Artists,* Vasari is considered to be the first

(A) humanist scholar to be interested in art
(B) art historian
(C) to be concerned with the question of aesthetics
(D) to question the seriousness of contemporary artists
(E) art collector

26. B Vasari's *Lives of the Artists* is generally considered to be the first work of art history. Although most art historians now reject many of Vasari's conclusions (he hated medieval art and thought too highly of his own paintings), he is recognized for providing the first systematic study of art.

27. The Catholic Church banned the work of which of the following humanist writers?

(A) Sir Thomas More
(B) Ulrich von Hutton
(C) Erasmus
(D) Rabelais
(E) Petrarch

27. C During the Catholic Counter-Reformation, the church placed the writings of the great Northern humanist Erasmus on the Index of Prohibited Books, a list that the church established as a means of countering religious heresy. Erasmus was a Catholic, although his writings were deemed to be suspect because they questioned such Catholic traditions as the special role of the clergy and practices like the veneration of religious relics. Erasmus's writings were thought to have laid the foundations for Luther's challenge to the church. Erasmus had in fact maintained a correspondence with Martin Luther and was sympathetic to some of Luther's ideas, but in the end, he rejected Luther's theology because he could not accept Luther's notion that man did not have free will.

QUESTIONS	EXPLANATIONS

28. Subsistence farming in the sixteenth century meant that

(A) there were significant surpluses
(B) famine was reduced significantly
(C) an agricultural revolution was imminent
(D) farming had changed little since the ancient world
(E) people consumed what they raised in any given year

28. E In a subsistence economy, people consume what they raise in a given year. Thus, if the growing season is too wet or possibly too dry and the harvest is insufficient, there is no food from the previous year in storage to make up for the bad harvest, and people go hungry. By the seventeenth century, the Netherlands, soon followed by Great Britain, became the first European area to move away from subsistence farming. The introduction of scientific farming in both these regions allowed for certain foodstuffs to be stored, providing a backup resource should an unexpected problem with the harvest arise. The end of subsistence farming would bring to an end the endemic famines that had been a part of European life since medieval times.

29. The majority of victims of the European witch craze were

(A) Protestants
(B) children
(C) women
(D) Catholics
(E) men

29. C It has been estimated that 90 percent of those who were executed as witches during the European witch craze of the sixteenth and seventeenth centuries were women. Why this was the case is still being debated, although some historians suggest that simple misogyny, the hatred of women, may have been a primary factor. Other historians suggest that women may have been more associated with certain traditional practices in the countryside that were tied to the pre-Christian pagan past and that when such practices came under scrutiny as a result of the Protestant Reformation and the Catholic Counter-Reformation, women were the natural suspects.

QUESTIONS	EXPLANATIONS

30. Napoleon's 1801 Concordat with the Catholic Church

(A) brought to a permanent close the church-state conflict in France

(B) once again made Catholicism the state church of France

(C) brought about an expulsion of French Protestants

(D) led the papacy to support the ideals of the French Revolution

(E) left the church under the supervision of the state

30. **E** Napoleon was nothing if not a clever politician, and he recognized that one of the most significant problems the governments formed after the French Revolution faced was their outright hostility toward the Catholic Church. Although Napoleon himself was an atheist, he thought that coming to an understanding with the church would lead to greater acceptance of his government. In 1801, he worked out a Concordat, or agreement, with Pope Pius VII. Napoleon did not give up much: He dropped the calendar that had been instituted in 1793 that eliminated Sundays and other Christian holidays. The papacy accepted the loss of church lands that had been confiscated during the Revolution and the fact that Catholic clergy within France would remain under the control of the state, which would continue to pay their salaries. The Concordat allowed the pope to select French bishops, but he could only choose from a list of individuals chosen by Napoleon.

31. The Congress of Vienna attempted to lessen the possibility of French expansion by

(A) leaving foreign troops on French soil

(B) granting Prussia land on the left bank of the Rhine

(C) demanding that the French dismantle their military

(D) providing the Russians with a corridor through German territory to reach the French border

(E) annexing large tracts of French territory

31. **B** Although there were foreign troops on French soil in the immediate aftermath of the Napoleonic wars (A), these troops were withdrawn following the Bourbon restoration in 1815. The search for a more permanent means of containing French power ensued and eventually entailed giving land on the left bank of the Rhine River to Prussia. The idea was that the powerful Prussian state would serve as a barrier to French territorial expansion. This was to have significant but unexpected consequences for European history. This new Prussian territory on the left bank of the Rhine turned out to be rich in coal and iron and provided the foundations of Prussian industrial expansion in the second half of the nineteenth century. When Prussia struggled with Austria for the leadership of Germany, Prussian industrialization played a significant role in its victory over the Austrians; it also helped in the eventual unification of Germany under Prussian leadership.

QUESTIONS	EXPLANATIONS
32. The Utopian Socialists were labeled as such by Marx mainly because (A) he couldn't imagine how such plans could be funded (B) he hated their plans for agricultural communities (C) he thought that they were primarily anarchists (D) he believed that their ideas were unsystematic and unscientific (E) he viewed with disdain any ideas that failed to account for bourgeois avarice	32. **D** Marx labeled the work of individuals such as Saint-Simon, Charles Fourier, and Robert Owen as "Utopian Socialism" because he believed that they were proposing a form of socialism that was unsystematic as compared to the scientific socialism that he touted. He despised their plans to establish little agricultural or industrial communities that were geared toward improving the lives of their members. Marx felt that such plans did not address the real issue, which was the control of the state by the capitalist class and the role of class struggle in eventually bringing about a proletarian revolution and the eventual elimination of the state.
33. The primary purpose of the Chartist movement of the 1840s was to (A) get working men the eight-hour day (B) convince working men to unionize (C) get the House of Commons to pass the Six Acts of the People's Charter (D) form a political party that would challenge the Whig and Tory political dominance (E) tap into the revolutionary potential of the English working class	33. **C** The Chartist movement of the 1840s was primarily geared toward getting the House of Commons to pass the Six Acts of the People's Charter. The charter consisted of demands for universal male suffrage, annual parliamentary elections, the end of property requirements for holders of parliamentary seats, equal electoral districts, payment for members of the House of Commons, and the secret ballot. Many workers probably believed that passage of the Six Acts would help lead to an amelioration of the harsh economic conditions that were common in Great Britain in the 1840s. The movement hit its peak in 1848, the year of vast revolutionary activity across Europe. In that year, the Chartists were able to get 3 million individuals to sign a petition calling for the passage of the Six Acts. A massive meeting was called in London to present the petition to the House of Commons, which summarily ignored it. At this point, Chartism went into a rapid decline and basically disappeared from British political life.

QUESTIONS	EXPLANATIONS

34. The Boulanger Affair almost destroyed the

(A) French Third Republic
(B) French-British commercial treaty of 1860
(C) Second Republic
(D) Fourth Republic
(E) Second Empire

34. A The Boulanger Affair threatened to destroy the French Third Republic that was created following the collapse of the Second Empire in 1870. Georges Boulanger was an ambitious general who some on the political right in France began to see as a useful tool for destroying the hated Third Republic. In 1889, some began to openly propose that Boulanger stage a coup d'état, and although Boulanger encouraged such talk, he refused to take immediate action, exactly why is not clear. Two years later, the Third Republic decided to bring charges of treason against him, which encouraged him to flee to Belgium, where he shot himself to death.

35. Bismarck's *Kulturkampf* was an attack on which of the following?

(A) German Social-Darwinists
(B) The Catholic Church
(C) The German Social Democratic Party
(D) German Liberals
(E) The Lutheran Church

35. B Following the unification of Germany under Prussian leadership in 1871, Bismarck turned his attention to German Catholics. He viewed Catholics with concern since they had an allegiance to an institution that extended beyond the borders of the new German Reich: the Catholic Church. Bismarck therefore regarded them as a potential threat to the state, and in 1873, he launched the *Kulturkampf*, a campaign against Catholics. Catholic priests had to study in German schools and universities. State officials could block the appointment of any clergyman they disliked, and eventually when the bishops protested, Bismarck either arrested them or threw them out of Germany. By the end of the 1870s, Bismarck dropped his campaign against Catholics because it had little effect and because he also wanted their political support against his next opponent—the German Social Democratic Party.

QUESTIONS	EXPLANATIONS

36. "To arrive at complete certainty, this is the attitude that we should maintain: I will believe that the white object I see is black if that should be the desire of the hierarchical church, for I believe that linking Christ our Lord the Bridegroom and His Bride the Church, there is one and the same Spirit, ruling and guiding us for our souls' good. For our Holy Mother the Church is guided and ruled by the same spirit, the Lord who gave the Ten Commandments."

This passage comes from the pen of

(A) Martin Luther
(B) Erasmus
(C) Ignatius Loyola
(D) Galileo
(E) John Calvin

36. C Ignatius Loyola, the Spanish noble who formed the Society of Jesus (Jesuits) in the sixteenth century, wrote this passage. It comes from his *Spiritual Exercises*, a book that provided the tools for the individual to connect with God through meditations and contemplative prayers. Such ideas were of concern to Catholic authorities because they were battling the Protestants over the issue of what role the church plays in the individual's salvation. Loyola wrote the passage to show that he offered complete and total obedience to the pope and to the Catholic Church. Satisfied that Loyola was not interested in challenging official church doctrines, the Catholic Church officially recognized the Society of Jesus in 1540.

37. The French Wars of Religion involved all of the following EXCEPT

(A) aristocratic resentment at royal authority
(B) antagonism between Calvinists and Catholics
(C) a weakened monarchy following the death of Henry II
(D) Spanish interference in French political affairs
(E) the refusal of the *politiques* to view France as anything other than a purely Catholic nation

37. E The French Wars of Religion are a bit of a misnomer because there were more than religious issues at play in the conflict. Many French nobles resented the growing power of the French monarchy (A), and the monarchy itself was in crisis following the accidental death of Henry II in 1559, which left his young son to govern in his stead (C). The Spanish interfered in the French Wars of Religion (D) partly to aid French Catholics and partly because the weakening of France by means of a civil war played to the interests of Spain, which had fought the French throughout the sixteenth century. Religious issues certainly played a role in the conflict (B), as there were growing tensions throughout France between Catholics and Calvinists. This leaves choice (E). The *politiques* were a loosely defined group of French Catholic writers who argued that it was better to recognize the rights of French Calvinists than to destroy the French nation with a destructive civil war.

QUESTIONS	EXPLANATIONS

38. The Restoration of Charles II to the throne in 1660 indicates that many Englishmen

   (A) hoped that Calvinism would remain a viable part of English religious life
   (B) were unsympathetic to the ideas of John Locke
   (C) had never chosen sides in the struggle between king and parliament
   (D) had a deep affection for the Stuart dynasty
   (E) were tired of what they perceived to be the anarchism of the English Republic

38. **E** By 1660, there was a general consensus among the English elite that the monarchy should be restored. This wish for restoration was a result of the heavy-handed rule of Oliver Cromwell, who governed England during its years as a republic from 1649, following the execution of King Charles I, until his own death in 1658. Throughout these years, Cromwell dismissed from Parliament those with whom he disagreed and generally ruled in a rather arbitrary manner. Cromwell had wanted his son, Richard, to succeed his position as Lord Protector, but two years after his death, General George Monck, who commanded an English army that was stationed in Scotland, brought his troops to London, dissolved Parliament, and threw Richard out of office. The elections that were held immediately afterward voted in a new parliament that asked Charles II, the son of the executed Charles I, to come back to England to be crowned king; his coronation took place on April 23, 1661.

39. Charles de Gaulle encouraged France to develop its own nuclear force because

   (A) he remained concerned about Soviet intentions
   (B) he wanted France still to be considered a great power
   (C) he doubted America's will to use its nuclear weapons in times of war
   (D) the conflict in Indochina would hinge on whether the French had nuclear arms
   (E) the expense of a nuclear force allowed the French to reduce the size of their conventional forces

39. **B** Perhaps the greatest concern for Charles de Gaulle was that in the postwar world, France would no longer be considered a great power. He refused to accept the idea of a bipolar world, one with only two great powers—the United States and the Soviet Union. De Gaulle therefore committed France to the building of its own nuclear arsenal.

QUESTIONS	EXPLANATIONS
40. In the immediate post–World War II period, most Western European states (A) continued to limit their spending on social service programs (B) expanded social services only for the poor and elderly (C) began to scale back on their more generous entitlement programs (D) greatly expanded their social service programs for all their citizens (E) focused on industrial expansion at the expense of social spending	40. **D** The end of the Second World War saw a new commitment among the nations of Western Europe to provide social services for their citizens. European nations developed cradle-to-grave social programs that provided free medical care and extensive benefits for the unemployed. Although each nation implemented its own programs with varying degrees of generosity, European nations shared a common goal of providing social services. This goal reflected a wish to avoid the social tensions that erupted after World War I from citizens on the bottom of the social ladder receiving an inadequate amount of attention. In recent years, many of these social programs have come under attack as European countries seek to emulate the United States by providing fewer social services in exchange for a much lower tax rate.
41. In the 1970s, one of the biggest threats facing the Italian government was the (A) escalation of political terrorism (B) collapse of the lire (C) reemergence of fascism as a political force (D) increasing strength of the Italian Communist Party (E) inability to increase industrial output	41. **A** After extreme political movements representing both the left and right failed to bring about a genuine restructuring of society in the late 1960s, some individuals who had been involved in these movements turned to terrorism. In West Germany, the Baader-Meinhof gang, an extreme left-wing group, unleashed a terror campaign aimed at toppling the state. In Italy, the Red Brigades attacked political and business leaders and in 1978 carried out their most audacious attack—the kidnapping and murder of former Italian premier, Aldo Moro. By the 1980s, the number of terrorist movements had declined because many of their members were arrested and also because they had failed to shake the foundations of the stable democracies of Western Europe.

QUESTIONS	EXPLANATIONS

42. Following the Conservative Party victory in 1979, the process began in Great Britain of

  (A) ending the National Health Service
  (B) once again using gold to back up the British pound
  (C) trying to loosen some of the ties with the United States
  (D) selling off many nationalized industries
  (E) trying to revive certain declining industries

42. **D** Although the Conservative Party under the leadership of Prime Minister Margaret Thatcher may have wanted to privatize the National Health Service (A), it realized that such a step would be political suicide and did not attempt it. Instead, it decided to sell off many of the industries that had been nationalized by the Labour government in the period from 1945 to 1951. Beginning in 1979, Prime Minister Thatcher sold such public concerns as British Airways, British Telecom, and British Steel to private investors.

43. The Price Revolution of the sixteenth century was primarily caused by

  (A) the influx of precious metals from the New World
  (B) currency devaluation
  (C) counterfeit currency
  (D) increased population
  (E) increased production

43. **D** Although choice (A) used to be considered the prime cause of the Price Revolution, historians today generally agree that although the influx of precious metals may have added to the sharp rise in prices, it was actually caused by a significant growth in the European population in the period from 1480 to 1560. Why this population growth occurred is not clear, but it certainly played a role in placing greater demands for goods, most particularly grains and wool, and therefore led to a sharp increase in prices, leading to what is known as the Price Revolution.

44. During the English Revolution, the Levellers advocated the idea that

  (A) all private property should be abolished
  (B) the economic playing field needed to be leveled to allow for greater opportunities for the poor
  (C) the monarchy had to be restored
  (D) all men should have the vote regardless of whether they own property
  (E) there was a contract between the government and the people

44. **D** The Levellers were one of several radical groups that emerged during the English Revolution. Although their name, which was given to them by their political opponents, seems to imply that they were interested in abolishing private property, that was not the case. The Levellers supported universal male suffrage, a radical view in an age that believed ownership of property was essential for political participation. The Levellers were active in Oliver Cromwell's New Model Army and eventually Cromwell had to subdue those regiments in which Leveller support was strong, and in some cases, he even had some of their leaders shot.

QUESTIONS	EXPLANATIONS
45. Spanish decline by the end of the seventeenth century was primarily caused by (A) religious zealotry (B) royal incompetence (C) too many foreign military commitments (D) Ottoman aggression in the Mediterranean (E) a lack of adequate revenue	45. **C** Spain enjoyed a brief golden age in the sixteenth century, a period in which it was the most powerful state in Europe. By the end of the century, signs of decay began to appear, and by the mid-seventeenth century Spain found itself in an almost irreversible decline. The main reason for this decline was that Spain had far too many military commitments, which ultimately consumed all its resources, resulting in little internal investment. In the sixteenth century, Spain was involved in long, drawn out struggles with the Ottoman Empire, France, England, and, perhaps most costly of all, their attempt to put down the revolt in the Netherlands. In the seventeenth century, Spain was involved in the Thirty Years War at a great financial expense to the country. By mid-century, France recognized this constant drain on the Spanish treasury as an opportunity to supplant Spain as the greatest power in Europe.
46. Louis XIV built his great palace of Versailles for all of the following reasons EXCEPT (A) to control the aristocracy (B) to show on a grand scale the wealth and power of the French monarchy (C) to rule outside the confines of Paris (D) to make it a center of French culture (E) to allow for better communications with his people	46. **E** Louis XIV constructed the palace of Versailles between 1669 and 1686 as a tool for ruling his state. Controlling the aristocracy (A) was a problem that French kings had struggled with for centuries. Louis managed this problem by inviting the nobility to share in the pleasures of court life. More than 10,000 nobles lived in or around the palace where they were distracted from thoughts of plotting rebellion against the king by intricate court ceremonies. The palace itself was built on a scale that showed off the wealth and power of the king (B) and was intentionally built outside of Paris (C) because Paris was a notoriously difficult city for French monarchs to control. The crown sponsored theatrical productions by the playwrights Molière and Racine, which helped make Versailles the cultural center not only of France but for all of Europe (D). The correct answer is (E): Louis XIV had little interest in better communications with his people. Absolute monarchy did not depend on the support of the public at large, and Louis tried not to concern himself with the lives of his more common subjects.

QUESTIONS	EXPLANATIONS

47. Which of the following individuals became known as the father of the experimental method?

(A) Descartes
(B) Francis Bacon
(C) Robert Boyle
(D) John Locke
(E) Richard Hooker

47. **B** Although he never conducted an experiment in his life, Francis Bacon is known as the father of the experimental method. In *Novum Organum* (1620), Bacon argued that to understand the natural world it was necessary to conduct careful scientific experiments. No one today would be shocked by such views, but when Bacon made this argument, he essentially was rejecting the philosophy of most of his contemporaries, who believed that all there was to know about the natural world could be found in the writings of the Ancient Greeks.

48. The two crises over Morocco in the early twentieth century almost brought about war between

(A) England and France
(B) England and Morocco
(C) France and Germany
(D) Italy and Germany
(E) Italy and France

48. **C** In 1904, Great Britain and France settled a number of colonial disputes by signing a series of agreements that were collectively called the *Entente Cordiale*. These agreements did not create a formal treaty of alliance between the two countries but were clearly a sign that France and Great Britain saw Germany as a potential enemy. The First Moroccan Crisis took place in 1905 and was instigated by Germany's desire to test whether the British would really back France in a crisis. The crisis started when the kaiser landed in Morocco, which was not formally a French colony, but was a French protectorate, meaning that France maintained a loose sort of control over its politics and strong economic control over the nation. The kaiser claimed that Germany should be given the same rights to engage in commercial activity with Morocco as France. This enraged the French (no one seemed to care what the Moroccans thought), but France's economic control over Morocco was confirmed at an international conference in 1906, settling the issue. This First Moroccan Crisis had the opposite effect of what the Germans intended; it brought France and Great Britain even closer together. Great Britain was horrified by the bellicose attitude of the Germans. The Second Moroccan Crisis took place in 1911 when Germany sent a gunboat to Morocco to supposedly protect German civilians living in Morocco, which was then engaged in a revolt against French domination. This served to provoke both France and Great Britain; however, the issue was settled nonviolently by giving Germany some small pieces of land in the French Congo. The Second Crisis led to even greater military cooperation between Britain and France, eventually bringing these two nations together as allies during the First World War.

49. Virginia Woolf's *A Room of One's Own* became an important piece of feminist writing for pointing out

(A) why women needed to advance their own political agenda outside mainstream British politics

(B) why women needed the vote

(C) how women could achieve equality only when the divorce laws are changed

(D) why women found it difficult to be taken seriously as writers and intellectuals

(E) that modern society had opened up new opportunities for women

49. **D** In 1929, Virginia Woolf published *A Room of One's Own* based on a series of lectures she had presented at Cambridge. In the work, she questioned why it was that women were not taken seriously as writers and intellectuals. Her conclusion stated that women needed to find a space of their own, away from male-dominated institutions, where they could create freely. To do this, they needed something that often did not exist for Victorian women—an independent income.

Source: Imperial War Museum

50. The preceding poster reveals the extent to which women

(A) were encouraged to leave the factories when their husbands came home

(B) were a critical part of the war effort

(C) needed to be careful while working in munitions factories

(D) were underutilized until the end of the war

(E) needed to be convinced to work in the factories because they were uninterested in the war effort

50. **B** During the First World War, women became an integral part of the war effort by working as nurses at the front or by filling jobs at home that previously were held by men. Many women worked in munitions factories, a job that was extremely dangerous, although the poster does not reveal that side of it. The poster shows women's commitment to the war effort and how their labor was essential for victory. Women were quickly removed from the factories once the war ended, and public posters in the ensuing years emphasized that women should focus on their homes and raising their children.

QUESTIONS	EXPLANATIONS
51. At the start of the First World War, the various Socialist parties in Europe (A) waited to see if the war would be over quickly before committing to a particular response (B) refused to vote for war credits for their governments (C) quickly organized the Third International to rebuild socialism as a political force (D) supported their nation's war efforts (E) voted to support the war only if certain critical demands were immediately met	51. **D** Prior to the outbreak of the First World War, Socialist parties throughout Europe claimed that they would never support a capitalist war. When war began in the summer of 1914, however, the Socialists supported their own nations' war effort. In Germany, the Socialists justified voting for war credits for the government by claiming that they were involved in a great struggle against Russian autocracy. French socialists backed up their decision to support their government by claiming the war was a struggle against German militarism. Socialist internationalism, the idea that workers know no national borders, was severely tested in 1914 and was defeated by the forces of nationalism.
52. Which group was most dramatically affected by the German hyperinflation of 1923? (A) unionized workers (B) the peasantry (C) the urban poor (D) the middle class (E) landowning families	52. **D** While no one could entirely avoid the effect of the German hyperinflation of 1923, the middle class was hit the hardest. Unionized factory workers in Germany generally had their wages indexed to the rate of inflation and so could manage to ride out the storm. For the middle class, however, the hyperinflation was a disaster, since as a group, these people tended to be careful savers and therefore witnessed the rapid loss of a lifetime of savings.
53. "Oh highest and most marvelous felicity of man! To him it is granted to have whatever he chooses, to be whatever he wills." The above quote represents most closely the view of (A) a Northern humanist scholar (B) someone from the Middle Ages (C) a Protestant preacher (D) a Catholic priest (E) an Italian Renaissance scholar	53. **E** The passage comes from Pico della Mirandola's *Oration on the Dignity of Man*. In the work, Pico, a humanist scholar, describes humans as free and able to make their own choices regarding their destiny. The *Oration* is often cited as an example of the optimism in human potential that was common in the Italian Renaissance. By contrast, in the Middle Ages, humanity was regarded as essentially negative: Man was a sinner and therefore in dire need of the church to provide salvation.

QUESTIONS	EXPLANATIONS

54. After a radical beginning marked by violence, Anabaptist communities

(A) fell apart after the execution of their leaders
(B) lost interest in the Reformation when they realized that Luther did not agree with them
(C) turned their attention inward, rejecting violence and the influence of outsiders
(D) attacked the ideas of the Mennonites
(E) fled to England where there was religious toleration

54. C Anabaptists rejected the notion of infant baptism, insisting that baptism should only be performed on adults who were fully aware of the consequences of their actions. In 1532, a radical group of Anabaptists took control over the German city of Munster. They imposed a rather odd theocratic government, allowing for polygamy and killing those who refused to go along with Anabaptist rule. After a year and a half, Catholic and Lutheran princes joined forces to send troops to put down Anabaptist rule in Munster. After the forces ended their rule over Munster, many Anabaptists moved toward pacifism, particularly in the Netherlands where a group under the leadership of Menno Simons renounced the use of violence. This community lived peacefully in the Netherlands; some moved to North America where they became known as Mennonites.

55. The fact that the Portuguese were able to dominate in the Indian Ocean was due to their ability to

(A) arrange diplomatic missions
(B) export valuable commodities from home
(C) mount cannons on their ships
(D) use religion as a tool to convert their opponents
(E) defeat the Spanish on the open seas

55. C When the Portuguese sailed into the Indian Ocean at the end of the fifteenth century, they came into contact with navies from the Islamic world. Although the Portuguese were brilliant navigators, the real reason why they were able to dominate the Indian Ocean and establish colonies on the western coast of India was that they enjoyed technological supremacy over their opponents. One example of this was their ability to mount cannons on their ships, which gave them a huge advantage over their opponents.

QUESTIONS	EXPLANATIONS

56. During the reign of Edward VI—Henry VIII's only surviving son—England

(A) continued to reject Protestantism in favor of Catholicism
(B) focused primarily on foreign disputes to limit the domestic impact of religious disputes
(C) became a center for religious toleration
(D) maintained the Church of England as it had been established under Henry VIII
(E) witnessed the introduction of Protestant ideas into the Church of England

56. **E** The Church of England created by Henry VIII through his Act of Supremacy in 1534 was not formed to follow Protestant doctrines. Henry had no interest in Luther's concept of salvation by faith alone and the Bible being the sole source of faith. Rather surprisingly, considering his lack of interest in Protestant theology, Henry provided Protestant tutors for his son, the future Edward VI. When Edward became king in 1547 at the age of nine, he and his royal advisors began to shift the Church of England in the direction of Protestantism. By the time of his death in 1553, the Church of England was clearly following Protestant theology on most major issues.

57. The Later Baroque style is known for

(A) its restrained use of color
(B) the intensity of its religious message
(C) its rigorous realism
(D) its soothing contemplative qualities
(E) its extreme ornamentation

57. **E** The Late Baroque period, often referred to as the Rococo style, placed tremendous emphasis on extreme ornamentation. The Early Baroque style focused on religious intensity and a restrained palate of colors; the Later Baroque style, however, rejected such constraints and was awash in bright colors and highly decorative elements.

58. Eduard Bernstein, the father of Marxist revisionism, believed that

(A) Marxism as a political force would be finished unless it learned how to deal with the issue of unemployment
(B) workers would not need to seize power by revolutionary tactics because their goals could be achieved through democratic means
(C) workers needed to primarily think of themselves as wage slaves before they could become proper Marxists
(D) European nations would have to adjust themselves to Marxism and not the other way around
(E) Marxism as a political force was over

58. **B** In 1898, Eduard Bernstein published *Evolutionary Socialism*, in which he argued that capitalism was not in its final death throes, as Marx had believed, and that Socialists needed to come to terms with the continuing strength of capitalism. Furthermore, the spread of universal male suffrage throughout much of western Europe meant that the triumph of the proletariat could be achieved through the ballot box and not only through violent means as Marx had contended. Bernstein's revisionist views were officially rejected by the German Social Democratic Party (SPD), although as a matter of course, the party practiced what Bernstein had preached: The SPD was not engaged in genuine revolutionary activities, and it did direct its attention toward achieving its goals within the German Parliament.

QUESTIONS	EXPLANATIONS
59. Anarchists believed that individuals will be free only when (A) the state is geared toward better meeting the needs of workers (B) the individual accepted that freedom is in the mind and not possible in a physical sense (C) the state is abolished (D) the teachings of Marx are accepted (E) the individual is free to return to the simple rural life	59. **C** Anarchists believed that the state should be abolished and that small cooperatives of factory workers or farmers should be organized in place of the state. Anarchism was never as popular as socialism among the working people of Europe, although it did become influential in both France and Italy, while the Spanish province of Andalusia contained the largest anarchist movement in all of Europe. The last decades of the nineteenth century saw a wave of violence by anarchist groups; not all anarchists, however, favored the use of bloodshed to overthrow the state.
60. Theodore Herzl argued that because of the increased anti-Semitism in Europe it would be necessary for Jews to (A) try to blend into the larger European population (B) recommit themselves to religious tradition (C) create a homeland of their own (D) go to the United States where there was religious freedom (E) organize associations to come to the aid of their hard-pressed brethren	60. **C** Two specific events convinced the journalist Theodore Herzl that it was necessary for Jews to leave behind the vehement anti-Semitism found in Europe and create a homeland of their own. These events were the election of a mayor in Vienna who ran on an openly anti-Semitic platform and the 1894 treason conviction of the Jewish Captain Dreyfus in France. The quest for a Jewish homeland, which was labeled Zionism, provided the foundation for the eventual creation of the Jewish state of Israel in 1948.
61. Sigmund Freud believed that humans are (A) influenced by their subconscious feelings and emotions (B) not influenced by the subconscious mind though it would be better if they were (C) sometimes influenced by their sexual drives (D) capable of making rational choices only when they are free of parental authority (E) eminently rational and therefore fully aware of their subconscious thoughts	61. **A** Freud believed that because the human mind is rational, there had to be an explanation for the irrational world of dreams. He concluded that dreams contained unconscious desires and emotions that the individual did not want to be aware of on a conscious level. Freud's most important ideas on the role of dreams can be found in his *The Interpretation of Dreams* (1900).

62. Voltaire's *Candide* reveals that Enlightenment thought was not always

(A) tolerant
(B) clearly focused on philosophical matters
(C) light-hearted
(D) opposed to traditional ideas
(E) optimistic

62. **E** One of the common clichés concerning the Enlightenment of the eighteenth century was that it was fundamentally optimistic. There is some justification for this view, because the Enlightenment's belief in the power of human reason did seem to imply that people were free to shape their own destinies as long as they trusted their rational minds and avoided the dogma of the past. Yet Voltaire's *Candide* (1759) reveals another side of enlightened thought: When young Candide takes a horrifying journey through a harsh world he is constantly reminded of the cruelties that humans can inflict on one another. At the end of the book, Candide is left to understand that the only possible satisfaction that the individual can achieve is by "cultivating one's own garden" or finding solace in one's personal affairs.

63. The loss of significant colonial possessions in the Seven Years War played a role in France's decision to

(A) impose a mercantilistic system on its remaining colonies
(B) aid the American colonies in their struggle with the British
(C) focus its attention on continental affairs
(D) ally itself with the Austrians to counter the British
(E) join with Prussia and Russia in an anti-British alliance

63. **B** French support for the American colonists proved to be decisive during the American Revolution. The French agreed to support the Americans in 1778 not because they had any sympathy for the ideals of the American Revolution, but rather as a means of striking back at the British, who had won a tremendous victory over the French in the Seven Years War (1756–1763). French naval support proved to be critical to the defeat of the British at Yorktown in 1781. In the end, the French basically achieved their goal to strike back at Great Britain, as the loss of their American colonies was a terrible blow for the British. However, this victory over Great Britain came at a heavy price for the French monarchy; the high costs of their military assistance to the Americans put them increasingly in debt. This proved to be one of the reasons why Louis XVI found himself in such a financial bind on the eve of the French Revolution.

64. *The law locks up both man and woman*
Who steals the goose from off the common
But lets the greater felon loose
Who steals the common from the goose.

This poem is primarily critical of English

(A) common law
(B) poaching laws
(C) hunting and fishing restrictions
(D) enclosure laws
(E) royal wealth

64. **D** Beginning in the sixteenth century, wealthy land-owners were allowed by acts of Parliament to take the common fields that were found in almost every agricultural community throughout England and fence them off, or enclose them, giving them exclusive use of this land. Many farmers who owned only small plots of land had grazed their animals in the common fields; therefore, these lands had been important for their survival. Once these lands were enclosed—a process that hit its peak in the eighteenth century—many small farmers found they couldn't live off their own land. The poem reveals the bitterness that these farmers felt when they found themselves forced to sell off their small farms because they could not make a living without use of the common fields.

65. The appointment of Lord Bute in 1761 as chief minister to George III

(A) solidified George's hold over the House of Commons
(B) seemed to violate the idea that the king should select ministers who had a power base in Parliament
(C) came when the king was suffering from a bout of insanity
(D) directly caused the American Revolution
(E) was quickly followed by political stability throughout the following decade

65. **B** The selection by George III of his friend Lord Bute to be chief minister was controversial, but not because the king had selected his own minister—in the eighteenth century this was one of the privileges enjoyed by the monarchy. It was controversial because by this time monarchs were expected to select individuals who had significant support in either the House of Lords or the House of Commons. Bute, a Scottish nobleman, was not a member of Parliament and had little political influence. For this reason, certain members of Parliament deemed his selection inappropriate.

66. During the French Revolution, *assignats*, the new paper money, were backed by

(A) church property
(B) noble property
(C) gold
(D) silver
(E) tax revenues

66. **A** In 1790, the French National Assembly made the decision to deal with the national debt by issuing paper money, or *assignats,* that were to be backed by the value of the lands confiscated from the Catholic Church.

QUESTIONS	EXPLANATIONS

67. "Sire! We must do from above what the French have done from below!"

Who said the above words?

(A) Johann Fichte
(B) Count Steuben
(C) Friedrich Hegel
(D) Baron Stein
(E) General Blucher

67. **D** Following the devastating defeat of Prussian forces by the French at the Battle of Jena (1806), Baron Stein, one of the chief ministers to King Frederick William III, urged Prussia to begin a series of fundamental reforms. The above quote reveals that the monarch was to implement these reforms, unlike in France where revolutionary activity by the people had brought about political change. Stein urged the king to abolish serfdom within Prussia and to allow middle-class men to become officers, previously the sole preserve of the nobility.

Source: Houghton-Mifflin

68. This drawing, which appeared on the cover of a songbook, best reveals

(A) the Victorian love of music
(B) Victorian sentimentality
(C) the Victorian cult of domesticity
(D) a reverence for the countryside
(E) Victorian prosperity

68. **C** The family that appeared on the cover of the songbook was the British royal family. Queen Victoria and her husband Prince Albert are presented along with their four children in a setting designed to emphasize the quiet bliss of family life. The Victorian cult of domesticity was an ideal that said personal satisfaction could best be located within the confines of the family, and Queen Victoria and her family were seen as its chief proponents. Like much of Victorian England, the reality was somewhat different than the projected image. Victoria, while deeply in love with her husband, had children only because she saw it as part of her responsibilities as queen and had a rather distant relationship with all of them.

QUESTIONS	EXPLANATIONS

69. The Black Hundreds

(A) were armed Russian anarchist bands
(B) were Socialist revolutionaries
(C) attempted to restore tsarist authority in Russia following the 1905 Revolution
(D) were armed bandits who stole to fill Bolshevik coffers prior to the First World War
(E) attempted to restore the tsar following the November 1917 Revolution

69. C The Black Hundreds were Russian nationalists who organized armed bands to commit atrocities against those they deemed to be enemies of the tsar. The Black Hundreds were part of the conservative backlash that followed on the heels of the 1905 Russian Revolution. They were viciously anti-Semitic and committed numerous atrocities against Jewish communities, including the murder of thousands of individuals, crimes that Nicholas II refused to prosecute. In fact, Nicholas was thrilled by the behavior of the Black Hundreds and encouraged their murderous rampages.

70. In 1924, Ramsey MacDonald became the first British Prime Minister

(A) who was a Catholic
(B) who was from Scotland
(C) from the Labour Party
(D) who had served in the First World War
(E) who received a salary

70. C Despite the fact that the Labour Party was not the largest party in the House of Commons in 1924, Ramsey MacDonald was given the opportunity to become the first Prime Minister from the Labour Party. The majority party, the Conservatives, had lost a vote in the House of Commons on the issue of economic protection and after that needed some time out of office to regroup. MacDonald's government fell several months later in part because by then the Conservatives were ready to come back into office and because MacDonald's government had taken the unpopular step of officially recognizing the Soviet Union.

71. Hitler won the support of the German military following

(A) his promise to remilitarize Germany
(B) the destruction of the S.A.
(C) his breaking of the Versailles Treaty
(D) the destruction of the Communist Party
(E) his commitment to wipe out European Jewry

71. B Ernst Röhm, the commander of the S.A., the Nazi Party's private army, wanted to establish a new German army with the S.A. as the base and with himself as its commander. This angered the officers of the German General Staff, who viewed Röhm and his S.A. as little more than street thugs, and they watched with concern as the S.A. grew to almost 3 million strong. Hitler wanted the support of the German military to consolidate his power, so he decided to sacrifice Röhm and the S.A. On June 30, 1934, the "night of the long knives," Röhm and most of the S.A. leadership were executed. In return, the army agreed to take an oath of personal loyalty to Hitler.

QUESTIONS	EXPLANATIONS

72. Which of the following nations was the last to grant women the right to vote?

(A) France
(B) Sweden
(C) Italy
(D) Switzerland
(E) Finland

72. **D** In 1971, Swiss women were granted the right to vote and to stand for parliament in a national referendum. This was a different outcome than in 1959 in which a 2 to 1 majority defeated a similar measure. While the 1971 referendum only covered national as opposed to canton elections, most Swiss cantons allowed for female suffrage in the immediate aftermath, with the exception of two cantons that didn't allow women to vote until the end of the 1980s.

73. The term "Phony War" refers to

(A) the French response to the German advance in 1940
(B) the way the British viewed the war in 1940
(C) the American attitude toward the war until the attack on Pearl Harbor
(D) the inability of Britain and France to come to the aid of the Poles
(E) the surprisingly little action on the Western Front following the fall of Poland

73. **E** Germany began the Second World War with a Blitzkrieg strike through Poland. Although they fought bravely, the Poles were easily defeated within the month of September. The French and British did little to aid the Poles. Following the collapse of Poland, there was no action on the Western Front during the remainder of the fall and the winter, a period that became known as the "Phony War" because of the inactivity on the war front. The "Phony War" came to a sudden end on May 10, 1940, when German soldiers invaded neutral Belgium, the first stage in the eventual conquest of France, which took place in June.

QUESTIONS	EXPLANATIONS

74. The government of Venice during the Renaissance may most accurately be labeled a

(A) constitutional monarchy
(B) dictatorship
(C) republic
(D) autocracy
(E) democracy

74. C Venice had a unique constitution, which, although widely respected throughout Europe, was never imitated. Venice was a republic, but one in which few Venetians were allowed to participate. Only about 2,500 wealthy individuals had the right to sit on the Great Council and to elect members of the Senate, who had to be of noble descent. The Senate in turn elected the Doge, the head of state who held the office for life. Increasingly, the Doge became more of a ceremonial position and the men who sat on the Senate held the real power in the state.

75. Luther's decision to marry Katherine Von Bora was an example of

(A) the means by which Luther reached the decision to challenge the church on the issue of the sacraments
(B) how clergy could misinterpret Catholic teachings on the sacrament of marriage
(C) a personal decision that involved no religious principles
(D) the changing role of the clergy in Protestant churches
(E) how traditional matchmaking remained significant in rural German communities

75. D One of the major changes brought about by Martin Luther's challenge to the Catholic Church was that he disagreed with it about the role of the clergy. For Catholics, the clergy plays a critical role; by administering the sacraments, it is the conduit through which the individual achieves salvation. Therefore, the Catholic Church believes that the clergy, in keeping with its special role, needs to be a separate caste, which in part is achieved through its vows of chastity. Luther, on the other hand, believed that all one needs for salvation is faith and that the clergy plays absolutely no role in whether one is to receive God's grace. Ministers may be teachers and help lead their flock toward faith, but they are not essential to salvation. Luther saw no reason why the clergy could not marry just like everyone else. Although he thought of himself as a confirmed bachelor, he did marry Katherine Von Bora in part to show the changing role of the clergy in the Lutheran church and partly for the companionship of marriage.

QUESTIONS	EXPLANATIONS
76. At the Council of Trent, the Catholic Church (A) agreed to work with Protestant theologians to come to an acceptable compromise (B) accepted Protestant positions on most issues, though still refused to allow for clerical marriage (C) decided to wait to formulate a position on most of the issues addressed by the Protestants (D) rejected Protestant positions on the sacraments, on the giving of wine to the laity during communion, and on clerical marriage (E) focused on producing a new catechism that could effectively counteract Protestant ideas	76. **D** The Council of Trent met in three sessions between 1545 and 1563 and serves as the centerpiece of the Catholic Counter-Reformation. The Catholic Church agreed to stop such controversial practices as the selling of indulgences and religious offices; it rejected, however, Protestant teachings on such critical issues as the question of salvation. The Catholic Church maintained its traditional theology that salvation is based on faith as well as works, as opposed to the Protestant idea that faith alone is needed for salvation. The Catholic hierarchy that gathered at Trent also rejected the following: the idea of giving the laity (the congregation) the wine as well as the wafer during the mass, the Protestant teachings on the role of the clergy, and the proposal to allow clergy to marry.
77. In the early 1950s, the French government tried to (A) ban the use of "Americanisms" like *le week-end* (B) ban the importation of Coca-Cola for fear it would damage the French wine industry (C) stop stores from using any language other than French in their store windows (D) ban the importation of American dairy products such as Velveeta (E) ban all British products from French stores unless they could be reinspected for contaminants	77. **B** Under pressure from the powerful French wine lobby, the government in the early 1950s attempted to ban the importation of Coca-Cola. After a short period the ban was lifted, but in France Coca-Cola remained a symbol of the spread of American culture throughout the world for the next several decades.
78. German chancellor Willy Brandt resigned in 1974 after it was revealed that (A) he had failed to acknowledge his Nazi past (B) his political party had received political funding from the American CIA (C) the West German economic miracle was fundamentally flawed (D) one of his aides was a spy for the East Germans (E) he was hiding a serious illness	78. **D** Willy Brandt hated fascism and fled Germany at the start of the Second World War and went on to serve bravely with the Norwegian resistance. He later became the Mayor of Berlin and in 1969, as head of the Social Democratic Party, became the German Chancellor. Brandt played a very important role in trying to establish better relations between West Germany and the Soviet Union. Brandt resigned from office in 1974 when it was discovered that one of his closest aides was a spy for East Germany.

QUESTIONS	EXPLANATIONS

79. German unification in October 1990

   (A) occurred with remarkably few problems since the West Germans had planned for this moment for decades

   (B) was achieved at an economic cost far higher than expected

   (C) led to renewed calls to redraw the postwar boundaries of Germany and its Eastern European neighbors

   (D) was secretly opposed by the United States

   (E) was strongly opposed by the French

79. B Although the West Germans had laid out plans for the eventual unification of Germany, when it finally happened in 1990, it occurred with such remarkable speed that the West Germans were quite unprepared. The East German economy was in far worse shape than previously realized, and the government of the newly unified Germany found itself having to spend much more than expected to modernize the economy and infrastructure of the eastern half of the country. The economic costs were also extremely high because of a controversial decision by the government to exchange the weak currency of East Germany on a one-to-one basis with the very strong currency of West Germany. This exchange was to aid the people of East Germany in their adjustment to life in the new Germany; however it proved to be extremely costly.

80. The formation of the Northern League in the early 1990s is a reflection of

   (A) the continuing strength of fascism in Italy

   (B) the failure of Italian governments to deal with substantive issues

   (C) the strength of separatist tendencies in Italy

   (D) the continuing political legacy of Garibaldi

   (E) Northern Italy's declining economic influence within the Italian Republic

80. C Creating an Italian nation required that the separatist tendencies that were part of the history of the Italian peninsula since the time of the fall of the Roman Empire had to come to an end. This unification was exceedingly difficult because in many ways Northern Italy is a very different place from Southern Italy. In 1861, as a result of the work of Cavour and Garibaldi, one Italian nation was formed, though the strong regional differences that existed throughout Italy remained unchanged. In recent years, this problem has received renewed attention. Some residents of the prosperous north feel that too much of their taxes are directed toward the much poorer south; money, due to corruption and various inefficiencies, does little to aid the squalid economic situation in the south. In the early 1990s, this sentiment was behind the creation of the Northern League, a political party based in Florence that claimed as its major goal the secession of the northern parts of Italy from the rest of the country.

THE DBQ EXPLAINED

The Document-Based Question (DBQ) section begins with a mandatory 15-minute reading period. During these 15 minutes, you'll want to (1) come up with some information not included in the given documents (your outside knowledge) to include in your essay; (2) get an overview of what each document means; (3) decide what opinion you are going to argue; and (4) write an outline of your essay.

The DBQ in Practice Test 1 concerns the issue of human rights during the French Revolution. You should be prepared to discuss how the French Revolution advanced the cause of human rights and also explain the ways that some individuals wanted a more narrow definition of who should be eligible to enjoy these rights. You will need to know something about human rights in France prior to the outbreak of the Revolution in 1789 and also know how the concept of human rights changed over the course of the Revolution.

The first thing you want to do, BEFORE YOU LOOK AT THE DOCUMENTS, is to brainstorm for a minute or two. Try to list everything you remember about the issue of human rights in France both prior to the French Revolution and after. This list will serve as your reference to the outside information you must provide to earn a top grade.

Next, read over the documents. As you read them, take notes in the margins and underline those passages that you are certain you are going to use in your essay. If a document helps you remember a piece of outside information, add that information to your brainstorming list. If you cannot make sense of a document or it argues strongly against your position, relax! You do not need to mention every document to score well on the DBQ.

Here is what you might assess in the time you have to look over the documents.

THE DOCUMENTS

Document 1

This excerpt comes from an article on Natural Law written by Diderot, which appeared in his *Encyclopedia*. You should note the date of the passage, 1755, which means it was written several decades prior to the French Revolution.

The passage refers to the term "Natural Rights," which it defines as those inalienable rights you enjoy as a human being, so long as the enjoyment of those rights does not impose on the rights of others. There is also the notion that these rights, because they are natural rights, are enjoyed by all of humanity without distinction as to time or place.

Document 2

This document also dates prior to the French Revolution and should be duly noted; you will need to address the question of rights prior to the French Revolution in your essay. The passage is an excerpt from a Royal Edict of Toleration granting certain rights to Calvinists within France.

The passage refers to King Louis XIV, who, in a rather grudging manner, granted that certain rights are to be extended to French Calvinists for the present.

The document makes it clear, however, that the right of public worship would remain the sole preserve of Catholics. Calvinists are to be granted only those things that "natural right" no longer allows the French government to deny them: the right to publicly register their births, marriages, and deaths.

Document 3

Document 3 comes from *What Is the Third Estate?*, a pamphlet written by the Abbé Siéyès, who is identified as a leading author during the French Revolution.

The passage refers to the role of the Third Estate (the commoners) and contends that the Third Estate is essentially the French nation. Should the privileged order (the nobility) be removed from France, the Third Estate would not decline but would rise up "free and flourishing." The passage also contains the rather sharp line: "everything would be infinitely better without the other two orders," an attack on the privileges of both the clergy and the nobility.

Again, the date of the passage should be duly noted. In this case it is 1789, the year of the French Revolution.

Document 4

Of all the documents in this DBQ, this should be the one with which you are most familiar. This is the *Declaration of the Rights of Man and Citizen* and therefore one of the documents that certainly was discussed in class while you were studying the French Revolution.

You'll notice that the document begins with the idea, "Men are born and remain free and equal in rights." Think about how this idea is linked to the issues raised in Document 1. Article 4 is also linked to Document 1 in that it says, "each man has no limits except those which assure to the other members of the society the enjoyment of the same rights." What specific rights is the author discussing here? Article 2 tells us these rights are "liberty, property, security, and resistance to oppression."

Document 5

This passage comes from a committee report prepared in 1789 by members of the National Assembly who submitted the report to the entire National Assembly during the debate over who should be allowed to vote. The committee decided that there had to be some restrictions on voter eligibility. They had to be French citizens, meet certain residency requirements, and have reached the age of maturity (the exact age is not spelled out in the document and the assumption throughout the document is that voters will be exclusively male). The committee also decided that the vote should be restricted to those who had enough income that they paid taxes that were equal to the wages paid to the average worker for three days of work. In addition, servants were excluded from the vote.

Document 6

Document 6 comes from a pamphlet written by the Bishop of Nancy that was about whether Jews should be granted the full rights of citizens. The Bishop is clearly unsympathetic to Jews, who he claims had "strayed into our midst" and therefore should still be considered foreigners, not French. He does allow that Jews should be provided with their personal liberty and enjoy certain property rights. Political rights, however, were out of the question.

Document 7

Document 7 serves as a nice counterbalance to Document 6. This passage comes from a speech given in 1791 by a member of the National Assembly during the debate on extending full political rights to Jews. Unlike the Bishop of Nancy, who refused even to consider Jews French citizens, the speaker, Adrien Jean Françoise Duport, argues that Jews should enjoy the full rights of citizenship. For Duport it was clear that, "freedom of worship no longer permits any distinction to be made between the political rights of citizens on the basis of their beliefs."

Document 8

Document 8 is the decree from the National Assembly declaring the abolition of slavery in all French colonies and that all men, without distinction of color, who reside in the colonies are French citizens and enjoy all rights that that entails. You might notice that this document is dated February 1794, five years after the start of the French Revolution and a number of years after the debate on extending political rights to Jews.

Document 9

Document 9 comes from the pen of Olympe De Gouges, who is identified as a self-educated woman who wrote pamphlets and plays that dealt with political topics. Notice that the title of her work is *The Declaration of the Rights of Woman*, an obvious play on the title *Declaration of the Rights of Man* (Document 4). Keep this in mind for your essay because there are some obvious comparisons that can be made between the two documents.

In this passage by De Gouges, she has obviously taken the natural rights language found in the *Declaration of the Rights of Man* and twisted it to argue for the rights of women. Women, according to De Gouges, were like men born free and equal in rights. This also meant that women, as seen in Article 13, also shared in the same public responsibilities as men, such as the payment of taxes and eligibility for forced public labor in times of emergency. These responsibilities, however, also bring with them certain rights, and therefore women should have equal access to government offices and employment.

Document 10

The passage found in Document 10 serves as a counterbalance to Document 9. The document contains parts of a speech delivered in the National Assembly in favor of a decree banning women from forming political clubs. The document touts some very sexist ideas such as, "women are hardly capable of lofty conception and serious cogitations." The speaker also asks men if they really wanted to see women take part in political assemblies if it meant that women would abandon their natural sense of feminine discretion and would lead them to neglect their families.

OUTSIDE INFORMATION

We have already discussed much more than you could possibly include in a 45-minute essay. Do not worry. You will not be expected to mention everything or even most of what we have covered in the section above. You will, however, be expected to include some outside information; that is, information not mentioned directly in the documents.

Here is some outside information you might incorporate in your essay.

- During the Enlightenment—the intellectual movement that dominated eighteenth-century thought—the idea of natural rights, or what we might call today human rights, became highly significant. There was a question, however, as to what exactly was meant by natural rights. For the seventeenth-century English philosopher John Locke those natural rights that the individual should enjoy were life, liberty, and property; however, his definition of who should enjoy such rights was narrow and did not extend to women, slaves, and those without property. In France, the question of natural rights was also debated. The philosopher Rousseau took perhaps the most radical position when he suggested that natural rights extend to all men. Rousseau, however, did not consider that natural rights extended to women.

- In France, the Bourbon monarchy prior to 1789 gave certain rights that were not considered to be natural rights but were rather special privileges extended by the monarchy to specific groups or individuals. For example, the nobility was exempt from the payment of most taxes. This was a right that was extended to them as a special caste within France and was certainly not a privilege held by all. Because such grants of rights or privileges were not grounded on the notion of being natural rights, they had the distinct problem that they could be revoked. For example, in 1685 Louis XIV revoked the Edict of Nantes, a list of privileges that Calvinists had received from an earlier French monarch.

- In 1763, the philosopher Voltaire wrote *Treatise on Toleration*, a work inspired by the execution of Jean Calas, a Calvinist who was wrongfully accused of murdering his son because of the son's supposed desire to convert to Catholicism. Voltaire argued that religious toleration was necessary because it was a natural right that should not be impinged on by government. Calvinists were not the only religious minority in France that lacked a legal standing. After Louis XIV's seventeenth-century conquest of Alsace and Lorraine, lands that were formerly part of the Holy Roman Empire, France suddenly had a significant Jewish population. These individuals were banned from most occupations and were restricted in terms of where they could live.

- The question of human rights was front and center at the start of the French Revolution. In 1789, the Third Estate refused to meet as a separate legislative body because they were tired of the fact that the other two estates enjoyed special privileges that were not extended to commoners. For the remainder of the revolutionary period (1789–1799), the question of how far human rights should be extended was a hotly debated issue. For every argument made in favor of extending rights to some previously denied group, counter-arguments could be made as to reasons why legal restrictions should remain in place.

- Defining who was a citizen and therefore entitled to enjoy the rights and privileges that came with citizenship was a primary issue throughout the revolutionary period. From 1789 to 1792, France was a constitutional monarchy, while the constitution drawn up in 1791 limited full political participation to men who owned property. When France became a republic in 1792, full political rights were extended to all men regardless of whether they owned property. During the revolutionary period, a backlash against this sentiment erupted known as the Directory (1795–1799), when once again only men who possessed property were granted the right to full political participation.

- *The Declaration of the Rights of Man* said that no one should be disturbed for holding contrary opinions including, the document specifically noted, religious opinions. Whether religious minorities should be granted full political rights was another question, however, and heated opposition existed in some quarters about granting such rights to Calvinists and Jews. By 1791, the question had been resolved by making it clear that political rights were not to be denied to anyone on the basis of one's religious beliefs.

- The struggle for human rights for slaves was in many ways a more difficult issue to resolve than the question of human rights for religious minorities. This was in part because money was at stake, as so much of the economy of the French colonies was connected to slave labor. Initially, the National Assembly eliminated slavery in France (where it had already died out as an institution) but gave in to a heavy lobbying effort by white plantation owners in their Caribbean colony of Hispaniola and allowed it to stay there. This instigated Toussaint L'Ouverture to lead a slave revolt on the island. By 1794, the National Convention did away with slavery in all French colonies, though L'Ouverture's rebellion resulted in France losing the eastern half of the island of Hispaniola, which became the independent nation of Haiti.

- Although wealthy French women played an important role as sponsors of Enlightenment authors, the question of rights for women was not central to Enlightenment thought. At no point following the French Revolution did the National Assembly pay any notice to the idea of extending political rights to women, and, by 1793, women were banned from even participating in political clubs. Women did receive some rights in some non-political areas, such as the right to initiate divorce proceedings and to inherit property.

CHOOSING A THESIS STATEMENT

This DBQ is not asking you to take a side in a debate. Instead, you can stick with a central theme such as discussing how the question of human rights was fundamental to the entire history of the French Revolution. You might try to show how these rights were defined in different ways at various points during the Revolutionary period, or you might attempt to show that the initial debate over the question of political rights was never fully resolved. Another way to approach the question is by comparing human rights prior to the French Revolution to how it was defined during the course of the French Revolution.

Planning Your Essay

Unless you read extremely quickly, you probably will not have time to write a detailed outline for your essay during the 15-minute reading period. However, it is worth taking several minutes to jot down a loose structure of your essay because it will actually save you time when you write! First, decide on your thesis, and write it down in the test booklet. (There is usually some blank space below the documents.) Then, take a minute or two to brainstorm all the points you might put in your essay. Choose the strongest points and number them in the order you plan to present them. Lastly, note which documents and outside information you plan to use in conjunction with each point. If you organize your essay in advance of writing, the actual writing process will go much more smoothly. More important, you will not write yourself into a corner, suddenly finding yourself making a point you cannot support or heading toward a weak conclusion (or worse still, no conclusion at all).

For example, if you wanted to discuss how the question of human rights was defined in increasingly broad terms as the Revolution progressed, you could brainstorm a list of ideas and issues that you want to raise in your essay such as:

Rights before the French Revolution

Enlightenment and Natural Rights

Royal Absolutism

Calling of the Estates General

Special privileges for specific estates

Property and political rights

Political rights for religious minorities

Abolishment of slavery

Limited rights granted to women

Next, you would want to figure out which of your brainstorm ideas could be the main idea of paragraph number one, which ones could be used as evidence to support a point, and which should be eliminated. You should probably begin your first paragraph with your thesis, and then discuss what was meant by rights prior to the French Revolution. Since the first two items on your brainstorming list can be used in conjunction with a discussion of rights prior to 1789, your list might look this way:

Rights before the French Revolution	*1*
Enlightenment and Natural Rights	*1-evidence*
Royal Absolutism	*1-evidence*
Calling of the Estates General	
Special privileges for specific estates	
Property and political rights	
Political rights for religious minorities	
Abolishment of slavery	
Limited rights granted to women	

What else would you want to mention in this paragraph? You should certainly refer to Documents 1 and 2. Document 1 reveals the way in which the writers of the Enlightenment addressed the issue of natural rights, and Document 2 is a nice example of how privileges could be extended to specific groups in France, though only through royal grant.

Your second paragraph could deal with the issue of political rights at the very onset of the French Revolution, when the Estates General was called in 1789. Your list could now look like this:

Rights before the French Revolution	*1*
Enlightenment and Natural Rights	*1-evidence*
Royal Absolutism	*1-evidence*
Calling of the Estates General	*2*
Special privileges for specific estates	*2-evidence*
Property and political rights	
Political rights for religious minorities	
Abolishment of slavery	
Limited rights granted to women	

In this paragraph, you should certainly incorporate Document 3, which challenges the entire concept of specific rights being granted to the first two estates to the complete exclusion of the third. You can also reference Document 4, the *Declaration of the Rights of Man*, which reveals that after the calling of the Estates General in May 1789, by July of that same year special rights based on social caste were eliminated from French political life.

Proceed in this way until you have finished planning your strategy. Try to fit as many of the documents into your argument as you can, but do not stretch too far to fit one in. An obvious, desperate stretch will only hurt your grade. Also, remember that history is often intricate and that the readers of your exam want to see that you respect the intrinsic complexity behind many historical events.

THE FREE-RESPONSE ESSAY QUESTIONS EXPLAINED

Because you only have 35 minutes to plan and write each of these essays, you will not have time to work out elaborate arguments. That's okay; nobody is expecting you to read two questions, choose one, remember all the pertinent facts about the subject, formulate a brilliant thesis, write an essay about it, and then repeat the process. Here is what you do. First, choose your question; brainstorm for two or three minutes, and edit your brainstorm ideas. Then, number those points you are going to include in your essay in the order you plan to present them. Last, think of a simple thesis statement that allows you to discuss the points your essay will make.

QUESTION 1 — RENAISSANCE ART

1. Analyze how Renaissance art was a reflection of the new humanistic learning of the period.

About the Structure of Your Essay

This is not a question to answer if you fell asleep when your teacher pulled out his or her slides of Renaissance art. If you cannot think of any specific works of art to cite, stay clear of this question. On the other hand, for those of you who have a broad knowledge of Italian Renaissance art, this question offers you a good opportunity to set this knowledge within the context of one of the major themes of the Renaissance—the intellectual contributions made by humanist scholars.

One way of tackling this question is by providing a discussion of Italian humanism in the first part of your essay. In the second half of the essay, try to link the goals of Renaissance artists with the ideas of the humanists. Try to cite a number of artistic works (though there is no need to go overboard and refer to every work that you ever studied), and relate the artwork to the themes you laid out in the first part of your essay.

For the first part of your essay, the discussion of Italian humanism, you should probably discuss the following:

- In a narrowly defined way, humanism refers to a form of education that became popular during the course of the Italian Renaissance (c. 1350–1550). Students who followed the humanist program pursued a course of study that mimicked what a Roman or Greek youth would have studied in the classical world. A humanist scholar in the fifteenth century would have studied Latin and Greek grammar, arithmetic, logic, geometry, astronomy, music, and rhetoric.

- The humanist education entailed a rejection of medieval scholarship, or what is commonly referred to as scholasticism. Writers in the scholastic tradition, most notably the greatest scholastic of them all, Thomas Aquinas (1225–1274), applied reason to the study of theology. Aquinas believed that the writings of the great Greek philosopher Aristotle, a pagan, could be applied to the study of religion. Humanist scholars, on the other hand, believed that classical authors could be appreciated on their own merits without Christianizing their ideas. Although the scholastic scholar used logic as a means of supporting the ultimate truth, the existence of God, humanist scholars sought out the classical authors for a host of moral questions knowing that the answer may not necessarily be supported by Christian theology.

- Petrarch, the fourteenth-century writer who is considered to be the father of Renaissance humanism, believed that an individual's knowledge of the classical past should be used for private satisfaction only. Many humanists, however, believed in using their skills to serve the city-state and to use their classical education as a tool to help answer contemporary questions.

- Inspired by their reading of classical literature, most humanist scholars took a positive view of human nature, as opposed to the medieval view, which emphasized the sinfulness of mankind. The humanists emphasized free will and the potential for self-improvement. They also possessed an interest in the natural world as opposed to their medieval predecessors, who feared the natural world and were therefore far more reluctant to explore nature.

For the second half of the essay, you could discuss the ways in which artists were inspired by the humanist program and cite some specific pieces of art to buttress your argument.

- Some artists who were active during the Italian Renaissance, particularly those artists who had come from wealthy or noble families, received a humanist education. However, Michelangelo, for example, was not formally educated in the humanist tradition, but was self-taught and familiar with the works of Plato, whose writings on eternal ideas—such as beauty—influenced the way in which he approached his art.

- In keeping with the humanist interest to better grasp the world around them, Renaissance artists worked to add greater realism to their art. In the 1420s, the single-point perspective developed, which allowed for the creation of a three-dimensional space and, thus, greater artistic realism. Renaissance artists, also in keeping with humanist ideas, became highly interested in depicting nature with detail and accuracy that were completely lacking in medieval art.

- Renaissance artists were directly inspired by the classical past, much in the same way that humanist scholars looked to the classical world for inspiration. When Brunelleschi wanted to build a dome for the cathedral of Florence (the Duomo), he turned to classical architecture to help him solve some of the complex problems that arose in building such a vast structure. One cannot look at Michelangelo's *David* without recognizing that Michelangelo was fully aware of classical sculpture.

- Neo-Platonism, the humanist idea that the mind could extend beyond the constraints of the flesh and contemplate such eternal ideas as beauty and truth, inspired many Renaissance artists. Botticelli's *Birth of Venus* is full of Neo-Platonic symbolism, which was in keeping with the intellectual interests of his patrons, the Medici family.

QUESTION 2 — ENGLISH REVOLUTION

2. Describe and analyze at least TWO factors that led to the English Revolution of 1642.

About the Structure of Your Essay

The causes of the English Revolution are rather involved since they straddle a number of different areas. One can find political, social, economic, and religious issues behind the outbreak of revolution in 1642. You would certainly be very hard pressed in a 30-minute essay to fully discuss all these issues. Fortunately, the question asks you to focus on only a select number of possibilities.

Your essay should mention at least some of the following:

- Financial problems were a critical issue for the English monarchy. The cost of governing had gone up dramatically over the course of the sixteenth century, although many members of Parliament could not accept the idea that the king could need almost annual grants of money from Parliament. They assumed that the crown must be wasteful, so to keep the government functioning, James I (r. 1603–1625) was forced to sell noble titles and sold monopolies to individuals who then had the sole right in England to sell items like coal. King James had stated early in his reign his goal of reforming the system of royal finance, but parliament grew concerned that such a plan would mean additional taxes and scuttled any discussion of the issue.

- The question of prerogative rights was central to the English Revolution. What political rights were inherently the king's and what political rights were inherently Parliament's? The English Constitution, that blending of written law and unwritten tradition, lacked a precise answer to this question. Both king and parliament grappled with this issue. Members of the House of Commons began to support the idea during the reign of James I that the king's ministers should be acceptable to Parliament. During the reign of James's son Charles I (r. 1625–1649) Parliament began to argue that the king's ministers should be responsible to Parliament by allowing both houses to select and remove royal ministers.

- Parliament was concerned over its lack of input in foreign affairs. During the reign of Elizabeth, her parliaments began to press her on certain foreign policy points, though Elizabeth insisted they had no right to speak on such questions. Increasingly, James and his parliaments saw themselves at odds over foreign affairs. Parliament wanted English involvement in the Thirty Years War; James wisely knew that this was a conflict that England should not enter.

- The early seventeenth century was a period of economic difficulty in England and throughout much of Europe; high inflation and a series of poor harvests were among the most significant problems. Although not perhaps a direct cause of the English Revolution, this economic downturn played a role in undermining the social stability that had been so critical for the success of the Tudors and which apparently was lacking in the time of the early Stuart monarchs.

- Religious issues were critical for the outbreak of revolution in 1642. In fact, earlier in our own century, the English Revolution was more commonly referred to as the Puritan Revolution. The Puritans, a faction within the Church of England, wanted to see their church move more in the direction of Calvinism. They disliked the fact that the Church of England had a religious hierarchy that included bishops and archbishops. They wanted to see religious authority in the hands of local synods, or councils, as was the case in Geneva and other centers of Calvinism. Additionally, Puritans wanted to see the Church of England purged of anything that to them smacked of Catholicism, which they hated with an incredible intensity. Although a minority within England, the Puritans were a very important minority, as many of their adherents were wealthy, and had a large representation in the House of Commons.

  The problem was that neither James I nor Charles I had any interest in the Puritan agenda. James had been raised in the Calvinist Church of Scotland, but when he became King of England, he immediately began to prefer the practices of the Church of England because he believed that its ornate ceremonial and hierarchical structure were important buttresses of the English monarchy. His son was even more hostile to the Puritans. During his reign, Charles I increasingly began to support another faction within the Church of England, the Arminians. The Arminians rejected such Calvinist doctrines as predestination and the lack of human free will, but supported church services that emphasized ornate ceremony and the importance of the clerical hierarchy. Charles eventually selected William Laud, a leading Arminian, as his Archbishop of Canterbury, thus enraging Puritan sentiment.

- When Charles came to the throne in 1625, the problems that his father had had with Parliament grew significantly worse, and by 1629, Charles decided to rule without a parliament. This "personal rule" was to last 11 years until Charles was forced to call a parliament in 1640 to raise money to deal with a rebellion in Scotland, which broke out when Charles wanted to introduce the Church of England's prayer book into the Calvinist Church of Scotland. By 1641, Parliament had passed what was known as the "Grand Remonstrance," a document of 204 clauses that listed all parliamentary grievances over the past decade. It demanded that the king name ministers in whom Parliament could trust and called for a bill to totally reform the Church of England along more Puritan lines. In response, Charles tried to seize five of the leaders of Parliament. This attempt failed and he left London in January of 1642 to raise his royal standard at Nottingham and to show he was ready to go to war.

  Parliament responded to this action by passing its most radical plan, which demanded that supreme authority in the government should be in the hands of Parliament. Royal advisors were to be subject to parliamentary approval and all military and ecclesiastical appointments were to be approved by Parliament. Clearly the king could never accept such demands, and by the end of the summer of 1642 the nation was locked in a civil war between king and parliament.

Question 3 — Impact of the Industrial Revolution

3. Discuss the impact of the Early Industrial Revolution on the British working class.

About the Structure of Your Essay

This is a straightforward question that seeks to draw out your knowledge of a particular aspect of the Industrial Revolution—in this case, <u>not</u> the ways in which the factory system developed and the inventions that brought about this significant change in production. This is not the essay to show off your detailed understanding of the inner workings of James Watt's steam engine. Instead, for this essay, you need to show your understanding of what these changes meant for those who were most dramatically impacted—the workers. Therefore, you might want to begin with a thesis that captures a sense of the magnitude of the changes for these individuals in the period from c. 1760–1850. You can then brainstorm a list of changes, focusing on various factors, such as where workers labored and the conditions under which they were employed. Impact on family life, housing, health, and leisure time can also be covered. You can discuss the ways in which the working class attempted to respond to changes that often must have seemed overwhelming.

Your essay should mention at lease some of the following:

- Many first generation factory workers were previously small-scale farmers. For such individuals, factory work was going to be a dramatic switch from what they had previously known. While no one has ever considered farming to be an easy way of life, farmers at least had the dignity of controlling the daily order of their lives. With the advent of industrialization, however, the self-discipline of the farm was going to be replaced with the externally imposed discipline of the factory manager. One design feature found in many early factories were large clocks near the entrance, a very visible indication of the new significance of structured time.

- Farmers worked brutally long hours during both the planting and harvest seasons, but there were other, quieter times during the year as well when there was less work to do and more time to enjoy life. Such practices were not to be found in the factories, where work didn't reflect the various pace of the seasons and those workers who tried to keep the tradition of "St. Monday," a means of extending leisure time so that Monday was another day off, often found themselves out of a job.

- Workers toiled under conditions that were often dangerous. Safety played little role in the design of early factories, with workers often paying a horrific price in lost limbs and damaged health.

- The pre-industrial family often functioned as a single working unit, working in close proximity on tasks that may have been gender specific but were interconnected. While no one should idealize this situation, it can be argued that it was replaced with something worse, with the family still in need of income but no longer able to work together as a unit towards that goal, with the father, mother, and children all possibly working in completely different environments. Also, while child labor existed well before there were factories, there does seem to be something far worse when children as young as six worked incredibly long under the eye of a foreman rather than a parent.

- The movement of a rural population to the cities was also going to bring significant problems, particularly since little thought was expended on urban planning in the period of the Early Industrial Revolution. A new phenomenon—slums, where you had an exclusively working class population living in abject squalor—began to emerge on the urban landscape. This was such a direct by-product of industrialization that visitors from the pre-industrialized continent would visit places like St. Giles in London to see what these slums were all about (although if they had stayed home they wouldn't have had that long to wait since European cities would develop slums of their own in the second half of the nineteenth century). Urban life was shaped by cholera and typhoid epidemics, stemming from the poor quality of the drinking water, while housing was often ramshackle and grossly overcrowded.

- British workers also had to deal with a government that was far from sympathetic. Ranging from the banning of unions, to the Poor Law of 1834, which treated those seeking relief in so awful a manner as to discourage all but the most desperate from seeking assistance, Parliament showed itself to be uninterested in the needs of workers. The one exception to this record was the Factory Act (1833), an attempt to mitigate one of the worst abuses—child labor—but even here, many workers must have been displeased, since the income earned by their children was important for the upkeep of the family.

You can also discuss the development of a self-conscious working class identity that was rooted in shared hardships. This working class identity can be found in the following:

- Communal attendance at Methodist chapels. Methodist ministers preached in urban areas where the Church of England basically maintained no institutional presence. Methodism also provided important lessons for the working class in encouraging literacy as well as organizational skills that would later prove to be useful for working class organizations.

- Friendly Societies were a way to get around the laws against unionization (in effect until 1824)

- Solidarity was established through the development of working class political organizations, the most important being the Chartist movement of the 1830s and '40s. Workers believed that the best way to mitigate the hardships in their lives was to have some influence over the political process. While the first working class men did not receive the vote until the Second Reform Bill of 1864, the previous decades had witnessed many attempts at organizing as a social class for political change, which made this later victory not only possible but in many ways inevitable.

QUESTION 4—CONTAINMENT OF REVOLUTION

4. Discuss how the great powers of Europe attempted to stem the tide of revolution in the period from 1815 to 1830.

About the Structure of Your Essay

This essay is asking you to deal with the political backlash that swept through Europe following the final defeat of Napoleon in 1815. The ensuing fifteen years witnessed an attempt by the major European powers to place the revolutionary genie back in the bottle with varying degrees of success. You should begin your essay with a discussion of the Congress of Vienna (1814–1815) and how the nations of Europe attempted to turn back the clock to a time before everything was disrupted by the events of the French Revolution of 1789. From there you should discuss the repressive steps taken in many of the capitals in Europe to ensure that revolutionary sentiments were kept under control. Finally, in the last part of your essay, you should write about some of the revolutions that broke out in places like Spain, Italy, France, and Russia, despite, or perhaps because of the concerted effort to contain all revolutionary ideas.

Your essay should mention at least some of the following signs of political backlash against revolutionary sentiment:

- At the Congress of Vienna there was an attempt by the five major powers in attendance (Prussia, Austria, Great Britain, Russia, and France) to ensure that the ideas of the French Revolution would remain contained so that they would not contaminate the rest of Europe. To that end it was agreed (with the sole dissent of Great Britain), that the great powers had the right to interfere in the internal affairs of other nations to contain the possibility of revolution. The Congress of Vienna refused to address such issues as nationalism and political reform, two issues that had been stirred up by the French Revolution and were now deemed too dangerous to even contemplate.

- A new, conservative political ideology began to emerge in the years following the defeat of Napoleon. Rather than the more nuanced conservatism found in the writing of Edmund Burke, who believed that gradual, evolutionary change could be beneficial for the state, this new breed of conservatism was arch-reactionary. One prominent writer of this tradition was Joseph de Maistre, a Frenchman who had fled France during the Revolution. De Maistre believed that all political sovereignty came from God, while also writing that "the first servant of the king should be the executioner."

- Monarchs across Europe established secret police forces (modeled on Napoleon's) in order to deal with suspected revolutionaries. They also committed resources to create government agencies to deal with the censoring of books and newspapers. Workers were banned from forming unions and political meetings were made illegal.

- Across Europe there was a tremendous religious revival in the years after 1815. Religious institutions had gone into decline as a result of the Enlightenment and the French Revolution. After 1815, there was a concerted effort by the European states to bring about a revival of religion, since it was believed that organized religion was an important bulwark of the conservative state.

Your essay should also deal with the various revolutionary movements that emerged in the period from 1815 to 1830, despite the attempt to contain all signs of revolutionary ardor.

- Ferdinand VII, the King of Spain, was restored to his throne in 1814 following the withdrawal of French troops from his country. During his years in exile, he promised that should he regain the throne of Spain, he would abide by a constitution that had been written by a group of Spanish liberals. By 1820, seeing that the king was not going to honor his promise, a group of army officers and liberals revolted and forced the king to accept the constitution. Two years later a French army, with the tacit support of Prussia, Austria, and Russia, swept into Spain and restored Ferdinand to absolute rule.

- In 1822, a revolt broke out in Naples when the members of a secret society called the *Carbonari*, which had initially formed to fight against Napoleon, decided to overthrow King Ferdinand I, the Neapolitan King, after the king refused to implement liberal reforms such as the granting of a constitution. The Austrians—who were horrified by the developments in Naples, which they feared could spread to their own territories—rushed troops to the south of the Italian peninsula to put down the revolt.

- In Greece, a revolt broke out against the rule of the Ottoman Turks in 1821. This revolt captured the imagination of liberals across Europe, since Ancient Greece was the home of democracy. Britain, France, and Russia came to the aid of the Greek rebels, not because they were inspired by liberal sentiment or even by the idea of Greek nationalism, but because they all saw it as being in their best interest to weaken the Ottoman Turks. By 1832, the Greeks had won their independence, though the newly created Greek state became a monarchy and was certainly not a bastion of liberal values.

- In December 1825, a group of liberal army officers attempted to establish a republic in Russia. The rebels failed to inspire more soldiers to join them, and the "Decembrists," as they came to be known, were caught and executed.

- In France, Louis XVIII (the brother of the executed Louis XVI) was restored to the throne for a second time in 1815, following the final defeat and exile of Napoleon. Upon his return, he granted the French people a charter, which established France as a constitutional monarchy. After his death in 1824 he was followed by his more reactionary younger brother, Charles X, who did his best to undermine the constitutional guarantees that Louis XVIII had established. By 1830, liberal dissatisfaction with the king's contempt for the constitution led to a rebellion that resulted in the exile of Charles X and the crowning of Louis-Philippe, a cousin of Charles X and a man who had a reputation for being a liberal.

QUESTION 5 — ECONOMIC AND SOCIAL COOPERATION IN THE POSTWAR PERIOD

5. Analyze and discuss why governments and workers in Western Europe in the aftermath of the Second World War sought to achieve a new level of cooperation, ushering in a period of economic, political, and social stability as well as an improved standard of living for the working class?

About the Structure of Your Essay

This is one of the most significant developments in the postwar period—the implied end of the class struggle as preached by revolutionary socialists like Marx and its replacement with an implied social contract between governments and workers. For this essay, you will need to discuss what factors motivated various Western European governments to pay more heed to the needs of their working class citizens and why the workers themselves were willing to accept this unprecedented commitment to such life-enhancing developments as cradle-to-grave social services and an overall improvement in the average worker's standard of living when earlier calls for such improvements went unaddressed.

Your essay should mention at least some of the following:

- Fear of a return to the radical politics of the interwar years, when workers embraced extremist political ideologies such as Fascism or Communism, leading to the horrors of the Second World War. Politics in the postwar period was going to be dominated by less ideologically driven centrist parties that could more effectively serve as a bridge between employers and workers.

- There was a general sense that the 1920s and '30s were decades of lost opportunity in which some of the pre-World War I economic and social issues should have been addressed rather than allowed to get worse, leading back to the issue of political radicalization from the previous bullet point.

- The fear of a return to the economics of the Great Depression with its dramatic drop in productivity and high unemployment. Knowledge that damage to the global economic order during the First World War played a role in the Depression made European states more willing to work towards new solutions to avoid a similar development after the Second World War.

- Much of the old elite was discredited by their fascination and at times collaboration with either Fascism or other forms of far-right politics. While the postwar period did not witness the mass removal of the old elite from their position of economic dominance, it left them more willing to cooperate with their workers, if at times only in the hope that this new attitude might allow amnesia to set in regarding the past.

- The brutal emergence of a Communist-dominated Eastern Europe and the threat this meant for the rest of Europe encouraged a much greater spirit of cooperation throughout the West.

- The military and economic commitment that the United States would show to Europe in the period after the Second World War through actions such as the distribution of Marshal Plan money gave European governments the confidence to enter into what they would have previously deemed to be dangerous concessions to workers.

- For many of the reasons listed above, unions also moderated their demands. A tacit agreement was worked out across Western Europe between owners, workers, and government. Workers gave up their dream of a proletarian future in exchange for governmental policies that would encourage full employment, living wages, and a fully panoply of social services.

- The expansion of governmental economic planning during the war years led to the acceptance of its continuance once the war was over. Previously troubled industries such as the coalmines and steel were often nationalized, while the export-driven-model for economic expansion, fueled by governmental currency controls, was accepted by all sides as the best recipe for economic growth.

- Workers no longer had to live in dread of the great economic scourge of the 1930s—unemployment—since governments pursued policies that supported full employment while also increasing benefits for those unable to find work.

- Workers were the main beneficiaries from the implementation of cradle-to-grave social programs, involving such items as universal health care and state-sponsored day care. Wages didn't increase significantly for most Europeans until the mid 1950s, but their quality of life had already improved as a result of governmental intervention.

QUESTION 6 — COLLAPSE OF THE EASTERN BLOC

6. Analyze the reasons behind the collapse of the Eastern Bloc and the demise of the Soviet Union.

About the Structure of Your Essay

One way of approaching this question is by beginning and concluding your essay with a focus on events within the Soviet Union. This approach is justified by the fact that the collapse of the Eastern Bloc must be understood within the context of changes within the Soviet Union. Your essay should begin with the rise of Mikhail Gorbachev in 1985 to the post of general secretary of the Communist Party and leader of the Soviet Union. Gorbachev's reforms, including *glasnost* and *perestroika*, should be discussed along with their repercussions within the Soviet Union. From there you should deal with the remarkable changes in Eastern Europe, when all of a sudden Gorbachev's refusal to bolster faltering Communist regimes in Eastern Europe brought about the collapse of Communist rule throughout the entire former Eastern Bloc. Finally, bring your essay back to the topic of the Soviet Union and address the momentous collapse of the Soviet state in 1991.

Your essay should mention at least some of the following:

- In 1985, Mikhail Gorbachev succeeded Konstantine Chernenko as general secretary of the Communist Party. Right away he showed he was not part of the old guard of Soviet bureaucrats. While he believed that the Communist Party should still dominate the political life of the Soviet Union, Gorbachev introduced what became known as *glasnost*, allowing for greater freedom of expression, while also providing for a new openness in government. Seeing that the Soviet economy was in frightful condition, Gorbachev introduced *perestroika*, an attempt to restructure the economy to make it more efficient and to make it more responsive to the needs of Soviet consumers.

- Rather than bringing satisfaction to most Soviet citizens, *glasnost* and *perestroika* made people hunger for more substantial changes. This feeling possibly intensified following the nuclear accident at Chernobyl in 1986. While *glasnost* led to Soviet citizens being informed (though not without some delay) of the magnitude of the disaster, the accident seemed to confirm what many individuals instinctively knew: Communist rule in the Soviet Union was not succeeding.

- Foreign policy issues also caused additional strains on the Soviet Union. Increased American spending on defense during the presidency of Ronald Reagan, as well as Reagan's call for the building of the "Star Wars" missile defense system, made it readily apparent to Gorbachev that the Soviet Union could never keep up militarily with the United States and that attempting to do so would be a terrible strain on the Soviet economy. Additionally, the Soviet Union's participation in the war in Afghanistan following its invasion of that country in 1979 revealed the relative weakness of the Soviet military as well as increasing dissatisfaction among Soviet citizens for their political leaders. By 1988, Gorbachev was withdrawing Soviet troops from the war zone, but the damage to Soviet prestige was already done.

- In a speech in 1989, Gorbachev announced that he rejected the Brezhnev Doctrine, the idea that the Soviet Union would send in troops to its allies in the Eastern Bloc of nations to support Communist regimes that were in trouble. The Brezhnev Doctrine had been used to justify sending Soviet troops into Czechoslovakia in 1968 during the Prague Spring. Now Gorbachev was directly repudiating the actions of the Soviet Union in 1968, as well as its behavior in 1956, when Soviet tanks were rushed into Hungary following the creation of a reform-minded Communist leadership in that country.

- With the Soviet Union making it clear that it would not interfere in the domestic issues of the Eastern Bloc countries, communist rule began to falter. In Poland, the once banned Solidarity trade union was able to take political advantage of the terrible economic crisis facing the nation. In 1989, the Polish government, facing default on their loans from the West, found themselves with no other choice other than to negotiate with the leaders of Solidarity. The Communist Party agreed to allow free elections, and Solidarity won all the contested seats in the legislature. Bowing to the will of the people, the Communists allowed Tadeusz Mazowiecki, a Solidarity leader, to become the first non-Communist leader of Poland since the end of the Second World War.

- In Hungary, just as in Poland, dismal economic conditions such as high inflation and low productivity led the Communist Party of Hungary to begin to implement reforms not just in the economic arena, but also in the realm of politics. By the end of 1989, Hungary had achieved a peaceful transition to a multiparty democracy.

- In East Germany, the leader of the Communist Party, Erich Honecker, tried to maintain a hard line against reform. However, a visit by Gorbachev in which he was wildly acclaimed for his commitment to *glasnost*, as well as the impact of reform in Hungary and Poland, led to Honecker's forced retirement with his place taken by a somewhat more moderate member of the East German Politburo. The new East German leader, Otto Krenz, tried to implement some changes, though his announcement that East Germans were free to go to the West began a mass exodus. Krenz was forced to announce a complete overhaul of the East German state, including the introduction of multiparty elections, while in November 1989 he gave orders to tear down the Berlin Wall. When elections were finally held in early 1990, the electors favored candidates who wanted to see Germany reunified. On October 3, 1990, with the permission of the Soviet Union, the two Germanys were reunited.

- The Czechoslovakian Communist Party following the Prague Spring of 1968 had been one of the most oppressive in Eastern Europe. Beginning in November 1989, partly due once again to terrible economic conditions as well as news from the rest of the Eastern Bloc, Communist rule collapsed over the course of several weeks. Czechoslovakia had always had a vibrant group of intellectuals who were against the Communist state, and it was this group, under the leadership of the playwright Václav Havel, which formed a government by the end of December 1989. Havel labeled this a "Velvet Revolution" because of its surprisingly peaceful nature.

- Communist rule would also collapse in Romania, Bulgaria, and Albania. Events in Romania were unique because of the violent nature of the process. The Communist Party leader Nicholae Ceausescu used force in an attempt to remain in power, but his regime was toppled by the end of 1989, though not before the death of more than 1,000 Romanians. In Bulgaria and even in Albania, the most backward and reactionary of all the Communist states of Eastern Europe, the Communist governments collapsed with startling swiftness, though in both of those nations the transition to democracy has not been smooth.

- Following the remarkable changes in Eastern Europe, events began to move swiftly in the Soviet Union. One of the reasons for the collapse of the Soviet state was the nationality problem. The Soviet Union, like the tsarist regime that preceded it, was an empire in which Russians dominated over many other nationalities. By 1991, Gorbachev recognized the impossibility of maintaining Russian control over the Baltic states of Estonia, Latvia, and Lithuania, as well as the republics of central Asia. Increasingly, it was clear that Russia would be a separate state, though the type of government it would have was still not resolved.

- Gorbachev had begun implementing political reforms back in 1990, when he convinced the Central Committee of the Communist Party to accept multiparty elections. However, his reputation as a reformer was increasingly challenged by Boris Yeltsin, the president of the Russian Republic. Yeltsin quickly became the darling of those who wanted to see more rapid movement on the question of political reform as well as the shift toward a market economy.

- In August 1991, a coup was staged by Communists who wanted to see Gorbachev's reforms halted. These were the very same men that Gorbachev had recently brought into his government, as he became increasingly concerned that political reforms were moving too fast. Gorbachev, who was on vacation in the Crimea, was placed under house arrest. The moment, however, belonged to Boris Yeltsin, who stood on a tank before the besieged Russian parliament building and called for Russians to stand up to the plotters. Two days later the coup collapsed.

- Yeltsin was able to use the coup to drive the final nails into the coffin of the Communist Party. On December 15, 1991, the Soviet Union, born out of the 1917 Russian Revolution, ceased to exist. In its place was the rather awkwardly named Commonwealth of Independent States.

18

Practice Test 2

EUROPEAN HISTORY

Three hours and five minutes are allotted for this examination: fifty-five minutes for Section I, which consists of multiple-choice questions and two hours and ten minutes for Section II, which consists of essay questions. Fifteen minutes of Section II are devoted to a mandatory reading period, primarily for the document-based essay question in Part A. Section I is printed in this examination booklet; all Section II essay questions are printed in a separate green booklet. In determining your grade, the two sections are given equal weight.

SECTION I

Time—55 minutes

Number of questions—80

Percent of total grade—50

Because this section of the examination contains 80 multiple-choice questions, please be careful to fill in only the ovals that are preceded by numbers 1–80 on your answer sheet.

General Instructions

DO NOT OPEN THIS BOOKLET UNTIL YOU ARE INSTRUCTED TO DO SO.

INDICATE ALL YOUR ANSWERS TO QUESTIONS IN SECTION I ON THE SEPARATE ANSWER SHEET. No credit will be given for anything written in this examination booklet, but you may use the booklet for notes or scratchwork. After you have decided which of the suggested answers is best, COMPLETELY fill in the corresponding oval on the answer sheet. Give only one answer to each question. If you change an answer, be sure that the previous mark is erased completely.

Example: Sample Answer

Chicago is a   Ⓐ ● Ⓒ Ⓓ Ⓔ

(A) state
(B) city
(C) country
(D) continent
(E) village

Many candidates wonder whether they should guess the answers to questions about which they are not certain. In this section of the examination, as a correction for haphazard guessing, one-fourth of the number of questions you answer incorrectly will be subtracted from the number of questions you answer correctly. It is improbable, therefore, that mere guessing will improve your score significantly; it may even lower your score, and it does take time. If, however, you are not sure of the best answer but have some knowledge of the question and are able to eliminate one or more of the answer choices as wrong, your chance of getting the right answer is improved, and it may be to your advantage to answer such a question.

Use your time effectively, working as rapidly as you can without losing accuracy. Do not spend too much time on questions that are too difficult. Go on to other questions and come back to the difficult ones later if you have time. It is not expected that everyone will be able to answer all the multiple-choice questions.

SECTION I

Time—55 minutes

80 Questions

<u>Directions:</u> Each of the questions or incomplete statements below is followed by five suggested answers or completions. Select the one that is best in each case and then fill in the corresponding oval on the answer sheet.

1. The Great Reform Bill of 1832 granted the vote in Great Britain to

(A) women
(B) the working class
(C) middle-class men
(D) Catholics
(E) all men over the age of 21

2. All of the following artists worked in the Impressionist style EXCEPT

(A) Edgar Dégas
(B) Camille Pissarro
(C) Édouard Manet
(D) Théodore Géricault
(E) Claude Monet

3. After the failure of the revolutions of 1848, many Italian Liberals looked to Piedmont for political leadership because

(A) it maintained the liberal constitution that had been granted in 1848
(B) the King of Piedmont was respected for his leadership abilities
(C) Pope Pius IX encouraged them to turn to Piedmont
(D) Piedmont promised Italian nationalists that they would lead the fight for a united Italy
(E) Piedmont had a long tradition as a reform-minded state

4. Social Darwinists believed that

(A) Darwinism was inapplicable to the study of societies
(B) nations operate under the principle of natural selection
(C) colonialism was wrong
(D) "survival of the fittest" applied to animals, not nations
(E) much could be learned from the cultures of Africa and Asia

5. The term "civic humanists" refers to those individuals who

(A) taught civics to other humanist scholars
(B) emphasized the role of cities in classical civilization
(C) wanted to remove themselves from public life
(D) wanted to use their humanist learning in the service of their city-states
(E) feared the encroachment of politics on their learning

6. The sack of Rome in 1527 played a significant role in the

(A) elimination of the papacy as a political force in Italian affairs
(B) end of the High Renaissance
(C) Protestant Reformation
(D) Counter-Reformation
(E) economic collapse of southern Italy

7. The chief reason for the importation of African slaves into the New World was

(A) the lack of European laborers who wanted to emigrate
(B) Spanish desire to eliminate the Portuguese as competitors for empire
(C) primarily political in origin
(D) the severe population losses among indigenous Central and South American populations as a result of smallpox
(E) the refusal by the Church to allow the enslavement of the newly Christianized people of the New World

GO ON TO THE NEXT PAGE

8. Sir Thomas More accepted martyrdom at the hands of Henry VIII because

   (A) he would not swear the Oath of Supremacy
   (B) he thought this would convince Henry of the errors of his ways
   (C) Erasmus convinced him that it was correct to seek martyrdom
   (D) he was already deathly ill
   (E) he could not imagine any sort of criticism of the Catholic Church

9. One of the most troubling aspects for Lutherans regarding the radical religious sects that appeared during the sixteenth-century Reformation was that the sects

   (A) practiced a form of egalitarianism between men and women
   (B) were strict sabbatarians
   (C) often lapsed back toward Catholicism
   (D) focused solely on the scriptures as authority
   (E) continued to practice infant baptism

10. Mussolini began his political career as

   (A) a Socialist
   (B) an anarchist
   (C) a monarchist
   (D) a liberal
   (E) a Fascist

11. In the 1920s and 1930s Czechoslovakia differed from the other states of Eastern Europe by

   (A) being a member of the League of Nations
   (B) being a constitutional monarchy
   (C) enjoying Russian support
   (D) being the only state to maintain a democratic form of government
   (E) being the first to embrace fascism

12. Pablo Picasso's masterpiece *Guernica* commemorates

   (A) the bombing of a Basque town during the Spanish Civil War
   (B) the expulsion of French troops from Spain during the Napoleonic Wars
   (C) the end of the Spanish Civil War
   (D) the revival of the Spanish Republic in the 1920s
   (E) the loss of life in World War I

13. Which of the following nations saved almost its entire Jewish population from extermination during the Holocaust?

   (A) The Netherlands
   (B) France
   (C) Poland
   (D) Norway
   (E) Denmark

14. The expansion of Austrian Habsburg lands in the late seventeenth century resulted primarily from

   (A) victories over the Prussians
   (B) victories over the Ottoman Turks
   (C) a series of advantageous treaties
   (D) a political vacuum in France
   (E) the support of England

15. Tsar Peter the Great of Russia forced his nobles to shave their beards because he wanted

   (A) to be the only one in Russia with facial hair
   (B) to tax them for shaving implements
   (C) his nobles to be prepared for war
   (D) them to look like nobles in western Europe
   (E) to prepare them for a more modern constitutional monarchy

16. Voltaire's famous slogan "Crush the horrible thing" refers to

   (A) nationalism
   (B) reason
   (C) conservatism
   (D) absolute monarchy
   (E) religion

17. Central to the concept of mercantilism was the idea that

   (A) constitutional monarchies were economically more efficient than absolute monarchies
   (B) military might was the key harbinger of economic progress
   (C) economic goals must be linked to political goals
   (D) merchants should dominate the state
   (E) the state should play an active role in managing the economy

GO ON TO THE NEXT PAGE

18. Following the death of Franco in 1975, Spain evolved into a

    (A) republic
    (B) constitutional monarchy
    (C) military dictatorship
    (D) communist state
    (E) group of autonomous regions

19. The collapse of the Communist regime in Czechoslovakia was deemed a "Velvet Revolution" because

    (A) it occurred without warning
    (B) Czech intellectuals wore velvet strips on their sleeves to symbolize their opposition to the state
    (C) it occurred without violence
    (D) it brought about limited changes
    (E) the old Communist elite remained in control

20. In the 1990s, governments across Western Europe have begun to reassess

    (A) their over-reliance on imported oil
    (B) their commitment to NATO
    (C) their commitment to the Common Market
    (D) their need for economic assistance from the United States
    (E) their commitment to providing cradle-to-grave social services

21. Italy's "economic miracle" of the 1950s and 1960s

    (A) was not based on exports
    (B) made the nation reluctant to join the European Economic Community (EEC)
    (C) led to the control of inflation
    (D) was mirrored by an increase in governmental efficiency
    (E) did not bring prosperity to the South

22. In the fifteenth century, Lorenzo Valla proved that the Donation of Constantine was a forgery by

    (A) showing that the paper was too new to be from the time of Constantine
    (B) providing other documents that contradicted what was supposedly stated in the Donation
    (C) revealing papal documents that discussed the forged nature of the document
    (D) showing that the language used in the document was not in use in the age of Constantine
    (E) guessing that Constantine never would have wanted to leave the West to the Church

23. Renaissance sculpture differed from medieval sculpture in that

    (A) it ignored religious themes
    (B) Renaissance artists made use of marble
    (C) it abhorred realism
    (D) it abandoned the classical tradition
    (E) it revived the classical tradition of sculpture in the round

24. Anabaptists believed in adult baptism based on

    (A) their reading of the New Testament
    (B) the teachings of Martin Luther
    (C) conjecture on the wishes of the apostles
    (D) Catholic teachings
    (E) medieval tradition

25. The diet of the average European in 1600 was primarily made up of

    (A) vegetables
    (B) meat
    (C) dairy
    (D) grains
    (E) legumes

26. As a result of the Council of Trent, the Catholic Church did all of the following EXCEPT

    (A) build seminaries for the training of priests
    (B) bring an end to the selling of indulgences
    (C) end the practice of simony
    (D) ban the cult of the saints
    (E) create a list of proscribed books

27. At the end of the French Wars of Religion, Henry IV converted from Calvinism to Catholicism because he

    (A) was threatened with death unless he converted
    (B) had genuine differences with Calvinist teachings
    (C) wanted to gain control over Paris
    (D) had undergone a genuine religious conversion
    (E) hoped to gain the support of Catholic Spain

GO ON TO THE NEXT PAGE

28. The revolt of the Greeks in 1821 against the Ottoman Empire attracted the attention of European liberals because

   (A) Greece was the home of democracy
   (B) the Greeks promised to institute universal male suffrage
   (C) it was the first rebellion in post-Napoleonic Europe
   (D) it marked the end of the repression instituted at the Congress of Vienna
   (E) Great Britain guaranteed Greek independence

29. The Frankfurt Parliament of 1848 marked an attempt to

   (A) respond to Prussian aggression
   (B) establish a German republic
   (C) create the Zollverein, or customs union
   (D) create a unified German state
   (E) tie all independent German cities into a confederation

30. Bon Marché in Paris was an early

   (A) public sporting event
   (B) café
   (C) apartment building with electric lights
   (D) joint-stock company
   (E) department store

31. The first person to isolate radium was

   (A) Louis Pasteur
   (B) Marie Curie
   (C) Max Planck
   (D) Ernest Rutherford
   (E) William Siemens

ASQUITH SURPRISED!

Asquith (astonished)--"That's funny, extremely funny. He doesn't seem to want to be killed."

32. The preceding cartoon

   (A) reveals the ambivalence of the Irish to Home Rule
   (B) is unsympathetic to Home Rule
   (C) is sympathetic to Home Rule
   (D) reveals optimism on the question of Home Rule
   (E) is cognizant of the political problems inherent in implementing Home Rule

33. Prussian power in the eighteenth century was primarily based on its

   (A) strong army
   (B) geographic location
   (C) well-trained diplomatic corps
   (D) military alliance with Great Britain
   (E) economic might

GO ON TO THE NEXT PAGE

34. Montesquieu, in his *Spirit of Laws*, was inspired by the system of government in

(A) Venice
(B) Russia
(C) Great Britain
(D) France
(E) the United States

35. The primary problem facing Louis XVI in the late 1780s was

(A) peasant unrest
(B) British naval expansion
(C) the poverty of the French nation
(D) the refusal of the Third Estate to pay taxes
(E) the bankruptcy of the monarchy

36. In *What Is the Third Estate?*, Abbé Siéyès called for

(A) the elimination of the Third Estate
(B) the creation of a republic
(C) the overthrow of the monarchy
(D) a dominant role for commoners in French political life
(E) the boycott by the Third Estate of the proceedings at Versailles

37. Mary Wollstonecraft's *Vindication of the Rights of Women* (1792) was the first book published in Great Britain to

(A) demand that women should be educated
(B) insist on the moral supremacy of women
(C) demand that women should have full political rights
(D) speculate on the advent of a political party for women
(E) demand that the monarchy should pass to the eldest child, regardless of whether they are male or female

38. The aristocracy created by Napoleon differed from that of the Ancien Régime in that

(A) titles were not passed down to heirs
(B) nobles were allowed to sit in a special legislative body
(C) all nobles enjoyed a tax-free status
(D) the Napoleonic code excluded them from appearing in court
(E) nobles were responsible for local government

39. Max Weber's *The Protestant Ethic and the Spirit of Capitalism* attempted to show

(A) how capitalism grew out of Protestant religious belief
(B) how capitalism was anathema to Protestantism
(C) why Protestants should embrace capitalism
(D) how John Calvin was indirectly the father of free markets
(E) what modern economies can learn from Protestant theology

40. The suffragettes gained much attention in Great Britain because

(A) most men started to accept female suffrage
(B) they were the first female political organization
(C) they seemed to be effective in galvanizing the support of women
(D) their violent acts seemed to be contrary to Victorian ideals concerning women
(E) they combined political and economic demands

41. The initial German reaction to French colonialism in Africa was

(A) distrust of French intentions
(B) anger
(C) tacit acceptance
(D) to look to Great Britain to block French expansion
(E) to build their own colonies

GO ON TO THE NEXT PAGE

Births per 1,000 of Total Population

Year	England and Wales	Scotland
1913	24.1	25.5
1914	23.8	26.1
1915	21.9	23.9
1916	20.9	22.9
1917	17.8	20.3
1918	17.7	20.3
1919	18.5	22.0
1920	25.5	28.1

42. What information can be concluded from the preceding table?

   (A) Better nutrition in Scotland led to a higher birthrate.
   (B) The number of illegitimate births declined during the war years.
   (C) There was a long-term decline in the birthrate in Great Britain dating back to the nineteenth century.
   (D) There was a post-war rise in the birthrate.
   (E) Because women worked in factories during the war, the birthrate declined.

43. The collapse of the Russian Provisional Government in November 1917 resulted from the government's

   (A) refusal to remove the Tsar
   (B) inability to collect taxes
   (C) refusal to call elections
   (D) banning of the Bolshevik Party
   (E) insistence on keeping Russia in the war

44. Spanish sailors returning from their voyages to the New World introduced which of the following diseases into Europe?

   (A) Smallpox
   (B) Venereal disease
   (C) Plague
   (D) Cholera
   (E) Polio

45. Martin Luther and Henrich Zwingli broke over the question of

   (A) salvation by faith
   (B) the primacy of the scriptures
   (C) the role of the clergy
   (D) Jesus's presence in the mass
   (E) infant baptism

46. The Church of England as initially established by Henry VIII in 1536 was

   (A) closely tied to Lutheranism
   (B) fundamentally Calvinist
   (C) dominated by the concept of salvation by faith alone
   (D) torn by religious skepticism
   (E) in many ways tied to traditional Catholic practices

47. There reigneth all abuse, carnal liberty, enormity, sin and Babylonical confusion. Take away kings, princes, rulers, magistrates, judges, and such estates of God's order, no man shall sleep in his own house or bed unkilled, no man shall keep his wife, children or possessions in quietness, all things shall be common; and there needs must follow all mischief and utter destruction both of souls, good and commonwealth.

   This homily, read from a pulpit in Elizabethan England, was primarily an attempt to convince people to

   (A) attend the services of the Church of England
   (B) accept the social hierarchy
   (C) accept Elizabeth as their Queen
   (D) challenge the status quo
   (E) guard their family and property

48. The influx of gold and silver into Spain in the sixteenth century failed to stimulate the economy for all of the following reasons EXCEPT

   (A) losses due to theft by corrupt officials
   (B) the high cost of maintaining a vast overseas empire
   (C) huge sums were needed to put down internal rebellions within Spain
   (D) high inflation
   (E) use of vast sums in foreign wars

GO ON TO THE NEXT PAGE

49. The primary significance of the Crimean War was that

(A) the Ottoman Empire lost control over Istanbul
(B) it revealed the impact of industrialization on warfare
(C) it marked the end of the Concert of Europe
(D) it left key issues in the Crimean region unresolved
(E) the French gained control over religious sites in the Holy Land

50. The Paris Commune of 1871 resulted from

(A) the declaration of German unification
(B) the anarchy caused by the Franco-Prussian War
(C) the collapse of the Third Republic
(D) tensions in France between Bonapartist and Bourbon supporters
(E) financial speculation in the Paris stock market

51. Bismarck's greatest fear for Germany was that

(A) France and Russia would form a military alliance
(B) Austria-Hungary would go to war with Serbia
(C) France and Great Britain would form a military alliance
(D) the Russians would seize Istanbul
(E) the Emperor would lead Germany into war

52. The building of a large German navy in the first decade of the twentieth century greatly antagonized

(A) Italy
(B) France
(C) Great Britain
(D) Russia
(E) the United States

53. By 1917, the biggest problem facing the French army was

(A) a shortage of shells
(B) the anticipated withdrawal of British forces from the Western Front
(C) Germany's capture of Verdun
(D) mass desertion
(E) the refusal of some soldiers to fight

54. President Wilson's "Fourteen Points" called for all of the following EXCEPT

(A) national self-determination
(B) the creation of the League of Nations
(C) decolonization in Africa
(D) a peace without reparations
(E) the end of secret treaties between nations

55. Renaissance humanists were primarily interested in the Roman politician Cicero because of

(A) his moral courage
(B) his detailed explanation of the crisis of the Late Roman Republic
(C) his denunciation of Caesar's tyranny
(D) medieval monks who had preserved his work
(E) the beauty of his Latin prose

56. Carnival was an important social outlet in Early Modern Europe because

(A) it liberated people, if only for a short time, from hierarchical society
(B) it was critical to economic growth
(C) it brought religious fervor to a frenzy
(D) it lessened tensions between Catholics and Protestants
(E) it was the only time during the year that townspeople didn't have to work

57. "We came here to serve God and King, but also to get rich."

The above quote best represents the views of a

(A) Renaissance humanist
(B) Spanish conquistador
(C) Jesuit missionary
(D) Florentine merchant
(E) supporter of the royalist side in the English Revolution

58. The Thirty Years War resulted from all of the following EXCEPT

(A) the Counter-Reformation
(B) the growing power of the Habsburgs
(C) Lutheran dissatisfaction with the Peace of Augburg
(D) religious conflict in Bohemia
(E) the expansion of Calvinism in the Holy Roman Empire

GO ON TO THE NEXT PAGE

59. The "Diggers," a group that emerged during the English Revolution, believed that

 (A) the monarchy must be based on popular support
 (B) England needed to become a theocracy
 (C) enclosure laws needed to be enforced
 (D) private ownership of land should be abolished
 (E) property belonging to supporters of Charles I should be redistributed to the landless

60. In the seventeenth century, the Netherlands became a haven for

 (A) former monarchs
 (B) religious minorities
 (C) political radicals
 (D) those seeking relief from high taxation
 (E) former mercenaries

61. The Irish Easter Rebellion of 1916 witnessed an attempt to

 (A) create an independent Irish republic
 (B) force the British out of Northern Ireland
 (C) recognize Catholic rights in Northern Ireland
 (D) force the British to step back from their plan to partition Ireland
 (E) provide dominion status for the southern counties

62. The New Economic Policy of 1921 marked an attempt in the Soviet Union to

 (A) impose stringent new controls over the Russian economy
 (B) appease the left wing of the Communist Party
 (C) step back from War Communism
 (D) redirect the Soviet state toward a market economy
 (E) provide the economic wherewithal to win the Civil War

63. The British General Strike of 1926 was sparked by problems in which industry?

 (A) Shipbuilding
 (B) Coal
 (C) Textiles
 (D) Transport
 (E) Iron

64. The Popular Front government formed in France in 1936 was an attempt to

 (A) reconcile with the British
 (B) appease the Germans
 (C) unite the parties of the left against fascism
 (D) create a coalition government bringing in parties from across the political spectrum
 (E) unite the parties of the right against socialism

65. Mussolini's Lateran Pact with the Catholic Church

 (A) revealed Mussolini's own deeply held religious beliefs
 (B) made Catholicism the official state religion in Italy
 (C) led to official Catholic support of Mussolini's fascist movement
 (D) restored the Vatican as an independent state
 (E) allowed Mussolini a veto over all clerical appointments

66. The "Great Fear" in the summer of 1789 was the result of rumors that

 (A) the harvest was far smaller than expected
 (B) the great French estates were not to be broken up and redistributed among the peasants
 (C) the monarchy was about to be restored
 (D) aristocrats were plotting to attack peasants
 (E) French farms would be collectivized

GO ON TO THE NEXT PAGE

67. During the Jacobin domination of France in 1793, the government did all of the following EXCEPT

(A) institute the metric system
(B) make all property communal
(C) change the calendar
(D) set price limits on bread
(E) attempt to move the people away from their allegiance to Catholicism

68. In his *Reflections on the Revolution in France* (1790), Edmund Burke was critical of

(A) British failure to formulate an effective response to events in France
(B) the removal of Louis XVI from the throne
(C) France's inability to evolve from constitutional monarchy to republic
(D) France's refusal to honor its national debt
(E) the rapid diminishing of the authority of the monarchy and the Church

69. Early nineteenth-century Luddites were known for

(A) political liberalism
(B) Chartism
(C) organizing the first British Labor unions
(D) breaking machinery
(E) republicanism

70. Metternich, the Austrian Chancellor who dominated the Congress of Vienna, was extremely fearful of

(A) nationalism
(B) the return of the Bourbons
(C) the impact of industrialization
(D) particularism among the Italian states
(E) Russian intentions in Europe

71. The murder of socialist leader Giacomo Matteotti ultimately provided Mussolini with the opportunity to

(A) overthrow the monarchy
(B) seek out a deal with opposition political leaders
(C) purge the ranks of his Fascist party
(D) eliminate all political opposition in Italy
(E) work on a political and military alliance with Nazi Germany

72. After receiving German and Italian support in the Spanish Civil War, Franco responded in World War II

(A) by joining with the Allies against the Fascist powers
(B) by aiding Germany and Italy with arms
(C) by remaining neutral
(D) by secretly attacking British convoys in the Atlantic
(E) by offering to serve as a facilitator for peace talks

73. Winston Churchill stood out among his colleagues in the Conservative Party for being firmly against

(A) implementing the gold standard
(B) the blockade against the Spanish Republic during the Civil War
(C) recognition of the Soviet Union
(D) the formation of a coalition government with the Labour Party
(E) appeasement with the Germans

74. The Wannsee Conference in January 1942 set the stage for

(A) Operation Barbarossa
(B) the entry of the United States into World War II
(C) the elimination of European Jewry
(D) creation of allied occupation zones in Germany
(E) German and Japanese military cooperation

75. Which of the following best describes the attitude of the French toward nuclear weapon development in the period following World War II?

(A) They felt protected by the American nuclear weapon umbrella.
(B) They committed themselves to the creation of their own small independent nuclear arsenal.
(C) They researched but never developed nuclear weapons.
(D) They joined with Third World nations and worked toward the banning of nuclear weapons.
(E) They were committed to matching the Russian nuclear arsenal.

GO ON TO THE NEXT PAGE

76. Martin Luther attended the Diet of Worms without fear of losing his life because

   (A) he possessed a sizable army
   (B) he was protected by the Elector of Saxony
   (C) he thought the Catholic Church would support his ideas
   (D) he enjoyed the support of the Holy Roman Emperor
   (E) he went in disguise

77. Oliver Cromwell's New Model Army differed from the Cavalier forces under Charles I by

   (A) its emphasis on cavalry
   (B) deemphasizing the role of religion
   (C) its recruitment of continental mercenaries
   (D) providing regular pay for soldiers and for paying for supplies taken from farmers
   (E) remaining on the defensive

78. In France in the seventeenth century, "nobles of the sword" differed from "nobles of the robe" in that the former were

   (A) wealthier
   (B) part of the old traditional landed nobility dating back to the Middle Ages
   (C) given special privileges in the Estates General
   (D) allowed to maintain manorial courts on their estates
   (E) banned from engaging in commerce

79. The Holy Roman Emperor was a weak title because

   (A) it was an elected monarchy
   (B) the Austrian Habsburgs controlled the throne
   (C) it was selected by the papacy
   (D) France was the power behind the throne
   (E) the religious authority of the Emperor was superior to the political

80. The seventeenth-century English scientist William Harvey discovered

   (A) that alchemy was a false science
   (B) the elliptical orbit of the Earth around the sun
   (C) how blood circulates within the human body
   (D) the circumference of the Earth
   (E) the function of the liver

STOP
END OF SECTION I

IF YOU FINISH BEFORE TIME IS CALLED, YOU MAY CHECK YOUR WORK ON THIS SECTION.
DO NOT GO ON TO SECTION II UNTIL YOU ARE TOLD TO DO SO.

EUROPEAN HISTORY

SECTION II

You will have 15 minutes to read the contents of this essay question booklet. You are advised to spend most of the 15 minutes analyzing the documents and planning your answer for the document-based question in Part A. You should spend some portion of the time choosing the two questions in Part B that you will answer. You may make notes in this booklet. At the end of the 15-minute period, you will be told to break the seal on the free-response booklet and to begin writing your answers on the lined pages of that booklet. Do not break the seal on the free-response booklet until you are told to do so. Suggested writing time is 45 minutes for the document-based essay question in Part A. Suggested planning and writing time is 35 minutes for each of the two essay questions you choose to answer in Part B.

BE SURE TO MANAGE YOUR TIME CAREFULLY.

Write your answers in the <u>free-response</u> booklet with a <u>pen</u>. The essay question booklet may be used for reference and/or scratchwork as you answer the free-response questions, but no credit will be given for the work shown in the essay question booklet.

DO NOT OPEN THIS BOOKLET UNTIL YOU ARE TOLD TO DO SO.

EUROPEAN HISTORY

SECTION II

Part A

(Suggested writing time—45 minutes)

Percent of Section II score—45

<u>Directions:</u> The following question is based on the accompanying Documents 1–10. (Some of the documents have been edited for the purpose of this exercise.) Write your answer on the lined pages of the free-response essay booklet.

This question is designed to test your ability to work with historical documents. As you analyze the documents, <u>take into account both the sources and the author's point of view.</u> Write an essay on the following topic that integrates your analysis of the documents; in no case should documents simply be cited and explained in a "laundry list" fashion. You may refer to historical facts and developments not mentioned in the documents.

1. Discuss and analyze the views of those who saw Chartism as a revolutionary movement versus those who saw it as essentially moderate.

Historical Background:

In the 1830s and 1840s, a new movement swept across the British political landscape. Chartism, a movement whose ostensible purpose was the passage of a six-point political program known as the Charter, brought thousands of working-class people to various Chartist meetings and led several million individuals to sign petitions. Historians of Chartism have debated whether the movement was revolutionary, in that it was willing to use violence to bring about radical changes to the British political system, or whether it was essentially non-revolutionary, with little desire to change the political and social structure of Great Britain, but simply wanted to achieve full political rights for working-class individuals.

Document 1

Resolved, That the Members of the Working Men's Association fully concurring in the great principles of Universal Suffrage, Annual Parliaments, the Ballot, and all the other essentials to the free exercise of Man's political rights— and hearing that a meeting is to be held at Glasgow on the 21st of May in furtherance of those objects do request our Honorary Members Mr. Thos. Murphy and the Revd Dr Wade to present to that meeting our pamphlet entitled the 'People's Charter' being the outline of an act to provide for the just representation of the people of Great Britain in the Commons House of Parliament—embracing the principles of Universal Suffrage, No Property Qualifications, Annual Parliaments, Equal Representation, Payment of Members, and Vote by [secret] Ballot prepared by a committee of twelve persons six members of parliament and six members of the Working Men's Association.

Minutes of the London Working Men's Association, May 15, 1838

GO ON TO THE NEXT PAGE

Document 2

This question of Universal Suffrage was a knife and fork question after all; this question was a bread and cheese question, notwithstanding all that had been said against it; and if any man ask him what he meant by Universal Suffrage, he would answer, that every working man in the land had a right to have a good coat to his back, a comfortable abode in which to shelter himself and his family, a good dinner upon his table, and as much wages for that work as would keep him in plenty, and afford him the enjoyment of all the blessings of life which a reasonable man could desire.

Speech by Joseph Stevens, at Chartist rally in Manchester, September 24, 1838

Document 3

It is also upon all sides agreed that this is a fearful remedy, which, like hazardous, extreme, and painful operations in surgery, is only to be brought into action in very extreme cases, when all ordinary courses of treatment have failed. Physical force is a thing not to be lightly had recourse to; it is the last remedy known to the Constitution . . .

Article in the *Chartist*, the movement newspaper, May 12, 1839

Document 4

It is of no use to refuse to look our difficulties in the face. The fact is, that, be it from listlessness, ignorance, want of thought, incapacity to reason as to political causes and effects, or satisfaction with things as they are, the great majority of the working men of the metropolis [London] are altogether indifferent as to representation. They feel certain evils, and they complain of them, but they do not apply themselves to consider whence they proceed.

In the country, we believe, it is far otherwise. . . We are sorry to have to report that in the metropolis, where the lead should have been taken, there is nothing doing; and unless the metropolis be set working, all agitation elsewhere is useless.

Article in the *Chartist*, the movement's newspaper, June 30, 1839

Document 5

...The pride of the nation, he's noble and brave
He's the terror of tyrants, the friend of the slave,
The bright star of freedom, the nobles of men,
We'll rally around him again and again.

Though proud daring tyrants his body confined,
they never could alter his generous mind;
We'll hail our caged lion, now free from his den
And we'll rally around him again and again...

Poem in honor of Chartist leader Feargus O'Connor

GO ON TO THE NEXT PAGE

Document 6

Last evening, a Chartist tea party and ball, as previously announced by placard were given in the Carpenters' Hall, by 'The committee for the erection of Hunt's monument.' The room and gallery were densely crowded, and an amateur band was in attendance. John Murray presided. After tea, the Rev. James Scholefield entered the room, and announced that Mr. Feargus O'Connor was unable to attend, as he was, in conjunction with other Chartists, engaged in considering what measures were best to be adopted in the present crisis [the call for a general strike].

Leeds Mercury, August 20, 1842

Document 7

Year after year have passed away, and even now our wishes have no prospect of being realized, our husbands are over wrought, our houses half furnished, our families ill-fed, and our children uneducated—the fear of want hangs over our heads, the scorn of the rich is pointed towards us; the brand of slavery is on our kindred, and we feel the degradation. We are a despised caste, our oppressors are not content with despising our feelings, but demand the control of our thoughts and wants!—want's bitter bondage binds us to their feet, we are oppressed because we are poor.

Address of the "Female Political Union," a Chartist organization, to their "Fellow-Countrywomen,"
February 9, 1839

Document 8

Glory to the Proletarians of Paris, they have saved the Republic!

How long, Men of Great Britain and Ireland, how long will you carry the damning stigma of being the only people in Europe who dare not will their freedom?

Patience! The hour is nigh! From the hill-tops of Lancashire, from the voices of hundreds of thousands has ascended to Heaven the oath of union, and the rallying cry of conflict. Englishmen and Irishmen have sworn to have THE CHARTER, or VIVE LA REPUBLIQUE!

Editorial in the *Northern Star*, a Chartist newspaper, March 25, 1848

Document 9

London is in a state of panic from the contemplated meeting of the Chartists, 200,000 strong on Monday; for myself, nothing that happened would in the least surprise me: I expect a revolution within two years: there may be one within three days. The *Times* is alarmed beyond all measure. I have it from good authority that the Chartists are determined to have their wishes granted.

Letter from middle-class merchant to his wife, April 1848

GO ON TO THE NEXT PAGE

Document 10

Lord John Russell presents his humble duty to your Majesty, and has the honor to state that the Kennington Common Meeting has proved a complete failure.

About 12,000 or 15,000 persons met in good order. Feargus O'Connor, upon arriving upon the ground in a car, was ordered by Mr. Mayne [the Commissioner of Police] to come and speak to him. Upon being told that the meeting would not be prevented, but that no procession would be allowed to pass the bridges, he expressed the utmost thanks, and begged to shake Mr. Mayne by the hand...

The mob was in good humor, and any mischief that now takes place will be the act of individuals; but it is to be hoped the preparations made will daunt those wicked but not brave men.

Letter from Lord John Russell, the Prime Minister, to Queen Victoria describing the Chartist march on Parliament to present their third petition, April 10, 1848

END OF PART A

EUROPEAN HISTORY

SECTION II

Part B

(Suggested writing time—70 minutes)

Percent of Section II score—55

Directions: You are to answer TWO questions, one from each group of three questions below. Make your selections carefully, choosing the questions that you are best prepared to answer thoroughly in the time permitted. You should spend five minutes organizing or outlining each answer. In writing your essays, use specific examples to support your answer. Write your answers to the questions on the lined pages of the free-response booklet. If time permits when you finish writing, check your work. Be certain to number your answer as the questions are numbered below.

Group 1:   Choose ONE question from this group. The suggested writing time for this question is 30 minutes.

1.   Which factors explain why European states in the fifteenth and sixteenth centuries were interested in the building of colonial empires?

2.   Discuss the term "Enlightened Absolutism" as it applies to certain rulers in eastern Europe and Russia in the eighteenth century.

3.   Discuss some of the new technologies that emerged during the Second Industrial Revolution of the nineteenth century.

Group 2:   Choose ONE question from this group. The suggested writing time for this question is 30 minutes.

4.   Describe and analyze how Martin Luther differed with Catholic teachings on the question of salvation and the sacraments.

5.   Analyze the domestic problems faced by TWO of the great European powers in the decade immediately prior to the outbreak of the First World War.

6.   Discuss why the period from 1870 to 1914 can be considered a "golden age" for Europe's middle class.

END OF EXAMINATION

19

Practice Test 2: Answers and Explanations

QUESTIONS	EXPLANATIONS
1. The Great Reform Bill of 1832 granted the vote in Great Britain to (A) women (B) the working class (C) middle-class men (D) Catholics (E) all men over the age of 21	1. **C** The Great Reform Bill of 1832 was the first of a series of bills that expanded the suffrage in Great Britain to groups that had previously been excluded from the political process. With the development of industrialization, middle-class men enjoyed significant wealth, but prior to 1832 they could not vote in a society that linked political participation to the ownership of land.
2. All of the following artists worked in the Impressionist style EXCEPT (A) Edgar Dégas (B) Camille Pissarro (C) Édouard Manet (D) Théodore Géricault (E) Claude Monet	2. **D** Théodore Géricault (1791–1824) worked in the Romantic style. His most famous work is his *Raft of the Medusa* (1819), which portrayed a group of men on a raft after their ship sank. Romantic artists used the contrast of light and dark images and stirring action to reveal the deep undercurrent of emotion lurking within all people.
3. After the failure of the revolutions of 1848, many Italian Liberals looked to Piedmont for political leadership because (A) it maintained the liberal constitution that had been granted in 1848 (B) the King of Piedmont was respected for his leadership abilities (C) Pope Pius IX encouraged them to turn to Piedmont (D) Piedmont promised Italian nationalists that they would lead the fight for a united Italy (E) Piedmont had a long tradition as a reform-minded state	3. **A** Although every state in Italy responded to the popular rebellions of 1848 by granting liberal constitutions, only the Kingdom of Piedmont maintained its liberal constitution following the political repression that swept Italy in the aftermath of the failed revolutions. With nowhere else to turn, Italian Liberals began to look to Piedmont for political leadership and it was the Kingdom of Piedmont that eventually unified all of the Italian peninsula under its rule.

4. Social Darwinists believed that

   (A) Darwinism was inapplicable to the study of societies
   (B) nations operate under the principle of natural selection
   (C) colonialism was wrong
   (D) "survival of the fittest" applied to animals, not nations
   (E) much could be learned from the cultures of Africa and Asia

4. **B** Social Darwinists believed that natural selection provided the critical explanation for why some nations triumphed over others. Herbert Spencer, one of the leading Social Darwinists, coined the phrase "survival of the fittest" to explain struggle between states. Social Darwinism was used as a justification for European imperialism, since superior Europeans had every right to dominate the less evolved civilizations of Africa and Asia.

5. The term *civic humanists* refers to those individuals who

   (A) taught civics to other humanist scholars
   (B) emphasized the role of cities in classical civilization
   (C) wanted to remove themselves from public life
   (D) wanted to use their humanist learning in the service of their city-states
   (E) feared the encroachment of politics on their learning

5. **D** Although Petrarch, the father of humanism, felt that scholarship should not be pursued for practical means, some of his followers in the humanist community in Florence wanted to use their refined classical education in the service of their state. These civic humanists worked in government offices such as the chancellery and used their fine knowledge of Latin to write correspondence on behalf of the Florentine state.

6. The sack of Rome in 1527 played a significant role in the

   (A) elimination of the papacy as a political force in Italian affairs
   (B) end of the High Renaissance
   (C) Protestant Reformation
   (D) Counter-Reformation
   (E) economic collapse of southern Italy

6. **B** In 1527, the mercenary army of the Holy Roman Emperor Charles V rampaged throughout Rome after not receiving their pay. The crisis brought on by the sack of the city—while certainly not the sole reason the High Renaissance ended—played a critical role in its demise. This event marked the end of a brief period when popes such as Julius II made Rome the center of Renaissance culture through the patronage of artists like Michelangelo and Raphael.

QUESTIONS	EXPLANATIONS

7. The chief reason for the importation of African slaves into the New World was

   (A) the lack of European laborers who wanted to emigrate

   (B) Spanish desire to eliminate the Portuguese as competitors for empire

   (C) primarily political in origin

   (D) the severe population losses among indigenous Central and South American populations as a result of smallpox

   (E) the refusal by the Church to allow the enslavement of the newly Christianized people of the New World

7. D While Europeans had few compunctions about enslaving the indigenous people of Central and South America, these populations were decimated by smallpox, a disease that the Spanish and Portuguese brought with them from Europe. The need for laborers led to the importation of slaves from Africa. Africans, like Europeans, had been exposed for many centuries to smallpox and were therefore able to work in the mines and plantations without being wiped out by the disease, though their lives were shortened as a result of brutal treatment and overwork.

8. Sir Thomas More accepted martyrdom at the hands of Henry VIII because

   (A) he would not swear the Oath of Supremacy

   (B) he thought this would convince Henry of the errors of his ways

   (C) Erasmus convinced him that it was correct to seek martyrdom

   (D) he was already deathly ill

   (E) he could not imagine any sort of criticism of the Catholic Church

8. A More, like his friend Erasmus, was part of a Northern humanist tradition that was critical of certain practices of the Catholic Church. Nonetheless, More remained deeply committed to the church and therefore refused to swear the Oath of Supremacy, an oath of loyalty to Henry as head of the Church of England. For More, the only head of the Church was the Pope. In 1535, Henry VIII executed More because More held this position.

9. One of the most troubling aspects for Lutherans regarding the radical religious sects that appeared during the sixteenth-century Reformation was that the sects

   (A) practiced a form of egalitarianism between men and women

   (B) were strict sabbatarians

   (C) often lapsed back towards Catholicism

   (D) focused solely on the scriptures as authority

   (E) continued to practice infant baptism

9. A Lutherans found many of the religious practices of the various radical sects to be troubling. One of the most disturbing, however, was that many of the sects allowed for female preachers, and in general, they lived in a manner that suggested equality among the sexes, a practice that was offensive to the more traditional Lutherans.

QUESTIONS	EXPLANATIONS

10. Mussolini began his political career as

(A) a Socialist
(B) an anarchist
(C) a monarchist
(D) a liberal
(E) a Fascist

10. **A** Perhaps surprisingly, Mussolini began his career as a Socialist journalist. In his early years he was influenced by his father, an ardent Socialist, who named his son after the Mexican revolutionary Benito Juarez. Mussolini broke with the Italian Socialist Party over his desire to see Italy enter World War I, and in the immediate aftermath of the war he created a new political organization—the National Fascist Party. Mussolini was not the only leader to move from socialism to fascism; Oswald Mosley, the leader of the British Union of Fascists, had earlier served in the House of Commons as a member of the Labour Party.

11. In the 1920s and 1930s Czechoslovakia differed from the other states of Eastern Europe by

(A) being a member of the League of Nations
(B) being a constitutional monarchy
(C) enjoying Russian support
(D) being the only state to maintain a democratic form of government
(E) being the first to embrace fascism

11. **D** While most of the nations of Eastern Europe became dictatorships of one form or another in the postwar period, Czechoslovakia maintained a thriving democracy. One of the many tragedies of the British and French policy of appeasement toward Nazi Germany was that they betrayed Czechoslovakia, a democratic state like their own. Following this betrayal the British and French had to struggle to find another ally in Eastern Europe. They settled on Poland, a state where, in 1926, the army overthrew the democratically elected government.

12. Pablo Picasso's masterpiece *Guernica* commemorates

(A) the bombing of a Basque town during the Spanish Civil War
(B) the expulsion of French troops from Spain during the Napoleonic Wars
(C) the end of the Spanish Civil War
(D) the revival of the Spanish Republic in the 1920s
(E) the loss of life in World War I

12. **A** On April 26, 1937, during the Spanish Civil War, Italian and German planes attacked the town of Guernica to terrorize the population of this city, which was located in an area that was controlled by those who were loyal to the Spanish Republic. The Italians and Germans knew that a large number of people would be outside because it was the traditional market day. This was the first aerial bombing of an exclusively civilian target and was a harbinger of the terror tactics used by the Germans in their blitzkrieg warfare during World War II. In response to this brutal attack on civilians, the Spanish artist Pablo Picasso painted a massive canvas showing the horror of modern warfare.

QUESTIONS	EXPLANATIONS
13. Which of the following nations saved almost its entire Jewish population from extermination during the Holocaust? (A) The Netherlands (B) France (C) Poland (D) Norway (E) Denmark	13. **E** Although the story that the King of Denmark put on a yellow star to symbolize his connection with the Jews of Denmark is not true (he only threatened to take this step to embarrass the Germans), the Danes did succeed in rescuing most of their fellow Jewish citizens. When word got out in October 1943 that the German forces occupying Denmark were going to round up Danish Jews to send them to concentration camps in Eastern Europe, the Danes organized a large number of boats to send the Jews to neutral Sweden.
14. The expansion of Austrian Habsburg lands in the late seventeenth century resulted primarily from (A) victories over the Prussians (B) victories over the Ottoman Turks (C) a series of advantageous treaties (D) a political vacuum in France (E) the support of England	14. **B** In the fifteenth and sixteenth centuries the powerful empire of the Ottoman Turks swept over large parts of eastern Europe. As late as 1683, an Ottoman army was at the gates of Vienna. However, the overextended Ottomans now found themselves dealing with the growing power of the Austrian Habsburgs, and over the next several years the Habsburgs regained control over Hungary and began to push the Ottomans out of the Balkan region.
15. Tsar Peter the Great of Russia forced his nobles to shave their beards because he wanted (A) to be the only one in Russia with facial hair (B) to tax them for shaving implements (C) his nobles to be prepared for war (D) them to look like nobles in western Europe (E) to prepare them for a more modern constitutional monarchy	15. **D** Although Peter the Great loved a close shave as much as any man, the real reason why he wanted his nobles to be without facial hair was that as part of his program to modernize Russia, he wanted his nobles to look like the unshaved nobles of western Europe.

QUESTIONS	EXPLANATIONS
16. Voltaire's famous slogan, "Crush the horrible thing," refers to (A) nationalism (B) reason (C) conservatism (D) absolute monarchy (E) religion	16. **E** Voltaire was extremely antagonistic toward organized religion, which he felt blocked humans from enjoying true freedom and the pursuit of reason. His own religious beliefs leaned toward Deism, in that he believed that there was a creator, though this creator stepped away from his creation and never revealed himself to mankind. Voltaire became known across Europe as a champion of religious toleration after his spirited defense of Jean Calas, a Protestant who was wrongfully accused of killing his son because he had declared his intention of converting to Catholicism.
17. Central to the concept of mercantilism was the idea that (A) constitutional monarchies were economically more efficient than absolute monarchies (B) military might was the key harbinger of economic progress (C) economic goals must be linked to political goals (D) merchants should dominate the state (E) the state should play an active role in managing the economy	17. **E** Mercantilism was based on the idea that government should play a direct role in the allocation of economic resources within the state. In France, where mercantilism was widely practiced during the reign of Louis XIV, Colbert—Louis's financial minister—sponsored such enterprises as commercial trading companies and textile and porcelain factories. Adam Smith in *The Wealth of Nations* attacked the idea of mercantilism and instead advocated that governments should practice laissez-faire, to keep their hands off the working of the economy.
18. Following the death of Franco in 1975, Spain evolved into a (A) republic (B) constitutional monarchy (C) military dictatorship (D) communist state (E) group of autonomous regions	18. **B** Franco selected Juan Carlos, the son of the last King of Spain, to succeed him as head of state in Spain, with the expectation that Juan Carlos would continue Franco's tradition of authoritarian political leadership. Fortunately, Juan Carlos was sympathetic to the ideas of democracy, and in the years following Franco's death, he helped establish a constitutional monarchy for the Spanish state.

QUESTIONS	EXPLANATIONS
19. The collapse of the Communist regime in Czechoslovakia was deemed a "Velvet Revolution" because (A) it occurred without warning (B) Czech intellectuals wore velvet strips on their sleeves to symbolize their opposition to the state (C) it occurred without violence (D) it brought about limited changes (E) the old Communist elite remained in control	19. **C** Over a period of two weeks at the end of 1989, the entire political structure in Czechoslovakia was dramatically altered, as the repressive Communist regime collapsed and was replaced by a democratically elected government. It was the playwright and political activist Václav Havel who labeled this change a "Velvet Revolution" because it occurred without bloodshed.
20. In the 1990s, governments across Western Europe have begun to reassess (A) their over-reliance on imported oil (B) their commitment to NATO (C) their commitment to the Common Market (D) their need for economic assistance from the United States (E) their commitment to providing cradle-to-grave social services	20. **E** In the years following World War II, governments across Western Europe felt the need to provide extensive social services for their citizens, partly in response to the horrendous social problems that existed in the period between the two world wars. More recently, countries—such as Great Britain during the Prime Ministership of Margaret Thatcher (1979–1990)—have begun to reassess this need for cradle-to-grave coverage. Even countries such as Germany and France, which for most of the 1990s have been reluctant to curtail their spending on social programs, have begun to reevaluate whether, in this age of global economic competition, they can continue to heavily tax their businesses and citizens to provide such comprehensive services.
21. Italy's "economic miracle" of the 1950s and 1960s (A) was not based on exports (B) made the nation reluctant to join the European Economic Community (EEC) (C) led to the control of inflation (D) was mirrored by an increase in governmental efficiency (E) did not bring prosperity to the South	21. **E** Despite efforts at land reform and public works projects, the South of Italy did not generally benefit from the remarkable expansion of the economy in the decades following the Second World War.

QUESTIONS	EXPLANATIONS

22. In the fifteenth century, Lorenzo Valla proved that the Donation of Constantine was a forgery by

(A) showing that the paper was too new to be from the time of Constantine
(B) providing other documents that contradicted what was supposedly stated in the Donation
(C) revealing papal documents that discussed the forged nature of the document
(D) showing that the language used in the document was not in use in the age of Constantine
(E) guessing that Constantine never would have wanted to leave the West to the Church

22. **D** Valla is one of the fathers of critical textual analysis, a process in which one approaches the text with close questions regarding the language being used. Valla used this technique to prove that the Donation of Constantine, a document that purported to show that the Roman Emperor Constantine had left the western part of his empire under the control of the papacy, could not have been a classical document. Valla proved this by revealing that the document referred to the word feudalism, a term that was not in use in the age of Constantine.

23. Renaissance sculpture differed from medieval sculpture in that

(A) it ignored religious themes
(B) Renaissance artists made use of marble
(C) it abhorred realism
(D) it abandoned the classical tradition
(E) it revived the classical tradition of sculpture in the round

23. **E** One concept that disappeared in medieval sculpture was the classical practice of creating works that were freestanding sculpture in the round. Medieval sculpture is primarily found attached to the wall, such as in the large number of sculptural works surrounding the entry portal of a church. Renaissance artists, inspired by their knowledge of classical art, brought back the practice of sculpture in the round.

24. Anabaptists believed in adult baptism based on

(A) their reading of the New Testament
(B) the teachings of Martin Luther
(C) conjecture on the wishes of the apostles
(D) Catholic teachings
(E) medieval tradition

24. **A** In their reading of the New Testament, Anabaptists found that Jesus was clearly an adult when he was baptized at the hands of John the Baptist. Believing the Bible to be their only authority on matters of faith, the Anabaptists took this to mean that they too should be baptized not as infants, who are unaware of the meaning of the event, but as adults, who have consciously accepted Jesus into their lives. For holding such beliefs, Anabaptists were brutally persecuted by both Catholics and Lutherans, two groups that insisted that infant baptism was the right way to baptize.

QUESTIONS	EXPLANATIONS

25. The diet of the average European in 1600 was primarily made up of

(A) vegetables
(B) meat
(C) dairy
(D) grains
(E) legumes

25. **D** Roughly 80 percent of the caloric consumption of the average European in 1600 came from the consumption of grain. The low amount of protein in such a diet was one reason that maternal and infant mortality were so high during childbirth.

26. As a result of the Council of Trent, the Catholic Church did all of the following EXCEPT

(A) build seminaries for the training of priests
(B) bring an end to the selling of indulgences
(C) end the practice of simony
(D) ban the cult of the saints
(E) create a list of proscribed books

26. **D** During the Catholic Reformation, the church attempted to address many of the problems that had hampered it in its struggle with Protestantism. At the Council of Trent (1545–1563) the church ended the practice of selling indulgences as well as simony, the selling of clerical offices. The church acknowledged that there were gaps in clerical education and established seminaries in every diocese, while also establishing a list of books that Catholics were to avoid. The Catholic Church did not, however, ban the cult of the saints, the use of saints as intermediaries between humans and God. Some Catholics such as Erasmus had earlier advocated an end to such practices, on the basis that it distracted from the essential teachings of the church, but such ideas were rejected at the Council of Trent.

27. At the end of the French Wars of Religion, Henry IV converted from Calvinism to Catholicism because he

(A) was threatened with death unless he converted
(B) had genuine differences with Calvinist teachings
(C) wanted to gain control over Paris
(D) had undergone a genuine religious conversion
(E) hoped to gain the support of Catholic Spain

27. **C** Henry IV made many religious shifts during his life. In 1593, he made a permanent break with Calvinism and embraced Catholicism, although his reasons for doing so were less than edifying. Paris was a stronghold of Catholic sentiment and refused to acknowledge the Calvinist Henry as its king. Henry therefore decided that "Paris was worth a mass" and converted to Catholicism to gain control over the French capital.

QUESTIONS	EXPLANATIONS

28. The revolt of the Greeks in 1821 against the Ottoman Empire attracted the attention of European liberals because

(A) Greece was the home of democracy
(B) the Greeks promised to institute universal male suffrage
(C) it was the first rebellion in post-Napoleonic Europe
(D) it marked the end of the repression instituted at the Congress of Vienna
(E) Great Britain guaranteed Greek independence

28. **A** The years following the Congress of Vienna in 1815 were tough for liberals throughout Europe because of the strength of the conservative backlash. When the Greeks revolted against their Ottoman overlords, it captured the imagination of many despairing liberals. Their sentiments were motivated by a romanticized and completely unrealistic view of the rebellion that was based on the fact that Ancient Greece was the home of democracy. Lord Byron, the Romantic poet, was so inspired by the struggle that he went to Greece to help the rebels, but he died, not from battlefield wounds (he never saw action), but from a fever. When the Greeks formally achieved independence in 1832, they invited a Bavarian prince to become their king and established a state that was quite unreceptive to liberal ideas.

29. The Frankfurt Parliament of 1848 marked an attempt to

(A) respond to Prussian aggression
(B) establish a German republic
(C) create the Zollverein, or customs union
(D) create a unified German state
(E) tie all independent German cities into a confederation

29. **D** In 1848, the year of revolutions across Europe, liberals from all the various German states met in Frankfurt to create a unified German state. When they offered the new German crown to the King of Prussia, he refused it. Eventually the delegates left Frankfurt without having achieved the stated goal of unifying the various German states. This task would be achieved several decades later under the guidance of Bismarck.

30. Bon Marché in Paris was an early

(A) public sporting event
(B) café
(C) apartment building with electric lights
(D) joint-stock company
(E) department store

30. **E** In the second half of the nineteenth century, department stores began to spring up in the major cities of Europe and the United States—one sign of the growing significance of middle-class consumers. These stores sold a wide variety of goods at set prices, and departed from the traditional haggling of the market. Bon Marché was one of the most ornate of the new department stores, possessing a beautiful glass ceiling and decorative statues along the sales floor.

31. The first person to isolate radium was

    (A) Louis Pasteur
    (B) Marie Curie
    (C) Max Planck
    (D) Ernest Rutherford
    (E) William Siemens

31. **B** In 1910, Marie Curie isolated radium, a radio-active element. She eventually won two Nobel Prizes for her scientific contributions.

ASQUITH SURPRISED!

Asquith (astonished)--"That's funny, extremely funny. He doesn't seem to want to be killed."

32. The preceding cartoon

    (A) reveals the ambivalence of the Irish to Home Rule
    (B) is unsympathetic to Home Rule
    (C) is sympathetic to Home Rule
    (D) reveals optimism on the question of Home Rule
    (E) is cognizant of the political problems inherent in implementing Home Rule

32. **B** This cartoon appeared in a pro-Ulster Unionist newspaper. The cartoonist was not very subtle in attempting to show how British Prime Minister Herbert Asquith and Catholic leader John Redmond planned to destroy Ulster when they attempted to create Home Rule for Ireland. In September 1914, Parliament passed a Home Rule bill, but strong opposition from Protestant Ulstermen and the onset of World War I delayed any action. It wasn't until 1922 that the Irish Free State in the south was created while the six northern provinces remain a part of the United Kingdom.

QUESTIONS	EXPLANATIONS

33. Prussian power in the eighteenth century was primarily based on its

(A) strong army
(B) geographic location
(C) well-trained diplomatic corps
(D) military alliance with Great Britain
(E) economic might

33. **A** Prussian power essentially rested on its powerful army. Because of its lack of natural defenses (such as the British enjoyed with the English Channel) and its physical location next to powerful neighbors such as Russia and Sweden, most of the resources of the Prussian state were spent on the military. Prussia was the first nation to establish a system of military reserves, therefore making military service a standard part of life for most Prussian men. Some commentators in Europe saw Prussia as a new Sparta, a state where everything was subsumed by military need.

34. Montesquieu, in his *Spirit of Laws*, was inspired by the system of government in

(A) Venice
(B) Russia
(C) Great Britain
(D) France
(E) the United States

34. **C** Montesquieu visited Great Britain in 1729 and was fascinated by the British system of government. Like many of the writers of the early Enlightenment, he thought Great Britain offered a standard of political freedom and religious toleration that should be emulated on the continent.

35. The primary problem facing Louis XVI in the late 1780s was

(A) peasant unrest
(B) British naval expansion
(C) the poverty of the French nation
(D) the refusal of the Third Estate to pay taxes
(E) the bankruptcy of the monarchy

35. **E** The chief problem facing the monarchy in the 1780s was bankruptcy. Bankruptcy occurred as a result of several factors, including the aid provided by the French to the American colonists during their revolution and France's inability to tax the wealthy nobility and the Church. Eventually in 1789, the financial desperation of Louis XVI led him to take the dramatic step of calling an Estates General, the first since 1614, in the hope that this body would agree to raise much needed revenue. This decision turned out to be a major miscalculation by the monarch and set the stage for the French Revolution.

QUESTIONS	EXPLANATIONS

36. In *What Is the Third Estate?*, Abbé Siéyès called for

(A) the elimination of the Third Estate
(B) the creation of a republic
(C) the overthrow of the monarchy
(D) a dominant role for commoners in French political life
(E) the boycott by the Third Estate of the proceedings at Versailles

36. **D** Louis XVI's 1788 decision to organize a meeting of an Estates General in the following year led to the publication of a torrent of pamphlet literature addressing the political and economic crisis facing the French state. One of the most famous of these pamphlets was written by a minor clergyman, Abbé Sieyes, who argued that while the Third Estate (commoners) was the heart of the nation, they had not previously enjoyed political influence within France.

37. Mary Wollstonecraft's *Vindication of the Rights of Women* (1792) was the first book published in Great Britain to

(A) demand that women should be educated
(B) insist on the moral supremacy of women
(C) demand that women should have full political rights
(D) speculate on the advent of a political party for women
(E) demand that the monarchy should pass to the eldest child, regardless of whether they are male or female

37. **C** The French Revolution inspired a number of women across Europe to think about the issue of rights for women. One of the most enthusiastic supporters of the French Revolution was the Englishwoman Mary Wollstonecraft (1759–1797), who went to France to view the new freedom first hand. Wollstonecraft returned to England disappointed that women's rights were not being fully addressed by the revolutionary governments. This inspired her to write the *Vindication of the Rights of Women*, in which she argued that women in England should be given the right not just to vote, but also to hold political office.

38. The aristocracy created by Napoleon differed from that of the Ancien Régime in that

(A) titles were not passed down to heirs
(B) nobles were allowed to sit in a special legislative body
(C) all nobles enjoyed a tax-free status
(D) the Napoleonic code excluded them from appearing in court
(E) nobles were responsible for local government

38. **A** Some traditional Jacobin supporters were horrified when Napoleon restored noble titles in France, but we should not view this as a complete return to the days of Louis XVI. The Napoleonic aristocracy differed from that of the Ancien Régime in that titles were awarded for service to the French state and were not to be passed down to heirs. Additionally, titleholders were given no special privileges under the law, such as the tax-free status that was enjoyed by nobles under the Bourbon monarchy.

QUESTIONS	EXPLANATIONS
39. Max Weber's *The Protestant Ethic and the Spirit of Capitalism* attempted to show (A) how capitalism grew out of Protestant religious belief (B) how capitalism was anathema to Protestantism (C) why Protestants should embrace capitalism (D) how John Calvin was indirectly the father of free markets (E) what modern economies can learn from Protestant theology	39. **A** Max Weber (1864–1920) was one of the fathers of sociology, a field that seeks to scientifically study society. In 1905, he published *The Protestant Ethic and the Spirit of Capitalism* in which he argued that the roots of capitalism could be found among sixteenth- and seventeenth-century Calvinists. Their "worldly asceticism," a term that indicates that Calvinists invested their profits back into their businesses rather than merely enjoying the fruits of their labors, made them the first capitalist entrepreneurs.
40. The suffragettes gained much attention in Great Britain because (A) most men started to accept female suffrage (B) they were the first female political organization (C) they seemed to be effective in galvanizing the support of women (D) their violent acts seemed to be contrary to Victorian ideals concerning women (E) they combined political and economic demands	40. **D** After they formed in 1903, the Women's Social and Political Union (popularly known as the suffragettes) gained public attention for breaking shop windows, heckling speakers at political meetings, and going on hunger strikes after being arrested. Such behaviors, which the suffragettes believed were the only way to gain the vote for women, drew particular attention since they contradicted the Victorian concept of women, which emphasized their domesticity and docility.
41. The initial German reaction to French colonialism in Africa was (A) distrust of French intentions (B) anger (C) tacit acceptance (D) to look to Great Britain to block French expansion (E) to build their own colonies	41. **C** Bismarck had no interest in the creation of German colonies in Africa or Asia. Instead he thought that a colonial empire might be just the thing to pacify the French, who were still bitter following the loss of the provinces of Alsace and Lorraine to Germany following the Franco-Prussian War. After Bismarck was removed from the Chancellery office in 1890, Kaiser Wilhelm II set Germany on a course of colonial expansion, thus adding to the tensions with France and Great Britain.

Births per 1,000 of Total Population

Year	England and Wales	Scotland
1913	24.1	25.5
1914	23.8	26.1
1915	21.9	23.9
1916	20.9	22.9
1917	17.8	20.3
1918	17.7	20.3
1919	18.5	22.0
1920	25.5	28.1

42. What information can be concluded from the preceding table?

(A) Better nutrition in Scotland led to a higher birthrate.
(B) The number of illegitimate births declined during the war years.
(C) There was a long-term decline in the birthrate in Great Britain dating back to the nineteenth century.
(D) There was a postwar rise in the birthrate.
(E) Because women worked in factories during the war, the birthrate declined.

42. **D** Remember not to overanalyze charts. The only thing that definitely can be concluded from this table is that in the years following the end of the war in 1919, the birthrate in Great Britain increased. None of the other answers can be backed up with the numbers found in this chart.

43. The collapse of the Russian Provisional Government in November 1917 resulted from the government's

(A) refusal to remove the tsar
(B) inability to collect taxes
(C) refusal to call elections
(D) banning of the Bolshevik Party
(E) insistence on keeping Russia in the war

43. **E** The Provisional Government (the government formed following the abdication of the tsar) made the difficult decision to keep Russia in World War I. This turned out to be a costly mistake, since by 1917 Russia was extremely war weary. The continued failure of Russian forces on the Eastern Front helped set the stage for the second Russian Revolution of 1917—this one under the leadership of the Bolshevik leader Lenin. Lenin gained many followers by simply promising to take Russia out of the war, which he promptly did in early 1918.

QUESTIONS	EXPLANATIONS

44. Spanish sailors returning from their voyages to the New World introduced which of the following diseases into Europe?

(A) Smallpox
(B) Venereal disease
(C) Plague
(D) Cholera
(E) Polio

44. **B** Sailors have always had the reputation of being promiscuous and in this case they brought back to Europe a nasty surprise. Spanish sailors had contracted venereal disease in the New World, something that had been unknown in Europe until the sixteenth century.

45. Martin Luther and Henrich Zwingli broke over the question of

(A) salvation by faith
(B) the primacy of the scriptures
(C) the role of the clergy
(D) Jesus's presence in the mass
(E) infant baptism

45. **D** Luther and Zwingli agreed on many points of theology including the concept of salvation by faith alone. Nevertheless, when the two men met they vehemently disagreed on the question of Jesus's presence in the mass. Luther believed that Jesus was present in the mass since he was present everywhere, while Zwingli believed that Jesus was only symbolically present in the mass since he was in heaven.

46. The Church of England as initially established by Henry VIII in 1536 was

(A) closely tied to Lutheranism
(B) fundamentally Calvinist
(C) dominated by the concept of salvation by faith alone
(D) torn by religious skepticism
(E) in many ways tied to traditional Catholic practices

46. **E** Henry VIII had little interest in Protestant theology and even wrote a pamphlet attacking the beliefs of Martin Luther. When the king broke with Rome in 1534, he established a Church of England that in many ways maintained Catholic teachings on questions concerning salvation and the sacraments.

QUESTIONS	EXPLANATIONS

47. There reigneth all abuse, carnal liberty, enormity, sin and Babylonical confusion. Take away kings, princes, rulers, magistrates, judges, and such estates of God's order, no man shall sleep in his own house or bed unkilled, no man shall keep his wife, children or possessions in quietness, all things shall be common; and there needs must follow all mischief and utter destruction both of souls, good and commonwealth.

This homily, read from a pulpit in Elizabethan England, was primarily an attempt to convince people to

(A) attend the services of the Church of England
(B) accept the social hierarchy
(C) accept Elizabeth as their Queen
(D) challenge the status quo
(E) guard their family and property

47. **B** The maintenance of the social hierarchy was an important goal for the elites in Early Modern Europe, and the Church played an important role in maintaining this hierarchy by teaching obedience to one's social superiors. Many Elizabethan homilies stressed similar ideas like the one shown above, which stresses that if you undercut support for the King, nobles, and judges, the sanctity of your property and family will come under threat.

48. The influx of gold and silver into Spain in the sixteenth century failed to stimulate the economy for all of the following reasons EXCEPT

(A) losses due to theft by corrupt officials
(B) the high cost of maintaining a vast overseas empire
(C) huge sums were needed to put down internal rebellions within Spain
(D) high inflation
(E) use of vast sums in foreign wars

48. **C** While Spain was not always well served by its kings in the sixteenth century, Spain, unlike France, avoided the horrors of internal civil war. However, the huge sums of money carried from the New World to Spain did little to enrich the country. Most of the funds were used to finance the endless wars that Spain found herself engaged in against the Ottomans, the French, the English, and against the Dutch rebels.

QUESTIONS	EXPLANATIONS

QUESTIONS

49. The primary significance of the Crimean War was that

    (A) the Ottoman Empire lost control over Istanbul

    (B) it revealed the impact of industrialization on warfare

    (C) it marked the end of the Concert of Europe

    (D) it left key issues in the Crimean region unresolved

    (E) the French gained control over religious sites in the Holy Land

50. The Paris Commune of 1871 resulted from

    (A) the declaration of German unification

    (B) the anarchy caused by the Franco-Prussian War

    (C) the collapse of the Third Republic

    (D) tensions in France between Bonapartist and Bourbon supporters

    (E) financial speculation in the Paris stock market

51. Bismarck's greatest fear for Germany was that

    (A) France and Russia would form a military alliance

    (B) Austria-Hungary would go to war with Serbia

    (C) France and Great Britain would form a military alliance

    (D) the Russians would seize Istanbul

    (E) the Emperor would lead Germany into war

EXPLANATIONS

49. **C** The Crimean War (1854–1856) was a sordid little affair in which none of the major participants fought very skillfully. Its primary historical significance was that it marked the end of the Concert of Europe, the idea that the major European powers needed to work in conjunction with one another. This was a concept that grew out of the Congress of Vienna. The fact that France and Great Britain were involved in a war with Russia, while the Prussians and Austrians remained neutral, revealed that the Concert was over and a new era of European rivalries was about to begin.

50. **B** Following the humiliating defeat of French forces in the Franco-Prussian War, the people of Paris refused to surrender to the Prussians. When the new republican government, which had been formed following the abdication of Napoleon III and was based at Versailles, insisted that the Parisians lay down their arms, the people of Paris formed their own radical government known as the Commune. This led to a civil war in France. The war ended when Paris was finally taken by the republican forces, which then "celebrated" their victory by executing thousands of communards during what came to be known as "bloody week."

51. **A** Throughout his time as German chancellor, Bismarck worked deliberately to ensure that France and Russia would not form an anti-German alliance. In 1873, he formed the Three Emperors league with Austria-Hungary and Russia to ensure cooperation among the three states. Six years later, however, he felt forced to establish the Dual Alliance with Austria-Hungary to stop the expansion of Russian influence in the Balkans. Although Bismarck hoped that the Dual Alliance would lead the Russians to establish better relations with Germany, it instead led tsarist Russia to seek out an alliance with a different ally—Republican France. By 1894, Bismarck's greatest fear was realized when Russia and France worked out a formal alliance to provide for mutual cooperation in the event of a German attack on either country.

QUESTIONS	EXPLANATIONS
52. The building of a large German navy in the first decade of the twentieth century greatly antagonized (A) Italy (B) France (C) Great Britain (D) Russia (E) the United States	52. **C** German-British relations remained quite good following the establishment of the German Empire in 1871. However, all that began to change in the last years of the nineteenth century when Germany decided to pursue a dramatic expansion of its navy. Fearing that their dominance over the seas was being threatened, the British sought to establish better relations with France, their traditional rival.
53. By 1917, the biggest problem facing the French army was (A) a shortage of shells (B) the anticipated withdrawal of British forces from the Western Front (C) Germany's capture of Verdun (D) mass desertion (E) the refusal of some soldiers to fight	53. **E** Although French soldiers did not desert en masse, by 1917 many soldiers refused to leave their trenches and advance toward the German lines because they felt that their officers were simply throwing away their lives. Several hundred soldiers were shot for disobeying orders. Recently, descendants of some of these men have petitioned the French government to grant the soldiers posthumous pardons. Their argument is that the men were willing to defend French soil, but simply could not accept being used in attacks in which they would be certainly wiped out by German machine guns.
54. President Wilson's "Fourteen Points" called for all of the following EXCEPT (A) national self-determination (B) the creation of the League of Nations (C) decolonization in Africa (D) a peace without reparations (E) the end of secret treaties between nations	54. **C** Although President Wilson called for self-determination for the people of eastern Europe, he did not match this with a similar call for the people of Asia and Africa. During the interwar years, the colonial powers increased their power over their colonial holdings. The process of decolonization didn't start until the end of World War II.

QUESTIONS	EXPLANATIONS
55. Renaissance humanists were primarily interested in the Roman politician Cicero because of (A) his moral courage (B) his detailed explanation of the crisis of the Late Roman Republic (C) his denunciation of Caesar's tyranny (D) medieval monks who had preserved his work (E) the beauty of his Latin prose	55. **E** Cicero was a brilliant Latin stylist whose graceful way with the language was widely admired and imitated by humanist scholars. Sometimes the term Ciceronian Latin was used in the Renaissance to distinguish the elegance of Cicero's Latin from, what the humanists deemed, the more crass Latin of the Middle Ages.
56. Carnival was an important social outlet in Early Modern Europe because (A) it liberated people, if only for a short time, from hierarchical society (B) it was critical to economic growth (C) it brought religious fervor to a frenzy (D) it lessened tensions between Catholics and Protestants (E) it was the only time during the year that townspeople didn't have to work	56. **A** Carnival played an important role in Early Modern Europe by providing people—at least for a short period—with a break from the strict rules of traditional hierarchical society. Carnival took place in the days leading up to Lent. It was a time when men dressed as women and vice versa, and when people felt free to mimic and satirize their social betters with no fear of retribution.
57. "We came here to serve God and King, but also to get rich." The above quote best represents the views of a (A) Renaissance humanist (B) Spanish conquistador (C) Jesuit missionary (D) Florentine merchant (E) supporter of the royalist side in the English Revolution	57. **B** Many of the conquistadors, the tough soldiers from Spain who conquered the New World, saw themselves as both servants of the Spanish crown as well as the Catholic Church. Ultimately, however, the conquistadors—many of whom came from the poorer regions of Spain—hoped that their time fighting in Central and South America would allow them to become wealthy men.

58. The Thirty Years War resulted from all of the following EXCEPT

(A) the Counter-Reformation
(B) the growing power of the Habsburgs
(C) Lutheran dissatisfaction with the Peace of Augburg
(D) religious conflict in Bohemia
(E) the expansion of Calvinism in the Holy Roman Empire

58. **C** The Thirty Years War (1618–1648) was a complex struggle that involved a variety of factors including the growing clash between a Catholic Church that had been reinvigorated by the Counter-Reformation, as well as a dynamic and aggressive Calvinism. Another issue was the growing fear of many independent rulers within the Holy Roman Empire that the Habsburgs were planning to extend their power within the Empire. On the other hand, Lutherans would not have been dissatisfied with the Peace of Augsburg (1559), since it fully recognized the rights of Lutherans to practice their faith in those states governed by Lutheran rulers.

59. The "Diggers," a group that emerged during the English Revolution, believed that

(A) the monarchy must be based on popular support
(B) England needed to become a theocracy
(C) enclosure laws needed to be enforced
(D) private ownership of land should be abolished
(E) property belonging to supporters of Charles I should be redistributed to the landless

59. **D** The Diggers (the name was given to them by their enemies) were one of a number of radical groups that appeared during the English Revolution. Diggers believed that all property should be communal and went so far as to establish small communities that practiced this belief. Ultimately, it was radical groups like the Diggers who scared men of property into calling for the restoration of the monarchy, which occurred when Charles II took the English throne in 1660.

60. In the seventeenth century, the Netherlands became a haven for

(A) former monarchs
(B) religious minorities
(C) political radicals
(D) those seeking relief from high taxation
(E) former mercenaries

60. **B** Unlike the rest of Europe, where religious intolerance was the rule of the day, the Netherlands was unique in serving as a haven for persecuted religious minorities. Jews who were expelled from Spain found a home in the Netherlands, as did Anabaptists, who fled the Holy Roman Empire because of persecution from both Catholics and Protestants.

QUESTIONS	EXPLANATIONS

61. The Irish Easter Rebellion of 1916 witnessed an attempt to

(A) create an independent Irish republic
(B) force the British out of Northern Ireland
(C) recognize Catholic rights in Northern Ireland
(D) force the British to step back from their plan to partition Ireland
(E) provide dominion status for the southern counties

61. A Frustrated by the failure to achieve an independent state for Ireland, members of the Irish Republican Army staged a rebellion on Easter Day in an attempt to forcibly achieve their goals. Although the rebellion received little support from the Irish populace, the brutality exhibited by the British at the end of the failed rebellion helped increase support among the Irish for a complete break with Great Britain.

62. The New Economic Policy of 1921 marked an attempt in the Soviet Union to

(A) impose stringent new controls over the Russian economy
(B) appease the left wing of the Communist Party
(C) step back from War Communism
(D) redirect the Soviet state toward a market economy
(E) provide the economic wherewithal to win the Civil War

62. C War Communism was a rapid attempt to create a Marxist economy in Russia during the years of the Civil War. It involved massive confiscation of property and created a great deal of ill will among the Russian people. Following the end of the Civil War and the rebellion of the Kronstadt sailors, who were protesting the harshness of War Communism, the political leadership under the direction of Lenin decided to implement the New Economic Policy. This policy allowed for small-scale, privately owned factories and shops and granted the right to farmers to sell some of their produce on the open market.

63. The British General Strike of 1926 was sparked by problems in which industry?

(A) Shipbuilding
(B) Coal
(C) Textiles
(D) Transport
(E) Iron

63. B With profits falling due to a decline in exports, mine owners announced in 1925 that they intended to reduce wages. In response, the government promised that for nine months it would subsidize the miners' wages to bring them back to their previous level. With the nine-month period coming to an end, the owners outlined new terms for employment including a longer workday and wage cuts. The Trades Union Congress, an umbrella organization of British unions, announced a general strike on May 3 in support of the miners. The General Strike lasted for nine days, after which only the miners stayed out on strike, with some not returning to work until November.

64. The Popular Front government formed in France in 1936 was an attempt to

    (A) reconcile with the British
    (B) appease the Germans
    (C) unite the parties of the left against fascism
    (D) create a coalition government bringing in parties from across the political spectrum
    (E) unite the parties of the right against socialism

64. **C** Following the early 1934 rioting of far-right Frenchmen, the parties of the French left decided that they needed to cooperate to save the republic. The rise of a fascist government in Germany during the previous year created an urgency in this need for cooperation. When the next elections took place in May 1936, the "Popular Front," an electoral alliance between Socialists and Communists, won a resounding victory over the parties of the right. Léon Blum became the first Socialist to be named Prime Minister of France, although this Popular Front Government would only remain in office for a little longer than one year.

65. Mussolini's Lateran Pact with the Catholic Church

    (A) revealed Mussolini's own deeply held religious beliefs
    (B) made Catholicism the official state religion in Italy
    (C) led to official Catholic support of Mussolini's fascist movement
    (D) restored the Vatican as an independent state
    (E) allowed Mussolini a veto over all clerical appointments

65. **D** Although Mussolini himself was an atheist, he sought out better relations with the Catholic Church. The Lateran Pact of 1929 restored Vatican City to the papacy (the papacy had lost this territory when the city of Rome was absorbed into the Italian monarchy in 1870), and in return, the papacy recognized the existence of the state of Italy. Popes to this day continue to rule Vatican City, the smallest nation in the world.

66. The "Great Fear" in the summer of 1789 was the result of rumors that

    (A) the harvest was far smaller than expected
    (B) the great French estates were not to be broken up and redistributed among the peasants
    (C) the monarchy was about to be restored
    (D) aristocrats were plotting to attack peasants
    (E) French farms would be collectivized

66. **D** Rumors played an important role in the French Revolution. Perhaps none were so significant as those that spurred the "Great Fear" during the summer of 1789. Seemingly, anarchy was taking place at Versailles as the king had to deal with a new National Assembly. This situation led to rumors throughout the countryside that nobles were using the king's troubles to their advantage and were plotting to drive off the peasants from their land. In response to the rumors, peasants organized armed bands and burned a number of aristocratic estates.

QUESTIONS	EXPLANATIONS
67. During the Jacobin domination of France in 1793, the government did all of the following EXCEPT (A) institute the metric system (B) make all property communal (C) change the calendar (D) set price limits on bread (E) attempt to move the people away from their allegiance to Catholicism	67. **B** The Jacobins did implement a number of dramatic changes into French life during their short period of control over the government from 1793 to 1794, including establishing a new calendar and a "Cult of Reason" to lessen people's attachments to the Catholic Church. Although they did establish a law of maximum prices to control the price of bread, they were not economically radical and therefore did not propose to make all property communal.
68. Edmund Burke in his *Reflections on the Revolution in France* (1790) was critical of (A) British failure to formulate an effective response to events in France (B) the removal of Louis XVI from the throne (C) France's inability to evolve from constitutional monarchy to republic (D) France's refusal to honor its national debt (E) the rapid diminishing of the authority of the monarchy and the Church	68. **E** Burke was horrified by what he believed were the excesses of the French Revolution. Within the British political landscape, he was a moderate reformer who was attached to the Whig political faction. Burke believed, however, that political change needed to evolve slowly as was the case in Britain, where the constitutional monarchy had developed over the course of several centuries. Burke predicted that the rapid creation of a constitutional monarchy in France, along with severe constraints on the Catholic Church, were bound to lead to even more radical changes and to increased violence.
69. Early nineteenth-century Luddites were known for (A) political liberalism (B) Chartism (C) organizing the first British Labor unions (D) breaking machinery (E) republicanism	69. **D** The Luddites were handloom weavers who, in the period from 1811 to 1812, destroyed hundreds of the new machines that were depriving them of work. We still use the term Luddite to describe those individuals who reject the use of new technology.

70. Metternich, the Austrian Chancellor who dominated the Congress of Vienna, was extremely fearful of

    (A) nationalism
    (B) the return of the Bourbons
    (C) the impact of industrialization
    (D) particularism among the Italian states
    (E) Russian intentions in Europe

70. **A** Metternich knew that the greatest danger to the Austrian Empire was the new power of nationalist sentiment that was sweeping Europe following the French Revolution and Napoleonic wars. The Austrian Empire was a polyglot state made up of numerous ethnic nationalities and Metternich recognized—true to what eventually happened in the early twentieth century—that nationalism was the greatest threat to the survival of the empire.

71. The murder of socialist leader Giacomo Matteotti ultimately provided Mussolini with the opportunity to

    (A) overthrow the monarchy
    (B) seek out a deal with opposition political leaders
    (C) purge the ranks of his Fascist party
    (D) eliminate all political opposition in Italy
    (E) work on a political and military alliance with Nazi Germany

71. **D** Even though the outcry over the 1924 murder of Matteotti by Fascist thugs almost threatened to topple Mussolini's government, Mussolini used the crisis to increase his control over Italian political life. Soon after the murder, Mussolini banned all political parties except his own National Fascist Party and silenced what remained of the independent Italian press.

72. After receiving German and Italian support in the Spanish Civil War, Franco responded in World War II

    (A) by joining with the Allies against the Fascist powers
    (B) by aiding Germany and Italy with arms
    (C) by remaining neutral
    (D) by secretly attacking British convoys in the Atlantic
    (E) by offering to serve as a facilitator for peace talks

72. **C** Despite receiving substantial military assistance from the Fascist powers during the Spanish Civil War, Franco ignored the entreaties of Hitler and wisely kept Spain out of World War II. Spain was exhausted following its Civil War, and Franco had doubts about the potential for an Axis military victory.

QUESTIONS	EXPLANATIONS

73. Winston Churchill stood out among his colleagues in the Conservative Party for being firmly against

(A) implementing the gold standard
(B) the blockade against the Spanish Republic during the Civil War
(C) recognition of the Soviet Union
(D) the formation of a coalition government with the Labour Party
(E) appeasement with the Germans

73. E The Conservative Party was dominated by appeasers like Prime Minister Neville Chamberlain, who believed that some sort of accommodation could be worked out with Hitler. Winston Churchill, however, recognized from the beginning the evil inherent in Nazism and realized that eventually Britain would have to go to war with Germany. When war did break out, Churchill emerged as Prime Minister, in part because he was one of the few conservative politicians who was not tainted by being associated with appeasement.

74. The Wannsee Conference in January 1942 set the stage for

(A) Operation Barbarossa
(B) the entry of the United States into World War II
(C) the elimination of European Jewry
(D) creation of allied occupation zones in Germany
(E) German and Japanese military cooperation

74. C Although what was exactly said at the Wannsee Conference is unknown, it is clear that this meeting of Nazi leadership, which took place in the Berlin suburb of Wannsee, set in motion the destruction of European Jewry. Prior to this point the murder of Jews had been a haphazard affair; after Wannsee the Nazis established a series of death camps in eastern Europe to more efficiently handle the task of extermination.

75. Which of the following best describes the attitude of the French toward nuclear weapon development in the period following World War II?

(A) They felt protected by the American nuclear weapon umbrella.
(B) They committed themselves to the creation of their own small independent nuclear arsenal.
(C) They researched but never developed nuclear weapons.
(D) They joined with Third World nations and worked toward the banning of nuclear weapons.
(E) They were committed to matching the Russian nuclear arsenal.

75. B It was President Charles de Gaulle who insisted that France had to maintain its own nuclear weapon arsenal. While France's *force de frappe* was not intended to match the massive American and Soviet nuclear arsenal, de Gaulle saw nuclear weapons as an essential part of maintaining France as a major power in the postwar world.

QUESTIONS	EXPLANATIONS

76. Martin Luther attended the Diet of Worms without fear of losing his life because

(A) he possessed a sizeable army
(B) he was protected by the Elector of Saxony
(C) he thought the Catholic Church would support his ideas
(D) he enjoyed the support of the Holy Roman Emperor
(E) he went in disguise

76. **B** Unlike the unfortunate Jan Hus, who attended the Council of Constance in 1415 and was burned at the stake for holding heretical views, Martin Luther attended the Diet of Worms in 1521 with the backing of a powerful noble. This noble, the Elector of Saxony, was skeptical of some of Luther's teachings, but thought that he should be allowed to speak his peace. After Worms, Luther was placed under the ban of the Empire, which meant that anyone could freely take his life. Supporters of the Elector Frederick safely escorted Luther to Wartburg Castle where he worked on his translation of the New Testament into German.

77. Oliver Cromwell's New Model Army differed from the Cavalier forces under Charles I by

(A) its emphasis on cavalry
(B) deemphasizing the role of religion
(C) its recruitment of continental mercenaries
(D) providing regular pay for soldiers and for paying for supplies taken from farmers
(E) remaining on the defensive

77. **D** Cromwell insisted on strict discipline within his army. While the Cavalier forces under King Charles I plundered supplies from the countryside, Cromwell recognized that he could gain the goodwill of many Englishmen who were not attached to either side in the struggle by having a well-behaved army. To that end, he implemented regular pay for his men to stop them from plundering and insisted that they pay for all supplies.

78. In France in the seventeenth century, "nobles of the sword" differed from "nobles of the robe" in that the former were

(A) wealthier
(B) part of the old traditional landed nobility dating back to the Middle Ages
(C) given special privileges in the Estates General
(D) allowed to maintain manorial courts on their estates
(E) banned from engaging in commerce

78. **B** The "nobles of the sword" were the traditional landed nobility, who employed genealogists to trace their family trees back to the time of Charlemagne. The "nobles of the robe," on the other hand, were the service nobility—middle-class individuals who had been ennobled by the king as a reward for their loyal service to the French state. Not surprisingly, the older nobility looked down their noses at these newly minted nobles.

QUESTIONS	EXPLANATIONS

79. The Holy Roman Emperor was a weak title because

    (A) it was an elected monarchy
    (B) the Austrian Habsburgs controlled the throne
    (C) it was selected by the papacy
    (D) France was the power behind the throne
    (E) the religious authority of the Emperor was superior to the political

79. **A** In the Early Middle Ages, elected monarchies were more the norm than the exception, but over time in places such as France the practice gave way to hereditary titles. The Holy Roman Empire, however, retained its electoral practices with seven German rulers serving as an electoral college. This practice tended to result in the selection of emperors who promised not to interfere with the independence of the German states.

80. The seventeenth-century English scientist William Harvey discovered

    (A) that alchemy was a false science
    (B) the elliptical orbit of the Earth around the sun
    (C) how blood circulates within the human body
    (D) the circumference of the Earth
    (E) the function of the liver

80. **C** Harvey was one of a number of extraordinary English scientists in the seventeenth century. Earlier scientists had believed that both the liver and the heart pumped blood throughout the body. Harvey showed that the heart and its valves were solely responsible for the process of circulation.

THE DBQ EXPLAINED

The Document-Based Question (DBQ) section begins with a mandatory 15-minute reading period. During these 15 minutes, you'll want to do the following: (1) come up with some information not included in the given documents (your outside knowledge) to include in your essay; (2) get an overview of what each document means; (3) decide what opinion you are going to argue; and (4) write an outline of your essay.

This DBQ deals with the issue of Chartism and is asking you to determine whether Chartism should be viewed as a revolutionary movement or as a moderate movement. You will need to have some knowledge of British politics in the nineteenth century to handle this question and at least a little familiarity with Chartism, although don't be too concerned if your knowledge of Chartism is somewhat limited.

The first thing you want to do, BEFORE YOU LOOK AT THE DOCUMENTS, is to brainstorm for a minute or two. Try to list everything you remember about both Chartism and British politics in the first half of the nineteenth century. This list will serve as your reference to the outside information you must provide to earn a top grade.

Next, read over the documents. As you read them, take notes in the margins and underline those passages that you are certain you are going to use in your essay. If a document reminds you of a piece of outside information, add that information to your brainstorming list. If you cannot make sense of a document or it argues strongly against your position, relax! You do not need to mention every document to score well on the DBQ.

Here is what you might see in the time you have to look over the documents.

THE DOCUMENTS

Document 1

This first document lays out the six points of the Charter. They are as follows:

1. universal suffrage

2. no property requirement for members of Parliament

3. annual parliaments

4. equal representation (meaning that all areas of the nation would be equally represented)

5. payment of members

6. vote by secret ballot

You'll notice that the document refers to the idea of the Charter providing for the "just representation of the people of Great Britain...," an indication that the goal is the political inclusion of working-class individuals rather than the complete overhaul of the system.

Document 2

This excerpt from a speech by Joseph Stevens given at a Chartist rally addresses one of the central issues behind the rise of Chartism. For Stevens, the Charter is all about providing people with the basic needs of life such as food and shelter. Clearly for Stevens (and for many other Chartists), the possession of political rights were the means by which British workers were going to achieve a better standard of living.

Document 3

This article, which appeared in a Chartist newspaper, appears to be aimed at those Chartists who were advocating the need for armed violence. While implying that it is within an Englishman's right to rebel and is, in fact, "the last remedy known to the Constitution," the article strongly rejects the use of physical force as an option in the current situation.

Interestingly, one of the arguments used against the use of arms has little to do with morality and everything to do with the potential for success. The author points out that to succeed, armed revolts would have to be staged concurrently throughout the land, and that even if they are staged concurrently there would still be only a "slender chance" for success. Perhaps reluctantly, the author does concede that those who have arms should hold onto them, although they should only be used in self-defense.

Document 4

This article also appeared in the *Chartist*—the largest and most important newspaper of the movement—and deals with the lack of interest in Chartism displayed by working men in London. The article deals with a standard complaint of grassroots organizations: People are good at complaining, but completely indifferent when it comes to actually doing anything to bring about change. The author points out that while it does appear that there is more activity taking place in the rest of Britain, without the active participation of those in the city the movement is doomed to fail.

Document 5

This document is a poem in honor of Feargus O'Connor. Besides noticing how nicely everything rhymes, you should be aware that the document refers to the earlier imprisonment of O'Connor, who, at the time the poem appeared in print, was free to continue with his labors on behalf of the Chartists.

Document 6

Document 6 contains a portion of a newspaper article detailing the events at a Chartist social gathering. You should note that the gathering consists of a tea party and ball, activities that clearly imitate the social activities of the upper classes and appear far from revolutionary. Feargus O'Connor (the same individual lionized in Document 5) was unable to attend the tea party because he and some of the other Chartists had to attend to the issue of the calling of a general strike (certainly not many middle-class tea parties were interrupted for similar reasons).

Document 7

While male Chartists split over the question of whether the right to vote should be extended to women, women were actively engaged in the Chartist movement, both as a source of support for male Chartists and as active participants in their own right. This document, from a female Chartist organization, should be viewed in conjunction with Document 2, because, like the earlier document, it focuses on the economic hardships of working-class life, rather than placing an emphasis on the political struggle.

Document 8

Get in the habit of noticing the dates provided in your documents. In this instance it contains some critical information that will allow you to see this document within context. Here we have an editorial that appeared in the *Northern Star* on March 25, 1848. In February of that year King Louis-Philippe was overthrown, and France became a republic. By March, revolution began to sweep across the German and Italian states.

With these events as the background, the editorialist seems to be advocating that it is time for similar action in Great Britain. The question comes down to "Reform or Revolution," and the author appears ready to have revolution in the event that reform fails. In fact, he ends with the threatening statement "THE CHARTER, OR VIVE LA REPUBLIQUE!," a call for the complete overhaul of the British political system should the Charter not be granted. Nevertheless, despite this seemingly stirring call for action, there is still some of that old British caution being displayed here: You might have noticed that the final paragraph begins with the word "patience."

Document 9

Make note that the author of this letter is a middle-class man and that the letter reveals some of the fears that his class must have felt about a working-class movement that they neither understood nor sympathized with. Also, the source for his information is the *Times,* the most important newspaper of the establishment and again not necessarily a source for genuine understanding of the Chartist movement.

Document 10

The source for Document 10 is also extremely important. In this case it is Lord John Russell, the Prime Minister, who was writing to Queen Victoria to inform her of events in London following a massive Chartist rally that took place in the spring of 1848. Russell clearly wants to show his monarch that he dominated the situation and that the preparations made by his government provided for complete control over the crowd.

Even if some of what Russell writes needs to be taken with a grain of salt, it does appear that the meeting broke up without any violence. In general, it was far from the revolutionary insurrection feared by many (including the author of Document 9).

OUTSIDE INFORMATION

We have already discussed much more than you could possibly include in a 45-minute essay. Don't worry. You will not be expected to mention everything or even most of what we have covered in the section above. You will, however, be expected to include some outside information; that is, information not mentioned directly in the documents.

Below is some outside information you might have used in your essay.

- The ostensible goal of Chartism was the passage of the People's Charter, a document that called for universal suffrage for all men over the age of twenty-one, the end of property requirements for those holding seats in Parliament, annual parliaments, equal electoral districts, and payment of those holding seats in Parliament. Chartists organized massive petitions that were presented on several occasions to the House of Commons, although the House of Commons did nothing to act on them. The largest and final petition was presented in 1848 with around 3 million signers.

- Five of the demands of the Chartists are today a part of the British constitution. The only one that has never been enacted was the idea of annual parliamentary elections, a radical idea that went back to the constitutional struggles of the seventeenth century. Today the life of a parliament is five years.

- The late 1830s and the 1840s were a particularly difficult period, one known to historians as the "hungry forties." Economic difficulties may account for the rise of Chartism, particularly if the movement is viewed as one whose primary goal was the establishment of political rights for working-class individuals so that as a group they could have some say over the economic conditions that ruled their lives. Economic conditions may also account for the decline of Chartism after 1848, since these were years of growing economic prosperity and therefore may have led to an easing of political demands.

- Working-class individuals were angered over the passage of the Great Reform Bill (1832), which provided political rights for middle-class individuals, but ignored the rights of the working class. Additionally, there was a tremendous amount of working-class frustration with certain bills passed by this new "reformed" Parliament, including the 1834 Poor Law, which treated those suffering from poverty with great harshness.

- 1848 was a year of revolutionary activity throughout Europe. In France, the monarchy was replaced by a republic and revolutions spread across Europe. You should know from your studies of this period, however, that England and Russia were the two European states that were exempt from revolutionary activity in that year.

- There were two dominant factions within Chartism. The majority can be labeled "moral force" Chartists; they wanted to peacefully campaign for the passage of the People's Charter. "Physical force" Chartists were a smaller faction found primarily in the cities of Northern England; they advocated the possible use of violence should their demands not be met. William Lovell was the leader of the moral force Chartists, while Feargus O'Connor was the main figure in the opposing faction.

- Chartism as a movement declined rapidly in the years after 1848. Working-class men increasingly looked to labor unions as a source for economic change rather than mass political movements, though working-class political activity did not disappear. The British political system would prove to be more flexible than many had imagined, and in 1867 male working-class householders received the vote, while in 1884 their counterparts in the countryside received the same.

CHOOSING A THESIS STATEMENT

This DBQ is asking you to take sides in a debate. On the basis of the documents, a much stronger case could be provided for taking the position that Chartism should be viewed as a movement for political change that was *not* fundamentally revolutionary. Keep in mind that while there are strong historical arguments for taking the other side (and a number of books and articles have taken the position that Chartism *was* inherently revolutionary), you must base your argument on the documents provided on the exam. The documents provided truly lean toward the nonrevolutionary aspects of the movement.

PLANNING YOUR ESSAY

Unless you read extremely quickly, you probably will not have time to write a detailed outline for your essay during the 15-minute reading period. However, it is worth taking several minutes to jot down a loose structure of your essay because it will actually save you time when you write! First, decide on your thesis and write it down in the test booklet. (There is usually some blank space below the documents.) Then take a minute or two to brainstorm all the points you might put in your essay. Choose the strongest points and number them in the order you plan to present them. Lastly, note which documents and outside information you plan to use in conjunction with each point. If you organize your essay in advance of writing, the actual writing process will go much more smoothly. More important, you will not write yourself into a corner, suddenly finding yourself making a point you cannot support or heading toward a weak conclusion (or worse still, no conclusion at all).

For example, to deal with the issue of whether Chartism was revolutionary you might want to organize a brainstorm list like the following:

Political demands of the Chartists

Six points of the Charter

Economic issues

Chartism and women

Violence and non-violence

Hunger

Actions taken by the Chartists

End result of Chartist activities

Next, you would want to figure out which of your brainstorm ideas could be the main idea of paragraph number one, which ones could be used as evidence to support a point, and which should be eliminated. You should probably begin your first paragraph with your thesis, and then discuss the specific political demands of the Chartists in an attempt to show that the Chartists were interested in being included in the British political system and were not seeking its destruction. In this case, your list might look this way:

Political demands of the Chartists	1
Six points of the Charter	1-evidence
Economic issues	
Chartism and women	
Violence and non-violence	
Hunger	
Actions taken by the Chartists	
End result of Chartist activities	

If paragraph one is going to deal with the political demands of Chartism, you should certainly refer to Document 1 because it lays out the Chartist program. You might want to use your second paragraph to deal with the economic issues behind Chartism. This approach is a way to show that economic deprivation played a major role in leading working-class individuals toward political activity, not for the purposes of destroying British society, but to ensure that there was food on their tables. You could therefore make use of Documents 2 and 7, both of which deal with the economic deprivations behind Chartism. In this case your list would look like this:

Political demands of the Chartists	1
Six points of the Charter	1-evidence
Economic issues	2
Chartism and women	2-evidence
Violence and non-violence	
Hunger	2-evidence
Actions taken by the Chartists	
End result of Chartist activities	

Proceed in this way until you have finished planning your strategy. Try to fit as many of the documents into your argument as you can, but do not stretch too far to fit one in. Don't be concerned, for example, if you can't find a use for the poem in honor of Feargus O'Connor. An obvious, desperate stretch will only hurt your grade. Also, remember that history is often intricate and that the readers of your exam want to see that you respect the intrinsic complexity behind many historical events.

THE FREE-RESPONSE ESSAY QUESTIONS EXPLAINED

Because you only have 35 minutes to plan and write each of these essays, you will not have time to work out elaborate arguments. That's okay; nobody is expecting you to read two questions, choose one, remember all the pertinent facts about the subject, formulate a brilliant thesis, write an essay about it, and *then* repeat the process. Here are the steps you should follow. First, choose your question, brainstorm for two or three minutes, and edit your brainstorm ideas. Then, number the points you are going to include in your essay in the order you plan to present them. Finally, think of a simple thesis statement that allows you to discuss the points your essay will make.

QUESTION 1 — AGE OF EXPLORATION

1. Which factors explain why European states in the fifteenth and sixteenth centuries were interested in the building of colonial empires?

About the Structure of Your Essay

This is a very straightforward type of essay in that it allows you to organize a list of factors that can be used to explain the reasons for European expansion in the Early Modern period. This list can then be used as the organizational basis for your essay.

Your essay should mention at least some of the following:

- Rivalry among the states of Europe played a major role in the age of expansion. Spain sponsored Columbus in part because the Portuguese had made great advances along the western coast of Africa, and the Spanish, their rivals, wanted to find an alternative route to the East. Once the Spanish set about creating a colonial empire, they were soon followed by France, their traditional enemy. The French were followed by the English and Dutch. China, on the other hand, possessed a major navy in the fourteenth century, but because it was a monolithic empire without any direct rivals, the Chinese felt no pressure to extend their influence overseas by establishing a colonial empire. China would go so far as destroying its navy in the fifteenth century, an action that is hard to imagine any European nation emulating.

- Religion was a factor in the age of exploration and conquest in that many of the explorers and conquistadors thought that they were serving God by bringing Christianity to the so-called heathens. Such views are clearly found in the diaries that Columbus kept during his journeys.

- Economic factors were critical in explaining European expansion in Early Modern Europe. The spice trade with the East was extremely lucrative; whichever state could find a sea route that would bypass the long overland passage would enjoy a tremendous economic advantage. Additionally, Europe in the fifteenth century was extremely short on precious metals such as gold and silver, thus creating a tremendous desire to find other sources for these extremely valuable commodities.

- The fifteenth and sixteenth centuries witnessed the rise of the powerful Ottoman Empire, a militaristic state that dominated trade in the eastern Mediterranean. The great rivalry between Catholic Spain and the Islamic Ottomans spurred on Spain to locate a route to the Far East that could bypass its great enemy.

- States that have new technologies tend to make use of them. Some of the new items that were discovered during this period made ocean-going voyages feasible for the first time. These included galleons, the first ships powered entirely by sail, as well as new navigational tools such as the compass and sextant. European states also enjoyed new military technologies such as the ability to mount guns on ships.

QUESTION 2 — ENLIGHTENED ABSOLUTISM

2. Discuss the term "Enlightened Absolutism" as it applies to certain rulers in eastern Europe and Russia in the eighteenth century.

About the Structure of Your Essay

In this essay, you might want to make a strong thesis statement, perhaps along the lines of arguing that while those rulers who are labeled as "Enlightened Absolutists" often spoke about enlightened ideas, for the most part they failed to implement any substantive changes within their realms. On the other hand, you could list some of their actual achievements (such as in the area of religious toleration), while pointing out that powerful elements within their states such as the church or nobility blocked any possibility for further reform.

Your essay should mention at least some of the following:

- Most of the leading writers of the Enlightenment, such as Voltaire and Diderot, wanted change to come about not through the advent of republics, but rather through "enlightened monarchs" who would seek to reform their ideas on the basis of the concepts of enlightened reason.

- The monarchs who historians are mostly referring to when using the term. "Enlightened Absolutists" are Catherine the Great, the Empress of Russia (1762–1796), Joseph II of Austria (1741–1790), and Frederick the Great, the King of Prussia (1740–1786).

- These Enlightened Absolutists certainly read the works of the leading writers of the Enlightenment. Frederick the Great read Voltaire and was so impressed that he invited him to stay at his court. Catherine also read Voltaire, as well as Diderot, and when the latter desperately needed money to get out of debt, Catherine bought his extensive library and then generously lent it back to him.

- Joseph of Austria was influenced by the Enlightenment's call for religious toleration. Joseph granted Jews the right to worship (though they had to pay special taxes for the privilege), while Protestants were given the right to hold positions at the court in Vienna. On the other hand, Frederick refused to grant similar rights to the Jews of his realm and did nothing to grant rights to religious minorities in Russia.

- Writers of the Enlightenment had discussed the need for humane treatment for the accused. Both Joseph and Frederick banned the use of judicial torture within their realms, while Frederick went so far as to ban capital punishment. Both rulers also relaxed the strict censorship that existed in their states, although at times they still banned works they considered critical of their rule.

- All three enlightened monarchs attempted to expand the number of individuals receiving an education, not so as to create free-thinkers, but rather that they might have more trained individuals to serve as bureaucrats. Although none of the states implemented anything close to universal public education, they did greatly increase the number of individuals who went to school. These students, however, almost exclusively came from the higher classes.

- Frederick, in his youth, had toyed with the concept of enlightened statecraft based on just relations among states. However, when he saw the opportunity, he launched an unprovoked attack on the Habsburg territory of Silesia.

- Joseph of Austria ended the practice of owning serfs, although the newly freed peasants found that freedom came with the price of greatly increased taxes. Joseph discovered that further reform in the countryside was impossible due to the strong resistance of the nobility.

- None of these rulers took steps toward making their states constitutional monarchies. Catherine toyed with the idea of granting a constitution, but in the end, she and her fellow absolutists showed little interest in doing anything that would place actual limits on their power.

QUESTION 3 — SECOND INDUSTRIAL REVOLUTION

3. Discuss some of the new technologies that emerged during the Second Industrial Revolution of the nineteenth century.

About the Structure of Your Essay

This is one of those essay questions where you are probably best off brainstorming a list and then working off that list to create a structured essay. In this case, try to list all the various technologies that first made their appearance during the Second Industrial Revolution (1870–1900). Besides simply naming the new technologies, you should also mention the ways in which they transformed people's lives. Don't worry about leaving some things out. After all, with only 30 minutes to write your essay, there is a limit to how many items you can discuss in any sort of detail.

Your essay should mention at least some of the following new technologies:

- The Second Industrial Revolution is sometimes referred to as the "Age of Steel." Although steel production predates the Second Industrial Revolution, it was Henry Bessemer who, in the 1850s, came up with a way of producing steel from pig iron by using pressurized air to reduce its carbon content. This "Bessemer process" revolutionized the steel industry by making steel far cheaper to produce.

- Major developments took place in the harnessing of electricity. Thomas Edison developed the lightbulb in 1879, and within a decade electrical power plants were operating in several European capitals. The use of electric power transformed life for millions as electric lights made urban life much safer. At the same time, electric trolleys could move large numbers of people quickly and efficiently through the ever-expanding cities. Electric elevators made it possible to build skyscrapers, and new electric appliances, such as refrigerators and sewing machines, were transforming domestic life.

- In the 1880s, Karl Benz invented the internal combustion engine, thus leading to the invention of the automobile. By the end of the century, more advanced engines and improved roads were making cars a practical means of transportation, at least for the rich, who were the only ones who could afford this apparatus.

- A communications revolution took place with the invention of the telephone by Alexander Graham Bell in 1876.

- New sources of entertainment were also developed during this period. Thomas Edison invented the gramophone in 1876, and the first motion pictures were shown in 1895. Relate these inventions to the demands of the new mass culture.

4. Describe and analyze how Martin Luther differed with Catholic teachings on the question of salvation and the sacraments.

About the Structure of Your Essay

This is another type of question you will commonly see on the AP exam. It forces you to make a comparison between two different points of view. There are two ways to possibly approach this: The first involves making a point-by-point comparison of where Luther differed with Catholic teachings on these fundamental issues. The second method involves laying out the various Catholic teachings in the first part of your essay, then moving on to address Luther's teachings in a separate section, and finally providing a conclusion where you highlight some of the differences.

Your essay should mention at least some of the following:

- Catholic beliefs on the issue of salvation center on the idea that grace comes from a combination of faith and works. Faith was based on the belief in the physical incarnation of God as Jesus Christ along with his resurrection. Works meant performing the sacraments as well as charitable acts.

- For Catholics, faith comes from two sources: The Bible is obviously a central source, while Catholic teachings also stress that faith must come from what we might label "the traditions of the Church." This includes the writings of certain ancient fathers of the Church, such as St. Augustine or St. Jerome. Their writings have been declared canonical, along with decisions made at councils of the church, such as at the Council of Nicea in 325, where the Catholic teachings on the Trinity were established. Papal decrees also are part of this source for faith.

- The Catholic Church is a sacramental church. There are seven sacraments (baptism, mass, ordination, last rites, marriage, penance, and confirmation), and they may only be performed by an ordained clergyman. The sacraments are considered means toward grace in that by partaking of them you are performing acts that aid you in your quest for salvation.

- For Catholics, the mass requires the participation of an ordained priest who performs the miracle of the mass (turning the wafer and the wine into the blood and body of Christ), in a process known as transubstantiation.

- Martin Luther argued that salvation comes from faith alone and that works (either sacramental or charitable) do not play a role in achieving salvation. Luther believed that God's sacrifice of Jesus on the cross was so great that there is nothing that man can do to deserve salvation. Instead, salvation is the free gift of God to you, provided that you have faith.

- Faith for Luther came only from the Bible. He refused to believe that there could be any other source for that faith, and he argued that decisions from church councils were often contradicted by later church councils or by papal decrees.

- Luther did not think that sacraments were a means toward grace; he instead viewed them as symbols of God's gift of grace. He eliminated five of the sacraments that he felt were not biblical in origin, while retaining baptism and communion (mass). Communion was performed in a different manner as well; since Luther believed that Jesus was already present in the mass, there was no need for the Catholic practice of transubstantiation.

- As a result of his disagreement with the Catholic Church over the sacraments, Luther also viewed the role of the clergy in a very different manner. For Catholics, the clergy are a separate celibate caste who are integral to their salvation because they are the only ones who administer the sacraments and can perform the mass. Luther, on the other hand, brought the clergy down to the level of the lay person and insisted that since they did not have any special role to play in terms of one's salvation, it was unnecessary for them to remain celibate.

QUESTION 5 — DOMESTIC TENSIONS ON THE EVE OF WORLD WAR I

5. Analyze the domestic problems faced by TWO of the great European powers in the decade immediately prior to the outbreak of the First World War.

About the Structure of Your Essay

The years immediately prior to World War I were notable for the domestic problems faced by the great powers: Germany, Austria-Hungary, Russia, France, Italy, and Great Britain. Since the question is asking you to deal with two of these states, it would be to your advantage to quickly consider a list of domestic concerns for each of these states and then decide which two states on your list look most promising when it comes to writing your actual essay.

Depending on which two nations you decide to focus, your essay should mention at least some of the following:

- On the surface, Germany was the great behemoth of Europe, possessing the strongest army, a growing navy and an unmatched industrial base. Despite these apparent strengths, on the eve of the First World War, Germany was facing a potential political crisis, with more than one nationalistic politician stating that Germany needed a "blood cure" (war) to divert public attention. The constitution that Bismarck established for the new German state in 1871 did not create a constitutional monarchy along British lines. While the national parliament, the Reichstag, was elected by universal male suffrage, its powers were severely circumscribed. The chief minister of the state, the Chancellor, was selected by the Kaiser and not dependent upon the support of the Reichstag.

  Despite being in many ways a conservative, militaristic society, Germany also had the largest Socialist party in all of Europe, and the Socialists were the single largest political party in the Reichstag by 1912. The problem was that while the party could bring hundreds of thousands of people out in the street for demonstrations and garner around a third of the popular vote, by itself it could not bring about desperately needed political reform. The party rejected the revisionist Socialist views of Eduard Bernstein, who argued that a Socialist state could be achieved without a violent revolution. Yet, the S.P.D., while clinging to revolutionary rhetoric, became a parliamentary party rather than a revolutionary one. Kaiser Wilhelm, however, remained convinced that the party was committed to the destruction of his state and lived in dread of the eventual day when the Socialists would put their revolutionary rhetoric into action.

  German Liberals, who perhaps should have been the leaders of the move to a genuine parliamentary system, found themselves split among a number of splinter parties as they argued over issues such as protective tariff. Meanwhile, in the decade before the war, the right witnessed a surge in small parties that espoused beliefs that foreshadowed the program of the Nazi party.

  Germany faced other domestic problems on the eve of the war. Many Germans bemoaned the declining world of the independent farmers, who were being crushed by a decline in food prices, and of craftsmen, who were threatened by the rise of large industrial concerns. Small shopkeepers also were threatened by large department stores. All of these problems contributed to the rise of anti-Semitic parties, which deflected blame from the government and encouraged Germans to blame the negative changes that were coming to their lives on Jewish retailers and bankers. While not as considerable as that facing Austria-Hungary, Germany had its own nationality problem with many voicing concern that Polish families were buying farmland from impoverished Prussian Junkers, while the higher birthrate among Polish families portended a potential demographic crisis in the east. Meanwhile in Alsace and Lorraine, territories that Germany had seized as part of their victory in the Franco-Prussian War in 1871, a population that was ostensibly ethnically German would have preferred to substitute French rule for that of the heavy-handed Germans.

- In Austria-Hungary, the Emperor Franz-Joseph saw himself as the father of his people, but he couldn't have been a proud parent when considering the behavior of his "children." The Emperor saw his throne as being above the nationality problem and to some extent affection for the Emperor made this true. However, the aging Franz-Joseph (he was born in 1830) couldn't live forever, and there was a sense that his demise would soon be followed by the collapse of his empire. The establishment of the dual monarchy of Austria-Hungary in 1867 had not solved the nationality problem and, in some ways, had made it worse as other nationalities strove to match the status achieved by the Hungarians. Within Hungary, the Magyars, who made up half of the population, essentially ignored minority rights. With only five percent of the male population in Hungary allowed to vote, Magyar magnates controlled a political machine that ensured their dominance over the political and cultural life in the Hungarian kingdom. While there were those within the empire who were advocates of breaking the empire into a federation of nationalities, the grim reality in Hungary revealed that this would not solve the problem since each federation would have had its own nationality problem. The nationality question dominated all other issues within the empire and right on the eve of the war there was a major political problem in Bohemia over the question of whether to teach German or Czech in the public schools.

While the army and civil service were two institutions that were reasonably successful in providing some sense of common imperial identity, other attempts to match this success failed. Universal male suffrage, adopted in 1907, led to even greater conflict in the Austrian parliament, the Reichsrat, as each nationality was represented by its various partisans. The institution itself was to become infamous for the unbelievably poor behavior of the parliamentary representatives as they cursed, threw things, and spit on their rivals. Eventually this tentative experiment in parliamentary rule was deemed a failure, and the Emperor shut down the parliament at the beginning of the war.

Of all the seemingly implacable problems facing Austria-Hungary, it was the South Slav issue that was most pressing on the eve of the First World War. The establishment of an independent Serbian state in 1878 out of a former piece of the Ottoman Empire was not a major problem for Austria-Hungary except for the fact that it was a state built on the issue of nationality, in this case, a Serbian national identity. At the same time the Serbian state was born, Austria-Hungary took administrative control over the province of Bosnia, a territory that had a significant ethnic Serbian population. Relations between the two states remained good until 1903 when the pro-Austrian Serbian dynasty was replaced by a group of army officers who wished to see Serbia pursue a more nationalistic program and ally themselves with their fellow Slavs in Russia. Ensuing tensions between Austria-Hungary and Serbia led to the so-called "Pig War," an economic war in which Austria-Hungary refused to import Serbia's main export—pigs. In 1908, Austria-Hungary broke an earlier promise it had made to Russia and formally incorporated Bosnia into the empire. This step was undertaken not out of a desire to add more Slavs to their already polyglot empire, but rather to forestall a possible expansion of Serbian power into the territory. The step infuriated the Russians, who, because they were just recovering from their war with Japan and the Revolution of 1905, were unable to respond with vigor, though they vowed that next time they would not stand down if there was a similar Austro-Hungarian provocation in the Balkans. By the summer of 1914, tensions between Austria-Hungary and Serbia were at a fevered pitch, with Archduke Franz Ferdinand on his way to Sarajevo to inspect the army divisions that would be used for a potential invasion and occupation of Serbia.

- In the years before the war, Russia remained something of an enigma in that it combined political backwardness with an economy that was making impressive advances. The nation had begun to industrialize by the 1890s, and, on the eve of the First World War, the potential size of its economy was becoming apparent. In 1914, Russia was the fourth largest industrial power on Earth, having overtaken France in indices of heavy industry. Rather than begin with smaller industrial concerns, Russian industrialization had occurred on a massive scale with gigantic factories sprouting up in the area in and around St. Petersburg, a city that, in this period, was facing an acute housing shortage and sanitation problems. The booming economy in the years prior to the war also brought about a high rate of inflation and significant social tensions resulting from an exploited workforce, with a significant number of workdays lost to strikes. There was also serious unrest in the countryside, where many peasants continued to try to scrape by on inadequate land holdings and grappled with declining agricultural prices.

  Politically, the tsarist system of royal absolutism seemed incredibly anachronistic at the start of the twentieth century. An unsuccessful war with Japan in 1904 would reveal the numerous failings of the political system and would help bring about the revolution of 1905. The tsarist state survived, but just barely, in part because the army stayed loyal, while the opposition to the tsar was scattered among many different groups. As a concession to those clamoring for change, Nicholas II was forced to accept a parliament, or Duma, but he treated it with disdain and by 1907 had packed it with sympathetic representatives. In order to restore its popularity following the Revolution, the government turned to anti-Semitism and nationalism as unifying forces, but even these proved problematic—as an empire that stretched across two continents populated by numerous peoples with different languages and cultures, Russia had a serious national identity problem.

- It can be argued that of all the great powers, France was in the best shape domestically on the eve of the war. Even so, the Third French Republic did face some significant domestic conflicts prior to the First World War, including the fact that many Frenchmen still questioned the legitimacy of the republic itself. The Third Republic that was officially created in 1875 was in some ways conceived by accident when it became clear that restoring the monarchy, a move many Frenchmen would have preferred, was fraught with difficulties. In the years that followed, prime ministers came and went but no single party was able to dominate the legislature. Unlike the other great European powers, French economic output was fairly stagnant in the decade prior to the war. As a result of this lack of growth, France encountered significant labor unrest with the number of work days lost to strikes increasing every year leading up to 1914.

  The fallout from the Dreyfus Affair, in which a Jewish officer had been falsely accused of selling military secrets to the Germans, overshadowed life in the Third Republic even after Dreyfus's pardon in September of 1899. *Action Française*, a right-wing newspaper, continued to push an anti-Semitic program, something that received a favorable response among a significant portion of the French populace, particularly as France's Jewish population increased with refugees escaping from the horrors of tsarist Russia. Other religious issues were equally contentious, such as the question of the role of the Catholic Church. Although church and state were officially separated in 1905, that decision continued to rankle the more religiously inclined. In the years immediately prior to the war, the Third Republic also grappled with the question of maintaining a three-year military service commitment for French conscripts (necessary in order to keep up with Germany's vastly larger population) as well as the controversial question of whether to introduce an income tax to pay for larger military expenditures and a minimal system of old-age pensions.

- The Italian economy was growing at a nice clip in the years prior to 1914, but the economy still could not keep up with the needs of a rapidly growing population. The industrialized north suffered from a wave of strikes, which, due to the relative weakness of the Italian trade union movement in comparison with its German or British counterparts, provided an opening for extremist groups such as the Syndicalists, which threatened to use the tool of the general strike to bring down the capitalist system. Meanwhile, in the largely agricultural south of Italy, life had hardly changed since the eighteenth century and was still a land of great estates and a hard-pressed peasantry. The desperate poverty of the region would eventually lead to entire villages packing up and emigrating to the United States.

  Parliamentary politics in Italy had never been a particularly enlightening sight, and, on the eve of the war, the entire system appeared to be breaking down. When Italy entered the war on the side of the Entente in 1915, the parliament was not even consulted. As in France, there was a significant anti-clerical element in Italian politics. While the growing Catholic Center Party benefited from the fact that the papacy still refused to recognize the Italian state, it came to realize that it would be useful to have a party that reflected church desire in order to stop the passage of bills allowing for such things as divorce. As a possible way out of the political quagmire, the government turned its attention to imperial affairs, such as the worthless conquest of Libya in 1911. For more ardent Italian nationalists, this action was not enough, and they clamored for the conquest of *Italia irredenta* (unredeemed Italy); that is, areas occupied by ethnic Italians living under Austro-Hungarian rule.

- Great Britain was facing a number of significant issues on the eve of the First World War. On the front burner in the decade prior to the First World War was the question of the extension of the suffrage to women. In the first half of the nineteenth century, Liberals often argued that voting should be limited to men of property, but once the vote was granted to working-class male householders in the reform bills of 1867 and 1884, it opened up the possibility of a further extensions to include women. In the second half of the century a number of women's suffrage societies emerged that worked for the vote through peaceful means, such as organizing petitions meant to influence Members of Parliament. By 1900, a new, more violent element emerged with the formation of the Women's Social and Political Union (W.S.P.U.), led by Emmeline Pankhurst. Pankhurst's group, often referred to as suffragettes, was quite different from the earlier suffrage societies in that the members felt justified in using means such as arson as a tool for bringing attention to the plight of women. When some suffragettes were arrested for violent acts, they staged hunger strikes in prison and in general brought negative publicity to the government of Liberal Prime Minister Herbert Asquith.

  Great Britain struggled over the place of the unelected House of Lords in a nation that was increasingly heading towards democracy. The focal point for this struggle came in 1909 when the Liberals introduced a bill to provide for old-age pensions. In order to finance the plan, David Lloyd George, the Chancellor of the Exchequer, proposed raising income taxes, death duties, and taxing landed wealth. The bill passed the House of Commons, but stalled in the House of Lords, where the Lords broke with tradition for the first time in over two hundred years and rejected a money bill. As punishment for this unprecedented behavior, the Liberal government pushed a bill to limit the House of Lords' power to a suspending veto lasting two parliamentary sessions. When the House of Lords refused to pass a bill that would effectively strip it of its powers, Prime Minister Asquith threatened to have the king instantly create several hundred new lords in order to stack the upper house of Parliament and pass the bill. With this the House of Lords passed the bill.

Yet the most serious crisis facing the British government on the eve of the First World War was the question of Home Rule for Ireland. The Liberal Party had first broached the subject when Prime Minister William Gladstone introduced a Home Rule bill in 1884. The bill failed to win support among the faithful party and, in fact, led to a split within the Liberal Party that helped bring about a long period of Conservative dominance over British politics. By 1914, Asquith was ready to try again to bring about Home Rule. Fearing the domination of Catholics, the Protestants of Ulster began to take up arms to resist home rule, while the Catholic population began to arm in response. Civil war looked almost certain in Ireland, and, to make matters worse, some British army officers indicated that they would refuse to obey if ordered to disarm the Ulster Protestants.

QUESTION 6 — "GOLDEN AGE" FOR THE MIDDLE CLASS

6. Discuss why the period from 1870 to 1914 can be considered a "golden age" for Europe's middle class.

About the Structure of Your Essay

Although it would come to an end in the overwhelming catastrophe of the First World War, the period from 1870 to 1914 was an age in which Europe's middle class seemed to be in the ascendancy. You can structure this essay by taking into consideration the various political, economic, social, and cultural developments of the period and the ways in which they often benefited the middle class. You can also consider to what extent this "golden age" was the conscious byproduct of the efforts, wants, and needs of the middle class and therefore argue that the middle class served as the primary agent of change, as well as how at times the middle class was simply the unconscious beneficiary of larger societal forces over which it had no control.

Your essay should mention at least some of the following:

- If this was an age of the middle class, its nearest rival, the aristocracy, was clearly in decline. A sustained agricultural depression in part fueled by growing overseas imports led to a decline in the value of land, the most important source of aristocratic wealth.

- The middle class underwent a significant expansion in size during this period. A new, lower middle class developed in this period made up of show clerks, lower civil servants, and teachers. Within the upper reaches of the middle class there was further growth, as the Second Industrial Revolution in the period after 1850 ushered in a new age of mass manufacturing.

- Growing professional status for middle class professions. The decades before the war witnessed a proliferation of licensing exams and the establishment of formal associations, leaving those without these credentials, as in the case with law and medicine, with no avenue for employment.

- Increasingly, cities could be seen as the playground for the middle class, with working class populations pushed to the far edges, or in the case of Baron Haussmann's renewal plan for Paris, entirely outside the city in poor suburbs that encircled the more desirable urban center. While witnessing significant growth in population during this period, cities also became much safer with the establishment of professional police forces and first gas, then later electric lights. This enabled people to go out at night safely and allowed for the enjoyment of the theatres and other cultural venues built for this enlarged middle class audience.

- Beginning with the French Revolution but increasing in this period, careers in government were more often based on merit rather than high social birth. The adoption of competitive examinations for government posts in Great Britain, for example, benefited a middle class that was pursuing the growing educational opportunities of the period rather than the more traditional elites.

- The period from 1870 to 1914 ushered in the first mass consumer society, with the middle class again being the primary beneficiary through its rising buying power. Department stores are just one example of a changing consumer environment in which those with money had more opportunities to purchase along with a more diverse assortment of goods.

- The middle class was increasingly confronted with varied choices for leisure activities. Foreign travel, for instance, previously the preserve of the landed classes, became available to a broader audience as entrepreneurs such as Thomas Cook introduced package tours to overseas destinations to a curious but price conscious middle class.

- While household tasks were exceedingly difficult and labor intensive, the middle class had no cause for concern, since even those toward the bottom of the middle class economic scale could afford at least one servant, with more prosperous households having large numbers of domestic servants. This state of affairs would come to an end with the First World War with the rise in working class wages.

- The middle class would achieve a measure of political dominance in most western European nations in this period, supplanting the rule of the old landed aristocracy. One example of this transformation can be found in the British Parliament, where by the end of the century it became almost impossible for a Prime Minister to run the government sitting in the House of Lords.

Index

War Crimes Tribunal, 250
War of Spanish Succession, 88
War of the Austrian Succession, 119
War of the Roses, 89
warfare revolution, 82
Warsaw Ghetto, 247
Warsaw pact, 247, 248
Washington, George, 160, 236
water frame, 164
Waterloo, 147
Watt, James, 164
Way of Perfection (St. Teresa), 46
wealth production, 163, 210
Weber, Max, 108
Weimar Republic, 190, 213, 218
Wellington, Duke of, 146, 147
Whigs, 94, 123, 140
"White" forces, 214
White Man's Burden (Kipling), 197
White Mountain, Battle of, 85
white terror, 147
Wilberforce, Wilbur, 163
Wilhelm II, Kaiser, 198, 205
Wilkes, John, 123
William and Mary, 94, 113
William I, King of Prussia, 170, 171
William III, King of England, 94
William IV, King of Prussia, 161
William of Orange, 88, 95
William Pitt the Younger, 139
William the Statholder, 94
Wilson, Woodrow, 209, 210, 220, 222
"Window on the West" (Russia), 121
Wittenberg, 45, 66
Wollstonecraft, Mary, 117
women
    divorce, 190
    dowries, 99
    education, 189–190

Enlightenment and, 117–118
family role, 99
fascism and, 216
feminism, 190
French Revolution and, 137, 141
Holy Roman Empire rulership, 119, 120
humanism and, 60
property rights, 98, 190
religion and, 45–48, 99
Victorian sensibilities, 186
voting, 117, 138, 190, 209, 243
women's rights movement, 186
Women's Social and Political Union, 190
woodcuts, 63
Woolf, Virginia, 60
Wordsworth, William, 192
workers' revolt, 159
workhouses, 159
working class, 165–166, 186–189
World War I. *See* First World War
World War II. *See* Second World War
Wright Brothers, 182
Wycliffe, John, 65

Yalta conference, 235, 237
Yeltsin, Boris, 249–250
Young Italy movement, 169
"Young Turks," 174
Yugoslavia, 238, 250

zemstvos, 174
"Zero Hour," 227
Zimbabwee, 239
Zimmerman telegram, 208
Zinoviev, Gregory, 215
Zola, Emile, 194
Zollverein, 164, 170
Zurich, 69
Zwingli, John, 69

Bibliography

If you want more information about the AP European History Exam and additional practice materials, the following is a list of publications that might be useful to you. Your history teacher or your school's history department should have some of them; others can be found in your local library. Here is a list of official College Board publications that your school should own.

- *2006, 2007 Advanced Placement Course Description: European History*—In addition to a description of the exam and a list of themes in modern European history with which students should be familiar, this publication also contains sample free-response and multiple-choice questions with an answer key.

- *AP CD-ROM in European History, 1999: Home Version*—This disc contains video-guided tours, audio, music, and slide shows in order to introduce students to all aspects of the exam. It includes test-taking and study-skill tips, essay tutorials, and multiple-choice practice on three full-length tests taken from actual AP Exams. It's possible your school has the Network License version instead of the Home Version. If that's the case, you should be able to access the program at school.

- *Free-Response Questions*—Free-response questions from the past several years are currently available for free download in .pdf format from the College Board website at:
  www.collegeboard.com/student/testing/ap/prep_free.html

- *2004 AP European History Released Exam*—Approximately every four years, the College Board releases a complete copy of an exam. Answers are provided for the multiple-choice section, and sample essays are included along with comments from graders. The 1999 and 1994 exams are also currently available for purchase.

- *AP Teacher's Guide in European History, 2007*—Although it is called a "teacher's guide," anyone can buy it from the College Board, so there is no reason your teacher should not let you read it. It contains material mainly of use to those preparing to teach an AP course, although you may find some useful material in the guide on which areas to emphasize in your own studies.

If your school doesn't have copies of the materials just mentioned, you can purchase any of them directly by visiting the College Board's website at **store.collegeboard.com**, by calling College Board Publications at 212-713-8165, or by sending an e-mail to **store_help@collegeboard.org**.

The following are some books that can help reinforce and enhance your knowledge of European History. You don't necessarily need to read them from cover to cover, but if you are interested in exploring a topic in more depth, these books are a good place to begin.

- *A History of Modern Europe*, 2 vols. By John Merriman (W.W. Norton & Company)— This is a wonderful survey of European history. It is both thorough and highly readable. If you are familiar with the material found in these two volumes, you will be extremely well-prepared for your exam.

- *The Norton History of Modern Europe* contains seven volumes, all of which are excellent:
  - *The Foundations of Early Modern Europe, 1460–1559*, by Rice & Grafton
  - *The Age of Religious Wars, 1559–1715* by Dunn
  - *Kings and Philosophers, 1689–1789*, by Krieger
  - *Eighteenth-Century Europe: Tradition and Progress, 1715–1789*, by Woloch
  - *The Revolutionary Era, 1789–1850*, by Breunig & Levinger
  - *The Age of Nationalism and Reform, 1850–1890*, by Rich
  - *The End of the European Era: 1890 to the Present*, by Gilbert & Large

- *A General History of Europe*, published by Longman, is another collection of wonderful studies, each written by a prominent historian. The following are the volumes within the series that contain material pertinent to the AP European History Exam. Some of them are very old and may be difficult to locate.
  - *Europe in the Fourteenth and Fifteenth Centuries*, by Hay
  - *Europe in the Sixteenth Century*, by Koenigsberger
  - *Europe in the Seventeenth Century*, by Pennington
  - *Europe in the Eighteenth Century 1713–1783*, by Anderson
  - *Europe 1780–1830*, by Ford
  - *Europe in the Nineteenth Century 1830–1880,* by Hearder
  - *Europe 1880–1945*, by Roberts

I'm hesitant to recommend specific websites for two reasons: First, web pages seem to come and go at the speed of light, and second, while there are a number of web pages that have been set up as part of an AP class project, I believe that your study time is better spent in doing the more old-fashioned thing—reading books. If you must see what other AP classes have put on the web, go to any of the major search engines and search under a phrase such as "AP European History."

ABOUT THE AUTHOR

Kenneth Pearl received his Ph.D. in European History from the Graduate Center of the City University of New York in 1998. He is an Associate Professor in the History Department at Queensborough Community College.

The Princeton Review

1

YOUR NAME: _____
(Print)   Last   First   M.I.

SIGNATURE: _____   DATE: ___ / ___ / ___

HOME ADDRESS: _____
(Print)   Number and Street

_____
City   State   Zip Code

PHONE NO.: _____
(Print)

IMPORTANT: Please fill in these boxes exactly as shown on the back cover of your test book.

2. TEST FORM

3. TEST CODE   **4. REGISTRATION NUMBER**

6. DATE OF BIRTH

Month		Day		Year

JAN, FEB, MAR, APR, MAY, JUN, JUL, AUG, SEP, OCT, NOV, DEC

5. YOUR NAME

First 4 letters of last name — FIRST INIT — MID INIT

7. SEX
MALE
FEMALE

The Princeton Review
© The Princeton Review, Inc.
FORM NO. 00001-PR

Start with number 1 for each new section. If a section has fewer questions than answer spaces, leave the extra answer spaces blank.

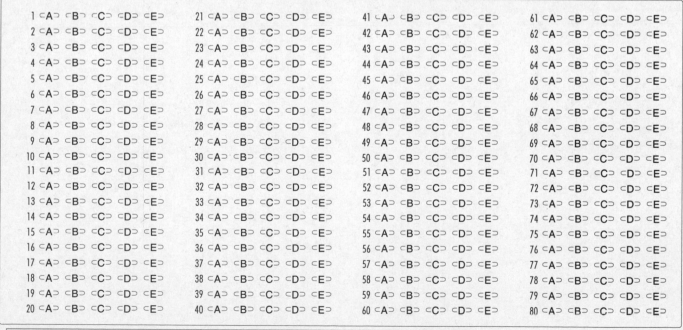

DO NOT MARK IN THIS AREA

The Princeton Review

1

YOUR NAME: _____
(Print)   Last   First   M.I.

SIGNATURE: _____   DATE: ___ / ___ / ___

HOME ADDRESS: _____
(Print)   Number and Street

_____
City   State   Zip Code

PHONE NO.: _____
(Print)

IMPORTANT: Please fill in these boxes exactly as shown on the back cover of your test book.

2. TEST FORM

_____

6. DATE OF BIRTH

Month		Day		Year
⊂ ⊃ JAN				
⊂ ⊃ FEB				
⊂ ⊃ MAR	⊂0⊃	⊂0⊃ ⊂0⊃	⊂0⊃
⊂ ⊃ APR	⊂1⊃	⊂1⊃ ⊂1⊃	⊂1⊃
⊂ ⊃ MAY	⊂2⊃	⊂2⊃ ⊂2⊃	⊂2⊃
⊂ ⊃ JUN	⊂3⊃	⊂3⊃ ⊂3⊃	⊂3⊃
⊂ ⊃ JUL		⊂4⊃ ⊂4⊃	⊂4⊃
⊂ ⊃ AUG		⊂5⊃ ⊂5⊃	⊂5⊃
⊂ ⊃ SEP		⊂6⊃ ⊂6⊃	⊂6⊃
⊂ ⊃ OCT		⊂7⊃ ⊂7⊃	⊂7⊃
⊂ ⊃ NOV		⊂8⊃ ⊂8⊃	⊂8⊃
⊂ ⊃ DEC		⊂9⊃ ⊂9⊃	⊂9⊃

3. TEST CODE

⊂0⊃ ⊂A⊃ ⊂0⊃ ⊂0⊃ ⊂0⊃
⊂1⊃ ⊂B⊃ ⊂1⊃ ⊂1⊃ ⊂1⊃
⊂2⊃ ⊂C⊃ ⊂2⊃ ⊂2⊃ ⊂2⊃
⊂3⊃ ⊂D⊃ ⊂3⊃ ⊂3⊃ ⊂3⊃
⊂4⊃ ⊂E⊃ ⊂4⊃ ⊂4⊃ ⊂4⊃
⊂5⊃ ⊂F⊃ ⊂5⊃ ⊂5⊃ ⊂5⊃
⊂6⊃ ⊂G⊃ ⊂6⊃ ⊂6⊃ ⊂6⊃
⊂7⊃ ⊂7⊃ ⊂7⊃ ⊂7⊃
⊂8⊃ ⊂8⊃ ⊂8⊃ ⊂8⊃
⊂9⊃ ⊂9⊃ ⊂9⊃ ⊂9⊃

4. REGISTRATION NUMBER

⊂0⊃ ⊂0⊃ ⊂0⊃ ⊂0⊃ ⊂0⊃ ⊂0⊃ ⊂0⊃
⊂1⊃ ⊂1⊃ ⊂1⊃ ⊂1⊃ ⊂1⊃ ⊂1⊃ ⊂1⊃
⊂2⊃ ⊂2⊃ ⊂2⊃ ⊂2⊃ ⊂2⊃ ⊂2⊃ ⊂2⊃
⊂3⊃ ⊂3⊃ ⊂3⊃ ⊂3⊃ ⊂3⊃ ⊂3⊃ ⊂3⊃
⊂4⊃ ⊂4⊃ ⊂4⊃ ⊂4⊃ ⊂4⊃ ⊂4⊃ ⊂4⊃
⊂5⊃ ⊂5⊃ ⊂5⊃ ⊂5⊃ ⊂5⊃ ⊂5⊃ ⊂5⊃
⊂6⊃ ⊂6⊃ ⊂6⊃ ⊂6⊃ ⊂6⊃ ⊂6⊃ ⊂6⊃
⊂7⊃ ⊂7⊃ ⊂7⊃ ⊂7⊃ ⊂7⊃ ⊂7⊃ ⊂7⊃
⊂8⊃ ⊂8⊃ ⊂8⊃ ⊂8⊃ ⊂8⊃ ⊂8⊃ ⊂8⊃
⊂9⊃ ⊂9⊃ ⊂9⊃ ⊂9⊃ ⊂9⊃ ⊂9⊃ ⊂9⊃

7. SEX
⊂ ⊃ MALE
⊂ ⊃ FEMALE

The Princeton Review
© The Princeton Review, Inc.
FORM NO. 00001-PR

5. YOUR NAME

First 4 letters of last name				FIRST INIT	MID INIT
⊂A⊃	⊂A⊃	⊂A⊃	⊂A⊃	⊂A⊃	⊂A⊃
⊂B⊃	⊂B⊃	⊂B⊃	⊂B⊃	⊂B⊃	⊂B⊃
⊂C⊃	⊂C⊃	⊂C⊃	⊂C⊃	⊂C⊃	⊂C⊃
⊂D⊃	⊂D⊃	⊂D⊃	⊂D⊃	⊂D⊃	⊂D⊃
⊂E⊃	⊂E⊃	⊂E⊃	⊂E⊃	⊂E⊃	⊂E⊃
⊂F⊃	⊂F⊃	⊂F⊃	⊂F⊃	⊂F⊃	⊂F⊃
⊂G⊃	⊂G⊃	⊂G⊃	⊂G⊃	⊂G⊃	⊂G⊃
⊂H⊃	⊂H⊃	⊂H⊃	⊂H⊃	⊂H⊃	⊂H⊃
⊂I⊃	⊂I⊃	⊂I⊃	⊂I⊃	⊂I⊃	⊂I⊃
⊂J⊃	⊂J⊃	⊂J⊃	⊂J⊃	⊂J⊃	⊂J⊃
⊂K⊃	⊂K⊃	⊂K⊃	⊂K⊃	⊂K⊃	⊂K⊃
⊂L⊃	⊂L⊃	⊂L⊃	⊂L⊃	⊂L⊃	⊂L⊃
⊂M⊃	⊂M⊃	⊂M⊃	⊂M⊃	⊂M⊃	⊂M⊃
⊂N⊃	⊂N⊃	⊂N⊃	⊂N⊃	⊂N⊃	⊂N⊃
⊂O⊃	⊂O⊃	⊂O⊃	⊂O⊃	⊂O⊃	⊂O⊃
⊂P⊃	⊂P⊃	⊂P⊃	⊂P⊃	⊂P⊃	⊂P⊃
⊂Q⊃	⊂Q⊃	⊂Q⊃	⊂Q⊃	⊂Q⊃	⊂Q⊃
⊂R⊃	⊂R⊃	⊂R⊃	⊂R⊃	⊂R⊃	⊂R⊃
⊂S⊃	⊂S⊃	⊂S⊃	⊂S⊃	⊂S⊃	⊂S⊃
⊂T⊃	⊂T⊃	⊂T⊃	⊂T⊃	⊂T⊃	⊂T⊃
⊂U⊃	⊂U⊃	⊂U⊃	⊂U⊃	⊂U⊃	⊂U⊃
⊂V⊃	⊂V⊃	⊂V⊃	⊂V⊃	⊂V⊃	⊂V⊃
⊂W⊃	⊂W⊃	⊂W⊃	⊂W⊃	⊂W⊃	⊂W⊃
⊂X⊃	⊂X⊃	⊂X⊃	⊂X⊃	⊂X⊃	⊂X⊃
⊂Y⊃	⊂Y⊃	⊂Y⊃	⊂Y⊃	⊂Y⊃	⊂Y⊃
⊂Z⊃	⊂Z⊃	⊂Z⊃	⊂Z⊃	⊂Z⊃	⊂Z⊃

Start with number 1 for each new section. If a section has fewer questions than answer spaces, leave the extra answer spaces blank.

1 ⊂A⊃ ⊂B⊃ ⊂C⊃ ⊂D⊃ ⊂E⊃   21 ⊂A⊃ ⊂B⊃ ⊂C⊃ ⊂D⊃ ⊂E⊃   41 ⊂A⊃ ⊂B⊃ ⊂C⊃ ⊂D⊃ ⊂E⊃   61 ⊂A⊃ ⊂B⊃ ⊂C⊃ ⊂D⊃ ⊂E⊃
2 ⊂A⊃ ⊂B⊃ ⊂C⊃ ⊂D⊃ ⊂E⊃   22 ⊂A⊃ ⊂B⊃ ⊂C⊃ ⊂D⊃ ⊂E⊃   42 ⊂A⊃ ⊂B⊃ ⊂C⊃ ⊂D⊃ ⊂E⊃   62 ⊂A⊃ ⊂B⊃ ⊂C⊃ ⊂D⊃ ⊂E⊃
3 ⊂A⊃ ⊂B⊃ ⊂C⊃ ⊂D⊃ ⊂E⊃   23 ⊂A⊃ ⊂B⊃ ⊂C⊃ ⊂D⊃ ⊂E⊃   43 ⊂A⊃ ⊂B⊃ ⊂C⊃ ⊂D⊃ ⊂E⊃   63 ⊂A⊃ ⊂B⊃ ⊂C⊃ ⊂D⊃ ⊂E⊃
4 ⊂A⊃ ⊂B⊃ ⊂C⊃ ⊂D⊃ ⊂E⊃   24 ⊂A⊃ ⊂B⊃ ⊂C⊃ ⊂D⊃ ⊂E⊃   44 ⊂A⊃ ⊂B⊃ ⊂C⊃ ⊂D⊃ ⊂E⊃   64 ⊂A⊃ ⊂B⊃ ⊂C⊃ ⊂D⊃ ⊂E⊃
5 ⊂A⊃ ⊂B⊃ ⊂C⊃ ⊂D⊃ ⊂E⊃   25 ⊂A⊃ ⊂B⊃ ⊂C⊃ ⊂D⊃ ⊂E⊃   45 ⊂A⊃ ⊂B⊃ ⊂C⊃ ⊂D⊃ ⊂E⊃   65 ⊂A⊃ ⊂B⊃ ⊂C⊃ ⊂D⊃ ⊂E⊃
6 ⊂A⊃ ⊂B⊃ ⊂C⊃ ⊂D⊃ ⊂E⊃   26 ⊂A⊃ ⊂B⊃ ⊂C⊃ ⊂D⊃ ⊂E⊃   46 ⊂A⊃ ⊂B⊃ ⊂C⊃ ⊂D⊃ ⊂E⊃   66 ⊂A⊃ ⊂B⊃ ⊂C⊃ ⊂D⊃ ⊂E⊃
7 ⊂A⊃ ⊂B⊃ ⊂C⊃ ⊂D⊃ ⊂E⊃   27 ⊂A⊃ ⊂B⊃ ⊂C⊃ ⊂D⊃ ⊂E⊃   47 ⊂A⊃ ⊂B⊃ ⊂C⊃ ⊂D⊃ ⊂E⊃   67 ⊂A⊃ ⊂B⊃ ⊂C⊃ ⊂D⊃ ⊂E⊃
8 ⊂A⊃ ⊂B⊃ ⊂C⊃ ⊂D⊃ ⊂E⊃   28 ⊂A⊃ ⊂B⊃ ⊂C⊃ ⊂D⊃ ⊂E⊃   48 ⊂A⊃ ⊂B⊃ ⊂C⊃ ⊂D⊃ ⊂E⊃   68 ⊂A⊃ ⊂B⊃ ⊂C⊃ ⊂D⊃ ⊂E⊃
9 ⊂A⊃ ⊂B⊃ ⊂C⊃ ⊂D⊃ ⊂E⊃   29 ⊂A⊃ ⊂B⊃ ⊂C⊃ ⊂D⊃ ⊂E⊃   49 ⊂A⊃ ⊂B⊃ ⊂C⊃ ⊂D⊃ ⊂E⊃   69 ⊂A⊃ ⊂B⊃ ⊂C⊃ ⊂D⊃ ⊂E⊃
10 ⊂A⊃ ⊂B⊃ ⊂C⊃ ⊂D⊃ ⊂E⊃   30 ⊂A⊃ ⊂B⊃ ⊂C⊃ ⊂D⊃ ⊂E⊃   50 ⊂A⊃ ⊂B⊃ ⊂C⊃ ⊂D⊃ ⊂E⊃   70 ⊂A⊃ ⊂B⊃ ⊂C⊃ ⊂D⊃ ⊂E⊃
11 ⊂A⊃ ⊂B⊃ ⊂C⊃ ⊂D⊃ ⊂E⊃   31 ⊂A⊃ ⊂B⊃ ⊂C⊃ ⊂D⊃ ⊂E⊃   51 ⊂A⊃ ⊂B⊃ ⊂C⊃ ⊂D⊃ ⊂E⊃   71 ⊂A⊃ ⊂B⊃ ⊂C⊃ ⊂D⊃ ⊂E⊃
12 ⊂A⊃ ⊂B⊃ ⊂C⊃ ⊂D⊃ ⊂E⊃   32 ⊂A⊃ ⊂B⊃ ⊂C⊃ ⊂D⊃ ⊂E⊃   52 ⊂A⊃ ⊂B⊃ ⊂C⊃ ⊂D⊃ ⊂E⊃   72 ⊂A⊃ ⊂B⊃ ⊂C⊃ ⊂D⊃ ⊂E⊃
13 ⊂A⊃ ⊂B⊃ ⊂C⊃ ⊂D⊃ ⊂E⊃   33 ⊂A⊃ ⊂B⊃ ⊂C⊃ ⊂D⊃ ⊂E⊃   53 ⊂A⊃ ⊂B⊃ ⊂C⊃ ⊂D⊃ ⊂E⊃   73 ⊂A⊃ ⊂B⊃ ⊂C⊃ ⊂D⊃ ⊂E⊃
14 ⊂A⊃ ⊂B⊃ ⊂C⊃ ⊂D⊃ ⊂E⊃   34 ⊂A⊃ ⊂B⊃ ⊂C⊃ ⊂D⊃ ⊂E⊃   54 ⊂A⊃ ⊂B⊃ ⊂C⊃ ⊂D⊃ ⊂E⊃   74 ⊂A⊃ ⊂B⊃ ⊂C⊃ ⊂D⊃ ⊂E⊃
15 ⊂A⊃ ⊂B⊃ ⊂C⊃ ⊂D⊃ ⊂E⊃   35 ⊂A⊃ ⊂B⊃ ⊂C⊃ ⊂D⊃ ⊂E⊃   55 ⊂A⊃ ⊂B⊃ ⊂C⊃ ⊂D⊃ ⊂E⊃   75 ⊂A⊃ ⊂B⊃ ⊂C⊃ ⊂D⊃ ⊂E⊃
16 ⊂A⊃ ⊂B⊃ ⊂C⊃ ⊂D⊃ ⊂E⊃   36 ⊂A⊃ ⊂B⊃ ⊂C⊃ ⊂D⊃ ⊂E⊃   56 ⊂A⊃ ⊂B⊃ ⊂C⊃ ⊂D⊃ ⊂E⊃   76 ⊂A⊃ ⊂B⊃ ⊂C⊃ ⊂D⊃ ⊂E⊃
17 ⊂A⊃ ⊂B⊃ ⊂C⊃ ⊂D⊃ ⊂E⊃   37 ⊂A⊃ ⊂B⊃ ⊂C⊃ ⊂D⊃ ⊂E⊃   57 ⊂A⊃ ⊂B⊃ ⊂C⊃ ⊂D⊃ ⊂E⊃   77 ⊂A⊃ ⊂B⊃ ⊂C⊃ ⊂D⊃ ⊂E⊃
18 ⊂A⊃ ⊂B⊃ ⊂C⊃ ⊂D⊃ ⊂E⊃   38 ⊂A⊃ ⊂B⊃ ⊂C⊃ ⊂D⊃ ⊂E⊃   58 ⊂A⊃ ⊂B⊃ ⊂C⊃ ⊂D⊃ ⊂E⊃   78 ⊂A⊃ ⊂B⊃ ⊂C⊃ ⊂D⊃ ⊂E⊃
19 ⊂A⊃ ⊂B⊃ ⊂C⊃ ⊂D⊃ ⊂E⊃   39 ⊂A⊃ ⊂B⊃ ⊂C⊃ ⊂D⊃ ⊂E⊃   59 ⊂A⊃ ⊂B⊃ ⊂C⊃ ⊂D⊃ ⊂E⊃   79 ⊂A⊃ ⊂B⊃ ⊂C⊃ ⊂D⊃ ⊂E⊃
20 ⊂A⊃ ⊂B⊃ ⊂C⊃ ⊂D⊃ ⊂E⊃   40 ⊂A⊃ ⊂B⊃ ⊂C⊃ ⊂D⊃ ⊂E⊃   60 ⊂A⊃ ⊂B⊃ ⊂C⊃ ⊂D⊃ ⊂E⊃   80 ⊂A⊃ ⊂B⊃ ⊂C⊃ ⊂D⊃ ⊂E⊃

NOTES

NOTES

NOTES

AP Exams

Cracking the AP Biology Exam,
2008 Edition
978-0-375-76640-4 • $18.00/C$22.00

Cracking the AP Calculus AB & BC Exams,
2008 Edition
978-0-375-76641-1 • $19.00/C$23.00

Cracking the AP Chemistry Exam,
2008 Edition
978-0-375-76642-8 • $18.00/C$22.00

**Cracking the AP Computer Science
A & AB Exams,** 2006–2007 Edition
978-0-375-76528-5 • $19.00/C$27.00

**Cracking the AP Economics (Macro &
Micro) Exams,** 2008 Edition
978-0-375-42841-8 • $18.00/C$22.00

**Cracking the AP English Language and
Composition Exam,** 2008 Edition
978-0-375-42842-5 • $18.00/C$22.00

Cracking the AP English Literature Exam,
2008 Edition
978-0-375-42843-2 • $18.00/C$22.00

**Cracking the AP Environmental
Science Exam,** 2008 Edition
978-0-375-42844-9 • $18.00/C$22.00

Cracking the AP European History Exam,
2008 Edition
978-0-375-42845-6 • $18.00/C$22.00

Cracking the AP Physics B Exam,
2008 Edition
978-0-375-42846-3 • $18.00/C$22.00

Cracking the AP Physics C Exam,
2008 Edition
978-0-375-42854-8 • $18.00/C$22.00

Cracking the AP Psychology Exam,
2008 Edition
978-0-375-42847-0 • $18.00/C$22.00

**Cracking the AP Spanish Exam,
with Audio CD,** 2008 Edition
978-0-375-42848-7 • $24.95/$29.95

Cracking the AP Statistics Exam,
2008 Edition
978-0-375-42849-4 • $19.00/C$23.00

**Cracking the AP U.S. Government
and Politics Exam,** 2008 Edition
978-0-375-42850-0 • $18.00/C$22.00

Cracking the AP U.S. History Exam,
2008 Edition
978-0-375-42851-7 • $18.00/C$22.00

Cracking the AP World History Exam,
2008 Edition
978-0-375-42852-4 • $18.00/C$22.00

SAT Subject Tests

**Cracking the SAT Biology E/M
Subject Test,** 2007–2008 Edition
978-0-375-76588-9 • $19.00/C$25.00

Cracking the SAT Chemistry Subject Test,
2007–2008 Edition
978-0-375-76589-6 • $18.00/C$22.00

Cracking the SAT French Subject Test,
2007–2008 Edition
978-0-375-76590-2 • $18.00/C$22.00

Cracking the SAT Literature Subject Test,
2007–2008 Edition
978-0-375-76592-6 • $18.00/C$22.00

**Cracking the SAT Math 1 and 2
Subject Tests,** 2007–2008 Edition
978-0-375-76593-3 • $19.00/C$25.00

Cracking the SAT Physics Subject Test,
2007–2008 Edition
978-0-375-76594-0 • $19.00/C$25.00

Cracking the SAT Spanish Subject Test,
2007–2008 Edition
978-0-375-76595-7 • $18.00/C$22.00

**Cracking the SAT U.S. & World History
Subject Tests,** 2007–2008 Edition
978-0-375-76591-9 • $19.00/C$25.00